ECONOMIC ANTHROPOLOGY

Readings in Theory and Analysis

ECONOMIC ANTHROPOLOGY
Readings in Theory and Analysis

edited by

EDWARD E. LeCLAIR, JR.
RENSSELAER POLYTECHNIC INSTITUTE

HAROLD K. SCHNEIDER
LAWRENCE UNIVERSITY

HOLT, RINEHART AND WINSTON, INC.
NEW YORK   CHICAGO   SAN FRANCISCO
ATLANTA   DALLAS   MONTREAL
TORONTO   LONDON

PREFACE

When this book was in the planning stage, the only book offering a general treatment of the field of economic anthropology was Melville Herskovits' *Economic Anthropology* (1952) which was a revised version of a book originally published as *The Economic Life of Primitive Peoples* (1940). A valuable and pioneering work in its time, developments in the field were making it increasingly obsolete.

Under such circumstances, a book of the sort that we were planning was almost its own justification: there was a clear gap in the available literature which we thought we could fill.

It is commonplace in society that multiple recognition of needs and accompanying efforts to fill those needs is more common than not. So it was that as we worked on this volume, three new books dealing generally with economic anthropology made their appearance (rumors of still another have not yet been confirmed). We are no longer filling a gap; rather, we are in the position of passengers trying to board a crowded bus. As we examined those on board it became more and more apparent that although the bus was filling up, we held a reserved seat which no one else had claimed.

Two of the books, those by Belshaw (1965) and Nash (1966) reflected the thinking of a single individual in each case. Without passing any judgments on the merits of the books in question, it was clear that what we were planning was quite different from what they had accomplished.

The third of the books, that by Dalton (1967), might, since it was also a reader, have covered substantially the same ground we had staked out for ourselves. However, it did not. Only one paper appears both in Dalton's book and in our own, that by Nash (1961, see below, pp. 311–322); in addition, Dalton includes material from Malinowski's *Argonauts of the Western Pacific* (1922, 1961) as we do, but for the most part, it is different material. Otherwise, the selection of readings in the two books is different. This perhaps offers testimony to the richness of the literature in what is a relatively undeveloped subdiscipline of anthropology. In many respects, the two volumes complement rather than compete with each other.

Moreover, Dalton's reader reflects essentially a single theoretical point of view, while we attempted, in our selections of readings, to present as many as possible of the varying views which not only have marked the development of economic anthropology over time, but which continue to flourish.

Thus, despite the minor flowering of general works in economic anthropology which has occurred over the past two years, we continue to feel that we have something to offer which is not otherwise available.

Anyone familiar with the literature of the field can perhaps readily get some sense of our plan and purpose in this book by reviewing the table of contents. For those who might encounter this book in an early stage of their acquaintance with the field, a brief statement of plan and purpose might be of use.

In the Introduction, we undertake a critical review of the conceptual development of economic anthropology from Malinowski to the present. This review provides the rationale for the bulk of the selections in Part Two. In Part Two, Sections I, II, IV and V contain the major writings in this development in their chronological order. Missing, somewhere near the end of this sequence, is any major reply from a "substantivist" source of the criticisms made against the "substantivist" position in readings 10, 11, and 12. It is missing only because to the best of our knowledge no such reply has ever been published.

Section III of Part Two and reading 15 represent very limited attempts to indicate some of the fundamental properties of the modes of analysis that are characteristic of contemporary economic thought. We could offer no more than an indication here for this book is not intended to be economics for anthropologists, but a review of economic anthropology.

Similarly, Reading 14 is included as a limited indication of the thinking among certain sociologists on economic matters. To try to do more in this direction once again would go beyond the scope of the present book. A good extended statement of the sociological view in these matters may be found in a recent book by Smelser (1963).

While there is a clear rationale supporting readings in Part Two, Part Three is necessarily somewhat diffuse in its content and therefore less structured. Our purpose in Part Three was to give a limited sampling of an increasingly rich literature of description, and an analysis of specific economic systems or parts of systems. We make no particular claims and offer no special defense for the particular readings which appear in Part Three. Perhaps our purposes could have been adequately served by thirteen totally different readings. The readings included appealed to us on a variety of grounds which need not be detailed.

It is characteristic of anthropology that theory and descriptive analysis often seem to be separate, unrelated realms of discourse. This is true even of Malinowski on the *kula*, whose theoretical statements are interspersed with descriptive material in his *Argonauts of the Western Pacific*. Yet even here, the theoretical remarks have a curious quality of detachment from the surrounding material, standing as *obiter dicta*, stimulated by but not wholly related to the data in which they are embedded.

This raises the question of whether the really meaningful theory may not be that incidentally contained in the selections of Part Three rather than in the self-consciously theoretical papers of Part Two. On the whole, we think not. The various papers in Part Two raise significant questions and deal with them in a significant way. It is our position that the material included in Part Two, certainly the earlier papers, have influenced the way ethnologists have looked at their materials. But this is something which one must intuit on the basis of an examination of a large body of material and it cannot be clearly and concisely demonstrated within the limitations of space which bound this reader.

To complete this brief review of what we have tried to do, in Part Four we consider a number of theoretical issues which for reasons of space or the availability of materials could not be treated or treated adequately in the readings proper. And here, once again, we try to indicate, but do no more than indicate, some of the fundamental properties of the mode of thinking which characterizes contemporary economic thought.

We were wrestling with an effort at summation, closure and prognostication for economic anthropology when we heard Richard Salisbury read the initial version of Reading 30 at the Annual Meetings of the American Anthropological Association in Pittsburgh in 1966. In this, Salisbury had already done very effectively what we were trying to do and so before the day was out we sought and received permission to incorporate his paper in our reader.

Earlier we commented that the reader recently edited by Dalton (1967) reflected essentially a single theoretical point of view. We hold a different theoretical position, that called the "formalist" point of view by Scott Cook (1966). This view dominates the discussion in Parts One and Four. We make no apologies for this. But subject to limitations of space, which made it impossible to include in this volume everything we might have wished to include, we have attempted to include a broad representation of the various points of view which have in the past and now exist in economic anthropology. In this, the "now" ends roughly near the end of 1966; with the special exception of the Salisbury paper, materials published after that time could not be included.

Of material not included we were especially regretful that for reasons largely beyond our control we could not include any of the writings of Polly Hill, Sol Tax, Cyril S. Belshaw, or Claude Meillasoux.

With the foregoing caveats, we hope and think that we have succeeded in presenting a well-balanced selection of readings. We know that if we have not, our colleagues will let us know and that future editions, if any, will benefit.

With exceptions to be noted, all readings are here reprinted as originally published. The only major exception is in the case of Reading 11. The original version contained an analytical appendix which was discarded as being superfluous in the present context. Throughout we revised citations to the style used in the *American Anthropologist* except in the case of Reading 5. In this case citation practice was so at variance to current usages that we thought it best to retain the original forms. In the case of readings from books, we eliminated references to preceding or subsequent material in the same book and we did not use any of the illustrations printed in Malinowski (1922, 1961) and eliminated references to such illustrations.

This book is the result of a joint, collaborative effort which began in late 1962. Our correspondence over these years has been voluminous and at two critical points we managed to get together, despite the distance which separated us, for several days each time to discuss not only what should be included and what left out, but also to discuss what we ourselves would say. These meetings turned into short, intensive workshops in which the ideas we each held were sharpened and polished by the abrasive of the criticism of the other. Throughout we were motivated by deeply held conviction that the modes of thought characteristic of formal economics will lead to new depths of understanding of man and his works.

It would be difficult to specify authorship of Part One. Schneider wrote a first draft which was rewritten by LeClair and later revised by LeClair on the basis of comments from Schneider and others. Many passages in the final version were carried over basically unchanged from the original Schneider draft; other portions were substantially changed. Part Four and Section II of Part Five were drafted by LeClair and revised and rewritten by LeClair on the basis of comments from Schneider and others.

We owe a great deal to a great many people, to some because of general contributions to our intellectual development, to others because of specific assistance with respect to this book. Among the latter, our first and foremost debt is to the publishers and authors who were so generous in giving permission to reprint the materials which are the core of the book. Specific acknowledgements are made on the first page of each reading.

We owe a common debt to the late Melville J. Herskovits, under whom we both studied anthropology, doing so at about the same time, so that he was responsible, in a sense, for bringing us together. Herskovits did much to shape our thinking, perhaps at times in ways he would not have approved. This book might appropriately be dedicated to his memory.

We owe much to David P. Boynton of Holt, Rinehart and Winston, Inc., without whose patient encouragement this book would not have come into existence. We must further say that the existence of the book is a reflection of a courageous and imaginative publishing program which Dave Boynton, with the advice of George and Louise Spindler, is conducting in anthropology and which we believe to be making an important contribution to the vitality of the field.

Frank Cancian, Scott Cook and Richard F. Salisbury read early versions of Parts One and Four and commented extensively on them. They and others also reviewed and commented on the proposed readings. These comments have made this a better book than it would otherwise have been. Needless to say, we are solely responsible for any deficiencies the book may have.

Mrs. Nannette Hadley, Secretary to the Department of History and Political Science at Rensselaer Polytechnic Institute, carried the burden of preparing the final manuscript. The skill and patience with which she carried on this task, while simultaneously carrying on her other assigned duties, removed from LeClair a burden which he might have found unmanageable. Also deserving of recognition is Mrs. Betty West, Science Hall Faculty Secretary of Lawrence University, who gave unselfishly of her time in preparing some portions of the manuscript in its earlier stages.

Troy, N.Y.   E.E.LeC., Jr.
Appleton, Wis.   H.K.S.

August 1968

CONTENTS

PART FIVE ECONOMIC ANTHROPOLOGY:
Retrospect and Prospect 475

ECONOMIC ANTHROPOLOGY

Readings in Theory and Analysis

part one

INTRODUCTION
THE DEVELOPMENT
OF ECONOMIC ANTHROPOLOGY

Nineteenth century anthropology—and even early twentieth century anthropology—tended to equate "economy" with technology to the virtual exclusion of all else. In commenting on this aspect of what might, for lack of a better term, be called early economic anthropology, Raymond Firth, in a passage reprinted in this book (see p. 71) quotes from a chapter on "Economic Life" in a monograph by Fay-Cooper Cole as follows: "To relieve the itch, the jucie of the *kabatiti* . . . is applied to the skin," and "cracked feet are treated with carabao dung." (Firth 1952:130; the quotations are from Cole 1922:410.) Statements of this kind still might be appropriately included in any respectable ethnography, but they would be frankly labeled technology—or even folk medicine. Economic life is now properly considered to be something else again.

There are, as we shall see, substantial disputes both in economics and in anthropology concerning the proper subject matter of economics, and the nature of economic systems and how they should be studied. But today, all agree on at least this much: that economic activity, properly considered, is a social process of some sort or other. It might be necessary to take technology into account in considering certain aspects of an economic system, but technology is not the economic system itself.

If this notion is generally accepted among anthropologists today, major credit for successful propagation of the idea among anthropologists of his generation must go to Bronislaw Malinowski. His account of the *kula* ring among the Trobriand Islanders of the western Pacific near New Guinea represented one of the first systematic attempts, and certainly the first searching attempt, to examine economic activity as a social phenomenon (Malinowski 1922).[1] Barton and Seligman had written on the *kula* as early as 1910 (Seligman 1910); Barton's account of Ifugao economics (1922) did not fall into the technology trap, but Malinowski's work was by far the most influential in this field.

The Anti-economics of Bronislaw Malinowski

Malinowski did not consider the *kula* exchange to be an economic activity, though what he did consider to be economic activity was associated with it on

---

[1] Citations to follow are from the Dutton paperback edition of 1961.

occasion. As Malinowski saw it, the *kula* was a system of ritual exchange, a "passing from hand to hand of two meaningless and quite useless objects . . ." (1961:86). In taking this position, Malinowski sought to emphasize what he considered to be the noneconomic character of the exchange. Moreover, he suggests over and over again that the natives were suppressing their natural economic instincts in carrying out the *kula*. The following passage is typical:

> Although, like every human being, the Kula native loves to possess and therefore desires to acquire and dreads to lose, the social code of rules, with regard to give and take by far overrides his natural acquisitive tendency (1961:96).

How then can we claim that Malinowski was anthropology's first true economic anthropologist? In assessing Malinowski's contribution to economic anthropology, Firth (1964:209–228) notes that Malinowski was concerned with the social context of economic activity. Malinowski pointed out how such activity may be socially motivated, how complex the economic activity of "savages" could be, how elaborate trade might get, and how complex the holding of rights and wealth are. Malinowski went beyond the normal concerns of conventional economics to show how the economic activity was intimately associated with other aspects of the culture; in the context of the Trobriand case, he showed how magical practices served a positive function in the economic system by instilling confidence and hope in the individual who was setting out on a trading expedition.

Though Malinowski was a pioneer in the field of economic anthropology, he had certain shortcomings. As Firth points out in his evaluation of Malinowski's contribution, Malinowski was essentially a common sense descriptive economist. He failed to consider value in relation to price, concentrating primarily on factors of demand; in analyzing the *kula* he failed to indicate how values are arrived at, and he ignored the concept of scarcity, which is central to modern economic thought. In general, he failed to adequately appreciate the range of economic theory as it might apply to his data.

Indeed, the matter goes beyond this. Malinowski was hostile rather than indifferent to most of economic theory as he understood it. It is difficult to get a clear idea of where Malinowski got his notions of the economic theory of his day, as his documentation is scanty. But a close reading of his work makes it clear that at best, his conception of the prevailing economic thought of his time was out of date; at worst, it was distorted and mistaken. He focused his attention on an already outmoded concept of an "economic man," and, as in the passage quoted above, repeatedly asserted that primitive man in general, and his Trobriand Islanders in particular, are not motivated by self-interest (see especially Malinowski 1961:60–62).

In taking this position, Malinowski set a fashion for much subsequent ethnographic writing, in which anthropologists gleefully documented cases which were asserted to be clear examples of "natives" acting in other than their own self-interest.

Malinowski himself failed to see a contradiction in his own view or in his statement of the view. In summing up his views on the "noneconomic" character of Trobriand choices, he writes as follows:

> [The Trobiander] is not guided primarily by the desire to satisfy his wants, but by a very complex set of traditional forces, duties and obligations, beliefs in magic, social ambitions and vanities. He wants, if he is a *man*, to achieve social distinction as a *good gardener* and a good worker in general (1961:62; italics in the original).

In two consecutive sentences, Malinowski first tells us that man is not motivated by his wants, then tells us that he is motivated by his wants. This makes sense only if we see the term "wants" in its first occurrence as being defined differently from "wants" in its second occurrence. This is the heart of the problem. (For a further discussion of the problem of "economic man" see below, pp. 456–457.)

In this way, Malinowski established a fashion in anthropology of denigrating conventional economic theory. To do so, however, was equivalent to the situation which would have obtained in personality and culture studies if anthropologists had systematically rejected Freudian or other psychological theories. By following Malinowski, anthropologists were systematically and uncritically cutting themselves from the one body of theory which sought to illuminate economic phenomena.

Economics Becomes Respectable

Malinowski established a fashion, but as is well known, there are always those who do not behave in accordance with established fashion. Richard Thurnwald had been using a peculiar variant of economic theory growing out of the German school of economic history in analyzing "primitive" economies even before 1922. But it was not until 1932 that any of his work appeared in English and then it had relatively little impact. Though then still heavily under the influence of Malinowski, Firth foreshadowed his later positions as early as 1929. W. E. Armstrong's application of the conventional concept of interest to the analysis of Rossell Island money (1924, 1928) remained no more than an enduring curiosity.

There were a few others of like mind but during the decades of the twenties and thirties, their work was no more than straws in the wind. Then as the thirties came to an end and the forties began, these straws coalesced into something far more substantial. Within a few months of each other, three anthropologists published books which, collectively, were to establish the respectability of economic theory in the minds of most anthropologists.

They were Firth and D. M. Goodfellow, both of whom had been students of

Malinowski, and Melville J. Herskovits. Working from somewhat different perspectives, and adopting positions which differed somewhat in detail but not in basic substance, all three argued that the conventional economic theory of the day was generally valid, or at least that its premises were valid. From this they argued that anthropologists could learn much by applying conventional theory to the settings of primitive economic systems.

Firth and Goodfellow rooted their theoretical discussions, as Malinowski had done, in the context of an analysis of the economic system of a particular group, Firth (1939), in that of the Polynesian island of Tikopia and Goodfellow (1939), in that of the Bantu of South Africa. Herskovits, on the other hand, worked in a cross-cultural perspective, combing the anthropological literature for materials to support his various positions (Herskovits 1940, 1952).

What was it that Firth, Goodfellow and Herskovits were advocating, each in his own way? There will be much discussion in the pages that follow of what is involved here, and each of these men will speak in their own words. But for purposes of the present discussion it is useful briefly to outline some of the thrust and meaning of formal conventional theory.

In essence it is a theory of rational choice built around a principle known as the "calculus of maximization." It assumes that people make choices among alternatives in a rational fashion, according to determinable principles; "rational" is defined by the theory. Out of this simple initial premise is built, largely by deduction, a highly elaborated set of propositions which, in their initial formulation, purport to show how an economic system, such as that existing in the United States, functions. In effect, Firth, Goodfellow, and Herskovits were arguing that the basic premises of this system of thought were valid everywhere and not merely in Western industrial-commercial societies.

But none of these men were professional economists and none of them were able or willing—and quite properly so—to ignore their basic anthropological underpinnings. For this and other reasons, none were willing to follow the logic of their positions as far as it could lead them, though Goodfellow, who was not nearly as well-known as are Firth and Herskovits, went considerably further than did the other two.

For example, the logic of the premises of formal economics is that economic theory is a way of looking at behavior. One can "economize" with respect to any scarce resource. But we find Firth writing, as late as 1952:

> Situations continually tend to arise . . . in which some sacrifice of economic benefits is judged necessary to maintain or raise one's social status, or to help give reality to social ideals which one thinks are important (Firth 1952:153; see also below, p. 86).

Given the premises of neoclassical economic theory—the theory with which people like Firth and Herskovits were more or less familiar—it is difficult to know how to give operational meaning to the phrase "economic benefits." Economizing is the allocation of scarce resources among alternative ends. One presumes that by "economic benefits" Firth means something like profits or a full belly as opposed to prestige or one's social status. But for the economist, ends cannot be distinguished along these lines. An individual might readily give up a full belly in order to secure an added measure of social status, and indeed, the anthropological literature contains numerous cases of this sort of decision. Here the individual is not choosing something noneconomic over something economic. He is allocating his resources between nourishment and status, accepting somewhat less nourishment in the interest of having somewhat more social status. If the observer thinks that he would have allocated his resources differently, this does not make the observee's behavior noneconomic. *Chacun à son gout*, to each his own, and one man's meat is another man's poison.

In another dimension, Herskovits was much influenced by the writings of Thorstein Veblen, though Veblen's ideas had long since faded from the mainstream of economic thought. This led him into a consideration of "the topsy-turvy realm of prestige economics" (Herskovits 1952:415) and into the quicksands of "economic surplus" as an explanatory device. This last has given rise to a seemingly interminable controversy in economic anthropology (which will be discussed more fully below, see pp. 469-470) though it is not an idea which has any place in contemporary economic theory.

Still another consequence of the fact that these were anthropologists writing about economics rather than economists writing economics, was in their awareness of an emphasis on social and cultural factors in the economic system. Economists traditionally could and did take the economic system as something of an isolate in the total social system. It could be studied in its own terms, and it was simpler to do so. By the same token, economists did not delve too much into ends in themselves; operating within a single cultural context, they could take ends as they were and felt no need for explaining them. Operating within a single social framework, they could afford to concentrate their attention on the economic system. Thus, the social and cultural systems were "givens," parameters which did not need to be taken into account in the analysis. (On the other hand, as economists have become preoccupied with problems of economic development, they have come into contact with social and cultural systems different from their own; they have therefore become acutely conscious of problems in this area.)

Anthropologists are constantly shifting their attention from culture to culture, from social system to social system. And so we find Firth writing:

> The choice, the behaviour, the values of any one person are conditioned by other people . . . The less any individual acts in isolation, the more he must be responsive to choices, or the expectation of choices, by others. Economic organization is set in a social framework . . . (Firth 1952:124; see also below, p. 66).

An economist would not deny these propositions. It is merely that these propositions have traditionally been irrelevant to his concerns; but they are not irrelevant to the concerns of an anthropologist, and may not be irrelevant to the concerns of an economic anthropologist.

The fact that economic organization is indeed set in a social framework, and the implications of this fact, remains one of the great unfinished tasks of economic anthropology. At the same time, Goodfellow is worth quoting in this connection:

> Even if the savage, therefore, could be said to be "dominated by custom," this, far from meaning that he did not dispose economically of his resources, might mean just the opposite; for custom may best be regarded as the mechanism through which this essential aim is achieved (Goodfellow 1939:16; see also below, p. 64).

In concluding this part of the discussion, it is well to point out that the theory of maximization, which is at the heart of neoclassical economic theory, says nothing about what is maximized. Neoclassical theory generally assumed that profit was maximized, but this represents an application of maximization theory, not maximization theory itself. An individual maximizes something, or different things at different times—presumably those things which he values. General maximization theory could be applied in any case.

The New Economic Anthropology in Action

The work of Firth and Herskovits in 1939–1940 (Goodfellow was not so widely read) set a new fashion in economic anthropology to replace the negativism of Malinowski. If the new fashion was not all that it might be, at least it was a large step in the right direction. Anthropologists began systematically to "apply" economic theory to the economies that they studied.

Herskovits had said that "practically every economic mechanism and institution known to us is found somewhere in the nonliterate world." (1952:488.) Anthropologists now embarked on a search for these analogues, these parallels, these similarities. If this was not quite economic theory reborn in a cross-cultural setting, it at least made use of conventional concepts where they seemed to fit.

These efforts were obviously most successful where the forms of economic organization were similar to those of the Western world. One of the notable examples of such a successful application of conventional economic concepts was *Penny Capitalism* by Sol Tax (1953). But the new fashion was more often to manifest itself in more subtle ways. The snide remarks about economic man were vanishing, there were alterations in emphasis and treatment, often involving no more than a few lines of text, in hundreds of articles and monographs. Economic anthropology began to grow in sophistication.

At the same time, many of these new economic anthropologists have, like Firth, been unable to cut themselves entirely loose from their anthropological underpinnings. There remains in many of them a preoccupation with social and cultural factors in the economic equation, a preoccupation which, as we have pointed out, was not traditionally found in conventional economic inquiry.

Typical in this group is Manning Nash. Nash recognizes the universality of decision-making behavior and even the profit orientation, and the applicability of conventional theoretical concepts in dealing with these things. But he sees the decision-making process as strictly circumscribed by the social structure. For example:

> What is distinctive about peasants in primitive societies are not the habits of mind about advantage, nor an ability to calculate costs and benefits of a course of action, nor even an absence of a motive of gain; but rather the possession of a set of concrete social organizations which directly channel economic choice, on the one hand, and a set of sanctions which operate to keep economic deviants in physical as well as moral jeopardy on the other (Nash 1961:186, see also below, p. 311).

However, one can well ask whether these facts are true only of "peasants in primitive societies." That the economist has not typically concerned himself with possible social and cultural constraints in studying Western industrial economies does not mean that such constraints do not exist. It means simply that their impact has not been analyzed. And by the same token there is no reason for supposing that they need necessarily be taken into account in a purely economic analysis of the economic activities of "peasants in primitive societies." If one wishes to take them into account in an analysis, so be it, but then the analysis is going beyond the purely economic.

It may be mentioned in passing that this same "economy plus society" syndrome appears, as might be expected, in the emerging field of economic sociology, especially as developed by Parsons and Smelser. In reviewing Parsons and Smelser's *Economy and Society* (1956) Harry W. Pearson indicates that "perhaps the most important achievement of this new statement by Professor Parsons and Mr. Smelser lies in their emphasizing the priority of a state of equilibrium for the society as a whole over that of the economy considered in isolation" (Pearson 1957:316; see also below, p. 241).

An explicit element in the Parsonian view of the relation between economy and society is the idea that the social system, of which the economy is a part, is designed to maintain itself in some kind of meaningful equilibrium. This view seems to be implicit in the passage from Nash quoted above. While the view has many adherents it is by no means generally accepted, as comments by Hagen and Krupp, which appear in this volume, will indicate. (See pp. 100–109 and 243–256.)

The Ghost of Malinowski Reincarnated

If the Firth-Goodfellow-Herskovits reaction to Malinowskian negativism had a quality of inevitability about it, then some sort of counterreaction was perhaps also inevitable. This counterreaction was mounted originally from outside the ranks of anthropology, though anthropologists were involved in the later stages of its development. It was led by an economic historian named Karl Polanyi, a name now at least as familiar in anthropology as in his own field. The work which had the greatest impact on economic anthropology was *Trade and Market in the Early Empires* (Polanyi *et al.* 1957) which Polanyi co-edited and to which he contributed.

In essence, Polanyi has simply denied, as Malinowski had denied 35 years earlier, the relevance of current economic theory to any but contemporary market economies. His denial was more reasoned in its foundations and broader in its scope than that of Malinowski. Polanyi was only incidentally concerned with "primitive" society; the main focus of his interest in *Trade and Market in the Early Empires* was the classical civilizations of antiquity.

While he acknowledged a debt to Malinowski (Polanyi 1957:252; see also below, p. 129) it is only in respect to a "form of integration" concept which shall be discussed presently. The reincarnate seldom knows much of his earlier life.

The basis of Polanyi's denial of the relevance of conventional or formal economic theory to any but market economies was his discovery of "two meanings of economic." The evidence is that Polanyi considered this an original formulation; in fact, it had been much debated in economics as many as forty years ago and the debate was over by the early thirties (see Robbins 1932 and below, pp. 88–100). Polanyi was aware of the debate—he cites Robbins—but he does not refer to any of the earlier economists whose writings might have supported his position, though Robbins mentions many of them.

Polanyi's two "meanings" are the "substantive" meaning and the "formal" meaning of "economic." The distinction can best be made in his own words:

> The substantive meaning of economic derives from man's dependence for his living upon nature and his fellows. It refers to the interchange with his natural and social environment, in so far as this results in supplying him with the means of material want satisfaction.
>
> The formal meaning of economic derives from the logical character of the means-ends relationship, as apparent in such words as "economical" or "economizing." It refers to a definite situation of choice, namely that between the different uses of means induced by an insufficiency of those means. If we call the rules governing choice of means the logic of rational action, then we may denote this variant of logic, with an improvised term, as formal economics" (Polanyi 1957:243; see also below, pp. 122).

Polanyi then asserts that there is no necessary connection between the two meanings. On the surface, this is true. The substantive meaning, if it has any acceptability at all, does not necessarily imply that man's "interchange with his natural and social environment" involves choice.

Having come this far, Polanyi goes one step further: he asserts that in societies other than market-oriented societies, men are in fact not confronted with making choices in the sense of the "formal" meaning of "economic." However, many critics have pointed out, in one way or another, that this is not a logical question, rather it is an empirical one. Even the most ardent of contemporary economic theoreticians would agree, and some of them specify, that the theory of choice is not applicable to those situations in which choice is not present. But it is quite another thing to *assume* choice away in whole classes of situations.

Polanyi readily concedes that choice-making is a characteristic of market-oriented societies. There is nothing in logic which requires that choice-making be absent from nonmarket-oriented societies. There are elaborate arguments in the writings of Polanyi and some of his followers designed to sustain the proposition that nonmarket economies are not characterized by choice-making. But it must be emphasized once again that this is an empirical, not a logical question.

Polanyi then proceeds to talk about the "forms of integration" of economies. He sees three such forms: reciprocity, redistribution and markets. Once again, he concedes that where markets offer the form of integration, classical economic theory is appropriate. But he denies that the market form is found in any but contemporary "Western" society; he argues that the "reciprocity" form is characteristic of "tribal" societies—in a later work (1966), he substitutes the word "primitive" for "tribal"—while the redistributive form is characteristic of "archaic" societies. In asserting the latter, Polanyi and his associates find it possible to talk of "market-less trade." For most economists, trade and exchange necessarily imply the existence of markets. If there is trade there is a market, whether or not there is an associated marketplace.

One strong element in the Polanyi position—and this has undoubtedly accounted for some of his appeal to some anthropologists—is a strong ideological antipathy to modern market systems. His general position was first developed at length in *The Great Transformation* (1944) and was given trenchant exposition in "Our Obsolete Market Mentality" (1947). Polanyi argued in effect that the invention of market organization, which he sees as having come relatively late in Western society, corrupted society in that it has removed the economic sphere from its integration with the rest of society. The persistent denial of choice or the existence of the market (hence "market-less trade") in earlier societies cannot be unrelated to this ideological bias and to what Cook (1966; see also below, pp. 208–288) calls the essential romanticism of this point of view. Given the entire structure of Polanyi's system of thought, it is necessary to define markets out of existence in earlier societies in order to preserve the perception of earlier societies as in some sense ideal.

Polanyi's work had only minor and scattered impact upon anthropology until 1961 when George Dalton published a paper which attempted to introduce the Polanyian view into a specifically anthropological context. The paper was largely a theoretical and philosophical argument, with little reference to the ethnological literature. The appearance of Dalton's paper (reprinted below, pp. 143–167) produced a rash of equally theoretical critiques on the whole point of view in anthropological literature.

The first of these critiques was by Robbins Burling in his "Maximization

Theory and the Study of Economic Anthropology" (Burling 1962; see also below, pp. 168–187). Burling accepted the basic distinction between the substantive and the formal meanings of "economic" but then went on to argue that maximizing behavior is in fact a universal phenomenon. He argues from this that maximization theory is universally applicable.

Burling's article was followed shortly by one by LeClair (1962; see also below, pp. 187–207). LeClair refuses to accept, as Burling does, the validity of the formal-substantive distinction and argues that scarcity and choice are probably universal, and therefore formal economics is probably universally applicable. He then attempts to move "formalist" economic anthropology beyond the "applicationist" or analogic level by suggesting that there is probably a general theory of economic structure and process. If there is, contemporary economic theory as known to the economist represents a special case of this general theory. Other special theories need to be worked out to fit other institutional settings; once some of these have been done, the outlines of a general theory might become clear. LeClair then goes on to suggest a program for the analysis of different economic systems which would permit such systematic cross-cultural comparisons.

In a sense, LeClair's proposals represent an effort to preserve the best of both worlds. They recognize that there are differences among societies in their economic structures and processes—no one denies this of course, but the fact becomes dominant for such as Malinowski and the substantivists—but insist on drawing upon what is most useful in formal economics as it has been developed for contemporary market-oriented societies.

Some Other Issues, Briefly Mentioned

Although the core of the present theoretical controversy in economic anthropology turns on the relevance of formal economic theory to nonmarket situations, there are other related issues which pop up from time to time. Some of them have already been mentioned. There is induction versus deduction. Anthropology has typically been inductive, while formal economics is essentially deductive. In general, the substantivists tend to be inductively oriented, which accounts for some of the appeal of the doctrine for anthropologists. Two papers in this volume, those by Hagen and Krupp (see pp. 100–109 and 243–256), attempt to put the canons of deductive procedure into proper perspective. Moreover, Krupp performs an additional useful service in attempting to clarify the issues in a current debate concerning the character of equilibrium models, which are prominent features of formal economic models.

The distinction employed by Krupp is between functionalist and mechanistic equilibrium models. In a mechanistic model, the equilibrium point can be any point determined by the system and by the parameters governing it; in a functional model, the equilibrium point is determined by some guiding principle— in particular, a rule stating that the system is designed to perpetuate itself. Mechanistic models have been characteristic of formal economics; functional models at varying levels of sophistication have been characteristic in certain branches of sociology and anthropology.

There is, as we have pointed out from time to time, the issue of the degree to which the economy can be considered in isolation from the rest of the society or culture. Functionalists, and perhaps substantivists as well, would tend to deny the isolability of the economy, even for purposes of analysis. At its extreme, such a view might hold that the economy was in some sense subordinate to society or culture. In one sense, it must necessarily be subordinate, as every aspect of society or culture is, in a sense, subordinate to every other; in another sense, the idea is simply without meaning.

There are some additional issues in economic anthropology which have not as yet been mentioned here, and which will not be touched upon in the selections which follow. We have not been able to include among the selections, for example, any part of the voluminous debate over the concept of economic surplus. Nor have we been able to include a full exposition of the idea of "multi-centric economies" which has been most fully developed by Paul Bohannan (1963:246–265).

Nowhere in the selections which follow is there any mention of the most significant development in economic theory in the past thirty-five years: the development of "Keynesian" economics. This is neither oversight nor deliberate exclusion. Economic anthropologists—using that term broadly—simply have not paid much attention to it. There is virtually no mention of Keynesian theory in the anthropological literature, with the single notable exception of Salisbury's ingenious use of it in his study of a changing New Guinea culture (1962).

Nor, finally, is there any discussion of money as such, though some of the papers skirt around some of the questions involved.

These and other neglected topics will be briefly considered in the closing section of this book.

part two

THEORETICAL PAPERS

· section I
THE BEGINNING: MALINOWSKI

1 MALINOWSKI ON THE *KULA*
Bronislaw Malinowski

The coastal populations of the South Sea Islands, with very few exceptions, are, or were before their extinction, expert navigators and traders. Several of them had evolved excellent types of large sea-going canoes, and used to embark in them on distant trade expeditions or raids of war and conquest. The Papuo-Melanesians, who inhabit the coast and the outlying islands of New Guinea, are no exception to this rule. In general they are daring sailors, industrious manufacturers, and keen traders. The manufacturing centres of important articles, such as pottery, stone implements, canoes, fine baskets, valued ornaments, are localised in several places, according to the skill of the inhabitants, their inherited tribal tradition, and special facilities offered by the district; thence they are traded over wide areas, sometimes travelling more than hundreds of miles.

Definite forms of exchange along definite trade routes are to be found established between the various tribes. A most remarkable form of intertribal trade is that obtaining between the Motu of Port Moresby and the tribes of the Papuan Gulf. The Motu sail for hundreds of miles in heavy, unwieldy canoes, called *lakatoi*, which are provided with the characteristic crab-claw sails. They bring pottery and shell ornaments, in olden days, stone blades, to Gulf Papuans, from whom they obtain in exchange sago and the heavy dug-outs, which are used afterwards by the Motu for the construction of their *lakatoi* canoes.[1]

Further East, on the South coast, there lives the industrious, sea-faring population of the Mailu, who link the East End of New Guinea with the central coast tribes by means of annual trading expeditions.[2] Finally, the natives of the islands and archipelagoes, scattered around the East End, are in constant trading relations with one another. We possess in Professor Seligman's book an excellent

From the book Argonauts of the Western Pacific *by Bronislaw Malinowski. Published by E. P. Dutton & Co., Inc. and reprinted with their permission and with the permission of Routledge and Kegan Paul Ltd. (Pagination given below from the Dutton paperback edition, 1961.)*

[1] The *hiri*, as these expeditions are called in Motuan, have been described with a great wealth of detail and clearness of outline by Captain F. Barton, in Seligman, 1910.

[2] "The Mailu" (Malinowski 1915:612–629).

description of the subject, especially of the nearer trades routes between the various islands inhabited by the Southern Massim.[3] There exists, however, another, a very extensive and highly complex trading system, embracing with its ramifications, not only the islands near the East End, but also the Louisiades, Woodlark Island, the Trobriand Archipelago, and the d'Entrecasteaux group; it penetrates into the mainland of New Guinea, and exerts an indirect influence over several outlying districts, such as Rossel [sic] Island, and some parts of the Northern and Southern coast of New Guinea. This trading system, the Kula, is the subject I am setting out to describe in this volume, and it will be seen that it is an economic phenomenon of considerable theoretical importance. It looms paramount in the tribal life of those natives who live within its circuit, and its importance is fully realised by the tribesmen themselves, whose ideas, ambitions, desires and vanities are very much bound up with the Kula.

(pp. 1–2)

Half of the natives' working life is spent in the garden, and around it centres perhaps more than half of his interests and ambitions. And here we must pause and make an attempt to understand his attitude in this matter, as it is typical of the way in which he goes about all his work. If we remain under the delusion that the native is a happy-go-lucky, lazy child of nature, who shuns as far as possible all labour and effort, waiting till the ripe fruits, so bountifully supplied by generous tropical Nature, fall into his mouth, we shall not be able to understand in the least his aims and motives in carrying out the Kula or any other enterprise. On the contrary, the truth is that the native can and, under circumstances, does work hard, and work systematically, with endurance and purpose, nor does he wait till he is pressed to work by his immediate needs.

In gardening, for instance, the natives produce much more than they actually require, and in any average year they harvest perhaps twice as much as they can eat. Nowadays, this surplus is exported by Europeans to feed plantation hands in other parts of New Guinea; in olden days it was simply allowed to rot. Again, they produce this surplus in a manner which entails much more work than is strictly necessary for obtaining the crops. Much time and labour is given up to æsthetic purposes, to making the gardens tidy, clean, cleared of all debris; to building fine, solid fences, to providing specially strong and big yam-poles. All these things are to some extent required for the growth of the plant; but there can be no doubt that the natives push their conscientiousness far beyond the limit of the purely necessary. The non-utilitarian element in their garden work is still more clearly perceptible in the various tasks which they carry out entirely for the sake of ornamentation, in connection with magical ceremonies, and in obedience to tribal usage. Thus, after the ground has been scrupulously cleared and is ready for planting, the natives divide each garden plot into small squares, each a few yards in length and width, and this is done only in obedience to usage, in order to make the gardens look neat. No self-respecting man would

[3] *Op. cit.*, Chap. xl.

dream of omitting to do this. Again, in especially well trimmed gardens, long horizontal poles are tied to the yam supports in order to embellish them. Another, and perhaps the most interesting example of non-utilitarian work is afforded by the big, prismatic erections called *kamkokola*, which serve ornamental and magical purposes, but have nothing to do with the growth of plants.

Among the forces and beliefs which bear upon and regulate garden work, perhaps magic is the most important. It is a department of its own, and the garden magician, next to the chief and the sorcerer, is the most important personage of the village. The position is hereditary, and, in each village, a special system of magic is handed on in the female line from one generation to another. I have called it a *system*, because the magician has to perform a series of rites and spells over the garden, which run parallel with the labour, and which, in fact, initiate each stage of the work and each new development of the plant life. Even before any gardening is begun at all, the magician has to consecrate the site with a big ceremonial performance in which all the men of the village take part. This ceremony officially opens the season's gardening, and only after it is performed do the villagers begin to cut the scrub on their plots. Then, in a series of rites, the magician inaugurates successively all the various stages which follow one another—the burning of the scrub, the clearing, the planting, the weeding and the harvesting. Also, in another series of rites and spells, he magically assists the plant in sprouting, in budding, in bursting into leaf, in climbing, in forming the rich garlands of foliage, and in producing the edible tubers.

The garden magician, according to native ideas, thus controls both the work of man and the forces of Nature. He also acts directly as supervisor of gardening, sees to it that people do not skimp their work, or lag behind with it. Thus magic is a systematising, regulating, and controlling influence in garden work. The magician, in carrying out the rites, sets the pace, compels people to apply themselves to certain tasks, and to accomplish them properly and in time. Incidentally, magic also imposes on the tribe a good deal of extra work, of apparently unnecessary, hampering taboos and regulations. In the long run, however, there is no doubt that by its influence in ordering, systematising and regulating work, magic is economically invaluable for the natives.[4]

Another notion which must be exploded, once and for ever, is that of the Primitive Economic Man of some current economic text books. This fanciful, dummy creature, who has been very tenacious of existence in popular and semi-popular economic literature, and whose shadow haunts even the minds of competent anthropologists, blighting their outlook with a preconceived idea, is an imaginary, primitive man, or savage, prompted in all his actions by a rationalistic conception of self-interest, and achieving his aims directly and with the minimum of effort. Even *one* well established instance should show how preposterous is this assumption that man, and especially man on a low level of culture, should be

---

[4] I have dealt with the subject of garden work in the Trobriands and with its economic importance more fully in an article entitled "The Primitive Economics of the Trobriand Islanders," Malinowski, 1921.

actuated by pure economic motives of enlightened self-interest. The primitive Trobriander furnishes us with such an instance, contradicting this fallacious theory. He works prompted by motives of a highly complex, social and traditional nature, and towards aims which are certainly not directed towards the satisfaction of present wants, or to the direct achievement of utilitarian purposes. Thus, in the first place, as we have seen, work is not carried out on the principle of the least effort. On the contrary, much time and energy is spent on wholly unnecessary effort, that is, from a utilitarian point of view. Again, work and effort, instead of being merely a means to an end, are, in a way an end in themselves. A good garden worker in the Trobriands derives a direct prestige from the amount of labour he can do, and the size of garden he can till. The title *tokwaybagula*, which means "good" or "efficient gardener," is bestowed with discrimination, and borne with pride. Several of my friends, renowned as *tokwaybagula*, would boast to me how long they worked, how much ground they tilled, and would compare their efforts with those of less efficient men. When the labour, some of which is done communally, is being actually carried out, a good deal of competition goes on. Men vie with one another in their speed, in their thoroughness, and in the weights they can lift, when bringing big poles to the garden, or in carrying away the harvested yams.

The most important point about this is, however, that all, or almost all the fruits of his work, and certainly any surplus which he can achieve by extra effort, goes not to the man himself, but to his relatives-in-law. Without entering into details of the system of the apportionment of the harvest, of which the sociology is rather complex and would require a preliminary account of the Trobriand kinship system and kinship ideas, it may be said that about three quarters of a man's crops go partly as tribute to the chief, partly as his due to his sister's (or mother's) husband and family.

But although he thus derives practically no personal benefit in the utilitarian sense from his harvest, the gardener receives much praise and renown from its size and quality, and that in a direct and circumstantial manner. For all the crops, after being harvested, are displayed for some time afterwards in the gardens, piled up in neat, conical heaps under small shelters made of yam vine. Each man's harvest is thus exhibited for criticism in his own plot, and parties of natives walk about from garden to garden, admiring, comparing and praising the best results. The importance of the food display can be gauged by the fact that, in olden days, when the chief's power was much more considerable than now, it was dangerous for a man who was not either of high rank himself, or working for such a one, to show crops which might compare too favourably with those of the chief.

In years when the harvest promises to be plentiful, the chief will proclaim a *kayasa* harvest, that is to say, ceremonial, competitive display of food, and then the straining for good results and the interest taken in them are still higher. We shall meet later on with ceremonial enterprises of the *kayasa* type, and find that they play a considerable part in the Kula. All this shows how entirely the real native of flesh and bone differs from the shadowy Primitive Economic Man, on whose imaginary behaviour many of the scholastic deductions of abstract economics are based.[5] The Trobriander works in a roundabout way, to a large extent for the sake of the work itself, and puts a great deal of æsthetic polish on the arrangement and general appearance of his garden. He is not guided primarily by the desire to satisfy his wants, but by a very complex set of traditional forces, duties and obligations, beliefs in magic, social ambitions and vanities. He wants, if he is a *man*, to achieve social distinction as a *good gardener* and a good worker in general.

I have dwelt at this length upon these points concerning the motives and aims of the Trobrianders in their garden work, because, in the chapters that follow, we shall be studying economic activities, and the reader will grasp the attitude of the natives best if he has it illustrated to him by various examples. All that has been said in this matter about the Trobrianders applies also to the neighbouring tribes.

(pp. 58–62)

Having thus described the scene, and the actors, let us now proceed to the performance. The Kula is a form of exchange, of extensive, inter-tribal character; it is carried on by communities inhabiting a wide ring of islands, which form a closed circuit. . . . Along this route, articles of two kinds, and these two kinds only, are constantly travelling in opposite directions. In the direction of the hands of a clock, moves constantly one of these kinds—long necklaces of red shell, called *soulava*. In the opposite direction moves the other kind—bracelets of white shell called *mwali*. Each of these articles, as it travels in its own direction on the closed circuit, meets on its way articles of the other class, and is constantly being exchanged for them. Every movement of the Kula articles, every detail of the transactions is fixed and regulated by a set of traditional rules and conventions, and some acts of the Kula are accompanied by an elaborate magical ritual and public ceremonies.

On every island and in every village, a more or less limited number of men take part in the Kula—that is to say, receive the goods, hold them for a short time, and then pass them on. Therefore every man who is in the Kula, periodically though not regularly, receives one or several *mwali* (arm-shells), or a *soulava* (necklace of red shell discs), and then has to hand it on to one of his partners, from whom he receives the opposite commodity in exchange. Thus no man ever keeps any of the articles for any length of time in his possession. One transaction does not finish the Kula relationship, the rule being "once in the Kula, always

[5] This does not mean that the general economic conclusions are wrong. The economic nature of Man is as a rule illustrated on imaginary savages for didactic purposes only, and the conclusions of the authors are in reality based on their study of the facts of developed economics. But, nevertheless, quite apart from the fact that pedagogically it is a wrong principle to make matters look more simple by introducing a falsehood, it is the Ethnographer's duty and right to protest against the introduction from outside of false facts into his own field of study.

in the Kula," and a partnership between two men is a permanent and lifelong affair. Again, any given *mwali* or *soulava* may always be found travelling and changing hands, and there is no question of its ever settling down, so that the principle "once in the Kula, always in the Kula" applies also to the valuables themselves.

The ceremonial exchange of the two articles is the main, the fundamental aspect of the Kula. But associated with it, and done under its cover, we find a great number of secondary activities and features. Thus, side by side with the ritual exchange of arm-shells and necklaces, the natives carry on ordinary trade, bartering from one island to another a great number of utilities, often unprocurable in the district to which they are imported, and indispensable there. Further, there are other activities, preliminary to the Kula, or associated with it, such as the building of sea-going canoes for the expeditions, certain big forms of mortuary ceremonies, and preparatory taboos.

The Kula is thus an extremely big and complex institution, both in its geographical extent, and in the manifoldness of its component pursuits. It welds together a considerable number of tribes, and it embraces a vast complex of activities, inter-connected, and playing into one another, so as to form one organic whole.

Yet it must be remembered that what appears to us an extensive, complicated, and yet well ordered institution is the outcome of ever so many doings and pursuits, carried on by savages, who have no laws or aims or charters definitely laid down. They have no knowledge of the *total outline* of any of their social structure. They know their own motives, know the purpose of individual actions and the rules which apply to them, but how, out of these, the whole collective institution shapes, this is beyond their mental range. Not even the most intelligent native has any clear idea of the Kula as a big, organised social construction, still less of its sociological function and implications. If you were to ask him what the Kula is, he would answer by giving a few details, most likely by giving his personal experiences and subjective views on the Kula, but nothing approaching the definition just given here. Not even a partial coherent account could be obtained. For the integral picture does not exist in his mind; he is in it, and cannot see the whole from the outside.

The integration of all the details observed, the achievement of a sociological synthesis of all the various, relevant symptoms, is the task of the Ethnographer. First of all, he has to find out that certain activities, which at first sight might appear incoherent and not correlated, have a meaning. He then has to find out what is constant and relevant in these activities, and what accidental and inessential, that is, to find out the laws and rules of all the transactions. Again, the Ethnographer has to *construct* the picture of the big institution, very much as the physicist constructs his theory from the experimental data, which always have been within reach of everybody, but which needed a consistent interpretation. I have touched on this point of method in the Introduction, but I have repeated it here, as it is necessary to grasp it clearly in order not to lose the right perspective of conditions as they really exist among the natives.

In giving the above abstract and concise definition, I had to reverse the order of research, as this is done in ethnographic field-work, where the most generalised inferences are obtained as the result of long inquiries and laborious inductions. The general definition of the Kula will serve as a sort of plan or diagram in our further concrete and detailed descriptions. And this is the more necessary as the Kula is concerned with the exchange of wealth and utilities, and therefore it is an economic institution, and there is no other aspect of primitive life where our knowledge is more scanty and our understanding more superficial than in Economics. Hence misconception is rampant, and it is necessary to clear the ground when approaching any economic subject.

Thus in the Introduction we called the Kula a "form of trade," and we ranged it alongside other systems of barter. This is quite correct, if we give the word *"trade"* a sufficiently wide interpretation, and mean by it any exchange of goods. But the word "trade" is used in current Ethnography and economic literature with so many different implications that a whole lot of misleading, preconceived ideas have to be brushed aside in order to grasp the facts correctly. Thus the *a priori* current notion of primitive trade would be that of an exchange of dispensable or useful articles, done without much ceremony or regulation, under stress of dearth or need, in spasmodic, irregular intervals—and this done either by direct barter, everyone looking out sharply not to be done out of his due, or, if the savages were too timid and distrustful to face one another, by some customary arrangement, securing by means of heavy penalties compliance in the obligations incurred or imposed.[6] Waiving for the present the question how far this conception is valid or not in general—in my opinion it is quite misleading—we have to realise clearly that the Kula contradicts in almost every point the above definition of "savage trade." It shows us primitive exchange in an entirely different light.

The Kula is not a surreptitious and precarious form of exchange. It is, quite

[6] By "current view," I mean such as is to be found in text-books and in passing remarks, scattered through economic and ethnological literature. As a matter of fact, Economics is a subject very seldom touched upon either in theoretical works on Ethnology, or in accounts of field-work. I have enlarged on this deficiency in the article on "Primitive Economics," Malinowski, 1921.

The best analysis of the problem of savage economy is to be found, in spite of its many shortcomings, in K. Bücher's "Industrial Evolution," English Translation, 1901. On primitive trade, however, his views are inadequate. In accordance with his general view that savages have no national economy, he maintains that any spread of goods among natives is achieved by non-economic means, such as robbery, tributes and gifts. The information contained in the present volume is incompatible with Bücher's views, nor could he have maintained them had he been acquainted with Barton's description of the Hiri (in Seligman, 1910).

A summary of the research done on Primitive Economics, showing incidentally, how little real, sound work has been accomplished, will be found in Pater W. Kopper, 1915–16:611–651, and 971–1079. The article is very useful, where the author summarises the views of others.

on the contrary, rooted in myth, backed by traditional law, and surrounded with magical rites. All its main transactions are public and ceremonial, and carried out according to definite rules. It is not done on the spur of the moment, but happens periodically, at dates settled in advance, and it is carried on along definite trade routes, which must lead to fixed trysting places. Sociologically, though transacted between tribes differing in language, culture, and probably even in race, it is based on a fixed and permanent status, on a partnership which binds into couples some thousands of individuals. This partnership is a lifelong relationship, it implies various mutual duties and privileges, and constitutes a type of inter-tribal relationship on an enormous scale. As to the economic mechanism of the transactions, this is based on a specific form of credit, which implies a high degree of mutual trust and commercial honour—and this refers also to the subsidiary, minor trade, which accompanies the Kula proper. Finally, the Kula is not done under stress of any need, since its main aim is to exchange articles which are of no practical use.

From the concise definition of Kula given at the beginning of this chapter, we see that in its final essence, divested of all trappings and accessories, it is a very simple affair, which at first sight might even appear tame and unromantic. After all, it only consists of an exchange, interminably repeated, of two articles, intended for ornamentation, but not even used for that to any extent. Yet this simple action—this passing from hand to hand of two meaningless and quite useless objects—has somehow succeeded in becoming the foundation of a big inter-tribal institution, in being associated with ever so many other activities. Myth, magic and tradition have built up around it definite ritual and ceremonial forms, have given it a halo of romance and value in the minds of the natives, have indeed created a passion in their hearts for this simple exchange.

The definition of the Kula must now be amplified, and we must describe one after the other its fundamental characteristics and main rules, so that it may be clearly grasped by what mechanism the mere exchange of two articles results in an institution so vast, complex, and deeply rooted.

First of all a few words must be said about the two principle objects of exchange, the arm-shells (*mwali*) and the necklaces (*soulava*).

(pp. 81–86)

. . . These objects are not owned in order to be used; the privilege of decorating oneself with them is not the real aim of possession.

Indeed—and this is more significant—by far the greater number of the arm-shells, easily ninety per cent., are of too small a size to be worn even by young boys and girls. A few are so big and valuable that they would not be worn at all, except once in a decade by a very important man on a very festive day. Though all the shell-strings can be worn, some of them are again considered too valuable, and are cumbersome for frequent use, and would be worn on very exceptional occasions only.

This negative description leaves us with the questions: why, then, are these objects valued, what purpose do they serve? The full answer to this question will emerge out of the whole story contained in the following chapters, but an approximate idea must be given at once. As it is always better to approach the unknown through the known, let us consider for a moment whether among ourselves we have not some type of objects which play a similar rôle and which are used and possessed in the same manner. When, after a six years' absence in the South Seas and Australia, I returned to Europe and did my first bit of sightseeing in Edinburgh Castle, I was shown the Crown Jewels. The keeper told many stories of how they were worn by this or that king or queen on such and such occasion, of how some of them had been taken over to London, to the great and just indignation of the whole Scottish nation, how they were restored, and how now everyone can be pleased, since they are safe under lock and key, and no one can touch them. As I was looking at them and thinking how ugly, useless, ungainly, even tawdry they were, I had the feeling that something similar had been told to me of late, and that I had seen many other objects of this sort, which made a similar impression on me.

And then arose before me the vision of a native village on coral soil, and a small, rickety platform temporarily erected under a pandanus thatch, surrounded by a number of brown, naked men, and one of them showing me long, thin red strings, and big, white, worn-out objects, clumsy to sight and greasy to touch. With reverence he also would name them, and tell their history, and by whom and when they were worn, and how they changed hands, and how their temporary possession was a great sign of the importance and glory of the village. The analogy between the European and the Trobriand *vaygu'a* (valuables) must be delimited with more precision. The Crown Jewels, in fact, any heirlooms too valuable and too cumbersome to be worn, represent the same type as *vaygu'a* in that they are merely possessed for the sake of possession itself, and the ownership of them with the ensuing renown is the main source of their value. Also both heirlooms and *vaygu'a* are cherished because of the historical sentiment which surrounds them. However ugly, useless, and—according to current standards—valueless an object may be, if it has figured in historical scenes and passed through the hands of historic persons, and is therefore an unfailing vehicle of important sentimental associations, it cannot but be precious to us. This historic sentimentalism, which indeed has a large share in our general interest in studies of past events, exists also in the South Seas. Every really good Kula article has its individual name, round each there is a sort of history and romance in the traditions of the natives. Crown Jewels or heirlooms are insignia of rank and symbols of wealth respectively, and in olden days with us, and in New Guinea up till a few years ago, both rank and wealth went together. The main point of difference is that the Kula goods are only in possession for a time, whereas the European treasure must be permanently owned in order to have full value.

Taking a broader, ethnological view of the question, we may class the Kula valuables among the many "ceremonial" objects of wealth; enormous, carved and decorated weapons, stone implements, articles of domestic and industrial nature, too well decorated and too clumsy for use. Such things are usually called "ceremonial," but this word seems to cover a great number of meanings and much that has no meaning at all. In fact, very often, especially on museum labels, an article is called "ceremonial" simply because nothing is known about its uses and general nature. Speaking only about museum exhibits from New Guinea, I can say that many so-called ceremonial objects are nothing but simply over-grown objects of use, which preciousness of material and amount of labour expended have transformed into reservoirs of condensed economic value. Again, others are used on festive occasions, but play no part whatever in rites and ceremonies, and serve for decoration only, and these might be called *objects of parade.* Finally, a number of these articles function actually as instruments of a magical or religious rite, and belong to the intrinsic apparatus of a cere-mony. Such and such only could be correctly called *ceremonial.* During the *So'i* feasts among the Southern Massim, women carrying polished axe blades in fine carved handles, accompany with a rhythmic step to the beat of drums, the entry of the pigs and mango saplings into the village. As this is part of the ceremony and the axes are an indispensable accessory, their use in this case can be legitimately called "ceremonial." Again, in certain magical ceremonies in the Trobriands, the *towosi* (garden magician) has to carry a mounted axe blade on his shoulders, and with it he delivers a ritual blow at a *kankokola* structure.

The *vaygu'a*—the Kula valuables—in one of their aspects are overgrown objects of use. They are also, however, *ceremonial* objects in the narrow and correct sense of the word. This will become clear after perusal of the following pages, and to this point we shall return in the last chapter.

It must be kept in mind that here we are trying to obtain a clear and vivid idea of what the Kula valuables are to the natives, and not to give a detailed and circumstantial description of them, nor to define them with precision. The comparison with the European heirlooms or Crown Jewels was given in order to show that this type of ownership is not entirely a fantastic South Sea custom, untranslatable into our ideas. For—and this is a point I want to stress—the comparison I have made is not based on purely external, superficial similarity. The psychological and sociological forces at work are the same, it is really the same mental attitude which makes us value our heirlooms, and makes the natives in New Guinea value their *vaygu'a.*

(pp. 88–91)

The main principle underlying the regulations of actual exchange is that the Kula consists in the bestowing of a ceremonial gift, which has to be repaid by an equivalent counter-gift after a lapse of time, be it a few hours or even minutes, though sometimes as much as a year or more may elapse between payments.[7]

---

[7] In order not to be guilty of inconsistency in using loosely the word "ceremonial" I shall define it briefly. I shall call an action ceremonial, if it is (1) public; (2) carried on under observance of definite formalities; (3) if it has sociological, religious, or magical import, and carries with it obligations.

But it can never be exchanged from hand to hand, with the equivalence between the two objects discussed, bargained about and computed. The decorum of the Kula transaction is strictly kept, and highly valued. The natives sharply distinguish it from barter, which they practise extensively, of which they have a clear idea, and for which they have a settled term—in Kiriwinian: *gimwali*. Often, when criticising an incorrect, too hasty, or indecorous procedure of Kula, they will say: "He conducts his Kula as if it were *gimwali*."

The second very important principle is that the equivalence of the counter-gift is left to the giver, and it cannot be enforced by any kind of coercion. A partner who has received a Kula gift is expected to give back fair and full value, that is, to give as good an arm-shell as the necklace he receives, or vice versa. Again, a very fine article must be replaced by one of equivalent value, and not by several minor ones, though intermediate gifts may be given to mark time before the real repayment takes place.

If the article given as counter-gift is not equivalent, the recipient will be disappointed and angry, but he has no direct means of redress, no means of coercing his partner, or of putting an end to the whole transaction. What then are the forces at work which keep the partners to the terms of the bargain? Here we come up against a very important feature of the native's mental attitude towards wealth and value. The great misconception of attributing to the savage a pure economic nature, might lead us to reason incorrectly thus: "The passion of acquiring, the loathing to lose or give away, is the fundamental and most primitive element in man's attitude to wealth. In primitive man, this primitive characteristic will appear in its simplest and purest form. *Grab and never let go* will be the guiding principle of his life."[8] The fundamental error in this reasoning is that it assumes that "primitive man," as represented by the present-day savage, lives, at least in economic matters, untrammelled by conventions and social restrictions. Quite the reverse is the case. Although, like every human being, the Kula native loves to possess and therefore desires to acquire and dreads to lose, the social code of rules, with regard to give and take by far overrides his natural acquisitive tendency.

This social code, such as we find it among the natives of the Kula is, however, far from weakening the natural desirability of possession; on the contrary, it lays down that to possess is to be great, and that wealth is the indispensable appanage of social rank and attribute of personal virtue. But the important point is that with them to possess is to give—and here the natives differ from us notably. A man who owns a thing is naturally expected to share it, to distribute it, to be its trustee and dispenser. And the higher the rank the greater the obligation. A chief will naturally be expected to give food to any stranger, visitor, even loiterer from another end of the village. He will be expected to

[8] This is not a fanciful construction of what an erroneous opinion might be, for I could give actual examples proving that such opinions have been set forth, but as I am not giving here a criticism of existing theories of Primitive Economics, I do not want to overload this chapter with quotations.

share any of the betel-nut or tobacco he has about him. So that a man of rank will have to hide away any surplus of these articles which he wants to preserve for his further use. In the Eastern end of New Guinea a type of large basket, with three layers, manufactured in the Trobriands, was specially popular among people of consequence, because one could hide away one's small treasures in the lower compartments. Thus the main symptom of being powerful is to be wealthy, and of wealth is to be generous. Meanness, indeed, is the most despised vice, and the only thing about which the natives have strong moral views, while generosity is the essence of goodness.

This moral injunction and ensuing habit of generosity, superficially observed and misinterpreted, is responsible for another wide-spread misconception, that of the *primitive communism of savages*. This, quite as much as the diametrically opposed figment of the acquisitive and ruthlessly tenacious native, is definitely erroneous, and this will be seen with sufficient clearness in the following chapters.

(pp. 95–97)

The Kula—it becomes, I hope, more and more clear—is a big, complicated institution, insignificant though its nucleus might appear. To the natives, it represents one of the most vital interests in life, and as such it has a ceremonial character and is surrounded by magic. We can well imagine that articles of wealth might pass from hand to hand without ceremony or ritual, but in the Kula they never do. Even when at times only small parties in one or two canoes sail overseas and bring back *vaygu'a*, certain taboos are observed, and a customary course is taken in departing, in sailing, and in arriving; even the smallest expedition in one canoe is a tribal event of some importance, known and spoken of over the whole district. But the characteristic expedition is one in which a considerable number of canoes take part, organised in a certain manner, and forming one body. Feasts, distributions of food, and other public ceremonies are held, there is one leader and master of the expedition, and various rules are adhered to, in addition to the ordinary Kula taboos and observances.

(pp. 101–102)

Before we proceed to the next stage, we must pause in following the events of a Kula expedition, and consider one or two points of more general importance. I have touched in the narrative, but not dwelt upon, certain problems of the sociology of work. At the outset of the preceding chapter it was mentioned that canoe-building requires a definite organisation of work, and in fact we saw that in the course of construction, various kinds of labour were employed, and more especially towards the end, much use was made of communal labour. Again, we saw that during the launching ceremony payment was given by the owner to the expert and his helpers. These two points therefore, the organisation of labour and communal labour in particular, and the system of payment for experts' work must be here developed.

ORGANISATION OF LABOUR. First of all, it is important to realise that a Kiriwinian is capable of working well, efficiently and in a continuous manner. But he must work under an effective incentive: he must be prompted by some duty imposed by tribal standards, or he must be lured by ambitions and values also dictated by custom and tradition. Gain, such as is often the stimulus for work in more civilised communities, never acts as an impulse to work under the original native conditions. It succeeds very badly, therefore, when a white man tries to use this incentive to make a native work.

This is the reason why the traditional view of the lazy and indolent native is not only a constant refrain of the average white settler, but finds its way into good books of travel, and even serious ethnographic records. With us, labour is, or was till fairly recently, a commodity sold as any other, in the open market. A man accustomed to think in terms of current economic theory will naturally apply the conceptions of supply and demand to labor, and he applies them therefore to native labour. The untrained person does the same, though in less sophisticated terms, and as they see that the native will not work well for the white man, even if tempted by considerable payment and treated fairly well, they conclude that his capacity for labour is very small. This error is due to the same cause which lies at the bottom of all our misconceptions about people of different cultures. If you remove a man from his social milieu, you *eo ipso* deprive him of almost all his stimuli to moral steadfastness and economic efficiency and even of interest in life. If then you measure him by moral, legal or economic standards, also essentially foreign to him, you cannot but obtain a caricature in your estimate.

But the natives are not only capable of energetic, continuous and skilful work; their social conditions also make it possible for them to employ organised labour. At the beginning of Chapter IV, the sociology of canoe-building was given in out-line, and now, after the details of its successive stages have been filled in, it is possible to confirm what has been said there, and draw some conclusions as to this organisation of labour. And first, as we are using this expression so often, I must insist again on the fact that the natives are capable of it, and that this contention is not a truism, as the following considerations should show. The just mentioned view of the lazy, individualistic and selfish savage, who lives on the bounties of nature as they fall ripe and ready for him, implicitly precludes the possibility of his doing effective work, *integrated into an organised effort by social forces*. Again, the view, almost universally accepted by specialists, is that the lowest savages are in the pre-economic stage of individualistic search for food, whereas the more developed ones, such as the Trobrianders, for instance, live at the stage of isolated household economy. This view also ignores, when it does not deny explicitly, the possibility of socially organised labour.

The view generally held is that, in native communities each individual works for himself, or members of a household work so as to provide each family with the necessities of life. Of course, a canoe, even a *masawa*, could obviously be made by the members of a household, though with less efficiency and in a longer time. So that there is *a priori* nothing to foretell whether organised labour, or the unaided efforts of an individual or a small group of people should be used in the work. As a matter of fact, we have seen in canoe-building a number of men engaged in performing each a definite and difficult task, though united to one purpose. The tasks were differentiated in their sociological setting; some of the workers were actually to own the canoe; others belonged to a different community, and did it only as an act of service to the chief. Some worked in order to derive direct benefit from the use of the canoe, others were to be paid. We saw also that the work of felling, of scooping, of decorating, would in some cases be performed by various men, or it might be performed by one only. Certainly the minute tasks of lashing, caulking and painting, as well as sail-making, were done by communal labour as opposed to individual. And all these different tasks were directed towards one aim: the providing the chief or headman with the title of ownership of a canoe, and his whole community with its use.

It is clear that this differentiation of tasks, co-ordinated to a general purpose, requires a well developed social apparatus to back it up, and that on the other hand, this social mechanism must be associated and permeated with economic elements. There must be a chief, regarded as representative of a group; he must have certain formal rights and privileges, and a certain amount of authority, and also he must dispose of part of the wealth of the community. There must also be a man or men with knowledge sufficient to direct and co-ordinate the technical operations. All this is obvious. But it must be clearly set forth that the real force which binds all the people and ties them down in their tasks is obedience to custom, to tradition.

(pp. 156–158)

Here, however, it seems necessary to make another digression from the straight narrative of the Kula, and give an outline of the various forms of trade and exchange as we find them in the Trobriands. Indeed, the main theme of this volume is the Kula, a form of exchange, and I would be untrue to my chief principle of method, were I to give the description of one form of exchange torn out of its most intimate context; that is, were I to give an account of the Kula without giving at least a general outline of the forms of Kiriwinian payments and gifts and barter.

In Chapter II,[9] speaking of some features of Trobriand tribal life, I was led to criticise the current views of primitive economic man. They depict him as a being indolent, independent, happy-go-lucky, yet at the same time governed exclusively by strictly rational and utilitarian motives, and logical and consistent in his behaviour. In this chapter again, in Division II, I pointed out another fallacy implied in this conception, a fallacy which declares that a savage is capable only of very simple, unorganised and unsystematic forms of labour. Another error more or less explicitly expressed in all writings on primitive eco-

[9] See above, pp. 18–21, 27, eds.

nomics, is that the natives possess only rudimentary forms of trade and exchange; that these forms play no essential part in the tribal life, are carried on only spasmodically and at rare intervals, and as necessity dictates.

Whether we have to deal with the wide-spread fallacy of the primitive Golden Age, characterised mainly by the absence of any distinction between *mine* and *thine*; or whether we take the more sophisticated view, which postulates stages of individual search for food, and of isolated household catering; or if we consider for the moment the numerous theories which see nothing in primitive economics but simple pursuits for the maintenance of existence—in none of these can we find reflected even a hint of the real state of affairs as found in the Trobriands; namely, that *the whole tribal life is permeated by a constant give and take*; that every ceremony, every legal and customary act is done to the accompaniment of material gift and counter gift; that wealth, given and taken, is one of the main instruments of social organisation, of the power of the chief, of the bonds of kinship, and of relationship in law.[10]

These views on primitive trade, prevalent though erroneous, appear no doubt quite consistent, that is, if we grant certain premises. Now these premises seem plausible, and yet they are false, and it will be good to have a careful look at them so that we can discard them once and for all. They are based on some sort of reasoning, such as the following one: If, in tropical conditions, there is a plenty of all utilities, why trouble about exchanging them? Then, why attach any value to them? Is there any reason for striving after wealth, where everyone can have as much as he wants without much effort? Is there indeed any room for value, if this latter is the result of scarcity as well as utility, in a community, in which all the useful things are plentiful? On the other hand, in those savage communities where the necessities of life are scarce, there is obviously no possibility of accumulating them, and thus creating wealth.

Again, since, in savage communities, whether bountifully or badly provided for by nature, everyone has the same free access to all the necessities, is there

[10] I am adducing these views not for any controversial purposes, but to justify and make clear why I stress certain general features of Trobriand Economic Sociology. My contentions might run the danger of appearing as gratuitous truisms if not thus justified. The opinion that primitive humanity and savages have no individual property is an old prejudice shared by many modern writers, especially in support of communistic theories, and the so-called materialistic view of history. The "communism of savages" is a phrase very often read, and needs no special quotation. The views of individual search for food and household economy are those of Karl Bücher, and they have directly influenced all the best modern writings on Primitive Economics. Finally, the view that we have done with Primitive Economics if we have described the way in which the natives procure their food, is obviously a fundamental premise of all the naïve, evolutionary theories which construct the successive stages of economic development. This view is summarised in the following sentence: ". . . . In many simple communities, the actual food quest, and operations immediately arising from it, occupy by far the greater part of the people's time and energy, leaving little opportunity for the satisfaction of any lesser needs." This sentence, quoted out of "Notes and Queries on Anthropology," p. 160, article on the "Economics of the Social Group," represents what may be called the official view of contemporary Ethnology on the subject, and in perusing the rest of the article, it can be easily seen that all the manifold economic problems, with which we are dealing in this book, have been so far more or less neglected.

any need to exchange them? Why give a basketful of fruit or vegetables, if everybody has practically the same quantity and the same means of procuring it? Why make a present of it, if it cannot be returned except in the same form?[11]

There are two main sources of error at the bottom of this faulty reasoning. The first is that the relation of the savage to material goods is a purely rational one, and that consequently, in his conditions, there is no room for wealth or value. The second erroneous assumption is that there can be no need for exchange if anyone and everyone can, by industry and skill, produce all that represents value through its quantity or its quality.

As regards the first proposition, it is not true either with regard to what may be called primary wealth, that is, food stuffs, nor with regard to articles of luxury, which are by no means absent in Trobriand society. First as to food-stuffs, they are not merely regarded by the natives as nourishment, not merely valued because of their utility. They accumulate them not so much because they know that yams can be stored and used for a future date, but also because they like to display their possessions in food. Their yam houses are built so that the quantity of the food can be gauged, and its quality ascertained through the wide interstices between the beams. The yams are so arranged that the best specimens come to the outside and are well visible. Special varieties of yams, which grow up to two metres length, and weigh as much as several kilograms each, are framed in wood and decorated with paint, and hung on the outside of the yam houses. That the right to display food is highly valued can be seen from the fact that in villages where a chief of high rank resides, the commoners' storehouses have to be closed up with coco-nut leaves, so as not to compete with his.

All this shows that the accumulation of food is not only the result of economic foresight, but also prompted by the desire of display and enhancement of social prestige through possession of wealth.

When I speak about ideas underlying accumulation of food stuffs in the Trobriands, I refer to the present, actual psychology of the natives, and I must emphatically declare that I am not offering here any conjectures about the "origins" or about the "history" of the customs and their psychology, leaving this to theoretical and comparative research.

Another institution which illuminates the native ideas about food storage is the magic called *vilamalya*, performed over the crops after harvest, and at

---

[11] These views had to be adduced at length, although touched upon already in Chapter II, Division IV, because they imply a serious error with regard to human nature in one of its most fundamental aspects. We can show up their fallacy on one example only, that of the Trobriand Society, but even this is enough to shatter their universal validity and show that the problem must be re-stated. The criticised views contain very general propositions, which, however, can be answered only empirically. And it is the duty of the field Ethnographer to answer and correct them. Because a statement is very general, it can none the less be a statement of empirical fact. General views must not be mixed up with hypothetical ones. The latter must be banished from field work; the former cannot receive too much attention.

one or two other stages. This magic is intended to make the food last long. Before the store-house is filled with yams, the magician places a special kind of heavy stone on the floor, and recites a long magical spell. On the evening of the same day, after the food houses have been filled, he spits over them with medicated ginger root, and he also performs a rite over all the roads entering into the village, and over the central place. All this will make food plentiful in that village, and will make the supplies last long. But, and this is the important point for us, this magic is conceived to act, not on the food, but on the inhabitants of the village. It makes their appetites poor, it makes them, as the natives put it, inclined to eat wild fruit of the bush, the mango and bread fruit of the village grove, and refuse to eat yams, or at least be satisfied with very little. They will boast that when this magic is performed well, half of the yams will rot away in the storehouses, and be thrown on the *wawa*, the rubbish heap at the back of the houses, to make room for the new harvest. Here again we meet the typical idea that the main aim of accumulating food is to keep it exhibited in the yam houses till it rots, and then can be replaced by a new étalage.

The filling of the storehouses involves a double display of food, and a good deal of ceremonial handling. When the tubers are taken out of the ground they are first displayed in the gardens. A shed of poles is erected, and covered with *taitu* vine, which is thrown thickly over it. In such arbours, a circle is pegged out on the ground, and within this the *taitu* (the ordinary small yams of the Trobriands which form the staple harvest) are carefully piled up into a conical heap. A great deal of care is lavished on this task, the biggest are selected, scrupulously cleaned, and put on the outside of the heap. After a fortnight or more of keeping the yams in the garden, where they are much admired by visiting parties, the owner of the garden plot summons a party of friends or relatives-in-law, and these transport them into a village. As we know already, from Chapter II, such yams will be offered to the owner's sister's husband. It is to his village that they are brought, where again they are displayed in conical heaps, placed before his yam house. Only after they have thus remained for several days—sometimes up to a fortnight—are they put into the storehouse.

Indeed, it would be enough for anyone to see how the natives handle the yams, how they admire big tubers, how they pick out freaks and sports and exhibit them, to realise that there is a deep, socially standardised sentiment centring round this staple product of their gardens. In many phases of their ceremonial life, big displays of food form the central feature. Extensive mortuary distributions called *sagali*, are, in one of their aspects, enormous exhibitions of food, connected with their re-apportionment. At harvest of the early yams (*kuvi*) there is an offering of first fruits to the memory of the recently dead. At the later, main harvest of *taitu* (small yams), the first tubers are dug out ceremonially brought into the village and admired by the whole community. Food contests between two villages at harvest, in olden days often followed by actual fighting, are also one of the characteristic features which throw light on the natives' attitude towards edible wealth. In fact, one could almost speak of a "cult of food" among these natives, in so far as food is the central object of most of their public ceremonies.

In the preparation of food, it must be noted that many taboos are associated with cooking, and especially with the cooking pots. The wooden dishes on which the natives serve their food are called *kaboma*, which means "tabooed wood." The act of eating is as a rule strictly individual. People eat within their family circles, and even when there is public ceremonial cooking of the taro pudding (*mona*) in the big clay pots, especially tabooed for this purpose, they do not eat in one body, but in small groups. A clay pot is carried into the different parts of the village, and men from that part squat round it and eat, followed afterwards by the women. Sometimes again the pudding is taken out, placed on wooden dishes, and eaten within the family.

I cannot enter here into the many details of what could be called the social psychology of eating, but it is important to note that the centre of gravity of the feast lies, not in the eating, but in the display and ceremonial preparation of the food. When a pig is to be killed, which is a great culinary and festive event, it will be first carried about, and shown perhaps in one or two villages; then roasted alive, the whole village and neighbours enjoying the spectacle and the squeals of the animal. It is then ceremonially, and with a definite ritual, cut into pieces and distributed. But the eating of it is a casual affair; it will take place either within a hut, or else people will just cook a piece of flesh and eat it on the road, or walking about in the village. The relics of a feast such as pigs' jaws and fish tails, however, are often collected and displayed in houses or yam stores.[12]

The quantity of food eaten, whether in prospect or retrospect, is what matters most. "We shall eat, and eat till we vomit," is a stock phrase, often heard at feasts, intended to express enjoyment of the occasion, a close parallel to the pleasure felt at the idea of stores rotting away in the yam house. All this shows that the social act of eating and the associated convivality are not present in the minds or customs of the Trobrianders, and what is socially enjoyed is the common admiration of fine and plentiful food, and the knowledge of its abundance. Naturally, like all animals, human or otherwise, civilised or savage, the Trobrianders enjoy their eating as one of the chief pleasures of life, but this remains an individual act, and neither its performance nor the sentiments attached to it have been socialised.

It is this indirect sentiment, rooted of course in reality in the pleasures of eating, which makes for the value of food in the eyes of the natives. This value again makes accumulated food a symbol, and a vehicle of power. Hence the need for storing and displaying it. Value is not the result of utility and rarity, intel-

---

[12] As a matter of fact, this custom is not so prominent in the Trobriands as in other Massim districts and all over the Papuo-Melanesian world, cf. for instance Seligman, 1910:56.

lectually compounded, but is the result of a sentiment grown round things, which, through satisfying human needs, are capable of evoking emotions.

The value of manufactured objects of use must also be explained through man's emotional nature, and not by reference to his logical construction of utilitarian views. Here, however, I think that the explanation must take into account, not so much the user of these objects, as the workman who produces them. These natives are industrious, and keen workers. They do not work under the spur of necessity, or to gain their living, but on the impulse of talent and fancy, with a high sense and enjoyment of their art, which they often conceive as the result of magical inspiration. This refers especially to those who produce objects of high value, and who are always good craftsmen and are fond of their workmanship. Now these native artists have a keen appreciation of good material, and of perfection in craft. When they find a specially good piece of material it lures them on to lavish on it an excess of labour, and to produce things too good to be used, but only so much the more desirable for possession.

The careful manner of working, the perfection of craftmanship, the discrimination in material, the inexhaustible patience in giving the final touches, have been often noted by those who have seen natives at work. These observations have also come under the notice of some theoretical economists, but it is necessary to see these facts in their bearing upon the theory of value. That is, namely, that this loving attitude towards material and work must produce a sentiment of attachment to rare materials and well-worked objects, and that this must result in their being valued. Value will be attached to rare forms of such materials as the craftsman generally uses: classes of shell which are scarce, lending themselves especially to fashioning and polishing; kinds of wood which are also rare, like ebony; and more particularly, special varieties of that stone out of which implements are made.[13]

We can now compare our results with the fallacious views on Primitive Economic Man, sketched out at the beginning of this Division. We see that value and wealth exist, in spite of abundance of things, that indeed this abundance is valued for its own sake. Great quantities are produced beyond any possible utility they could possess, out of mere love of accumulation for its own sake; food is allowed to rot, and though they have all they could desire in necessities, yet the natives want always more, to serve in its character of wealth. Again, in manufactured objects, and more especially in objects of the *vaygu'a* type, it is not rarity within utility which creates value, but a rarity sought out by human skill within the workable materials. In other words, not those things are valued, which being useful or even indispensable are hard to get, since all the necessities of life are within easy reach of the Trobriand Islander.

---

[13] Again, in explaining value, I do not wish to trace its possible origins, but I try simply to show what are the actual and observable elements into which the natives' attitude towards the object valued can be analysed.

But such an article is valued where the workman, having found specially fine or sportive material, has been induced to spend a disproportionate amount of labour on it. By doing so, he creates an object which is a kind of economic monstrosity, too good, too big, too frail, or too overcharged with ornament to be used, yet just because of that, highly valued.

Thus the first assumption is exploded, "that there is no room for wealth or value in native societies." What about the other assumption, namely, "That there is no need to exchange if anyone can by industry and skill, produce all that represents value through its quantity or its quality?" This assumption is confuted by realising a fundamental fact of native usage and psychology: the love of give and take for its own sake; the active enjoyment in possession of wealth, through handing it over.

In studying any sociological questions in the Trobriands, in describing the ceremonial side of tribal life, or religion and magic, we constantly meet with this give and take, with exchange of gifts and payments. I had occasion several times to mention this general feature, and in the short outline of the Trobriand sociology in Chapter II, I gave some examples of it. Even a walk across the island, such as we imagined in that chapter, would reveal to an open-eyed Ethnographer this economic truth. He would see visiting parties—women carrying big food baskets on their head, men with loads on their shoulders—and on inquiring he would learn that these were gifts to be presented under one of the many names they bear, in fulfilment of some social obligation. Offerings of first fruits are given to the chief or to relatives-in-law, when the mango or bread fruit or sugar cane are ripe. Big quantities of sugar cane being borne to a chief, carried by some twenty to thirty men running along the road, produce the impressions of a tropical Birnam Wood moving through the jungle. At harvest time all the roads are full of big parties of men carrying food, or returning with empty baskets. From the far North of Kiriwina a party will have to run for some twelve miles to the creek of Tukwa'ukwa, get into canoes, punt for miles along the shallow Lagoon, and have another good walk inland from Sinaketa; and all this is in order to fill the yam house of a man who could do it quite well for himself, if it were not that he is under obligation to give all the harvest to his sister's husband! Displays of gifts associated with marriage, with *sagali* (food distributions), with payments for magic, all these are some of the most picturesque characteristics of the Trobriand garden, road and village, and must impress themselves upon even a superficial observer.

The second fallacy, that man keeps all he needs and never spontaneously gives it away, must therefore be completely discarded. Not that the natives do not possess a strongly retentive tendency. To imagine that they differ from other human beings in this, would be to fall out of one fallacy into the opposite one also already mentioned, namely that there is a sort of primitive communism among the natives. On the contrary, just because they think so much of giving, the distinction between mine and thine is not obliterated but enhanced; for the presents are by no means given haphazardly, but practically always in fulfilment of definite obligations, and with a great deal of formal punctilio. The very fundamental motive of giving, the vanity of a display of possession and power, *a limine* rules out any assumption of communistic tendencies or institutions. Not in all cases, but in many of them, the handing over of wealth is the expression of the superiority of the giver over the recipient. In others, it represents subordination to a chief, or a kinship relation or relationship-in-law. And it is important to realise that in almost all forms of exchange in the Trobriands, there is not even a trace of gain, nor is there any reason for looking at it from the purely utilitarian and economic standpoint, since there is no enhancement of mutual utility through the exchange.

Thus, it is quite a usual thing in the Trobriands for a type of transaction to take place in which A gives twenty baskets of yams to B, receiving for it a small polished blade, only to have the whole transaction reversed in a few weeks' time. Again, at a certain stage of mortuary ritual, a present of valuables is given, and on the same day later on, the identical articles are returned to the giver. Cases like that described in the *kabigidoya* custom, where each owner of a new canoe made a round of all the others, each thus giving away again what he receives, are typical. In the *wasi*—exchange of fish for yams, to be described presently— through a practically useless gift, a burdensome obligation is imposed, and one might speak of an increase of burdens rather than an increase of utilities.

The view that the native can live in a state of individual search for food, or catering for his own household only, in isolation from any interchange of goods, implies a calculating, cold egotism, the possibility of enjoyment by man of utilities for their sake. This view, and all the previously criticised assumptions, ignore the fundamental human impulse to display, to share, to bestow. They ignore the deep tendency to create social ties through exchange of gifts. Apart from any consideration as to whether the gifts are necessary or even useful, giving for the sake of giving is one of the most important features of Trobriand sociology, and, from its very general and fundamental nature, I submit that it is a universal feature of all primitive societies.

I have dwelt at length on economic facts which on the surface are not directly connected with the Kula. But if we realise that in these facts we may be able to read the native's attitude towards wealth and value, their importance for the main theme becomes obvious. The Kula is the highest and the most dramatic expression of the native's conception of value, and if we want to understand all the customs and actions of the Kula in their real bearings we must, first and foremost, grasp the psychology that lies at its basis.

(pp. 166–176)

We have at last arrived at the point when the real Kula has begun. So far, it was all preparations, and sailing with its concomitant adventure, and a little bit of preliminary Kula in the Amphletts. It was all full of excitement and emotion, pointing always towards the final goal, the big Kula in Dobu. Now we have at last reached the climax. The net result will be the acquisition of a few dirty, greasy, and insignificant looking native trinkets, each of them a string of flat, partly discoloured, partly raspberry-pink or brick-red discs, threaded one behind the other into a long, cylindrical roll. In the eyes of the natives, however, this result receives its meaning from the social forces of tradition and custom, which give the imprint of value to these objects, and surround them with a halo of romance. It seems fit here to make these few reflections upon the native psychology on this point, and to attempt to grasp its real significance.

It may help us towards this understanding to reflect, that not far from the scenes of the Kula, large numbers of white adventurers have toiled and suffered, and many of them given their lives, in order to acquire what to the natives would appear as insignificant and filthy as their *bagi* are to us—a few nuggets of gold. Nearer, even, in the very Trobriand Lagoon, there are found valuable pearls. In olden days, when the natives on opening a shell to eat it, found a *waytuna*, as they called it, a 'seed' of the pearl shell, they would throw it to their children to play with. Now they see a number of white men straining all their forces in competition to acquire as many of these worthless things as they can. The parallel is very close. In both cases, the conventionalised value attached to an object carries with it power, renown, and the pleasure of increasing them both. In the case of the white man, this is infinitely more complex and indirect, but not essentially different from that of the natives. If we would imagine that a great number of celebrated gems are let loose among us, and travel from hand to hand—that Koh-i-noor and Orloff and other celebrated diamonds, emeralds and rubies—were on a continuous round tour, and to be obtained through luck, daring and enterprise, we would have a still closer analogy. Even though the possession of them would be a short and temporary one, the renown of having possessed them and the mania of 'collectioneering' would add its spur to the lust for wealth.

(pp. 351–352)

At one or two places in the previous chapters, a somewhat detailed digression was made in order to criticise the view about the economic nature of primitive man, as it survives in our mental habits as well as in some text books—the conception of a rational being who wants nothing but to satisfy his simplest needs and does it according to the economic principle of least effort. This economic man always knows exactly where his material interests lie, and makes for them in a straight line. At the bottom of the so-called materialistic conception of history lies a somewhat analogous idea of a human being, who, in everything he devises and pursues, has nothing but his material advantage of a purely utilitarian type at heart. Now I hope that whatever the meaning of the Kula might be for Ethnology, for the general science of culture, the meaning of the Kula will consist in being instrumental to dispel such crude, rationalistic conceptions of primitive mankind, and to induce both the speculator and the observer to deepen the analysis of economic facts. Indeed, the Kula shows us that the whole conception of primitive value; the very incorrect habit of calling all objects of value 'money' or 'currency'; the current ideas of primitive trade and primitive ownership—all these have to be revised in the light of our institution.

(p. 516)

2 ECONOMIZING AND RATIONAL BEHAVIOR

Melville J. Herskovits

The elements of scarcity and choice, which are the outstanding factors in human experience that give economic science its reason for being, rest psychologically on firm ground. It is a truism that wants are capable of a degree of expansion the end of which has not been reached by any known society. Wants, that is, apparently manifest a certain dynamic quality, which seems to derive from the inventiveness and receptivity of man, and are ultimately to be referred to the cumulative nature of human culture itself. Each generation takes for granted the cultural setting of the society into which it is born. And each, because of the creative restlessness of man, adds its contribution to the total culture of the group it comprises.

It is important for us, at this point, to consider the breadth of social effort included under the term "economizing." How wide this is becomes evident in reading the many discussions of the scope of economics and its relation to the term from which the discipline derives its name. Knight holds that common definitions are too inclusive: "The term economic has come to be used in a sense which is practically synonymous with intelligent or rational." "It is in accord with good linguistic usage," he continues, "to think and speak of the whole problem of living as one of economy, the economical use of time, energy, etc.—*resource* of every sort." Yet he stresses the point that "the restrictions which mark off the modestly limited domain of economic science within the inclusive sphere of knowledge as a whole" must be clearly understood (Knight 1933:1–2).

This limitation is indicated by Benham, who states that "the rationale of economic activity is to satisfy human wants by producing consumers' goods." He explains: "People are continually deciding how they will use their time and energy and property and how they will spend their money. . . . It is these decisions which determine the nature and extent of economic activity" (1936: 5–6). A philosopher, assessing the nature of the economizing experience, states:

"We can start with one agreed quality: Economizing is a way of doing things; first, of thinking about them, then, of acting; in sum, of arranging or choosing them. It is imposed on us by scarcity of means in relation to expanding desires. In this sense, it is purposive, a process which we direct and develop creatively; for we can agree that choice involves this" (Macfie 1949:20). This mode of circumscribing the term emphasizes conscious choice, stresses the essential role of alternatives between which to choose, and relates the whole to the problem of attaining efficiency through choosing.

Like any phenomenon that exists in time, the development of the wants of a people is irreversible. Small, isolated nonliterate societies may sometimes seem to the observer to live in terms of a degree of stability and conservatism that belies this. But there is no study of cultural change in process, or of contact between peoples having different cultures, which does not document the proposition that a people give over an item in their cultural store only when it becomes apparent to them that a more desirable substitute—iron implements for stone tools, for example—is at hand, or when circumstances beyond their control dictate this. There is nothing more difficult to accept than a lowered standard of living.

Our primary concern in these pages is to understand the cross-cultural implications of the process of economizing. We may begin our analysis by considering the concept of a free good. It is a commonplace in economic theory, for example, that no economic value can be assigned to a sunset or the view of a mountain, since these are to be had for the taking. It is only when a given good is not available in quantities to supply every desire for it that the economizing process comes into play. Even in the case of the utilization of what would seem to be a free good, however, some economic factors may enter. There may be more than enough animals available, and no restrictions on the member of the tribe as to where and what he will hunt; but choices will nonetheless have to be made. These considerations cannot be overlooked if the free good is not to lie, inert, as a theoretical concept and not as a functioning element in the daily life of the people.

It is generally recognized by economists that even the utilization of air, an example of a free good often cited, entails economizing. This is apparent if we consider so simple an example of economic behavior as occurs when an Australian aborigine decides to build a fire and a wind-screen. In this case, a choice is made between the cold (free) air of the night and the warmed (economic) air available only after the energy needed to collect wood, kindle the fire (no mean task where a fire-drill must be used), and build the screen, has been expended. It is apparent, in these instances, that the question of whether a resource is free or economic is not a simple concept. An understanding of these critical cases confirms empirically the economic principle that the applicability of the concept depends on the ends sought. Where choice enters so that the satisfactions derived are to be maximized, the free good becomes an economic one.

Beyond whatever free goods may be available, even to members of societies with the smallest numbers, the simplest technologies and the most direct economic systems, the far greater number of goods are not free. Even the provision of basic needs, food and shelter and clothing and implements, must inevitably involve choice; moreover, these choices are dictated not only by the alternatives between available items, but by the patterns of the culture of the individual who, in the final analysis, must do the choosing. Choice between alternatives is limited not only by the goods and services available to satisfy wants. The nature of the available goods and of the wants they are to satisfy is likewise restricted. Economizing, that is, is carried on in a cultural matrix. The matter has been phrased cogently in considering the economy of southern Bougainville, Solomon Islands: "At the present, in answer to the problem of discrepancy between needs and resources, it is sufficient to recall that these needs are *cultural* rather than *nutritional*, and to state the conviction that there will always be discrepancies between cultural needs and available resources" (Oliver 1949:18). Social conventions, religious beliefs, aesthetic conceptions, and ethical prescriptions all function in shaping the wants of peoples and the times and places and circumstances in which they can be satisfied.

We shall see how, for example, certain West African peoples conventionally and traditionally expend food so liberally on feasts that must be given during the dry season that at the beginning of the rainy season, when hard labor of breaking the ground for the new planting has to be performed, there is an actual inadequacy of caloric intake that could easily be supplied if food resources had been conserved. It must be emphasized that there is no question of lack of foresight, for it is well established that these peoples are aware of the alternate possibility. It is rather a question of economic choice dictated by the drive to maximize satisfactions in terms of the traditional values of the culture.

As another instance, we may consider the utilization of land among the Kogi (or Kagaba) Indians who inhabit the Sierra Nevada range of northeastern Colombia. Because of the steepness of the mountains and the degree of erosion, this agricultural people is faced with a scarcity of land that forces each family to work patches in the lowland and highland areas, moving from one to another at considerable cost of expenditure in time and energy. In these mountain ranges, however, are many terraces, built by the earlier inhabitants, where numerous archaeological remains suggest a stable and considerable population. These terraces, each of which might provide on the average about two and a half acres of arable land, are not used, but the difficult mountain-sides and tiny patches in the valleys, often far removed from the habitation, are cultivated instead. The reason is a supernatural one: "There are many spirits of the dead there," they say. Except when they place offerings at these places, they avoid them, thus "depriving themselves of their best land" and "being forced to plant in patches far from each other, patches which at times are steep and very small" (Dolmatoff 1950:97–101).

One of the principles of early economic theory was to regard the individual as the point from which all development of theoretical principles must begin. We have come to realize that the individual never exists alone; that a society, as it has been put, is more than an aggregate of Robinson Crusoes; and that social interaction in terms of cultural tradition dictates reconsideration of the earlier starting-point. The process of economizing, we recognize, is essentially based on the broader organization of society. Yet the individual cannot be left out of the picture, for all forms of social behavior, in the final analysis, must be referred to the behavior of individual members of a given society in specific situations.

This is why we must be on our guard against permitting the pendulum of reaction against the older point of view to swing to a point where we reify the common elements in the behavior of individuals into a construct that is conceived as existing by and of itself. There is much truth in the statement by Polanyi: "The outstanding discovery of recent historical and anthropological research is that man's economy, as a rule, is submerged in his social relationships." However, anyone who has had first-hand experience among nonliterate, non-machine, and non-pecuniary peoples, can but wonder at the validity of the statement which succeeds the sentence just quoted: "He does not act so as to safeguard his individual interest in the possession of material goods; he acts so as to safeguard his social standing, his social claims, his social assets. He values material goods only in so far as they serve this end" (1944:46).

Paulme has drawn conclusions concerning this point, based on her research among the Dogon of West Africa, which depict somewhat more realistically the interaction between individual and social factors in the economic process. "It is clear," she says, "that individual advantage, understood as the realization of the greatest possible gain with the expenditure of a minimum of effort is not the sole force that causes men to work in the society we are studying. Each person is motivated, more or less consciously, in more or less indirect ways, by the desire for the well-being, wealth and prestige of the community as a whole" (Translated from Paulme 1940:194). All choices, that is, however they may be influenced by considerations of social standing, social claims, and social assets, are ultimately the choices of individuals.

In short, we must not reject Economic Man only to substitute Society as an exclusive formula for understanding economic behavior and as a base-point for analysis. Economizing is never carried on *unilaterally*. The choices of the individual must always be limited by the resources of his society and the values of his culture. But the factors of variation to be found even within the smallest, most homogenous, and most conservative society must not be lost sight of. The economic unit, we must conclude, is the individual operating as a member of his society, in terms of the culture of his group.

This implies that any analysis of the schedule of wants of a given society which projects these wants against the supply of goods and services available to satisfy them must be supplemented by introducing a third term into the equation; the cultural definition of wants and the conventions that dictate how and when they are to be regarded as adequately satisfied. It is in terms of these factors that we will consider the economic systems of nonliterate, non-machine, and, often, non-pecuniary peoples treated in this book.

2

The means by which the ends of the economizing process, however defined, are achieved, comprise universals in human experience. They therefore provide the basis for all generalizations concerning the nature and functioning of economic systems, whatever their form and whatever the particular mechanisms they may use to convert these means into satisfying the wants that make up the socially sanctioned ends toward whose fulfillment a given economy is directed.

We may move, first of all, to those human and ecological factors that provide the goods and services which satisfy the demands of living, both biological and psychological, and that are at the core of any economic system. In some form, these factors are present everywhere; without their interaction life as we know it could not exist.

Initially, the elements that are given by the world as it is constituted must be considered: the natural resources derived from the habitat, and the labor power of men themselves, the prime mover in the utilization of what is provided by the natural setting. As Knight has phrased it, these are the "ultimate" resources, from which, through intermediate steps that vary in number with economies of different degrees of complexity, come the consumption goods that make possible the gratification of wants (Knight 1933:41).

But these do not tell the whole tale, for everywhere there must be the technical knowledge that permits men to take advantage of the resources to which they must look for the raw materials of their economy, and those tools they devise to permit them to utilize their labor effectively in exploiting the natural resources of the territories they inhabit. Their technologies, however crude, are expressed in the form of goods which are to be thought of, in the less complex economies, as capital goods of varying degrees of permanency. Clearing a waterhole can be interpreted in this way, despite the simplicity of the technique whereby the improvement of the natural resource is achieved, and the slight amount of time and energy that is expended in achieving this end. A bow and arrow is likewise an intermediate good of this sort. The effort capitalized in its making brings return in the greater effectiveness of its maker when hunting the game he needs for subsistence, or for prestige, or for other desired ends.

Yet while all these factors—natural resources, man-power, technical knowledge, and capital equipment—must be present in the productive processes of any functioning economy, the weighting of each in making the whole a going concern may differ widely. It is not chance that economists in their discussions have found it necessary to stress these prime factors, and especially to make explicit the role of "ultimate" resources. In a pecuniary, machine economy such as that of Europe and America, they are easily lost sight of in the face of the wealth of technical knowledge and the complexities of capital investment, with their resulting equipment which pours forth the enormous quantities and variety of goods that satisfy the needs of the people living in these societies.

In the non-pecuniary, non-machine societies with which we will be concerned, almost the exact opposite obtains. The factors of natural resources and man-power stand out in bold relief. One must search and interpret if the phenomenon of capitalization is to be taken into account; the technological equipment is direct and relatively simple and at once apparent; the intermediate steps between the utilization of raw materials and the production of a consumption good are few. We shall see, in considering the simplest economies, how close to the subsistence level a society can be. Among nonliterate peoples in general, both the inventory of goods and services and the range of wants to be satisfied, as expressed in the standards of living of the people, are relatively restricted. The margin between available resources and physical survival, in the simplest of these economies, such as are found among the South African Bushmen, or the Indians of the Great Basin region of western United States, or the inhabitants of Tierra del Fuego, is slender indeed. The scarcity of available goods in societies living on this level holds the factor of choice to the narrowest of ranges; the wants are to a considerable degree biological and are of the order of survival itself. Here, in short, the need to economize does not have to be analyzed in forms of mathematical formulae; it is apparent, in all its stark biological implications, for the most casual traveler to observe.

These simplest economies, however, are few in number. They shade imperceptibly into systems in which increasing command of technology and greater capital equipment cause the factors of natural resources and labor-power again to be obscured by the secondary aspects of the total equipment for production. Even so, it is rare in these intermediate societies to find individuals as completely removed from the primary factors as, let us say, are the urban dwellers of Europe and America, though such persons are sporadically to be found. The apparatus to care for wants is capable of greater productivity, and the wants to be satisfied are correspondingly expanded. The margin which permits the expenditure of labor-power for the production of services as well as goods is greater, and this in turn leads to a greater degree of specialization.

In these societies, too, the entrepreneurial function, where it is to be discerned at all, is at a minimum. The men who, in terms of the economies of Euroamerican society, direct industrial enterprises, decide what is to be produced and how, hire workmen and direct what they shall do, borrow money to acquire capital goods or land holdings, and assume the risks inherent in their ventures, do not exist, in the sense of the word as used by economists, in non-pecuniary, non-industrialized societies. For in these societies, production and distribution involve little of the profit motive, and labor is only in special instances for hire.

Attempts that have been made to discern the entrepreneur in a South Seas chief or in a Bantu household head afford examples of this. Firth's statement, that he employs the term, "in default of finding a better," is to the point. "It must be taken in its simplest sense," he cautions, "of the person primarily responsible for an undertaking, and is not intended to imply propositions about risk-taking and profit-reception. For the Tikopia economy the term covers ownership of the final product, responsibility for payment of the workers if such is to be made, and usually some actual participation in the work" (Firth 1939:134n). In the case of the Bantu, Goodfellow, commenting on the fact that "the function of consumers to release part of their resources for further general production has scarcely existed," concludes that, "there has been little room for the function of the entrepreneur in managing such resources" (Goodfellow 1939:80).

We come here to a point that cannot be stressed too early in our discussion. This concerns the *generalized* nature of the mechanisms and institutions that mark the economies of all the nonliterate, non-machine societies. It is a point that will recur as a basic theme of this book, and will be extensively documented in the pages that follow. It explains the difficulties that arise when we attempt to apply the more refined concepts of economics to these societies, or when we attempt to test some of the more debated hypotheses of economic theory by reference to them. The example given above of the nature of a capital good in such an economy makes the point; it could be equally well made if the question of the character of rent or interest were raised. In addition, the intimate interlarding of economic motivations with these of a religious or artistic nature further complicates the analysis.

Nonetheless, however generalized and however difficult to disentangle from their cultural matrix, the basic elements of the apparatus to care for wants are present in every economy. We may conceive of the totality of economic systems as lying on a kind of continuum. At one pole we find the societies living closest to the subsistence level, with the exploitation of natural resources slight, a slender endowment of technical knowledge, and implements few and simple. At the other end we place the great literate population aggregates, with their machine technologies, producing vast stores of goods and supporting a great variety of specialists to satisfy the wants of the people. Between these extremes lie the many societies having intermediate degrees of economic complexity and technical resource. As we move from the less to the more complex, the choices that are afforded between alternative possibilities become greater, the range of wants to be satisfied wider. But in every case choices must be made.

3

The mechanisms of production represent only the initial steps in the total system whereby the goods and services that meet the needs of a people are made available to them. The apparatus that utilizes the resources at hand to care for wants must be linked with some mode of distributing what has been produced if the members of a group are to be able to make their choices among the goods and services that represent the alternative possibilities presented to them. And as with the mechanisms of production, the distributive system, though a universal in human social life, takes on a vast number of forms. These vary from the highly specialized and complex modes of distribution found in the pecuniary, mechanized societies of Europe and America to the generalized and diffuse forms found among small, isolated, nonliterate groups.

How rudimentary the distributive mechanism can be is realized when we consider those societies where the economic unit is the self-sufficient family. It has, indeed, been held that there could be no distributive mechanism present at all in such situations, since "logically . . . each household would provide for its own industrial wants. No products would be exchanged in such a society. Productive effort would be directed solely to the satisfaction of the wants of the household" (Usher 1920:4). In terms of our discussion, this implies that the distributive element of these economies is simply omitted, and the middle term of the progression from production through distribution to consumption falls out. In actuality, however, this never happens. An exchange of goods and services may not occur *between* households. Yet from the fact that no human society exists wherein at least the division of labor along sex lines is absent, it follows that within the smallest, most self-sufficient households some kind of exchange of services, and of the goods produced by these services, must be postulated. For there can be no division of labor without a resulting economic exchange. The universality of the fact of division of labor, even if only on sex lines, underscores the essential soundness of the reasoning which has made of exchange and distribution basic factors in all economic theory.

This is apparent, for example, when we consider the distribution system of the Lunga and other tribes of the Kimberly Division of Western Australia, who have this kind of family-band subsistence economy.

> The husband must from time to time give kangaroo to his wife's parents and brothers; besides this he always distributes a little among his blood relatives. Most of what the woman has obtained is consumed by herself, husband and children; if she has a little extra she takes some to her mother, sister, mother's mother, father, in fact to any close relative. She on another occasion receives similar offerings from them, and also meat from her male relatives, which she shares with her husband and children. These gifts are not compulsory as are her husband's to her people. They are dictated by tribal sentiment and her own affection for these individuals; by kinship system which finds concrete expression not only in attitudes and linguistic usage, but also in the exchange of the limited food resources and the material and ritual objects which are found in the community. Kinship as seen in Australia is practical altruism or enlightened self-interest (Kaberry 1939:33).

A somewhat analogous state of affairs is found among the cattle-keeping Swazi of South Africa, where "economically the family is the unit in production and consumption" and where, in pre-contact times, trade was non-existent (Marwick 1940:43–44; 177–178).

The simplicity of the distributive mechanism in societies such as these, or as are to be found in the Amazon basin, stands in sharp contrast to the manner in which goods are distributed to the ultimate consumer in the industrialized societies of Europe and America. Here the economic problem resolves itself into an analysis of market operations which are so vast and which present such a multiplicity of choice that they seem to differ in kind rather than in degree when compared to the household economies of many nonliterate peoples.

From one point of view, indeed, the difference actually is one of kind. In the simplest economic systems, no pecuniary factor enters. What elementary types of exchanges of goods and services occur are on the basis of an immediate, *ad hoc* kind of give and take. Because of this, the problems raised in assessing the nature and forms of exchanges, and the kinds of choices that are made, take on a new and particular shape. The market is present in such rudimentary form that it exists by definition only; no least common denominator of value obtains; there is a face-to-face relationship between producer and consumer.

We must not, however, lose sight of the intermediate societies, such as those of Central America or West Africa, in stressing the economies of the simplest sort. In these more complex systems, where the market, distinguishable as such in its institutionalized forms, and based on exchanges involving the use of pecuniary media—money—is present, the complexity of the process that marks the movement of goods and services to the ultimate consumer in industrial communities is almost entirely lacking. This derives from the fact that even among nonliterate peoples, whose economies are of this order of complexity, the individual controls a substantial proportion of the techniques employed by his group in the basic tasks of getting a living, in addition to whatever specialized skills he may possess in the production of capital and consumption goods. Here again, then, it follows that even in such societies, as far as the necessities of life are concerned, distribution is in large measure a process of allocating what has been produced by members of the household to those who constitute its personnel. Such commercial transactions as do take place, except among social aggregates large enough to permit a degree of specialization rare in nonliterate societies, are again personal, direct, and specific.

Moreover, to the extent that the market in such societies does possess an objective and formal existence, it is a mechanism that facilitates the exchange of goods between members of different communities rather than between those who belong in the same group. This proposition will be amply documented in later pages. Here it need only be pointed out that where the degree of specialization in production is slight, no market-place is needed to effectuate whatever few exchanges of goods may be consummated. By far the greater number of cases of market operations we shall encounter will be those in which members of different villages or tribes exchange such commodities as each produces in excess of its own needs for such other goods as its members do not themselves manufacture.

In the absence of pecuniary mechanisms and the element of profit in the transactions of the market, it follows that the problem of the relation between supply and demand takes on unexpected turns. The West African woman trader who will not lower the price of the commodity she sells when business is dull

—and this is an economy where values have for centuries been expressed in the quantitative terms of the prevalent form of money—presents a difficult enough problem. But where the total supply of commodities, even of subsistence goods, available to the members of a given society is severely limited, the question of fluctuations in value becomes pointless.

Economic theory, on the whole, is not geared to consider the problem of demand schedules where the alternatives are so restricted that there is no margin between utility and disutility—or to put it in other terms, where the choices are so few that no curve of indifference can be drawn between satisfactions and costs, where costs are always maximized, since individuals must work or starve. In situations such as these, the utility of any good recognized by the culture as having utility is maximized in its mere possession, where it is a tool; or in the very opportunity to consume it, if it is a commodity such as food. There is no inducement to trade it for something else, since there are no costs (disutilities) to be taken into account.

Thus food, to a South African Bushman or a native of Tierra del Fuego, who lives always in a state of potential hunger, is always of maximum value, since it is essential to the maintenance of life itself. And since there is little surplus of energy or resources available for other activities than the food quest, it follows that whatever commodities, such as clothing, weapons, and the like are produced, likewise have constant maximum value and are not subject to exchanges essential to the existence of a market in any sense of the term. Differential utilities do enter, as, for example, where an Australian aborigine cannot kill an animal that has food value for him, despite his hunger, because of a system of totemic belief that taboos the animal. Here the disutility of the animal as food is matched by its utility as a supernatural and social agent. But in setting the standards of utility in such a case no distributive mechanism, no market factor, enters, and the utilities are of the all-or-none variety.

In the vastly greater number of non-machine societies, in which people are not pressed against the iron wall of subsistence needs, and the range of choice widens, the factor of differential utility is present. A hungry man may choose between fowl and game for his meal, or between yams and taro. A less hungry one may make his choice between work and leisure, food and effort. A person confronted with a problem beyond his means of solving may employ the services of a diviner or of a worker of magic. But even here the measurement of differential utilities in terms of price based on the fluctuations of the market in response to the factors of supply and demand may be discerned but dimly, if at all. In these societies the market is not free; it is a market in which "prices"— evaluations in whatever terms—are "administered" by custom.

It is not a question of which food is cheaper, and of balancing this against a desire for a change to taro after having eaten too many yams. Both foods, in all likelihood, will be equally available; they may well be perfect substitutes, as concerns effort required to grow them as well as concerns preference in taste. But money cost will be of no importance because it is not a factor. Or again, the decision where to seek advice will be made on the basis of entirely extra-pecuniary considerations—that is, without weighing costs against satisfactions. Our man may have lost faith in the skill of his diviner, or he may have decided that the situation calls for a magic charm rather than the intervention of the gods. Choice is thus dictated by differentials in utility; but the utility is not measured in terms of alternate costs (prices) by the one who makes the choice, and is not measurable in quantitative terms by the student.

We have again reached the point where we must take into account the fact that the economic institutions and mechanisms that are sharply differentiated in the machine societies become blurred and generalized in nonliterate cultures. There can, for example, be no question that the functioning of price mechanisms in the economic systems of Europe and America can be studied in the objective terms of economic theory, which has tellingly employed it as affording a precise measure of the choices made in the market by consumers. Its place in popular thinking likewise reflects its importance as an isolate in the economy. "No judgements are more closely associated with our daily living than judgements of price and the judgements of material values that underlie the structures of market prices," Usher has observed. "Because they are commonplaces of our living we are prone to think of them as simple and obvious, though they are no less complex than any other value judgements" (Usher 1949:146).

But what of the price mechanism in societies where cost is but one of a number of considerations dictating economic behavior? Or where it does not figure at all? Where the producer is the consumer of the goods he produces or of the greater proportion of what he produces, where market dealings are determined by all kinds of non-economic factors? Here the problem of ascertaining why given choices are made and how the economic devices that help maximize satisfactions actually function calls for an attack that will take into account the cross-cultural variations in the nature of the data.

4

We have seen that the scarcity of goods in the face of the wants of a given people at a given time is a universal fact of human experience; that no economy has been discovered wherein enough goods are produced in enough variety to satisfy all the wants of all the members of any society. This is true whether the group is small or large, the mechanisms of its economic system simple or complex. More important, it is true whether the society is undisturbed and the differences in its way of life from one generation to another slight, or whether it is in a state of dynamic change. The dissimilarities between any society and any other in these respects is one of degree and not of kind. The general principle, therefore, stands, despite the many changes that are rung on the basic theme manifested in the particular forms it assumes in functioning economies.

It can also be taken as cross-culturally acceptable that, on the whole, the individual tends to maximize his satisfactions in terms of the choices he makes. Where the gap between utility and disutility is appreciable, and the producer or consumer of a good or service is free to make his choice, then, other things being equal, he will make his choice in terms of utility rather than disutility. One need not accept the hedonism of classical economics to recognize the validity, on broad lines, of the proposition, at least in the terms in which we have phrased it here.

Yet it should be apparent that the two basic postulates of economic science— the allocation of scarce resources among alternative ends and the conscious determination of the choices made in maximizing satisfactions—are not of the same order. The first is a statement of fact that can be objectively verified. In pecuniary, machine economies this can be done by means of price analysis which shows how the market responds to scarcities or overproduction of given commodities. In non-pecuniary, non-machine, and nonliterate societies we can have recourse to ethnographic descriptions of the range of goods produced by a people and record the choices that are actually reached. The empirical nature of analyses that press the point further, inquiring into the kind of resources a people can draw on, and how they are utilized in producing ultimate consumption goods, is likewise apparent. The forms taken by competitive striving for a good in short supply, if competitive patterns are present, and the degree to which this striving stimulates to further production, can also be objectively described. We can determine whether bidding will be in terms of prestige or price. We can ascertain whether a failure to increase supply is due to lack of ultimate resources, or to non-economic causes of a social or religious order. Or, where the response to increased demand is increase in supply, we can find out how this increase has occurred and, given time and resources for adequate investigation of the problem, the extent to which the supply has increased.

The second proposition, however, lies in the realm of values, not only in the technical sense of economic science, but in the broader philosophical connotation of those ultimate sanctions to behavior that give meaning to life. It is possible to bring objective proof, that is, as to *what* men do in the way of economizing; the question *why* they do it rests on subjective and cultural factors. It is significant that so much of that aspect of economic theory that bears on this latter point derives from assumptions of a psychological nature. It is more than a figure of speech when economists speak of "rationalizing" production or distribution. The usage derives logically and semantically from the prominence traditionally given the view that man, in his economic behavior, acts rationally.

The earlier concept of Economic Man, the most extreme expression of this position, has long since been given over by economists, together with any conclusions that may have been drawn concerning the relevance of this concept as indicative of Human Nature in the large. The influence of the earlier economic historians was important in bringing about this changed point of view. They indicated the need to take time and place into full account if the economies of earlier periods of western European society were to be understood. The process of refining the conception of the role of rational choice has continued, with stress being laid on non-economic choices to be made in "the business of living," or by successively eliminating more and more variables in drawing assumptions so that the choices to be made rationally are restricted not only as to time and place but to the economic as against other aspects of living, as well.

We may take as an example the case of the Kwakiutl of the Northwest Coast of North America, whose economy has been the subject of much study, earlier in terms of its dramatic prestige give-away rituals termed potlatches, and in later years concerning the productive and social system that made this institution possible. As a result of these investigations, an inner dynamic of considerable significance for the point under discussion has been revealed. Codere has phrased the matter in these terms: "In what might be called their 'economic life' the Kwakiutl are virtuoso technicians and extravagant producers and storers. It is in their 'social life' that they 'economize'." In this society, that is, a basic aim was the attainment and maintenance of position, to be achieved only through the expenditure of valuable goods. This was carried on by certain financial mechanisms—investment, credit, and the payment of interest, which, as it is phrased, "maximized the potlatch." The underlying drive in this complex system, therefore, "is to be found in the relation of the arbitrarily determined scarcity of potlatch positions to the superabundance of some economic goods" (Codere 1950:68).

The factor of rational choice, even when its applicability is narrowed, still remains as an element in the basic postulates of economic science. Price movements may theoretically be predicted without reference to the behavior of individuals on the basis of fluctuations of supply and demand in an assumed economic universe involving perfect competition, or where it is assumed that competition is not perfect, and monopolistic factors enter. Yet underlying the argument is the human factor. Thus Boulding, in explaining "the method of economic analysis," states that it begins "with very simple assumptions concerning human behavior." He goes on "to discover what consequences would follow for the economic system as a whole if these assumptions were true" before bringing these findings "into closer relation to real life by introducing qualifications of our original assumptions and seeing how they affect the picture as we see it" (Boulding 1941:15). In other words, it is the individual, the ultimate producer and consumer, who is the prime economic mover. His mode of rationally choosing the economically more advantageous alternatives, expressed in price, is considered so fundamental that it is often not even verbalized, to say nothing of being questioned.[1]

From the cross-cultural point of view, however, it is this assumption that is at the crux of the analysis, no matter how qualified or restricted it may be. For the economic anthropologist deals with the total range of human societies. Many of the questions he must ask thus arise from the fact that the economies with which he deals present a vastly greater range of differences than the earlier

---

[1] Cf., Knight's statement concerning the categories to be distinguished in the "interpretative aspect of social phenomena." Here, introducing his final two categories, he writes: "But what is finally, or almost uniquely, distinctive of human phenomena is the aspect of conscious purpose, or rationality" (Knight 1941, reprinted in Herskovits 1952:512).

systems of western Europe and the Mediterranean, which themselves had enough of a special quality to cause the economic historians to raise comparable questions concerning early statements of the universality of economic mechanisms.

It is essential at this point to consider the problem of rationality in the light of our knowledge of the psychology of culture. The concept of culture, it will be remembered, includes all phases of the learned, traditionally sanctioned behavior of human beings. These phases are conceived as aspects of culture, which are universals in the ways of life of all human groups—technology, economics, social organization, political structures, religious beliefs and institutions, language, art, music, and literary modes of expression being the broadest categories. These universal aspects, in their institutionalized forms, are different in all of the many different societies found over the earth. Yet each of these *forms* represents the working out, in terms of its own particular historical stream, of universal *processes* of cultural dynamics which have brought about the results to be observed in the life of any given people at any given point in time. Thus, for example, we may say that the process of interchange of cultural items between two peoples will result from contact between them; but what forms will be taken over in a given case—whether material or non-material elements, for example— will depend on the nature of the contacts, the varied emphases laid by the two bodies of traditions concerned, and the like. It follows that since the economic aspect of a given culture is but a part of the total range of culture, any valid principles that apply to the whole must likewise apply to any part of the whole.

From the psychological point of view, culture is behavior in the broadest sense of the term—overt acts and their implicit sanctions. The mechanism that gives stability to a culture is the learning-conditioning process. An infant is born into a society that is a going concern. In his education, he is conditioned to behave, within the limits of variation sanctioned by his group, like the other members of his society. This process is called *enculturation*. Not only motor habits, but also modes of conceptualizing and evaluating are learned—and learned so thoroughly that, for the most part, they are taken for granted, and seem to the enculturated individual to be as immutable as the contours of his physical environment. Later in life, through the process of invention or because of contact with other peoples, reenculturation may occur. But basic motor-habits and, above all, value-systems and other sanctions are extremely tenacious, and are modified slowly, if at all.[2] More than this, these value-systems and other sanctions are taken for granted and form the basis for judgments of all sorts.

The pertinence of this last fact for an understanding of the nature of rational behavior is at once apparent. We may accept the findings of psychology concerning the role of emotions and other non-cognitive mechanisms in influencing behavior. In addition to these mechanisms, however, we find in the enculturative process a further qualifying element—the patterns of thought that are laid down in accordance with the value-systems of the group to which the individual

[2] Cf. Herskovits (1948), 17–42, for a more extended discussion of this phenomenon.

belongs. The question of rationality, then, at once poses itself: rational in terms of what system of thought and behavior?

Granting the force of the enculturative conditioning, it is apparent that this forms the principal basis for judgment, for choice, for rational behavior in any given situation where alternatives are presented. In the light of the principle that the *process*, though universal, may manifest itself in different *forms*, we can understand why peoples hold so stubbornly to their own value-judgments. This brings us to *cultural relativism*, which stresses the validity of the most diverse kinds of value-systems for the peoples who live in accord with them. It derives from the following proposition in cultural psychology: "Judgments are based on experience, and experience is interpreted by each individual in terms of his own enculturation."[3] Its documentation is vast, and derives principally from much research that has established the devotion of every people to their own way of life, and the extent to which the malfunctioning of culture can be ascribed to a break-down in the value-systems of a people.

The principle of relativism is nothing new. In economics, it has been present for many years, though its voice was never strong and has become stilled with the passage of time. The elder Keynes, in his classical work on the nature and method of economics, turns continually to the problem. The major presentation of relativism is to be found in a section entitled, significantly, "On the Limits of the Validity of Economic Doctrines," though various passages elsewhere are devoted to considering the "relativity of economic definitions" (J. N. Keynes 1897:293–307; 15n. 1; 64; 163–167). It is as true of economic conditions, as of social conditions in general," he says, "that they are ever subject to modification. They vary with the legal form of society, and with national character and institutions" (J. N. Keynes 1897:295).

He likewise points out how the earlier German economic historians combatted the principle of the "absolutism of theory." His analysis, in terms of "abstract" and "concrete" economics, recalls the point just made concerning the differences between process and form. He does not in any sense cede the importance of what he terms "abstract analysis"; he quite properly stresses the need to ascertain the underlying least common denominators, and then to discover how they manifest themselves in differing concrete situations. But the "inferences which possess the character of universality"—the processes assumed to occur—are to be understood through the study of the varying forms they take.[4]

This relativistic approach to the comparative study of economic behavior and

[3] Herskovits, op. cit., 63; see pp. 61–78 for an elaboration of the implications of this proposition.

[4] It is not without significance, in this connection, that almost the only economist who has attempted to systematize a comparative, cross-cultural approach to economics has been R. Mukerjee, the relativism of whose point of view is made explicit in Ch. XV of his work. It may, at this point, also be indicated that the phrase "comparative economics," which he attempted to study in broad terms of reference, in the terminology of economics is restricted to the comparative analysis of the economic systems of free enterprise, communism, and fascism.

institutions provides the epistemological foundation essential if the differences between different ways of life are not to be analyzed and assessed in terms of principles that derive from a single culture—in this case, our own. The point of view this latter engenders is called enthnocentrism, the roots of which, in Euroamerican cultures, will be considered in the next chapter. Here it need merely be pointed out that this is a habit of thought that must be guarded against if understanding of any modes of behavior and value-systems other than those of one's own group is to be attained.

The principle of maximizing satisfactions by the conscious exercise of choice between scarce means is valid because we find that this does occur in all societies. The cross-cultural perspective, however, gives us pause when defining "rationality."[5] We are tempted to consider as rational the behavior that represents only the typical reactions to be expected of those who order their lives in terms of the economic systems of Europe and America, where it is rational to defer the gratification of wants, to accumulate resources, to produce more goods and multiply services. Yet, as we shall abundantly see, there are many cultures, if not a majority of them, where the deferment of wants is held to be disadvantageous, where best judgment dictates that resources be expended, where there is no tradition of expanding production and increasing services. None the less, in societies having traditions of this sort, choices are not only made, but debated. It will be our task in the pages that follow, then, to discern the economic universals in human society by sampling the many forms in which they are manifest.

3 THE APPLICABILITY OF ECONOMIC THEORY TO SO-CALLED PRIMITIVE COMMUNITIES
D. M. Goodfellow

It has long been recognized that the formulations of economic theory have in them a certain universality. Many are the references in standard works which may legitimately be taken to show that the writers believe themselves to be handling "Laws of Human Nature", or facts so fundamental that, explored though they might be upon the basis of Western communities, their value would be found to hold in any community whatever.

Yet extremely little exploration has been made in the fitting of economic

From Principles of Economic Sociology *by D. M. Goodfellow, London, Routledge & Kegan Paul Ltd., 1939, pp. 3–17. Reprinted by permission.*

[5] This is implicit in a discussion of the subject by Diesing (1950:16–23), though the question of economic relativism as regards the nature of economic rationality is not taken up as such. Yet it should be noted that in discussing the normative aspects of economic behavior, he distinguishes, as one of these, "norms of property, manners, or taste, which appear to the individual in exemplary actions and the approval or disapproval of other people."

formulae to those types of society which are taken to differ so fundamentally from our own as to merit the term "primitive". This at once indicates a line of sociological study which not only may be fruitfully undertaken, but which, in the interests alike of economics and of other branches of social study, must sooner or later be faced. Does the method of modern economic theory apply equally to the Trobriander and to the Londoner? to the peasant of Eastern Europe and to the Chinese aristocrat? The question is far indeed from being an idle one. The very form in which we have put it reveals the chaos in which we should find ourselves should a negative answer be returned or even should any doubt remain in our minds. The aim of this book is to show that the concepts of economic theory must be taken as having universal validity, and that, were this not so, the result would be not only scientific confusion but practical chaos.

The practical weight of the problem is easily indicated. Our economic relationships now embrace in the most vital way peoples of very divergent cultures; trade is conducted and employment carried out between the most primitive of human creatures, such as the natives of the Andaman Islands or the Aborigines of Australia, and the most highly organized of London and New York firms. We have no doubt whatever that these Western businesses conduct their activities according to the dicta of modern economics, for these dicta were arrived at very largely by studying such businesses. But, should it happen that the assumptions of economic theory fail to fit the other term of the equation, that they give no guidance to the future conduct of the Andaman or the Aborigine, then the scope and usefulness of economic theory become so restricted that, in order to give guidance in the affairs of the modern world, the economist has before him no less a task than that of devising a "new economics" which would apply to the primitive people. The inevitable further task of establishing some correlation between the two "systems" of economics would then be so vast that we choose not to attempt to consider it.

Actually, once it is baldly stated, the proposition that there should be more than one body of economic theory is absurd. If modern economic analysis, with its instrumental concepts, cannot cope equally with the Aborigine and with the Londoner, not only economic theory but the whole of the social sciences may be considerably discredited. For the phenomena of social science are nothing if not universal. The groups, the behaviour, the fundamental social relationships such as those of kinsmen and neighbours, are qualitatively the same the world over. Wherever we look at Mankind we see motives of accumulation, of competitive display, of obligations towards kinsfolk, of religious organization and political activity; these, and such, make up the body of fact with which social science must deal. The fundamental differences between "civilized" and "savage", so dear to nineteenth-century sociologists, have now been so effectively exploded that we need not here waste space upon them. Quantitative differences between cultures most certainly exist; the people of one will have mechanical machinery while those of another may lack even the wheel; in one case literacy will be so common that almost everyone reads a morning newspaper, while in another case even the wise men of the people may have nothing corresponding to written characters. But if we turn our attention to these quantitative differences we shall find at the very outset that we are robbed of our hard-and-fast line between the savage and the civilized. Within one complex modern community such as the United States of America we must find many grades of culture; we shall find many people using machines but very few capable of originating them; we shall find people who can merely spell out the headlines of newspapers in their own language, and others who can write creatively. Turning to Europe, we find that under the term "European culture" we include such divergent peoples as the truly Western product of the great European capitals and the simplest of peasants who, at any rate until very recent years, must have been classed as much nearer, in cultural affinity, to the African tribesman, the subject of this volume, than to the highly sophisticated member of the great urban communities.

When it is asked, indeed, whether modern economic theory can be taken as applying to primitive life, we can only answer that if it does not apply to the whole of humanity then it is meaningless. For there is no gulf between the civilized and the primitive; one cultural level shades imperceptibly into another, and more than one level is frequently found within a single community. If economic theory does not apply to all levels, then it must be so difficult to say where its usefulness ends that we might be driven to assert that it has no usefulness at all.

Yet when, as inevitably happens, the social anthropologist and the economist begin to compare notes, a tendency shows signs of arising whereby the former may claim that economics, which he describes as "Western exchange economics", cannot quite apply to his primitive peoples, while the latter, although he regards his system as consisting of logical deductions from universal truths, finds himself in doubt as to whether these may correspond sufficiently to actual fact among peoples who are termed primitive. The problem, we believe, arises almost entirely from the difficulty of co-ordinating social studies. Economist and social anthropologist have one thing in common, the source of their strength and of their weakness; they are specialists. Each has carried his study to a high stage of validity and effectiveness; the very degree of their success makes it difficult for one to know what the other is doing. Hence the especial need for a study in co-ordination. The social anthropologist has the keenest need and desire to understand the economic aspect of the cultures upon which he works; the economist is no less desirous of testing and applying his equipment in every conceivable social setting. But, on the first approaches which they may make to each other, it is only too likely that they will be found to use terms in slightly different ways and to be unfamiliar with the exact nature of each other's working concepts.

The fundamental propositions of economics have probably not been in the mind of the anthropologist when he was making his enquiries; hence he is in the position of having to take these propositions, which, admittedly, were formulated with Western exchange communities in mind, and to test them out against the facts which he gathered in "the field". It is not surprising that this task has not so far been undertaken in a systematic way; nor is it surprising that, as appears to the present writer, the few efforts so far made do not show every sign of following the most fruitful lines. Yet we have conceded too much in saying that modern economic theory has been formulated with Western exchange systems in mind. It has been shown that Robinson Crusoe has something more than a strictly methodological significance; that an individual in his position would indeed feel the pressure of needs upon resources, would in fact make choices between the applications of his various resources, would encounter varying returns and would have to choose between present and future and between work and leisure. Wicksteed, on the other hand, has shown how the greater part of the apparatus of economic theory may be evolved without going outside a single household. This being so, it would be surprising if modern economic theory failed to apply to the peoples known as primitive.

We shall find that any difficulty which may arise in seeing that the savage disposes of his resources along ordinary economic lines, will arise through misconceptions very similar in character to those which, for a time, prevented the realization that people of low cultures conduct their affairs according to definite principles of law. It is not necessary here to recall how the savage was believed to have nothing corresponding to civil law, to be a blind slave of custom and, in general, not to be amenable to the legal principles which had been formulated in Western communities. It has now been shown very clearly that although the savage may not have formulated legal systems, yet he is in no way lacking in means of defining and enforcing obligations; in fact, that early legal theorists were misled by the absence of written codes and of formal courts. The "automatic obedience to custom", once the reality of savage law had been established, was seen to be a simple error; the savage obeys his customs, not automatically, but just as other people do; because there are sanctions which secure his obedience and because the whole of his training gives him the values which make him a good member of his own society. Legal principles were found to apply just as clearly in South Seas communities as in our own. It has been necessary to refer to the great step forward embodied in this realization because an analogous step must be taken with regard to economic theory.

It is almost superfluous to point out that the *forms* taken by the agencies of production in Western economics are almost undiscoverable in those of savage communities. Rent, wages, interest and profit assumed great importance in nineteenth-century economic discussions because they could, to some extent, be distinguished as separate shares given to separate bodies of people. In a primitive community we do not expect to find them in clearly distinguishable forms, although we shall find their distinct beginnings in Bantu societies. Likewise, special organizations to carry out cultivation or manufacture need not be expected among the Bantu; the functions are always actively carried out, but often by organizations, of which the family or household is the most important, which exist to carry out almost all necessary functions, including the religious, the legal, the political, and the educational, and which conduct manufacture and agriculture alongside of these other activities. Anything resembling a modern mercantile firm is, among the Bantu, conspicuous by its absence. Yet distribution is conducted and the elements of sale by specialists are by no means lacking. To attempt to apply the categories of production, exchange, distribution, and of rent, wages, interest and profit, to Bantu society would be to choose the most difficult of all approaches. Yet we must remember that these categories are not inapplicable among the people whom we study. It is often possible, as will be seen in forthcoming pages, to distinguish shares of product given to people on account of their labour, or their organizing power, for the use of their land or cattle, or even as a surplus corresponding to profit, accruing to them through the uncertainties of the situation. Yet we mention this point now mainly for three reasons: first, because the difficulty of discovering the *forms* of modern economic life may well lead to a mistaken belief that the *functions* of that life are not to be discoverable among our less advanced people; second, because these forms are not without their relevance for primitive communities; third, and most important, because modern economic theory has supplied us with a technique which transcends these forms and has the great merit of being applicable to the economic aspect of life, simply as an aspect, and independently of the forms prevalent in any given culture.

First among the principles which we must use in studying the economic aspect of Bantu life is that of the indirect satisfaction of wants, with which is closely associated the fact of division of labour. It is as true of African society as of any other that the people do not work each to satisfy his or her own needs. The division of labour is elementary, being largely dominated by such natural or social facts as differences in age, sex, or rank. Yet, no matter how elementary the division may be, it is a fact that we see people manufacturing goods and rendering services because they expect these to be valued sufficiently highly by other members of the community. In a Bantu household the women are able to concentrate on certain services and the men upon others. A woman produces more grain than she and her children will wish to consume; the way in which the surplus is used to feed her husband and his unmarried brothers is dependent upon these men valuing the women's produce in some ascertainable way, and, in return, performing their own services, which in their turn are evaluated by the women. Even if this evaluation were conducted without any conscious effort, it would still establish an effective relationship. But, as we shall see, the people appear to be very conscious of the importance of the reciprocity, as is best seen when one party believes the other to fail in his or her duties, when scarcity or plenty changes the value of either set of services, or when people are contemplating a marriage and carefully compute the value of the services which the prospective partner is likely to render. When grain is plentiful in a community, the value of an extra wife may noticeably diminish, while in time of scarcity, when baskets of grain take on a very high value in relation to other commodities, the women will be justly valued as standing between the household and starvation.

If this indirect principle, controlling the investment of working power in accordance with the estimated value of the product, can be seen, as we hold it can, even in the relationship between the women and the men of a household, then it may be seen even more clearly in situations depending upon a wider sphere of exchange. More specific exchange takes place also within a given household, as when one person may specialize in tending cattle and will certainly be rewarded accordingly. It is clear that the principle of the indirect rendering of services is as real in Bantu society as in Western. Each person, or group, carries out productive activities upon the basis of an estimate of the demand of other persons for the product; this demand thereby originates the activity and values the units of product according to the urgency of the needs which they satisfy and the possibility of securing equal satisfaction by the use of substitutes, which, in their turn, will be produced upon such a demand coming into evidence.

It is in this way that we begin to see the concept of wants as controlling the means of their satisfaction. The legal principle operates alongside of this principle of economic indirectness, and is indispensable to it. There must be effective sanctions for the carrying out of obligations; it is the economic principle which lies at the root of the obligations. The fact that this division of labour is quantitatively very much less than in a Western community in no way lessens its importance. The principle is just as valuable to the more primitive community as to the more complex, and we cannot begin to appreciate the universal applicability of economic method until we grasp this fact.

The principle of economic indirectness is, in turn, but part of the wider one of the economic application of resources. The question is whether the savage can be said so to dispose of his resources as to feel that no unit would have given greater satisfaction if put to a different use. This concept is at the basis of modern economic method. As we shall see later, it is to be taken simply as a methodological assumption, and not as a statement having content. Can we assume that the savage so disposes of his total resources as to obtain the maximum satisfaction? Our reply is an unhesitating affirmative, in the sense, and in the sense only, in which we should reply in the affirmative if asked whether the assumption is useful in Western communities. There can be no doubt that the Bantu enjoys a flow of resources which he must apply to the satisfaction of a series of needs. He has labour power and land, then cattle, grain, and other disposable commodities, continuously coming to hand; he has the needs for nutrition, for warmth, for government, for religious experience and for many similar things which we are yet to examine more closely. It should be evident that the diversion of an undue proportion of his goods to the satisfaction of any one need will leave the others unsatisfied, and a feeling of frustration in the man. It must have been easy for him (in the old days) to devote so much time to house-building or removing, when the time was needed for the fields, that the family would be left short of food. It must have been easy to kill valuable animals for sacrifice to such an extent that the household was left short of flesh and milk at another season. It will be seen throughout this book that economic choice is constantly exercised by the individual both in disposing of resources for consumption and in the disposal of resources for further production. An individual who disposes unsuccessfully of his supplies will enjoy less satisfactions than his neighbours; a household which ineffectively applies its resources to the creation of further commodities will likewise see its members less well supplied with consumable produce than are their neighbours. The assumption of the economic disposal of resources appears to work. Yet it is just here that doubts have arisen.

These doubts may be comprehensively stated under some four headings. There is first the question as to whether the alleged carefree nature of the savage may rule out effective economical disposal of his resources. Little time need be wasted on this proposition, although it is well to note it, for, mistaken though it is in itself, it suggests one or two genuine points. The fiction of the lazy savage has by now been thoroughly exploded; some of the most lowly peoples have been found to be industrious gardeners and tireless craftsmen. Yet proof of these activities is no proof of a keen desire to dispose carefully of units of resources. With the savage as with ourselves, a point must arrive at which his main satisfaction will be derived from not worrying too much about the way in which he may consume his worldly wealth. An Englishman sooner or later reaches the point at which he decides that, in order to expend his income so as to get the maximum of satisfaction from the last sixpence, he would have to give to the matter much more than sixpennyworth of care and attention. It may be suggested that peoples of different cultures are willing to go to different degrees of trouble in the careful planning of their expenditure. This is a matter upon which we can have only personal impressions. It is probable, however, that some peoples, of whom the Latins of South America are reputedly an example, may put much less stress upon the economic disposal of their resources than do certain other peoples, generally supposed to reside in more Northern climes. It is also certain, among individuals, that some, even within a group of acquaintances, are much more economically minded than others. Yet we should never suppose from this that the assumptions of economic theory apply to some individuals and not to others, or that they break down when applied to the South American whose main occupation appears, at least to the superficial observer, to be to lie in the sun.

The uneconomically minded person, so-called, is simply a person who puts a relatively high value upon his time and attention; he does not squander these upon attention to details. If part of his resources are expended in ways other than they would have been had he devoted more attention to the matter, the fact still remains that his whole resources, including his powers of attention, have been disposed of in the ways which give him his greatest satisfaction. He may have paid a good deal for his carefreeness, but this in no way breaks down the basic assumptions of economic theory. The possibility always remains that he will change his habits, and we cannot suppose that such a change would suddenly bring him within the scope of economic principles. Thus, even if the Trobrianders or the Bantu happened to be very careless in their domestic economies, this fact would not invalidate our contention that the main body of economic theory applies to them just as much as to ourselves.

Yet all our evidence points to the fact that even these widely divergent peoples are relatively careful in spending their resources. There is overwhelming evidence that they dislike waste; a Bantu family has very efficient means of making its resources go as far as possible. Social mechanisms show this, in that the head of the household has ultimate control of the great majority of food stores. The housewives cannot draw upon these without his knowledge or permission. The need for economic disposal along careful lines is often paramount, for the penalty for neglect may be starvation. A herd of cattle, likewise, is certainly not squandered by any Bantu owner; all evidence points to the fact that he most carefully weighs the alternative uses to which his animals might be put; some will be used for a sacrifice, some for a wedding portion, some to relieve a necessitous relative, some as gifts (*i.e.* taxes) to the chief. It is no mere form of words to say that cattle are highly valued among the Bantu; this statement points to one of the central facts of their lives, and its meaning lies in their *behaviour*, which carries out an extremely careful disposal of these objects of wealth, so that *the central assumption* of economic theory is readily applicable.

A more important objection to the application of modern economic assumptions to peoples such as the Bantu is that their lives are so dominated by custom that they cannot be said to exercise free economic choice. The present writer has not yet seen this objection clearly stated in print, but he does find a tendency to say that, of course, free choice, as known in Western communities, does not exist among savages. It is held of some of the poorer tribes that they are so near the margin of subsistence that they cannot exercise economic choice, while it appears to be a tacit assumption of many writers about primitive peoples that an entity called custom controls their lives in such a way that they dispose of their resources with but little willed choice.

With regard to both of these points, we should say that we are already thoroughly familiar with them in discussions of Western economic life. Very large numbers of Western and European people spend their lives very near what may be called subsistence level. Peasants and unskilled labourers have normally just enough resources to meet what appear to be elementary physical needs. Yet we never say that economic theory does not apply to these people, and in this we are right, for, no matter how scant the resources may be, they still must be disposed of along economic lines. We might even go further and say that the fewer the resources, the more need there is for the housewife to expend them carefully, thus adding to the total family income of real satisfactions through the increased exertion on her part. It is doubtful even whether the fact that Western wages are paid in the form of money gives to the European labourer any freedom to waste his resources which is denied to the Bantu, whose income is in the form of readily usable products. Just as the European labourer's income may be expended in "worthless" ways, so the Bantu who is near the starvation level may well consume all his resources at a feast which will bring him no return, or exchange them for trinkets. Even the savage who is normally near starvation has freedom of choice to "waste" those resources which he has, and a correspondingly greater need to apply them with due care.

But by no means all Bantu tribes are, or were in the past, on what is called the "margin of subsistence". Yet it appears to have been assumed that they, in common with other primitive peoples, have been so dominated by custom that free economic choice has not been to them the reality which it is to us. The supposition has been that "custom" may make primitive peoples behave in ways unlike those which we know in the Western world. It might appear that the savage has held expensive feasts because these were customary; has kept large herds of cattle because custom so dictated; has given part of his crops away against his own interest, because it was customary to do so; has allowed his chief to plunder him, again because it was the custom.

Any such statements or suppositions are entirely meaningless. Custom is merely another name for behaviour, and these statements merely state that such-and-such behaviour is carried out; they solve no problems. All that social scientists can do is to observe the ways in which human beings behave. When any piece of behaviour is repeatedly observed, it is described and given a name, so that it may be observed and discussed upon future occasions. A custom is therefore a unit of behaviour, isolated for purpose of observation. When customs are carried out in very well marked ways by considerable groups of people, on specific occasions, they become those organized activities which have sometimes been called Institutions. Thus to say that savage behaviour is customary, or even dominated by custom, is to be guilty of tautology. To say that he pays taxes to his chief because of "custom", is merely to say that he pays them. We shall see throughout this work that organized custom remains a most useful concept in describing Bantu behaviour so as to appreciate its economic aspect, but we must never suppose that a piece of conduct is disposed of as soon as we have called it a "custom".

We shall find that resources are indeed disposed of according to the dictates of social values and rules of behaviour, describable in terms of custom. In this way we hope to obtain a full appreciation of the economic aspect of Bantu life. It will be found that this, instead of invalidating the assumption of the economic disposal of resources, gives us the terms on which this disposal takes place.

Two threads are clearly visible: on the one hand, society lays down the main lines along which resources must be disposed of; on the other hand, the individual or the group is left free to achieve the social ends by his own planning. We may say that this gives us economic disposal in two different senses. In one, the society or the culture lays down the broad rules for the economic disposal, and in the other, the individual or his group manages his own resources in conformity with social rule. But these together only give a total management of resources along strictly economic lines. Any economic management must be with a view to realizing values already in the minds of the people. These values are themselves a cultural product, and are inculcated into each individual almost from the first hours of life. A man grows up to value certain social forms and activities, be they the ceremonies at the crises of life or the more continuous conventions of daily existence. One of the main lessons of his life is to dispose of his resources so as to realize these valued things to the highest degree possible. Thus in behaving in the customary ways, he exhibits no conduct presenting any new difficulties to the assumptions of modern economists. It would be quite as true to say that the people of America or Europe are so dominated by custom that they cannot dispose economically of their resources. Exploring the point with a primitive people in mind, we are brought to realize that we are dealing with a sociological principle of universal import. All over the world, people are not free to dispose of their resources, as it were, *de novo*. Everywhere the main lines of expenditure are laid down; the aim of the individual's choice is to realize the maximum satisfaction along these lines.

The principle of economic disposal is an essential part, or aspect, of any cultural scheme. One of the basic facts to be observed in any culture, however primitive, is that it has mechanisms whereby the individual is taught not to waste; to acquire values in consonance with those of his fellow-beings, and to manage his affairs according to those values. Even if the savage, therefore, could be said to be "dominated by custom", this, far from meaning that he did not dispose economically of his resources, might mean just the opposite; for custom may best be regarded as the mechanism through which this essential aim is achieved. Customary behaviour is simply the entity of which we are now studying the economic aspect.

A further way in which it is sometimes argued that the savage so behaves as to render economic assumptions less illuminating when applied to him, is that in which he may be said to fail to perceive small units of commodities, or to have a large *minimum sensible*. It may be said that time means little to him, therefore that if it is customary for him to devote a certain number of days to a piece of work or to a ceremony, he will do so without further calculation. The same may be said of the units in terms of which he thinks; if it is customary for him to make a gift of a certain number of baskets of grain on a certain occasion, then that he will do so. Against any such argument we can but invoke all the factual evidence of the best modern anthropology. It has been shown again and again that the savage can be careful to the last basket of grain and that he can bargain to the last goat-skin. Further, that if the goat-skin is too valuable, some extra small service will be expected in return to make the bargain even. Perhaps the most effective demonstration of the futility of such an argument is afforded by the introduction of currency by Europeans. When this occurs, the people will be found to balance their accounts and their bargains down to the smallest coin available.

It remains only, in this connection, to answer the argument that savages may not behave in ways consistent with their self-interest. The Trobriand Islanders have been quoted as giving away a large part of their produce to their wives' brothers instead of keeping it for themselves. This behaviour, so far from exemplifying disinterested, non-economic action, merely indicates an extension of kinship ties. It is quite on a par with a European father giving a large part of his income to his own wife or children. To introduce such considerations and to try to prove from them that savage behaviour may be of so peculiar a nature that it actually reverses ordinary economic assumptions is regarded by the present writer as fantastic.

4 THE SOCIAL FRAMEWORK OF ECONOMIC ORGANIZATION
Raymond Firth

The anthropologist is interested in the structure and organization of economic activity for two reasons: most social relations have an economic coefficient; many social relations are primarily concerned with economic values. But the anthropologist is not setting out to discover the principles of economics in the sense of the abstract body of theory which attempts to explain economic aspects of human behaviour at the most general, universal level. His task is to examine how these principles work in specific social or cultural contexts. The principles of economics which are truly general or universal in their application are few. Most of those which purport to be general have been constructed primarily within the framework of ideas of an industrial, capitalist system. This means a machine technology, a monetary medium of exchange, an elaborate credit system using stocks and shares and banking institutions, developed private enterprise, and a social structure of an individualistic, Western kind. The anthropologist struggles with a diversity of types. Many are peasant systems, with money used for a limited range of transactions, a simple technology with hardly any machinery, and methods of enterprise, co-operation, credit, and income-getting very different from those in a Western economy. Some are truly primitive, with no monetary medium at all to facilitate the processes of exchange, distribution, and storage of wealth. The anthropologist's problem, then, is one of applying or translating economic principles in novel contexts. He is even deprived for the most part of the common means of measurement available to his economist colleague. Without money there is

From Elements of Social Organization *by Raymond Firth, London, C. A. Watts & Co. Ltd., 1952, pp. 122–154. Reprinted by permission.*

no simple means of reckoning prices. Even where money is used, its limited range inhibits easy measurement of the bulk of economic relations. Although the passage of time can be quite carefully expressed, it is rare for any system of regularly spaced units of less than a day to be used. So any close calculation of labour expenditure, as in man-hours, is possible only by field observation. All this has one advantage: that the anthropologist is not so subject to the possible distortion of monetary preoccupations. He is looking at the interplay of "real" units of man-power and materials, output and income, not veiled by the "money illusion" of a Western economy. He finds it necessary to examine the picture of economic relationships in the kind of frame in which the people themselves have set it. What results has he achieved? And what is their relation to the study of economics as ordinarily understood?

First consider the nature of economic organization, in its broadest scope.

Economic organization is a type of social action. It involves the combination of various kinds of human services with one another and with non-human goods in such a way that they serve given ends. This means an arrangement of these elements in a system, by limiting the kinds of relations that can potentially exist between them. Such combination or limitation does not occur mechanically, but by giving values to the goods and services. Choice is exercised in the light of these values. From among the available means those are chosen which seem most appropriate to the given ends. From among possible ends those are taken which seem to be most realizable by the available means. Choice at some level of consciousness is required for most types of action. Its implications for economic organization lie where the emphasis is on disposal of resources. There can be other emphases—on the nature of the social relations involved, or of the action as such. Moral choice or aesthetic choice, for instance, are concerned with actions and relations rather than with use of resources.

Choices are not discrete, unrelated. They form a system, they have continuity. Each is related to the others which succeed it, behaviourally—not only in a time-sequence but in an action sequence. They are related also conceptually, in terms of values—that is, in regard to a series of qualities assigned to the relations involved in action.

In all this, the fact of sociality is vitally important. The choice, the behaviour, the values of any one person are all conditioned by other people. They, too, are exercising their choices. They compete for a common set of resources. By their very existence they are significant elements in the individual's total appreciation of his own position. Relations with them are then assigned specific qualities—values. This is so in part because the actions of these other persons give sense to the conceptual and symbolic system of the individual. His notions of economic reality are confirmed by seeing the type of choice made by others around him. The less any individual acts in isolation, the more he must be responsive to choices, or the expectations of choices, by others. Economic organization is set in a social framework—of relations between persons and between groups, expressed in different conceptual ways and with different emphases, as values, symbols, rules of conduct, patterns of behaviour. To take a very obvious example—the operation of a monetary system. Money is a symbol. It represents in a measurable way some command over goods and services. It can operate effectively only so long as there is general confidence that it is a valid symbol in the economic system concerned, and is so recognized by others. This confidence can be shaken by events arising from within the system—as a very rapid increase in the volume of money in circulation. But it can also be shaken by events from without the economic system—as by a legal pronouncement that this money is no longer valid; or by a new moral conviction of, say, religious origin that is wrong to use money at all. The confidence of every individual in the monetary system is a matter of delicate adjustment, and is a function of his wider confidence in his fellows. This is maintained not merely by seeing them use money, and seeing the material equivalent for what money he himself uses: it rests also on his belief in the general consistency of their conduct, on his expectations that there will be general consensus of views even in spheres where money is not used. One aspect of this is seen in the demarcation of such spheres. It is only by taking into account the general social framework of relations and evaluations that one can accept the Western exchange codes. One pays money for a meal in a restaurant but not for one in a private house, for a cow but not for a wife. Yet these are conventions of primarily a moral order. There are non-Western systems where money is handed over in return for the private meal, and for the wife, and where both transactions are justified on moral grounds.

It is against this social framework that the anthropologist takes up his economic study.

The basic concept of economics is the allocation of scarce, available resources between realizable human wants, with the recognition that alternatives are possible in each sphere. However defined, economics thus deals with the implications of human choice, with the results of decisions. Choices, wants, and their implications in action involve personal relations, social relations. If social anthropology examines forms of social relations in the more primitive societies, economics examines certain types of social relations—for example, production and exchange relations—in all societies. This is done with a rigour rarely if ever reached in anthropological propositions. In so far as the science of economics can be said to put forward principles that are truly universal, it could have more justification for being called the science of man than has anthropology, which might be called the science of kinds of men.

The relation of social anthropology to economics can really be shown best by examples. The problem is complicated by the asymmetrical development of the two sciences. Whereas some institutional fields of relationships given conventional recognition, above all kinship, are almost wholly the subject-matter of social anthropology, the economic field is already pre-empted. The most significant generalizations—that is, those which explain the widest spheres of action and link very many elements of apparently disparate kind—are the property of economic science. What, then, can be done in the name of economic anthropology?

If we examine economic propositions we see that all but the most formal and abstract are expressed in terms of institutionalized concepts. There may be no reference to particular commodities, no time and place coefficients. There may be even deliberate avoidance of the monetary expression of relations in favour of expression in output units, investment units, labour units, and other "real" quantities. But the concepts of output involve more or less explicitly stated notions of the business firm as an entity; of an industry as a series of such localized entities using much the same kinds of resources and technical processes and bringing out a comparable product; of the entrepreneur with the specialized function of conducting economic operations in such a *milieu*. The concepts of investment likewise involve notions of a market in which buying and selling are characteristic operations and in which there is sufficient continuity of requirement, in replacement of equipment at least, to allow of reasonable alternatives in choice. Usually there is a far more substantial content in the propositions—they involve ideas of foreign trade, government taxation and expenditure, accumulation of money balances, limited liability in industrial and commercial operations. Moreover, this is set against a specific background of socially oriented notions of community life—involving autonomous national entities; a distinction between public and private services; the operation of government as a legislative as well as an executive machine. Many of these concepts are alien to the kinds of economy the anthropologist has to describe.

This contextualization of economic theory is obvious and necessary. It is primarily Western, not only, as some would argue, because of the need for a theory to give social and moral validity to the series of economic changes which found their outlet in the industrial revolution. The anthropologist is perhaps more prone than most other social scientists to a tacit historicism. Yet even should one accept much of the criticism of such a standpoint, in its more extreme forms, the way in which the trend of economic theory has followed the march of economic fact cannot be ignored.[1] But the cogency of the argument implied in most economic analysis, that the complexities of the Western institutional field offer the most attractive intellectual exercise and the greatest possibilities of mensurational refinement, must be recognized. One can expect an economist, then, to have only limited sympathy with Radhakamal Mukerjee's complaint of the neglect of non-Western economic forms (1922:

[1] It has probably been the rise of the Soviet and Fascist economies and the prospects of democratic socialism elsewhere, rather than theoretical preoccupations, which has led to the many recent analyses of the economic problems involved in central planning and restriction of freedom of individual choice in a socialist State. And this also, combined with the difficulties attending a programme of investment in technically underdeveloped countries, may lead to more intensive theoretical investigation of peasant economic systems, including moneyless ones.

II, 86. Cf. also Firth 1929:2–4 and Firth 1939:23–28. Cf. Weber 1947:192),
which has been repeated by anthropologists. The role of the anthropologist here
is rather that of a watch-dog—to see that no one takes away the reality of the
economic systems of primitive peoples by default. Of this there has been some
danger.

But the anthropological function is more relevant from a theoretical angle.
Economic propositions and processes of economic analysis tend always to
involve assumptions about social behaviour. One of the great achievements of
modern economic theory is the success with which it has eliminated such
extraneous matter, and based its reasoning upon a very small amount of primary
data about human existence. The main premises are: the varied and expansible
nature of human objectives of conduct—the multiplicity of ends; the limitation
of means for satisfying them—the fact of scarcity; and the need to choose
between them—the exercise of preference. Thus equipped, the economist can
afford to ignore the character of specific ends, except by way of illustration.
From this point of view the argument of Herskovits, that economists have
neglected the psychological factor in assessing the determinants of value (Herskovits 1940:210), is a misunderstanding. The "psychological factor" is introduced
much farther back, in the assumptions of demand and choice as such. To investigate the psychological and social determinants of particular evaluations,
to chart the value system of a society empirically, are important tasks. But
they cannot be imposed on the theoretical economists in a concrete way. When,
however, economic theory moves from the realm of pure abstraction to analysis
and description of the behaviour of people in any specific society, then
additional assumptions must be inserted into the argument. The objection that
can be legitimately raised against some aspects of economic analysis is that
such assumptions, which should be explicit and based upon empirical study, are
often only half-explored and based upon some vague general notions of
what is the local norm of behaviour.

In ordinary economic analysis the "impersonal system of markets and
prices" serves as a medium by which allocation of resources among different
possible uses is arranged, through the competition of users, expressed in monetary terms. The system is recognized to be in fact not one of really free
movement. Competition is imperfect; combinations of producers, of traders,
restrict fluctuations in commodity prices, and trade unions restrict wage rates.
A theory of imperfect competition may take such "frictions" into account in a
highly abstract way. But something more is needed if the economic system
described is to be part of the real world. Whenever an attempt is made to
assess magnitudes, whether in the expenditure patterns of people with small
incomes, in the relation of co-operation and rivalry of capital and labour, in
the decisions of the directors of a joint-stock company, in the whole sphere
of incentives to production, assumptions have got to be made. These need the
empirical data which the sociologist and historian should help to supply.
Such data provide a basis for assumption as to what people will really do in

response to changes in their economic conditions, and, in particular, by how much their behaviour will be likely to vary. Highly technical devices, such as indifference curves, are claimed to rule out the psychological elements of utility or satisfaction from the exercise of preferences. But they have to rely ultimately on some observational foundation—if they are to be anything more than logical manipulations. For the economic propositions derived from them to be capable of reference to reality it is necessary to assume, as Hicks points out, that there are no "kinks" in the curves or that the kinks can be ignored. This means an assumption that there is enough regularity in the system of wants and in the productive system for inferences about possible equilibrium to be made. Just as the older economists based their principle of diminishing marginal utility on some appeal to everyday experience, so also Hicks, after pointing out that this assumption about regularity is the simplest possible, says, "In fact, its accordance with experience seems definitely good" (Hicks 1939:24 and *passim*). But how does one arrive at the idea that it is good or correct to assume a regularity in the system of wants? Only ultimately from some observation of the behaviour of people.

The implications of this for economic anthropology are clear. Part of the task of the anthropologist is to assist in translating general propositions of economic theory into terms that will apply to the particular types of society in which he is interested, and which do not ordinarily come under the economist's observation. To do this he must expose the social factors which are of most relevance in the preference scales of the members of the society. He must make clear—ultimately, if possible, by quantitative demonstration—the regularities and irregularities in the system of wants. If in a primitive community a fishing-canoe is an important item of wealth, ranking high in the scale of exchange values, then the anthropologist must make clear just what is the position when such a canoe is destroyed on the death of a close agnatic kinsman. He must indicate that this competing use for an item of capital has very definite restrictions placed upon it by social convention. It is not simply a sporadic, incalculable individual act. There is predictable regularity in the complex adjustments concerned with breaking up the craft or saving it from destruction.

In essence, then, the antropologist accepts as valid the body of economic doctrine. Ordinarily he can absorb only a very small part of it into his conceptual apparatus for the study of primitive society. But he attempts to push it farther into the empirical field by securing evidence to give content to economic propositions in social situations where the economist's assumptions about human behaviour must be reformulated. It cannot be said that the results are yet very satisfactory. One reason for this is undoubtedly a lack of clear ideas or formulation by many anthropologists as to the nature of economic data.

Most social relations have an economic aspect. The exercise of choice in social situations involves economy of resources in time and in energy. In this sense a marriage has an economic aspect in all the decisions and relations of daily life, even in sex congress, quite apart from the exchanges of goods and services that may go on. But by a convention the science of economics concerns itself with those fields of choice which involve goods and services, and primarily those which have a price put upon them. In this sense relations between persons in virtue of their association in the production or exchange of these goods and services are "economic" relations. Anthropologists have frequently missed the point of such relations. We need demonstrate only briefly that economics is not technology. To read in the chapter entitled "Economic Life" in a well-known ethnographic monograph such statements as, "To relieve the itch, the juice of the *kabatiti* . . . is applied to the skin" or that "cracked feet are treated with carabao dung," (Cole 1922:410) reminds one how wrongly classified has been much of what is called economic treatment in most of the classical records of field research. Yet even in the examples mentioned a little interesting economic information might have been given about the amount of time and effort spent on collecting and applying the remedies; the frequency with which they were found to be used by the people; whether they were ever borrowed for a consideration; whether there were other remedies easier to come by, but not preferred. Failure to realize the nature of the problems has led to the omission of a whole range of data on output, on costs, on incomes, on circulation of valuables, and other economic aspects which could have given form and precision to a dreary collection of facts. The castigation which Robbins gave to Alfred Marshall's "spineless platitudes about manures" would clearly be even more merited if applied to some anthropologists who have written under the heading of Economics. Apart from this, there is still a tendency among modern anthropologists to frame their definitions of economics in terms of goods, or material goods, to the exclusion of services. Yet the anthropologist, above all, is in a position to appreciate Frank H. Knight's dictum that the economic magnitude is not goods, but service. A tendency to neglect the basic factor of choice in the allocation of resources betrays an equal unfamiliarity with guiding ideas of the economic discipline.

If, then, economics deals with the principles of the use of resources in general, economic anthropology deals with concomitant social relations, the specific ways in which the principles are exemplified in a range of given social situations. Economic anthropology is an empirical study, and a comparative one. But what social situations are its subject-matter? The definition obtained on this question is no more precise than that of the scope of social anthropology —that on the whole it is the more primitive societies that are the proper study.[2] The first criterion, then, is an empirical one—simplicity of technology. A second criterion, also empirical, is to some extent related to the first, but arises in part from the abstentions of the economists themselves. The tendency of

[2] Radcliffe-Brown gives different delimitations. In an article on social structure (Radcliffe-Brown 1952) social anthropology is the study of human society, equivalent to comparative sociology. In a comment on Leslie White's views (1949:503) he describes the science as the study of primitive or preliterate societies.

economics is to claim the complete realm of choice in the allocation of resources as their province, but in practice to restrict their analyses to price
situations, where there is money measurement. Pigou, for instance, after
correcting Marshall to include the operations of a barter economy in the
subject-matter of economics, in fact pays little attention to such operations in
his analyses. The reason is that the technical difference is regarded as embodying
also a conceptual difference. Further, an evaluation containing moral and
possibly aesthetic elements gives approval to the efficiencies provided by a
monetary system.[3] Such an evaluative approach to the existence of money as an
effective calculating medium of exchange draws strength in contemporary conditions from the conviction of many economists that the price mechanism is a
necessary instrument in the economic system of any developed community, and
that planning of the major structure of the economy by the State, if ever it can
be effective, must employ such an instrument. The close connection of the
political and economic arguments means that statements about a moneyless
economy by those who are not anthropologists have usually to be read in a
special context. We read that co-operation and exchange cannot function
effectively without a money system. We are also told that a moneyless economy,
which could not orient its production on the basis of profitability, would have
to make its decisions as to what and how much should be produced either
according to tradition or to arbitrary dictatorial regulation (Pigou 1935:33, 70;
Weber 1947:166, 190; Shils 1948: 36–50). But we need not make immediate
protest. If it were a primitive economy that was under discussion, an anthropologist would have to make two points. First, the concept of what is effective
functioning of an exchange and co-operative system depends on what criteria
are applied. For many primitive societies, taking the small magnitude of the
society and the ends of the people into consideration, a claim for effectiveness
might well be made. Secondly, granting the difficulties of measuring efficiencies
in a non-monetary economy, goods and services are in fact measured against
one another, and there is no evidence that efficiency declines without effective
check. The problem of decision as to how much shall be produced in a primitive
economy is decided in terms of at least four considerations. Dictation by
individual leaders does occur, though usually in a modified form of a decision
which is basically representative of group interests—as that a feast of a
certain magnitude shall be held, and food accumulated accordingly. Again,

[3] Pigou heads a chapter "The Need for Money in Voluntary Private Dealings," (1935).
Cf. J. E. Meade: "There can be no doubt that money and the pricing system are among
the greatest social inventions of mankind. Properly used, they should be capable of giving
to each individual a general command over his *fair* share of the community's resources; of
allowing each individual to decide for himself—where private choice is *appropriate*—in what
form he will exercise this command; of allowing initiative to individual producers and
merchants to produce what is most wanted, in the most economical manner, in the markets
where supplies are most needed; in short, of combining *freedom*, *efficiency* and *equity* in
social affairs" (1948:34).

traditional norms help to decide the level of production—expressed in the form of immediate conventions of day-to-day work. Apart from these two elements, mentioned by Max Weber, a non-monetary economy does provide for a great deal of direct matching of goods and services, in which ideas of comparative worth of time, labour, and other components of preference scales operate. Finally, the concept of technical efficiency in an economic situation is partially replaced by that of social efficiency. The lack of a money index in the comparative rating of goods and services means imprecision. But it does not imply either the lack of rational calculation or an unregulated system of handling expenditure of resources.

Exposition of this last point can best be done by examining more deeply some of the general characteristics of the simpler economic systems, especially by contrast with a highly differentiated industrial system. It should first be made clear that just as the term "preliterate" has little value as an empirical defining character in contemporary conditions, where some system of primary education is creeping into all remote communities, so also the term "non-monetary" is for the most part a conceptual and not empirical criterion for distinguishing economic systems. In the whole Pacific region, for instance, only a few isolated communities on islands such as Tikopia, and in the heart of New Guinea, are entirely without money of a Western type. When the economist talks, then, of the "natural economy" of primitive communities— that is, the obtaining or exchanging of goods and services without using money in the transactions—this is to be regarded as a label—not to the anthropologist an attractive one—for a section of an economic system. Like the term "subsistence economy", it describes an emphasis, a conceptual category, not an economic totality. (It should be clear from earlier analysis that the term "natural" cannot be held to imply an economy springing direct from the uninhibited wants of the primitive individual. These wants are highly socialized, and the exchange system operates in a set of social conventions, often employing also symbolic media.) But where there is a monetary medium facilitating exchanges and serving as a measure of economic activity, the system of transactions in which this medium is used is apt to be restricted. Many exchanges of goods and services take place which fall outside the monetary sphere and yet must be reckoned as an integral part of the economic system. The price system which does exist in such conditions may be, as Weber argues, of a highly traditionalized type, with relative inflexibility in rates over long periods, and considerable resistance on the part of producers and consumers to variation in these rates. This is not always the case. There may be a distinct contrast between the traditional rates for some types of service and the highly flexible rates for others. In the Malay peasant economy, side by side with firmly established conventions of paying harvesters of the rice crop a tenth of what they gather, irrespective of the current price of rice, and of making conventional money gifts at feasts, there is a most sensitive bargaining system in the buying and selling of fish, with prices varying from site to site and hour to hour. Fluctuations in supplies and requirements, and in the expectations of profit, are geared into a mechanism of almost "pure" market relationships. In such peasant conditions the manifestations of a price economy and a "natural" economy can occur side by side. But more important is that economic behaviour in many types of relation, as, for instance, attitudes towards saving or lending, can be equated as between price and non-price systems. Such behaviour is a function of the social structure, with its emphasis on the village community and the kinship group.

A summary of the principal features of the economy of such peasant systems, whether monetary or non-monetary, outside the immediate Western orbit, would be as follows:

The relative simplicity of technology, with little use of machinery, means the lack of a high degree of economic specialization. With it goes the lack of allocation of resources to technical development as such. The economic mechanism is not highly sensitive to the possibility of technical change, and such change is slight and slow.

The actual productive unit is small. Even in a large community such as an African or Malay state, where the network of producers may be wide, their combinations at one time and place as units of differentiated function are of limited scale.

There is no constantly expanding market for capital, ever seeking fresh avenues of investment, though capital goods exist, and there are effective notions of their use and maintenance.

Correspondingly, there is no widespread entrepreneur system ever seeking to create new demands. Entrepreneurs usually play some part in the organization of goods and services, but they normally plan to fulfil traditional wants, and they are not restricted to this occupation.

The system of control of capital goods follows different conventions from those with which we are familiar in a Western economic system. The social limits to accumulation differ, by providing more specific and more regular institutionalized avenues for disbursement, as by a feast; or by prohibiting certain kinds of increment—as Muslims are forbidden to take interest from their fellows. Traditional means of levelling out or mitigating inequalities in the possession of capital exist, as by enforced lending on request—with the sanction of public disapproval on refusal—or by the recognition of communal rights which are basic to the whole social order.

In terms of personnel, the agents of production are often not clearly separable in practice. Instead of the separation familiar in the scheme of a capitalist economy—of entrepreneur, workmen, organizing manager, capitalist—the provider of the major capital is commonly a manual worker himself. Other workers may put up some of the capital, directly or indirectly, severally or jointly, as by contributing food to the undertaking. This makes for a different scheme of economic relationships. It tends to obviate friction between the parties. It also allows for different expectations as to the outcome if change in circumstances should affect the rewards of production.

Partly as a result of this, the organization of production tends to be based not merely on a system of cash rewards, where money is used in exchange. Wage relations as such may not exist. The workers may get their return by simple profit-sharing, and may be drawn to contribute their services by a range of incentives, including kinship, or ties of loyalty to a chief. The ties between producers tend to reach out beyond their common interest in the act of production and its rewards alone. A production relationship is often only one facet of a social relationship.

Emerging from this, the system of distribution of the results of production tends to be a complex one, and not easily separated into a classical economist's scheme of rent, interest, wages, profits—granted that this formal division is now breaking down in modern economic analysis.

The peasant system may be much simpler, as, for instance, by rewarding all the agents of production together at a common meal or feast. Or it may be much more complex, and assign to each a reward which is calculated in accordance with his social contribution rather than his economic contribution. For example, take the building of a house in the simple community of Tikopia. The workers comprise a few skilled craftsmen and a number of ordinary assistants. The former get special payment in bark-cloth, mats, and other valuables in recognition of their skill, though not directly proportioned to the relative amounts of time they have put in. The assistants get their payment at a common meal which they share with the skilled builders. Any man who comes along gets his share of the meal, no matter how little work he may have done. As a special section of producers, come the husbands of the sisters and daughters of the men for whom the house is being built. They each bring to the work a bundle of firewood and some coconuts or other raw food. This is their contribution to the meal, in virtue of their marriage obligations, which extend to attendance in a similar capacity at all social events of the group into which they have married. They have also to act as cooks for the occasion. In their turn, they also receive as reward a portion of the cooked food in due course, and possibly other goods too.

The principle recognized by the economist, of reward proportioned to total productivity, is not easy to recognize here. Such a principle does exist in this type of system. But its operation is conditioned by other factors—social factors. In such circumstances economic relations can be understood only as part of a scheme of social relations. What I have said about the peasant society studied by the anthropologist is very much what the historian has described in other language for the economic life of the Middle Ages. One can translate this into various propositions. One may say that in such a peasant economy economic ties are personalized—that is, relationships as economic agents depend on the social status and relationships of the persons concerned. Put another way, labour is given as a social service, and not simply an economic service. Its reward is therefore apt to be calculated in terms of the total social situation, and not merely the immediate economic situation. Economic means tend to be translated into social ends.

Contrast this with economic relations in an industrial system. In the latter the individual has normally a high degree of anonymity, of impersonality in the economic situation. Even if he is not merely a number on a pay-roll, it is his function as an energy factor, a provider of capital, or of organizing capacity that is of prime importance. As such it is his specific industrial characteristics, not his total social characteristics, that matter. He is deemed to be replaceable. It is the magnitude and quality of his contribution to the economic process, irrespective of his personal status or position in the society, that defines him. In primitive communities the individual as an economic factor is personalized, not anonymous. He tends to hold his economic position in virtue of his social position. Hence, to displace him economically means a social disturbance.

Another general characteristic, linked with this, is the overt entry of group elements into individual choice. In a Western economic system the role of an individual may be affected by his group position. A worker's choice of employment is guided by his wife's attitude to the conditions of his work, its cleanliness, occupational risks, or security. His choice of whether to work or stay at home if he is ill is governed largely by the family reaction to his condition. But in a large range of decisions in economic aspects of his behaviour a person is guided by the immediate advantage to himself. His choice is made in consultation with others concerned directly in the economic process, but not with those external to it. But in a primitive system personal choice operates more overtly in a social, not merely economic, *milieu*. In the smaller scale communities it may be even difficult to find outsiders; all the members are involved, in one way or another, in an economic situation, as co-holders of resources, co-producers, or co-sharers in the rewards of production through various social channels.

The contrast can be seen still further in the relations between economic and moral standards. In our modern Western society they often clash or their inconsistencies are unresolved. "Business is business" and "love thy neighbour" are normally parallel lines which never attempt to meet, and the State or voluntary organizations have to bridge the gap. In a peasant society business is often keen enough. But since the relationship is often more than a purely economic one, provision for moral obligations can be made within the economic framework itself, which is integrated with the social framework. Hence what appears to be a paradox—that in an African or Oriental peasant economy there may be no unemployment problem, no radical class struggle, no gap between the hungry and the well-fed.

It is important, then, in economic anthropology to examine the economic role of a person in a particular situation against his social role, and against that of the system of groups of which he is a member. Economic anthropology deals primarily with the economic aspects of the social relations of persons. The factors in economic process are considered not as abstract entities, as units of labour or capital or purchasing power, but as social entities, in terms of the relations of persons controlling or using these units. The economic anthropologist has a dual role: to analyse and classify the processes of combining goods and services in circumstances where money does not enter largely into the combination system; and to examine the way in which the necessary relations involved in such handling of goods and services affect the system of social relations. As an adjunct to this the anthropologist can help to provide for the proper social contextualization of economic propositions.

One can see that the generalizations offered here are very far from the kind of proposition which the economist is apt to use when he talks of primitive economic systems. Quite a lot of economic theory is still in the "nuts-and-apples" stage when it comes to assumptions about a non-monetary economy. In line with this is the treatment of "Crusoe economics." Crusoe is taken as the illustration of the isolated economic man. But the modern economist is often more profoundly read in Lewis Carroll than in Daniel Defoe. "Alice" he quotes to some purpose. But he often seems curiously unaware that Robinson Crusoe is less remarkable for his economy of isolation than for his adventures into trade and colonization. And when Robinson's economic ventures came to nought it was mainly—as he says himself—because of his failure to take into account his own human frailty and the complexity of other men's motives! It is true that Robinson Crusoe and the Marshallian savage are only expository devices. They are not intended to mirror real life. But they carry with them some of the implications of crudity which the Westerner is only too prone to attribute to his primitive contemporary. If the economist does not distort the ethnographic image, he does at times seem to behave as if there were no reality to furnish one.

Much of my argument so far has been necessarily abstract. It can now be taken up more concretely. One of the central themes in understanding an economic system is the nature of the incentives which move people to action. A brief consideration here of incentives in the use of labour and in the use of capital, in some primitive and peasant economic systems will show how many economic incentives are culturally defined and often of a symbolic character.

To the economist of a quarter of a century ago the nature of incentive in industry was not unimportant, but it was treated as being outside his immediate concern. He did not necessarily assume that the only incentive that mattered was money. But he did assume that the main element that mattered for his purposes was money, partly because it was the easiest to measure. In more recent years problems of incentive occupy a prominent place in discussions of output, by business men and economists alike.[4] There is much difference of view as to how far in modern industry the level of output of wage labourers is dependent on the relative weight of such factors as the amount of the money wage, the amount and nature of outlets for spending, the amenities of the work, or the compatible character of managing and employing agencies. One point of view is that the size of the wage-packet remains the most important factor still in the incentive to work. A more sophisticated opinion stresses not the amount of the money wage, but the availability of the consumption goods to be bought by it. Here the wants of a man's wife and family are held to be an important determinant. Again, it is argued that at present levels of prices the ordinary working man is not much interested in further increments to total money wages. What he wants, it is said, is a weekly income of a certain definite size to meet his usual requirements, and he is not willing to work to get more. In effect, these latter views tend to minimize the importance of the opportunities for saving as incentives in modern conditions. Some empirical research has been carried out to try to determine the relative importance of these and other propositions. But the results so far seem to be applicable to particular rather than to general industrial conditions. An example of interest in this connection is an inquiry into restriction of output in an American factory, conducted by a group of anthropologists who worked there for many months as "participant observers." Their general conclusion was that output restriction has been looked upon hitherto far too much as a technical and economic problem to be solved by devices such as production control and incentive pay. But basic to the whole problem of output in that factory was the idea of the workers about the differences between their goals and those of the management, and the conviction of the importance of group loyalty within the workers' organization. The problem seemed, then, to be one primarily of social relations, not economic relations (Collins, Dalton and Roy 1946. See also Firth 1948). Such results may do little more than confirm existing impressions. But they reinforce the need to give some assessment of this sociological element among the factors composing entrepreneurial costs and expectations.

For the peasant and primitive economic systems which he has studied the anthropologist has accumulated a great deal of qualitative data on labour

---

[4] See: Lionel Robbins, "The propositions of the Theory of Variation [i.e., Laws of Supply and Demand] do not in the least involve the assumption that men are actuated *only* by considerations of money gains and losses. They involve only the assumption that money plays *some* part in the valuation of the given alternatives. . . . Money may not be regarded as playing a predominant part in the situation contemplated. So long as it plays some part then the propositions are applicable" (1932:90).

Cf. S. Moos: "One of the foremost tasks facing the economist today is an investigation into the problem of incentives," (1945:17). Sir Sydney Chapman: "The mistake of identifying monetary actuation with personal initiative lies at the root of the error I have been trying to expose. Initiative . . . in the social system (it) is the motive force. The one-sided 'economic incentive' theory was sometimes advanced to account for its operation in business matters. But nobody who had pondered over the matter could suppose for a moment that the thought of what paid one best was the primary fact and strenuous application merely the product or an expression of it" (1946:51–56).

incentives in production. With the possibilities of money measurement largely absent, he has had to concentrate on the more direct objectives of work. He has shown how the individual's work in such conditions is motivated by his conceptions of the wants of his family, of his obligations to his kinsfolk and the community in which he lives, of the chances of gaining prestige in socially prescribed and valued ways, of the dictates of a magical and religious system. Even where monetary rewards for labour are largely current, he has noted that work may be undertaken for other than money symbols. For instance, to revert to the Irish peasantry referred to in the first chapter—there is a form of non-monetary co-operation known as *coor*, in tasks such as mowing, turf-cutting, or potato-planting. No wage payment or other cash equivalent is involved. The help is given as part of the reciprocities of kinship relations—to a second cousin, an uncle, or other member of an extended kin group. The expression in English is that So-and-So "has a right to help," meaning that he has an obligation to do so. In an industrial community such rights are not likely to be of great importance in the scheme of production relations. But in a peasant community they may account for a substantial part of the agricultural services. In the olden days in Ireland a working team of wider scope, called *meithal*, was drawn from the community in the same way to mow and harvest for the village priest or for an old couple without children; or to re-settle an evicted family. Here, too, the contribution was given by each person as a social service, without reciprocity being sought. As with the *coor*, the incentive was of a social, even of a moral, kind, and the material element did not overtly appear.

The principle is not precisely that of the old slogan, "From each according to his ability, to each according to his needs." It is crossed by another, "From each according to his status obligations in the social system, to each according to his rights in that system." Putting it another way, powerful incentives to work lie in the individual's membership of a social group. He dare not relax lest he lose many of the benefits of membership. In distribution, the apportionment of the rewards for work, short-term effects can be distinguished from long-term effects. In the short run it is the impact of the social obligation that is most marked, the frequent rendering of the service without apparent equivalent return. In the long run contributions and rewards may be assumed to even out. The system operates because, in addition to the immediate social satisfactions gained, some material reward is often eventually obtained. Concretely, the work which A does for B as a social obligation is paid back in the long run by gifts which C makes to D. Here B may be the father-in-law of A, D the son of A, and C the brother of B. Or B and C may be the brothers-in-law of A, and D the son of A. The recognition of the long-term trend towards equivalence of service is one of the most important incentives to work in a primitive or peasant society.[5] In societies with strongly demarcated kin groups, such as exist in most of the primitive field, one may speak figuratively of

[5] Some of the effects of this were worked out well by B. Malinowski (1922, 1926).

vertical, lateral, and diagonal service relations. In a system with patrilineal lineages, for example, there are vertical service relations between father and son and between other people of different kinship grades in the same group. Lateral service relations occur between people of the same kinship grade, in the same group, as brothers: or in different groups, as brothers-in-law. Diagonal service relations occur between people of different kinship grades in different groups, as between mother's brother and sister's child. The combination of such service relations is one of the most important networks in the economic organization of such a type of community. It represents one of the exemplifications of the principle of basic compensation which is a fundamental aspect of social organization.

This brings out also the importance of the moral imperative of much economic activity. Behind a person's work, mirroring the allocations of his labour, are obligations bearing as it were a moral electric charge. Positively and negatively, his conduct is regulated by the right and wrong of giving and of receiving, of paying a material equivalent for one type of service and a verbal equivalent for another type, of using one kind of object for food and of avoiding the use of another superficially as good. Even in our own Western society there are strong conventions as to the propriety, amounting to the morality, of work and the return that should be made for it. Work in itself in general is regarded as good, and idleness as morally wrong. Most people have definite ethical views about others giving "a fair day's work" for the pay received. With the fixing of hours of work in many occupations has grown up the idea that "overtime" is a concession, and that it is a matter of right, not merely economic demand, that entitles a person to get pay at more than average rates. And many religious people, while supporting the morality of work in general, regard it as immoral to do work on the Sabbath—though they are not all agreed as to what activity comes under that category. There is also the convention that certain kinds of work, known as "personal service," demand a special acknowledgement over and above ordinary wage-return. Most people seem to give tips not because they expect better service or because they themselves think it morally right, but out of deference to the moral views of others, including the recipients. Examination of industrial disputes would probably show that moral indignation plays a considerable and very real part in exacerbating the issues between the parties, and that concepts of moral justice rank side by side with economic pressures and legal requirements in effecting a settlement. Far more than we ordinarily suppose, economic relations rest upon moral foundations. If it were not so, Communism in the industrial field would be without one of its most powerful weapons. In a primitive society the moral design is very different from that in a Western society, and the pattern of economic relations is therefore supported at different points.

One of the points of difference is the use made of status concepts. In the West we have learnt from Veblen and from the behaviour of industrial magnates the role of "conspicuous consumption" as a motivating force in economics. This is one of the facets of status acquisition. In a Western society the process is comparatively unsystematized. Lavish entertainment and public gifts may lead a man to honours. But they are not recognized as constituting a ladder in themselves, giving their own title to the donor. In primitive and peasant societies there is much variation of practice. But the tendency is for feasts and other forms of large-scale consumption and display to be schematized, set in a series each with its own name, and each giving in succession a right to the feast-holder to take a specific title of honour, to wear certain reserved ornaments, to build a more lofty house than his fellows have, or to exercise other privileges. The *potlatch* of the Haida, Tlinkit, and other Indians of the American North-West coast; the Feasts of Merit of the Chins of Burma; the *Pai* of the Chinese Shans; the *anga* of the Tikopia; the *gawai* of the Borneo Dyak are all examples of the allocation of large-scale resources in goods and labour with primary reference to status yields. This involves not merely the use of surpluses above daily requirements. It involves the creation of surpluses for the purpose, the orientation of the energies and wealth of the feast-holder and his community for months or even years in advance. Such a system is bound in with the obligation system discussed earlier, of kinship and other bonds, which are given economic expression in the preparations for these feasts. But the status incentive is of much wider application. Some of these large-scale consumption occasions confer no particular title or insignia on the donors. But these feasts are a means of heightening their prestige among their neighbours, or at least of maintaining their status by rendering an equivalent for past services. Moreover, in the general conduct of affairs, in the everyday handling of resources and the application of labour to enterprises, maintenance of status in the eyes of others is important.

It is this which explains the great measure of conformity to obligation which occurs. It can be argued that in a small-scale personalized economy such as we have been discussing there are many opportunities of shirking work. The kinship system and other structural arrangements will ensure that no man starves. Is it not true that a sense of insecurity is a necessary drive to induce a man to work and give of his best? But in such an economy it is taken for granted that most people will fulfil their obligations. This normal expectation is based largely upon the status factor. If a man does not do his share of work, and especially the tasks which fall to him individually because of his kinship and other social obligations, then his reputation suffers. Apart from direct stimulus by taunts and jeers, a lowered prestige in the eyes of others is apt to wound his pride. And desire for prestige in the positive sense may well lead a man to proceed to excess in fulfilment of his obligations. (Stakhanovite methods in the Soviet economy have utilized this principle.)

The material incentive must be considered in conjunction with other criteria. The Bemba of Northern Rhodesia have not been very keen cultivators in the past. This has been due in part to the lack of a tradition of good gardening, a lack of good leadership, and a lack of workmates owing to the absence of many young

men at the mines. Poor nutrition is perhaps also partly responsible. The practice among these people is that agricultural work for someone else gives a legitimate claim to food. But distinctions are made on the basis of nearness of kinship. A close kinsman will continue to be fed even though he be a wastrel and
do practically no work at all. A young son-in-law risks not only his meals but
even his bride if he should turn out to be incorrigibly lazy. A distant kinsman
has service and material reward equated as closely as possible; he has to earn his
food by his work to such a degree that the line between a co-operating kinsman
and a temporary labourer is a fine one (Richards 1939:143).

The interweaving of incentives can be seen in a case where money is largely
used in the economy as a reward for work. In one Canadian Indian community
it was noted that the incentives to work included prominently a recognition of
the need to settle one's debts in order to be able to get supplies to go trapping
with in the following autumn; the desire to provide for one's family; the un-
willingness to excite community disapproval by neglect of family obligations.
All these could be expressed in ordinary monetary terms through the money
earned. On the other hand, the prestige element operated in the exhibition of a
fear of failure and the shame attendant on it. If the chances of success were very
dubious, then this tended to result in a slackening off of work and exaggeration
of the risk factor to a degree almost irrespective of the rate of return. The tendency for the Indian was then to select work which promised a ready success,
which was likely to evoke favourable public opinion, and which was in general
significant to his immediate value scheme. The Indian was correspondingly unwilling to work for the Hudson Bay Company, since not only did he judge the
wage rates to be too low, but the work tended to lack meaning in his scheme of
values. It included in particular a concentration on routine and a conflict with
his leisure season which did not fit his other social and economic patterns
(Honigman 1949:23–28).

In discussing economic incentive the anthropologist is sometimes tempted to
deny the value of material inducements and to stress to the exclusion of them
the non-material factors. This is a mistake. In many cases the incentive to work
is primarily the desire to get food and shelter, granted that in every case the
form that these things take is culturally defined. In other cases the incentives,
whether status-seeking or other, are given expression in material terms. But
when allowance is made for this, granted that there are prospects of equal return
to courses *a* and *b*, why is course *a* consistently chosen rather than course *b*?
And, granted that course *a* offers prospects of greater return than course *b*, why
is course *b* nevertheless consistently chosen? At this stage of the study the answer
can be given only in reference to social and moral standards lying behind
particular economic systems. Some indication of it has been made already. The
questions can be looked at further in reference to some aspects of the use of
capital, in particular as regards the taking of interest.

Throughout most economic discussions it is implied that to obtain the use of
capital some interest payments are necessary. It is also held that receipt of

interest is morally justified. The basic point I wish to make is simply this. The ideas about capital and the way in which it should be used and rewarded are not merely economic concepts; they are also social concepts. They are not rooted in the nature of economic activity itself; they vary from one society to another.

First consider the concept of interest as such. Just as Marxism revolts against capitalism in general, so mediæval Christendom and Islam revolted against interest specifically. But the West, forced by the expansion of its economic programme, has come to justify the taking of interest, and, in fact, always did distinguish in practice between common usury and the results of an apparently productive investment of capital. Islam, on the other hand, still carries the moral law overtly through into the commercial sphere. The fulminations of the Koran against "the devourer of usury" are regarded in many Muslim circles as being as valid today as they were 1300 years ago. The word used in the Koran for interest or usury is *riba*, meaning increase in anything, or addition—that is, the additional amount which a debtor pays to a creditor in consideration of time to use the money. According to Moslem jurists, *riba* is the extortion of wealth without legal or lawful consideration. And the taker of *riba*, its giver, the scribe of the deed, and the witnesses to it have been pronounced by the Prophet to be alike cursed in their sin.

What, then, are the arguments for this forbidding of interest. Islam does not forbid the giving of credit in general. The essence of its objection to the taking of interest is that the creditor receives an increment on his loan and that this increment is a fixed periodic sum. If, on the other hand, one puts one's money into a business as a partner and takes a profit by sharing in the risks of the undertaking, this is legitimate; the increment on one's money is uncertain. One may get no increment, and indeed may lose one's capital invested. As Imam Razi, a well-known Muslim scholar, writes: "The creditor's deriving a profit from every investment in business is uncertain, whereas this 'additional amount' from the debtor to the creditor is certain" (Razi as quoted in Qureshi 1945:52).

Now, these words of the Egyptian scholar are almost identical with those used to me by a Malay fisherman, and those of R. H. Tawney in speaking of the mediæval prohibition on pure interest. The Malay fisherman argued that if one lends money on a boat and takes half the weekly earnings of the boat in return (quite apart from principal) this is not a "tax on money" or "the child of money" (i.e., interest), "because it is uncertain." One week the provider of capital may get a good increment on his loan, the next week he may get nothing. To the Malays, then, the process is one of profit-sharing and not of interest-taking. Now compare Professor Tawney. "The essence of usury was that it was certain, and that whether the borrower gained or lost, the usurer took his pound of flesh. Mediæval opinion, which has no objection to rent or profits provided that they are reasonable . . . has no mercy for the debenture holder. His crime is that he takes a payment for money which is fixed and certain and such a payment is usury" (Tawney 1926, 1938:II, i. Cf. Weber 1930:202 and Firth 1946: 169–176).

The coincidence, of course, is not fortuitous. The Egyptian jurist and the Malay fisherman approach the subject of economics from opposite angles, but they both share a simple faith in the rightness of the Koran. The mediæval churchmen built on different religious foundations. But the same basic social and economic conditions apply in both cases. Both societies have an essentially peasant basis to their social structure, and trade rather than industry as their major outlet for economic enterprise. What Tawney says of the mediæval West, "That the doctrine of interest received its character in an age in which most loans were not part of a credit system but an exceptional expedient, and in which it could be said that he who borrows is always under stress of necessity," would seem to apply largely to the contemporary East as well. The prohibition of interest, then, is not just the result of an arbitrary moral attitude about the use of money. It is linked with a type of society in which the use of money in certain ways is apt to result in clearly perceptible personal hardship, and in the drying up of that fount of compassion which should remain fresh in every human being.

In modern Islam, as in mediæval Christendom, these doctrines have not passed without either challenge or evasion. The Christian story is well known. In Islam there are two parallel movements, both responsive to the economic situation, but in different ways. One is that of plain side-stepping of the Prophet's injunctions. I knew of cases in Malaya where lenders of money secretly stipulated and received a fixed increment on their loan. Or in order to be able to defend it before the courts, if necessary, they lent a smaller sum than was written down for repayment on the document agreed to by the borrower. The courts, which disallow any case brought where there was a bargain for payment of interest, would have no evidence that less than the agreed sum for repayment had in fact been handed over. On the other hand, some Muslim modernists argue for a more refined interpretation of the Prophet's views. Some Muslims defend the taking of interest and say that what the Prophet really disallowed was "usury." This is combated by the more orthodox, who argue that usury is commonly regarded as an exorbitant rate of interest, but that ideas as to exorbitance vary greatly at different times and there is no essential difference between the two concepts. Another view is that simple interest is allowed, but not compound interest. But this again is regarded by most Muslim jurists as very specious. Many modern Muslims of the educated class regard even ordinary interest on bank deposits as illegitimate for them.[6] It has been said rather ingeniously that although many of them do in fact accept the addition of interest to their bank deposits, this is to be regarded as "a personal weakness" analogous to that of not saying one's prayers regularly at the prescribed times. A strictly orthodox view of the role of banks in an Islamic State would be that they can function provided that they

[6] I am indebted to Mrs. Barbara Fisher for the information that in 1901, the first year in which Savings Banks were opened in Egypt, of 4,197 total Egyptian depositors, being largely Muslims, 390 Muslims refused interest on their deposits (presumably on religious grounds). For the most part the depositors were urban residents (and therefore likely to be more sophisticated than ordinary peasants). (From H.M. Agent and Consul-General's Report, 1901, in *Accounts and Papers*, 1902, vol. CXXX.)

pay no interest to depositors and charge no interest to their clients—in other words, they would treat all deposits as Western banks treat current accounts, and depositors would use them for security, and not profit.

The prohibition on *riba* was also extended by the Prophet to such transactions of exchange whereby quantities of gold, silver, wheat, barley, dates, and salt are exchanged for more or less of the *same kind* of commodity. Trade in general is encouraged, but this prohibition puts a bar on concealed interest-taking and direct dealing in futures. But here again there is a difference of opinion among the learned men of Islam. Some wish to extend this prohibition in modern times to all commodities. Others, holding to the letter of the law, argue that one may not reason by analogy, and that it is only the six commodities specifically mentioned by the Prophet which are so affected.

A sophisticated view of the orthodox Muslim position in which many of the points just made are examined in detail has recently been put forward by an academic economist who has been economic adviser to the Government of the Nizam of Hyderabad (Qureshi 1945). His thesis is briefly that many of the ills of capitalist society are mainly due to interest and that Islam has made a contribution to the solution of world ills by the definite prohibition of interest. He quotes Western historical precedents in support of his contention. Aristotle's comparison of money to a barren hen which laid no eggs is cited; likewise the mediæval objections to interest. To him, as perhaps to others, the age of faith has given place to the age of science, but not necessarily to that of reason. He defends the position further by arguing somewhat ingenuously that Western economists are not agreed on the nature and theory of interest, that Keynes and others have regarded the rate of interest as a highly conventional phenomenon, and that the rate of interest in Western countries is progressively becoming lower. Hence it is theoretically possible and practically by no means out of the question that the minimal rate of interest may be a zero rate. His general conclusion is that that which Islam has forbidden on religious grounds should be abandoned on economic grounds. The certainty, regular accumulation, and lack of expenditure of effort characteristic of interest-taking militate socially and economically against it. To him, as to most Muslims, the proper method of using capital is the partnership system in which capital co-operates with labour, and gets a profit on the joint result. This profit should be allocated in an agreed proportion—one-third, one-quarter, etc.—of the joint product, and not as fixed percentage of the principal sum invested. This is the Muslim *mazarebat*, the profit-sharing enterprise.

Islam has thus not illegalized all transactions which produce income without labour. In fact, in addition to the profits of co-partnership, it allows rent from houses and agricultural land. What it objects to is a situation where only one party bears sacrifice or the risk, and the other remains immune, or practically so.

To a nineteenth-century audience such arguments would have sounded like the sheerest idealism, or a sentimental antiquarianism. Today perhaps we are not so sure. We do not accept the fiat of Mahomet as an argument for not charging interest. We accept the view that it may be necessary to give interest in order to obtain the use of capital. But we have seen that the rate of interest in itself is not necessarily a measure of the willingness of people to lend money, provided that the security is sound. And we can conceive of social circumstances in which loans can be made—or perhaps should be made—either at a rate so low as to be called uneconomic or even interest free. It would be difficult for a nation which has had the advantage of lend-lease from the United States during the war and of Marshall Aid after the war, to argue otherwise. And I think it is undoubted that the practice of making interest-free loans of smaller magnitude either as a general social gesture, or in order to assist economic recovery or expansion to the ultimate benefit of the lender, is a practice which has increased during the present century.

Our concern, however, is not with the possibilities of an interest-free economy as such. It is with the basis of choice in this type of economic action. What we have shown is that, faced by prospects of apparently equal return, the good Muslim prefers profit to interest, a share in the risks of an undertaking to a passive usury; moreover, he is prepared in some cases to forego return on his capital. No absence of monetary incentive is implied by this, but a positive desire for conformity to moral and religious ideals.

This bears on the problem of rationality in economic action. Rational behaviour involves the adaptation of means to a recognized goal as closely as possible in terms of the available knowledge. In the economic sphere in particular it has been interpreted, as by Max Weber, to mean the deliberate systematic adjustment of economic means to attain the objective of pecuniary profit. It will be clear from discussion earlier in this chapter that many of the economic actions of primitive peoples, including their feasts and other large-scale consumption efforts, appear to lack an immediate rationality. But they do in the long run meet the ends of material gain. Even where this is not so, rational conceptions have not been abandoned. Their scope has only been extended to embrace the social system, and not merely the economic system. The economic system has no intrinsic meaning for an individual. It derives its evaluations ultimately from his interpretation of social concepts. Situations continually tend to arise, then, in which some sacrifice of economic benefit is judged necessary to maintain or raise one's social status, or to help give reality to social ideals which one thinks are important. Economic activity is subordinate to social ends. It is only by studying those ends that one can see how particular economic systems work. Failure to do so may impair the effectiveness of many of the attempts now being made to stimulate the productive organization of primitive and peasant peoples by process of investment from the Western world.

In this field of problems the social framework may be conceived as a system of choices in situations where the emphasis is other than on the "prudent allocation of resources." This framework affects choices in the economic sphere in several ways. To some extent it limits the number of combinations of his resources open to any individual—social and moral values inhibit his range of action. On the other hand, by providing him with well-recognized norms of conduct it aids him in selection of fields for the use of his resources. Many of them, for instance, he puts into strengthening the position of his family. Moreover, it aids him to some degree in prediction. He knows in advance how the exercise of much economic choice by other people will be made, and this allows of easier planning of his own choices. Social codes give him clues to what other people will do. But what is particularly important is that the social framework confirms his choices, and gives them that basic meaning without which the economic process could not continue. The economist is apt to think of the social framework as consisting mainly of the controls exercised by law—e.g., in regard to the holding of property, in minimization of force or fraud. The anthropologist thinks of this framework as essentially one of values giving meaning to the economic system.

ON ECONOMICS
AND ON MODELS

5 THE SUBJECT MATTER OF ECONOMICS
Lionel Robbins

1. The object of this Essay is to exhibit the nature and significance of Economic Science. Its first task therefore is to delimit the subject-matter of Economics— to provide a working definition of what Economics is about.

Unfortunately, this is by no means as simple as it sounds. The efforts of economists during the last hundred and fifty years have resulted in the establishment of a body of generalisations whose substantial accuracy and importance are open to question only by the ignorant or the perverse. But they have achieved no unanimity concerning the ultimate nature of the common subject-matter of these generalisations. The central chapters of the standard works on Economics retail, with only minor variations, the main principles of the science. But the chapters in which the object of the work is explained still present wide divergences. We all talk about the same things, but we have not yet agreed what it is we are talking about.*[1]

From An Essay on the Nature and Significance of Economic Science by Lionel Robbins, New York, St. Martin's Press and London, Macmillan & Co. Ltd., 1932, pp. 1–23. Reprinted by permission.

* Footnotes are given exactly as they appear in the original. No bibliographic information other than that which is contained in the footnotes as reproduced here is to be found in the original work. (eds.)

[1] Lest this should be thought an overstatement I subjoin below a few characteristic definitions. I have confined my choice to Anglo-Saxon literature because, as will be shown later on, a more satisfactory state of affairs is coming to prevail elsewhere. "Economics is a study of mankind in the ordinary business of life; it examines that part of individual and social action which is most closely connected with the attainment and with the use of the material requisites of well-being" (Marshall, *Principles*, p. 1). "Economics is the science which treats phenomena from the standpoint of price" (Davenport, *Economics of Enterprise*, p. 25). "The aim of Political Economy is the explanation of the general causes on which the material welfare of human beings depends" (Cannan, *Elementary Political Economy*, p. 1). "It is too wide a definition to speak of Economics as the science of the material side of human welfare." Economics is "the study of the general methods by which men co-operate to meet their material needs" (Beveridge, *Economics as a Liberal Education, Economica*, vol. i., p. 3). Economics, according to Professor Pigou, is the study of economic welfare, economic welfare being defined as "that part of welfare which can be brought directly or indirectly into relation with the measuring rod of money" (*Economics of Welfare*, 3rd edition, p. 1). The sequel will show how widely the implications of these definitions diverge from one another.

This is not in any way an unexpected or a disgraceful circumstance. As Mill pointed out a hundred years ago, the definition of a science has almost invariably, not preceded, but followed the creation of the science itself. "Like the wall of a city it has usually been erected, not to be a receptacle for such edifices as might afterwards spring up, but to circumscribe an aggregate already in existence."[2] Indeed, it follows from the very nature of a science that until it has reached a certain stage of development, definition of its scope is necessarily impossible. For the unity of a science only shows itself in the unity of the problems it is able to solve, and such unity is not discovered until the interconnection of its explanatory principles has been established.[3] Modern Economics takes its rise from various separate spheres of practical and philosophical enquiry—from investigations of the balance of trade—from discussions of the legitimacy of the taking of interest.[4] It was not until quite recent times that it had become sufficiently unified for the identity of the problems underlying these different enquiries to be detected. At an earlier stage, any attempt to discover the ultimate nature of the science was necessarily doomed to disaster. It would have been waste of time to have attempted it.

But once this stage of unification has been reached not only is it not waste of time to attempt precise delimitation; it is waste of time not to do so. Further elaboration can only take place if the objective is clearly indicated. The problems are no longer suggested by naïve reflection. They are indicated by gaps in the unity of theory, by insufficiencies in its explanatory principles. Unless one has grasped what this unity is, one is apt to go off on false scents. There can be little doubt that one of the greatest dangers which beset the modern economist is preoccupation with the irrelevant—the multiplication of activities having little or no connection with the solution of problems strictly germane to his subject. There can be equally little doubt that, in those centres where questions of this sort are on the way to ultimate settlement, the solution of the central theoretical problems proceeds most rapidly. Moreover, if these solutions are to be fruitfully applied, if we are to understand correctly the bearing of Economic Science on practice, it is essential that we should know exactly the implications and limitations of the generalisations it establishes. It is therefore with an easy conscience that we may advance to what, at first sight, is the extremely academic problem of finding a formula to describe the general subject-matter of Economics.

2. The definition of Economics which would probably command most adherents, at any rate in Anglo-Saxon countries, is that which relates it to the study of the causes of material welfare. This element is common to the definitions of

[2] *Unsettled Questions of Political Economy*, p. 120.

[3] "Nicht die 'sachlichen' Zusammenhänge der 'Dinge' sondern die *gedanklichen* Zusammenhänge der *Probleme* liegen den Arbeitsgebieten der Wissenschaften zugrunde" (Max Weber, *Die Objectivität sozialwissenschaftlicher und sozialpolitischer Erkenntnis, Gesammelte Aufsätze zur Wissenschaftslehre*, p. 166).

[4] See Cannan, *Review of Economic Theory*, pp. 1–35, and Schumpeter, *Epochen der Methoden- und Dogmengeschichte*, pp. 21–38.

Cannan[5] and Marshall,[6] and even Pareto, whose approach[7] in so many ways was so different from that of the two English economists, gives it the sanction of his usage. It is implied, too, in the definition of J. B. Clark.[8]

And, at first sight, it must be admitted, it certainly does appear as if we have here a definition which for practical purposes describes the object of our interest. In ordinary speech there is unquestionably a sense in which the word "economic" is used as equivalent to "material". One has only to reflect upon its signification to the layman in such phrases as "Economic History" or "a conflict between economic and political advantage", to realise the extreme plausibility of this interpretation. No doubt there are some matters falling outside this definition which seem to fall within the scope of Economics, but at first sight these may very well seem to be of the order of marginal cases inevitable with every definition.

But the final test of the validity of any such definition is not its apparent harmony with certain usages of everyday speech, but its capacity to describe exactly the ultimate subject-matter of the main generalisations of the science.[9] And when we submit the definition in question to this test, it is seen to possess deficiencies which, so far from being marginal and subsidiary, amount to nothing less than a complete failure to exhibit either the scope or the significance of the most central generalisations of all.

Let us take any one of the main divisions of theoretical Economics and examine to what extent it is covered by the definition we are examining. We should all agree, for instance, that a theory of wages was an integral part of any system of economic analysis. Can we be content with the assumption that the phenomena with which such a theory has to deal are adequately described as pertaining to the more material side of human welfare?

Wages, in the strict sense of the term, are sums earned by the performance of work at stipulated rates under the supervision of an employer. In the looser sense

[5] *Wealth*, 1st edition, p. 17.

[6] *Principles*, 8th edition, p. 1.

[7] *Cours d'Economie Politique*, p. 6.

[8] *Essentials of Economic Theory*, p. 5. See also *Philosophy of Wealth*, ch. i. In this chapter the difficulties discussed below are explicitly recognised, but, surprisingly enough, instead of this leading to a rejection of the definition, it leads only to a somewhat surprising attempt to change the significance of the word "material".

[9] In this connection it is perhaps worth while clearing up a confusion which not infrequently occurs in discussions of terminology. It is often urged that scientific definitions of words used both in ordinary language and in scientific analysis should not depart from the usages of everyday speech. No doubt this is a counsel of perfection, but in principle the main contention may be accepted. Great confusion is certainly created when a word which is used in one sense in business practice is used in another sense in the analysis of such practice. One has only to think of the difficulties which have been created by such departures in regard to the meaning of the term capital. But it is one thing to follow everyday usage when appropriating a term. It is another thing to contend that everyday speech is the final court of appeal when defining a science. For in this case the significant implication of the word *is* the subject-matter of the generalisations of the science. And it is only by reference to these that the definition can finally be established. Any other procedure would be intolerable.

in which the term is often used in general economic analysis, it stands for labour incomes other than profits. Now it is perfectly true that some wages are the price of work which may be described as conducive to material welfare—the wages of a sewage collector, for instance. But it is equally true that some wages, the wages of the members of an orchestra, for instance, are paid for work which has not the remotest bearing on material welfare. Yet the one set of services, equally with the other, commands a price and enters into the circle of exchange. The theory of wages is as applicable to the explanation of the latter as it is to the explanation of the former. Its elucidations are not limited to wages which are paid for work ministering to the "more material" side of human well-being—whatever that may be.

Nor is the situation saved if we turn from the work for which wages are paid to the things on which wages are spent. It might be urged that it is not because what the wage-earner produces is conducive to other people's material welfare that the theory of wages may be subsumed under the description, but because what he gets is conducive to his own. But this does not bear examination for an instant. The wage-earner may buy bread with his earnings. But he may buy a seat at the theatre. A theory of wages which ignored all those sums which were paid for "immaterial" services or spent on "immaterial" ends would be intolerable. The circle of exchange would be hopelessly ruptured. The whole process of general analysis could never be employed. It is impossible to conceive significant generalisations about a field thus arbitrarily delimited.

It is improbable that any serious economist has attempted to delimit the theory of wages in this manner, however much he may have attempted thus to delimit the whole body of generalisations of which the theory of wages is a part. But attempts have certainly been made to deny the applicability of economic analysis to the examination of the achievement of ends other than material welfare. No less an economist than Professor Cannan has urged that the political economy of war is "a contradiction in terms",[10] apparently on the ground that, since Economics is concerned with the causes of material welfare, and since war is not a cause of material welfare, war cannot be part of the subject-matter of Economics. As a moral judgment on the uses to which abstract knowledge should be put, Professor Cannan's strictures may be accepted. But it is abundantly clear, as Professor Cannan's own practice has shown, that, so far from Economics having no light to throw on the successful prosecution of modern warfare, it is highly doubtful whether the organisers of war can possibly do without it. It is a curious paradox that Professor Cannan's pronouncement on this matter should occur in a work which, more than any other published in our language, uses the apparatus of economic analysis to illuminate many of the most urgent and the most intricate problems of a community organised for war.

This habit on the part of modern English economists of describing Economics as concerned with the causes of material welfare, is all the more curious when

---

[10] Cannan, *An Economist's Protest*, p. 49.

we reflect upon the unanimity with which they have adopted a non-material definition of "productivity". Adam Smith, it will be remembered, distinguished between productive and unproductive labour, according as the efforts in question did or did not result in the production of a tangible material object. "The labour of some of the most respectable orders in the society is, like that of menial servants, unproductive of any value and does not fix or realise itself in any permanent subject or vendible commodity which endures after that labour is past. . . . The sovereign, for example, with all the officers both of justice and war who serve under him are unproductive labourers. . . . In the same class must be ranked some both of the gravest and most important, and some of the most frivolous professions: churchmen, lawyers, physicians, men of letters of all kinds; players, buffoons, musicians, opera singers, opera dancers, etc. . . ."[11] Modern economists, Professor Cannan foremost among them,[12] have rejected this conception of productivity as inadequate.[13] So long as it is the object of demand, whether privately or collectively formulated, the labour of the opera singers and dancers must be regarded as "productive". But productive of what? Of material welfare because it cheers the business man and releases new stores of energy to organise the production of material? That way lies dilettantism and *Wortspielerei*. It is productive because it is valued, because it has specific importance for various "economic subjects". So far is modern theory from the point of view of Adam Smith and the Physiocrats that the epithet of productive labour is denied even to the production of material objects, if the material objects are not valuable. Indeed, it has gone further than this. Professor Fisher, among others, has demonstrated conclusively[14] that the income from a material object must in the last resort be conceived as an "immaterial" use. From my house equally as from my valet or the services of the opera singer, I derive an income which "perishes in the moment of its production".

But, if this is so, is it not misleading to go on describing Economics as the study of the causes of material welfare? The services of the opera dancer are wealth. Economics deals with the pricing of these services, equally with the pricing of the services of a cook. Whatever Economics is concerned with, it is *not* concerned with the causes of material welfare as such.

The causes which have led to the persistence of this definition are mainly historical in character. It is the last vestige of Physiocratic influence. English economists are not usually interested in questions of scope and method. In nine cases out of ten where this definition occurs, it has probably been taken over quite uncritically from some earlier work. But, in the case of Professor Cannan, its retention is due to more positive causes; and it is instructive to attempt to

---

[11] *Wealth of Nations* (Cannan's ed.), p. 315.

[12] *Theories of Production and Distribution*, pp. 18–31; *Review of Economic Theory*, pp. 49–51.

[13] It is even arguable that the reaction has gone too far. Whatever its demerits, the Smithian classification had a significance for capital theory which in recent times has not always been clearly recognised. See Taussig, *Wages and Capital*, pp. 132–151.

[14] *The Nature of Capital and Income*, ch. vii.

trace the processes of reasoning which seem to have rendered it plausible to so penetrating and so acute an intellect.

The rationale of any definition is usually to be found in the use which is actually made of it. Professor Cannan develops his definition in close juxtaposition to a discussion of "the Fundamental Conditions of Wealth for Isolated Man and for Society",[15] and it is in connection with this discussion that he actually uses his conception of what is economic and what is not. It is no accident, it may be suggested, that if the approach to economic analysis is made from this point of view, the "materialist" definition, as we may call it, has the maximum plausibility. This deserves vindication in some detail.

Professor Cannan commences by contemplating the activities of a man isolated completely from society and enquiring what conditions will determine his wealth—that is to say, his material welfare. In such conditions, a division of activities into "economic" and "non-economic"—activities directed to the increase of material welfare and activities directed to the increase of non-material welfare—has a certain plausibility. If Robinson Crusoe digs potatoes, he is pursuing material or "economic" welfare. If he talks to the parrot, his activities are "non-economic" in character. There is a difficulty here to which we must return later, but it is clear *prima facie* that, in this context, the distinction is not ridiculous.

But let us suppose Crusoe is rescued and, coming home, goes on the stage and talks to the parrot for a living. Surely in such conditions these conversations have an economic aspect. Whether he spends his earnings on potatoes or philosophy, Crusoe's getting and spending are capable of being exhibited in terms of the fundamental economic categories.

Professor Cannan does not pause to ask whether his distinction is very helpful in the analysis of an exchange economy—though, after all, it is here that economic generalisations have the greatest practical utility. Instead, he proceeds forthwith to consider the "fundamental conditions of wealth" for society considered as a whole irrespective of whether it is organised on the basis of private property and free exchanges or not. And here again his definition becomes plausible: once more the aggregate of social activities can be sorted out into the twofold classification it implies. Some activities are devoted to the pursuit of material welfare: some are not. We think, for instance, of the executive of a communist society, deciding to spend so much labour-time on the provision of bread, so much on the provision of circuses.

But even here and in the earlier case of the Crusoe Economy, the procedure is open to what is surely a crushing objection. Let us accept Professor Cannan's use of the terms "economic" and "non-economic" as being equivalent to conducive to material and non-material welfare respectively. Then we may say with him that the wealth of society will be greater the greater proportion of time which is devoted to material ends, the less the proportion which is devoted to

---

[15] This is the title of ch. ii. of *Wealth* (1st edition).

immaterial ends. We may say this. But we must also admit that, using the word "economic" in a perfectly normal sense, there still remains an economic problem, both for society and for the individual, of choosing between these two kinds of activity—a problem of how, given the relative valuations of product and leisure and the opportunities of production, the fixed supply of twenty-four hours in the day is to be divided between them. *There is still an economic problem of deciding between the "economic" and the "non-economic".* One of the main problems of the Theory of Production lies half outside Professor Cannan's definition.

Is not this in itself a sufficient argument for its abandonment?[16]

3. But where, then, are we to turn? The position is by no means hopeless. Our critical examination of the "materialist" definition has brought us to a point from which it is possible to proceed forthwith to formulate a definition which shall be immune from all these strictures.

Let us turn back to the simplest case in which we found this definition inappropriate—the case of isolated man dividing his time between the production of real income and the enjoyment of leisure. We have just seen that such a division may legitimately be said to have an economic aspect. Wherein does this aspect consist?

The answer is to be found in the formulation of the exact conditions which make such division necessary. They are four. In the first place, isolated man wants both real income and leisure. Secondly, he has not enough of either fully to satisfy his want of each. Thirdly, he can spend his time in augmenting his real income or he can spend it in taking more leisure. Fourthly, it may be presumed that, save in most exceptional cases, his want for the different constituents of real income and leisure will be different. Therefore he has to choose. He has to economise. The disposition of his time and his resources has a relationship to his system of wants. It has an economic aspect.

This example is typical of the whole field of economic studies. From the point of view of the economist, the conditions of human existence exhibit four fundamental characteristics. The ends are various. The time and the means for achieving these ends are limited and capable of alternative application. At the same time the ends have different importance. Here we are, sentient creatures with bundles of desires and aspirations, with masses of instinctive tendencies all urging us in different ways to action. But the time in which these tendencies can be expressed is limited. The external world does not offer full opportunities for their complete achievement. Life is short. Nature is niggardly. Our fellows have other objectives. Yet we can use our lives for doing different things, our materials and the services of others for achieving different objectives.

---

[16] There are other quarrels which we might pick with this particular definition. From the philosophical point of view, the term "material welfare" is a very odd construction. "The material causes of welfare" might be admitted. But "material welfare" seems to involve a division of states of mind which are essentially unitary. For the purposes of this chapter, however, it has seemed better to ignore these deficiencies and to concentrate on the main question, namely, whether the definition can in in any way describe the contents of which it is intended to serve as a label.

Now *by itself* the multiplicity of ends has no necessary interest for the economist. If I want to do two things, and I have ample time and ample means with which to do them, and I do not want the time or the means for anything else, then my conduct assumes none of those forms which are the subject of economic science. Nirvana is not necessarily single bliss. It is merely the complete satisfaction of *all* requirements.

Nor is the mere limitation of means *by itself* sufficient to give rise to economic phenomena. If means of satisfaction have no alternative use, then they may be scarce, but they cannot be economised. The Manna which fell from heaven may have been scarce, but, if it was impossible to exchange it for something else or to postpone its use,[17] it was not the object of any activity with an economic aspect.

Nor again is the alternative applicability of scarce means a complete condition of the existence of the kind of phenomena we are analysing. If the economic subject has two ends and one means of satisfying them, and the two ends are of equal importance, his position will be like the position of the ass in the fable, paralysed halfway between the two equally attractive bundles of hay.[18]

But when time and the means for achieving ends are limited *and* capable of alternative application, *and* the ends are capable of being distinguished in order of importance, then behaviour necessarily assumes the form of choice. Every act which involves time and scarce means for the achievement of one end involves the relinquishment of their use for the achievement of another. It has an economic aspect.[19] If I want bread and sleep, and in the time at my disposal I cannot have all I want of both, then some part of my wants of bread and sleep must go unsatisfied. If, in a limited lifetime, I would wish to be both a philosopher and a mathematician, but my rate of acquisition of knowledge is such that I cannot do both completely, then some part of my wish for philosophical or mathematical competence or both must be relinquished.

Now not all the means for achieving human ends are limited. There are things in the external world which are present in such comparative abundance that the use of particular units for one thing does not involve going without other units for others. The air which we breathe, for instance, is such a "free" commodity. Save in very special circumstances, the fact that we need air imposes no sacrifice

---

[17] It is perhaps worth emphasising the significance of this qualification. The application of technically similar means to the achievement of qualitatively similar ends *at different times* constitute alternative uses of these means. Unless this is clearly realised, one of the most important types of economic action is overlooked.

[18] This may seem an unnecessary refinement, and in the first edition of this essay I left it out for that reason. But the condition that there exists a hierarchy of ends is so important in the theory of value that it seems better to state it explicitly even at this stage.

[19] Cp. Schönfeld, *Grenznutzen und Wirtschaftsrechnung*, p. 1; Hans Mayer, *Untersuchungen zu dem Grundgesetze der wirtschaftlichen Wertrechnung* (*Zeitschrift für Volkswirtschaft und Sozialpolitik*, Bd. 2, p. 123).

It should be sufficiently clear that it is not "time" as such which is scarce, but rather the potentialities of ourselves viewed as instruments. To speak of scarcity of time is simply a metaphorical way of invoking this rather abstract concept.

of time or resources. The loss of one cubic foot of air implies no sacrifice of alternatives. Units of air have no specific significance for conduct. And it is conceivable that living creatures might exist whose "ends" were so limited that all goods for them were "free" goods, that no goods had specific significance.

But, in general, human activity with its multiplicity of objectives has not this independence of time or specific resources. The time at our disposal is limited. There are only twenty-four hours in the day. We have to choose between the different uses to which they may be put. The services which others put at our disposal are limited. The material means of achieving ends are limited. We have been turned out of Paradise. We have neither eternal life nor unlimited means of gratification. Everywhere we turn, if we choose one thing we must relinquish others which, in different circumstances, we would wish not to have relinquished. Scarcity of means to satisfy ends of varying importance is an almost ubiquitous condition of human behaviour.[20]

Here, then, is the unity of subject of Economic Science, the forms assumed by human behaviour in disposing of scarce means. The examples we have discussed already harmonise perfectly with this conception. Both the services of cooks and the services of opera dancers are limited in relation to demand and can be put to alternative uses. The theory of wages in its entirety is covered by our present definition. So, too, is the political economy of war. The waging of war necessarily involves the withdrawal of scarce goods and services from other uses, if it is to be satisfactorily achieved. It has therefore an economic aspect. The economist studies the disposal of scarce means. He is interested in the way different degrees of scarcity of different goods give rise to different ratios of valuation between them, and he is interested in the way in which changes in conditions of scarcity, whether coming from changes in ends or changes in means—from the demand side or the supply side—affect these ratios. Economics is the science which studies human behaviour as a relationship between ends and scarce means which have alternative uses.[21]

4. It is important at once to notice certain implications of this conception. The conception we have rejected, the conception of Economics as the study of the causes of material welfare, was what may be called a *classificatory* conception. It marks off certain kinds of human behaviour, behaviour directed to the procuring of material welfare, and designates these as the subject-matter of Economics. Other kinds of conduct lie outside the scope of its investigations.

[20] It should be clear that there is no disharmony between the conception of end here employed, the terminus of particular lines of conduct in acts of final consumption, and the conception involved when it is said that there is but one end of activity—the maximising of satisfaction, "utility", or what not. Our "ends" are to be regarded as proximate to the achievement of this ultimate end. If the means are scarce they cannot all be achieved, and according to the scarcity of means and their relative importance the achievement of some ends has to be relinquished.

[21] Cp. Menger, *Grundsätze der Volkswirtschaftslehre*, 1te Aufl., pp. 51–70; Mises, *Die Gemeinwirtschaft*, pp. 98 *seq.*; Fetter, *Economic Principles*, ch. i.; Strigl, *Die ökonomischen Kategorien und die Organisation der Wirtschaft*, *passim*; Mayer, *op. cit.*

The conception we have adopted may be described as *analytical*. It does not attempt to pick out certain *kinds* of behaviour, but focuses attention on a particular *aspect* of behaviour, the form imposed by the influence of scarcity.[22] It follows from this, therefore, that in so far as it presents this aspect, any kind of human behaviour falls within the scope of economic generalisations. We do not say that the production of potatoes is economic activity and the production of philosophy is not. We say rather that, in so far as either kind of activity involves the relinquishment of other desired alternatives, it has its economic aspect. There are no limitations on the subject-matter of Economic Science save this.

Certain writers, however, while rejecting the conception of Economics as concerned with material welfare, have sought to impose on its scope a restriction of another nature: They have urged that the behaviour with which Economics is concerned is essentially a certain type of social behaviour, the behaviour implied by the institutions of the Individualist Exchange Economy. On this view, that kind of behaviour which is not specifically social in this definite sense is not the subject-matter of Economics, Professor Amonn in particular has devoted almost infinite pains to elaborating this conception.[23]

Now it may be freely admitted that, within the wide field of our definition, the attention of economists is focused chiefly on the complications of the Exchange Economy. The reason for this is one of interest. The activities of isolated man, equally with the activities of the exchange economy, are subject to the limitations we are contemplating. But, from the point of view of isolated man, economic analysis is unnecessary. The elements of the problem are given to unaided reflection. Examination of the behaviour of a Crusoe may be immensely illuminating as an aid to more advanced studies. But, from the point of view of Crusoe, it is obviously *extra-marginal*. So too in the case of a "closed" communistic society. Again, from the point of view of the economist, the comparison of the phenomena of such a society with those of the exchange economy may be very illuminating. But from the point of view of the members of the executive, the generalisations of Economics would be uninteresting. Their position would be analogous to Crusoe's. For them the economic problem would be merely whether to apply productive power to this or to that. Now, as Professor Mises has emphasised, given central ownership and control of the means of production, the registering of individual pulls and resistances by a mechanism of prices and costs is excluded by definition. It follows therefore that the decisions of the

---

[22] On the distinction between analytical and classificatory definitions, see Irving Fisher, *Senses of Capital* (*Economic Journal*, vol. vii., p. 213). It is interesting to observe that the change in the conception of Economies implied by our definition is similar to the change in the conception of capital implied in Professor Fisher's definition. Adam Smith defined capital as a kind of wealth. Professor Fisher would have us regard it as an aspect of wealth.

[23] See his *Objekt und Grundbegriffe der theoretischen Nationalökonomie*, 2Aufl. The criticisms of Schumpeter and Strigl on pp. 110–125 and pp. 155–156 are particularly important from this point of view. With the very greatest respect for Professor Amonn's exhaustive analysis, I cannot resist the impression that he is inclined rather to magnify the degree of his divergence from the attitude of these two authors.

executive must necessarily be "arbitrary".[24] That is to say, they must be based on *its* valuations—not on the valuations of consumers and producers. This at once simplifies the form of choice. Without the guidance of a price system, the organisation of production must depend on the valuations of the final organiser, just as the organisation of a patriarchal estate unconnected with a money economy must depend on the valuations of the patriarch.

But in the exchange economy the position is much more complicated. The implications of individual decisions reach beyond the repercussions on the individual. One may realise completely the implications for oneself of a decision to spend money in this way rather than in that way. But it is not so easy to trace the effect of this decision on the whole complex of "scarcity relationships"— on wages, on profits, on prices, on rates of capitalisation, and the organisation of production. On the contrary, the utmost effort of abstract thought is required to devise generalisations which enable us to grasp them. For this reason economic analysis has most utility in the exchange economy. It is unnecessary in the isolated economy. It is debarred from any but the simplest generalisations by the very *raison d'être* of a strictly communist society. But where independent initiative in social relationships is permitted to the individual, there economic analysis comes into its own.

But it is one thing to contend that economic analysis has *most interest and utility* in an exchange economy. It is another to contend that its subject-matter is *limited* to such phenomena. The unjustifiability of this latter contention may be shown conclusively by two considerations. In the first place, it is clear that behaviour outside the exchange economy is conditioned by the same limitation of means in relation to ends as behaviour within the economy, and is capable of being subsumed under the same fundamental categories.[25] The generalisations of the theory of value are as applicable to the behaviour of isolated man or the executive authority of a communist society, as to the behaviour of man in an exchange economy—even if they are not so illuminating in such contexts. The exchange relationship is a *technical* incident, a technical incident indeed which gives rise to nearly all the interesting complications, but still, for all that, subsidiary to the main fact of scarcity.

In the second place, it is clear that the phenomena of the exchange economy itself can only be explained by *going behind* such relationships and invoking the operation of those laws of choice which are best seen when contemplating the behaviour of the isolated individual.[26] Professor Amonn seems willing to admit

[24] See Mises, *Die Gemeinwirtschaft*, pp. 94–138. In his *Economic Planning in Soviet Russia*, Professor Boris Brutzkus has well shown the way in which this difficulty has been exemplified in the various phases of the Russian experiment.

[25] See Strigl, *op. cit.*, pp. 23–28.

[26] Professor Cassel's dismissal of Crusoe Economics (*Fundamental Thoughts*, p. 27) seems unfortunate since it is only when contemplating the conditions of isolated man that the importance of the condition that the scarce means must have alternative uses if there is to be economic activity, which was emphasised above, leaps clearly to the eye. In a social economy of any kind, the mere multiplicity of economic subjects leads one to overlook the possibility of the existence of scarce goods with no alternative uses.

that such a system of pure Economics may be useful as an auxiliary to Economic Science, but he precludes himself from making it the basis of the main system by postulating that the subject-matter of Economics must be defined in terms of the problems discussed by Ricardo. The view that a definition must describe an existing body of knowledge and not lay down arbitrary limits is admirable. But, it may legitimately be asked, why stop at Ricardo? Is it not clear that the imperfections of the Ricardian system were due to just this circumstance that it stopped at the valuations of the market and did not press through to the valuations of the individual? Surely it is the great achievement of the more recent theories of value to have surmounted just this barrier?[27]

5. Finally, we may return to the definition we rejected and examine how it compares with the definition we have now chosen.

At first sight, it is possible to underestimate the divergence between the two definitions. The one regards the subject-matter of economics as human behaviour conceived as a relationship between ends and means, the other as the causes of material welfare. Scarcity of means and the causes of material welfare—are these not more or less the same thing?

Such a contention, however, would rest upon a misconception. It is true that the scarcity of materials is one of the limitations of conduct. But the scarcity of our own time and the services of others is just as important. The scarcity of the services of the school-master and the sewage man have each their economic aspect. Only by saying that services are material vibrations or the like can one stretch the definition to cover the whole field. But this is not only perverse, it is also misleading. In this form the definition may *cover* the field, but it does not describe it. For it is not the *materiality* of even material means of gratification which gives them their status as economic goods; it is their relation to valuations. It is their relationship to given wants rather than their technical substance which is significant. The "materialist" definition of Economics therefore misrepresents the science as we know it. Even if it does not definitely mislead as to its scope, it necessarily fails to convey an adequate concept of its nature. There seems no valid argument against its rejection.

At the same time, it is important to realise that what is rejected is but a definition. We do not reject the body of knowledge which it was intended to describe. The practice of those who have adopted it fits in perfectly with the

---

[27] The objections outlined above to the definition suggested by Professor Amonn should be sufficient to indicate the nature of the objections to those definitions which run in terms of phenomena from the standpoint of price (Davenport), susceptibility to the "measuring rod of money" (Pigou), or the "science of exchange" (Landry, etc.). Professor Schumpeter, in his *Wesen und Hauptinhalt der theoretischen Nationalökonomie*, has attempted with never to be forgotten subtlety to vindicate the latter definition by demonstrating that it is possible to *conceive* all the fundamental aspects of behaviour germane to Economic Science as having the form of exchange. That this is correct and that it embodies a truth fundamental to the proper understanding of equilibrium theory may be readily admitted. But it is one thing to generalise the notion of exchange as a *construction*. It is another to use it in this sense as a *criterion*. That it *can* function in this way is not disputed. But that it throws the maximum light on the ultimate nature of our subject-matter is surely open to question.

alternative definition which has been suggested. There is no important generalisation in the whole range of Professor Cannan's system, for instance, which is incompatible with the definition of the subject-matter of Economics in terms of the disposal of scarce means.

Moreover, the very example which Professor Cannan selects to illustrate his definition fits much better into our framework than it does into his. "Economists", he says, "would agree that 'Did Bacon write Shakespeare?' was not an economic question, and that the satisfaction which believers in the cryptogram would feel if it were universally accepted would not be an economic satisfaction. . . . On the other hand, they would agree that the controversy would have an economic side if copyright were perpetual and the descendants of Bacon and Shakespeare were disputing the ownership of the plays."[28] Exactly. But why? Because the ownership of the copyright involves material welfare? But the proceeds may all go to missionary societies. Surely the question has an economic aspect simply and solely because the copyright laws supposed would make the use of the plays scarce in relation to the demand for their use, and would in turn provide their owners with command over scarce means of gratification which otherwise would be differently distributed.

6 ANALYTICAL MODELS IN THE STUDY OF SOCIAL SYSTEMS[1]

Everett E. Hagen

As judged by the history of the physical, biological, and social sciences, study in any field is apt to begin with a none-too-ordered description of phenomena in the field, followed by a cataloguing of them on bases that seem to make sense. As understanding grows, the systems of classification become more closely related to the functioning of interacting elements. Gradually, generalizations about functioning are reached which are useful in predicting future events. As the generalizations gain rigor, they take the form of analytical models of the behavior of the elements being studied. An analytical model is a mental construct consisting of a set of elements in interrelation, the elements and their interrelations being precisely defined.

The first stage in the analysis of functioning is usually study of processes at narrowly defined points within the general area of the science. Attention is focused on how the elements at the point being examined would function in the

[28] *Wealth* (1st edition), ch. i.

Reprinted from The American Journal of Sociology, *Vol. LXVII, Sept. 1961, pp. 144–151, by permission of The University of Chicago Press. Copyright* © *by The University of Chicago.*

[1] I am grateful to Robert Solow for comments on the first draft of this paper.

absence of change elsewhere. Then a mental model of the processes at this point is formed, which is a simplification of reality that retains only the features essential for predicting similar processes elsewhere. Such analysis of a narrowly defined point in a system may be termed "partial analysis."

Later comes the development of more comprehensive analytical models, which in some sense encompass a complete system rather than simply one point in relationships. Such a model is termed a "general system" or "analytical model"; its construction and use are "general analysis" or "system analysis." There is no sharp distinction between partial and general models, for analysis of a general system also holds in abeyance change beyond certain boundaries. As a science is able to move to more and more comprehensive systemic analysis, its power increases greatly.

Since the work of Willard Gibbs in the physical sciences and mathematics some three-quarters of a century ago, thinking in the physical sciences has been self-consciously in terms of models. Since Walras, theoretical analysis in economics also has rapidly come to be stated exclusively in terms of models. The analytical model has only recently become prominent in the other social sciences, however, probably mainly because of their greater complexity but also because of their slighter contact with the general science of relationships among magnitudes, that is, mathematics.

In the evolution of theory, concepts found useful at various stages are later discarded as analysis grows in rigor. In the study of social systems, many early concepts, for example, those which reified society, have been sloughed off. But certain concepts and methodologies remain which, it seems, are incompatible with rigorous analysis of causal relationships.

Logical Requirements of General System Analysis

The following requirements of general system analysis are of most interest here:

1. An analytical model is defined by defining the elements and their interrelations.[2] The relationships among the elements of a system are statements of the alternative values (magnitudes) or states of one of the elements associated with alternative values or states of one or more of the other elements. Because the elements are assumed to vary in magnitude or state, they are termed variables—which, broadly, includes constants—that is, the variation in some may be zero. If two variables are related in this way, each is said to be a function of the other without regard to the direction of causation between them. While the flow of causation between any two elements may be in one direction and not

[2] Physical scientists refer to a set of elements in interaction as an "analytical system" or simply a "system." They include as systems entities of the real world. I use the term analytical model to emphasize that the concept relevant in theoretical analysis is one of an intellectual construct.

For definitions of systems and discussions of their properties, see von Bertalanffy; Boulding 1956, Hall and Fagen; Ashby 1958; Thrall, Coombs and Davis.

the other, among all of the elements taken as a group, apart from the impact of forces from outside the system, all depend on all. Let it be noted clearly that this concept of mutual interdependence or interaction does not involve circular reasoning or indeterminacy.[3]

2. The variables of a system must exist either in conceptually measurable amounts, or in one or another set of definable states. It is impossible to conceive of variation in one element associated with variation in another if the two cannot be conceived of as varying by measurable amounts, or from one state or structural form to another. If a variable (such as "community spirit" or "love of family") is not defined so as to be conceptually measurable or as existing in one or another set of definable states, it cannot have a precise reasoning, in an analytical model or otherwise.

A variable is a single dimension of an entity, not the entity itself. Thus a variable is not a physical body but one of its qualities, for example, length; in a model of society, it is not an individual, but, say, each value and each need (motive) attributed to him and each component of his perception of the nature of the world. The individual as a group of interacting elements may be a subsystem within the model.

3. For use in analysis, a system must be "closed." A system which is interacting with its environment is an "open" system: all systems of "real life" are therefore open systems. For analysis, however, it is necessary in the intellectual construct to assume that contact with the environment is cut off[4] so that the operation of the system is affected only by given conditions previously established by the environment and not changing at the time of analysis, plus the relationships among the elements of the system.

Elements of the system whose magnitudes are wholly determined by the environment, and which are therefore constant rather than variable so long as the system is insulated from change in the environment, are termed parameters. For example, in some analyses in economics the size of the population and per capita income are parameters, that is, it is assumed that they remain constant.

In the process of analysis a closed system is not assumed to remain closed. Only extremely limited analysis is possible except as the theorist opens the system to a change in the environment, and observes its effect. Thus in a model of a society, the sequence of effects when some one type of relationship with other societies is changed may be analyzed.

4. It is often useful to construct a model which is in equilibrium, and in stable rather than unstable equilibrium.

Equilibrium in its simplest sense refers to a condition in which the variables

[3] Henderson's mechanical example provides a beautifully simple visual illustration of mutual dependence or interaction: Henderson (1937:14).

[4] Technically, that there is no exchange of energy in any form, in the broadest definition of the term energy, to include, for example, information. For this reason, Ashby (1958) suggests that instead of being termed "closed," such a system should be termed "energy-tight," "information-tight," or "noise-tight," the last term of course coming from the terminology of the modern study of communication.

in the system are in such a relationship to each other that all remain constant in value, not by assumption, but by their interaction.

If the magnitude of a variable has been changed by a temporary change in the magnitude of some external force that affects the system, its change will necessarily cause at least temporary changes in the magnitudes of other variables, because of the functional relationships among them. (If change in one variable affects no other variable, then that one variable is not in any significant sense a part of the system.) These changes will in turn react on the magnitudes of the variable which first changed, and of each other. The equilibrium of the system is stable if the final result of this interaction, after an initial temporary disturbance, is a return to the initial values. The equilibrium is unstable if a temporary disturbance causes the values of some or all variables to move cumulatively farther from the initial equilibrium.

The equilibrium of a system may, of course, be stable with respect to one type of disturbance and not with respect to another. Further, the equilibrium of a system may be stable with respect to a small disturbance ("stability in the small") but not with respect to a large disturbance ("stability in the large"). Stability of equilibrium, moreover, implies only that the equilibrium values of the variables will remain unchanged as long as the system remains closed except for temporary "disturbances." If permanent changes in the environment are communicated to the system, there will be corresponding permanent changes in the equilibrium values of variables in the system (that is, the values they will have when the system has settled down into the new equilibrium).

To illustrate equilibrium and related concepts, suppose that deposits in a certain commercial bank are at a "normal" level, and a rumor that the bank is unsafe (a "disturbance") arises. The rumor causes a few depositors to withdraw their money (a movement away from equilibrium). If the total network of circumstances is such that the withdrawals do not lead to a spread of anxiety, but instead the outflow stops, and the funds are redeposited, then by definition the equilibrium was stable; if the initial withdrawals cause a run on the bank so that it fails, the equilibrium was unstable. The bank's equilibrium might be stable with respect to a rumor that a nearby bank was about to close, but not with respect to the unexplained disappearance of the cashier.

The stability of equilibrium is caused, not by (a) the degree of confidence depositors had in the bank, nor by (b) the magnitude of the net demand for withdrawals by depositors, nor by (c) the ability and willingness of the bank to supply funds taken alone, but by the interrelationships among the three—the magnitude of rise in net demand for withdrawals caused by a given decrease in confidence; the ability of the bank to supply an increase of this magnitude in the demand for funds, and the seeming lack of concern with which it does so; the effect of withdrawals of this magnitude in causing further decline in confidence; and the effect of the bank's readiness to supply funds (and the attitude of its officers) in increasing confidence.

Suppose that total income in the community increased because of opening of a new factory. With this change in one of the parameters, deposits in the bank may be expected to rise to a new higher level, at which their value will be in a new stable equilibrium.

Comparison of the equilibrium positions of the variables of a model under two differing values of one or more of the parameters—in the example above, comparison of the level of bank deposits at the two different levels of income— is termed *comparative statics* in economics. There is no comparable term in the other social sciences.

If one or more of the parameters of a system goes through a process of con- tinuing change—for example, if total income in the community steadily increases —the values of the variables at which they are in equilibrium may be expected to change continuously. We may then refer to a "moving equilibrium."

It is especially important, in the application of models to the study of societies, to note that the presence or absence of equilibrium in a system and the stability or instability of equilibrium are results of the interrelationships among the vari- ables. Equilibrium or its absence, and its stability or instability, cannot be caused by the nature of one variable considered without relation to the others. If we knew the interrelationships accurately we could tell in advance whether equi- librium would be restored after a given temporary disturbance. Stability of equilibrium is not merely an *ex post facto* fact.

5. It may also be fruitful to study a system which is not in equilibrium.

Often we are concerned only with the conditions for equilibrium. We may solve a set of equations to determine the value each variable will have in equi- librium. But we may also be interested in a sequence of change, in time, in the values of the variables. A change in the position of one variable has an effect on one or more other variables only after a time interval.[5] For example, a change in birth rates will affect the age composition of the population throughout many generations. A change in the environment in which the children of a group are brought up will affect their personalities as adults only after the lapse of years necessary for them to become adults, and through their impact on their children, will continue to cause alteration in adult personality for generations thereafter.[6]

A new equilibrium will be reached only after a time interval.

In contrast to comparative statics, analysis may be made of the path of change of the several variables of the system (presumably from one equilibrium to another) when a change in a parameter occurs. Such analysis is termed "dynamics," and a model whose process of change is being analyzed is said to

[5] It is sometimes said that, when we consider only the conditions of equilibrium, our analysis is as though the causal effect of change in each variable on each other were instantaneous. This statement may give some "feel" of the nature of analysis of equi- libriums, but it is not literally correct. Nothing happens instantaneously, and analysis does not really assume so.

[6] We select a length of time in which we assume one step of change occurs and treat this as the unit time period. Where the value of a variable is determined by the values of other variables in past periods, and not by the values of other variables in the same time period, the value of the variable is said to be "predetermined," and the variable is said to be a "predetermined variable."

be a dynamic model. The term "diachronic analysis" in anthropology is apparently identical in meaning with dynamic analysis.

It is unfortunate that the terms *dynamic* and *dynamics* are used in this sense with reference to analytical models and in quite a different sense in contemporary psychology. Both usages are so well entrenched that they must be lived with. Freudian psychology introduced, or gave increased emphasis to, two elements in psychological theory. One was the study of the formation of personality, that is, change in personality. This is a study of "personality dynamics" in a sense precisely analogous to that in which the term "dynamics" is used above; hence, the terms "personality dynamics" and "dynamic psychology" came to be applied. The other new element was emphasis on unconscious motivation. These two new elements appeared at once, and by terminological inaccuracy, "dynamic" became a synonym for "motivational." Thus the terms "personality structure" and "personality dynamics" are sometimes used interchangeably, and the term "personality dynamics" is also used to refer to the study of the influences which cause a person to behave as he does.

Sociology has taken over, somewhat out of context, this extension of psychological terminology. Parsons, for example, frequently refers to dynamic factors or processes in any social system, including one which is in stationary equilibrium. And, on the other hand, sociology has no technical terms for the distinction between a social system in equilibrium and one in movement not in equilibrium. Parsons discusses such movement; he entitles the relevant chapter of *The Social System* simply "The Processes of Change in Social Systems." In this essay, to prevent confusion, I shall avoid the psychological-sociological use of the term *dynamics*.

6. When the system moves to a new position of equilibrium, not all the variables necessarily change in value. The interrelationships of the system may be such that, in spite of permanent change in one or more parameters, some of the variables, after being temporarily disturbed, will return to their initial magnitudes. This is the condition termed homeostasis: it is usually illustrated by organic or mechanical examples. If the temperature in the environment of an organism falls, the fall will cause heat to drain more rapidly from the organism, which, in turn, will activate a mechanism which will increase the body's generation of heat, so that unless the fall in external temperature is too great, the temperature of the organism, after a temporary fall, returns to normal.

Homeostasis (or an analogue, if it is preferred to reserve the term for reference to biological or mechanical cases) may also be illustrated by an example from economics. Suppose that in a certain city, the price charged for putting new rubber heels on a pair of shoes is 75 cents. Suppose that the city now grows rapidly; because shoe-repair shops find themselves flooded with business, they can and do obtain 90 cents for putting new rubber heels on shoes, and obtain similarly increased prices for other shoe repairing. The increased profit margin, however, draws more artisans into the shoe-repair business, so that after a time the supply of these services increases so much that it is no longer possible to obtain more than 75 cents for putting on heels. The new equilibrium of the price of equipping a pair of shoes with rubber heels is the same as the old: a "negative feedback mechanism" has restored the former price.

Note, however, that one variable (the body temperature or the price for supplying a pair of rubber heels) could return to its old value only if another one (the bodily consumption of energy and generation of heat, or the quantity of shoe-repair services available) changed permanently in magnitude. This is an aspect of homeostasis sometimes overlooked. Homeostasis with respect to one variable necessarily implies an altered position of another—"heterostasis"— for as long a period as the changed external condition that brought the homeostatic mechanism into play prevails.[7]

Concepts and Methodology

It will be obvious that these requirements of analytical models are necessary characteristics of the interrelationships within any set of variables in any field. Hence concepts concerning society which contradict them are either logically mistaken or, at best, not useful. Concepts which either contradict the logical requirements or, at best, are ambiguous are found, however, in the writings not merely of lesser students but of some of the most creative and influential of recent theorists.

Some of these errors or instances of imprecise formulation of concepts may have arisen originally from a state of mind characteristic of the early stages of anthropology and sociology, social constancy being regarded as good, and social change (perhaps because it created tensions, or because it was imposed, willy-nilly, from without), as bad. Some may have arisen from concentration on social structure rather than on social processes. Perhaps the explanation of their persistence is that the study of societies has not yet fully reached the stage of precise definition of variables. In any event, the social sciences are now moving toward greater precision in the definition of variables, analysis of functional relationships, and creation of models, and in this transitional phase it may be useful to call attention to some concepts that seem obsolescent.

1. In much sociological writing, the concept of society is viewed as necessarily involving stable equilibrium (either static or moving). Thus in *Toward a General Theory of Action*, Parsons writes, with Shils:

> The most general and fundamental property of a system is the interdependence of parts or variables. Interdependence consists in the existence of determinate relationships among the parts or variables as contrasted with randomness of variability. In other words, interdependence is *order* in the relationship among the components which enter into a system. This order must have a tendency to self-maintenance, which is very generally expressed in the concept of equilibrium. That is, if the system is to be permanent enough to be worth study, there must be a tendency to maintenance of order except under exceptional circumstances. It need not, however, be a

[7] The term *heterostasis* is from Davis (1958:8–13).

static self-maintenance or a stable equilibrium. It may be an ordered process of change—a process following a determinate pattern rather than random variability relative to the starting point. This is called a moving equilibrium and is well exemplified by growth. Furthermore, equilibrium, even when stable, by no means implies that process is not going on; process is continual even in stable systems, the stabilities residing in the interrelations involved in the process (Parsons and Shils 1954:107).

Note that the word *stable* here is used to refer to static as distinguished from moving equilibrium, and not to stable equilibrium in the sense in which the term is defined above.[8]

In this statement, it is not entirely clear whether the reference to moving equilibrium is to that concept as defined above (continuing shift in equilibrium caused by continuing change in an exogenous force) or to a dynamic process (change in time in the values of variables in the system caused by the relationships within the system). However, in the latter case the statement is tautologous, and means merely, "Do not study a system unless it is a system," for the only possible states of a system are equilibrium and dynamic. Hence, and because his own analytical models are purely static,[9] I conclude that Parsons is warning against formulation of models not in equilibrium.

Related is the implication, in the terms "dysfunction," "eufunctional," and "dysfunctional," by Merton and by Levy (Merton 1957:51; Levy 1952 *passim*), that tendency toward equilibrium is somehow good and toward disequilibrium somehow bad. While these authors may disavow the implication, the use of the prefixes *eu* and *dys* conveys an inescapable suggestion.

Parsons does not assert, it should be noted, that a society necessarily possesses stable equilibrium, but only that it is not worth studying unless it does. The restriction is thus logically permissible. It also has empirical relevance. Some societies certainly have had a tendency toward stability of equilibrium; their internal dynamics have at best brought rather slow change. But adherence to this model as the general case unnecessarily limits the domain of sociological theory, and excludes from sociological theory important problems that ought to be treated within it. First, it tends to exclude from the theoretical system consideration of what kind of force is necessary (and sufficient) to push the society away from the equilibrium and lead to the disruption of the social system. Second, it excludes study of the relationships within the society which will determine the nature of the sequence of change in time, once the equilibrium has been disturbed—or the nature of a sequence of change in time in a society conceived of as never having been in equilibrium, but rather under continuing change

---

[8] Parsons presents a similar formulation, though one which may be interpreted as presenting stable equilibrium as a basis for Parsons' work rather than as a general theoretical requirement (1951:481).

[9] Parsons discusses social change, not only in specific "empirical" discussions, but more generally in 1951:xi and in Parsons and Bales 1954:vii, but in each case this discussion is an addendum, not a part of the analytical system which he presents in *The Social System* and in *Toward a General Theory of Action*.

from its own dynamics. Virtually all societies in the world at present are in a process of change which, however it began, is best analyzed as continuing partly by virtue of the dynamics within the system itself. A model of stable equilibrium is not a satisfactory theoretical analogue for use in studying their behavior. If sociologists are to analyze change in a society as a whole, rather than merely to describe it loosely, they must go beyond models in equilibrium and construct models involving dynamic processes.

Further, even with regard to a society—or a model—in stable equilibrium, or changing only very slowly, study of the relationships that bring about the stability or quasi-stability may be extremely fruitful. It is illuminating to isolate the network of relationships which, if a temporary disturbance brings change within a society, determines whether the change will be cumulative or whether the system will return to the initial equilibrium. Out of studying precisely this question great advances in the understanding of societies, even of societies in stable equilibrium, may come.

2. Perhaps underlying these difficulties are undesirably vague definitions of *function*. The question of the meaning of the concept has been much speculated upon since Radcliffe-Brown's essay of 1935 (reprinted in Radcliffe-Brown 1952), yet in 1954 Parsons had not yet arrived at a precise meaning. Referring to testing the significance of processes, he states "That test of significance takes the form of the 'functional' relevance of the process. The test is to ask the question, what would be the differential consequences for the system of two or more alternative outcomes of a dynamic process."[10]

And in 1957, Merton defined function as "the observed consequences" of "a sociological item" for "the social or cultural system in which it is implicated,"[11] a statement which in addition to being vague suggests that the nature of a single "item" can lead to stability or instability.

These statements are not incorrect, only vague. In them precisely what does the word *consequences* refer to?

These writers have made great contributions to sociological theory, as Radcliffe-Brown did to anthropology. It implies no lack of appreciation of their work to suggest that, in the most fruitful usage, only a quality can be a variable; only a variable has a functional relationship; a functional relationship consists of the change in the magnitude (or state) of one variable (not in a system)

---

[10] *The Social System*, pp. 21–22. The term *dynamic* here does not refer to change in the equilibrium of the system, but to a process of action by an individual or a group in a role. In neither *The Social System* nor *Toward a General Theory of Action* does Parsons define *function*.

[11] This definition is arrived at by joining phrases from two sentences, on the assumption that *function* and *dysfunction* as contrasting concepts are subcategories of the general concept *function*:

"We have observed two prevailing types of confusion enveloping several current conceptions of 'function':

"(1) The tendency to confine sociological observations to the *positive* contributions of a sociological item to the social or cultural system in which it is implicated; . . .

"Functions are those observed consequences which make for the adaptation or adjustment of a given system; and dysfunctions, those observed consequences which lessen the adaptation or adjustment of the system." (Merton 1949:51).

associated with change in the magnitude (or state) of another; and no single variable, but only the functional relationships among variables can lead to stability (adaptation, adjustment) or instability in a system.

Though system analysis is used more in psychological theory than in that relating to societies or communities as wholes,[12] failure to state theory relating to social systems in terms of variables, functions, and a general system has not been for lack of sophistication. Rather, the difficulty has been one of substantive complexity. The applicability of functional analysis, in the mathematical sense, in any science does not become apparent to students of that science until they have been able to arrive at a certain precision and breadth of understanding of causal relationships. This is why each discipline slowly and stumblingly rediscovers concepts concerning method already discovered long ago in other disciplines— why, for example, economics clumsily and painfully groped its way to the concept of marginal productivity and only subsequently realized that it was merely applying elementary calculus to its problems; and why anthropologists groped toward the concepts of synchronic and diachronic analysis, and not all anthropologists realize fully even today that they are referring to static and dynamic analysis of an analytical system. Scholars are not apt to realize the applicability of the concepts of variable, function, and general system until they understand functional relationships in their field of study well enough so that their images of the phenomena in their field of analysis begin to resemble variables in interaction.

Freudian and post-Freudian analysis of personality formation has made it possible to formulate plausible and useful models of individual personality and its formation. If we incorporate these subsystems in models of society, the time when we may formulate useful though heroically simplified models of society in equilibrium and of societal change does not seem far off. Even a model which, with respect to many functional relationships, merely indicated that between two certain variables a relationship must exist, while admitting ignorance of its nature, could be a highly useful vehicle for the furthering of substantive analysis.

7 SOCIAL BEHAVIOR AS EXCHANGE
George C. Homans

The Problems of Small-Group Research

This essay will hope to honor the memory of Georg Simmel in two different ways. So far as it pretends to be suggestive rather than conclusive, its tone will be Simmel's; and its subject, too, will be one of his. Because Simmel, in essays such as those on sociability, games, coquetry, and conversation, was an analyst

---

[12] For a recent discussion by a psychologist which takes aim beyond the boundaries of his discipline, see Miller 1955.

Reprinted from The American Journal of Sociology, *Vol. LXII, 1958, pp. 597–606, by permission of The University of Chicago Press. Copyright © 1958 by The University of Chicago.*

of elementary social behavior, we call him an ancestor of what is known today as small-group research. For what we are really studying in small groups is elementary social behavior: what happens when two or three persons are in a position to influence one another, the sort of thing of which those massive structures called "classes," "firms," "communities," and "societies" must ultimately be composed.

As I survey small-group research today, I feel that, apart from just keeping on with it, three sorts of things need to be done. The first is to show the relation between the results of experimental work done under laboratory conditions and the results of *quasi-* anthropological field research on what those of us who do it are pleased to call "real-life" groups in industry and elsewhere. If the experimental work has anything to do with real life—and I am persuaded that it has everything to do—its propositions cannot be inconsistent with those discovered through the field work. But the consistency has not yet been demonstrated in any systematic way.

The second job is to pull together in some set of general propositions the actual results, from the laboratory and from the field, of work on small groups—propositions that at least sum up, to an approximation, what happens in elementary social behavior, even though we may not be able to explain why the propositions should take the form they do. A great amount of work has been done, and more appears every day, but what it all amounts to in the shape of a set of propositions from which, under specified conditions, many of the observational results might be derived, is not at all clear—and yet to state such a set is the first aim of science.

The third job is to begin to show how the propositions that empirically hold good in small groups may be derived from some set of still more general propositions. "Still more general" means only that empirical propositions other than ours may also be derived from the set. This derivation would constitute the explanatory stage in the science of elementary social behavior, for explanation *is* derivation (see Braithwaite 1953). (I myself suspect that the more general set will turn out to contain the propositions of behavioral psychology. I hold myself to be an "ultimate psychological reductionist," but I cannot know that I am right so long as the reduction has not been carried out.)

I have come to think that all three of these jobs would be furthered by our adopting the view that interaction between persons is an exchange of goods, material and non-material. This is one of the oldest theories of social behavior, and one that we still use every day to interpret our own behavior, as when we say, "I found so-and-so rewarding"; or "I got a great deal out of him"; or, even, "Talking with him took a great deal out of me." But, perhaps just because it is so obvious, this view has been much neglected by social scientists. So far as I know, the only theoretical work that makes explicit use of it is Marcel Mauss's *Essai sur le don*, published in 1925, which is ancient as social science goes.[1]

---

[1] Translated by I. Cunnison as *The Gift* (Glencoe, Ill.: Free Press, 1954).

It may be that the tradition of neglect is now changing and that, for instance, the psychologists who interpret behavior in terms of transactions may be coming back to something of the sort I have in mind.[2]

An incidental advantage of an exchange theory is that it might bring sociology closer to economics—that science of man most advanced, most capable of application, and, intellectually, most isolated. Economics studies exchange carried out under special circumstances and with a most useful built-in numerical measure of value. What are the laws of the general phenomenon of which economic behavior is one class?

In what follows I shall suggest some reasons for the usefulness of a theory of social behavior as exchange and suggest the nature of the propositions such a theory might contain.

An Exchange Paradigm

I start with the link to behavioral psychology and the kind of statement it makes about the behavior of an experimental animal such as the pigeon (Skinner 1953). As a pigeon explores its cage in the laboratory, it happens to peck a target, whereupon the psychologist feeds it corn. The evidence is that it will peck the target again; it has learned the behavior, or, as my friend Skinner says, the behavior has been reinforced, and the pigeon has undergone *operant conditioning*. This kind of psychologist is not interested in how the behavior was learned: "learning theory" is a poor name for his field. Instead, he is interested in what determines changes in the rate of emission of learned behavior, whether pecks at a target or something else.

The more hungry the pigeon, the less corn or other food it has gotten in the recent past, the more often it will peck. By the same token, if the behavior is often reinforced, if the pigeon is given much corn every time it pecks, the rate of emission will fall off as the pigeon gets *satiated*. If, on the other hand, the behavior is not reinforced at all, then, too, its rate of emission will tend to fall off, though a long time may pass before it stops altogether, before it is *extinguished*. In the emission of many kinds of behavior the pigeon incurs *aversive stimulation*, or what I shall call "cost" for short, and this, too, will lead in time to a decrease in the emission rate. Fatigue is an example of a "cost." Extinction, satiation, and cost, by decreasing the rate of emission of a particular kind of behavior, render more probable the emisison of some other kind of behavior, including doing nothing. I shall only add that even a hard-boiled psychologist puts "emotional" behavior, as well as such things as pecking, among the unconditioned responses that may be reinforced in operant conditioning. As a statement of the propositions of behavioral psychology, the foregoing is, of course, inadequate for any purpose except my present one.

We may look on the pigeon as engaged in an exchange—pecks for corn—

---

[2] In social anthropology D. L. Oliver is working along these lines, and I owe much to him. See also Newcomb 1956:575–586.

with the psychologist, but let us not dwell upon that, for the behavior of the pigeon hardly determines the behavior of the psychologist at all. Let us turn to a situation where the exchange is real, that is, where the determination is mutual. Suppose we are dealing with two men. Each is emitting behavior reinforced to some degree by the behavior of the other. How it was in the past that each learned the behavior he emits and how he learned to find the other's behavior reinforcing we are not concerned with. It is enough that each does find the other's behavior reinforcing, and I shall call the reinforcers—the equivalent of the pigeon's corn—*values*, for this, I think, is what we mean by this term. As he emits behavior, each man may incur costs, and each man has more than one course of behavior open to him.

This seems to me the paradigm of elementary social behavior, and the problem of the elementary sociologist is to state propositions relating the variations in the values and costs of each man to his frequency distribution of behavior among alternatives, where the values (in the mathematical sense) taken by these variable for one man determine in part their values for the other.[3]

I see no reason to believe that the propositions of behavioral psychology do not apply to this situation, though the complexity of their implications in the concrete case may be great indeed. In particular, we must suppose that, with men as with pigeons, an increase in extinction, satiation, or aversive stimulation of any one kind of behavior will increase the probability of emission of some other kind. The problem is not, as it is often stated, merely, what a man's values are, what he has learned in the past to find reinforcing, but how much of any one value his behavior is getting him now. The more he gets, the less valuable any further unit of that value is to him, and the less often he will emit behavior reinforced by it.

The Influence Process

We do not, I think, possess the kind of studies of two-person interaction that would either bear out these propositions or fail to do so. But we do have studies of larger numbers of persons that suggest that they may apply, notably the studies by Festinger, Schachter, Back, and their associates on the dynamics of influence. One of the variables they work with they call *cohesiveness*, defined as anything that attracts people to take part in a group. Cohesiveness is a value variable; it refers to the degree of reinforcement people find in the activities of the group. Festinger and his colleagues consider two kinds of reinforcing activity: the symbolic behavior we call "social approval" (sentiment) and activity valuable in other ways, such as doing something interesting.

The other variable they work with they call *communication* and others call *interaction*. This is a frequency variable; it is a measure of the frequency of emission of valuable and costly verbal behavior. We must bear in mind that, in general, the one kind of variable is a function of the other.

Festinger and his co-workers show that the more cohesive a group is, that is,

3 Skinner 1953:297–329. The discussion of "double contingency" by T. Parsons and E. A. Shils could easily lead to a similar paradigm (1951:14–16).

the more valuable the sentiment or activity the members exchange with one another, the greater the average frequency of interaction of the members (Back 1950:21–36). With men, as with pigeons, the greater the reinforcement, the more often is the reinforced behavior emitted. The more cohesive a group, too, the greater the change that members can produce in the behavior of other members in the direction of rendering these activities more valuable (Schachter, Ellertson, McBride, and Gregory 1951:229–238). That is, the more valuable the activities that members get, the more valuable those that they must give. For if a person is emitting behavior of a certain kind, and other people do not find it particularly rewarding, these others will suffer their own production of sentiment and activity, in time, to fall off. But perhaps the first person has found their sentiment and activity rewarding, and, if he is to keep on getting them, he must make his own behavior more valuable to the others. In short, the propositions of behavioral psychology imply a tendency toward a certain proportionality between the value to others of the behavior a man gives them and the value to him of the behavior they give him (Skinner 1953:100).

Schachter also studied the behavior of members of a group toward two kinds of other members, "conformers" and "deviates" (Schachter 1951:190–207). I assume that conformers are people whose activity the other members find valuable. For conformity is behavior that coincides to a degree with some group standard or norm, and the only meaning I can assign to *norm* is "a verbal description of behavior that many members find it valuable for the actual behavior of themselves and others to conform to." By the same token, a deviate is a member whose behavior is not particularly valuable. Now Schachter shows that, as the members of a group come to see another member as a deviate, their interaction with him—communication addressed to getting him to change his behavior—goes up, the faster the more cohesive the group. The members need not talk to the other conformers so much; they are relatively satiated by the conformers' behavior: they have gotten what they want out of them. But if the deviate, by failing to change his behavior, fails to reinforce the members, they start to withhold social approval from him: the deviate gets low sociometric choice at the end of the experiment. And in the most cohesive groups—those Schachter calls "high cohesive-relevant"—interaction with the deviate also falls off in the end and is lowest among those members that rejected him most strongly, as if they had given him up as a bad job. But how plonking can we get? These findings are utterly in line with everyday experience.

Practical Equilibrium

At the beginning of this paper I suggested that one of the tasks of small-group research was to show the relation between the results of experimental work done under laboratory conditions and the results of field research on real-life small groups. Now the latter often appear to be in practical equilibrium, and by this I mean nothing fancy. I do not mean that all real-life groups are in equilibrium. I certainly do not mean that all groups must tend to equilibrium. I do not mean that groups have built-in antidotes to change: there is no homeostasis here. I do not mean that we assume equilibrium. I mean only that we sometimes *observe* it, that for the time we are with a group—and it is often short—there is no great change in the values of the variables we choose to measure. If, for instance, person A is interacting with B more than with C both at the beginning and at the end of the study, then at least by this crude measure the group is in equilibrium.

Many of the Festinger-Schachter studies are experimental, and their propositions about the process of influence seem to me to imply the kind of proposition that empirically holds good of real-life groups in practical equilibrium. For instance, Festinger *et al.* find that, the more cohesive a group is, the greater the change that members can produce in the behavior of other members. If the influence is exerted in the direction of conformity to group norms, then, when the process of influence has accomplished all the change of which it is capable, the proposition should hold good that, the more cohesive a group is, the larger the number of members that conform to its norms. And it does hold good (Festinger, Schachter, and Back 1950:72–100).

Again, Schachter found, in the experiment I summarized above, that in the most cohesive groups and at the end, when the effort to influence the deviate had failed, members interacted little with the deviate and gave him little in the way of sociometric choice. Now two of the propositions that hold good most often of real-life groups in practical equilibrium are precisely that the more closely a member's activity conforms to the norms the more interaction he receives from other members and the more liking choices he gets from them too. From these main propositions a number of others may be derived that also hold good.[4]

Yet we must ever remember that the truth of the proposition linking conformity to liking may on occasion be masked by the truth of other propositions. If, for instance, the man that conforms to the norms most closely also exerts some authority over the group, this may render liking for him somewhat less than it might otherwise have been (Homans 1950: 244–248 and Bales 1953:450–456).

Be that as it may, I suggest that the laboratory experiments on influence imply propositions about the behavior of members of small groups, when the process of influence has worked itself out, that are identical with propositions that hold good of real-life groups in equilibrium. This is hardly surprising if all we mean by equilibrium is that all the change of which the system is, under present conditions, capable has been effected, so that no further change occurs. Nor would this be the first time that statics has turned out to be a special case of dynamics.

Profit and Social Control

Though I have treated equilibrium as an observed fact, it is a fact that cries for explanation. I shall not, as structural-functional sociologists do, use an assumed equilibrium as a means of explaining, or trying to explain, why the other

[4] For propositions holding good of groups in practical equilibrium see Homans, 1950 and Riecken and Homans 1954:786–832).

features of a social system should be what they are. Rather, I shall take practical equilibrium as something that is itself to be explained by the other features of the system.

If every member of a group emits at the end of, and during, a period of time much the same kinds of behavior and in much the same frequencies as he did at the beginning, the group is for that period in equilibrium. Let us then ask why any one member's behavior should persist. Suppose he is emitting behavior of value A_1. Why does he not let his behavior get worse (less valuable or reinforcing to the others) until it stands at $A_1 - \triangle A$? True, the sentiments expressed by others toward him are apt to decline in value (become less reinforcing to him), so that what he gets from them may be $S_1 - \triangle S$. But it is conceivable that, since most activity carries cost, a decline in the value of what he emits will mean a reduction in cost to him that more than offsets his losses in sentiment. Where, then, does he stabilize his behavior? This is the problem of social control. (Homans 1950:281–301).

Mankind has always assumed that a person stabilizes his behavior, at least in the short run, at the point where he is doing the best he can for himself under the circumstances, though his best may not be a "rational" best, and what he can do may not be at all easy to specify, except that he is not apt to think like one of the theoretical antagonists in the *Theory of Games*. Before a sociologist rejects this answer out of hand for its horrid profit-seeking implications, he will do well to ask himself if he can offer any other answer to the question posed. I think he will find that he cannot. Yet experiments designed to test the truth of the answer are extraordinarily rare.

I shall review one that seems to me to provide a little support for the theory, though it was not meant to do so. The experiment is reported by H. B. Gerard, a member of the Festinger-Schachter team, under the title "The Anchorage of Opinions in Face-to-Face Groups" (Gerard 1954:313–325). The experimenter formed artificial groups whose members met to discuss a case in industrial relations and to express their opinions about its probable outcome. The groups were of two kinds: high-attraction groups, whose members were told that they would like one another very much, and low-attraction groups, whose members were told that they would not find one another particularly likable.

At a later time the experimenter called the members in separately, asked them again to express their opinions on the outcome of the case, and counted the number that had changed their opinions to bring them into accord with those of other members of their groups. At the same time, a paid participant entered into a further discussion of the case with each member, always taking, on the probable outcome of the case, a position opposed to that taken by the bulk of the other members of the group to which the person belonged. The experimenter counted the number of persons shifting toward the opinion of the paid participant.

The experiment had many interesting results, from which I choose only those summed up in Tables 7–1 and 7–2. The three different agreement classes are made up of people who, at the original sessions, expressed different degrees of

TABLE 7–1   Percentage of Subjects Changing toward Someone in the Group

	Agreement	Mild Disagreement	Strong Disagreement
High attraction	0	12	44
Low attraction	0	15	9

TABLE 7–2   Percentage of Subjects Changing toward the Paid Participant

	Agreement	Mild Disagreement	Strong Disagreement
High attraction	7	13	25
Low attraction	20	38	8

agreement with the opinions of other members of their groups. And the figure 44, for instance, means that, of all members of high-attraction groups whose initial opinions were strongly in disagreement with those of other members, 44 per cent shifted their opinion later toward that of others.

In these results the experimenter seems to have been interested only in the differences in the sums of the rows, which show that there is more shifting toward the group, and less shifting toward the paid participant, in the high-attraction than in the low-attraction condition. This is in line with a proposition suggested earlier. If you think that the members of a group can give you much—in this case, liking—you are apt to give them much—in this case, a change to an opinion in accordance with their views—or you will not get the liking. And, by the same token, if the group can give you little of value, you will not be ready to give it much of value. Indeed, you may change your opinion so as to depart from agreement even further, to move, that is, toward the view held by the paid participant.

So far so good, but, when I first scanned these tables, I was less struck by the difference between them than by their similarity. The same classes of people in both tables showed much the same relative propensities to change their opinions, no matter whether the change was toward the group or toward the paid participant. We see, for instance, that those who change least are the high-attraction, agreement people and the low attraction, strong-disagreement ones. And those who change most are the high-attraction, strong-disagreement people and the low-attraction, mild-disagreement ones.

How am I to interpret these particular results? Since the experimenter did not discuss them, I am free to offer my own explanation. The behavior emitted by the subjects is opinion and changes in opinion. For this behavior they have learned to expect two possible kinds of reinforcement. Agreement with the group gets the subject favorable sentiment (acceptance) from it, and the experiment was designed to give this reinforcement a higher value in the high-attraction condition than in the low-attraction one. The second kind of possible reinforcement is what I shall call the "maintenance of one's personal integrity," which a subject gets by sticking to his own opinion in the face of disagreement with the group. The experimenter does not mention this reward, but I cannot make sense of the results without something much like it. In different degrees for different subjects, depending on their initial positions, these rewards are in competition with one another: they are alternatives. They are not absolutely scarce goods, but some persons cannot get both at once.

Since the rewards are alternatives, let me introduce a familiar assumption from economics—that the cost of a particular course of action is the equivalent of the foregone value of an alternative (Stigler 1952:99)—and then add the definition: Profit = Reward — Cost.

Now consider the persons in the corresponding cells of the two tables. The behavior of the high-attraction, agreement people gets them much in the way of acceptance by the group, and for it they must give up little in the way of personal integrity, for their views are from the start in accord with those of the group. Their profit is high, and they are not prone to change their behavior. The low-attraction, strong-disagreement people are getting much in integrity, and they are not giving up for it much in valuable acceptance, for they are members of low-attraction groups. Reward less cost is high for them, too, and they change little. The high-attraction, strong-disagreement people are getting much in the way of integrity, but their costs in doing so are high, too, for they are in high-attraction groups and thus foregoing much valuable acceptance by the group. Their profit is low, and they are very apt to change, either toward the group or toward the paid participant, from whom they think, perhaps, they will get some acceptance while maintaining some integrity. The low-attraction, mild-disagreement people do not get much in the way of integrity, for they are only in mild disagreement with the group, but neither are they giving up much in acceptance, for they are members of low-attraction groups. Their rewards are low; their costs are low too, and their profit—the difference between the two—is also low. In their low profit they resemble the high-attraction, strong-disagreement people, and, like them, they are prone to change their opinions, in this case, more toward the paid participant. The subjects in the other two cells, who have medium profits, display medium propensities to change.

If we define profit as reward less cost, and if cost is value foregone, I suggest that we have here some evidence for the proposition that change in behavior is greatest when perceived profit is least. This constitutes no direct demonstration that change in behavior is least when profit is greatest, but if, whenever a man's behavior brought him a balance of reward and cost, he changed his behavior away from what got him, under the circumstances, the less profit, there might well come a time when his behavior would not change further. That is, his behavior would be stabilized, at least for the time being. And, so far as this were true for every member of a group, the group would have a social organization in equilibrium.

I do not say that a member would stabilize his behavior at the point of greatest conceivable profit to himself, because his profit is partly at the mercy of the behavior of others. It is a commonplace that the short-run pursuit of profit by several persons often lands them in positions where all are worse off than they might conceivably be. I do not say that the paths of behavioral change in which a member pursues his profit under the condition that others are pursuing theirs too are easy to describe or predict; and we can readily conceive that in jockeying for position they might never arrive at any equilibrium at all.

Distributive Justice

Yet practical equilibrium is often observed, and thus some further condition may make its attainment, under some circumstance, more probable than would the individual pursuit of profit left to itself. I can offer evidence for this further condition only in the behavior of subgroups and not in that of individuals. Suppose that there are two subgroups, working close together in a factory, the job of one being somewhat different from that of the other. And suppose that the members of the first complain and say: "We are getting the same pay as they are. We ought to get just a couple of dollars a week more to show that our work is more responsible." When you ask them what they mean by "more responsible," they say that, if they do their work wrong, more damage can result, and so they are under more pressure to take care (Homans 1953:5–10). Something like this is a common feature of industrial behavior. It is at the heart of disputes not over absolute wages but over wage differentials—indeed, at the heart of disputes over rewards other than wages.

In what kind of proposition may we express observations like these? We may say that wages and responsibility give status in the group, in the sense that a man who takes high responsibility and gets high wages is admired, other things equal. Then, if the members of one group score higher on responsibility than do the members of another, there is a felt need on the part of the first to score higher on pay too. There is a pressure, which shows itself in complaints, to bring the *status factors*, as I have called them, into line with one another. If they are in line, a condition of *status congruence* is said to exist. In this condition the workers may find their jobs dull or irksome, but they will not complain about the relative position of groups.

But there may be a more illuminating way of looking at the matter. In my example I have considered only responsibility and pay, but these may be enough, for they represent the two kinds of thing that come into the problem. Pay is clearly a reward; responsibility may be looked on, less clearly, as a cost. It means constraint and worry—or peace of mind foregone. Then the proposition about status congruence becomes this: If the costs of the members of one group are higher than those of another, distributive justice requires that their rewards should be higher too. But the thing works both ways: If the rewards are higher, the costs should be higher too. This last is the theory of *noblesse oblige*, which we all subscribe to, though we all laugh at it, perhaps because the *noblesse* often fails to *oblige*. To put the matter in terms of profit: though the rewards and costs of two persons or the members of two groups may be different, yet the profits of the two—the excess of reward over cost—should tend to equality. And more than "should." The less-advantaged group will at least try to attain greater equality, as, in the example I have used, the first group tried to increase its profit by increasing its pay.

I have talked of distributive justice. Clearly, this is not the only condition determining the actual distribution of rewards and costs. At the same time, never tell me that notions of justice are not a strong influence on behavior, though we sociologists often neglect them. Distributive justice may be one of the conditions of group equilibrium.

Exchange and Social Structure

I shall end by reviewing almost the only study I am aware of that begins to show in detail how a stable and differentiated social structure in a real-life group might arise out of a process of exchange between members. This is Peter Blau's description of the behavior of sixteen agents in a federal law-enforcement agency (Blau 1955:99–116).

The agents had the duty of investigating firms and preparing reports on the firms' compliance with the law. Since the reports might lead to legal action against the firms, the agents had to prepare them carefully, in the proper form, and take strict account of the many regulations that might apply. The agents were often in doubt what they should do, and then they were supposed to take the question to their supervisor. This they were reluctant to do, for they naturally believed that thus confessing to him their inability to solve a problem would reflect on their competence, affect the official ratings he made of their work, and so hurt their chances for promotion. So agents often asked other agents for help and advice, and, though this was nominally forbidden, the supervisor usually let it pass.

Blau ascertained the ratings the supervisor made of the agents, and he also asked the agents to rate one another. The two opinions agreed closely. Fewer agents were regarded as highly competent than were regarded as of middle or low competence; competence, or the ability to solve technical problems, was a fairly scarce good. One or two of the more competent agents would not give help and advice when asked, and so received few interactions and little liking. A man that will not exchange, that will not give you what he has when you need it, will not get from you the only thing you are, in this case, able to give him in return, your regard.

But most of the more competent agents were willing to give help, and of them Blau says:

A consultation can be considered an exchange of values: both participants gain something, and both have to pay a price. The questioning agent is enabled to perform better than he could otherwise have done, without exposing his difficulties to his supervisor. By asking for advice, he implicitly pays his respect to the superior proficiency of his colleague. This acknowledgment of inferiority is the cost of receiving assistance. The consultant gains prestige, in return for which he is willing to devote some time to the consultation and permit it to disrupt his own work. The following remark of an agent illustrates this: "I like giving advice. It's flattering, I suppose, if you feel that others come to you for advice (Blau 1955:108).

Blau goes on to say: "All agents liked being consulted, but the value of any one of very many consultations became deflated for experts, and the price they paid in frequent interruptions became inflated" (Blau 1955:108). This implies that, the more prestige an agent received, the less was the increment of value of that prestige; the more advice an agent gave, the greater was the increment of cost of that advice, the cost lying precisely in the foregone value of time to do his own work. Blau suggests that something of the same sort was true of an agent who went to a more competent colleague for advice: the more often he went, the more costly to him, in feelings of inferiority, became any further request. "The repeated admission of his inability to solve his own problems . . . undermined the self-confidence of the worker and his standing in the group (Blau 1955:109).

The result was that the less competent agents went to the more competent ones for help less often than they might have done if the costs of repeated admissions of inferiority had been less high and that, while many agents sought out the few highly competent ones, no single agent sought out the latter much. Had they done so (to look at the exchange from the other side), the costs to the highly competent in interruptions to their own work would have become exorbitant. Yet the need of the less competent for help was still not fully satisfied. Under these circumstances they tended to turn for help to agents more nearly like themselves in competence. Though the help they got was not the most valuable, it was of a kind they could themselves return on occasion. With such agents they could exchange help and liking, without the exchange becoming on either side too great a confession of inferiority.

The highly competent agents tended to enter into exchanges, that is, to interact with many others. But, in the more equal exchanges I have just spoken of, less competent agents tended to pair off as partners. That is, they interacted with a smaller number of people, but interacted often with these few. I think I could show why pair relations in these more equal exchanges would be more economical for an agent than a wider distribution of favors. But perhaps I have gone far enough. The final pattern of this social structure was one in which a small number of highly competent agents exchanged advice for prestige with a large number of others less competent and in which the less competent agents exchanged, in pairs and in trios, both help and liking on more nearly equal terms.

Blau shows, then, that a social structure in equilibrium might be the result of a process of exchanging behavior rewarding and costly in different degrees, in which the increment of reward and cost varied with the frequency of the behavior, that is, with the frequency of interaction. Note that the behavior of the agents seems also to have satisfied my second condition of equilibrium: the more competent agents took more responsibility for the work, either their own or others', than did the less competent ones, but they also got more for it in the way of prestige. I suspect that the same kind of explanation could be given for the structure of many "informal" groups.

Summary

The current job of theory in small-group research is to make the connection between experimental and real-life studies, to consolidate the propositions that empirically hold good in the two fields, and to show how these propositions might be derived from a still more general set. One way of doing this job would be to revive and make more rigorous the oldest of theories of social behavior— social behavior as exchange.

Some of the statements of such a theory might be the following. Social behavior is an exchange of goods, material goods but also non-material ones, such as the symbols of approval or prestige. Persons that give much to others try to get much from them, and persons that get much from others are under pressure to give much to them. This process of influence tends to work out at equilibrium to a balance in the exchanges. For a person engaged in exchange, what he gives may be a cost to him, just as what he gets may be a reward, and his behavior changes less as profit, that is, reward less cost, tends to a maximum. Not only does he seek a maximum for himself, but he tries to see to it that no one in his group makes more profit than he does. The cost and the value of what he gives and of what he gets vary with the quantity of what he gives and gets. It is surprising how familiar these propositions are; it is surprising, too, how propositions about the dynamics of exchange can begin to generate the static thing we call "group structure" and, in so doing, generate also some of the propositions about group structure that students of real-life groups have stated.

In our unguarded moments we sociologists find words like "reward" and "cost" slipping into what we say. Human nature will break in upon even our most elaborate theories. But we seldom let it have its way with us and follow up systematically what these words imply (Survey Research Center 1953:115–127). Of all our many "approaches" to social behavior, the one that sees it as an economy is the most neglected, and yet it is the one we use every moment of our lives—except when we write sociology.

THE SUBSTANTIVIST REVOLUTION

8 THE ECONOMY AS INSTITUTED PROCESS
Karl Polanyi

Our main purpose in this chapter is to determine the meaning that can be attached with consistency to the term "economic" in all the social sciences.

The simple recognition from which all such attempts must start is the fact that in referring to human activities the term economic is a compound of two meanings that have independent roots. We will call them the substantive and the formal meaning.

The substantive meaning of economic derives from man's dependence for his living upon nature and his fellows. It refers to the interchange with his natural and social environment, in so far as this results in supplying him with the means of material want satisfaction.

The formal meaning of economic derives from the logical character of the means-ends relationship, as apparent in such words as "economical" or "economizing." It refers to a definite situation of choice, namely, that between the different uses of means induced by an insufficiency of those means. If we call the rules governing choice of means the logic of rational action, then we may denote this variant of logic, with an improvised term, as formal economics.

The two root meanings of "economic," the substantive and the formal, have nothing in common. The latter derives from logic, the former from fact. The formal meaning implies a set of rules referring to choice between the alternative uses of insufficient means. The substantive meaning implies neither choice nor insufficiency of means; man's livelihood may or may not involve the necessity of choice and, if choice there be, it need not be induced by the limiting effect of a "scarcity" of the means; indeed, some of the most important physical and social conditions of livelihood such as the availability of air and water or a loving mother's devotion to her infant are not, as a rule, so limiting. The cogency that is in play in the one case and in the other differs as the power of syllogism differs from the force of gravitation. The laws of the one are those of the mind; the laws of the other are those of nature. The two meanings could not be further apart; semantically they lie in opposite directions of the compass.

It is our proposition that only the substantive meaning of "economic" is capable of yielding the concepts that are required by the social sciences for an investigation of all the empirical economies of the past and present. The general frame of reference that we endeavor to construct requires, therefore, treatment of the subject matter in substantive terms. The immediate obstacle in our path lies, as indicated, in that concept of "economic" in which the two meanings, the substantive and the formal, are naively compounded. Such a merger of meanings is, of course, unexceptionable as long as we remain conscious of its restrictive effects. But the current concept of economic fuses the "subsistence" and the "scarcity" meanings of economic without a sufficient awareness of the dangers to clear thinking inherent in that merger.

This combination of terms sprang from logically adventitious circumstances. The last two centuries produced in Western Europe and North America an organization of man's livelihood to which the rules of choice happened to be singularly applicable. This form of the economy consisted in a system of price-making markets. Since acts of exchange, as practiced under such a system, involve the participants in choices induced by an insufficiency of means, the system could be reduced to a pattern that lent itself to the application of methods based on the formal meaning of "economic." As long as the economy was controlled by such a system, the formal and the substantive meanings would in practice coincide. Laymen accepted this compound concept as a matter of course; a Marshall, Pareto or Durkheim equally adhered to it. Menger alone in his posthumous work criticized the term, but neither he nor Max Weber, nor Talcott Parsons after him, apprehended the significance of the distinction for sociological analysis. Indeed, there seemed to be no valid reason for distinguishing between two root meanings of a term which, as we said, were bound to coincide in practice.

While it would have been therefore sheer pedantry to differentiate in common parlance between the two meanings of "economic," their merging in one concept nevertheless proved a bane to a precise methodology in the social sciences. Economics naturally formed an exception, since under the market system its terms were bound to be fairly realistic. But the anthropologist, the sociologist or the historian, each in his study of the place occupied by the economy in human society, was faced with a great variety of institutions other than markets, in which man's livelihood was embedded. Its problems could not be attacked with the help of an analytical method devised for a special form of the economy, which was dependent upon the presence of specific market elements.[1]

This lays down the rough sequence of the argument.

We will begin with a closer examination of the concepts derived from the two

---

[1] The uncritical employment of the compound concept fostered what may well be called the "economistic fallacy." It consisted in an artificial identification of the economy with its market form. From Hume and Spencer to Frank H. Knight and Northrop, social thought suffered from this limitation wherever it touched on the economy. Lionel Robbins' essay (1932), though useful to economists, fatefully distorted the problem. In the field of anthropology Melville Herskovits' recent work (1952) represents a relapse after his pioneering effort of 1940.

meanings of "economic," starting with the formal and thence proceeding to the substantive meaning. It should then prove possible to describe the empirical economies—whether primitive or archaic—according to the manner in which the economic process is instituted. The three institutions of trade, money and market will provide a test case. They have previously been defined in formal terms only; thus any other than a marketing approach was barred. Their treatment in substantive terms should then bring us nearer to the desired universal frame of reference.

The Formal and the Substantive Meanings of "Economic"

Let us examine the formal concepts starting from the manner in which the logic of rational action produces formal economics, and the latter, in turn, gives rise to economic analysis.

Rational action is here defined as choice of means in relation to ends. Means are anything appropriate to serve the end, whether by virtue of the laws of nature or by virtue of the laws of the game. Thus "rational" does not refer either to ends or to means, but rather to the relating of means to ends. It is not assumed, for instance, that it is more rational to wish to live than to wish to die, or that, in the first case, it is more rational to seek a long life through the means of science than through those of superstition. For whatever the end, it is rational to choose one's means accordingly; and as to the means, it would not be rational to act upon any other test than that which one happens to believe in. Thus it is rational for the suicide to select means that will accomplish his death; and if he be an adept of black magic, to pay a witch doctor to contrive that end.

The logic of rational action applies, then, to all conceivable means and ends covering an almost infinite variety of human interests. In chess or technology, in religious life or philosophy ends may range from commonplace issues to the most recondite and complex ones. Similarly, in the field of the economy, where ends may range from the momentary assuaging of thirst to the attaining of a sturdy old age, while the corresponding means comprise a glass of water and a combined reliance on filial solicitude and open air life, respectively.

Assuming that the choice is induced by an insufficiency of the means, the logic of rational action turns into that variant of the theory of choice which we have called formal economics. It is still logically unrelated to the concept of the human economy, but it is closer to it by one step. Formal economics refers, as we said, to a situation of choice that arises out of an insufficiency of means. This is the so-called scarcity postulate. It requires, first, insufficiency of means; second, that choice be induced by that insufficiency. Insufficiency of means in relation to ends is determined with the help of the simple operation of "earmarking," which demonstrates whether there is or is not enough to go round. For the insufficiency to induce choice there must be given more than one use to the means, as well as graded ends, i.e., at least two ends ordered in sequence of preference. Both conditions are factual. It is irrelevant whether the reason for which means can be used in one way only happens to be conventional or technological; the same is true of the grading of ends.

Having thus defined choice, insufficiency and scarcity in operational terms, it is easy to see that as there is choice of means without insufficiency, so there is insufficiency of means without choice. Choice may be induced by a preference for right against wrong (moral choice) or, at a crossroads, where two or more paths happen to lead to our destination, possessing identical advantages and disadvantages (operationally induced choice). In either case an abundance of means, far from diminishing the difficulties of choice, would rather increase them. Of course, scarcity may or may not be present in almost all fields of rational action. Not all philosophy is sheer imaginative creativity, it may also be a matter of economizing with assumptions. Or, to get back to the sphere of man's livelihood, in some civilizations scarcity situations seem to be almost exceptional, in others they appear to be painfully general. In either case the presence or absence of scarcity is a question of fact, whether the insufficiency is due to Nature or to Law.

Last but not least, economic analysis. This discipline results from the application of formal economics to an economy of a definite type, namely, a market system. The economy is here embodied in institutions that cause individual choices to give rise to interdependent movements that constitute the economic process. This is achieved by generalizing the use of price-making markets. All goods and services, including the use of labor, land and capital are available for purchase in markets and have, therefore, a price; all forms of income derive from the sale of goods and services—wages, rent and interest, respectively, appearing only as different instances of price according to the items sold. The general introduction of purchasing power as the means of acquisition converts the process of meeting requirements into an allocation of insufficient means with alternative uses, namely, money. It follows that both the conditions of choice and its consequences are quantifiable in the form of prices. It can be asserted that by concentrating on price as the economic fact *par excellence*, the formal method of approach offers a total description of the economy as determined by choices induced by an insufficiency of means. The conceptual tools by which this is performed make up the discipline of economic analysis.

From this follow the limits within which economic analysis can prove effective as a method. The use of the formal meaning denotes the economy as a sequence of acts of economizing, i.e., of choice induced by scarcity situations. While the rules governing such acts are universal, the extent to which the rules are applicable to a definite economy depends upon whether or not that economy is, in actual fact, a sequence of such acts. To produce quantitative results, the locational and appropriational movements, of which the economic process consists, must here present themselves as functions of social actions in regard to insufficient means and oriented on resulting prices. Such a situation obtains only under a market system.

The relation between formal economics and the human economy is, in effect, contingent. Outside of a system of price-making markets economic analysis loses most of its relevance as a method of inquiry into the working of the economy. A centrally planned economy, relying on nonmarket prices is a well-known instance.

The fount of the substantive concept is the empirical economy. It can be briefly (if not engagingly) defined as an instituted process of interaction between man and his environment, which results in a continuous supply of want satisfying material means. Want satisfaction is "material," if it involves the use of material means to satisfy ends; in the case of a definite type of physiological wants, such as food or shelter, this includes the use of so-called services only.

The economy, then, is an instituted process. Two concepts stand out, that of "process" and its "institutedness." Let us see what they contribute to our frame of reference.

Process suggests analysis in terms of motion. The movements refer either to changes in location, or in appropriation, or both. In other words, the material elements may alter their position either by changing place or by changing "hands"; again, these otherwise very different shifts of position may go together or not. Between them, these two kinds of movements may be said to exhaust the possibilities comprised in the economic process as a natural and social phenomenon.

Locational movements include production, alongside of transportation, to which the spatial shifting of objects is equally essential. Goods are of a lower order or of a higher order, according to the manner of their usefulness from the consumer's point of view. This famous "order of goods" sets consumers' goods against producers' goods, according to whether they satisfy wants directly, or only indirectly, through a combination with other goods. This type of movement of the elements represents an essential of the economy in the substantive sense of the term, namely, production.

The appropriate movement governs both what is usually referred to as the circulation of goods and their administration. In the first case, the appropriative movement results from transactions, in the second case, from dispositions. Accordingly, a transaction is an appropriative movement as between hands; a disposition is a one-sided act of the hand, to which by force of custom or of law definite appropriative effects are attached. The term "hand" here serves to denote public bodies and offices as well as private persons or firms, the difference between them being mainly a matter of internal organization. It should be noted, however, that in the nineteenth century private hands were commonly associated with transactions, while public hands were usually credited with dispositions.

In this choice of terms a number of further definitions are implied. Social activities, insofar as they form part of the process, may be called economic; institutions are so called to the extent to which they contain a concentration of such activities; any components of the process may be regarded as economic elements. These elements can be conveniently grouped as ecological, technological or societal according to whether they belong primarily to the natural environment, the mechanical equipment, or the human setting. Thus a series of concepts, old and new, accrue to our frame of reference by virtue of the process aspect of the economy.

Nevertheless, reduced to a mechanical, biological and psychological interaction of elements that economic process would possess no all-round reality. It contains no more than the bare bones of the processes of production and transportation, as well as of the appropriative changes. In the absence of any indication of societal conditions from which the motives of the individuals spring, there would be little, if anything, to sustain the interdependence of the movements and their recurrence on which the unity and the stability of the process depends. The interacting elements of nature and humanity would form no coherent unit, in effect, no structural entity that could be said to have a function in society or to possess a history. The process would lack the very qualities which cause everyday thought as well as scholarship to turn towards matters of human livelihood as a field of eminent practical interest as well as theoretical and moral dignity.

Hence the transcending importance of the institutional aspect of the economy. What occurs on the process level between man and soil in hoeing a plot or what on the conveyor belt in the constructing of an automobile is, *prima facie* a mere jig-sawing of human and nonhuman movements. From the institutional point of view it is a mere referent of terms like labor and capital, craft and union, slacking and speeding, the spreading of risks and the other semantic units of the social context. The choice between capitalism and socialism, for instance, refers to two different ways of instituting modern technology in the process of production. On the policy level, again, the industrialization of under-developed countries involves, on the one hand, alternative techniques; on the other, alternative methods of instituting them. Our conceptual distinction is vital for any understanding of the interdependence of technology and institutions as well as their relative independence.

The instituting of the economic process vests that process with unity and stability; it produces a structure with a definite function in society; it shifts the place of the process in society, thus adding significance to its history; it centers interest on values, motives and policy. Unity and stability, structure and function, history and policy spell out operationally the content of our assertion that the human economy is an instituted process.

The human economy, then, is embedded and enmeshed in institutions, economic and noneconomic. The inclusion of the noneconomic is vital. For religion or government may be as important for the structure and functioning of the economy as monetary institutions or the availability of tools and machines themselves that lighten the toil of labor.

The study of the shifting place occupied by the economy in society is therefore no other than the study of the manner in which the economic process is instituted at different times and places.

This requires a special tool box.

Reciprocity, Redistribution, and Exchange

A study of how empirical economies are instituted should start from the way in which the economy acquires unity and stability, that is the interdependence and recurrence of its parts. This is achieved through a combination of a very few patterns which may be called forms of integration. Since they occur side by side on different levels and in different sectors of the economy it may often be impossible to select one of them as dominant so that they could be employed for a classification of empirical economies as a whole. Yet by differentiating between sectors and levels of the economy those forms offer a means of describing the economic process in comparatively simple terms, thereby introducing a measure of order into its endless variations.

Empirically, we find the main patterns to be reciprocity, redistribution and exchange. Reciprocity denotes movements between correlative points of symmetrical groupings; redistribution designates appropriational movements toward a center and out of it again; exchange refers here to vice-versa movements taking place as between "hands" under a market system. Reciprocity, then, assumes for a background symmetrically arranged groupings; redistribution is dependent upon the presence of some measure of centricity in the group; exchange in order to produce integration requires a system of price-making markets. It is apparent that the different patterns of integration assume definite institutional supports.

At this point some clarification may be welcome. The terms reciprocity, redistribution and exchange, by which we refer to our forms of integration, are often employed to denote personal interrelations. Superficially then it might seem as if the forms of integration merely reflected aggregates of the respective forms of individual behavior: If mutuality between individuals were frequent, a reciprocative integration would emerge; where sharing among individuals were common, redistributive integration would be present; similarly, frequent acts of barter between individuals would result in exchange as a form of integration. If this were so, our patterns of integration would be indeed no more than simple aggregates of corresponding forms of behavior on the personal level. To be sure, we insisted that the integrative effect was conditioned by the presence of definite institutional arrangements, such as symmetrical organizations, central points and market systems, respectively. But such arrangements seem to represent a mere aggregate of the same personal patterns the eventual effects of which they are supposed to condition. The significant fact is that mere aggregates of the personal behaviors in question do not by themselves produce such structures. Reciprocity behavior between individuals integrates the economy only if symmetrically organized structures, such as a symmetrical system of kinship groups, are given. But a kinship system never arises as the result of mere reciprocating behavior on the personal level. Similarly, in regard to redistribution. It presupposes the presence of an allocative center in the community, yet the organization and validation of such a center does not come about merely as a consequence of frequent acts of sharing as between individuals. Finally, the same is true of the market system. Acts of exchange on the personal level produce prices only if they occur under a system of price-making markets, an institutional setup which is nowhere created by mere random acts of exchange. We do not wish to imply, of course, that those supporting patterns are the outcome of some mysterious forces acting outside the range of personal or individual behavior. We merely insist that if, in any given case, the societal effects of individual behavior depend on the presence of definite institutional conditions, these conditions do not for that reason result from the personal behavior in question. Superficially, the supporting pattern may *seem* to result from a cumulation of a corresponding kind of personal behavior, but the vital elements of organization and validation are necessarily contributed by an altogether different type of behavior.

The first writer to our knowledge to have hit upon the factual connection between reciprocative behavior on the interpersonal level, on the one hand, and given symmetrical groupings, on the other, was the anthropologist Richard Thurnwald, in 1915, in an empirical study on the marriage system of the Bánaro of New Guinea. Bronislaw Malinowski, some ten years later, referring to Thurnwald, predicted that socially relevant reciprocation would regularly be found to rest on symmetrical forms of basic social organization. His own description of the Trobriand kinship system as well as of the Kula trade bore out the point. This lead was followed up by this writer, in regarding symmetry as merely *one* of several supporting patterns. He then added redistribution and exchange to reciprocity, as further forms of integration; similarly, he added centricity and market to symmetry, as other instances of institutional support. Hence our forms of integration and supporting structure patterns.

This should help to explain why in the economic sphere interpersonal behavior so often fails to have the expected effects in the absence of definite institutional preconditions. Only in a symmetrically organized environment will reciprocative behavior result in economic institutions of any importance; only where allocative centers have been set up can individual acts of sharing produce a redistributive economy; and only in the presence of a system of price-making markets will exchange acts of individuals result in fluctuating prices that integrate the economy. Otherwise such acts of barter will remain ineffective and therefore tend not to occur. Should they nevertheless happen, in a random fashion, a violent emotional reaction would set in, as against acts of indecency or acts of treason, since trading behavior is never emotionally indifferent behavior and is not, therefore, tolerated by opinion outside of the approved channels.

Let us now return to our forms of integration.

A group which deliberately undertook to organize its economic relationships on a reciprocative footing would, to effect its purpose, have to split up into subgroups the corresponding members of which could identify one another as such. Members of Group A would then be able to establish relationships of reciprocity with their counterparts in Group B and vice versa. But symmetry is not restricted to duality. Three, four, or more groups may be symmetrical in regard to two or more axes; also members of the groups need not reciprocate with one another but may do so with the corresponding members of third groups toward which they stand in analogous relations. A Trobriand man's responsibility is toward his sister's family. But he himself is not on that account assisted by his sister's husband, but, if he is married, by his own wife's brother—a member of a third, correspondingly placed family.

Aristotle taught that to every kind of community (*koinōnia*) there corresponded a kind of good-will (*philia*) amongst its members which expressed itself in reciprocity (*antipeponthos*). This was true both of the more permanent communities such as families, tribes or city states as of those less permanent ones that may be comprised in, and subordinate to, the former. In our terms this implies a tendency in the larger communities to develop a multiple symmetry in regard to which reciprocative behavior may develop in the subordinate communities. The closer the members of the encompassing community feel drawn to one another, the more general will be the tendency among them to develop reciprocative attitudes in regard to specific relationships limited in space, time or otherwise. Kinship, neighborhood, or totem belong to the more permanent and comprehensive groupings; within their compass voluntary and semi-voluntary associations of a military, vocational, religious or social character create situations in which, at least transitorily or in regard to a given locality or a typical situation, there would form symmetrical groupings the members of which practice some sort of mutuality.

Reciprocity as a form of integration gains greatly in power through its capacity of employing both redistribution and exchange as subordinate methods. Reciprocity may be attained through a sharing of the burden of labor according to definite rules of redistribution as when taking things "in turn." Similarly, reciprocity is sometimes attained through exchange at set equivalencies for the benefit of the partner who happens to be short of some kind of necessities—a fundamental institution in ancient Oriental societies. In non-market economies these two forms of integration—reciprocity and redistribution—occur in effect usually together.

Redistribution obtains within a group to the extent to which the allocation of goods is collected in one hand and takes place by virtue of custom, law or *ad hoc* central decision. Sometimes it amounts to a physical collecting accompanied by storage-cum-redistribution, at other times the "collecting" is not physical, but merely appropriational, i.e., rights of disposal in the physical location of the goods. Redistribution occurs for many reasons, on all civilizational levels, from the primitive hunting tribe to the vast storage systems of ancient Egypt, Sumeria, Babylonia or Peru. In large countries differences of soil and climate may make redistribution necessary; in other cases it is caused by discrepancy in point of time, as between harvest and consumption. With a hunt, any other method of distribution would lead to disintegration of the horde or band, since only "division of labor" can here ensure results; a redistribution of purchasing power may be valued for its own sake, i.e., for the purposes demanded by social ideals as in the modern welfare state. The principle remains the same—collecting into, and distributing from, a center. Redistribution may also apply to a group smaller than society, such as the household or manor irrespective of the way in which the economy as a whole is integrated. The best known instances are the Central African *kraal*, the Hebrew patriarchal household, the Greek estate of Aristotle's time, the Roman *familia*, the medieval manor, or the typical large peasant household before the general marketing of grain. However, only under a comparatively advanced form of agricultural society is householding practicable, and then, fairly general. Before that, the widely spread "small family" is not economically instituted, except for some cooking of food; the use of pasture, land or cattle is still dominated by redistributive or reciprocative methods on a wider than family scale.

Redistribution, too, is apt to integrate groups at all levels and all degrees of permanence from the state itself to units of a transitory character. Here, again, as with reciprocity, the more closely knit the encompassing unit, the more varied will the subdivisions be in which redistribution can effectively operate. Plato taught that the number of citizens in the state should be 5040. This figure was divisible in 59 different ways, including division by the first ten numerals. For the assessment of taxes, the forming of groups for business transactions, the carrying of military and other burdens "in turn," etc., it would allow the widest scope, he explained.

Exchange in order to serve as a form of integration requires the support of a system of price-making markets. Three kinds of exchange should therefore be distinguished: The merely locational movement of a "changing of places" between the hands (operational exchange); the appropriational movements of exchange, either at a set rate (decisional exchange) or at a bargained rate (integrative exchange). In so far as exchange at a set rate is in question, the economy is integrated by the factors which fix that rate, not by the market mechanism. Even price-making markets are integrative only if they are linked up in a system which tends to spread the effect of prices to markets other than those directly affected.

Higgling-haggling has been rightly recognized as being of the essence of bargaining behavior. In order for exchange to be integrative the behavior of the partners must be oriented on producing a price that is as favorable to each partner as he can make it. Such a behavior contrasts sharply with that of exchange at a set price. The ambiguity of the term "gain" tends to cover up the difference. Exchange at set prices involves no more than the gain to either party implied in the decision of exchanging; exchange at fluctuating prices aims at a gain that can be attained only by an attitude involving a distinctive antagonistic relationship between the partners. The element of antagonism, however diluted, that accompanies this variant of exchange is ineradicable. No community intent on protecting the fount of solidarity between its members can allow latent hostility to develop around a matter as vital to animal existence and, therefore, capable of arousing as tense anxieties as food. Hence the universal banning of transactions of a gainful nature in regard to food and foodstuffs in primitive and archaic society. The very widely spread ban on higgling-haggling over victuals automatically removes price-making markets from the realm of early institutions.

Traditional groupings of economies which roughly approximate a classification according to the dominant forms of integration are illuminating. What historians are wont to call "economic systems" seem to fall fairly into this pattern. Dominance of a form of integration is here identified with the degree to which it comprises land and labor in society. So-called savage society, is characterized by the integration of land and labor into the economy by way of the ties of kinship. In feudal society the ties of fealty determine the fate of land and the labor that goes with it. In the floodwater empires land was largely distributed and sometimes redistributed by temple or palace, and so was labor, at least in its dependent form. The rise of the market to a ruling force in the economy can be traced by noting the extent to which land and food were mobilized through exchange, and labor was turned into a commodity free to be purchased in the market. This may help to explain the relevance of the historically untenable stages theory of slavery, serfdom and wage labor that is traditional with Marxism—a grouping which flowed from the conviction that the character of the economy was set by the status of labor. However, the integration of the soil into the economy should be regarded as hardly less vital.

In any case, forms of integration do not represent "stages" of development. No sequence in time is implied. Several subordinate forms may be present alongside of the dominant one, which may itself recur after a temporary eclipse. Tribal societies practice reciprocity and redistribution, while archaic societies are predominantly redistributive, though to some extent they may allow room for exchange. Reciprocity, which plays a dominant part in some Melanesian communities, occurs as a not unimportant although subordinate trait in the redistributive archaic empires, where foreign trade (carried on by gift and countergift) is still largely organized on the principle of reciprocity. Indeed, during a war emergency it was reintroduced on a large scale in the twentieth century, under the name of lend-lease, with societies where otherwise marketing and exchange were dominant. Redistribution, the ruling method in tribal and archaic society beside which exchange plays only a minor part, grew to great importance in the later Roman Empire and is actually gaining ground today in some modern industrial states. The Soviet Union is an extreme instance. Conversely, more than once before in the course of human history markets have played a part in the economy, although never on a territorial scale, or with an institutional comprehensiveness comparable to that of the nineteenth century. However, here again a change is noticeable. In our century, with the lapse of the gold standard, a recession of the world role of markets from their nineteenth century peak set in—a turn of the trend which, incidentally, takes us back to our starting point, namely, the increasing inadequacy of our limited marketing definitions for the purposes of the social scientist's study of the economic field.

Forms of Trade, Money Uses, and Market Elements

The restrictive influence of the marketing approach on the interpretation of trade and money institutions is incisive: inevitably, the market appears as the locus of exchange, trade as the actual exchange, and money as the means of exchange. Since trade is directed by prices and prices are a function of the market, all trade is market trade, just as all money is exchange money. The market is the generating institution of which trade and money are the functions.

Such notions are not true to the facts of anthropology and history. Trade, as well as some money uses, are as old as mankind; while markets, although meetings of an economic character may have existed as early as the neolithic, did not gain importance until comparatively late in history. Price-making markets, which alone are constitutive of a market system, were to all accounts non-existent before the first millennium of antiquity, and then only to be eclipsed by other forms of integration. Not even these main facts however could be uncovered as long as trade and money were thought to be limited to the exchange form of integration, as its specifically "economic" form. The long periods of history when reciprocity and redistribution integrated the economy and the considerable ranges within which, even in modern times, they continued to do so, were put out of bounds by a restrictive terminology.

Viewed as an exchange system, or, in brief, catallactically, trade, money and market form an indivisible whole. Their common conceptual framework is the market. Trade appears as a two-way movement of goods through the market, and money as quantifiable goods used for indirect exchange in order to facilitate that movement. Such an approach must induce a more or less tacit acceptance of the heuristic principle according to which, where trade is in evidence, markets should be assumed, and where money is in evidence trade, and therefore markets, should be assumed. Naturally, this leads to seeing markets where there are none and ignoring trade and money where they are present, because markets happen to be absent. The cumulative effect must be to create a stereotype of the economies of less familiar times and places, something in the way of an artificial landscape with only little or no resemblance to the original.

A separate analysis of trade, money and markets is therefore in order.

1. Forms of Trade

From the substantive point of view, trade is a relatively peaceful method of acquiring goods which are not available on the spot. It is external to the group, similar to activities which we are used to associating with hunts, slaving expeditions, or piratic raids. In either case the point is acquisition and carrying of goods from a distance. What distinguishes trade from the questing for game, booty, plunder, rare woods or exotic animals, is the two-sidedness of the movement, which also ensures its broadly peaceful and fairly regular character.

From the catallactic viewpoint, trade is the movement of goods on their way through the market. All commodities—goods produced for sale—are potential objects of trade; one commodity is moving in one direction, the other in the opposite direction; the movement is controlled by prices: trade and market are co-terminous. All trade is market trade.

Again, like hunt, raid or expedition under native conditions, trade is not so much an individual as rather a group activity, in this respect closely akin to the organization of wooing and mating, which is often concerned with the acquisition of wives from a distance by more or less peaceful means. Trade thus centers in the meeting of different communities, one of its purposes being the exchange of goods. Such meetings do not, like price-making markets, produce rates of exchange, but on the contrary they rather presuppose such rates. Neither the persons of individual traders nor motives of individual gain are involved. Whether a chief or king is acting for the community after having collected the "export" goods from its members, or whether the group meets bodily their counterparts on the beach for the purpose of exchange—in either case the proceedings are essentially collective. Exchange between "partners in trade" is frequent, but so is, of course, partnership in wooing and mating. Individual and collective activities are intertwined.

Emphasis on "acquisition of goods from a distance" as a constitutive element in trade should bring out the dominant role played by the import interest in the early history of trade. In the nineteenth century export interests loomed large— a typically catallactic phenomenon.

Since something must be carried over a distance and that in two opposite directions, trade, in the nature of things, has a number of constituents such as personnel, goods, carrying, and two-sidedness, each of which can be broken down according to sociologically or technologically significant criteria. In following up those four factors we may hope to learn something about the changing place of trade in society.

First, the persons engaged in trade.

"Acquistion of goods from a distance" may be practiced either from motives attaching to the trader's standing in society, and as a rule comprising elements of duty or public service (status motive) ; or it may be done for the sake of the material gain accruing to him personally from the buying and selling transaction in hand (profit motive).

In spite of many possible combinations of those incentives, honor and duty on the one hand, profit on the other, stand out as sharply distinct primary motivations. If the "status motive," as is quite often the case, is reinforced by material benefits, the latter do not as a rule take the form of gain made on exchange, but rather of treasure or endowment with landed revenue bestowed on the trader by king or temple or lord, by way of recompense. Things being what they are, gains made on exchange do not usually add up to more than paltry sums that bear no comparison with the wealth bestowed by his lord upon the resourceful and successfully venturing trader. Thus he who trades for the sake of duty and honor grows rich, while he who trades for filthy lucre remains poor—an added reason why gainful motives are under a shadow in archaic society.

Another way of approaching the question of personnel is from the angle of the standard of life deemed appropriate to their status by the community to which they belong.

Archaic society in general knows, as a rule, no other figure of a trader than that which belongs either to the top or to the bottom rung of the social ladder. The first is connected with rulership and government, as required by the political and military conditions of trading, the other depends for his livelihood on the coarse labor of carrying. This fact is of great importance for the understanding of the organization of trade in ancient times. There can be no middle-class trader, at least among the citizenry. Apart from the Far East which we must disregard here, only three significant instances of a broad commercial middle class in premodern times are on record: the Hellenistic merchant of largely metic ancestry in the Eastern Mediterranean city states; the ubiquitous Islamitic merchant who grafted Hellenistic maritime traditions on to the ways of the bazaar; lastly, the descendants of Pirenne's "floating scum" in Western Europe, a sort of continental metic of the second third of the Middle Ages. The classical Greek middle class preconized by Aristotle was a landed class, not a commercial class at all.

A third manner of approach is more closely historical. The trader types of antiquity were the *tamkarum*, the metic or resident alien, and the "foreigner."

The *tamkarum* dominated the Mesopotamian scene from the Sumerian beginnings to the rise is Islam, i.e., over some 3000 years. Egypt, China, India, Palestine, pre-conquest Mesoamerica, or native West Africa knew no other type of trader. The *metic* became first historically conspicuous in Athens and some other Greek cities as a lower-class merchant, and rose with Hellenism to become the prototype of a Greek-speaking or Levantine commercial middle class from the Indus Valley to the Pillars of Hercules. The *foreigner* is of course ubiquitous. He carries on trade with foreign crews and in foreign bottoms; he neither "belongs" to the community, nor enjoys the semi-status of resident alien, but is a member of an altogether different community.

A fourth distinction is anthropological. It provides the key to that peculiar figure, the trading foreigner. Although the number of "trading peoples" to which these "foreigners" belonged was comparatively small, they accounted for the widely spread institution of "passive trade." Amongst themselves, trading peoples differed again in an important respect: trading peoples proper, as we may call them, were exclusively dependent for their subsistence on trade in which, directly or indirectly, the whole population was engaged, as with the Phoenicians, the Rhodians, the inhabitants of Gades (the modern Cadix), or at some periods Armenians and Jews; in the case of others—a more numerous group—trade was only *one* of the occupations in which from time to time a considerable part of the population engaged, travelling abroad, sometimes with their families, or over shorter or longer periods. The Haussa and the Mandingo in the Western Sudan are instances. The latter are also known as Duala, but, as recently turned out, only when trading abroad. Formerly they were taken to be a separate people by those whom they visited when trading.

Second, the organization of trade in early times must differ according to the goods carried, the distance to be travelled, the obstacles to be overcome by the carriers, the political and the ecological conditions of the venture. For this, if for no other reason, all trade is originally specific. The goods and their carriage make it so. There can be, under these conditions, no such thing as trading "in general."

Unless full weight is given to this fact, no understanding of the early development of trading institutions is possible. The decision to acquire some kinds of goods from a definite distance and place of origin will be taken under circumstances different from those under which other kinds of goods would have to be acquired from somewhere else. Trading ventures are, for this reason, a discontinuous affair. They are restricted to concrete undertakings, which are liquidated one by one and do not tend to develop into a continuous enterprise. The Roman *societas*, like the later *commenda*, was a trade partnership limited to one undertaking. Only the *societas publicanorum*, for tax farming and contracting, was incorporated—it was the one great exception. Not before modern times were permanent trade associations known.

The specificity of trade is enhanced in the natural course of things by the necessity of acquiring the imported goods with exported ones. For under non-market conditions imports and exports tend to fall under different regimes. The process through which goods are collected for export is mostly separate from, and relatively independent of, that by which the imported goods are repartitioned. The first may be a matter of tribute or taxation or feudal gifts or under whatever other designation the goods flow to the center, while the repartitioned imports may cascade along different lines. Hammurabi's "Seisachtheia" appears to make an exception of *simu* goods, which may have sometimes been imports passed on by the king via the *tamkarum* to such tenants who wished to exchange them for their own produce. Some of the preconquest long-distance trading of the *pochteca* of the Aztec of Mesoamerica appears to carry similar features.

What nature made distinct, the market makes homogeneous. Even the difference between goods and their transportation may be obliterated, since in the market both can be bought and sold—the one in the commodity market, the other in the freight and insurance market. In either case there is supply and demand, and prices are formed in the same fashion. Carrying and goods, these constituents of trade, acquire a common denominator in terms of cost. Preoccupation with the market and its artificial homogeneity thus makes for good economic theory rather than for good economic history. Eventually, we will find that trade routes, too, as well as means of transportation may be of no less incisive importance for the institutional forms of trade than the types of goods carried. For in all these cases the geographical and technological conditions interpenetrate with the social structure.

According to the rationale of two-sidedness we meet with three main types of trade: gift trade, administered trade, and market trade.

Gift trade links the partners in relationships of reciprocity, such as: guest friends; Kula partners; visiting parties. Over millennia trade between empires was carried on as gift trade—no other rationale of two-sidedness would have met quite as well the needs of the situation. The organization of trading is here usually ceremonial, involving mutual presentation; embassies; political dealings between chiefs or kings. The goods are treasure, objects of élite circulation; in the border case of visiting parties they may be of a more "democratic" character. But contacts are tenuous and exchanges few and far between.

Administered trade has its firm foundation in treaty relationships that are more or less formal. Since on both sides the import interest is as a rule determinative, trading runs through government-controlled channels. The export trade is usually organized in a similar way. Consequently, the whole of trade is carried on by administrative methods. This extends to the manner in which business is transacted, including arrangements concerning "rates" or proportions of the units exchanged; port facilities; weighing; checking of quality; the physical exchange of the goods; storage; safekeeping; the control of the trading personnel; regulation of "payments"; credits; price differentials. Some of these matters would naturally be linked with the collection of the export goods and the repartition of the imported ones, both belonging to the redistributive sphere of the domestic economy. The goods that are mutually imported are standardized in regard to quality and package, weight, and other easily ascertainable criteria. Only such "trade goods" can be traded. Equivalencies are set out in simple unit relations; in principle, trade is one-to-one.

Higgling and haggling is not part of the proceedings; equivalencies are set once and for all. But since to meet changing circumstances adjustments cannot be avoided, higgling-haggling is practiced only on *other items than price*, such as measures, quality, or means of payment. Endless arguments are possible about the quality of the foodstuffs, the capacity and weight of the units employed, the proportions of the currencies if different ones are jointly used. Even "profits" are often "bargained." The rationale of the procedure is, of course, to keep prices unchanged; if they must adjust to actual supply situations, as in an emergency, this is phrased as trading two-to-one or two-and-a-half-to-one, or, as we would say, at 100 per cent or 150 per cent profit. This method of haggling on profits at stable prices, which may have been fairly general in archaic society, is well authenticated from the Central Sudan as late as the nineteenth century.

Administered trade presupposes relatively permanent trading bodies such as governments or at least companies chartered by them. The understanding with the natives may be tacit, as in the case of traditional or customary relationships. Between sovereign bodies, however, trade assumes formal treaties even in the relatively early times of the second millennium B.C.

Once established in a region, under solemn protection of the gods, administrative forms of trade may be practiced without any previous treaty. The main institution, as we now begin to realize, is the port of trade, as we here call this site of all administered foreign trade. The port of trade offers military security to the inland power; civil protection to the foreign trader; facilities of anchorage, debarkation and storage; the benefit of judicial authorities;

agreement on the goods to be traded; agreement concerning the "proportions" of the different trade goods in the mixed packages or "sortings."

Market trade is the third typical form of trading. Here exchange is the form of integration that relates the partners to each other. This comparatively modern variant of trade released a torrent of material wealth over Western Europe and North America. Though presently in recession, it is still by far the most important of all. The range of tradable goods—the commodities—is practically unlimited and the organization of market trade follows the lines traced out by the supply-demand-price mechanism. The market mechanism shows its immense range of application by being adaptable to the handling not only of goods, but of every element of trade itself—storage, transportation, risk, credit, payments, etc.—through the forming of special markets for freight, insurance, short-term credit, capital, warehouse space, banking facilities, and so on.

The main interest of the economic historian today turns towards the questions: When and how did trade become linked with markets? At what time and place do we meet the general result known as market trade?

Strictly speaking, such questions are precluded under the sway of catallactic logic, which tends to fuse trade and market inseparably.

2. Money Uses

The catallactic definition of money is that of means of indirect exchange. Modern money is used for payment and as a "standard" precisely because it is a means of exchange. Thus our money is "all-purpose" money. Other uses of money are merely unimportant variants of its exchange use, and all money uses are dependent upon the existence of markets.

The substantive definition of money, like that of trade, is independent of markets. It is derived from definite uses to which quantifiable objects are put. These uses are payment, standard and exchange. Money, therefore, is defined here as quantifiable objects employed in any one or several of these uses. The question is whether independent definitions of those uses are possible.

The definitions of the various money uses contain two criteria: the sociologically defined situation in which the use arises, and the operation performed with the money objects in that situation.

Payment is the discharge of obligations in which quantifiable objects change hands. The situation refers here not to one kind of obligation only, but to several of them, since only if an object is used to discharge more than one obligation can we speak of it as "means of payment" in the distinctive sense of the term (otherwise merely an obligation to be discharged in kind is so discharged).

The payment use of money belongs to its most common uses in early times. The obligations do not here commonly spring from transactions. In unstratified primitive society payments are regularly made in connection with the institutions of bride price, blood money, and fines. In archaic society such payments continue, but they are overshadowed by customary dues, taxes, rent and tribute that give rise to payments on the largest scale.

The standard, or accounting use of money is the equating of amounts of different kinds of goods for definite purposes. The "situation" is either barter or the storage and management of staples; the "operation" consists in the attaching of numerical tags to the various objects to facilitate the manipulation of those objects. Thus in the case of barter, the summation of objects on either side can eventually be equated; in the case of the management of staples a possibility of planning, balancing, budgeting, as well as general accounting is attained.

The standard use of money is essential to the elasticity of a redistributive system. The equating of such staples as barley, oil and wool in which taxes or rent have to be paid or alternatively rations or wages may be claimed is vital, since it ensures the possibility of choice between the different staples for payer and claimant alike. At the same time the precondition of large scale finance "in kind" is created, which presupposes the notion of funds and balances, in other words, the interchangeability of staples.

The exchange use of money arises out of a need for quantifiable objects for indirect exchange. The "operation" consists in acquiring units of such objects through direct exchange, in order to acquire the desired objects through a further act of exchange. Sometimes the money objects are available from the start, and the twofold exchange is merely designed to net an increased amount of the same objects. Such a use of quantifiable objects develops not from random acts of barter—a favored fancy of eighteenth century rationalism—but rather in connection with organized trade, especially in markets. In the absence of markets the exchange use of money is no more than a subordinate culture trait. The surprising reluctance of the great trading peoples of antiquity such as Tyre and Carthage to adopt coins, that new form of money eminently suited for exchange, may have been due to the fact that the trading ports of the commercial empires were not organized as markets, but as "ports of trade."

Two extensions of the meaning of money should be noted. The one extends the definition of money other than physical objects, namely, ideal units; the other comprises alongside of the three conventional money uses, also the use of money objects as operational devices.

Ideal units are mere verbalizations or written symbols employed as if they were quantifiable units, mainly for payment or as a standard. The "operation" consists in the manipulation of debt accounts according to the rules of the game. Such accounts are common facts of primitive life and not, as was often believed, peculiar to monetarized economies. The earliest temple economies of Mesopotamia as well as the early Assyrian traders practiced the clearing of accounts without the intervention of money objects.

At the other end it seemed advisable not to omit the mention of operational devices among money uses, exceptional though they be. Occasionally quantifiable objects are used in archaic society for arithmetical, statistical, taxational, administrative or other non-monetary purposes connected with economic life. In eighteenth-century Whydah cowrie money was used for statistical ends, and *damba* beans (never employed as money) served as a gold weight and, in that capacity, were cleverly used as a device for accountancy.

Early money is, as we saw, special-purpose money. Different kinds of objects are employed in the different money uses; moreover, the uses are instituted independently of one another. The implications are of the most far-reaching nature. There is, for instance, no contradiction involved in "paying" with a means with which one cannot buy, nor in employing objects as a "standard" which are not used as a means of exchange. In Hammurabi's Babylonia barley was the means of payment; silver was the universal standard; in exchange, of which there was very little, both were used alongside of oil, wool, and some other staples. It becomes apparent why money uses—like trade activities— can reach an almost unlimited level of development, not only outside of market-dominated economies, but in the very absence of markets.

3. Market Elements

Now, the market itself. Catallactically, the market is the *locus* of exchange; market and exchange are co-extensive. For under the catallactic postulate economic life is both reducible to acts of exchange effected through higgling-haggling and it is embodied in markets. Exchange is thus described as *the* economic relationship, with the market as *the* economic institution. The definition of the market derives logically from the catallactic premises.

Under the substantive range of terms, market and exchange have independent empirical characteristics. What then is here the meaning of exchange and market? And to what extent are they necessarily connected?

Exchange, substantively defined, is the mutual appropriative movement of goods between hands. Such a movement as we saw may occur either at set rates or at bargained rates. The latter only is the result of higgling-haggling between the partners.

Whenever, then, there is exchange, there is a rate. This remains true whether the rate be bargained or set. It will be noted that exchange at bargained prices is identical with catallactic exchange or "exchange as a form of integration." This kind of exchange alone is typically limited to a definite type of market institution, namely price-making markets.

Market institutions shall be defined as institutions comprising a supply crowd or a demand crowd or both. Supply crowds and demand crowds, again, shall be defined as a multiplicity of hands desirous to acquire, or alternatively, to dispose of, goods in exchange. Although market institutions, therefore, are exchange institutions, market and exchange are *not* coterminous. Exchange at set rates occurs under reciprocative or redistributive forms of integration; exchange at bargained rates, as we said, is limited to price-making markets. It may seem paradoxical that exchange at set rates should be compatible with any form of integration except that of exchange: yet this follows logically since only bargained exchange represents exchange in the catallactic sense of the term, in which it is a form of integration.

The best way of approaching the world of market institutions appears to be in terms of "market elements." Eventually, this will not only serve as a guide through the variety of configurations subsumed under the name of markets and market type institutions, but also as a tool with which to dissect some of the conventional concepts that obstruct our understanding of those institutions.

Two market elements should be regarded as specific, namely, supply crowds and demand crowds; if either is present, we shall speak of a market institution (if both are present, we call it a market, if one of them only, a market-type institution). Next in importance is the element of equivalency, i.e., the rate of the exchange; according to the character of the equivalency, markets are set-price markets or price-making markets.

Competition is another characteristic of some market institutions, such as price-making markets and auctions, but in contrast to equivalencies, economic competition is restricted to markets. Finally, there are elements that can be designated as functional. Regularly they occur apart from market institutions, but if they make their appearance alongside of supply crowds or demand crowds, they pattern out those institutions in a manner that may be of great practical relevance. Amongst these functional elements are physical site, goods present, custom and law.

The diversity of market institutions was in recent times obscured in the name of the formal concept of a supply-demand-price mechanism. No wonder that it is in regard to the pivotal terms of supply, demand and price that the substantive approach leads to a significant widening of our outlook.

Supply crowds and demand crowds were referred to above as separate and distinct market elements. In regard to the modern market this would be, of course, inadmissible; here there is a price level at which bears turn bulls, and another price level at which the miracle is reversed. This has induced many to overlook the fact that buyers and sellers are separate in any other than the modern type of market. This again gave support to a twofold misconception. Firstly, "supply and demand" appeared as combined elemental forces while actually each consisted of two very different components, namely, an amount of *goods*, on the one hand, and a number of *persons*, related as buyers and sellers to those goods, on the other. Secondly, "supply and demand" seemed inseparable like Siamese twins, while actually forming distinct groups of persons, according to whether they disposed of the goods as of resources, or sought them as requirements. Supply crowds and demand crowds need not therefore be present together. When, for instance, booty is auctioned by the victorious general to the highest bidder only a demand crowd is in evidence; similarly, only a supply crowd is met with when contracts are assigned to the lowest submission. Yet auctions and submissions were widespread in archaic society, and in ancient Greece auctions ranked amongst the precursors of markets proper. This distinctness of "supply" and "demand" crowds shaped the organization of all premodern market institutions.

As to the market element commonly called "price," it was here subsumed under the category of equivalencies. The use of this general term should help avoid misunderstandings. Price suggests fluctuation, while equivalency lacks this association. The very phrase "set" or "fixed" price suggests that the price, before being fixed or set was apt to change. Thus language itself makes it difficult to convey the true state of affairs, namely, that "price" is originally a rigidly fixed quantity, in the absence of which trading cannot start. Changing or fluctuating prices of a competitive character are a comparatively recent development and their emergence forms one of the main interests of the economic history of antiquity. Traditionally, the sequence was supposed to be the reverse: price was conceived of as the result of trade and exchange, not as their precondition.

"Price" is the designation of quantitative ratios between goods of different kinds, effected through barter or higgling-haggling. It is that form of equivalency which is characteristic of economies that are integrated through exchange. But equivalencies are by no means restricted to exchange relations. Under a redistributive form of integration equivalencies are also common. They designate the quantitative relationship between goods of different kinds that are acceptable in payment of taxes, rents, dues, fines, or that denote qualifications for a civic status dependent on a property census. Also the equivalency may set the ratio at which wages or rations in kind can be claimed, at the beneficiary's choosing. The elasticity of a system of staple finance—the planning, balancing and accounting—hinges on this device. The equivalency here denotes not what should be given *for* another good, but what can be claimed *instead* of it. Under reciprocative forms of integration, again, equivalencies determine the amount that is "adequate" in relation to the symmetrically placed party. Clearly, this behavioral context is different from either exchange or redistribution.

Price systems, as they develop over time, may contain layers of equivalencies that historically originated under different forms of integration. Hellenistic market prices show ample evidence of having derived from redistributive equivalencies of the cuneiform civilizations that preceded them. The thirty pieces of silver received by Judas as the price of a man for betraying Jesus was a close variant of the equivalency of a slave as set out in Hammurabi's Code some 1700 years earlier. Soviet redistributive equivalencies, on the other hand, for a long time echoed nineteenth century world market prices. These, too, in their turn, had their predecessors. Max Weber remarked that for lack of a costing basis Western capitalism would not have been possible but for the medieval network of saturated and regulated prices, customary rents, etc., a legacy of gild and manor. Thus price systems may have an institutional history of their own in terms of the types of equivalencies that entered into their making.

It is with the help of noncatallactic concepts of trade, money and markets of this kind that such fundamental problems of economic and social history as the origin of fluctuating prices and the development of market trading can best be tackled and, as we hope, eventually resolved.

To conclude: A critical survey of the catallactic definitions of trade, money and market should make available a number of concepts which form the raw material of the social sciences in their economic aspect. The bearing of this recognition on questions of theory, policy and outlook should be viewed in the light of the gradual institutional transformation that has been in progress since the first World War. Even in regard to the market system itself, the market as the sole frame of reference is somewhat out of date. Yet, as should be more clearly realized than it sometimes has been in the past, the market cannot be superseded as a general frame of reference unless the social sciences succeed in developing a wider frame of reference to which the market itself is referable. This indeed is our main intellectual task today in the field of economic studies. As we have attempted to show, such a conceptual structure will have to be grounded on the substantive meaning of economic.

9 ECONOMIC THEORY AND PRIMITIVE SOCIETY[1]
George Dalton

Economics is the study of that broad aspect of human activity which is concerned with resources, their limitations and uses, and the organization whereby they are brought into relation with human wants. In modern industrial societies economists have worked out an elaborate technique for the study of this organization, and have produced a body of generalizations upon it. It is still a matter of argument as to how far this technique and these generalizations can be applied in the study of primitive communities (Firth 1958:63).

Some ambiguities in the literature of economic anthropology result from a lack of clarity concerning the revelance of Western economic theory to the economic organization of primitive communities (Knight 1941; Herskovits 1940; 1941). Anthropologists concerned with primitive economy sometimes seek preparation by studying the economics of their own society in the hope of acquiring analytical categories, techniques, and useful insights. Such procedure seems especially reasonable because of the success formal economic theory has had in analyzing Western economy. However, it is not well enough understood that much economic theory is inapplicable to primitive economy.

From American Anthropologist *63:1–25. Reprinted by permission.*

The fact that the attention of economists has been focused so exclusively on just those aspects of our economy least likely to be found among non-literate folk has thus confused anthropologists who turned to economic treatises for clarification of problems and methods in the study of the economic systems of non-literate societies (Herskovits 1952:53).

This paper presents some reasons why economic theory cannot be fruitfully applied to the study of primitive communities and suggests an alternative approach to analytical treatment of primitive economy.

Economic Theory and Market Economy

The purpose of this section is to describe those special organizational features of Western economy which formal economic theory was created to analyze. And then to show why formal economic theory, so derived, cannot be used to analyze the essentially different structures and processes of primitive economic organization.

Both the method and content of economic theory were shaped by two central features of 19th century Britain: factory industrialism and market organization. Market exchange, as the principle of economy-wide integration, compels its participants to conform to very special rules. *Everyone derives his livelihood from selling something to the market.* Laborers must sell their labor, land-owners must sell the use of their land and natural resources, farm and factory owners must sell end products. The same market mechanism transacts the factor ingredients of production—labor, land, natural resources, finance, transportation—as well as finished goods and services of all varieties.

Market exchange refers not only to the existence of market places (sites wherein buyers and sellers congregate), but more importantly, to the organizational process of purchase and sale at money price which is the mechanism of transacting material products, labor, and natural resources. In Western economy such transactions frequently take place outside of market places. For example, labor is not brought to a market place to sell, but its use is bought and sold through the same price-making process that transacts produced items at a market place. Land too becomes such a marketed commodity, whose ownership or use is something bought and sold for a money price determined by the same forces of market exchange which determine prices of labor and material items. Indeed, the market forces of cost and demand which transact material items such as wheat are functionally linked with those that transact the labor and land resources producing wheat. A change in wheat price "feeds back" on the rent price of wheat land and the wage price of farm labor. Land and labor use become rearranged in response to such price changes because the landowners and laborers depend for their livelihood on the money price of their land and labor which, in turn, depends upon the sales price of the material product land and labor produce. This is what is meant by the market mechanism or market principle integrating—bringing together in mutually dependent fashion—the components of economy.

The distinguishing feature of a market-organized economy, then, is the special nature of interdependence: all material livelihood is derived from selling something through the market mechanism; resource and labor ingredients of production are organized for purchase and sale as are produced material items; market prices rearrange labor and resource uses. Economists sum up the essential process in the shorthand expression that market-made prices allocate resources among alternative output uses, and wage, profit, rent, and interest incomes among the resource owners.

What should be emphasized is that it is market organization which compels its participants to seek material self-gain: each must sell something of market value to acquire the material means of existence. The "economic man" of 19th century economics was not a myth, but a succinct expression of this institutional fact: the necessity for each of the atomistic units in an impersonal, market exchange system to acquire his livelihood through market sale.

Throughout the 19th century—from Malthus and Ricardo to Alfred Marshall —a body of formal economic analysis was developed primarily concerned with a single set of questions: what are the forces which determine prices in a market-organized, industrial economy? Such theoretical concentration on price mechanics was simply a reflection of the crucial integrative role of prices in determining outputs and incomes.

Moreover, the market system functioned in a self-regulating way. The "economy" was a cohesive entity apart from other subsystems in society. It is true that government protected property and enforced contracts, but neither government, family, nor religion controlled market organization or price results. Where social institutions did impinge on market forces, they did so only in an indirect way by affecting supply or demand conditions (such as the demand for fish in Catholic countries), and thereby prices. The market structure was self-regulating in the sense that it required the components of the system to move— land to change its use, labor to change its location or occupation—in response to price changes made in markets. Price changes induced buyers and sellers to "economize," that is, to seek monetary cost reduction, or monetary gain increase. Production methods as well as the choice of which items to produce were guided by market prices. A condition for undertaking production is that the producer must expect to make a profit, which is the money differential between two sets of prices: those that determine his costs of production, and those that determine his sales revenue.

When market organization is economy-wide it creates a "market society," in the sense that social organization has to adapt to market needs to allow the sustained provision of material goods, and of money incomes with which to acquire goods.

> A market economy can only exist in a market society . . . a market economy must comprise all the elements of industry, including labor, land, and money. . . . But labor and land are no other than the human beings themselves of which every society consists and the natural surroundings in

which it exists. To include them in the market mechanism means to subordinate the substance of society itself to the laws of the market (Polanyi 1944:71).

For example, that laborers are compelled to sell their labor for a market-determined wage, means that they must move to remunerative labor markets when their present employments and wages fall. The location of population thereby conforms to market-registered needs for labor.

Finally, a market economy is highly decentralized. It consists of a multitude of related but nonetheless individual purchase and sale transactions. The operational units are individual business firms buying resources and selling outputs, and individual families buying household goods and selling labor and other resources. Such decentralization reinforces the atomistic view of society as simply an aggregate of self-interested individuals.

The question arises, why is it believed that the body of economic theory derived from such a special institutional matrix has analytical relevance to all economies, including the primitive? The reasons are several.

The English originators of formal economic theory grounded their analyses on postulates which seemed structured in the *physical* universe, and therefore universally applicable (Polanyi 1944: chapter 10). In addition, the repeal of mercantilistic economic controls and the consequent formation of nationwide markets, allowed the classical economists to use an "economistic" approach—to focus on economy as separate from society, to regard economy as having such an inner consistency and autonomy as to allow the derivation of distinct economic laws which seemed to operate independently of social institutions.

Especially significant in the work of the classicists was the delineation of purely "economic" motivation (material self-gain), as both necessary and sufficient to induce laborers to conform to market needs. For example, in urging repeal of Poor Laws which guaranteed subsistence as a traditional social right, William Townsend based his argument on the assertion that the "natural" force of fear of hunger was the most efficacious inducement to work.

> Hunger will tame the fiercest animals, it will teach decency and civility, obedience and subjection, to the most perverse. In general it is only hunger which can spur and goad them on to labour; yet our laws have said they shall never hunger. The laws, it must be confessed, have likewise said, they shall be compelled to work. But then legal constraint is attended with much troubles violence and noise; creates ill will, and never can be productive of good and acceptable service: whereas hunger is not only peaceable, silent, unremitting pressure, but as the most natural motive to industry and labour, it calls forth the most powerful exertions (Townsend 1786, quoted in Polanyi 1944:113–114).[2]

With Malthus, too, immutable biology was the starting point for deriving economic laws: that the natural fertility of humans made food scare because of the pressure of population growth, led him to deduce his subsistence theory of wages. The conclusions of biology—that the populations of all plant and animal life are limited only by their food supplies—were projected to the social world.

Ricardo's postulate, the "law" of diminishing returns, was also a natural phenomenon from which he deduced his income distribution theory: if one or more ingredients of production, such as land, is fixed in quantity, then output growth will consist of diminishing increments. In a market economy, owners of the fixed ingredient (landlords) will gain at the expense of the others (laborers and entrepreneurs).

Utilitarianism provided the crowning sanction, again in the guise of universal law: self-interest as the well-spring of all human action. The quest for material self-gain need be the only regulator of an economic system based upon the physical nature of man and the universe.

> The general conception which Bentham had is one that is widely prevalent today. . . . I think we shall conclude before the course is over that the bulk of orthodox economic theory as we have it at the present time [1935] rests upon a conception of human nature which is not very different from that which Jeremy Bentham drew up in such formal shape (Mitchell 1949:92).

The parametric assumptions of early economic analysis appeared as physical facts. The derived laws of market economy were thereby given the authority of nature. It seemed that economic processes had separate physical laws of their own, divorced from social convention (Polanyi 1944:115).

The economistic approach which separated out economy from society and created a body of theoretical analysis of market industrialism received more refined expression later in the 19th century in the works of Stanley Jevons, Carl Menger, John B. Clark, and Alfred Marshall. What is important for our purposes is that the neo-classicists made theoretical refinements also derived, it seemed, from universal truths: that the condition of "natural scarcity" (insufficiency of resources relative to unlimited material wants), necessitated marginal choice if maximum fulfillment of material wants was to be attained.

It is important to note how the condition of "scarcity"—so relevant for market economy—became regarded as universal fact, and a further basis for assuming the universal relevance of economic theory.

The institutional necessity for individuals to pursue material self-gain in market economy, had ideological reflections in the form of generalizations about the nature of "man" in society. One such is the textbook homily that man's material wants are insatiable, a dictum that often implies the immutability of genetic impulse. If man's material wants are insatiable, then scarcity of enabling means exists by definition: no matter the absolute quantity of resources, they are scarce, that is, insufficient relative to the unlimited desire for the end products they produce. If man places great emphasis on fulfilling his insatiable material wants, then economizing, rational calculation results in order to arrange some preferred ordering of resource uses. But if such is ever the case in an actual community, it is a *socially* determined result: a result which obtains only in a society which places great value on material acquisition relative to other goal attainments, and whose institutional structure impels its members to behave accordingly (Mead 1937; Fusfeld 1957:343).

To the extent that the syllogistic chain—man's material wants are infinite, his material means are finite, maximum material acquisition therefore requires economizing calculation—is regarded as having universal relevance, it is incorrect and misleading. It confuses the universally correct, *biologically* derived postulate—man's existence requires continuous material sustenance—with a special type of *social* orientation: man's social organization impels him always to want more material goods than he has at the moment, and makes him value such material acquisition more than the fulfillment of other social goals with which it might be in conflict. If it is once seen that the degree of importance attached to material acquisition is most definitely determined by social institutions and values, then it immediately follows that the presence, absence, or existing degree of "scarcity" of enabling material means (in any society) also depends upon social, not physical, circumstances.[3]

It is not so, as some literature of economic anthropology asserts, that the postulates of scarcity and economizing calculation are of universal relevance.

> The elements of scarcity and choice, which are the outstanding factors in human experience that give economic science its reason for being, rest psychologically on firm ground. . . . Our primary concern in these pages is to understand the cross-cultural implications of the process of economizing (Herskovits 1952:3, 4).

It is an erroneous linking together of two different meanings of the concept "economic" which is at the root of the misleading assumption of universal scarcity, and the misleading conclusion that formal economic theory has relevance to all economies. Clarification of two points is necessary: what it is that all economic systems—Western and primitive alike—have in common; and the nature of those structural differences between them which makes Western economic theory inapplicable in the analysis of primitive economy.

Two Meanings of Economic[4]

The word "economic" has two distinct and independent meanings, both in common use, but differing essentially in the extent to which each can be fruitfully applied to real-world structures. In the substantive sense, economic refers to the provision of material goods which satisfy biological and social wants. The substantive meaning is perfectly general in applicability, because all communities, regardless of differences in natural environment, production techniques, or cultural traits, are composed of human beings whose bio-social existence depends upon the sustained provision of material items.

> The basic problem is universal: not only to have enough to eat to keep alive, but also to satisfy the demands of personal tastes, religious rules and a multitude of social obligations, all as important to the life of the group as mere subsistence is to the life of the organism (Herskovits 1952:294).

The broad agencies of material-means provision are everywhere the same: natural endowment and the cooperation of inhabitants.

> We may move first of all, to those human and ecological factors that provide the goods and services which satisfy the demands of living, both biological and psychological, and that are at the core of any economic system. In some form, these factors are present everywhere; without their interaction life as we know it could not exist (Herskovits 1952:8).

With unambiguous meaning, therefore, one can talk about the "economic" system of Imperial Rome, of the Kwakiutl Indians, of the Benedictine Order of Monks, of 19th century England, or of Soviet Russia—meaning nothing more than the organizational structures and processes through which material goods are provided; one need not assume anything beforehand about necessary techniques, motivations, or specific types of economic organization.

The existence of some type of *systematic* economic structure is implied for the following reasons: the exploitation of natural resources requires the use of technique for the acquisition or creation of material goods (horticulture, farming, hunting, manufacture). The use of technique and of natural resources, together with the need for distributing goods among all the inhabitants, require definite institutional arrangements—structured rules of the game—to assure continuity of supply, that is, to assure repetition of performance. The participants are mutually dependent for other reasons as well: the use of technique, division of labor, natural environment, and the fact that economic processes take place within a social community, all make necessary the utilization of some pattern of recognized rights and obligations. It is the rules which integrate the use of natural resources and technique and assure continuous co-operation in the provision of material goods that we call an economic "system."

The substantive meaning of economic, however, is not analytically informative in the investigation of specific economies because of the diversity of technical and institutional structure which exists. But it does have the merit of pointing up and explaining the general existence of organizational requirements for the sustained provision of material goods which must be fulfilled in any society. It is, of course, what anthropologists usually mean when they refer to the "economic" aspects of primitive society.

The second meaning of economic is described by the terms "economical" and "economizing." It denotes a special set of rules designed to maximize the achievement of some end or to minimize the expenditure of some means. Four aspects of this formal meaning of economic deserve emphasis.

(1) It has no necessary connection with the substantive meaning of economic. It would be prejudicial to assume that the organizational provision of material goods must be universally achieved through economizing calculation; whether such is the case for any specific economy can only be established by empirical investigation.

(2) Economizing calculation by no means need be confined to the creation, distribution, or use of material goods. It derives rather from the general logic of rational action which is appropriate to a large number of theoretical and empirical situations; these have in common explicit ends, delimited means, and definite rules of alternative choice for the achievement of the ends with the stated means. For example, economizing calculation unrelated to substantive economic organization appears in games such as chess, in military problems, and in preparing for academic examinations: each entails allocating specific means to achieve goal maximization.

(3) A primary field of Western economic analysis, price and distribution theory, is an application of the formal meaning of economic—economizing calculation—to a special set of conditions and organizational practices for the provision of material goods: that the acquisition of material items is valued greatly relative to other goal attainments; that factor resources are therefore scarce (insufficient in quantity to achieve all ends), are multipurposed (capable of fulfilling more than one end); that the ends for which the material means shall be used are graded (of differential preferment); that the hierarchy of preferred ends is known; and that the rules for relating the scarce, multi-purposed resource means to the graded ends be that (a) any material end shall be fulfilled with no more than the minimum resource means necessary for its fulfillment; (b) no means shall be provided for lesser ends before provision for greater ends is made (Robbins 1932).

(4) The fruitful application of economic theory derived from the formal meaning of economic, depends on the existence of a substantive, real-world economy so organized that at least some of the special postulates of the analysis are institutionally fulfilled. If the members of some society do not show an economizing predisposition in their use of means (they use more than the minimum necessary to achieve the end), their rules of social organization dictate that some means may be used only for one purpose (such as religion proscribing all but one kind of crop grown on land), or there is no condition of "scarcity" because extensive material acquisition is not socially regarded as of primary importance, then formal economic analysis is not capable of yielding insights if applied to that economy (Knight 1941; Herskovits 1941; Fusfeld 1957; Neale 1957b).

Western Market Industrialism and Primitive Economy

A distinguishing characteristic of market-organized industrialism is that both meanings of economic are relevant. The substantive economic structure through which material want satisfaction is provided for consists of a special set of economizing practices applied to scarcity situations. The participants need material goods to survive; the market structure compels economizing performance for their acquisition and provides integrating unity and stability to such performance. The institutional complex which integrates the system—which links together the efforts of each and assures the sustained provision of material goods—is the supply-demand-price mechanism. Conformity to the market rules is effected through competition and by structured motivation: the institutionalized pursuit of material self-gain through market participation. One has to abide by the market rules to acquire material livelihood in a market-organized economy.

It should be added that, as with competitive market organization, the use of machine technology imposes a similar need for economizing calculations. Regardless of who owns them, machines are expensive. In the context of private ownership and market organization, economizing is enforced by potential market penalties in the form of money losses. The competitive striving for profits—the source of material livelihood for owners—requires efficient machine use to minimize costs. In the context of state ownership and central planning, economical use is required for fulfillment of priority goals: output maximization, rapid growth, and the production of crucial output components such as military and capital goods. Both the United States and Soviet Russia use structured mechanisms of economizing such as cost accounting, contract obligation to assure continuous resource supply, hierarchical authority discipline within factory organization, and price and wage formation so as to economize on the use of most scarce factor resources.

That every society must have substantive economic organization to provide material means of existence does not mean that each must have that special set of market exchange institutions for the analysis of which formal economic theory was uniquely designed. Indeed, there is increasing evidence that the market integrated economy is historically and anthropologically rare.

> A considerable body of evidence runs contrary to the notions that human wants are unlimited, that financial incentives will transfer labor from nonindustrial to industrial pursuits and thus that the potential worker may be viewed as welcoming release from traditional restraints. Some of this evidence can be interpreted in terms of "rational conduct," but not in terms of economic maximization. The potential worker in underdeveloped areas is typically required to give up traditional forms of organization and reciprocal obligations that have combined to afford him security—both material and affective. The kinship system in any nonindustrial society is likely to provide a major barrier to individual mobility, because it is a social security system, because it is the focus of positive values and advantages, and because extended kin obligations are likely to reduce the effective appeal of individual rewards (Moore 1955b:158–159).

Karl Polanyi and his associates (Polanyi, Arensberg, Pearson 1957) have shown that there exist at least two nonmarket principles of integrative economic organization for the analysis of which conventional economic theory is inappropriate. But such is the tenacity of belief that market theory is universally relevant—even to nonmarket and nonindustrial structures—that one economist says the following:

> What are the qualities which, it is said, are possessed by the [primitive and archaic] economies for the study of which conventional analysis is not helpful? They are: inflexible or sluggish prices or exchange ratios; inelastic (sometimes absolutely inelastic) supply; inelastic (sometimes absolutely inelastic) demand.
>
> The specific instances enumerated by the authors—e.g., set rates, customary or statutory equivalencies, gift trade, administered trade, status-trading, trading partnerships, the influence of kinship, magic and etiquette on economic behavior, noncompeting groups—seem to fall into one or more of these boxes.
>
> . . . now, the conventional doctrine and techniques of formal economics have much to say about economies or markets in which inflexibilities and inelasticities occur. It is not true that economic analysis cannot perform useful predictive tasks in such economies (Rottenberg 1958:676).

The use of formal price theory concepts such as "inelastic demand" in reference to primitive economies indicates an implicit market orientation: the prejudgment of economic organization by way of a priori assumption that market structure—or its functional equivalent—exists universally. A market orientation assumes that economic theory is universally relevant because it assumes that scarcity situations are universal and everywhere compel materially self-gainful economizing, such as maximization of consumer utility and production at least cost.

It is true that economic theory has much to say about inelastic supply and demand conditions. But it is also true that what is said concerns economic sectors so organized that resource ingredients and product outputs are bought and sold through the market mechanism. As Herskovits rightly points out, economic theory requires market-determined prices to be applicable.

> The problem of how value flows from fluctuations in supply and demand, in its essentially mathematical character, needs the quantitative index of value contained in price as manifest in the market to permit its analysis (Herskovits 1952:49).

The import of the work of Polanyi and his associates is that the economy-wide market mechanism, its materially self-gainful economizing, and its monetized internal and external trade do not exist as integrative pattern in the primitive economies they consider. Rather, that the production and distribution of material goods are organized by transactional principles essentially different from market exchange.

> For in these societies, production and distribution involve little of the profit motive, and labor is only in special instances for hire (Herskovits 1952:11).

The process of distribution, in many tribes, is thus set in a non-economic [non-economizing] matrix, which takes the form of gift and ceremonial exchange (Herskovits 1952:155).

The integrative patterns which do exist widely in primitive economy are (1) reciprocity, that is, material gift and counter gift-giving induced by social obligation derived, typically, from kinship, as is the case with the Trobriand Islanders; and (2) redistribution, the channeling upward of goods or services to socially determined allocative centers (usually king, chief, or priest), who then redistribute either to their subordinates at large by providing community services, or in specific allotments to individuals in accordance with their political, religious, or military status. Redistribution, often accompanied by reciprocity, was the dominant principle in ancient Egypt, ancient Mexico, Dahomey, and in feudalistic societies generally (Malinowski 1922; Thurnwald 1932; Herskovits 1952: chapter 19; Mauss 1925; Firth 1958:65, 68–69).

> . . . *the whole tribal life is permeated by a constant give and take*; that every ceremony, every legal and customary act is done to the accompaniment of material gift and counter gift; that wealth, given and taken, is one of the main instruments of social organization, of the power of the chief, of the bonds of kinship, and of relationships in law (Malinowski 1922:167).

The importance to economic anthropology of the distinction between the substantive and formal meanings of economic should be further emphasized.

That all societies must have substantive economic organization means that there will be similarities (and therefore bases for comparison) even between two widely differing economies—say, the Trobriand Islands and present-day United States. Thus one could talk meaningfully about the creation, distribution, and use of material goods in each, as well as the roles of money and external trade, and the organization of land tenure. However—and this is the point to be underscored—the fact that the United States is pervasively market-organized and industrialized (and thereby amenable to analysis by formal economic theory), while the Trobriands is neither, *makes the differences in economic organization and processes between the two more important than the similarities*, especially so on matters of interest to the anthropologist.[5]

There are three ways to clarify the issue and reinforce the point: (1) To contrast the questions of economic interest to the anthropologist with those the economist asks in his own field. (2) To show that economic mechanisms, practices, and processes common to both primitive and Western economies are institutionalized differently and often function in different ways and for different purposes. (3) To cite examples which show how misleading results follow from the assumption that primitive economic organization is functionally equivalent to Western economy, and from the conclusion that primitive economy is amendable to analysis by formal economic theory.

The matters of interest to the anthropologist investigating the general aspects of primitive economy can be classified, perhaps, into some six overlapping categories.

(1) Technological processes. Are they horticulturalists, fishermen, gardeners, hunters, etc.? Which technical devices are used? How are canoes and houses built, land tilled, fish-traps made?

(2) What is the level of material subsistence and how secure is it?

(3) What the the ecological conditions? What is the natural endowment (climate, waterways, land acreage and fertility) from which livelihood is extracted?

(4) Which economic devices and processes are used and how do they work? Are there money uses? If so, for which types of transactions? Which goods are transacted without the use of money? Is there more than one kind of money used? Are there market places or external trade? If so, how are they organized and which items do they transact? Are there prices or equivalency ratios for goods which change hands? How are such determined?

(5) What is the place of the "economy" in the society? How are production processes, material goods transactions, labor services, and land utilization organized? How are they related to kinship structure, religion, political authority, and other social institutions? On what principles do things and labor services change hands and location? What is the nature of economic interdependence which allows division of labor to be practiced? What are the socially sanctioned motives which induce conforming participation in substantive economic activity? How is continuity assured in the supply of material items? How are the inefficient, the unusually efficient, and the recalcitrant treated?

(6) Are there distinct economic spheres with different operational principles and value norms in each (DuBois 1936; Steiner 1954; Polanyi 1957a; Bohannan 1959)? Is it meaningful in terms of the specific goods transacted, the processes and mechanisms which transact them, and the value judgments attached to such transactions by the participants, to distinguish between subsistence and prestige spheres? Are there treasure items or items of elite circulation? Is external trade carried out on the same principles as internal transactions?

Economists are not concerned directly with technology, social institutions, or physical environment. Such matters are regarded as given, in the sense of existing as part of the total environment of market-organized industrialism, within which economic mechanism functions.

> It is *precisely* the separate class of variables which it employs which for the economist, at any rate, distinguishes economics from the other sciences. Economics studies prices; quantities of commodities exchanged, produced, consumed; interest rates, taxes, tariffs: its basic abstraction is that of the commodity. It seeks to find reasonably stable relationships among these variables, but it is the variables not the relationships, which delimit the subject matter of the science (Boulding 1957:318).

Technology, physical environment, and social institutions are of interest only in special instances: when they affect the economic variables in which the economist is interested. Two examples will illustrate the point.

For problems of aggregate output determination and growth in a market-industrial economy, an important quantity is the money expenditure by business firms in purchasing new plant and equipment. By changing the complex of costs, proportions used of resource ingredients, and profit expectations, an innovation in technique of producing will affect yearly investment outlays and so is of interest to the economist. But the anthropologist's interest in technology is both more direct and somewhat different. The economist is not interested in how the machine is built and operated (or in the social organization of the factory) as is the anthropologist in how the fish-trap is built, operated, shared, and inherited.

More importantly, the same is true of social institutions. On the rare occasion when the economist considers kinship, religion, or government, he does so only for a special purpose: when they have significant impact on economic quantities; for example, the impact of governmental price-support programs on agricultural prices and incomes. Because the organization of market economy is a cohesive entity in itself, the economist can describe and analyze that range of processes of interest to economics without reference to the social.[6] In contrast, the close integration of social and economic institutions in primitive society makes it impossible for the anthropologist to describe the economic, without at the same time showing its relation to the social.

> Basically, the anthropologist is not asking the same set of questions as the economist. The business of anthropology is not economics; it is rather something that we might call "ethno-economics" . . . a statement of the categories of thought and language, the ideas, the principle of action, in terms of which a people institutionalize the business of getting a living. . . . For the anthropologist's task is to explain how people get a living, then to classify those modes . . . and theorize about the way they are linked with other cultural or social attributes (Bohannan 1958).

> The exchanges of archaic societies which he [Mauss] examines are total social movements or activities. They are at the same time economic, juridical, moral, aesthetic, religious, mythological, and sociomorphological phenomena. Their meaning can therefore only be grasped if they are viewed as a complex concrete reality (Evans-Pritchard 1954:vii).

Neither the problems of interest nor the methods of analysis are the same for economics and economic anthropology.

Economic Mechanisms

A point of some importance is that a number of economic mechanisms, practices, and processes—the use of money, external trade, division of labor, market places, debt, prices—occur both in Western economy and in the primitive. But to conclude that because both use them, their organization, functioning, or purpose in primitive economy must be essentially the same as in ours, is not warranted.[7] Yet such is sometimes implied in the literature of economic anthropology.

> . . . there can be no division of labor without a resulting economic exchange. The universality of the fact of division of labor, even if only on sex lines, underscores the essential soundness of the reasoning which has made of exchange and distribution basic factors in all economic theory (Herskovits 1952:13).

Surely one could not conclude that because division of labor is practiced in the United States, in Soviet Russia, and in the Trobriand Islands, the same principles of "exchange" are operative in each. All one can infer from the universality of division of labor is a tautology: wherever it is practiced there is structured interdependence, and there must be some institutional means for persons to acquire what they do not themselves produce.[8] The basic form of institutional means for such exchange in any economy can only be established by empirical investigation.

> And as with the mechanisms of production, the distribution system, though a universal in human social life, takes on a vast number of forms (Herskovits 1952:12).

Similarly, when we compare other Western economic mechanisms with what seem to be their counterparts in primitive economy, it becomes clear that the differences in their organization and functioning are more important than their similarities. Clarification of the point is especially necessary for understanding the nature of money uses, external trade, and market places in primitive economy (Polanyi 1957a).

In Western market economy, money is all-purpose money, the same money serving all transactional sectors as medium of exchange, standard of value, store of value, and as means of payment (for example, of debts). Few economic transactions take place without the use of money; and only one kind of money—conveniently interchangeable as check deposit, paper currency, and coin—is in general use. It is no accident that such is the case: the use of all-purpose money is a requisite for a market-organized economy because all labor and resource ingredients as well as finished outputs must bear price tags expressed in the same money in order for buyers and sellers to transact them through the market exchange mechanism. The use of the same money instrument makes physically different items both commensurable and "commodities," that is, things to be bought and sold whose value can be compared. (Indeed, money itself becomes a marketed commodity, the price of which is an interest rate.)

Where money is used in primitive economy, it is not all-purpose money; each kind can be used only for a special range of transactions, such as the use of cattle as a money object for acquiring a bride or paying bloodwealth, but not for acquiring food or craft products. In primitive economy a given money object often serves one use only, as when debts are calculated in terms of brass rods but actually paid in strips of cloth (Bohannan 1959). What should be emphasized is that the differences in money usage between primitive economy and the Western market system are indicators of underlying differences in transactional principles of economic integration (such as reciprocity, redistribution, and market exchange). The disposition of natural resources, material outputs, and labor are often compartmentalized separately in primitive economy. Frequently they are transacted without the use of money, and neither enter market places nor are transacted by the market mechanism of purchase and sale. Rather, they change hands and location in different economic spheres—in accordance with different sets of social rules, such as kinship obligation inducing gift exchange; political obligation inducing payment to central authority.

So, too, with other economic devices common to both primitive and Western economies. The uncritical application to primitive economy of such familiar Western categories as external trade and markets obscures essential differences. Usually they are not functional equivalents, but rather superficially similar practices not only organized differently, but often with different sociological as well as economic purposes (Firth 1958:63).

For example, in Western economy exports and imports are transacted through the same market principle which transacts internal exchanges, both economy-wide and local. In primitive economy, transactional mechanisms used in external trade are sometimes distinctly different from those used internally; moreover, external trade transactions of a nonmarket kind are frequently found. Some examples are the fish-yam and Kula gift trade of the Trobriands (Malinowski 1922) and politically administered trade in elite items so typical of West Africa (Arnold 1957). A further point of difference is that external trade in primitive economy is induced by the nonavailability of the import items at home. Indeed, such seems invariably to be the rationale for primitive external trade (Herskovits 1952:36–37, 181; Polanyi 1957a, 1957b). In contrast, external trade among Western market economies takes place on the least-cost principle: things *are* imported which can be produced at home if such imports are cheaper than the domestic equivalents. The market principle of least-cost economizing, which pervades internal production and sale, characterizes external trade as well.

Of special importance is the fact that where markets do exist in primitive economy, they almost invariably are restricted to produced material items: *rarely, if ever, do land or labor get transacted through the price-making mechanism of market exchange.* Prices made in local markets do not reallocate labor and other resource ingredients of production, as in Western market economy. Neither land usage nor labor location and occupation respond to market price changes, because subsistence livelihood does not depend on market sale. In primitive economy the market is local, specific, and contained; its price results do not "feed-back" into nonmarket spheres of economy. A primitive community often has a market place, but not a market system; that is, an economy-wide complex of resource and output market integration through which most people acquire their subsistence livelihood.[9]

It is indicative that in economic anthropology the term "market" always is used to mean "market-place": an actual site wherein goods change hands by purchase and sale (Neale 1957b). In Western economy, the term market is applied not only to specific marketplace sites such as a cluster of retail stores, and to sites where ownership changes hands but not the goods themselves (the New York Stock Exchange, the Chicago Wheat Pit), but also to the diffusive economic forces of market exchange: the pervasive supply-demand-price mechanism which systematically transacts resources, labor, and products regardless of what specific site—market bazaar, retail store, hiring firm—is the location of such transactions. Indeed, that where an economy-wide market mechanism exists the market place site is of little importance, is indicated by such concepts as the "market" for automobiles or for engineers' labor, meaning the mass of potential buyers or sellers of something, wherever they are located. A further indicator of the importance, complexity, and special role of the market mechanism in Western economy is that market forces are classified many ways: controlled and uncontrolled markets; factor ingredient and output markets: local, economy-wide, and international markets; competitive and oligopolistic markets.

In summary, Western industrial economy is organized through the market principle and the use of all-purpose money: they are pervasive, interrelated, and tend to homogenize most sectors of production and distribution. Market economy has been appropriately termed "uni-centric" because of the wide variety of material items and labor transacted in the sphere of market exchange (Bohannan 1959). In contrast, primitive economy is "multi-centric," and the dominant centers are organized through nonmarket patterns of integration, such as reciprocity and redistribution; special-purpose monies are in use, and market-place exchange (where it exists at all) is subordinate and contained (Polanyi 1957a).

A Money Economy Is A Market Economy

A point mentioned above which deserves separate elaboration concerns the anthropologist's use of the term "money economy" as a shorthand expression for the type of economic organization prevalent in the West. Thus Watson (*Tribal Cohesion in a Money Economy*, 1958) uses the term in describing how the Mambwe absent themselves temporarily from their villages to work for money wages in European industrial enterprises in Rhodesia; and Firth contrasts uni-centric Western "money economy" with primitive spheres of non-exchangeable goods:

> Another feature of such primitive transactions is the existence of what may be termed "spheres of exchange." There are various groups of goods and services, and exchange of one item can only take place with another item in the same group. In southeastern New Guinea, for instance, a very important series of exchanges takes place between the possessors of shell arm-rings and of necklaces of shell discs, while other important exchanges are of fish for vegetables. But the food items can only be exchanged against

each other, and so also the shell valuables. It would be unthinkable for a man who wished a shell valuable to offer in return yams or fish or other property not of a shell kind. There is no free market, no final measure of the value of individual things, and no common medium whereby every type of goods and services can be translated into terms of every other. A primitive economy thus presents a strong contrast to our money economy (Firth 1958:69).

The term money economy emphasizes a derivative rather than the dominant feature of Western economic structure. The use of all-purpose money is not an independent trait, but rather a requirement for the functioning of a market exchange economy. Continuity in supply of material goods in market economy is assured through several practices, one of which is the use of all-purpose money. It is only when land and labor as well as fabricated goods are organized as available commodities to be bought and sold through the market mechanism that a money economy exists. From the anthropologist's viewpoint, they enter the same transactional sphere of market exchange. Where all-purpose money is absent in primitive economy, it is because market exchange as the economy-wide principle of integration is absent.

. . . one cardinal feature of a primitive economic system is clearly the absence of money, of a price mechanism, and in many cases of a formal market (Firth 1958:70).

What is a "money economy" to an anthropologist appears as a "market economy" to an economist.

Economic Theory, Market Categories, and Primitive Economy

Those who attempt to analyze primitive economy with the economic theory and categories derived from Western market industrialism seem uniformly selective in their choice of specific theories to apply. Almost invariably, it is from one field of economic analysis, price theory, that they choose (Goodfellow 1939; Rottenberg 1958).

The question arises, if it is thought that Western price theory is relevant to primitive economy, why not other branches of Western theory—say, Keynesian income and employment theory—as well? The answer, perhaps, is that in the attempt to apply Keynesian theory to primitive economy it would become evident that the assumption of functional similarity of economic organization between the primitive and the West is empirically indefensible. In a word, it cannot be done.

The contribution of Keynes was to show why, *in a decentralized market economy* such as those of England and America in the early 1930's, the full employment rate of production is not automatically sustained. But rather that we experience sharp and deep output fluctuations. The basic reason is institutional: in a market economy, all incomes are derived from the sale of end-products to private households (consumption goods—C), business firms (investment goods—

I), government (governmental purchases—G), and foreigners (export goods —E) ; but there exists no automatic mechanism to assure that the total amount of such market purchases (effective demand) by C, I, G, and E will be sufficient to keep the labor and machine force fully employed. Moreover, the inter-dependence of the segments of market economy is such—each person acquires his livelihood by selling something to someone else—that a sharp reduction in one category of expenditure (say, business firm outlay on new machinery—I), inevitably induces spending cutbacks in other effective demand sectors (house-hold consumption good purchases—C) : those who earn their wage and profit incomes in producing machinery will be forced by income cuts to spend less on household goods.

One cannot apply such analysis to primitive economy because the basic institu-tional precondition is absent: the bulk of material income is not derived from, and therefore does not depend upon, market sales of output. In primitive econ-omy, mutual dependence is not structured through the market mechanism: the primitive does not depend for his material livelihood on sale of his labor for a money wage which he then uses to buy material items; "effective demand" for goods cannot shrink, as it does in market economy, because the aggregate amount of money incomes received for market sale of labor and other resources shrinks.

Functional Equivalence

One type of ambiguity in economic anthropology is the result of the assump-tion that primitive economic processes and devices are functionally equivalent to their Western counterparts. The temptation to make such assumption is great: primitive and Western communities alike must have substantive economic organ-ization to provide continuous material sustenance; and, as we know, both use superficially similar devices and processes, such as tools, money, external trade, and market places. But if such functional equivalence implies a more precise identity—either organizational equivalence or identical purpose—it is a highly misleading concept.

Two examples showing how the use of Western market categories transforms primitive economic practices into overly precise functional equivalents of market processes, and in so doing obscures the essential differences between market economy and the primitive, are given below. (Italics are added to point up the use of market exchange terms.)

> The economic system of the Indians of British Columbia is largely based on *credit*, just as much as that of civilized communities. In all his undertakings, the Indian relies on the help of his friends. He promises to pay them for this help at a later date. If the help furnished consists in valuables, which are measured by the Indians by blankets as we measure them by *money*, he promises to pay the amount so loaned with *interest*. The Indian has no system of writing, and therefore, in order to give security to the trans-action, it is performed publicly. The *contracting* of *debts*, on the one hand, and the paying of debts, on the other, is the potlatch. This economic

system has developed to such an extent that the *capital* possessed by all the individuals of the tribe combined exceeds many times the actual amount of *cash* that exists; that is to say, the conditions are quite analogous to those prevailing in our community: if we want to call in all our outstanding debts, it is found that there is not by any means money enough in existence to pay them, and the results of an attempt of all the *creditors* to call in their *loans* results in disastrous panic, from which it takes the community a long time to recover.

It must be clearly understood that an Indian who invites all his friends and neighbours to a great potlatch, and apparently squanders all the accumulated results of long years of labour, has two things in his mind which we cannot but acknowledge as wise and worthy of praise. His first object is to pay his debts. This is done publicly and with much ceremony, as a matter of record. His second object is to *invest* the fruits of his labours so that the greatest benefit will accrue from them for himself as well as for his children. The recipients of gifts at this festival receive these as loans, which they utilize in their present undertakings, but after the lapse of several years they must repay them with interest to the giver or to his heirs. Thus the potlatch comes to be considered by the Indians as a means of insuring the well-being of their children if they should be left orphans while still young (Boas 1898:681–682, quoted in Mauss 1925: 100).

Some differences between the Kwakiutl and the Western transactions are these: in Western market economy credit has a variety of functions, the most important of which is the financing of business enterprise through both short- and long-term loans. The recipients employ the amounts of all-purpose money borrowed in such materially productive ways (ways which enlarge output and sales revenue) as to be able to repay the loan, plus the interest charge, and still retain some profit from the use of the loan. Such is not the case with the Kwakiutl.

The debt-credit creation apparatus in Western economy is part of market institution. The rate of interest paid on loans is a variable rate, depending on supply and demand forces in the money markets.

There is no status constraint on borrowing in Western economy: one does not borrow solely from one's lineage group.

In the above quote, Kwakiutl blankets are special-purpose money used only for a limited range of transactions, and not used at all in some spheres of Kwakiutl economy; blankets are not all-purpose money used in all sectors of economy, as is money in market economy.

It is true that, both in market economy and in the Kwakiutl, the volume of outstanding "debt" may exceed the volume of existing "money"; however, the mechanisms through which both debt and money are created, as well as the conditions under which debt is called in for repayment, are entirely different; also different are the penalties for nonrepayment of "loans contracted," as well as the specificity of the loan obligation (Goldman 1937:188; Herskovits 1952: 238).

The imputation of *material* self-gain as dominant motive in giving gifts which must be returned with larger gifts is an injection of Western values. In Kwakiutl values, the chief motive is seeking honorific prestige, not material profit, as is demonstrated by the ultimate in the potlatch code of honor: the outright destruction of wealth to show one's aristocratic worth, and to crush a rival.

In Western market economy, the debtor always initiates a loan transaction; in the potlatch, it is the "creditor," who takes the initial step by forcing a rival to accept gifts.

The potlatch sphere transacts some goods which are unique to it, uses some special-purpose monies (coppers) not used in other spheres, and transacts goods and monies in accordance with principles which are distinct from those of the subsistence spheres of everyday livelihood: the major portion of a Kwakiutl's daily consumed material goods is not acquired through the potlatch (or with money used in the potlatch), but through other mechanisms and relationships, that is, in other economic spheres (Goldman 1937:181–182). In Western economy, the bulk of one's livelihood is acquired through market sale and purchase; almost all material goods and services enter the same market exchange sphere— subsistence goods, prestige goods, as well as the debt-credit services to which Boas compares the potlatch (Mauss 1925:33, 36, 39, 102; Goldman 1937:180).

In what surely must be the most vigorous attempt to apply economic theory to primitive economy, it is asserted:

> The aim of this book is to show that the concepts of economic theory must be taken as having universal validity, and that, were this not so, the result would be not only scientific confusion but practical chaos (Goodfellow 1939:3).

Repeated assertion of the credo—faith means salvation, doubt means chaos— is preliminary to exegesis.

> Actually, once it is baldly stated, the proposition that there should be more than one body of economic theory is absurd. If modern economic analysis with its instrumental concepts cannot cope equally with the Aborigine and with the Londoner, not only economic theory but the whole of the social sciences may be considerably discredited. For the phenomena of the social sciences are nothing if not universal. . . . When it is asked, indeed, whether modern economic theory can be taken as applying to primitive life, we can only answer that if it does not apply to the whole of humanity then it is meaningless. For there is no gulf between the civilized and the primitive; one cultural level shades imperceptibly into another, and more than one level is frequently found within a single community. If economic theory does not apply to all levels, then it must be so difficult to say where its usefulness ends that we might be driven to assert that it has no usefulness at all (Goodfellow 1939:4, 5).

But there is a gulf between the Western and the primitive; types of *economic organization* do not shade imperceptibly one into another; and it is not impossible to say where the usefulness of economic theory ends.

Economic theory was created to analyze the special structures, processes, and problems of market-organized industrialism, with its special features of all-purpose money, impersonal contract obligation, atomistic individualism, and the institutional necessity for individuals to acquire livelihood through market sale of labor, natural resources, and outputs. It is these which create the gulf between the primitive and the West. It would indeed be remarkable if economic theory *were* relevant to primitive economies which differed from the Western at essential points.

Confusion is compounded by reiterating the credo while, at the same time, offering evidence for disbelief: the economizing concepts of economic theory are applicable to Bantu economy despite the absence of machines, market exchange, all-purpose money, rent, interest, wages, profit, and the private business firm.

> . . . the functions are always actively carried out, but often by organizations, of which the family or household is the most important. . . . The difficulty of discovering the *forms* of modern economic life may well lead to a mistaken belief that the *functions* of that life are not to be discoverable among our less advanced people. . . . Modern economic theory has supplied us with a technique which transcends those forms and has the great merit of being applicable to the economic aspect of life, simply as an aspect, and independently of the forms prevalent in any given culture (Goodfellow 1939:7, 8).

It is illustrative that here again the root of ambiguity lies in the erroneous identification of the two meanings of economic: because Bantu society must provide for a sustained flow of material goods (the substantive meaning of economic, universally relevant), it is erroneously concluded that Bantu economy must consist of *economizing structures functionally equivalent* to those of market industrialism; and, therefore, that Bantu structures must also be amenable to analysis by market theory.

Economic Anthropology: Description and Analysis

The literature of economic anthropology displays a frequent dichotomy: excellent description of economic organization, processes, values, and technology, combined with inadequate theoretical analysis and generalization. Perhaps the dichotomy reflects the institutionalized preparation of anthropologists. Precise description of data in which the anthropologist immerses himself is a distinguishing feature of the profession (Evans-Pritchard 1954:viii). Theoretical analysis, however, is one step away from the data; and, as we have seen, the obfuscating preconceptions of the economics and the economy of the anthropologist's own culture make theoretical analysis of primitive economy yet more difficult and less successful.

> Admittedly, there is as yet no body of generalizations that treats "economic" behavior from the specifically anthropological point of view. . . . "Economic anthropology," to date, is not yet a reality. It is still freeing itself from the

> belief . . . that economic theory itself already has something to offer for
> an easy explanation of other economic systems than the market system of
> the recent West (Arensberg 1957:99, 100).

In conclusion, several points of emphasis will be summarized in order to delineate those important differences between primitive economy and Western market industrialism which makes formal economic theory incapable of yielding analytical insights when applied to primitive structures.

For economic anthropology, only the substantive meaning of economic is relevant. For any primitive community, one can only assume the existence of some kind of institutional apparatus through which material goods are acquired and distributed. One cannot assume as a universal the presence of any special economizing institutions such as those which distinguish market economies. It is not economizing calculation induced by "scarcity" which is universal, but rather the need for structured provision of material goods (Arensberg 1957:110).

It should be emphasized that no economic "system" is of one piece. Rather, that in any society—including our own, and most certainly the primitive—there exist spheres of economy with different principles of organization, different sanctions to induce conformity, different institutionalization of economic mechanisms, indeed, different moral values for judging worth and performance (Bohannan 1959:492). Even in our own economy, which is unusual for the variety of resources, outputs, and services transacted in the sphere of market exchange, there exist sectors such as family, government, and military organization, within which nonmarket patterns operate (Smelser 1959:173).

Primitive economy is different from market industrialism not in degree but in kind. The absence of machine technology, pervasive market organization, and all-purpose money, plus the fact that economic transactions cannot be understood apart from social obligation, create, as it were, a non-Euclidean universe to which Western economic theory cannot be fruitfully applied. The attempt to translate primitive economic processes into functional equivalents of our own inevitably obscures just those features of primitive economy which distinguish it from our own.

It is true that many economic mechanisms and practices either are universal or very frequently found in primitive, historical, and modern economies. But their presence is not prima facie evidence of organizational, operational, or functional similarity. Division of labor, money uses, external trade, and market places are best regarded as adaptable devices (like language and mathematics), capable of varied use for different purposes in a variety of organizational contexts. Here, the poverty of our terminology is a source of built-in ambiguity. Although categories such as land tenure and division of labor may be universals, their meanings are so colored by their special organization in our own economy that when used in reference to primitive economy they inadvertently impart the familiar, specialized meaning of our own. Conceptual categories are useful analytically only when they fit real-world structures; when diverse real-world structure is made to fit our specialized categories, distortion results.

The mistake of judging the men of other periods by the morality of our own day has its parallel in the mistake of supposing that every wheel and bolt in the modern social machine had its counterpart in more rudimentary societies (Maine, quoted in Bohannan 1957:iii).

A related point is that the reification of economic categories tends to create another type of ambiguity, as occurs when the Western investigator of primitive economy seeks answers to questions whose importance is derived from his own: how are governmental services financed? Who owns the means of production (Herskovits 1952:496)? It is neither possible nor desirable for the anthropologist to shed his cultural skin; but surely he can and should differentiate between primitive values and our own (Dalton 1960).

A matter of general theoretical significance to economic anthropology concerns the dominance and frequency of reciprocative and redistributive forms of economic integration. A distinguishing characteristic of primitive life is the fusion of social and economic institutions. Indeed, even the word "fusion" is distorting because it implies the bringing together of separate elements. It would be better to say that there is no awareness of the "economy" as a distinct set of practices apart from social institutions. Transactions of material goods in primitive society are expressions of social obligation which have neither mechanism nor meaning of their own apart from the social ties and social situations they express. In the Western meaning of the word, there is no "economy" in primitive society, only socio-economic institutions and processes.

Finally, it should be added that these matters are no longer of interest to anthropologists alone. Understanding primitive economy has become a necessity for those economists concerned with underdeveloped area transformation (Moore 1955b; Myrdal 1957; Keyfitz 1959; Shea 1959; Neale 1959). The phrase "economic growth" joints together two different kinds of change which go on simultaneously in underdeveloped areas: institutional transformation from indigenous socio-economic forms such as reciprocity and redistribution, to market-organized industrialism; and additions to real material output generated by the new economic and technical apparatus. Economists are concerned with inducing real output increases, anthropologists with reducing the social decimation inherent in rapid institutional departure from indigenous forms. Both must understand the nature of the primitive economies which are being dismantled as well as the economic and social characteristics of market industrialism. For the economist to assume that the problem is primarily quantitative—more machinery, more roads, more food—would be to blind himself to the social realities of economy as well as to the social miseries of culture disintegration.

> In primitive communities, the individual as an economic factor is personalized, not anonymous. He tends to hold his economic position in virtue of his social position. Hence to displace him economically means a social disturbance (Firth 1951:137).

Western economic theory has proved a powerful tool for making industrialized market systems grow. But primitive communities are neither industrialized nor market systems. One must start from ethno-economic analysis—with Malinowski, not Ricardo—in order to choose those transformation paths to industrialization which entail only the unavoidable social costs.

NOTES

[1] I am very grateful to Karl Polanyi of Columbia Universtiy and Paul Bohannan of Northwestern University for their helpful suggestions and criticisms. Much of this paper consists of an application of Professor Polanyi's work (1944; 1947; 1957) to the special problems considered. Part of the paper is drawn from my doctoral dissertation (Dalton 1959a).

[2] As Polanyi points out, hunger is natural in the sense of biological, but it is not synonymous with an incentive to produce. It becomes such an incentive if society makes eating specifically dependent upon that individual's producing, which early market economy in fact did. For views similar to those of Townsend, that only poverty and the fear of hunger could make the lower classes industrious, see Bendix (1956: 63–82); on the origins of laissez-faire market economy in England, see also Keynes (1926).

[3] In the economist's sense, "scarcity" does not mean physical shortage, but a condition of insufficiency relative to desire. Any item in market economy which has a money price is regarded as scarce. Scarcity is, so to speak, a fraction: the numerator is resource ingredients available, and the denominator is desire for material outputs. The social emphasis on material acquisition in the United States, ironically, makes factor resources very "scarce" in the most affluent society in the world.

[4] I am indebted to Karl Polanyi for his illuminating distinction between the two meanings of economic (Polanyi 1957b, 1959; Hopkins 1957).

[5] Compare the following two statements: "Whether we consider the motivations underlying the economic activities of peoples without writing or a machine industry, or the institutions that are the framework of the economic systems of nonliterate, non-industrialized societies, it is clear that these are directed toward the same ends and utilize substantially the same means to attain those ends, as do people who are equipped with writing, and with the superior technologies of the historic societies" (Herskovits 1952: 487). "Whether one looks at undeveloped areas or the most highly industrialized ones, a fundamental theoretical point is evident. That point is the great complexity of human motivation. Men will work for as many reasons as there are values to be served by such activity and will refuse to work where that serves his values. The fact that industrial systems emphasize values that are commanded in a market and incentives that provide monetary claims on a market should not blind us to the diversity of ends or the diversity of means for their satisfaction" (Moore 1955b:162).

[6] The degree of autonomy of market processes has been drastically reduced in Anglo-American systems, especially in the last thirty years. The experiences of depression and war have induced extensive structural reforms, increasing the number and variety of social controls over market processes. Some examples are minimum wage legislation and agricultural price supports; also, increased governmental spending and taxing for war, welfare, full employment, and growth purposes.

From the viewpoint of this paper, two results of increased market control in the West are that formal price theory is less usefully applicable to present-day Western economy, and the areas of similarity between economic organization in the West and in primitive society have been enlarged (Dalton 1959a: chapter 6; 1959b).

[7] One need only point out that both the Soviet and American systems employ money, division of labor, foreign trade, market places, etc., to indicate that similar economic mechanisms can be adapted to dissimilar organizational structures, and used for different purposes. The point was not obvious in the 19th century because all Western industrialized economies were integrated through the same pattern of market exchange (Neale 1957b; Pearson 1957c).

[8] Adam Smith's famous dictum—that division of labor is limited by the extent of the market—is, of course, true for market economy. It does *not* mean that the prior existence of market organization is a necessary condition for division of labor to be practiced. Division of labor based on sex seems to be universal.

[9] Max Weber contrasted primitive and archaic economies with the modern by singling out two features of market-organized industrial capitalism as historically unique: that the provision for a wide range of daily material needs is organized through market purchase and sale, and that, "Persons must be present who are not only legally in the position, but are also economically compelled, to sell their labor on the market without restriction" (Weber 1923:276–277).

· section V
THE FORMALIST
COUNTER-REVOLUTION

10 MAXIMIZATION THEORIES AND THE STUDY OF ECONOMIC ANTHROPOLOGY

Robbins Burling

Economics, along with religion, kinship, and all the other subjects that make up the table of contents of innumerable anthropological monographs, has long been confidently felt to include a tolerably well-defined type of human behavior. We manage to communicate with each other when we speak of economic activities, of economic motives, and of economic groups, even when we fail to give these phrases explicit definitions. Nevertheless, "economics" has had almost as many meanings to anthropologists as has "function," and the confusion between its various meanings has led to as much misunderstanding. At one time or another, anthropologists have given at least five meanings to the term: 1) the study of the *material* means to man's existence; 2) the study of the production, distribution, and consumption of goods and services; 3) the study of the things that economists study; 4) the study of systems of exchange however they are organized; and 5) the study of the allocation of scarce means to alternative ends. None of these definitions covers exactly the same area of behavior as any other. In the first half of this paper I will argue that the first definition refers to an area of behavior that is probably better called by a less ambiguous term, while the second is too general to have much meaning. The third turns out to be grossly illogical and ethnocentric. The fourth is perhaps too limited, although it would seem useful for certain purposes, and it is logically unassailable. In the second half of the paper, I will give special attention to the problems and possibilities of the fifth definition.

The Meanings of "Economics"

1) *Economics deals with the material means to man's existence.* Even economists have long claimed to equate the material side of life with economic behavior, so it is hardly surprising to find anthropologists following them. In our discussions, material life has figured in several different ways. Many an older monograph simply took economics to be synonymous with technology and care-

From American Anthropologist *64:802–821. Reprinted by permission.*

fully recorded such interesting data as how sleds are made, or how skins are tanned, under the heading of "economic life." This particular use of the term has pretty well gone out of style and without belaboring a point that has been made entirely adequately by others (e.g., Herskovits 1952:57), I think that it can be assumed that few of us are still likely to confuse economics with technology. Other aspects of material life, however, still regularly crop up in our discussions of economics. We all speak of the Australians as having a "hunting and gathering economy," or of the Bedouin as having a "pastoral economy," and many of us still speak of stages in economic development, or at least of the agricultural revolution, as being in the first instance an "economic revolution." These phrases all imply that economics is equivalent to the study of subsistence methods, an idea not so very far removed from defining it as technology. Economics also has sometimes been used in a slightly broader sense, equivalent to what others have called ecology, or the total way in which the culture is adjusted to its environment. This can include not only the ways in which nourishment can be extracted from the forests, or streams, or soil, but also the way in which feathers for ceremonial headdresses are obtained, or the way in which the environment is reflected in the mythology of the people.

These definitions all hinge upon the notion that economics is somehow concerned with *material* goods and it is this that has caused more confusion between anthropologists and economists than almost anything else. It is true that economists themselves have sometimes defined economics as "the study of the causes of material welfare" or the "study of [human action] connected with the attainment and with the use of material requisites of well being" (Herskovits 1952: 45–46). When they have done so, however, they have had to define "material" in such a broad way that it loses its ordinary meaning of visible tangible artifacts, and some economists have maintained that whether or not a good or service is material has nothing to do with whether it is economic. In a classic essay which deserves to be read by all anthropologists who feel that they have an interest in economics, the British economist Lionel Robbins devastated these materialist definitions (1935). He pointed out that economists regularly deal with many nonmaterial aspects of life. Wages may be paid to people who do material tasks and prices may be applied to material goods, but wages and prices are just as firmly assigned to nonmaterial events as well. The wages earned by an opera singer, and the price of a ticket to hear him perform, have nothing material about them, though they are surely economic. War is actually destructive of material goods, but to wage war successfully, one must certainly economize. But the real point is that we must repeatedly economize *between* material and nonmaterial ends. We must make repeated choices between goals, some of which are material while some are not. We must decide whether added leisure is more important to us than the extra money we could earn by working overtime. Would I rather have a new car or a trip to Europe? It is nonsense to pretend that all of these goals are "material," at least if "material" is intended to have any normal meaning at all, but if these choices are economic choices, and by any conventional use of the term by economists they most assuredly are, then the term economics embraces far more than simply material life. We can hardly speak of some of our goals as being "economic" and others as "noneconomic" if the very choice between the different goals is an economic decision and if we have to economize our resources in attaining our choices. Robbins points out that in a sense it is even possible to say that *none* of our goals are ultimately material. "Income from [even] a material object must in the last resort be conceived as 'immaterial' use. From my house equally as from my valet or the services of the opera singer, I derive an income which 'perishes in the moment of its production' " (Robbins 1935:8).

I am aware of only one attempt in which economists have been involved in recent years to take seriously the notion that the material side of life has any distinctive claim on economic theory. This is in the book *Trade and Market in the Early Empires* by Karl Polanyi and his associates (1957). The authors of the book explicitly reject most of traditional economics, at least as far as its potential applicability to societies other than our own is concerned. Polanyi makes a long needed distinction between economics in the substantive sense of the provision of material goods, and in the formal sense of rationalizing calculation or "economizing" (corresponding roughly to the first and fifth definitions considered in this paper). He seems to believe, however, that in modern Western society the two definitions cover much the same ground. "As long as the economy was controlled by [price-making markets] the formal and the substantive meanings [of 'economic'] would in practice coincide" (Polanyi 1957a:244). If this means that the two definitions cover the same areas of behavior, it is simply untrue, because our market organized economy does embrace many nonmaterial, nonsubstantive items, while on the other hand, as I will take pains to point out in detail later, some material goods are sometimes distributed outside the market system. Even in our own society the material side of life and the market system do not coincide, although they do overlap. Polanyi and his associates are right to distinguish the two definitions of economics and right to emphasize that in primitive societies they may not correspond. I believe that they are wrong to assume that they correspond any better in our society, and I feel that their discussion rather obscures the possibility that primitives may also "economize" (i.e., practice rationalizing calculation), even in the absence of a market. Furthermore, given the choice between the substantive and rationalizing definitions, I think it is unfortunate to use the word economic for the former, in defiance of most customary practice. If one wishes arbitrarily to define economics in this way, it is impossible to call him wrong, but except for Polanyi and his colleagues this is a use of the term which has very little to do with the work of practicing economists. Moreover, for anthropologists it is a terribly arbitrary decision to consider material goods to be economic, but services (which are certainly nonmaterial) to be noneconomic. What happens when one exchanges a material object for a nonmaterial service? Is one half of the transaction to be considered economic and the other noneconomic?

Technology, subsistence, and ecology are all important areas of study, and the real question as far as this paper is concerned is whether we wish to waste the term "economic" on them when other terms are available, and when they leave out so much which we usually feel belongs to "economics." The exchange of ceremonial jewelry, the inheritance of crests, or in our own society the possession of copyrights, are usually considered pretty unambiguously to be economic phenomena, even though they are hardly a part of subsistence activities or the "material side of life." My feeling is that it is better to call technology, subsistence, and ecology by their own terms, and not glorify them by the term "economic" which is better reserved for a broader concept. No doubt we will continue to understand each other when we speak of "economic activities," but if we wish to talk to economists and not just to each other, we had better realize that whether something is material or not is quite irrelevant.[2]

2) *Economics studies the production, distribution, and consumption of goods and services.* This is a widespread definition among anthropologists, and at first blush seems rather harmless. Although I have been emphasizing the attention that Polanyi and his associates give to material goods, they seem in the end to be particularly interested in the mechanics of distribution, though I have been unable to find a place where they come right out and admit this. Polanyi states, for instance, that when facing other societies than modern Western ones, economics must focus upon the "instituted process of interaction between man and his environment, which results in a continuous supply of want satisfying material means" (1957a:248). However, he pays no attention to the technical processes that this definition seems to imply but rather considers the methods by which goods are distributed, and he constructs a typology of distributive systems which he calls respectively "reciprocity," "redistribution," and "exchange."

Many anthropologists have also focused their attention on distribution. If they are interested in the distribution of material objects only, then they run into the kinds of unfortunate complications already referred to, but if they mean seriously to include with economics the distribution of *all* goods and services, whether material or not, then everything that man does fits the definition. We tend to think rather casually of some services as having a primarily political or kinship character, such as arbitrating disputes or teaching children good manners, but they are still services as are all social acts. When economics is defined as the production and distribution of goods and services, one usually has in mind some other implicit meaning of "economic" that makes some services economic and others not. In other words, "economics is the study of the distribution of *economic* goods and services," but this is no definition.[3] Since this definition does not isolate any type of behavior from any other type, it is quite useless unless one wants to say that economics and social organization are synonymous. Since I believe that few anthropologists are ready to say this, this definition had better be abandoned.

3) *Economic anthropology treats in primitive societies those areas of life which economists study in ours.* However uninspiring this definition sounds when

stated bluntly, I am convinced that it is the one which has dominated the thinking of most anthropologists who have tried to deal seriously with economics over the past decade or two. Anthropologists have felt that to talk about technology or subsistence or material culture is not enough, but nobody has really taken seriously the suggestion that the distribution of *all* goods and services should be included within the subject. Somehow it has been felt that we must discover what the economists are doing and then go forth and do likewise. Before we can do this we had better have a clear understanding not only of the economists' formal definition of their subject, which may or may not correspond to what they actually do, but also of their reasons for considering specific topics. It is this which leads me to a reasonably obvious but, among anthropologists at least, only sporadically perceived truth: Whatever formal definitions they may give to their science (and these vary considerably) economists actually study the operation of the price system in our own society and the exchange of priced goods and services through the market system.[4]

It is worth noting that in the introductory sections of their books, when abstract concepts and definitions of the subject are given, economists may give formulations which make no reference to money or markets, but which are set in completely general terms. In an aging but standard introductory text book of economics, Fairchild, Furniss, and Buck (1936: Chapter I) define most of the major concepts of economics without any reference to money at all: "Wealth consists of all useful material things owned by human beings." "Income consists of the benefits or services rendered by wealth or by free persons." "The undesirable events caused by wealth are called the disservices or costs of wealth." "The difference between the income and the cost of any article of wealth is its net income." Property is "the right to income; that is, the right to the benefits or services of wealth or free persons." "The value of anything is the quantity of any other thing that would be given in exchange for the first thing."[5] Once past their initial and formal definitions, however, economists have been perfectly clear about what their subject includes. Knight has declared that in practice the scope of economics is narrow, a situation he feels to be entirely proper. He says

> . . . there are many ways in which economic activity may be socially organized, but the predominant method in modern nations is the price system, or free enterprise. Consequently it is the structure and working of the system of free enterprise which constitutes the principal topic of discussion in a treatise on economics (Knight 1951:6).

Although Robbins, as will be seen below, gives a much broader definition of economics as a whole, even he feels that it is appropriate for economists to concentrate on the operation of "the exchange economy" (our system of markets as dominated by money prices) and recognizes that they have always done so. Robbins says that it is not incorrect to study other kinds of economy, but it is simply not particularly useful (1935:19).

There are, to be sure, good practical reasons for dealing with money and price. For one thing, price allows a form of quantification. One can specify whether price is going up or down, one can compute "total" value, and one can compare various commodities and services by means of the common denominator of dollars or pounds or rubles. As a result, economic discussion is for practical if not theoretical reasons limited to goods and services that are measured in money. But anthropologists ought to realize just how arbitrary the distinction between priced and unpriced commodities is, and how useless it is for their own work. We have not, however, for it is this distinction which makes us feel that a wage earner performs an economic service, while we leave a housewife's labor out of all of our national economic statistics. It is why food served in a restaurant is seen as an economic good, but food served hospitably to friends in one's home is not. It is why the services of a prostitute but not those of a wife are economic. It is why food bought in a store, but not the row of radishes in my back yard, enters into statistics of gross national product. It is what makes the distinction between professional and amateur athletics. Since we, in Western countries normally price food, housing, land, most manufactured products, and most labor outside of the household, we easily fall into the habit of considering these things to be economic in their nature. Since we do not price other goods, and services— hospitality, a housewife's labor, the care of children by their parents, brides, and Christmas presents—they are not considered economic. For certain practical purposes within our own society this is a useful if not theoretically unassailable approach. It does serve some useful purposes to calculate gross national product, and this can only be done by adding up values of things produced, and the only apparent common denominator to which these objects can be reduced is money value or price. Since a housewife's labor is not priced there is no conceivable way to add her labor into the total value of goods and services produced in our society, however uncomfortable we may feel about the logic of the figures that leave her out.

One can even make out a case that this concentration on the price system is not only practically, but even theoretically justifiable. Within our society the particular goods and services which are priced are treated in certain special ways. Money pricing and the operation of the markets gives a unity to a certain segment of our culture and this segment is important and deserves to be studied. But if economics is limited to a study of priced goods, it is an incredible contradiction in terms to speak of primitive economics, when we are dealing with a society without money. *What anthropologists have done, however, is to look upon the type of goods and services that we price and consider these to be economic even in other societies, instead of realizing that it is the phenomenon of pricing itself which gives these particular goods and services their unity.* Labor, manufactured goods, land, and the way in which these are allocated and exchanged are felt to be economic, even though they may no more be priced in some other society than is the labor of nursing an infant. Just because land is priced in our society is no reason to call it economic in another society where it is not priced, and yet land tenure is universally considered to fall within the scope of "economics." Some people, to be sure, price goods or services which we do not. Brides frequently are paid for, but because of our ethnocentric view that brides are not an economic commodity (because we do not happen to price them) anthropologists have resisted the idea that women can be bought and sold and have even suggested that it is somehow nicer to speak of "bride-wealth" than "bride-price."[6] This magic with words does not obscure the fact that in some parts of the world wealth is transferred in exchange for brides. In many places monetary compensation is paid to redress injuries such as theft, adultery, or even murder, though since we do not happen to feel that it is appropriate to price such transactions, we usually feel that they are not "economic."

I believe that it is fair to state that Herskovits, in the most extensive treatment of economic anthropology to date, adheres generally to the idea that anthropological economics is concerned in other societies with the same phenomena that economists deal with in ours (Herskovits 1952). He does recognize that economists concentrate on priced goods and services, but he does not conclude that this makes unreasonable the study of the same kinds of goods and services in other societies. He clearly feels that there is a category of behavior that is reasonably called "economic" and which can become the focus of special study (see for instance pp. 60–61). To judge by the topics with which he deals, this includes land tenure, ownership, trade, division of labor, and credit, even in societies where money is not used to organize them. It is true that he also extends his discussion to such things as gift and ceremonial exchange which we do not price, and to this extent he expands and makes more useful our conception of economics. But Herskovits does not deal with all the goods and services which are exchanged or produced in the society. He does not, for instance, deal with the care of children by their mother, or the services of a political leader and follower toward one another. He would have startled many people had he included these services, for they do not fit into our preconception of what economics embraces, but they are services which are just as much exchanged as are the services of a mutual-help team at harvesting. The only reason for considering the latter and not the former to be economic is that in *our* society we price agricultural labor, while we are not supposed to price political patronage or a mother's care.

It should be apparent that once we deal with any society other than our own, pricing is a totally useless means of distinguishing the economic aspect of society from the noneconomic aspects. If the unity of economics arises out of the fact that it deals with priced goods, then in some primitive societies it is silly to look for any behavior that can be called "economic." It is illogical to argue that other societies use other methods of distribution of these goods (which is, I believe, what Polanyi and associates assert) and that their substitutes for the market mechanism should be studied under the title of economics, if it is the market mechanism and its prices that give the particular goods and services of *our* economy their only unity. It is as if anthropologists from a matrilineal society insisted upon studying the matrilineal groupings of all other societies. One can, after all, isolate those kinsmen who are related to each other along the matriline, even in our own society. It simply happens to be nonsense to do so because we do not assign any duties or responsibilities on the basis of matrilineal descent. The association into a unified system of those goods and services which *we* price is just as arbitrary as the association of people into a matrilineage. It is silly to examine either system where it does not exist.

I was led to reject the "material" definition of economics because it seemed to me that technology, subsistence, and ecology are more conveniently called by some other term than "economic." I reject the definition which states that economics deals with the goods which are priced in our own society on different grounds: it is not a real category in any society but our own. It is, in fact, startlingly ethnocentric.

I believe that it is our felt but unstated knowledge of the areas of our life which are touched upon by our own price system that has made us hope for some unity in what we have called economics. If pricing is what gives unity to economics, perhaps we had better stop using the term at all unless we happen to be studying a society where money is important. Perhaps the most successful "economic" studies by anthropologists have been in areas where money is important—such as in Panajachel studied by Tax, and among the Malay fishermen studied by Firth. But if economics means a concern with the price system, then some societies simply have no economics. This would not offend me, but there are still some alternative uses of the term, which allow it to be applied to a less arbitrary category of culture, which deserve to be examined.

4) *Economics is the study of systems of exchange, whatever the particular institutional arrangements surrounding them may be.* I have pointed out that the justification for the traditional scope of economics in our society is that certain goods and services are united within one system by the common use of money when they are exchanged. Probably every society has some systems of exchange, and certainly we have several quite distinct systems ourselves. Hospitality is returned with considerable responsibility and calculated closely, although without the intermediacy of money. We even use expressions like "owing an invitation" or "working off our debts by throwing a cocktail party." The exchange of gifts and cards at various holidays forms another system. It would be as legitimate, though no doubt less important for conventional objectives, to study the way in which these gifts and countergifts are balanced, calculated, and agreed upon, as to study the transactions of a price-setting market. Once these systems of exchange are noted one can hardly help recognizing systems of exchange in other societies, although they may be quite different from any that we have in our own. Some of these are old stand-bys in the anthropological literature: the kula ring; the system of potlatches in the Northwest Coast; feast-giving, prestige, and power in Melanesia; brides and cattle in Africa.

It must be emphasized that the isolability of these various systems is only partial. It is usually possible to convert goods and services normally exchanged within one system into those of another. We do, of course, use money to purchase goods which we then use in entertaining, so that our market system and our hospitality system are interrelated, but this does not mean that the value of hospitality can be expressed in a money price, as is evident from our relative evaluation of the simple but warm hospitality of our less affluent acquaintances, and the sumptuous ostentation of the wealthy. Bohannan gives an unusually clear example of the partial independence and partial interdependence of three systems of exchange found among the Tiv: 1) subsistence goods consisting of food and various household objects which are exchanged freely with each other but less readily converted into other forms of wealth; 2) prestige goods consisting of iron bars, cattle, and slaves, and 3) women, which before the confusion brought about by the introduction of money constituted an exchange system of their own (Bohannan 1955).

The systematic comparison of different systems of exchange might prove extremely interesting. One could ask such questions as whether similar methods of calculation are used in them all, whether the same principles of rational alloca-tion are present, and to what extent the individual's motives vary. But it should be entirely clear that these systems of exchange do not necessarily include either material goods or money pricing. No one can predict ahead of time what systems will be found in any particular society. By this definition there is not *an* economic system but rather several economic systems in each society, and their character-istics can only be discovered through empirical observation.

Perhaps the definition of economics as the study of systems of exchange leads to the least complex and contradictory results of any of the five definitions sug-gested here, but it is limited. It seems paradoxical to suggest that a single society may have several economic systems. Why not simply call them exchange systems?

One final definition which arises out of certain fundamental principles of theoretical economics remains. This approaches more closely the way in which many economists in their more thoughtful and less practical moments define their subject, and here I return to the formulation of Lionel Robbins.

5) *Economics is the study of the allocation of scarce means to multiple objectives, or more broadly "the science which studies human behavior as a relationship between ends and scarce means which have alternative uses."* (Robbins 1935:16). Many anthropologists who have concerned themselves with economic problems have recently used similar definitions, including Firth in his latest discussion of anthropological economics, and Herskovits.[7] But these authors, after indicating choice, allocation, and "economizing" to be the core of economic behavior, slip back to a consideration of "economizing" among material objects and ends, or only among the objects which *we* include in our market system. It is this mistake that Robbins avoids and it is for this reason that I have found his essay so valuable and so much more satisfying logically than the formulations of most anthropologists who have dealt with these problems.

Robbins points out that there is no economic problem if unlimited means are available for achieving some goal, and furthermore we do not have to economize if something has no alternative use whatsoever. "When time and the means for achieving ends are limited, *and* capable of alternative application, *and* the ends are capable of being distinguished in order of importance, then behavior necessarily assumes the form of choice" (1935:14. Italics in the original). One must choose between scarce means and apply them to the variously valued ends. The unity of economic science, says Robbins, lies in the forms assumed by human behavior in disposing of scarce means.[8] Neither ends nor means can necessarily be measured in monetary terms, and neither need consist of material objects, and so economics defined in this way has no necessary connection with the use of money or material objects. Since we are disposing of scarce means in virtually everything we do, economics in this view focuses on a particular *aspect* of behavior and not on certain kinds of behavior (Robbins 1935:17). The woman organizing her housework, the man allocating his time between his family and his club, the child deciding whether to play baseball or fly a kite, the political leader distributing patronage, and the feast giver who "gives" away food in order to accumulate prestige, are making "economic" decisions whether or not money has anything to do with their choice, and whether or not they are dealing with "material" objects. If Robbins, like other economists, goes on to study those types of behavior in which the economic aspect (choice and allocation) can to a certain extent be measured in money, it is not because of the principles of economics, but because of expedient and supplementary assumptions about what kinds of behavior are more and less important or more easily analyzed. Clearly, in turning to a primitive society, this alternative of restricting ourselves to priced phenomena does not exist. The implications of seizing upon the "economizing" aspect of behavior, as central to the study of economics, are a good deal more far reaching than has sometimes been realized, and my major criticism of both Herskovits and Firth, for instance, in that neither follows out the implications of his own definitions. If all behavior involving allocation is economic, then the relationship of a mother to her baby is just as much an economic one, or rather has just as much of an economic aspect, as the relationship of an employer to his hired laborer. A farmer hoeing his yams is being no more economic than when he is chatting with his cronies in the men's house. The economic aspect of behavior—choice, allocation of scarce means, including time and energy and not just money—is present in all this behavior. From this point of view it is quite hopeless to speak of an institution or group as being economic in nature. All groups have an economic aspect.

It is possible to look upon a society as a collection of choice-making individuals, whose every action involves conscious or unconscious selections among alternative means to alternative ends. The ends are the goals of the individual colored by the values of his society toward which he tries to make his way. They may include prestige, love, leisure, or even money. The means are the technical skills and knowledge at his disposal, including skill at oratory or endurance at the hunt as well as technical knowledge as such. There are no specifically economic techniques or economic goals. It is only the relationship *between* ends and means, the way in which a man manipulates his technical resources to achieve his goals, that is economic.

Now, strictly speaking, given a set of technical skills and knowledge and given a set of scalable ends or values, there is only one best way to use one to reach the other. The economist is not usually interested in either ends or means themselves but rather in the way in which means are manipulated to reach ends, and he is above all interested in working out the most efficient possible way of achieving certain ends, given the means. It is at this point that economists are likely to express their lack of interest in the economics of primitive people, because the most economic procedure for a primitive is presumably no different than it is for anyone, granted of course that both ends and means may be different in another society than in our own. To most economists it hardly matters how the members of any particular society make their choices. If they are inefficient and do not direct their means to rational accomplishment of their ends, why then, so much the worse for the people.

In practice, of course, economists have not worried about the general problem of how all of the varied ends of an individual can be met. They have limited their problem by asking how a particular man, say an entrepreneur, can best accomplish the end of a large money profit—how can money be maximized. This has an air of unreality when applied to a primitive society. People work and try to achieve their goals. They want more food, or more wives, or more prestige, and they clearly work to achieve these aims, but the ends they have in mind are never so simple as those dealt with by economists who speak of high money profit. Of course, the entrepreneur's aims are not really so simple either, but the grossness of the oversimplification becomes inescapable when looking at a primitive society.

Polanyi and his associates recognize that "economics" has often been used in this sense, to refer to situations of choice in areas of limited means.[9] They argue that price setting markets are found only in a limited segment of human history. They seem to conclude that for this reason it is difficult to study choice-making in other societies, but their interests are simply not centered on choice-making. Nevertheless, it may be worthwhile to examine choice-making even in societies where money and price-setting markets are absent. One can hardly argue that "economization," the careful calculation of choices with an eye to one's prospects, is missing simply because the particular institutional framework which helps us to make *some* economizing decisions (the market) is missing. Primitives are presumably neither more or less rational than any of us, although they may use different institutions through which to express their rationality. Of course, the system of market regulated prices cannot be studied in the absence of market regulated prices, but it may still be useful to study rationalizing calculation. Furthermore, certain characteristics of price-regulating markets may be readily seen even in societies very different from our own and in very different institutional settings. Where doweries are substantial or bride-price is required, the amount to be paid may be a matter of careful bargaining. The total bride-price may depend upon the desirability of the girl, either personally or as derived from her family's social status. Instances of curtailment or increase in the amounts of cattle available for bride-price (through disease or otherwise) show that the price also depends upon the supply of cattle. It seems entirely reasonable to suggest that certain characteristics of our marketing system that go under the name of "the law of supply and demand" are applicable in a much broader context than our own markets. This possibility would be obscured if we have to limit the range of meaning of economics to a consideration of material goods, as suggested by Polanyi. If we can get back to the initial assumptions of economists about scarcity of means and unlimited wants we may find that they are still useful assumptions even in the absence of markets and prices.

Here, then, is a final area of behavior to which the term "economic" might apply, the area of choice and allocation of scarce resources to alternative goals. It would study an aspect of behavior, not a type of behavior, and it would be an aspect of behavior that has no more connection with the material aspects of life than with others, and no necessary connection with the objects which are priced in our society. One of the troubles with our understanding of the economics of primitive people has surely been that we have confused the various possible definitions of economics and have persuaded ourselves that allocation of resources was somehow more characteristic of behavior that deals with material goods than with other behavior, or that the use of money coincided with the use of material goods or that only by using money could we rationally economize. It is clear, however, that economizing calculation, material goods, and items exchanged through price-setting markets, each refer to something distinctly different.

Once we focus upon choice and allocation, it becomes apparent that there have been a number of strands of thought in the social sciences that have looked upon human behavior from this essentially economic view. For the rest of this paper I will investigate just one of the implications of regarding human behavior as if governed by an attempt to allocate scarce resources in a rational way. I find it convenient to call this the principle of "maximization," but it is closely related to the idea of "rationalizing calculation."

Maximization Theories

The notion that human behavior is somehow oriented toward a maximization of some desired end has appeared in a great range of social science theory. Maximization is, of course, a fundamental concept in economics, for a central axiom of that discipline is that human wants are unlimited, but that we constantly strive to maximize our satisfactions. More specifically, all of microeconomics, the study of how an entrepreneur or a firm should behave, assumes that he or it is trying to maximize money profit. Such questions as what will happen to profit if price is increased, or how a decrease in production will effect the ratio of income to costs, are at the heart of a great deal of economic theorizing, and they assume that the end in view is to make as much money as possible. Of course we know, and to give them their due I believe that economists know also, that not even entrepreneurs always strive to maximize money profit, but that sometimes they may prefer something else—leisure, conceivably even good human relations— rather than more money. This is not to deny that these entrepreneurs are trying to maximize something, but only states that they sometimes have to choose between money and some other desired end. The assumption that it is money that is being maximized is only a convenient simplification in line with the general attention of economists to those instances of choice and behavior in which money is involved.

Economics, however, is by no means the only branch of social science that has looked upon man as though he were maximizing something. Deeply imbedded in the Freudian conception of the personality lies the pleasure-pain principle. The id, in seeking to reduce tension, operates according to this "pleasure principle" always acting so as to maximize pleasure and minimize pain. The ego, mediating between the id and the outside world, is, to be sure, governed by an occasionally conflicting reality principle and must face the fact that pleasure is not to be achieved directly, but that the route toward satisfaction of the demands made by the id may be roundabout and involve the formulation of plans and complex procedures before final satisfaction is achieved. Freud even speaks of the suspension of the pleasure principle during this finagling toward the end of tension reduction. Finally, however, the goal of the ego is the same as that of the id, and this is the reduction of tension, or more generally the maximization of pleasure.

> Actually the substitution of the reality-principle for the pleasure-principle denotes no dethronement of the pleasure-principle, but only a safeguarding of it. A momentary pleasure, uncertain in its results, is given up, but only in order to gain in the new way an assured pleasure coming later (Freud 1925:18).

This Freudian personality is remarkably similar to the economic man. Both are striving for something, both are planning, both have an end in view, and both are trying by all the means at their disposal to reach the end and to get as much of it as possible. Of course, the ends in sight appear at first glance, at least, to be rather different, maximization of money income, or maximization of pleasure, and the contrast is especially strong when pleasure seems most closely related to sex. But sex is a very broad concept in the Freudian version of the personality, and, as has been said, money income is a convenient simplification so, broadly speaking, both individuals are striving in parallel ways toward parallel if not identical objectives.

Other maximization theories have appeared in the social sciences, though none have become incorporated into such elaborate theoretical systems as these. Part of the conception of society that Leach presents in his book, *Political Systems of Highland Burma*, involves the assumption that men generally seek for power. Leach says:

> . . . I consider it necessary and justifiable to assume that a conscious or unconscious wish to gain power is a very general motive in human affairs. Accordingly I assume that individuals faced with a choice of action will commonly use such choice so as to gain power (Leach 1954:10).

Quoted simply, and out of context, this is unfair to Leach, for immediately preceding this statement he also says, "As a general rule I hold that the social anthropologist is never justified in interpreting action as unambiguously directed toward any one particular end." Nevertheless, for his particular task, namely the analysis of the shifting power relationships of upper Burma, he finds it convenient to suggest that people generally strive to maximize their own power. As he goes on to analyze the situation, the power seeking by many individuals, each using whatever means the social environment offers to him, leads to shifting power relationships in the society as a whole, and this harmonizes with a more general conception of society as being given its dynamism by the multiple striving of all of its members, each seeking his own ends, each using the society where it is convenient, each going against the usual rules of the society where he feels he can get away with it and where it will be worthwhile in terms of his own goals. In fairness to Leach, it must be said that I do not interpret him as presenting power as the main or major motive of all men, and that if he were analyzing some other relationship than that of power he might focus on some other general motive that could be imputed to all men. Taken superficially, however, one might be tempted to raise power to the overriding position that similar exaggerations of money profit in economics, or of the biological urges of the id in psychology, have assumed. Harold Lasswell in his book, *Power and Personality*, considers the pursuit of power from a similar point of view and explicitly compares the interest of political science in the pursuit of power to the interest of economics in the pursuit of wealth. Lasswell, however, does not suggest that the pursuit of power overrides other goals in human behavior, but only that it is this particular pursuit that political science deals with (Lasswell 1948).

All three of these conceptions of human behavior focus on something that seems real, but something that is incomplete. People do not always try to maximize money, or basic biological satisfactions, or power, though all of these certainly do enter into our decisions, and, in a general way, the more we have, the happier we expect to be.

The most explicit theory of maximization which I know of is that of George Zipf, who wrote an incredible book called *Human Behavior and the Principle of Least Effort* (1949). Kluckhohn reviewed this book as being ". . . fertile and suggestive, mad, irrelevant" (1950:270), and indeed it was all of these things. Zipf believed that all of our behavior is oriented toward the minimization of effort. Now, taken literally, and the delight of Zipf's book is that he stated his principles with no leeway for ambiguity, this is nonsense. Athletic events and taking a walk to work up an appetite are hardly understandable within this framework. This among other flights of fancy has lead most people who have stumbled upon his book to reject his principles, even while recognizing the fertile mind which produced them and the remarkable collection of data which he believed would support them. However, even some of his principles may deserve an examination. Like the economist, the Freudian psychologist, or like Leach or Lasswell when they look at political behavior, Zipf assumes that people are trying to orient their behavior, that is, make their choices in such a way that they will obtain the greatest possible amount of something. Zipf recognizes, and in fact he spells out in detail, how a man in trying to minimize effort may be lead a long way around to reach his ultimate goal. It may pay in the long run (in terms of less effort) to stop work and make a new tool because, even though it takes effort to make the tool, the total effort expended may eventually be less when the tool is used. He discusses how various factors may make it more or less desirable to have many specialized tools or a few more generalized ones. He demonstrates with an enormous collection of data that the words we use most frequently are the shortest ones and says that in the long run this means a lesser expenditure of effort in speaking. He also points out that there is a point beyond which the planning to minimize effort is itself more costly of effort than the amount saved, and it is therefore extramarginal. One does best, in terms of saving energy, not to plan beyond that point. Now all this is rather neat, and it is reminiscent of the discussions of economists on how to maximize money income, except, of course, that it is so absurd to set up the minimization of effort as the overriding goal which guides all of our behavior. Perhaps it is no more extreme than the idea that maximization of income, or sex, or power is the main dynamo of human behavior, but the people who have suggested these other motivations have hedged more cautiously than Zipf did. Money income is a convenient simplification to the economist, "pleasure" is a broad enough concept to include all of our motivations, and Leach suggests power only for the particular purposes of a particular analysis. Zipf's mistake was to give himself no loophole, but to maintain that effort minimization was the one and primary motive of all human behavior. His lack of ambiguity, however, even though it may have led him to be rapidly rejected as a somewhat mad genius, allowed a more explicit formulation of the implications of a maximization theory than any of the others, except perhaps for technical economics.

All of these theories are disconcerting for much the same reason: all are too simple. Cleary the things we want are more complicated than expressed by any of these simple motivations. Certainly we are sometimes happy to avoid effort, and we often seek money or power, but these are not always sought after by all people. More significantly, we often have to choose *between* these things. We must decide whether leisure (minimum effort) is more or less important to us at the moment than an increase in money income, or whether power is to be sought after instead of either of these, and it is here that Zipf presents an intriguing argument. He points out that it is quite impossible to maximize two things at once. One might, for instance, offer a prize to the submarine commander who sinks the greatest number of ships in a given interval of time. Alternatively, one might offer the prize to whoever sinks a given number of ships in the shortest possible time: "Yet when we offer a prize to the submarine commander who sinks the *greatest number* of ships in the *shortest possible time*, we have a double superlative—a *maximum* number and a *minimum* time—which renders the problem completely meaningless and indeterminate, as becomes apparent upon reflection" (1949:3). Similarly, one cannot simultaneously try to maximize both sexual satisfaction and the acquisition of money, because there may come a time when there is a choice between the two, and to increase one will at the same time decrease the other. This is precisely the same argument that Robbins used in denying that economics could in principle be restricted to material ends, since one often has to decide between material and nonmaterial objectives. To scale one's ends and distinguish them in the order of importance implies some general standard against which the more specific goals can be measured. This presumably is what economists mean when they speak of achieving satisfactions as the ultimate goal.

Now to say that an individual strives to maximize his satisfactions is to state little more than a truism. Unless satisfactions are expressed in some more concrete form, such as money, they are ill defined and of course may shift from time to time for the same person and also be different for various individuals. All that is really said is that our behavior is goal-oriented and that the various immediate goals are themselves measurable with respect to one another and can be scaled. It certainly does not help us to predict human behavior, since the only way we know what is desired is to watch which choices people make. So, we are faced with a dilemma. If we state that people act so as to maximize something broad enough ("satisfactions") to subsume all our more specific goals, we say very little. If we state that we act so as to maximize one particular goal—power, money income, or whatever we choose, then usually we are incorrect. But the idea of maximization cannot be abandoned since any discussion of purposive or goal-oriented behavior, or any analysis of choice, does imply a maximization theory and we may as well make explicit a common notion in the social sciences, and for that matter in all of our everyday thinking. It does bring us closer to one of the basic postulates of economics.

Economists have assumed that our wants are infinite. This does not mean that any *particular* want is unlimited, and specifically the desire for material goods may conceivably not be unlimited. Western industrialism has increased material goods so greatly that one can at least imagine that the desire for these may eventually be satiated. Some goals, however, have inherent limitations. Power and prestige cannot be multiplied for everybody since the implication of more power or prestige for some people in a society is that others must have less. For every winner in the race for prestige, just as in a running race or football game, there is also a loser. As has long been pointed out, moreover, much of modern purchasing is not based so much on the desire for material objects, anyway, as for the prestige that it is hoped these objects—cars, swimming pools, or filled book cases—will bring. The principle that our wants are unlimited is a statement that is hardly susceptible of proof, but it may be a useful axiom which can be assumed to lie at the base of human behavior and which can bring sense to a good deal of man's actions. Similarly, it seems reasonable to accept the principle that the means of achieving our desires are limited so that we can only manipulate our means so as to satisfy as many of our wants as possible. Interpreted in this way and stripped of their connotation of money profit, these basic postulates of economics may be worth incorporating into a more general theory than that of market analysis.

From this point of view, we are "economizing" in everything we do. We are always trying to maximize our satisfactions somehow, and so we are led back to the notion that economics deals not with a type but rather with an aspect of behavior. This economic view of society becomes one way, or if one prefers, one model for looking at society. It is a model which sees the individuals of a society busily engaged in maximizing their own satisfactions—desire for power, prestige, sex, food, independence, or whatever else they may be, in the context of the opportunities around them, including those offered by their own culture. Since one makes choices partly with an eye to the expected choices of others, it is not unreasonable to view this pursuit of satisfactions as a great and continuing game of strategy. It makes no sense at all for anthropologists to try to limit economics to mean the pursuit of one particular goal.

If we now focus upon the individual who is caught in the web of his society, and who is trying to maximize his satisfactions, we are led to the investigation of his actual behavior in situations of choice. This is the crucial economic question. In the first place, one must allocate his own resources. A woman must allocate her attention between her husband and her children, and for that matter save a bit for her mother. Attention, like money or time, must be economized. Patronage must be allocated among followers. Admiration or prestige must be granted to some people, denied to others. Each person has at his disposal a certain amount of love, of admiration, and of power, as well as of labor or money or energy, and these must all be distributed. It is reasonable to suppose that they are distributed with the intention of maximizing one's own prestige in return for affection or social approval, and it is totally irrelevant whether money or material goods happen to be part of the equation in these various types of exchange, though in a sense we are acting so as to make a profit in all of this exchange behavior. We feel that the prestige gained is worth more than the food we give away, or that the power gained is worth the distribution of patronage, though of course the person with whom we are trading must feel differently, or we could never come to terms. This leads to a conception of social organization as a whole as a system of exchange, a broader concept than that of the particular and limited systems of exchange mentioned earlier.

George Homans not long ago suggested that an exchange model would be a useful one in uniting various lines of social science research:

> . . . [small-group research] would be furthered by our adopting the view that interaction between persons is an exchange of goods, material and non-material. This is one of the oldest theories of social behavior, and one that we still use every day to interpret our own behavior, as when we

say 'I found so-and-so rewarding'; or 'I got a great deal out of him'; or even 'Talking with him took a great deal out of me.' But, perhaps just because it is so obvious, this has been much neglected by social scientists (Homans 1958:597).

Homans goes on to consider several experiments in sociology and even in animal psychology and uses terms such as "cost," "value," and "profit" to describe them and even constructs the formula: Profit = Reward — Cost. He uses these terms in very much the same way that they are defined in the elementary economics textbook referred to earlier (Fairchild, Furniss, and Buck 1936), but Homans realizes that in his experiments as in much of life, these cannot possibly be measured in money. Exchange, like maximization, is certainly close to the heart of economics, and in fact an exchange model of society is remarkably similar to conventional economic analysis, even though it takes into account far more than our primitive notion of economics. It should be possible to speak of the supply of prestige, the demand for power, and the cost of authority. I see no reason why one should not even speak of the marginal utility of loving care. Each man can be regarded as an entrepreneur, manipulating those around him, trading his products of labor, attention, respect, etc., for the most he can get in return.

The trouble with this is, of course, that there seems too little prospect for quantification. The contrasting beauty, perhaps a spurious beauty, of traditional economics is that one can assign figures to the commodities and services that are exchanged, because they have prices, and one can then manipulate the figures. But unless the anthropologist uses concepts of economics, cost, value, demand, supply, etc. in a much broader context than is the custom of the economist, over a range of meaning far wider than that which is priced, he had better stop talking about economics.

The view of society as a system of exchange, and the view that men act so as to attempt to maximize satisfactions, are fundamentally economic ones and are close to the way in which economists look upon their subject matter. However, unlike anthropologists, economists have not ordinarily been interested in finding out *whether* people economize intelligently, but only in figuring out *how* they can economize more intelligently. This difference in objectives creates an almost unbridgeable gap between economics and anthropology, because an anthropologist is always most interested in the actual behavior of men in concrete situations. I think, however, that a clear conception of this broader "economic" or "exchange" view of society might, if followed out consistently, be of interest even to the economist. The problems that have to be wrestled with in describing a society in this manner make themselves known most insistently where money value is not used as a means of measurement. Once this problem is clearly faced, it is obvious that the same problem exists in our own society. There are many things which we do not price, and our behavior can never be understood if we focus only on those limited types of behavior which are priced. We must constantly choose between monetary and nonmonetary goals. Even if an economist is interested only in advising people how they ought to behave if they want to maximize their satisfactions (and not just their money income), he will have to take nonmonetary goals into account. From this point of view I think that anthropology could play its time-honored role of broadening the viewpoint of others and making even our own society more understandable, because of the attention it has directed towards differing cultures. Of course, we will have to get economists to listen to us first, but we cannot possibly expect economists to listen to us until we get some clear idea of what economic science is trying to achieve, and of what "economic" means. As long as we stumble along with the extraordinarily ethnocentric notion that somehow economics is primarily connected with food production, or with material culture or land tenure, or certain restricted types of labor, then we are missing any opportunity for fruitful communication with our economist colleagues.

NOTES

[1] This paper is the product of several frustrating attempts to teach a course with the title "Primitive Economics" and to decide what in the world that meant. My students deserve my thanks and apologies for letting me try out various ideas on them. I am also indebted to Edward B. Harper of Bryn Mawr College for suggestions and criticisms.

[2] For a discussion by an economist of the anthropological misinterpretation of "economies" and "subsistence," see Knight's review of Herskovits' *The Economic Life of Primitive Peoples*, reprinted in *Economic Anthropology*, especially pages 520–521 (Knight 1952).

[3] This absurd phrasing hardly exaggerates the position of some workers. Dalton says, "Few economic transactions [in Western market economy] take place without the use of money." If a transaction is economic because it involves money, then this is a glorious tautology. If "economic" is given some other meaning then the statement is untrue (Dalton 1961:13). A somewhat related statement is that of Polanyi: "Only in the presence of a system of price-making markets will exchange acts of individuals result in fluctuating prices that integrate the economy" (1957b: 252). But a price-making market is *defined* as an institutional arrangement in which the exchange acts of individuals result in fluctuating prices that integrate the market. It is wonderful to discover definitions.

[4] This point was clearly made by Dalton, although he emphasized the market exchange economy and somewhat minimized the place of money. He says: "The term money economy emphasizes a derivative rather than the dominant feature of Western economic structure. The use of all-purpose money is not an independent trait, but rather a requirement for the functioning of a market exchange economy" (Dalton 1961:15). I am not certain that I understand these sentences completely. They seem to say that money is both a prerequisite to, and a derivative of the market, but the point is surely that whenever we price goods in our society we speak of there being a market for these goods (or services). The two concepts are almost synonymous, and rather than focus on the somewhat abstract idea of the market, one may as well recognize that priced goods have formed the core of the materials which economists study.

It should also be pointed out that the phrase "all-purpose money" is an unfortunate one, and that there are plenty of things in our society (wives, hospitality) that cannot be purchased with money, and that we do not ordinarily price. As a result there is no market for these items. Our money is not "all-purpose" by any means.

[5] Only when these terms are defined does money finally come in and the authors state that ". . . value is almost always expressed in terms of money" (1936:23). This final statement is nonsense if the earlier definitions are taken seriously (are the value of wives, Christmas presents, or political patronage expressed in money?) for the earlier definitions are so general that they can be interpreted as applying to all aspects of social behavior.

[6] This foolishness was neatly disposed of by Robert F. Gray in a recent article which showed how impossible it is to avoid calling this a purchase (1960).

[7] The first words of Herskovits' first chapter are: "The elements of scarcity and choice are the outstanding factors in human experience that give economic science its reason for being" (1952:3). Similarly, Firth states: "[A modern economic anthropologist] examines the ways in which [the people he studies] conceive of and express their wants and dispose of their available resources in a given social milieu" (1959:25).

[8] Dalton also recognizes this to be one of the significant definitions that has been given to "economics" and he presents it in very much the same way. Unfortunately, after sensibly pointing out that economizing calculation is not limited to the creation and distribution of material goods, he goes on to say that economists deal with economizing calculation with respect to material goods and thereby seriously distorts the work of economists. Incredibly, after a short paragraph in which he uses the word "material" no less than four times in an attempt to define what Western economic analysis is all about, he gives a reference to Robbins' essay, although one of the major points that Robbins had to make was that economic analysis has no necessary connection with material goods (Dalton 1961:7).

[9] The core of Polanyi's theory is found in Chapter XIII of the book, which was written by Polanyi himself (Polanyi et al. 1957).

11 ECONOMIC THEORY AND ECONOMIC ANTHROPOLOGY
Edward E. LeClair, Jr.

Exactly 40 years ago, Bronislaw Malinowski published the book which was to have a powerful influence on the study of the economies of "primitive" peoples (Malinowski 1922). The influence was mixed. Malinowski did succeed in calling the attention of anthropologists to the fact that a consideration of the economic activities of nonliterate peoples required the consideration of much beyond their technologies. But his disdainful comments on what he conceived to be then contemporary economic thinking convinced many anthropologists that they had little to learn from conventional economics.

Nearly 20 years later, Raymond Firth and Melville J. Herskovits inde-

From American Anthropologist *64:1179–1203. Reprinted by permission.*

pendently sought to establish the respectability of economic theory in the eyes of anthropologists (Firth 1939; Herskovits 1940, 1952). Their view, which Firth sought to demonstrate with his materials from Polynesia, and which Herskovits sought to demonstrate with materials culled from a massive body of ethnographic material, was succinctly stated by Herskovits in the following terms:

> Considerations of sound analysis dictate that no comparison between our own and other economies be attempted without full realization of the effect on the main lines of economic development and the shaping of economic institutions exerted by the presence of a machine technology, the invasion of the evaluation process by pecuniary considerations, and the high development of business enterprise.
>
> Yet, practically every economic mechanism and institution known to us is found somewhere in the nonliterate world. . . .
>
> The distinctions to be drawn between literate and nonliterate economies are consequently those of degree rather than of kind (1952:487–88).

Although the point is difficult to demonstrate, it seems clear that ethnographic work in the last 20 years has been heavily influenced by this point of view. A handful of major economic studies (see Belshaw 1955, Foster 1942, and Tax 1953, for example), plus a number of shorter papers, reveal the impact of this position. But the full weight of the approach manifests itself in more subtle ways: in the altered organization, the new interpretation or phrasing, or the shift of emphasis that is to be found scattered through the ethnographic literature of the last 20 years.

In the last few years it has become apparent that a systematic reexamination of the position expressed by Herskovits was necessary. The postwar interest in the problem of economic development of under-developed areas has posed a number of new questions for research to answer. In addition, the insights gained in the past 20 years provide the material which is needed to make such a reexamination fruitful.

The results of such a reexamination could take us in one of two directions, one evolutionary and one revolutionary, or, more properly, counter-revolutionary.

An evolutionary development would leave the basic position unchallenged. Changes would involve a refinement of concepts and further development of analytical techniques. A revolutionary development would involve the substitution of a new basic premise.

In a recent paper, George Dalton has stated the revolutionary case (Dalton 1961).[1] In this paper, I propose to offer a rebuttal to Dalton's case, then to offer the case for an evolutionary development.

Critique of Dalton's Position

Dalton's basic point is that there are ". . . important differences between primitive market economy and Western market industrialism which makes formal economic theory incapable of yielding analytical insights when applied to primitive structures" (pp. 19–20). And, "Primitive economy is different from market industrialism not in degree but in kind" (p. 20).

Entirely apart from the fact that Herskovits has expressed an apparently well-founded contrary view, a judgment as sweeping as this is *prima facie* suspect. Nowhere does Dalton explicitly define the terms: "primitive market economy," "primitive structures," or "primitive economy." They are implicitly defined as non-Western, nonmarket, and nonindustrial. Whatever the definition, Dalton's assertion requires that these economies be assumed to have a high degree of similarity and unity in respect to those characteristics which are important for this issue. The weight of ethnographic evidence strongly suggests that such an assumption is not warranted. (See Tax and Mednick 1960.)

The foregoing questions only the extent to which Dalton's generalization is valid. It is also necessary to consider whether the generalization has any validity at all, and, if so, the conditions under which it may be valid. In order to examine this question, we must turn to the line of reasoning which Dalton offers in support of his generalization.

Space does not permit a point-by-point consideration of Dalton's argument. However, the core of the argument turns on a single fundamental issue: the nature and scope of economics—and by extension, of economic anthropology as well. In addition, several minor points require comment.

On the Nature and Scope of Economics

Throughout his discussion, Dalton equates "economic" (in one sense of the term) with "material." Thus, we are told: "Especially significant in the work of the classicists was the delineation of purely 'economic' motivation (material self gain) as both necessary and sufficient to induce laborers to conform to market needs" (p. 3).

Then, in discussing "two meanings of economic," the substantive and the formal, Dalton paraphrases Polanyi's definition as follows: "In the substantive sense, economic refers to the provision of material goods which satisfy biological and social wants" (p. 5).

Polanyi's own statement of the distinction is worth quoting in full:

> The substantive meaning of economic derives from man's dependence for his livelihood upon nature and his fellows. It refers to the interaction with his natural environment, insofar as this results in supplying him with the means of material want satisfaction.
>
> The formal meaning of economic derives from the logical character of the means-ends relationship, as apparent in such words as "economical" or "economizing." It refers to a definite situation of choice, namely, that between the different uses of means induced by an insufficiency of the means. If we call the rules governing choice of means the logic of rational action, then we may denote this variant of logic, with an improvised term, as formal economics.
>
> The two root meanings of economic, the substantive and the formal,

have nothing in common. The latter derives from logic, the former from fact (Polanyi, 1953, as reprinted in Fried 1959:162).

Whatever may have been the view of classical (19th century) economists, contemporary economists have long since adopted a broader view of the nature of human wants. Consider the following: ". . . there is a loose sense of the word utilitarian, implying a prosaic attachment to material ends, which has passed into common English" (Brinton 1948:197).

George Stigler has outlined the main assumptions underlying contemporary economic theory in the following terms:

> *First*, it is assumed that individuals (or, more properly, the heads of family units) have specific and complete information concerning the things they desire. By things we mean general ends of activity, such as the satisfaction of hunger and the attainment of prestige . . .
>
> *Second*, it is assumed that consumers know the technical means by which these general ends may be attained. More specifically, we are to know of the effects of pork chops on hunger and physical efficiency, and of a new car on our neighborhood position.
>
> *Third*, it is assumed that consumers utilize their information in such a way as to maximize the attainment of the ends they desire. This assumption is known, somewhat notoriously, as the concept of an "economic man." . . . The concept of an "economic man" does not imply (as almost all of its critics state) that the individual seeks to maximize money or wealth, that the human soul is a complex cash register. It does not affect the formal theory . . . in the least whether the individual maximizes wealth, religious piety, the annihilation of crooners or his waistline (1946:63–64).[2]

Other economists have made the same point in a variety of ways. Machlup, for example, insists that the fact "That a business man is motivated by considerations other than the maximization of money profits does not necessarily make his conduct 'uneconomic' " (1946:526).[3]

In short, economists no longer believe, if they ever did, that human wants are confined, in market societies, to material wants, nor do they *assume* this to be true of any society. Nor is an assumption of the materialistic nature of human wants a necessary element in contemporary economic theory.

The issue posed by these two differing views of economics—and "economic" —concerns the scope of economics, although neither Polanyi nor Dalton phrases the issue in these terms. In short, we may ask why there is a "felt need" for a substantive definition of economics.

As stated, Stigler's propositions do not imply or require that "economizing calculation . . . be confined to the creation, distribution, or use of material goods" (Dalton p. 7). Therefore, there may be problems of economizing with respect to, let us say, authority, or prestige, or religious merit; "goods and services" may include the services of the ritual specialist, the political specialist, or the esthetic specialist; in short, the purview of economics may extend to all human wants, rather than merely to material wants. If so, economics would seem to be a general social science concerned with the totality of social life.

This conclusion makes most social scientists acutely uncomfortable. It seems to deprive noneconomists of the integrity of their disciplines, and it appears to impose upon economists responsibilities which they are not prepared to accept. From a practical point of view, it is an entirely unreliable guide to what economists actually do or may do.

The latter point suggests that a substantive definition of economics is desirable. But we must first note that the imperialistic implications of the formal concept are more apparent than real. To suggest that economics may logically concern itself with all of social life does not imply that economics can satisfactorily *explain* all of social life. Certainly, no logical basis for such a view can be established.

But, if an economist, regarded as a specialist in the study of the economizing process, can offer useful or valid insights into the allocation of authority, there would seem to be no good reason why he should not be expected to do so. By the same token, if the political scientist can offer useful and valid insights into the operation of business firms by studying the mobilization, validation, and application of authority, again there is not good reason why he should not be expected to do so. If the notion of interdisciplinary research in the social sciences has any meaning, surely it means precisely this: that representatives of two or more disciplines, observing phenomena from different points of view, or employing different frames of reference, join forces to explain that which no one of them can adequately explain by himself.

We have already quoted Polanyi's substantive definition. Later he says: "The empirical economy . . . can be briefly . . . defined as an institutionalized process of interaction between man and his environment, which secures him material want satisfaction" (Polanyi, 1953, as reprinted in Fried 1959:166).

The use of the word "material" in these statements either restricts the scope of the concept unduly, or it is meaningless. Polanyi defines want satisfaction as "material" "if it directly or indirectly involves the use of material means to satisfy ends" (loc. cit.). By this definition, the following situations or activities are examples of "material want satisfaction": a performance of the New York Philharmonic—the instruments; a Kwakiutl potlatch—the coppers and blankets; gaining religious merit in Burma—a gift of grain to a Buddhist priest; gaining prestige in East Africa—building up a large herd of cattle: "the expression of a loving mother's devotion"—feeding the child; a funeral in Dahomey—goods are buried with the deceased; a wedding in North India—the bride brings a dowry to her husband's family; an assignation among the Siriono—the male gives the female some meat; the Kula ring activities—canoes, armbands, bracelets, etc.

All of the foregoing, and the list could be expanded almost without end, suggests that the use of the term "material" in the various definitions is meaningless, since it fails significantly to restrict the range of phenomena admitted as "economic."

Dalton's statement of the substantive concept appears more restrictive, since it "refers to the provision of material goods which satisfy . . . wants" (p. 5). Thus the "provision" of musical instruments would come within the purview of substantive economics, but their use in a performance would not. More generally, this implies that substantive economics includes only the fabrication, collecting, transport, storage, or other manipulation of material things, where the objective is to make them available for use for whatever purpose. Interpreted literally, this would exclude from the purview of substantive economics the whole realm of services: personal services of all kinds and most of the professions. All of these things become the occasion for market transactions. On these grounds alone, this interpretation is too restrictive.

If these definitions of the "substance" of economics do not serve, what will?

I have long since abandoned efforts to formulate a definition of the actual scope of economics which is both accurate and succinct. My best approximation is the question-begging statement that "economics is what economists do." Less accurate but more informative is the proposition that economists concern themselves largely with economizing as a social process and with those organizations, institutions, and groups which have specialized functions in relation to that process. In practice, this has meant a primary concern with market institutions together with other things to the extent that they have an influence on the market. Further accuracy of definition can be secured only by abandoning any effort at succinctness. However, an appreciation of many of the nuances of the foregoing can be secured by skimming any standard introductory economics texts.

It is essential to recognize the *ad hoc* character of any definition of this sort. In particular, a definition of this kind cannot become the basis for deductions concerning either the nature of economic systems or of the scope of the discipline.

The natural history of any discipline involves steady expansion of its scope, and it is at the frontiers of a discipline that a definition of this kind becomes least adequate. And while I prefer to regard economic anthropology as a sub-discipline of anthropology, it can equally well be regarded as a frontier sub-discipline of economics, one which must explore for itself, and *de novo*, its own proper scope.

The Meaning of Scarcity

Part of Dalton's case for the inapplicability of economic theory to primitive societies turns on the concept of scarcity.

The concept of scarcity is a central one in contemporary economics, for it is possible, if not customary, to define economics as the study of the consequences of scarcity, and of man's individual and social efforts to adjust to the fact of scarcity. Samuelson points out that if there were "no *economic goods*, *i.e.*, no goods that are relatively scarce . . . there would hardly be any need for a study of economics, of 'economizing' " (1958:17). "Scarcity," as economists use the term, means simply that goods are not freely available—all economic goods are scarce by definition.

Dalton argues as follows: "If man's material wants are insatiable, then scarcity of enabling means exists by definition . . . [But this] obtains only in a society which places great value of material acquisition relative to other goal attainments, and whose institutional structure impels its members to behave accordingly. . . . It is not so . . . that the postulates of scarcity and economizing calculation are of universal relevance" (p. 5). The foregoing implies that there is no scarcity of the means which are appropriate to "other goal attainments." But Dalton does not specify what "other goal attainments" he has in mind, nor the means which may be appropriate to them, nor does he identify any particular society in which the postulates of scarcity and economizing calculation are irrelevant. Consequently, the basis for his statement cannot be evaluated.

The economists' concept of marginal utility gives precision to the concept of scarcity. If a "good"—and the term is defined to include anything, whether tangible or intangible, which may satisfy a human want—is available in sufficient quantity that its marginal utility is zero, then that good may be said not to be scarce. If such a good is available in such quantities without the expenditure of resources, then it is a "free good." Of the goods which are not free, their scarcity or nonscarcity depends on the availability of the resources necessary to produce them, on the productivity of those resources, and on the desires or wants for the goods as reflected in the marginal utility schedules.

There is a great deal of evidence which suggests that the "wants" for some goods, notably the tangible goods which give sustenance, are expandable only to a limited degree. (Hence the proposition that the "demand" for agricultural goods is inelastic.) But there is a great deal of additional evidence to suggest that other wants are capable of expansion and elaboration without limit. The flowering of culture which seems more or less inevitably to accompany a basic solution to the food-producing problem in any society represents the most general kind of support for this proposition.

The general pattern of needs and wants, including relative priorities, can be inferred for any society by examining the allocation of resources, although the inference cannot be drawn in as straightforward a manner as might be supposed. It takes no more than a superficial examination of a number of such patterns to realize that the elaborations over the physiological needs include both "material" and "nonmaterial" wants in all societies. What also becomes apparent is that all needs-wants are mutually competitive, in that there is at least one category of means which is common to all. That category is human energy—what the economist refers to as "labor."

Thus we may restate the postulate of the universality of scarcity in the following terms: that men everywhere are confronted with the fact that their aspirations exceed their capabilities. This being the case, they must everywhere economize their capabilities in the interest of meeting their aspirations to the fullest extent possible.

Despite the foregoing, it must be recognized that there may be societies in which there is no scarcity, as the term has been defined here. If such societies exist, there will be no need for economizing, and a study of the "economy" will consist of a study of the technology plus a study of what we may call the sociology of production.

Markets and Market Places

Dalton makes two points on the subject of markets which require comment. One is in connection with the "materialistic" character of "economic," the other concerns markets themselves.

On the first, Dalton says: "What should be emphasized is that it is market organization which compels its participants to seek material self-gain: each must sell something of market value to acquire the material means of existence (p. 2).

Market organization is a particular kind of organization the purpose of which is to facilitate a particular kind of social interaction, namely, the exchange of goods and services. As such, it compels nothing beyond an adherence to its own rules and conventions. One of the conventions in most markets (but not all) is that transactions be made in terms of some medium of exchange (money). This means that anyone who wishes to offer something for sale in the market must expect to receive money for it, whether it is a bushel of wheat, a year's services as a college professor, or a book manuscript. By the same token, if you wish to purchase something in the market, you must expect to offer money for it whether it is a ticket to a concert, a dozen eggs, or a session with a psychoanalyst. It is also true, and inherent in the nature of the market organization, that the principal or only way that most people can secure the money necessary to buy things is to sell something first. The only other ways to get money are to receive it as a gift or a loan, with the latter simply begging the issue, or to steal it.

It is rather unfortunate that money income has come rather loosely to be regarded as "material self gain," regardless of what it may be spent for.

Dalton's second point on markets deals with their character. In attempting to show that apparently similar mechanisms which occur in both Western and primitive societies are actually different, Dalton asserts: ". . . in economic anthropology the term 'market' always is used to mean 'market place': an actual site wherein goods change hands by purchase and sale. . . . In Western economy, the term market is applied not only to specific market place sites . . . but also to the diffusive economic forces of market exchange . . ." (p. 14).

The first part of the foregoing statement is true, the second part is rather badly stated. Many economics texts fail to give a concise definition of the term "market." Those that do emphasize, in one way or another, its interactional aspect. The following are representative: "A market is usually defined as a group of buyers and sellers actively trading in a more or less homogeneous commodity" (Evans 1950:245). Or, " 'The market,' as we use the term, is a set of pressures exerted by actual or potential buyers and sellers for a total of related transactions" Harriss 1959:36–37).

It is clear that a distinction must be made between a "market," as defined above, and a "market place." We may then speak of a market as being "site-confined" or "site-free." In the first case, it is necessary for the buyers and sellers to be physically present in a particular place to "exert pressure" on the price. In the second case, this necessity does not arise, although a market place may exist in which most or all actual transactions do take place. Most markets in the United States are "site-free," although some markets may not be.

Dalton appears to infer, from anthropological use, that all "primitive" markets are site-confined. Although few anthropologists have considered markets with the foregoing distinction in mind, it is clear that many "primitive" markets are not site-confined, and I suspect that many which appear to be are not.

Three examples may establish the point:

1) The markets in and around Panajachel, Guatemala. Tax is at great pains to demonstrate how and to what extent the Indians of Panajachel keep themselves posted on price variations in and around their village and act accordingly (Tax 1953:13–19).

2) The wholesale-retail produce markets around Abomey, Dahomey. The market women know what prices must be paid at different wholesale farms, the farmers in turn keep themselves informed concerning the retail prices in the market and act accordingly (Herskovits 1938:I:56–62).

3) The "market" for armbands and necklaces which constitute the Kula Ring. Although any particular transaction is a matter of bilateral bargaining between a pair of trading partners, each one has a series of alternatives in mind, as well as detailed knowledge about the past history of transactions surrounding each item (Malinowski 1922:passim).

On Economists and Anthropologists

Dalton asserts that ". . . the difference in economic organization and processes between [primitive and Western economic systems] are more important than the similarities, especially so on matters of interest to the anthropologist" (p. 10). Then, after discussing the interests of anthropologists at some length, Dalton sums up with the assertion that "Economists are not concerned with technology, social institutions, or physical environment" (p. 11). This is in contrast to anthropologists, who are interested not only in these but in many other things as well. Having made this judgment, Dalton immediately qualifies it: "Technology, physical environment, and social institutions are of interest only in special instances: when they affect the economic variables in which the economist is interested" (p. 11). And, "On the rare occasion when the economist considers kinship, religion, or government, he does so only for a special purpose: when they have significant impact on economic quantities . . ." (p. 11).

Several points must be made concerning these arguments:

1) There should be nothing surprising in the discovery that economists and anthropologists have different interests.

2) If there is any difference in the interests of economists and economic anthropologists—regarded as a special branch of anthropology—it lies in the fact that the economist focuses his attention on Western society, the economic anthropologist on non-Western society. Both are presumably interested, by definition, in the structures and functioning of economic systems.

3) There is nothing surprising in the notion that economists are interested in technology, physical environment, social institutions—or anything else— only to the extent that they constitute significant variables in the economic process. It is standard scientific practice to consider only those variables which are believed to be relevant to the matter under study. Economic anthropologists are—or should be—subject to the same rules. That they should be is sometimes obscured by two facts: a) economic anthropologists are always general anthropologists as well; b) as general anthropologists, they have an interest in the interrelation between the economic systems and the other subsystems in the total socio-cultural system, an interest few economists share.

4) If there is a difference between the economic anthropologist and the economist in these matters, it lies in the economists' willingness (possibly excessive) to assume the irrelevance of "noneconomic" variables and in the economic anthropologists' willingness (possibly excessive) to assume that practically everything is relevant.

Concluding Remarks on Dalton

Several more general points and a number of additional specific criticisms could be made of Dalton's paper and the views it reflects. Generally, while rightly calling attention to the danger of allowing superficial similarities to mask fundamental differences, Dalton commits what I regard to be a more grievous error: allowing superficial differences to mask fundamental similarities.

Toward a New Approach to Economic Anthropology

Earlier in this paper, it was argued that an evolutionary development of economic anthropology now seems possible. Raymond Firth has outlined the objectives of such a development in the following terms: ". . . what is required from primitive economics is the analysis of material from uncivilized communities in such a way that it will be directly comparable with the material of modern economics, matching assumption with assumption and so allowing generalizations to be ultimately framed which will subsume the phenomena of both civilized and uncivilized, price and nonprice communities into a body of principles about human behavior which will be truly universal" (1939:29). Fulfillment of such an objective requires something more than the application of conventional concepts to unconventional situations. What is required instead is a search for the general theory of economic process and structure of which contemporary economic theory is but a special case.

At the present time, the existence of such a general theory can only be postulated. Nevertheless, there are good grounds for doing so. While the ethnographic literature is a record of the diversity of human experience, it also provides witness to the existence of characteristically human problems met in characteristically human ways. Were this not so, scientific anthropology could not exist as a generalizing discipline.

If such a general theory exists, it must underlie and be implicit in the special case. Accordingly, the search for such a theory logically can, and practically should, begin with the available special case. But it must be recognized that: 1) the general case may be obscurely buried in the specific details of the special case; 2) any tentative formulation of the general theory based entirely upon the single special case must be suspect until verified by other materials. In practice, such verification must accompany the formulation of the general case. Finally, the formulation of the general case will: 1) assist in the formulation of the large number of special cases which must be formulated to cover the varied economies to be found in the real world, and 2) permit controlled and systematic comparisons among all the special cases, including that of the Western market economy.

It would be premature to attempt to give even a tentative outline of a general theory of economic process. The following is intended to indicate what appears to me to be a promising approach to the problem of formulating such a general theory.[4] Some of the bases for the approach to be offered have already been indicated in the discussion of Dalton's paper. In order to insure consistency and clarity, the essential points will be repeated. In what follows, key propositions will be italicized; explanation and discussion will not be.

Some Basic Concepts and Definitions

Economics is the study of economizing.

Economizing is the allocation of scarce resources among alternative ends.

This proposition contains a redundancy the nature of which is indicated in the following proposition.

Resources subject to allocation are scarce by definition; resources are not scarce if they exist in such abundance as not to require allocation.

What constitutes a suitable operational definition of "subject to allocation" will vary from circumstance to circumstance. No effort to consider the possibilities will be made here.

"Wants" are defined as anything which human beings may desire or need.

The "ends" among which resources may be allocated are defined as the satisfaction of the various wants human beings may have.

One end is an alternative to another only in relation to the resources which may be used to satisfy them: they are alternatives when one or more of the resources which may be employed to satisfy one may also be used to satisfy the other.

It may be noted that the fundamental human resource is human energy. I find it difficult to imagine any human want being satisfied without the expenditure of human energy. However, this does not warrant the assumption, although it does create the expectation, that there are no human situations in which the necessity for economizing is totally absent.

"Goods" or "goods and services" include anything (but not merely any "thing") which may be used to satisfy a human want. Such "goods" may be either tangible or intangible.

"Production" is any activity which utilizes resources for the purpose of creating or providing goods, or making them available, where such activity is a necessary or desirable condition of availability. Production includes any and all activity which has this purpose or result.

Goods were defined first, and production was defined in terms of goods. It does not involve any circularity at this point to define goods in relation to production. This becomes useful and necessary because some *things* are produced which are not used directly to satisfy human wants. Rather, they are used as an adjunct to production activity. Hence, the following definition is necessary:

"Goods" which are not used directly to satisfy human wants, but are used as an adjunct to production activity, shall be referred to as "capital goods."[5]

Capital goods cannot be defined in terms of the properties of goods themselves, but rather in terms of the manner of their use. A particular thing may at some times be used as a capital good, at other times, it may be used directly to satisfy a human want.

"Consumption" is the direct utilization of a good in the satisfaction of human wants. Consumption is also an activity.

Consumption activities may be inseparable from production activities in some circumstances. Thus, to cite a trivial case, a man picking berries and eating them as he picks them is engaging in an activity which is simultaneously production and consumption. While it would be fruitless to attempt to distinguish that part of the activity which peculiarly constitutes production from that part which peculiarly constitutes consumption, the conceptual distinction is best retained. A rather different and less trivial case is illustrated by the public performance of a symphony by an orchestra. Here, the production activity and the associated consumption activity are quite distinct, but they must occur simultaneously.

A number of additional propositions could be advanced, propositions which would amplify or clarify those already made. Much more could be said in explanation, or to show the practical or operating significance of these concepts. However, we must turn to another aspect of the problem.

Economizing as a Social Process

All of the propositions advanced so far could apply to the economists' favorite hermit: Robinson Crusoe. However, hermitry is an exceptional state of affairs for human beings, and, while we may wish, from time to time, to consider economizing in its individual aspects, we will ordinarily be more concerned with economizing as it involves groups of people. For the time being, at least, we will consider economizing as a "social" process only inasmuch as it may involve human interaction of one sort or another. We shall see presently that, in fact, economizing may be a social process in a much more fundamental sense.

It is customary to speak of "economic *systems*." In accordance with previous definitions, such systems have as their function the provision of orderly procedures for resolving economizing problems which are social, at least in the sense mentioned above. The approach to the study of economic systems to be proposed here grows out of the consideration of two questions: 1) the implications of the notion that we are dealing with an economic *system*; 2) what are the detailed functions of an economic system.[6]

The idea that any society has an economic *system* implies that the organizations, institutions, practices, and beliefs of the society which are concerned with economic processes are something more than an unstructured aggregate. To postulate the existence of a system is to postulate first that a number of identifiable entities stand in some structural relationship to each other. If the system is a dynamic or operating one, it also implies that the parts interact dynamically to yield a "systemic" outcome. The understanding of a dynamic system requires an understanding of the structural articulation of the components of the system; it also requires an understanding of how the component events of the dynamic process articulate to produce the systemic outcome.

It follows from earlier propositions that the general function of an economic system is to provide an orderly mechanism for "social economizing." It is now useful to consider whether this general function may be resolved into a series of interrelated specific functions—to determine what social economizing problems exist. While there is no unanimity among economists concerning the specific functions of economic systems, there is fairly general agreement on three of them, and these may be used as the basis for further discussion. The three are as follows:[7]

1) To determine what goods are to be produced and in what relative quantities. This is the problem of *the product mix*.

2) To determine how these goods shall be produced—where the issue concerns the relative proportions of the "factors of production" (land, labor, and capital). This is the problem of *factor proportions*.

3) To determine how the total output of goods and services shall be shared among the members of the society. This is the problem of *distribution of product.*[8]

Once the functions of a dynamic system are defined, it becomes possible to make useful statements about the specific objectives of any intended analysis. In this case, it is clear that the systemic outcome would be expressed as statements concerning the identity and quantities of goods produced, the manner in which they are produced, and how they are shared among the

members of the society: e.g., what each individual's "income" is. Such statements can be made from a number of points of view, most of which are
mutually complementary. Space does not permit an exploration of the possibilities.

Components of an Economic System

The components of an economic system are individuals or groups of individuals when such groups are organized in some way. They fall into two clearly
definable classes: production units on the one hand, and consumption or
income-pooling units on the other.

A *"production unit" is any individual or group of individuals engaged in or
organized for the purpose of engaging in productive activity.*

A production unit may consist of a single individual, or of thousands of
individuals standing in an elaborate organizational relationship with each
other—as for example in the case of a large American corporation. Production
units may differ in a number of dimensions besides size, including the following: basis for recruitment of members, whether its productive functions are
generalized or specialized, whether it has functions other than productive
functions, its degree of permanence, and its internal organization.[9] The term
"production unit" as used here is roughly analogous to the economists' term
"business firm." More properly, a "business firm" is a particular institutional
form that a production unit may take. While production units may differ
within wide limits with respect to a number of variables, differences among
such units within a particular system may be confined to a smaller number of
variables and to a narrower range of limits. In short, we can expect to find
cultural patterning in the forms and scope of production units.

A *"consumption unit" (income-pooling unit) may consist of a single individual, or of a group of individuals, who pool their incomes for consumption
purposes, sharing the pooled income among the members of the group without
reference to production considerations.*

The terms "consumption unit" and "income-pooling unit" may be used
interchangeably and are roughly equivalent to the term "household" as used
by the economist. The terms suggested here are more descriptive, however.

Kinship appears to be the universal basis for the establishment of consumption units, and indeed, such units are ordinarily identical to family units
as such units are defined in the society in question. Thus, consumption units
seem always to consist of monogamous or polygamous nuclear families, or of
conjugal or consanguine joint families. This basic situation may be qualified
in a number of respects. First, units having large numbers of members may
demonstrate incomplete income pooling so that the unit may be seen as an
aggregate of more or less closely-linked sub-units. Second, income may regularly
be shared between or among units as the occasion may require. Third, there
are situations in many societies where, as a result of cultural definition or

because of the inherent characteristics of the situation, income may be communally consumed. All of these will be found to represent variations on a basic theme, however.

If the components of an economic system fall into two classes, the structural articulation of the system involves three possible classes of relationships: 1) relationships between or among consumption units; 2) relationships between or among production units; and 3) relationships between consumption units and production units. I do not believe that these relationships can be described in purely structural terms. That is, it does not seem possible to describe the structure of an economic system without making some statements, either explicit or implied, about associated social processes. Indeed, the units themselves are defined in terms of certain processes. We must therefore now consider economic processes.

Processes of an Economic System

The economic process involves three classes of events: production events, utilization events, and transfer events.

A "production event" is an act or series of acts the result or intended result of which is to make goods or services available for utilization.

The terms "production event" and "production" are not strictly synonymous. A production event may consist of a single act or a series of acts which are productive in intent. The production of a usable good may consist of a single production event, or a series of them. In general, a production event will be considered to have "terminated" when the "product" is given final form, or when an intermediate form becomes the subject of a transfer event. (See below.)

Reference to "intent" in the foregoing is designed to emphasize the fact that a production event may be abortive. A hunter who returns empty-handed must be considered nevertheless to have been engaged in productive activity. It may be necessary, of course, to distinguish between those production events which have the intended outcome and those which do not. One important datum for any system may well be the ratio between the two.

A "utilization event" is the utilization of a good or service. It may be a "consumption event": the utilization of goods for the direct satisfaction of human wants, or a "capital consumption event": the utilization of goods for productive purposes.

Production events and capital consumption events occur in or are carried out by production units; consumption events occur in or are carried out by consumption units.

Transfer events cannot conveniently be defined without prior discussion. The idea of a transfer event rests on the fact of rights in or control over utilizable goods or services. Such rights almost always come into being when production takes place. They may be defined in various ways, may be circumscribed, conditioned, limited, or otherwise modified by custom, convention, or circumstance, but I know of no society in which they do not regularly arise and are not regularly recognized.

A *"transfer event" shifts control over, or rights in, an economic good from one individual to another or from one group to another.*

Transfer events include such things as giving, bestowing, borrowing, lending, sale-purchase, barter, exchange, theft,[10] and appropriation. It is such events which provide the links between and among units in the structure of an economic system.

The Structure of an Economic System

Assuming that it is possible to devise symbolic-schematic devices for describing the structure of an economic system, two kinds of resultant models may be constructed for any system. Descriptive models are those in which an attempt is made to identify the specific units which exist, as well as describing all of the structural links among them. If such models are further expanded to take account of actual events over a period of time—if, in short, the dynamic functioning of the system is depicted—the result would be a highly specialized sociometric diagram. If an abstract-analytical model—the second possible type— the effort is made to express the fundamental properties of the system. Such a model could also be expanded to take account of the dynamic processes involved. In any case, the structural articulation of the system may be described, at some convenient level of abstraction, in terms of production units and their internal structure, of consumption units and their internal structure, and in terms of the kinds of transfer events which link the units together.

The Systemic Outcome and Its Determinants

The economic system and its processes are not an autonomous isolate, although, to this point, we have been discussing it as though it were. The structure of the system, the characteristic forms of its components, and the specific nature of the associated processes will be determined or influenced by a host of environmental, cultural, and social variables. The nature of the relationships that are involved can best be indicated by considering how the systemic outcome for the three functions may be influenced by the many variables.

PRODUCT MIX. The natural environment may influence what is produced in a number of ways. In particular, the environment contains within it a set of opportunities and associated limits. Put simply, this means that the environment, merely through the presence or absence of certain "raw materials" or natural characteristics, makes it possible or impossible to produce certain goods. The Plains Indians could not orient their subsistence around salmon fishing, nor could the Northwest Coast tribes hunt bison. In a similar fashion, the environment might lay down requirements: the Polar Eskimo could not survive without producing goods suitable for protecting them from the cold.

These opportunities, limits, and requirements are not absolute, nor are they strictly independent variables among themselves. The joint presence of two raw materials may make possible the production of something which would be impossible in the absence of either one of them. And that part of culture which is summed up in the term "technology" obviously plays a role in translating potentialities into realities. Pottery cannot be made in the absence of suitable clays; their presence does not guarantee that pottery will be made. An outstanding example of the operation of factors of this kind is the acquisition of the horse by the Plains Indians. With horses, they were able to exploit, in a decidedly new fashion, the bison that had always been there. And, of course, the whole history of mankind is a record of the development of techniques for greater and greater mastery of the potentialities of the environment.[11]

The combination or interaction of these two variables result in the existence of certain "production possibilities." For any given range of production possibilities, the goods which will be produced will be influenced by "consumer preferences": the sum total of wants and the relative intensity of the desire/need for various things. While it may be assumed that idiosyncratic differences in preferences are to be found everywhere, it is also clear that consumer preferences are culturally patterned. Furthermore, the range of such preferences must be limited by experience, which in turn depends upon what is possible. Finally, although there are many cases in which the range of choice is severely restricted, there are few, if any, cases in which there is no possibility for exercising choice.

One more determinant of the product mix must be mentioned: the economic system itself. Insofar as the system constitutes or provides a mechanism for converting consumer preferences into production decisions, it may influence the outcome of the process. Not every economic system has this capability; market systems do, and others may. What this means is that for any given set of production possibilities and any given set of consumer preferences, a change in the system would produce a change in the product mix.

Thus, we see that the product mix may depend upon four classes of variables: 1) environmental opportunities, limitations, and requirements; 2) technological possibilities; 3) consumer preferences; 4) the economic system itself. These variables are themselves interdependent to some degree, and, of course, the specific variables which apply in any specific case may differ widely from those which apply in another.

FACTOR PROPORTIONS. This problem, as defined by economists, is one which assumes that there are known alternative possibilities in the design of production events. To discuss this problem here in adequate detail would take us far afield. I will simply assert that environmental and technological variables may play a role in the solution of this problem, and, in some cases, the system will also. In addition, want-like preferences concerning desirable or undesirable activity may also be important in the final outcome. As before, the specific variables and their relative importance, as well as the functional interrelation among them, will vary from case to case.

DISTRIBUTION OF PRODUCT.   If, and only if, every member of a society were productive and fully self-sufficient in the satisfaction of his wants, the problem of distribution of product would not exist. Since every viable society must have in it members who are not productive—even if they are only children and infants—it is a universal problem, the only one of the three for which an a priori case for universality can be made. In practice, sharing exists universally because differential productivity of the members of a society is also universal.

In considering the problem of the sharing of total product, we may distinguish between the *"system" of distribution* and the *pattern of distribution*. The system of distribution consists of the methods and devices by which the share to be allocated to each individual is determined and perhaps also by which the share is placed in his control. The pattern of distribution is the result of the determination and can be expressed as lists of quantities of goods going to different individuals or groups of individuals. The system of distribution could be either determinate or indeterminate. A determinate system would be one in which, if the system were known, and the total quantities of all kinds of goods were known, the pattern could be predicted with great accuracy; an indeterminate system is one in which, perhaps because individuals are given options concerning what they will do with goods, the pattern of distribution cannot be predicted accurately, although it may be possible to predict it within certain definable margins of error. That is, it may be possible to say that some particular individual will get as much as some quantity but not more or as little as some other quantity but not less, without being able to say what quantity he would get between those limits until the distribution has been completed. A system may be determinate with respect to some distribution items and indeterminate with respect to others.

The system of distribution consists of all of the socially sanctioned claims that may be made by the members of the society against the total product or any part of it, together with any actions necessary on the part of the individual to validate these claims. A complete description of the system will consist of a list of all of these claims and of that which is necessary to validate them.

Any system of distribution must accomplish certain minimum objectives if the society using the system is to be viable. Assuming that total output is large enough, it must guarantee minimum subsistence to all or to a substantial proportion of the productive or potentially productive members of the society. If, after this basic kind of claim has been satisfied, there is some product left over, a system of claims will ordinarily be expected to provide subsistence in some fashion for those who are no longer productive. Thereafter, the distribution of product may have any one of many possible outcomes; however, the claims against this product will probably be defined and validated in such a way as to reward certain kinds of behavior which are highly valued by the society. This being the case, it would appear that a consideration of these claims will reveal much about the basic values of the society.

It should be clear from the foregoing that, subject to the indicated constraints necessary to maintain a viable society over a period of time, the principal variable in the solution of the sharing problem is cultural-evaluative. Environmental and technological variables will ordinarily play no role in the situation and may never do so. However, systemic variables, where they play a role in the determination of factor proportions and product mix, will probably play such a role here also. It should also be clear that the "system of distribution" concerns at least certain transfer events which involve a production unit and a consumption unit, or two or more consumption units. Thus, the "system" in effect consists of normative rules concerning certain transfer events, rules concerning the conditions under which certain transfer events must or should take place.

Concluding Remarks

The foregoing has been no more than a limited sketch of an approach to the problem of describing, analyzing, and understanding nonindustrial economic systems. Several additional general points must be made.

Insofar as Dalton is concerned with the uncritical application of the concepts of economics to apparently similar phenomena in "primitive" societies, his position has merit—although I think that the problem is not as serious or as widespread as Dalton implies. The approach outlined here, with its insistence upon a careful appraisal of the specific functional variables which are relevant to the situation under study, offers the promise, I think, of an escape from this difficulty without abandoning, as Dalton would have us do, everything which is potentially fruitful in contemporary economic thought. Since "primitive" societies are not a homogeneous class of socio-cultural entities, the relevance, applicability, or fruitfulness of any approach to their study must and can only be tested on the merits of each case, which means, ultimately, by the test of available data.

Implicit in this view is the painfully-acquired conviction that there are no royal highroads to general, cross-cultural understanding of economic systems and processes. The descriptive analysis of any single economic system will, in most cases, be a task of some magnitude, although its magnitude will diminish somewhat as concepts are tested and refined, and as experience is gained in their use. Comparative economics cannot mature either in its methods or in its substantive findings until a substantial number of such descriptive analyses have been made and perhaps revised, not once, but many times.

Finally, it must be emphasized that despite the apparent dogmatism with which they were stated, the propositions advanced here must be regarded as subject to revision. Progress in any science is testimony to the inadequacy of its antecedents, and so presumably it will be here. This does not mean, however, that any conceivable alternative set of propositions may be substituted for those given above. The present propositions were chosen with regard to four criteria: 1) compatibility with the main body of contemporary economic thought; 2) compatibility with a limited, essentially impressionistic-intuitive analysis of ethnographic material; 3) logical consistency; 4) the capacity to generate insights which will lead to the required conceptual refinements. The second criterion makes refinement necessary; the fourth, it is hoped, will make systematic and well-grounded refinement possible.

NOTES

[1] Hereafter, reference to Dalton 1961 will be by page number only.

[2] It should also be noted that the foregoing contains an implied assumption of human omniscience which is clearly not in accord with reality. Such an assumption represents a pedagogical and analytical simplification comparable to the assumption of a perfect vacuum in the theory of falling objects. No economist believes in the omniscience of human beings, and the validity of his theories does not stand or fall on the sharpness of these assumptions. The fallibility of human belief introduces a complexity into the theory—it does not invalidate it.

[3] Controversies on issues of this kind continue to recur within economics. See for example: Lester (1946), Machlup (1946), together with a series of comments and rejoinders by Lester, Machlup, Stigler, and others in various issues of the American Economic Review (March, 1946, *et seq.*). The persistence of such controversy may very well arise out of a peculiar characteristic of the formal properties of deductive systems in economics which distinguishes them from similar systems in the natural sciences—a difference which has been pointed out by Northrup (1948: 107–10, 235–54). Normally, deductive systems begin with logically arbitrary premises, and the validity of the system, including the premises, is tested by empirically verifying the emergent conclusions. In deductive systems in economics, on the other hand, it is the premises which are asserted to be valid; if they are, the validity of the conclusions necessarily follows. The difficulty lies not so much in the reversal of the normal sequence, but in the mode of verification of the validity of the premises. The premises by their nature find their verification in introspective data which is inherently not demonstrable. This means that just as there is no way of communicating to a blind man the concept of "blue" as a visual phenomenon, there is also no way to communicate to a skeptic the validity of the introspected data. When we realize that anthropologists generally have been prominent among skeptics in these matters, it is clear that this state of affairs has considerable significance for economic anthropology. Unfortunately, such has been the depth of conviction of those for whom the premises have validity that they have tended to ignore the possibility of settling the issue by attempting to verify, through publicly available data, the conclusions which stem from their premises. Those who are interested might find it revealing to reread the exchange between Knight and Herskovits (Herskovits 1952:507–31) with this view in mind.

[4] The approach outlined here was developed in connection with and as guidance for an exploratory study of nonindustrial economic systems. In large part, the study has as its purpose the clarification of conceptual and theoretical issues involved in the analysis of such systems. This study grows out of earlier work carried out as a Research Training Fellow of the Social Science Research Council (see LeClair 1953). The present study has had financial support from the Committee on Economic Growth of the Social Science Research Council. I wish to express my appreciation for the support which made this research possible. I wish also to express my special gratitude to Melville J. Herskovits, whose support and encouragement over a considerable period of time has meant much to me.

[5] "Capital goods" are not ordinarily defined in this way, although this definition is not inconsistent with the more usual ones.

[6] Portions of what follow are drawn from LeClair 1959 and 1960. My participation in the Workshop in Economic Anthropology (see *Current Anthropology* 1960:149–50) resulted in many alterations in my thinking—although my co-participants should not be charged with any responsibility for my views. I owe much to them and to the organizers and sponsors of the Workshop. The later paper led to a number of discussions which were of great benefit. Of particular value were lengthy and searching discussions with Harold K. Schneider and Lilo Stern.

[7] Characteristically, economists have generally considered this issue for pedagogical rather than for analytical reasons. Consequently, the issue has not received as careful attention as we might wish. It may conceivably be left for economic anthropologists to clarify the matter.

The list presented here follows Samuelson (1958:16). For longer and somewhat different lists, see Harriss (1959:6–8) and Frank (nd:1–2).

Beals and Hoijer (1959:415–16) discuss three "problems of economics" which have a close but superficial resemblance to the three "functions" given here. Since we define economics as the *study* of economizing, the Beals and Hoijer problems are not strictly equivalent to our functions.

[8] The italicized terms are ones which are conventionally used in economics. It must be kept firmly in mind that "distribution" is used here and in this context strictly in the sense of sharing or of allocation. Anthropologists tend most often to use it in the trading-marketing sense and have tended to overlook the other meaning.

[9] For a discussion of some of these variables, as well as a provocative study of some related problems, see Udy (1959).

[10] Theft belongs in this list because if it is successful it does constitute a *de facto* transfer of control, even though *de jure* rights presumably cannot be transferred in this way.

[11] Although it has so far been applied only to a limited variety of materials, the "ethnoecological" approach being developed for the study of swidden agriculture appears to be a promising development in the study of the consequences of the interaction of technology and environment. I am inclined to think that the approach can fruitfully be adapted to productive situations other than swidden agriculture. For a succinct statement of the approach, see Conklin (1961). I am indebted to Anthony Leeds for first calling my attention to this approach and for making available to me the results of his own work prior to publication. (See Leeds 1961.)

12 THE OBSOLETE "ANTI-MARKET" MENTALITY: A CRITIQUE OF THE SUBSTANTIVE APPROACH TO ECONOMIC ANTHROPOLOGY
Scott Cook

> *Analytic work begins with material provided by our vision of things, and this vision is ideological almost by definition. It embodies the picture of things as we see them, and wherever there is any possible motive for wishing to see them in a given rather than another light, the way in which we can see things can hardly be distinguished from the way in which we wish to see them. The more honest and naive our vision is, the more dangerous it is to the eventual emergence of anything for which general validity can be claimed. The inference for the social sciences is obvious, and it is not even true that he who hates a social system will form an objectively more correct vision of it than he who loves it. For love distorts indeed, but hate distorts still more.*
>
> Joseph Schumpeter

I. The Problem[1]

Economic anthropology, a major sub-area of anthropological inquiry, is plagued by a serious communication gap between its practitioners. Since the impact on the field of the writings of Karl Polanyi and his followers, a clear-cut dichotomy has emerged between scholars who maintain that "formal" economic theory is applicable to the analysis of "primitive" and "peasant" economies and those who believe that it is limited in application to the market-oriented, price-governed economic systems of industrial economies.[2] Prior to the publication of *Trade and Market in the Early Empires* (Polanyi, *et al.* 1957) the field of economic anthropology represented a single sphere of discourse, with the majority of its practitioners believing that formal economic theory could contribute to anthropological inquiry. However, after the publication of this substantivist *magnum opus*, the field underwent a bifurcation into two discrete spheres of discourse. Although several attempts have been made by various scholars to provoke a meaningful dialogue with the substantivists, their critiques have failed to elicit any such exchange of views.[3] Thus the field is presently characterized by a "split-level" dialogue in which the proponents of the two dominant views of economics-in-anthropology are talking past one another and are operating within separate spheres of discourse.

From American Anthropologist *68:323–345. Reprinted by permission.*

Many anthropologists are still apparently unfamiliar with the scope and content of the critiques of substantivist economics, while substantivist views continue to find expression in the literature without manifesting any noticeable concessions to the arguments of their critics (e.g., Dalton 1961; Dalton 1962; Bohannan and Dalton 1962; Bohannan 1963; Dalton 1964). The present critique is intended to supplement its predecessors by elaborating on the thesis that the substantivists' intransigency concerning the cross-cultural applicability of formal economic theory is a by-product of a romantic ideology rooted in an antipathy toward the "market economy" and an idealization of the "primitive."

II. A "Paradox" in the Recent Substantivist Literature

In their introduction to *Markets in Africa* Paul Bohannan and George Dalton (1962), two of the most articulate and sophisticated representatives of that group of economic anthropologists who take the writings of Karl Polanyi as their major theoretical point of departure, make an effort to adapt the typology of economies first formulated by Polanyi for the analysis of a series of extinct societies (1957a, b:250–256; 1959:168–174) to a body of concrete data from eight societies of contemporary Africa. The alteration of the original Polanyi typology reflects their attempt to cope with the fact that in Africa "those economic activities organized on the market principle are expanding with a concomitant attenuation of redistribution and reciprocity" (1962:24) or that "multicentric economies are in the process of becoming unicentric" (1962:25).[4] Moreover, these two authors commit themselves to the following prognosis: "It seems safe to predict that the process will continue, and that African economies are becoming like our own in the sense that the sectors dominated by the market principle are being enlarged" (1962:25). There is every reason to believe that the trend so succinctly described by Bohannan and Dalton for Africa is a process which has world-wide ramifications.

Unfortunately, neither of these substantivist writers deals with the obvious theoretical implications of the discerned developmental trend in empirical economies nor with its significance for future inquiry in economic anthropology. To cope theoretically with this trend would necessarily entail a basic revision of a key tenet in the substantivist ideological system—a concomitant of the simplistic dichotomy between "market" and "primitive-subsistence" economies, namely, the dogma that formal economic theory, being a creature of the market economy, is, *ipso facto*, inapplicable to the analysis of primitive-subsistence economies (Polanyi, *et al.* 1957; Polanyi 1959:166; Dalton 1961:25; Bohannan 1963:229–231). While the recent postulation of "subtypes" of primitive-subsistence or non-market economies (i.e., the "marketless" and the "peripheral market" types in Bohannan and Dalton 1962; Bohannan 1963; Dalton 1964) can be considered as an attempt by the substantivists to escape from the restrictions imposed by the polar dichotomization of economies, Dalton's position *vis-à-vis* formal economic theory remains essentially the same as that enunciated in 1961, although he has re-phrased it to fit the new typological accretions.[5]

One slight variation on the Polanyi theme which can be detected in the writings of Bohannan (1963:263–265) and Dalton (1964) is a concern with "transitional" or "peasant" economies. Nevertheless, a recent statement by Dalton leads one to believe that what the "market-economy" construct is in Polanyi's scheme, the "peasant economy" construct is in Dalton's i.e.; it is postulated as a type of economy studied by those economic anthropologists who successfully utilize concepts and principles from formal economic theory (Dalton 1965b:122–123).[6] In other words, it is merely a rhetorical device designed to preserve the integrity of the substantivist ideology.

The specific nature of the substantivist dilemma can now be pieced together in the form of a paradox. Confronted with a body of ethnographic data from contemporary African economies, Dalton (along with Bohannan) is forced to admit that they are "becoming more like our own in the sense that the sectors dominated by the market principle are being enlarged," while studies elsewhere have forced him to admit that "small-scale peasant societies . . . can be considered analytically with the concepts and questions from large scale American and European market economies" (1965b:122). Dalton persists, however, in reiterating Polanyi's thesis by asserting that those ethnographers who successfully utilize formal economic theory are doing so in peasant or market-dominated economies, not in primitive-subsistence (i.e., marketless or peripheral) economies. This argument implies that the latter type of economy is still the dominant focus of inquiry in economic anthropology, with substantive theory being the only legitimate analytic tool for economic anthropologists. It is undeniable that anthropology can still profit from the study of extinct societies as well as from the study of extant "primitive" societies; and, in the field of economics, substantive theory offers one meaningful approach to such studies. But given the fact that marketless subsistence economies are rapidly disappearing as ethnographic entities, being displaced by market-influenced or -dominated transitional and peasant economies, it seems rather pointless to persist, as Dalton does, in concocting tortured arguments in defense of a theory which was designed specifically for the analysis of these moribund types of economies (i.e., substantive economic theory).

III. Deduction, Induction and "Economic Man": The Substantivist Position *Vis-à-Vis* the Knight-Herskovits Exchange[7]

The exchange between Frank Knight and Melville Herskovits is one of the few in the literature between an economist and an anthropologist about the field of economic anthropology which revolves primarily around philosophical issues. Knight's main thesis was essentially that "any intelligent or useful exposition of facts imperatively requires an understanding of principles, while the need for facts in connection with the exposition of principles is far more tenuous" (Herskovits 1952:516). Herskovits' position reflected his indoctrination in the tradition of Boasian inductionism: "My point of view concerning scientific method is that findings must be based on fact, and that to depart from reality s to vitiate the tenability of conclusions" (1952:527). Although this exchange of views occurred a quarter of a century ago, it carries an important message or contemporary anthropological inquiry, in general, and for economic anthropology in particular.[8]

Not only has Knight's position in the dialogue been widely misunderstood and slighted by many anthropologists but, even more deplorable, has been their failure to discern the theoretical implications for economic anthropology inherent in Herskovits' change of attitude between 1941 and 1952 when his text *Economic Anthropology* (1952) was published. In the exchange with Knight, Herskovits demonstrated an inadequate knowledge of the economic literature which obviously impaired his understanding of the scope and methods of economic theory. This was reflected most vividly in his contemptuousness with regard to the 'economic man" construct on the grounds that the available evidence from all over the world indicated that its existence was purely mythical (1952:525). At his point in his career Herskovits' position *vis-à-vis* the "economic man" was similar to that later expressed by the substantivists (e.g., Polanyi, *et al.*, 1957: 239; Dalton 1961:2). However, this position was substantially modified in the 1952 edition of his text where it is clear that Herskovits had acquired more knowledge of the role of the "economic man" construct in the history of economic analysis, and had achieved greater insight into the importance of deductive reasoning in economic model-building (1952:8; 1952:19).[9]

How can one explain this change in attitude by Herskovits? Does it represent a basic intellectual conversion from "Boasian inductionism" to "Knightian deductionism"? This hypothesis can be rejected as incompatible with the tone and content of his voluminous writings which, until the time of his death, continued to manifest his inductive orientation. Fortunately, Herskovits provides us with two reasons for his change in attitude in the preface to *Economic Anthropology:* (1) new ethnographic data about the economies of non-literate, non-industrial, non-pecuniary societies which convinced him of the universality of the concepts and principles of economic theory (1952:vi); and (2) increased knowledge on his part of the scope and methods of economic theory and of economists' views about economic anthropology (1952:vi–vii). Thus, far from reflecting an intellectual conversion from inductionism to deductionism, Herskovits' attitudinal change was an affirmation of his own inductionist view of social science.

It seems to me that the followers of Polanyi could profit from a reexamination of the Knight-Herskovits exchange and its implications for theory and methodology in economic anthropology. Although they continue to espouse inductionistic canons of social scientific method, the substantivists are, in fact, guilty of a failure to cope with ethnographic and theoretical contributions in economics which contradict many of their own assumptions. Polanyi established a precedent in this regard with his terse and unelaborated condemnation of Herskovits' text: "In the field of anthropology, Melville Herskovits' recent work (1952) represents a relapse after his pioneering effort of 1940" (1959:164).

IV. The Romantic "Anti-Market" Syndrome: The Market as a Universal Bogey

Underlying and to some extent cross-cutting the major split among students of economic anthropology between those who believe that the difference between Western-type market and primitive-subsistence economies is one of degree, and those who believe it is one of kind (i.e., the substantivists) is a split of another dimension—that between the "Romanticists" and the "Formalists". The Formalists may be characterized as those who focus on abstractions unlimited by time and place, and who are prone to introspection or are synchronically oriented; they are scientific in outlook and mathematical in inclination, favor the deductive mode of inquiry, and are basically analytic in methodology (i.e., lean toward the belief that parts determine the whole). The Romanticists, on the other hand, may be characterized as those who focus on situations limited in time and space, and who are prone to retrospection or are diachronically oriented; they are humanistic in outlook and nonmathematical in inclination, favor the inductive mode of inquiry, and are basically synthetic in methodology (i.e., lean toward the belief that the whole determines its parts). In this section the concern will be to link Polanyi and his followers to the Romanticist tradition and to suggest certain implications of this linkage for economic anthropology.

Eric Wolf has recently described the "Romantic Syndrome" in its anthropological context as follows: "The anthropologist has shown a tendency . . . to construe . . . savage worlds as worlds *sui generis*, to hypostatize them into representatives of pristine designs for living, untouched by the hands of civilization from which he escaped . . ." (1964:11–12). Since World War II, according to Wolf, this romantic element in anthropology has diminished in scope, thus he speaks of the "decline of the romantic quest for pristine alternatives" (1964: 23). While this trend may be discernible in anthropology as a whole, it does not seem to be dominant in the field of economic anthropology where Polanyi's influence has been essentially a post-war phenomenon and shows no signs of diminution at present. Of course, it has not yet been demonstrated how Polanyi and the substantivists can be categorized as romanticists. To assist in this task I will turn to a recent article by Stanley Diamond (1964) who is one of the few anthropologists to view anthropology from the standpoint of intellectual history and the sociology of knowledge.

Diamond's thesis is that anthropology falls into the romantic stream of historical knowledge which is part of the "retrospective" tradition of the Enlightenment—a tradition which found its living laboratory in the Age of Discovery (1964:433). This tradition consists of ". . . the conscious search in history for a renewed and basic sense of the possibilities in human nature and of culture, not only in response to the fall of feudal ideology but in contrast to the nascent modern realities that were being created by the revolutionary bourgeoisie" (1964:432). The representative *par excellance* of this tradition was, in Diamond's opinion, Rousseau, and his characterization of the French social philosopher (1964:434–5) isolates certain motive forces and intellectual tendencies implicit in Polanyi's quest for a new thought pattern for modern industrial civilization (Polanyi 1947). Implicit in Polanyi's writings and inevitably adopted by other substantivist writers is a utopian model of primitive society which minimizes the role of conflict, coupled with a model of man which emphasizes innate altruistic and cooperative propensities while playing down self-interest, aggressiveness, and competitiveness.

In essence, Polanyi's view of human motivation is that the pursuit of self-interest in the form of material gain and profit is a concomitant of the rise of the "self-regulating" market economy in 19th century Europe and the United States. This development represented the emergence of a new historical type of society since in the "pre-market" situation (which Polanyi invariably equates with primitive society) men were motivated not by selfish propensities for economic gain but by simple, unadulterated subsistence needs (1947:112). The upshot of this argument is that the motive of material gain or profit is not "natural" to man and is operative only under special circumstances of time and place (1947:112). In other words, Polanyi views all human behavior prior to the 19th century institutionalization of the "self-regulating" market economy, or outside the market economy context in primitive society, as being devoid of the pursuit of self interest and as being inherently altruistic. Primitive Man, as inferred from Polanyi's writings, is incapable of acting to secure his own material advantage through the calculated manipulation of social relations (1944: 46).[10]

Polanyi's model of primitive society is based on two principles of behavior, reciprocity and redistribution, which he posits as ordering the processes of production and distribution in primitive economies (1957a:250–256; 1959: 168–172). These principles are in turn related to the institutional patterns of symmetry and centricity—the former associated with reciprocal economies and the latter with redistributive economies. It is in the explanation of these principles that Polanyi, in effect, idealizes primitive society and sociologizes the economic sector, i.e., contends that the economic system is "submerged" or "embedded" in social organization (1944:49).[11] Reciprocal systems characterized by symmetry and redistributive systems characterized by centricity are considered as sub-types of the non-market economy in Polanyi's scheme. However, when he compares and contrasts 'primitive', 'tribal' or 'subsistence' economies (i.e., non-market economies) with the 'market-economy' type, he always utilizes the reciprocal economy construct (e.g., 1957a:255).[12]

The following model of a market or exchange economy can be inferred from Polanyi's writings: The dominant principle of behavior is higgling-haggling (i.e., bargaining to arrive at a mutually satisfactory price) motivated by a desire for personal gain or profit; this inevitably involves mutual antagonism and ultimately provokes latent hostilities into overt expression and/or creates anxiety. In contrast, the inferred model of a non-market (i.e., reciprocal) economy is as follows: The dominant principle of behavior is reciprocity (i.e., the process of mutual give and take guided by a series of set equivalencies) motivated by generosity; this inevitably involves a mutually cooperative relationship which ultimately allays latent hostilities and creates solidarity.[13] While conflict is built into the market model, the reciprocal or non-market model precludes it.

At least two important relationships are glossed over in Polanyi's non-market economy model: (1) the norm of reciprocity is not incompatible with the self-interest or aggressiveness postulate (e.g., Gouldner 1960:171; Homans 1961: 61–4, 316–20; Blau 1964:88–114) ; (2) the principle of generosity in a recipro-cal economy can create conflict as well as contribute to solidarity, and can also be manipulated to secure an advantage over one's fellows (Levi-Strauss 1944:24; Homans 1961:316–20 *passim;* Sahlins 1963:42; Blau 1964:88–114 *passim*). In other words, "laying on obligations of reciprocity" (Sahlins 1962:1068) in a reciprocal economy is functionally equivalent to the selfish seeking of gain or profit in a market economy. Granted the fact that exchange at fluctuating prices in a market economy involves antagonism and that the social context of inter-action is more impersonal than that in a reciprocal economy, it must also be recognized that failure to reciprocate within the period stipulated or anticipated in a reciprocal economy usually produces conflict.[14] At the very least, failure to reciprocate is dysfunctional for embryonic reciprocity relationships. In view of these relationships the "fount of solidarity" postulate (Polanyi 1957a:255) in the extrapolated model of Polanyi's non-market economy is untenable.[15]

Polanyi contends, as a final proposition in his ideological scheme, that the market economy guided by its "ideological promoters," the Classical econo-mists, transformed the natural and human substance (i.e., land and labor) of 19th century Western society into commodities, thereby projecting "hunger" (fear of going without life's necessities) and "gain" (profit expectation) as economic motives into the saddle to ride man (1947:111–112). These two motives, working together, served as the propelling forces in the institutionaliza-tion of the market economy.[16] That Polanyi views this "transformation" as degrading to man, and the market system which produced it as the principal nemesis of human dignity and civilization is apparent from statements like the following: "Economic motives reigned supreme in a world of their own, and the individual was made to act on them under pain of being trodden under foot by the juggernaut market" (1947:110). Or, in still more dramatic prose:

> This latter field (i.e., economy) has been "separated out" of society as the realm of hunger and gain. Our animal dependence upon food has been bared and the naked fear of starvation permitted to run loose. Our humilitating enslavement to the 'material' which all human culture is designed to miti-gate, was deliberately made more rigorous . . .
>
> Only since the market was permitted to grind the human fabric into the featureless uniformity of selenic erosion has man's institutional creativeness been in abeyance. No wonder that his social imagination shows signs of fatigue (1947:115).

These are undeniably the words of a Romanticist in the Rousseauian tradition who feels alienated by an industrial civilization in which the division of labor is rejected as paralyzing, in which mechanism is dominant over organism and bureaucracy stifles individual spontaneity, and where life itself is perceived as routinized tedium. Like Rousseau, Polanyi does not advocate a return to any historically specific primitive condition, but he warns that unless present trends are reversed, contemporary man will be unable to "recover the elasticity, the imaginative wealth and power, of his savage endowment" (1947:115).

V. A Critique of Substantivist Views of Formal Economic Theory

In what is generally recognized as the most erudite and authoritative study of the development of economic science, Joseph Schumpeter (1954) delimits three sub-areas within the discipline: (1) economic analysis; (2) political economy; (3) economic thought. He defines economic analysis as "the intellectual effort that men have made in order to understand economic phenomena" or "the analytic or scientific aspects of economic thought" (1954:3). By a system of political economy he means "an exposition of a comprehensive set of economic policies that its author advocates on the strength of certain unifying (normative) principles such as the principles of economic liberalism, of socialism, etc." (1954: 38). Finally, economic thought in Schumpeter's terms is defined as "the sum total of all the opinions and desires concerning economic subjects, especially concerning public policy bearing upon these subjects that, at any given time and place, float in the public mind" (1954:38).[17]

The immediate relevance of these distinctions to a critique of substantive economics becomes clear only when we realize that Schumpeter, who fully accepted the idea of the pervasiveness of ideological bias in the history of economics, nevertheless suggested that "economic analysis" was less susceptible to the interests and attitudes of the market place than either "political economy" or "economic thought." Economic analysis alone displays a unique property of "scientific progress" which, according to Schumpeter, is analogous to "technological progress in the extraction of teeth between the times of, say J. S. Mill and our own" (1954:39). By failing to distinguish between these three aspects of economics Polanyi and his followers necessarily ignore two factors which are crucial to a proper understanding of the history of the discipline, as well as its present nature and scope: first, that when one looks at the content of the tool-kit of economic analysis, he discovers many conceptual tools that are ideologically neutral; second, that there are concepts or theories that, though they can be shown to be actually neutral, acquire a putative ideological importance because people erroneously believe that they are relevant to their ideologies (Schumpeter 1954:44).

Examining substantivist writings with Schumpeter's discussion as a point of departure, the following conclusions emerge: (1) Insofar as an attempt is made to document a historical and institutional linkage between economic theory (i.e., economic analysis) and the "market economy," the end result is the documentation of a linkage between a *particular system* of political economy (i.e., economic liberalism) and the *19th century European* market economy; (2) Generalizations regarding the historical and institutional limitations of formal economic theory refer to the latter as it stood in the late 19th and early 20th centuries, thus ignoring subsequent refinements, modifications and new additions to the science.

For example, in his role as chief theoretical spokesman for the substantivist approach to economics in anthropology, George Dalton sets out to "describe those special organizational features of Western economy which formal economic theory was created to analyze" (1961:1).[18] The only post-Classical economists singled out in Dalton's presentation are Jevons, Menger, Clark, and Marshall who were the founders of the Neoclassical tradition in economic analysis (1961: 4). Dalton fails to demonstrate precisely how the theoretical and conceptual contributions of these economists are products of and solely applicable to the market institution, nor does he bother to consider contributions to the economic literature subsequent to those of the founders of Neoclassical theory. Few would deny that this theory has been formulated with the Western market-economy model as a reference point but, as Schumpeter pointed out, many of the conceptual tools so formulated will be ideologically neutral and their conditioning by the interests and attitudes of the market will be tenuous at best. Moreover, the assertion that this theory is inapplicable to the analysis of non-market economies is verifiable only by empirical test—a procedure which the substantivists have never taken seriously.

Even if the substantivists provided an airtight case for the historical and institutional limitations of Classical and early Neoclassical theories, it would be stretching their arguments beyond all reasonable bounds to then assert that "all economic theory" is so limited. Dalton's use of the early Neoclassical economists as typical representatives of economic theory is tantamount to using Weber, Simmel, and Durkheim (for example) as typifying sociological theory. To carry this analogy one step further, it is tantamount to arguing that because sociological theory was formulated to analyze complex institutions and behaviors of Western industrial civilization (which is essentially correct) it is, *ipso facto*, inapplicable to the analysis of simple, non-industrial societies. Such an attitude implicitly condemns to the anthropological wastebasket a whole host of penetrating studies of simple societies which utilize a conceptual scaffolding derived from sociological theory. It seems to me that the burden of proof rests with the substantivists to demonstrate that what has been done with recognized success by anthropologists with sociological (and one might add, psychological) theory cannot also be done with economic theory.

Economists and economic analysis have, by and large, adapted to changing intellectual and institutional conditions so that what was true of them a hundred, fifty, or even ten years ago is not true of them today. This is why one has difficulty in viewing current expositions of economic theory in terms of the substantivist interpretation of it. Schumpeter has noted the following crucial fact about the history of economics: ". . . the subject matter of economics is itself a unique historical process so that, to a large extent, the economics of different epochs deal with different sets of facts and problems" (1954:5). Economic analysis copes with change in its subject matter through the "filiation of scientific ideas" which Schumpeter defines as the "processes by which men's efforts to understand economic phenomena produce, improve, and pull down analytic statements in an unending sequence" (1954:6). To overlook this central process in the history of economics, as the substantivists from Polanyi to Dalton do, is to distort contemporary economic analysis and to arbitrarily deny its status as a science.

The substantivists are unanimous in agreeing that the distinction between the "formal" and "substantive" meanings of economic is the greatest single conceptual contribution of Polanyi. Dalton, for example, acknowledges his indebtedness to Polanyi for "his illuminating distinction between the two meanings of economic" (1961:22). Even Robbins Burling who goes on to criticize certain implications of the semantic dichotomy refers to "a long needed distinction between economics in the substantive sense of the provision of material goods, and in the formal sense of rationalizing calculation or 'economizing'" (1962: 802).[19]

The only dissenting view of the Polanyi distinction which I have found in the anthropological literature is by LeClair in his formidable critique of the substantivist position when he asks "why there is a 'felt need' for a substantive definition of economics" (1962:1181). His curiosity over this point is shared by me, especially in view of the fact that economists have expended as much effort in writing about the definition and scope of economics as in regard to any other single issue, and that an enormous body of literature focused on this topic has been totally by-passed in substantivist discussions.[20] LeClair, however, assumes in his critique that Polanyi and Dalton, in making their distinction between the "two meanings of economic," are indeed paralleling comparable distinctions made by economists. But the failure of the substantivists to consciously tie-in their discussion with the "definition and scope" debate in economic discourse raises serious doubts in my mind concerning the "meaning" of their "two meanings."[21]

Polanyi did not separate out the two meanings as a simple intellectual exercise; his aim was "to determine the meaning that can be attached with consistency to the term 'economic' in the social sciences" (1957a:243). Given this goal, Polanyi's lack of reference to the economic literature relating to this problem is even more baffling. It is not surprising, then, that many complications arise in the course of his discussion, ranging from his doctrinaire denial of the universality of rational choice in man's economic life to the rationale underlying the "two meanings" distinction itself. Polanyi's statement of the issue enables us to separate a series of traits, and to arrange them in terms of a dichotomous typology in which the polar opposites are "substantive" and "formal":[22]

Substantive	*Formal*
1. derives from fact	1. derives from logic
2. implies neither choice nor insufficiency of means	2. set of rules referring to choice between alternative uses of insufficient means
3. power of gravity	3. power of syllogism
4. laws of nature	4. laws of mind

These two meanings obfuscate the nature of the relationship between economic theory as the science of economics and "economy" or "economic facts," which is no different than that between any science and its subject matter. It expresses in semantic terms what is essentially a relationship between phenomena of separate epistemological statuses. To obscure the relationship between economic theory and empirical reality is to place yet another artificial barrier between economists and anthropologists which, by exacerbating the current communication gap between these two sets of scholars, can only serve to impede meaningful research in the field of economic anthropology.[23]

Given Polanyi's sentiments regarding the price-regulated market economy, coupled with his attempt to set the historical and institutional limitations of formal economic theory, it follows that only the "substantive meaning of economic" can yield the concepts required by the social sciences for an investigation of all the empirical economies of the past and present (1957a:244). Simon Rottenberg has pointed out that Polanyi and other substantivists have examined the conventional assumptions of economic theory seeking to ascertain whether these have empirical counterparts in primitive economies, but warns that the "significant question is not whether real world duplicates can be found for the assumptions, but whether real-world observed experience duplicates theoretically derived predictions" (1958:677). Any careful reader of the substantivist literature must agree with Rottenberg that "the door to this area of inquiry was foreclosed by prejudgement" (1958:677).[24]

The substantivist attempt to delimit the boundaries within which economic theory proves ineffective as an analytical tool depends for its success or failure upon their handling of the "economizing" and "scarcity" postulates.[25] According to Polanyi, economic theory is analytically useful only in these economies in which economizing acts (i.e., sequences of rational choice in the allocation or use of resources) induced by scarcity situations are institutionalized (1957a:247; Polanyi, *et al.*, 1957:xvii). He argues that the presence or absence of scarcity is invariably a question of fact (1959:165). Although frequently denying the universal relevance of scarcity as a conditioning factor in economic action, the substantivists have never, to my knowledge, provided an ethnographic example of an empirical economy in which scarcity was without implications for economic decision-making (i.e., economizing).[26] Nor, as Smelser has observed, have they formulated a counter-postulate which better serves economic analysis than that based on the notion of "scarcity" (1959:176). As is so often the case in substantivist theorizing, the sole evidence which is offered in support of the series of propositions relating "economizing," "scarcity" and the applicability of economic theory is verbal acrobatics as illustrated in the following statement by Polanyi: "While the rules governing such acts (of economizing) are universal, the extent to which the rules are applicable to a definite economy depends upon whether or not that economy is, in actual fact, a sequence of such acts" (1957a:247).

Economists reject the thesis, developed by Polanyi and preserved by Dalton, that scarcity is solely a function of social organization (Dalton 1961:5). The basic assumption which economic analysis makes about the physical world is that the resources which it provides for human utilization are scarce (i.e., limited in relation to the demand for them). It is because of this scarcity that goods have to be shared out among the individual members of a social group, and it is the role of an economic system to perform this "sharing out" task. From the economist's point of view, if there were no scarcity and consequently no need for goods to be shared out among individuals, there would be no economic system (Stonier and Hague 1957:3). While economists view scarcity as an inherent condition in any human situation, they consider it to have relevance in economic theory only when associated with the concept of "economic good" (i.e., in order to get more of a given commodity, a quantity of some other commodity must be relinquished). Since a good is economically scarce only in relation to the demand for it, it follows that "scarcity always means scarce in relation to demand" (Stonier and Hague 1957:26). In economic theory, then, "scarcity" is a relative concept which reflects the interplay of biosocial (i.e., wants and the resources of time and energy required to satisfy them) and ecological (i.e., physical and natural environmental) determinants.

In recent years George Dalton has emerged as the most ardent and articulate spokesman for substantivist economics in anthropology (1961; 1962; 1964; 1965a). His influence on current thinking in economic anthropology among American anthropologists is substantial, if not dominant. Yet anyone who has followed the trend of controversy in this field will have realized that the persuasiveness of Dalton's arguments is a direct concomitant of his failure to treat adequately the criticisms which have periodically been directed against the substantivist approach. For example, in his 1961 article which is essentially an attempt to clarify certain ambiguities in earlier substantivist writings, Dalton devotes only one short paragraph in reply to Rottenberg's incisive critique (1958). Furthermore, he selectively limits his comments to only one of several issues raised by this critic which he dismisses arbitrarily as follows: "The use of formal price theory concepts such as 'inelastic demand' in reference to primitive economies indicates an implicit market orientation: the prejudgement of economic organization by way of an *a priori* assumption that market structure— or its functional equivalent—exists universally" (1961:9). In other words, Dalton is simply echoing Polanyi's ideological argument against the universal applicability of formal economic theory. His treatment of Smelser's major critique is even less adequate than that of Rottenberg's, since he alludes to it only once and that is to cite a minor point on which Smelser happens to agree with the substantivist position (1961:20). One sentence from Smelser's critique places Dalton's evasiveness in proper perspective: "It is as illegitimate to try to force a physical or material bias on all economic activity as it is to impose a fully-developed market analysis on all types of economy; both operations involve an ill-advised reductionism" (1959:177).

In his discussion of economic theory Dalton refers to "the textbook homily that man's material wants are insatiable, a dictum that often implies the immutability of genetic impulse" (1961:5) providing still another example of the substantivist penchant for overstatement. If economists really believed that human wants were insatiable they would provide the rationale for discontinuing one of their own major intellectual activities, namely, the study of consumer behavior—that branch of micro-economic theory devoted to the study of want-satisfaction. Indeed, many economists define their discipline as dealing with that aspect of the human activity of want-satisfaction in which the problem of scarcity of means is paramount (e.g., Roll 1937:9–13). As one economist expresses it: "The satisfaction of wants constitutes a major segment of human activity and economics is occupied with a study of this segment" (Bober 1955:7). Economists, then, do not hold to the simplistic dictum which Dalton attributes to them but believe, more realistically, that in any given situation man's wants will be more numerous than the means available for satisfying them; but that once choice as to the utilization of scarce means is exercised those wants which are deemed most satisfying or as having the highest marginal utility will be satisfied. Among other things, Dalton has chosen not to consider the important role which the time factor plays in economic analysis. The unqualified proposition that wants are insatiable would be true in economic theory only in a hypothetical situation in which the time factor was held constant or assumed to be unlimited. However, in economic model-building the limitation of the time factor is crucial to the analysis of most economic problems, as well as to the predictability of the model.

Wilbert E. Moore, a sociologist with substantivist leanings, has argued that "the essential difficulty in the concepts (of economic theory) as applied to primitive or agrarian societies is that their 'operational definition' is not the same as in a market system" (1955a:5). He further suggests that discussions of "primitive" or "peasant" economics commonly employ concepts that are essentially metaphorical, being borrowed from economic theory but without precise application where the assumptions of economic theory are inoperative (which, he neglects to mention, can only be determined by empirically testing the derivative principles and models). Moore's argument, like those of the substantivists in general, seems to minimize the inherent plasticity and logical integrity of the assumptions and concepts of economic theory (Walker 1943:136) which, after all, are ultimately derived from one simple, yet heuristically powerful, proposition: "The problem of maximizing satisfactions through the utilization of 'scarce means'—the need to economize in the broadest sense of the term—derives from the basic fact of the existence of wants in excess of the capacity to produce" (Herskovits 1952:266). Or, to state the proposition differently: Most members of every discrete human group have economically relevant wants that exceed the procurement means available to them. In band societies, simple tribal and peasant societies, these economically relevant wants lie predominantly, though not exclusively, in the subsistence realm; while in more complex societies such wants exist both within and beyond the bounds of the subsistence sphere.

In the development of economic principles through the use of models, any assumption is considered valid if it conveniently simplifies analysis, if it is not incompatible with other necessary assumptions and if it either conforms to reality, or can subsequently be discarded without making it impossible to revise accordingly the generalizations reached (Higgins 1959). This is the rationale underlying the economist's "method of successive approximations" to reality which is the core tool of economic theorizing and the *conditio sine qua non* of model-building. Economists, on the whole, are willing to sacrifice reality in making these assumptions in order to benefit heuristically from their simplicity. Given a set of simple assumptions about human behavior, the economist is better equipped to maneuver within the realm of deductive analysis. In effect, simple postulates relating to choice of means and ends (e.g., "scarcity," "economizing," "maximization") enable the economist to predict economic action in accordance with the canons of logical reasoning. The strength, not the weakness, of economic theory lies in its reliance upon such simple assumptions (Firth 1951:127).

Scientific knowledge of the external world is not achieved through doctrinaire or *a priori* rejections of basic assumptions simply because they fail to conform to certain preconceived notions of "reality." The successful practitioner of any science tests the validity of his operating assumptions indirectly by applying the models and principles derived from them to the analysis of concrete situations. He only begins to question the validity of these assumptions when and if the derivative models and principles fail to explain empirical phenomena. Dalton and the substantivists are deviating from the accepted canons of scientific inquiry when they argue for the *a priori* rejection of the basic assumptions and derivative models of economic theory. Their position is made even more untenable when they persist in advocating such doctrinaire views in open defiance of a growing body of ethnographic literature which provides ample evidence that concepts and models from economic theory do have relevance in the analysis of various types of non-market economies.

VI. Recapitulation and Conclusions

Karl Polanyi and his followers, the "Substantivist" school of economic anthropology, are unanimous in their judgement that economic theory—the skills practiced by the social scientists known as economists—is inapplicable to the study of "non-market" or "primitive" economies. They further assert that a new approach to the study of economics, substantive and inductive in orientation, must be developed to provide a cross-culturally valid methodology from which a "general economic theory" may eventually derive. In the preceding sections of this paper it has been demonstrated that these substantivist views emanate from an "anti-market" ideology which considers formal economic theory as a creature of the 19th century market economy and its intellectual apologists, the Classical economists. It was further suggested that substantivist beliefs rest upon a gross oversimplification of the history of Western economic thought as well as of the nature and content of contemporary economic analysis. Finally, on the basis of a critical analysis of the substantivist distinction between the "two meanings of economic" and their views *vis-à-vis* certain basic postulates of formal economic theory, it was suggested that their extreme conclusions derive from fallacious logic, pseudo-inductionism, and are ultimately reducible to the status of metaphysical propositions.

There are many aspects of the substantivist approach to economics, both positive and negative, which were not treated in this paper. The effort here has been to focus on the relationship between economic theory and anthropology and, in keeping with this aim, the discussion has been selectively limited to those aspects of the substantive approach which bear directly upon this focal concern. It should now be apparent that urging the total rejection of economic theory in anthropological inquiry is a position which is justifiable only in ideological terms and by dependence upon arbitrary chains of doctrinaire assertions. The selective use of models and concepts taken from the formidable tool-kit of economic theory in the analysis of non-market economies does not necessarily involve an "a priori assumption that market structure—or its functional equivalent—exists universally" as Dalton would have us believe. This is an unwarranted assertion generated by the "anti-market" ideology and, in making it, Dalton conveniently ignores key studies in economic anthropology which demonstrate conclusively that many of the principles and concepts of economic theory, given certain necessary but not critical modifications, do hold up in the analysis of non-market economic systems (e.g., Salisbury 1962; Pospisil 1963a).[27]

One proponent of the substantivist approach, visualizing the economic anthropology of the future, advocates that "the leading ideas that have to be developed further are those of Malinowski, Thurnwald, Benedict, DuBois and Mead, and not those of the economic theorists" (Fusfield 1957:354). For economic anthropologists to follow this advice would be building upon our weakest links with the two great founders of economic anthropology and, consequently, would stunt the growth of the discipline. From my perspective, a science of economic anthropology will emerge only as a "hybrid discipline"—representing the fusion of two trends: the study of economic theory by anthropologists (admirably begun by Firth more than 25 years ago and continuing today in the work of anthropologists like Salisbury and Nash), and the development of an anthropological perspective by economists (begun by scholars like Goodfellow and evident today in the work of development economists like E. E. Hagen, W. A. Lewis, B. Hoselitz, and B. S. Yamey). To a large extent, the economic anthropology of the future will be focused on development—the "peasantization" of the primitive and the "proletarianization" of the peasant. Regardless of his ideological or philosophical commitments, the contemporary anthropologist must adapt to one ineluctable condition: the human populations among which he must work are not static—change of revolutionary proportions is ubiquitous; norms, attitudes, and behaviors of the Western market economy are rapidly being disseminated throughout the world's culture areas by the many institutions of neo-imperialism.

Given this situation, the eventual emergence of a general theory of comparative economic systems depends largely upon how well economics can be anthropologized. The infusion of cultural relativism into the economist's world-view is long overdue; his discipline is the last stronghold of cultural parochialism and ivory-tower disdain of socio-cultural realities in the social sciences. Nevertheless, any *general theory* of comparative economics must ultimately come from the sophisticated model-building skills of the economist applied to data collected by systematic ethnographers who are aware of the relevant categories and conceptual tools of economic analysis. To conceive, as the substantivists do, of economics as subsistence activity plus material want satisfaction, and as being comprehensible exclusively in inductive terms, is to preclude the formulation of a viable science of comparative economic systems.[28]

It has been suggested that the primitive world which for so long had dominated the anthropological imagination is inevitably on the wane, being displaced by the world of the peasant and the proletarian. The substantivist position, rooted as it is in a profound resentment of this transition, unavoidably leads its adherents to a narrow and restricted role conception of the anthropologist in economic inquiry. In the words of Dalton: "Economists are concerned with inducing real output increases, anthropologists with reducing the social decimation inherent in rapid institutional departure from indigenous forms . . . One must start with ethnoeconomic analysis—with Malinowski, not Ricardo—in order to choose those transformation paths to industrialization which entail only the unavoidable social costs" (1961:21). Apparently, Dalton conceives of the anthropologist's role *vis-à-vis* the economist as analogous to that of the social worker *vis-à-vis* the sociologist. While one may sympathize with Dalton's sentiments on philosophical grounds, it is time for anthropologists to realize that the either/or ultimatum which he poses (i.e., Malinowski or Ricardo) is not the choice upon which the development of a science of economic anthropology depends. Surely, a more promising point of departure is from the writings of those economists who have made contributions to anthropological theory (e.g., J. S. Berliner 1962) and others (e.g., W. A. Lewis 1954; B. Higgins 1959; B. Hoselitz 1960; E. E. Hagen 1962) who have begun to cope in theoretical terms with the insights of Thurnwald, Malinowski and their present anthropological counterparts; and, finally, from the work of anthropologists like Melville Herskovits, Raymond Firth, Richard Salisbury, Manning Nash, Robbins Burling and others who have moved well beyond the contributions of Ricardo in their study of the literature of economic analysis. In conclusion, I can only repeat the words which Herskovits chose to express his vision of the future of economic anthropology: "It is my hope that the future will see further analysis of the points taken up here, so that the science of comparative economics may eventually emerge as a structure based on a foundation that is equally solid in its anthropological and economic postulates" (1952:531).

NOTES

[1] The writer is currently a Public Health Service Fellow (Fellowship #-Fl-MH-23, 929-02) with the Department of Anthropology at the University of Pittsburgh. This paper was originally drafted for presentation in a graduate seminar on "Models and Model-building in Anthropology" conducted during the Winter Trimester of 1964–65 by Dr. Leonard Kasdan. I wish to express my appreciation to Dr. Kasdan, Dr. Hugo Nutini, and David Gregory of the University of Pittsburgh and to Roger Peranio of the Carnegie Institute of Technology for their helpful comments and criticisms during the preparation of this manuscript.

[2] The former group includes D. M. Goodfellow (1939), Raymond Firth, K. F. Walker, Melville Herskovits, Richard Salisbury, Edward LeClair, Robbins Burling, J. S. Berliner, and others. The latter group includes Karl Polanyi, C. M. Arensberg, Daniel Fusfield, Walter Neale, George Dalton, Paul Bohannan, Wilbert Moore, and others. Another split among economic anthropologists is between those who believe that economics deals with a certain *type* of behavior and those who believe that it deals with an *aspect* of all behavior. This split is also found among economists and relates to the manner in which they interpet the roles of the "rationality," "economizing," and "maximization" postulates in model-building.

[3] Simon Rottenberg (1958), Edward LeClair (1962), Neil Smelser (1959), and Robbins Burling (1962) have written the major critiques.

[4] For a concise discussion of the terms "unicentric" and "multicentric" refer to Bohannan (1963:246–265).

[5] For example, he recently criticizes writers who generalize "from what is true in market-integrated economies, to all economies" and rejects two recent studies which argue the case for "economic man" in Africa (i.e., that "Africans respond to material incentives and choose among economic alternatives just as we do") on the grounds that ". . . all their examples come from type III economies, where Africans—like us—have come to depend for livelihood on market sale (of labor or cash crops) (1965a:63). It is interesting to speculate as to how Dalton would deal with recent studies by Salisbury (1962) and Pospisil (1963a) neither of which analyze "type III" economies, but which do point up similarities between actors in market and non-market economies.

[6] A somewhat ironical illustration of the "communication gap" between the two groups of scholars is provided by the fact that immediately following the expression of these views on "peasant economics" by Dalton is a review by Raymond Firth of Pospisil's *Kapauku Papuan Economy*—a thorough study of the economic life of a highland New Guinea tribe which certainly qualifies as having a "primitive" or "subsistence" economy. Yet Pospisil framed his study in terms of formal economic theory and, as Firth notes in the review, he found that ". . . the Kapauku use sale as the most important form of exchange, and their economic transactions are carried on in a highly individualistic manner, with the profit motive plainly manifest" (1965:123).

[7] While the "economic man" model has been the cause of considerable controversy among economists and between economists and their critics, it continues to serve as a useful heuristic device in economic analysis. For a discussion of the role of "economic man" in the history of economic analysis see Gide 1930:924–925; Grampp 1948; Chalk 1964:223–225. For some views by economic theorists on the role of

"economic man" in contemporary economic analysis see Robbins 1935:94–99; Roll 1937:1–37; Higgins 1947; Bober 1955:22–24; Boulding 1961:82–96; 1962.

[8] No one has more clearly discerned the implications of the Knight-Herskovits exchange for economic anthropology than W. E. H. Stanner (1962:x), although K. F. Walker (1943) anticipated many of Stanner's insights.

[9] Chalk (1964:223) has succinctly delimited two roles which "economic man" has played in the history of economic analysis: (1) as an abstract description of "human nature"; (2) as a heuristic model of human action.

[10] A substantial portion of the support which Polanyi provides for this argument is drawn from the writings of Thurnwald, Malinowski and Aristotle (1944:269; 1947:112). With regard to the two eminent founders of economic anthropology, their writings—while still stimulating and useful—can no longer be considered authoritative as general texts in the field. Studies in non-market economies such as those by Firth 1939, Salisbury 1962, and Pospisil 1963 have documented the proposition that economic relations among "primitive" peoples do involve motivational patterns and rational calculations not unlike those characterizing actors in market economies. With regard to Aristotle, Polanyi tends to minimize this ancient thinker's role as a cynical and astute observer of human activity as reflected in statements like the following: ". . . all men, or the generality at least, wish what is honorable, but, when tested, choose what is profitable" (Book VIII *Ethics*—Smith and Chase 1950:219). Polanyi bases his interpretation of Aristotle on the latter's role as a utopian political and social philosopher (1947:112). That Aristotle's writings reflect these two roles is shown by Heimann 1945:23.

[11] Polanyi inverts the approach of the classical economists since he is critical of them for subordinating "society" to "economy" (1944:45–46; 1947).

[12] The statement in reference (i.e., 1957a:255) serves to illustrate clearly Polanyi's tendency to equate "simplicity" with "temporal priority" in his discussions of social and economic institutions. Juxtaposed are "primitive"—a term which has no necessary temporal connotation, and "archaic"—a term which does possess such a connotation. (Elsewhere [1947:112] Polanyi juxtaposes "early" and "primitive".) The final sentence in this statement which includes the phrase ". . . from the realm of early institutions" implies that Polanyi is not talking about "contemporary" primitive societies at all but, rather, about "extinct" societies of the historical past. Thus, one can never be certain what the societal referent is in many of Polanyi's assertions about social and economic institutions.

[13] That "primitive communism" is still very much a live issue and is reconcilable with the substantivist belief system can be inferred from Dalton's recent note which begins euphemistically with the statement: "There is a kernel of truth in the notion of 'primitive communism' " (1964:380). Polanyi also flirts with this notion throughout his writings (e.g., 1944:44; 1947:112).

[14] Levi-Strauss (1944) has documented several cases among the Nambikuara in which "chiefs" were forced to relinquish their statuses because of their failure to be generous in the provisioning of their "companions." This crisis is always accompanied by a great deal of hostility and aggressiveness in the form of verbal abuse, threatening gestures, etc.; and the process itself threatens the existence of the Nambikuara band as an ongoing system.

[15] The value of Sahlins' contributions in the field of economic and political anthropology (1960; 1962; 1963) lies in his attempt to formulate models which are more

consistent with social reality. Concerning his position on the "gainful motive" or the "self-interest" postulate in the study of primitive economics see 1962:1068.

[16] For Polanyi's description of the transformation of the human economy necessitated by the rise of the market system see 1944:41.

[17] In Schumpeter's terms the "public mind" is never an undifferentiated or homogeneous entity but is the result of the class and group structure of a given community.

[18] The bulk of Dalton's discussion under the heading "Economic Theory and Market Economy" (1961:1–5) is essentially a summary of sections of Polanyi's earlier writings and is devoted to "documenting" a posited relationship between "the method and content of economic theory" and "two central features of 19th century Britain: factory industrialism and market organization" (Dalton 1961:1).

[19] Burling's attitude is puzzling since he is one of a handful of anthropologists who demonstrates an intimate acquaintance with Lionel Robbins' seminal essay on *The Nature and Significance of Economic Science* (1935) in which the opening chapter on "The Subject Matter of Economics" incorporates separate sections devoted respectively to "The 'Materialist's' Definition of Economics" and "The 'Scarcity' Definition of Economics." Although Polanyi accuses Robbins and others of committing the "economistic fallacy" (i.e., artificially identifying the economy with its market form) and further asserts that Robbins' essay ". . . fatefully distorted the problem" (of the study of the place occupied by the economy in human society) (1959:164), I fail to understand how Polanyi's distinction between the "formal" and "substantive" meanings of economic adds anything but confusion to Robbins' concise discussion.

[20] Writings by economists on the "scope and method" of economics can be traced back as, least to James Mill and through the writings of his son, John Stuart Mill, to John Neville Keynes, Lionel Robbins (1935), T. W. Hutchinson (1938), Frank Knight (1941), Joseph Schumpeter (1954), and down to such current writers as Kenneth Boulding (1958) and Benjamin Higgins (1959).

[21] Walter Neale, in a recent attempt by a substantivist to clarify some of the ambiguity associated with the concept of "economic," does relate Polanyi's substantive definition to others in the economic literature (1964:1300–1302). After citing Alfred Marshall's definition which focuses on the "material requisites of well-being," he admits that portions of it are "close to, if not identical with, the substantive definition . . ." (1964:1301). However, Neale unfortunately remains silent about the criticisms of Rottenberg, Smelser, LeClair and Burling and, in other respects, does not deviate from the Polanyi line (e.g., 1964:1302). Thus, the "split-level" dialogue is perpetuated as the Polanyites continue to exchange notes within their own closed sphere of discourse, without directly acknowledging or attempting to answer the views of their critics.

[22] Statements of this distinction are available in Polanyi (1957a:243–44; 1959:162–63) and, more recently in Dalton (1961:5–7) and Neale (1964:1302). Max Weber made the "formal-substantive" distinction in his discussion of "The Formal and Substantive Rationality of Economic Action" (1947:184–86). However, the extent to which Polanyi used Weber's discussion as a point of departure for his own is unclear.

[23] For a recent cogent statement by an economist on the relationship between economic theory and economic facts in model-building see G. G. Firth (1964).

[24] Neil J. Smelser in a major critical review article of *Trade and Market in the*

Early Empires, describes the "two meanings of economic" and then proceeds to suggest that this distinction and the inferences drawn from it come ". . . perilously close to throwing out the baby of *general economic analysis* with the *culture-bound market orientation* of traditional economics" (1959:175). To compound the confusion created by the "two meanings" discussion, Polanyi devises a bogey construct in the form of a "compound concept of the two meanings." According to him this concept is both current and past, popular and scientific in usage (1959:163). In this discussion, Polanyi switches his frame of reference from political economy and economic analysis and seems, instead, to be talking about something comparable to Schumpeter's "economic thought" or about "sociological analysis" (he cites Pareto, Durkheim, Weber (1947) and Parsons). Pervading the substantivist literature is this ambiguity concerning the intended referents of terms which are used loosely and interchangeably, e.g., "formal economics," "formal economic theory," "economic analysis," "formal meaning of economic," and "economic theory." Even when the context seems to indicate that the referent is "economic analysis," it is obviously not referring to that set of skills which contemporary economists practice, but to a set of assumptions and principles related to the Classical economists or to the founders of Neoclassical economics.

[25] In the economic literature to "economize" means to arrange, constitute, organize or turn to best account. The act of "economizing" implies two things: (1) a standard for measuring needs so that the greater or more highly valued may be distinguished from the lesser or less highly valued; together with (2) an acceptable method for apportioning time, energy, and resources in accordance with the results of this measurement. The mutual interdependence of "choice" and "standard of comparison" and the universality of these two minimal components of "economizing" has been expressed with great insight by Heimann (1945:4–5).

[26] LeClair makes the same point (1962:1184).

[27] Salisbury in his analysis of a New Guinea highland tribe, the Siane, though unable to identify any discrete empirical entity which he could label "economy" and without being able to quantify economic data in terms of the usual measuring rod of money, was nevertheless able to conduct an elaborate and penetrating study of what he calls "the economic aspects of Siane behavior" (i.e., those aspects in which there is allocation of scarce means, based on a rational calculation in terms of quantities of goods and services, and in which goods are produced, exchanged or consumed). Not only did Salisbury find several traditional western economic concepts useful in his analysis, but his formulation of categories of goods among the Siane in terms of demand elasticities is a convincing demonstration that economic concepts taken from "price theory" (which in the substantivist scheme is the most market-economy biased aspect of economic theory) can serve as valuable analytic tools in the study of non-market economies.

[28] The vision of a "science of comparative economic system" does not necessarily involve a commitment to the formulation of a cross-culturally valid "general" or "grand" theory of economic behavior. Such a theory may never be developed and, if and when it is, the logico-mathematical skills which are part of the economist's tool-kit will inevitably play a dominant role in its formulation. Given this situation, anthropologists should focus their skills on more concrete and readily achievable tasks. Currently, one of the most complex, least understood, and most potentially fruitful problem-areas in economic anthropology is the study of so-called "peasant"

or "intermediate" societies. It is in the study of such societies that an "empirically powerful body of middle range theory" (Nash 1961:186) will be developed in economic anthropology and it is here that the anthropologist can perform his most significant role as a student of economic behavior.

13 MAXIMIZATION AS NORM, STRATEGY, AND THEORY: A COMMENT ON PROGRAMMATIC STATEMENTS IN ECONOMIC ANTHROPOLOGY[1]

Frank Cancian

The impetus for this comment is Scott Cook's paper, "The Obsolete 'Anti-Market' Mentality: A Critique of the Substantive Approach to Economic Anthropology," in this issue. In it he shows (with more or less success depending on your point of view): 1. That most societies by now participate in active "market" economies, and that therefore any significance the substantivist position may have for the study of "non-market" economies is of little importance as a guide to present field research (Section II); 2. That the substantivists have not understood economic theory and are unfair and unscientific in their rejection of the possibility that it will be useful in the study of non-Western economies (Section III and V); 3. That the substantivists, and especially Polanyi as their leader, are "romanticists" who see primitives as altruistic and naturally cooperative (Section IV). Cook's paper, and the many that have gone before it[2] in this debate, show that many questionable statements have been made by both teams. The literature is heavy with lengthy quotes showing that "we" understand and "they" do not, but it often seems that the insolvable problems are being discussed while the basic issues from which they stem are never joined. In this paper I will not quote or cite extensively; further textual analysis will only make it more difficult for the next man. Rather I will try to suggest that there are at least two legitimate positions, and that the issues really at stake are not the ones that the combatants explicitly address themselves to. For the most part I will assume the reader is familiar with the literature being discussed.

Economic Anthropology

The formalists say that economics in the study of the allocation of scarce means to alternative ends. That is, it is the study of economizing, or the way in which people maximize personal satisfactions. Economists have some theories about how people do this, say the formalists, and there is no reason to think that these theories are not general enough to be helpful in the study of non-

Reproduced by permission of the American Anthropological Association from American Anthropologist *68:465–470 (April, 1966).*

Western societies. In fact, say the formalists, some scholars have shown that they are helpful in understanding events in non-Western societies.

No, say the substantivists, economic theory is based on the study of market economies where the point is maximization of profit by both parties to a transaction, and non-Western societies are not all like that, so the theory is not general enough and will not apply to non-Western societies. We must study the unique configurations of non-Western societies, their institutions. Economic anthropology is about the institutions surrounding the provision of the material necessities of existence to man.

But, says the formalist, you cannot prove that non-Western man does not maximize, he clearly is subject to some kinds of scarcity, if only the scarcity of human energy; and therefore he must allocate scarce means to alternative ends. And besides, "material" and "non-material" goods are often exchanged for each other, so you cannot hold to your definition of economic anthropology.

The bystander may think: Yes, but if everybody maximizes and the realms of material and non-material goods cannot be separated, economic anthropology must be the study of all human behavior, and that seems strange. I thought it was a small subfield of anthropology.

Insofar as this caricature is accurate, it should be clear that:

1. Some people seem to be interested in maximization processes, and others in the study of institutions, but they all say they are interested in whether economic theory is applicable to non-Western societies.

2. Neither approach, given its starting point, provides an intuitively satisfactory definition which delimits the field of economic anthropology, and the effort to do this is probably hopeless.

The controversy, it seems to me, has little to do with the applicability of economic theory to non-Western society. It has to do with the belief by one group that maximization is a good way to approach human behavior, and the belief by the other group that human institutions are varied and difficult to categorize, and that many "economic" ones are quite distinct from certain Western institutions in which maximization of something (usually "profit") is the norm. The root of the misunderstanding is best seen by examining three meanings of maximization.

Maximization as a Norm

There are certain Western institutions which involve maximization as a norm. For example, in a buying-selling situation both parties are expected, in fact enjoined, to allocate resources so as to maximize their profits. In this case, maximization is part of an institution; it is a norm. The buyer role and the seller role are institutionalized roles.

As I understand them, the substantivists argue that there are many institutions in which maximization is not a norm. Presumably this is true in any society. Furthermore, they say, in non-Western society, in many of the situations involving provision of the material necessities of life, it is not a norm for the parties to a transaction to maximize *material things* or any non-material things that may be exchanged for material things. This contention of the substantivists has nothing to do with whether the parties to the transaction are maximizing or not. The parties almost certainly may be seen as maximizing adherence to some norm or set of norms, but none of these norms is itself a prescription to maximize *in terms of the very objects being exchanged.*

This contrast is seen in two American institutions: buying in a store and giving a Christmas gift. In the store it is considered appropriate for the owner and the customer to maximize in terms of money (getting the most or giving the least), and this is the norm (in the context of other norms that bar fraud). In the exchange of Christmas gifts (in my American culture) it is appropriate to maximize equality of exchange. Given adjustments for obvious differences in resources, both parties to the exchange are most satisfied when they manage to guess correctly the level at which they are exchanging with each other. Individuals who grossly deviate from the established standard of the relationship, or people who imply that their gifts are uncommonly expensive, are not behaving appropriately and are sanctioned. Granted that, in contradiction of Polanyi's "romanticist" views, the exchange of Christmas gifts may be fully as antagonistic, competitive and unaltruistic as the purchase of an article in a store, what is interesting about the two situations in that in one maximization of the objects being exchanged is the norm, and in the other it is not.

When, in non-Western societies, substantial quantities of life-sustaining goods which would be considered "economic" goods in Western societies are transferred in the absence of a norm that both parties maximize the quantity of such goods finally in its possession, it is the absence of that norm that is interesting. The fact that the interaction may be seen as economizing or maximizing in terms of some set of means and ends like yams, kinship obligations and prestige does not obviate the normative or institutional differences.

Maximization as a Strategy

That the participants in a transaction can be seen as maximizing something is true by definition. Maximization is one of the standard restatements of the *a priori* truth that all human behavior is patterned; that all human behavior has a reason. This use of maximization as a scientific strategy involves seeking out the norms or motives (or whatever the investigator sees as the impetus of behavior) and attempting to rank order them so as to see the behavior as the (conscious or unconscious) maximization of these things. They become the ends being maximized. When using maximization as a scientific strategy, the investigator knows that his analysis is complete when he has stated the norms, motives, etc. and the conditions (means and their limits, the scarce factors) such that every act may be seen as a predictable maximization of the ends. If he cannot see the act as maximization, he immediately assumes that his statements of norms, motives, etc., and conditions are not yet correct and seeks to "balance the equation" so that it will work. He does not reject the idea that people will maximize, for it is the basis of his scientific strategy. It is in this sense that all people always maximize or economize. There can be no argument about it, but knowing this helps very little in achieving the end of predictions about empirical cases.

Maximization and Theories

The two principal formalist articles to appear in this journal (Burling 1962 and LeClair 1962) agree in seeing economizing or maximization as the scientific strategy characteristic of economic anthropology, but insofar as they propose concrete research programs they are quite different. Burling takes note of some theories that involve maximization of factors like power, and comments that single factor theories are usually untenable. He goes on to suggest that economic anthropology be the search for the multiple factors that people maximize, i.e., he proposes that studies of human behavior using maximization as a scientific strategy constitute economic anthropology and leaves it at that. LeClair, though his title is "Economic Theory and Economic Anthropology," does not refer to theory at all in the positive part of his paper. He states the economizing principle and then takes up a number of concepts used by economists and generalizes them so they may apply to all human behavior. When he comes to citing examples he very quickly shifts to a "material" definition of economics.

George Homans has used the idea of maximization in a theory that applies to all human behavior. A brief look at the problems Homans encounters in his *Social Behavior: Its Elementary Forms* (1961) will suggest that, whatever the virtues of the maximization idea, the research problems still lie in the area of the study of institutions.

For Homans "elementary" denotes that aspect of social behavior that is independent of institutions. He calls it "subinstitutional" (1961:6). Homans wishes to state general propositions about social behavior that are independent of cultural convention and individual differences. He uses concepts and ideas like "cost," "reward," "profit" and maximization and others about hunger, satiation and conditioning. In thinking about cost and reward he comes to the idea of value, and in thinking about measuring values he arrives at the idea that values vary according to the cultural and individual past of the person involved (1961:39–49). Mired again in institutional behavior, he deftly invokes the dictum that the best guess we can make is that the future will be like the past and that thus a person's future valuing will be like his past valuing, and often like the past valuing of other people who share his culture. This places Homans more squarely in the middle of institutional variations and is really no help in making the long step from his subinstitutional theory to measures of the values exhibited in human behavior. In the theory all valuing is placed on a single dimension according to its intensity; in behavior value is expressed in terms of local custom (disregarding the further complications introduced by variations in personal preference). The related problems of learning to read local customs and learning to equate local custom in one place with local custom in another place have no automatic solution that will permit Homans to test his theory. In this situation Homans merely states that he will be crude about measuring values and gets on with his task. In short, he does not solve the problem of operationalizing his subinstitutional theory.[3]

The formalists say that economic theory is not bound by the market principle, that it is logically free from limitations of time and place, that it is, in effect, subinstitutional. Insofar as this is true, the theory should be equally useful in the study of non-Western and Western societies; and, insofar as this is true, it faces the same problems of operationalization faced by Homan's theory and any other very abstract theory.

We cannot expect to borrow procedures for operationalization from the economists (as far as I know they are short on them anyway). The anthropological chestnut about the comparability of institutional forms in different cultures remains a lively topic of debate in discussion about cross-cultural research in anthropology. There is no reason to think that measures (operationalizations) devised by non-anthropologists (economists) for a part of our own culture (the economy) are less subject to difficulties than measures devised by anthropologists with a cross-cultural perspective. To the contrary in fact.

The Substantivists and the Formalists

In the controversy that has developed it appears that the formalists have been arguing for the use of economic theory in its subinstitutional form as a general scientific strategy, and that the substantivists have been arguing for the obvious differences among institutions associated with the transfer of the material necessities of life. The formalists have made sorties into the application of more concrete economic concepts and theory to non-Western society and the substantivists have made parallel sorties into the study of the social concomitants of types of exchange—both with some success. By the time they had done this, however, they could no longer talk with each other, and the basic problem of operationalizing subinstitutional theoretical propositions or (from the other point of view) building general theory about varied institutions was for the most part cast aside.

In the spirit of reconciliation it might be admitted that while Cook may be right about the dogmatism of the substantivists, he does not appreciate the distance between the abstractions of economic theory and the giving of Christmas gifts; and that while the substantivists are correct that maximization (of the material object being exchanged) is found as a norm only in some exchanges of material objects, they have not appreciated the usefulness of maximization as a scientific strategy in situations where maximization as a norm is not present.

There is no contradiction between: "Economics is the study of economizing. Economizing is the allocation of scarce resources among alternative ends" (LeClair 1962:1188), and "The economy, then, is an instituted process" (Polanyi 1957b:248).

NOTES

[1] I am grateful to my wife, Francesca Cancian, and to Roy D'Andrade for comments on an earlier draft of this paper.

[2] Here I am principally concerned with the formalists as they are represented by Burling (1962), Cook (1966) and LeClair (1962), and with the substantivists as they are represented by Dalton (1961) and Polanyi (1957b).

[3] For those familiar with Homans' charge that Talcott Parsons "has written the dictionary of a language that has no sentences" (1961:11), it is helpful to see Homans as a man who has written sentences in a language that has no dictionary.

· section VI
ECONOMIC SOCIOLOGY

14 PARSONS AND SMELSER ON THE ECONOMY
Harry W. Pearson

The publication of a greatly enlarged and revised version of Professor Talcott Parsons' "Marshall Lectures"[1] lends impressive support to our conviction that a discipline which may be called "economic sociology" is being newly established in the United States. The impetus for the widely current efforts in the direction of an economic sociology comes from the increasing array of empirical problems met by all social scientists who must face up to economies as social systems. The problems arise in two different areas of interest; those involving premarket economies, both literate and nonliterate, and those where contemporary departures from the pattern of a self-regulating system of markets pose the problem. Attempts to deal systematically with these distinctly separate empirical problems converge on a common interest: the establishment of a generally relevant theory of economic organization and development.

It is this interest that we have in mind in attempting to appraise the accomplishments of Talcott Parsons and Neil Smelser in their new book, *Economy and Society*, for, although the empirical problems with which this book deals are derived from a market-ordered economy, it represents a theoretical *tour de force* aimed in the direction of a general theory. Starting at the opposite pole, the book in which this chapter appears is concerned with the problems of primitive, early historical and nonwestern economies, but it too is regarded as a modest offering in the same direction. The opportunity to discuss the position now taken by Professor Parsons is therefore welcomed on general grounds. Our purpose is to clarify points held in common, differences in approach and fundamental disagreements in so far as both efforts come to grips with the problem of determining the shifting place of the economy in human society.

It is encouraging to find that there are important areas of agreement between these two books. A "functional" approach is common to both. Professor Parsons' sociology views society in terms of certain functional requirements all of which must be satisfied if that society is to continue and prosper. All of the specific units of the society—the "collectivities," institutions and roles—are seen as necessarily contributing to the fulfillment of these functional prerequisites; although they may, of course, be differentiated in terms of primary functions. The central analytical problem is that all the units of the whole society *"partici-pate* in the economy," but, because every concrete unit is multi-functional, none is "purely economic" (p. 14). Thus, although we feel that the authors' analysis is based on a mistaken quasi-identification of economic theory and sociology, *in principle* the Parsons-Smelser book conceives the problem of economy and society in the same way as it is here conceived. The fruitfulness of employing the basic conceptual tools of modern sociology in approaching the economy— especially the conception of cultural values embedded in institutions, roles and personalities (i.e., the "reality" of society)—is clearly demonstrated in the ease with which this new book is able to dispose of some hoary problems of economic theory which arise from that theory's "psychological and sociological atomism" (p. 23). A functionally defined economy is seen as performing *within* the structural context of society. Thus, "the goal of the economy is not simply the production of income for the utility of an aggregate of individuals. It is the maximization of production relative to the whole complex of institutionalized value-systems and functions of the society and its subsystems" (p. 22). We believe that the maximization principle introduces a bias into the definition of the economy's function, but again in principle there is agreement with many of the basic ideas in the present book.

While we thus find important areas of fundamental agreement and the under-lying concepts for the articulation of an economic sociology are clearly presented, the two efforts part company in their separate attempts to deal systematically with the problems. In fact they seem to move in almost opposite directions. This divergence may be due in large measure to the different location of the empirical problems which the two books set out to examine. But in so far as both make some claim to generality this reason cannot be accepted as decisive. More sig-nificant, is the fact that in the manner of attacking the problem, once it is stated, we are at opposite poles.

In the history of the attempt to locate the place of the economy in society— or, as we should prefer, of economies in societies—two distinct lines of approach can be discerned. Both take their cue from the entrance of the market system onto the scene of history.

One approach proceeds through what might be called "institutional" analysis. The economy in its concrete manifestations is here the subject of interest. Aris-totle, Marx, the German "Historical School," Menger in his posthumous work, the American "Institutionalists," to name but a few, resorted to this approach with varying degrees of success. It is also the method of the book in which this chapter appears. It was the appearance of the market system with its inherent tendency to separate the economic process from its societal integument which urgently raised the question of the different ways in which the organization of livelihood affects the community. And this is the parent interest of all those who followed this line of attack. The first essential of this method (here most attempts have foundered) is a definition of the economy that allows an analytical distinction between what is economic and what is not. This requires a statement of the economy's function and of the operations necessary to that function. The analysis of any particular economy, its development over time, or the comparison of different economies hinges here upon observation of the manner in which the economic operations are institutionalized. And this is an empirical problem. The ability to generalize and predict depends, with this method, upon the emergence of common patterns in the institutionalized operations. The forms of integration—reciprocity, redistribution and exchange as they are employed in the present book, for example—are typical of such empirically derived patterns.

There is another tradition of social thought which was brought to the consideration of our problem through an interest in, to use Weber's term, the *Zweckrational* orientation of modern western society, i.e., its heightened concern with the rational way of doing things whatever the ultimate ends. Represented most prominently by Weber, Marshall, Pareto, and Parsons, this strain of thought has therefore been concerned primarily with a certain "aspect" of social behavior, its development and organizational consequences. The link between this interest and the location of empirical economies in societies was provided by the advent of the market system which institutionalized economizing action so that the goods and person movements of the empirical economy tended to be ordered by individuals rationally choosing among alternative uses of scarce means. The interest of the scholars in this tradition thus turned very largely around the economy in its market form.

If this approach is consistently followed, it will become obvious, as Parsons has clearly shown, that economizing does not exhaust rational human experience, but is inevitably overlaid with other attitudes and orientations toward the just, the kind, the temperate, the politic, or otherwise "right" way of doing things (Cf. Parsons 1949. See also Diesing 1950; Macfie 1949; Streeten 1954). In logic, the ultimate step in the development of this approach would be the proper identification of *all* the "aspects" of social action. If this were possible—an attempt Weber himself declined to make—it might then seem feasible to employ the universal "aspects" in the analysis of operating social systems, economic as well as noneconomic. Crucial to the fruitfulness of this approach in the analysis of empirical problems would be the ability to relate in a meaningful way the universals to the actual social structure under consideration. If, for example, the economizing "aspect" of behavior is under scrutiny, then it must first be located in some structure or other—the family, the government, the economy.

Economy and Society represents the logically ultimate step in the tradition of this latter attempt to locate economizing action in its social setting. Professor Parsons long ago rejected the "institutional" approach. His decision grew out of the "dilemma," as he saw it, presented by the American "institutionalist" school of economics, especially in the work of Veblen (pp. 5–6). Parsons viewed the "institutionalists" as rejecting economic theory (i.e., the theory of economizing behavior) on the grounds of its failure to explain the concrete facts of economic life, and as attempting, in its stead, to propound "a complete theory of social development." He felt strongly that in such a theory the "economic aspect" of social action "loses its theoretical specificity altogether," hence his own rejection of "institutionalism" (p. 6). Unfortunately, his new statement of the problem does not resolve so much as raise to another level precisely the "dilemma" which is presented not only by the American "institutionalist" movement, but by the whole tradition of western social thought in its attempts to deal with the economy.

The aim of the Parsons-Smelser work is stated as the formulation of "economic theory's relation to the non-economic aspects of social life" (p. 5), and this is equated with "the relation of the economy to the total society" (p. 16). It thus continues in the direction established by Parsons in *The Structure of Social Action*. Yet, in another sense, as we are told, the position here is "distinctly different" (p. 6). The alternative to the institutional approach which Professor Parsons took in his earlier work was to follow Pareto (Cf. Parsons 1949:757ff), maintaining the general validity of economic theory, but admitting that it dealt only with "*some of the variables* which determine concrete social behavior in the 'economic' as in other spheres" (p. 6). The formal advance beyond Pareto in the new statement lies in the identification of *all* the "aspects" of social action ["on a cognate level" of abstraction] (pp. 5–6), and their inclusion in a general theory of action, applicable to *all* systems and subsystems of social interaction. Thus there are no special variables unique to economies as social systems, only "the general variables" of social theory, which are the universal "aspects." The economic case of the general theory is distinctive only in the sense that here "the concrete structures of different societies" are "most favorable empirically to 'purely economic' analysis." That is, economizing action tends to be located in the economy. The authors are aware that there are empirical economies where the social structure does not enforce economizing rationality to any important degree, and further that, "most so-called 'economic' processes must be regarded as resultants of economic and non-economic factors." The former condition, however, is that of the "completely routinized," "undifferentiated" economy with which they are not primarily concerned; the latter, i.e., the interplay of "economic" and "noneconomic" factors, is really the subject of the book (p. 6, n. 4; p. 42).

In developing their subject the authors identify four properties of social action as representing the universal functional requirements of social systems and subsystems. The "economic" aspect is said to arise out of the requirement of "adaptation" to an external environment in order that the goals of the system may be achieved. The function of this aspect is said to be, "the generalization of facilities for a variety of system and subsystem goals." The "facilities" are specified as "wealth" or "income" (pp. 18 ff). Their important feature is "their adaptability to . . . various uses" (p. 48). Thus the "economy" becomes a kind of value-neutral sphere of action devoted exclusively to making means available. Of the "noneconomic factors" with which "economic" processes are compounded, one is said to be "goal attainment," a requirement also growing out of the relationship between system and environment. It is distinguished from "adaptation," however, by its special function: "the *mobilization* of the necessary prerequisites for the *attainment* of given system goals of the society" (p. 48). Thus the attempt is made to distinguish between means and ends by making each a distinctive category of social action. In addition, the fact that these categories necessarily operate in a larger social environment is made the subject of two other system requirements. The process of attaining specific goals and making means generally available must be consistent with the values of the total social system, and it must be coordinated with other processes so as to avoid undue internal conflict among the parts. These two additional requirements are given the names "pattern maintenance" and "integration," respectively.

The means-ends distinction has, of course, long been basic to Professor Parsons' analysis of social action. And he has always identified "economic" action with "an intermediate position in the great chain of means and ends" (Parsons 1935:421; also Parsons 1934:522–529). That is, economic action was held to be directed toward maximizing the supply of generally available means (Parsons 1934:526). But Professor Parsons has, in the past, been careful to point out that economizing is a *norm* of action; its empirical relevance resting on the "circumstance that men do in fact try (not merely 'tend') to 'economize' " (Ibid. 520). And economizing has been distinguished from other types of action in terms of the different norms involved in each case. Thus political action, for example, has been identified as "a rational process of the attainment of ends through the acquisition and exercise of coercive power over other individuals and groups" (Ibid. 528). It is important, therefore, to emphasize (a point we shall return to) that in this new elaboration of his position, Professor Parsons has, with Mr. Smelser, taken an important step beyond his previous stand. For while economic ("adaptive") and political ("goal attainment") action are defined in essentially the same way as before, they now assume an entirely new significance by being classed not merely as types of action, but as *functional* prerequisites of any and all social systems.

The "most general proposition" of the authors regarding these categories is that "total societies *tend* to differentiate into subsystems (social structures) which are specialized in each of the four primary functions" (p. 47). Thus they argue that the empirical economy tends to be specialized according to the "adaptive" requirement of the society as a whole, maximizing the flow of "fluidly disposable means," or "utility," to the total social system (pp. 20–1). In other words, although, like every other "concrete" social system, the empirical economy is a composite of *all* the "aspects" of social action, it tends to be structurally differentiated according to its primary function the definition of which corresponds to economizing with scarce means.

This leaves us in the following position: Economizing rationality has been identified as one of the universal aspects of human social behavior. The actual appearance of such behavior, however, is said to depend upon the prior existence of social structures which favor action so oriented. If we are primarily interested in locating the types of social structure in which economizing is found, all of this seems unexceptionable. But if the method is to enhance our understanding of that system whereby men secure the means of their livelihood, then a bridge must be provided between economizing and the economy. Parsons and Smelser do indeed fashion such a bridge, but it is constructed out of conjecture, not the empiry of comparative analysis. Apparently by virtue of a familiar developmental law involving the tendency toward greater division of labor and its assumed correlative, exchange (p. 104, p. 141), the human economy is said to exhibit a tendency to differentiate according to the society's "adaptive" requirement, which is defined in terms of economizing with scarce means. It is a process consisting of instrumental activity designed to maximize the "economic value" of inherently scarce means.[2] By thus joining a formal category of action, economizing, with an empirical entity, the economy, the authors have committed a fateful error. Inevitably, the economy tends to be identified with its market form. The source of the error appears to lie in their having *confused the functional requirement of adaptation* to environment in the process of achieving system goals *with one of the modes of adaptation, namely, economizing.*

This leads us to suggest that the economic sociology of this new book is founded upon a confusion of two quite different methods of approach. The "Columbian map" by means of which the authors attempt to locate the universal aspects of social systems is capable of being read in two distinctly different ways, and these different interpretations are not adequately distinguished.

One reading implies a separation, for purposes of analysis, between goal states and the means of attaining them. It is a generalization of the means-ends distinction. The primary "function" of any particular system is, in this interpretation, defined in terms of specific "goals" of the subsystem. For example, at one point we are told, "the *goal* of the economy is to provide goods and services for consumption" (p. 42). Here we find no assumption regarding *how* the goal is to be achieved. Since every social structure must somehow reflect the requirement that it "adapt" to its environment, natural and social, there can be no objection to this reading of the "map." And the "exigencies" of that environment will necessarily shape the social structure. Thus societal values will leave their imprint and the necessity of integration with other structural units will be reflected. These are requirements of the social situation. The important feature of this interpretation is that it requires no unwarranted assumptions. Specific system goals and the mode of their attainment are here open to investigation. A social system is identified in terms of its goals, while its actual societal form is determined through study of the situation in which it functions.

Another interpretation, however, views the same "Columbian" classification in terms of certain types of social action. Here "adaptation" and "goal attainment" are defined as the locus of economizing and power, respectively, acquiring the names "economy" and "polity" (pp. 47–8). The analytical isolation of such spheres may be useful for some purposes, but they are, for that reason, not mere phantoms; *their actual appearance presupposes definite social structures.* That is, the social structure for economizing action can be clearly defined; it has definite requirements. A perfect market system is the embodiment, although certainly not the only one, of these requirements. The same may be said regarding the exercise of power, although here, of course, the typical social structure would be different. In any case, the correspondence between these types and actual social structures, the economy or government, for example, is problematical. It is precisely the problem for investigation, given this method of approach. To say that the empirical economy inevitably becomes more and more specialized in economizing is to posit a relationship between the livelihood process and a type of rationality which we must insist is not inherent.

The above criticism is relevant only in so far as the authors tend to generalize economic rationality as the typical economic process. A fatal blow to a general economic sociology, this false equation might be less serious given the principal subject of the book itself. For the authors are chiefly concerned with the "non-economic" aspects of the *market* economy, and here, it is true, their analytical subsystem, "economy," and the empirical economy do in fact *tend* to coincide.

It seems to us, however, that a fallacy of misplaced concreteness ramifies throughout the whole presentation. The "Columbian map" according to which all of the aspects of the total social system are identified is employed to "locate" specifically the noneconomic social environment with which the "economy" (read, "economizing" action) must somehow come to terms in its functioning. As a social system the economy itself is said to have pattern maintenance, integrative, adaptive and goal-attainment exigencies of its own to meet (pp. 40–3). It too is thus composed of analytical subsystems, which, it must be remembered, may not be identified with the firms, unions, banks, etc., of the empirical economy. The economy thus differentiated is bounded by the remaining three subsystems of the total society. In order for the economy to perform its total function all of its system members must somehow come to terms with the apposite member of the societal subsystem at that boundary. This "coming to terms" with the counterpart in a bordering subsystem is viewed as a series of "inputs" and "outputs" and their "exchange" between system members. In these terms each subsystem is regarded as "producing" an output and exchanging it for the output of its bordering system to their mutual advantage, and contributing, incidentally, to the equilibrium of the total system (Cf. Ch. III). The subsystems of society thus behave toward one another like persons in a price-making market.

The details of this scheme of analysis are much too elaborate to describe here, but it clearly represents a highly formalized attempt to illustrate the subordination of the economy to the functional requirements of the whole society. While every social scientist must applaud the basic objective, and even agree that important insights may be gained from such schematic outlines, the same basic criticism must be levelled against the details of this sociology of the market economy as against the general scheme itself. The temptation to reify the purely analytical categories is apparently too great to be resisted. Thus the authors insist that there must be "*some* correspondence between these economic differentiations and those of social structure . . . though the concrete social structures vary from one society to another" (p. 52). But this is precisely what cannot be concluded from their scheme. It is said, for example, that the "polity" is that sphere where power is employed to achieve collective system goals (p. 48). The importance of the "polity" vis-à-vis the "economy" lies in its making available credit facilities for purposes of capital investment. In other words, money is a "political" instrument. Formally, this is stated in terms of the exchange between the "economy" and the "polity" across their "adaptive" boundaries, "rights to intervene" being exchanged for the polity's "decision" to provide credit facilities for capital investment (Cf. Ch. III). Putting aside the difficulty of distinguishing between analytical categories and concrete structures here, what is primarily objectionable is the identification of the *general* interest of the "polity" in the economic process with only *one* of the markets in the total system, i.e., the money market. At this point of the analysis, where it is argued that "each of the four [societal subsystems] has one boundary which interchanges primarily with *one* of the other three cognate subsystems" (p. 297), the "Columbian map" is in danger of becoming a Procrustean bed. Does not the "polity," for example, *necessarily* have a similar "interest" in regulating the employment of labor and land in the productive process, i.e., in the economy's "goal attainment" sphere?

Perhaps the most important achievement of this new statement by Professor Parsons and Mr. Smelser lies in their emphasizing the priority of a state of equilibrium for the society as a whole over that of the economy considered in isolation. In this way the problem of an economic sociology finds its proper statement. We feel however that, in their analysis of the problem, they have maintained the "theoretical specificity" of economics at what may well be the inevitable cost of confusing economizing with the economy. But what is more, their interpretation of the mode of interrelationship between the "economic" and "noneconomic" aspects of social life, i.e., the economic sociology itself, is imbued with a bias which appears to have been derived from formal economic theory. Basic to their analysis is the contention that in all social interaction, "The amount of performance contribution is a function of the expectation (and in the long run, receipt) of sanction. . . . Conversely, amount of sanction or reward is a function of amount of performance contribution" (p. 10). It is then suggested, however, that the "conceptual structure in economics which defines the elements involved in an exchange transaction can be generalized to all cases of performance-sanction balancing" (p. 13). It is a daring theoretical move to apply the concept of inputs and outputs in equilibrium to the whole of society, but whatever the ultimate verdict of scholarship regarding this move, it is surely premature to apply the terminology of the supply-demand scheme of economic theory to the general balancing of performances and sanctions in social interaction.

The "economistic" character of the sociology here is perhaps most apparent in Chapter III, where an attempt is made to develop a sociology of markets. The economics of imperfect competition is shown to be limited by the narrow range of the imperfections considered. It is suggested that the degrees of "imperfection" of markets can be more fully understood if their qualitative differences are analyzed. And such differences are sociological in character. The sellers in the money market, for example, are located at a different point on the sociological compass than the sellers in the labor market. These suggestions, while not new, are presented with a clarity that excites anticipation of what is to come. But in the analysis built upon these insights a penchant for the formalisms of economic theory mars the whole scheme. The concepts of property, contract, and market are expanded to include "properties" in the "possession" of noneconomic subsystems, the "noncontractual" elements of contract, and the noneconomic modifications of market behavior, respectively. Persistent imperfections in the "economic" market are then explained by the allusion to a broader, hypothetical market which must always be in equilibrium if the economic market is not.

This is certainly an ingenious scheme, and no one will read the book without receiving important insights into the sociology of a market economy. But what have we learned about the actual mechanisms through which different markets are modified by the social situations in which they operate? Here, instead of maintaining the specificity of economic theory, the authors have so diffused it in application to phantom subsystems without shape or form that even the economist must object. A market is not a self-sufficing social system, but at least it presents us with a concrete mechanism which validates the abstractions of economic theory. It would seem that Professor Parsons and Mr. Smelser have indeed provided some relief from the one-sided rationalism of the economic theorist, but have they not conjured empty sociological boxes to replace their misnamed economic counterparts?

Weaknesses such as these which we find in the book, *Economy and Society*, lead us to suggest that Parsons and Smelser have not resolved the so-called "institutionalist dilemma," but only raised it to another level. Like the most sophisticated of the economic theorists, the authors do not set out to detail the operation of concrete economic systems. Several times they are at pains to point out the lack of correspondence between their categories and the real flesh and blood units of the economic system. Nevertheless, again like many economic theorists, they exhibit a persistent tendency to assume that there *must* be such a correspondence, and this assumption, when it is made, confuses the analysis, and bars the door to the understanding of how in fact social interaction in the economy is patterned.

Having in mind again the two traditions according to which western social scientists have attempted to place the economy in society, we suggest that the "dilemma" consists primarily of the question, What is it that we wish to know? If it is the problem, which occupied Weber and Pareto, of the degree to which the rationality of economizing with scarce means can be present in society, that is one thing. If we wish to generalize our understanding of the way in which substantive economic processes are institutionalized, that is another. Each will have its appropriate method. The two interests have been greatly confused because of their convergence on the presumed super-rational market economy of the eighteenth and nineteenth centuries. The market system in its ideal form is the very embodiment of that rationality of which economizing with scarce means is the essence. Economic analysis, as that discipline developed in the late nineteenth century, is the perfect theoretical statement of such action, *wherever it may actually be located in society*. But the unique convergence of substantive economic process, economizing rationality and economic theory is an event of history which cannot justify their being equated everywhere and always. And the attempt to locate the place of economies in societies which begins with the question of the relationship between economic theory and theory of other "aspects" of social action is doomed to failure unless the significance of this special case is clearly recognized.

NOTES

[1] Talcott Parsons and Neil Smelser, *Economy and Society* (1956). (The author wishes to express his sincere thanks to Professor Parsons and Mr. Smelser for providing the manuscript of *Economy and Society* so that this review might appear in the present book. Page proof was also kindly provided so that references to *Economy and Society* might be identified by the page on which they appear.)

[2] On the inherent scarcity of the means involved in the adaptive process, see also Parsons, Bales and Shils 1953:210; and Parsons and Shils (eds.) 1951:25, 197. See also Hopkins 1957:289ff. There are exceptions to this interpretation of adaptation. When the authors discuss the "adaptive exigencies" of "concrete economic structures," for example, they say that the economy must "adapt" to its ecological-technological and socio-cultural environment. And the nature of that natural-social environment then will explain the differentiation of the economy into its structural elements (industries, etc.) (Chap. II). Here, in other words, the mode of adaptation is left open to research.

15 EQUILIBRIUM THEORY IN ECONOMICS AND IN FUNCTIONAL ANALYSIS AS TYPES OF EXPLANATION
Sherman Roy Krupp

This paper discusses mechanistic theory in economics and functionalist theory in the other social sciences, emphasizing the different kinds of logical procedure they use. Functionalist theory focuses on the unity and directedness of a total system, while mechanistic theory tends to concentrate on the precise determination of the relationships between parts of a system. Functionalist theory assumes a system to have a basic organizing principle of goals and self-regulating

From Functionalism in the Social Sciences *edited by Don Martindale, Philadelphia, The American Academy of Political and Social Science, Monograph #5, pp. 65–83. Reprinted by permission.*

mechanisms. Mechanistic theory takes a system to be derived from the relationships between the parts. Both types of theory, organizing their explanations in different ways, develop equilibrating systems. The special properties of equilibrium are significantly determined by the nature of their individual logical procedures.

In economics, the properties of equilibrating systems have been systematically explored. The emphasis on stable equilibrium, which has been basic to functionalist theory, is regarded mainly as a special case of equilibrium. Unstable and dynamic systems are explored. As a result, homeostatic mechanisms of self-regulation are merely special kinds of forces and are not basic to equilibrium. The equilibrating systems of economic theory, unlike those of the other social sciences, are more neutral with respect to the goal-maintaining or integrating qualities of systems. In contrast, functional theory commonly predisposes analysis to those equilibrating forces which make for co-operation and harmony, and reduces the forces which move the system away from a stable equilibrium of high goal achievement.

Introduction[1]

Functional and Mechanical Theories Compared

The initial impetus to theory-building lies in the regularities we observe in the world around us. It is not necessarily the most implacable repetitions that engage our attention, however, but rather those phenomena which exhibit gross consistency and a tantalizing amount of irregularity. The effort to explain variation and regularity in a systematic way results in the production of theories. A great number of theories have been produced, and theories themselves may be examined from the point of view of the regularities they exhibit and the variations that occur. Theories differ in subject matter and scope, of course, but they can also differ in the kind of logical structure they employ. This paper will discuss two major kinds of theory, mechanistic and functionalist, paying particular attention to the different kinds of logical procedure that they use.[2]

The difference between mechanistic and functionalist theories may be informally described by noting that functionalist theory focuses on the unity and directedness of the total system, while mechanistic theories tend to concentrate on the precise determination of relationships between parts of the system. At the same time, both theories describe a network of relations between the variables or units of a system. Both provide a framework that allows the theorist to specify the conditions that produce particular outcomes. At least in principle, both theories are able to analyze the way the system works and to

[1] I should like to thank Ross Fagin, William Howton, Eugene Schneider, Milton H. Spencer, and Herbert Spitz for their helpful discussions and advice in the preparation of this paper. I am especially grateful to Mrs. Amy Goldin for her perceptive editorial services.
[2] Ernest Nagel, in his distinguished book, *The Structure of Science* (1961), systematically explores some of these differences. He contrasts the mechanical, the teleological, the statistical, and the genetic as modes of scientific explanation.

deduce or predict special outcomes of the system. Although they are built in different ways, both mechanistic and functionalist theories try to organize patterns of relationship between the variables into coherent systems.[3]

What are the structural differences between these two kinds of theory? Let us examine them in relation to a single problem. Take, for example, the transfer of heat between a body and its environment. The gross consistency is the tendency of body temperature to rise or fall in a direct relation to the temperature surrounding it. This direct correlation is particularly evident among cold-blooded animals. But all animals have a limited tolerance for heat and cold; there are extremes of temperature beyond which no creature can survive. In addition, some species exhibit a high degree of resistance to changes in environmental temperature; their bodies function to preserve the specific temperature they require for optimal functioning. These limits and variations of temperature exchange present modifications of the general tendency of bodies and environments to reach a common temperature. With the development of thermometry it becomes possible to regard the complex of relations between the temperature of a body and its environment as an equilibrating system. The constituent elements of the system must be isolated and defined, and the manner in which they relate to each other must be made as clear and precise as possible. The elements of the system that vary in relation to each other are called the units or variables of the system. The way a change in one variable brings about a change in another, the relations between the units, is described in terms of functions or equations. Finally, the conditions under which the system will operate must be specified.

For cold-blooded animals the physical laws of heat transfer may be observed to function with significant regularity. The body temperature of a snake, for example, will normally reveal a direct correlation with the temperature of its environment. Both heat loss and heat gain are measurable by the physical efficiency of the animal's body as a conductor. Viewed as an equilibrating system, this may be expressed by saying that a change in the temperature of the environment will induce a change in the temperature of the snake, and this change will continue in the same direction until both temperatures are the same. The general law of heat transfer postulates a movement to the state of zero differential, whether or not this point is actually reached. Since the snake's homeostatic adaptations are relatively few and simple—for example, it moves into and out of the sunlight—physical laws of heat transfer apply without much modification.

---

[3] By functionalism I do not mean to stress the kind of early formulations of Malinowski, Radcliffe-Brown, or Lloyd Warner which explained the persistence of traits and institutions by referring to the imputed needs of society. The individual did what he had to do to make the society work. Mainly, these frameworks were definitional and classificatory; they formulated a *naïve* teleology. By functionalism I will mean a generic model of thought basic to the more systematic constructions of Robert F. Bales, Chester Barnard, Marion Levy, Elton Mayo, Robert Merton, Talcott Parsons, Philip Selznick, Herbert Simon, and Ralph Stodgill. These frameworks contain implicit and explicit equilibrium analysis.

With warm-blooded animals, however, theory must allow for feedback systems and a generally greater complexity of relationships. The feedback systems tend to the continual restoration of a particular body temperature. Activity raises internal body temperature and rest lowers it. Sweating and panting are other homeostatic techniques and can accelerate the transfer of heat from the animal's body to its environment. Given the many heat-modifying techniques of warm-blooded animals, the most economical explanation is that the organism seeks the maintenance of a temperature that permits it to function with optimal efficiency. A theoretical system based on this assumption is teleological rather than mechanistic. That is, the coherence of the system is not achieved by compounding simple relations of parts, but by organizing the parts as functions of a goal-oriented whole.

The equilibrating system that adequately accounts for the phenomena of heat transfer among cold-blooded animals is mechanistic. The theory that accounts for the same phenomena among warm-blooded animals is equally an equilibrating system, but the orientation and structure of the theory is functionalist.

Our example of the difference between these two types of theory was taken from the biological sciences, both kinds appear in the social sciences as well. This paper will explore some similarities and differences between functional theories in the social sciences and the equilibrating method of economics. Economics, more than any other social science, has tried to organize the relationships with which it deals in the form of mechanistic equilibrium theories. It is less commonly recognized that functionalism also provides many of the elements of equilibrating systems. Functionalist theories characteristically modify equilibrating systems by introducing confining assumptions about the conditions, relations, variables, and solutions of the system. The consequences of this practice will be examined in the final section of the paper.

The Basic Concepts of Mechanical and Functional Systems

Mechanical equilibrium theories vary in structure. Economics generally uses the postulate-deductive form of equilibrium theory which begins with a few simple axioms and combines them to form a group of concepts that are logically interrelated. These concepts provide the basic terms of the system and describe the primary general relations between them. The atom would be such a basic term, and gravity such a relation. The primary concepts also provide the dimensions of the system; that is, the kinds of change in which the elementary units are liable, such as variations of mass, position, velocity, and time. Finally, the rules of composition or aggregation describe the limits beyond which the elementary concepts do not apply. The speed of light acts as such a limit on the Newtonian laws of motion.[4]

---

[4] Charles Dunbar Broad (1925) classically outlines the doctrines of mechanism and its alternatives. See esp. pp. 3–94.

Once the primary concepts have been stated, relatively complex processes may be formulated. In economics, the elementary unit is the utility of objects for individuals; the general relation is the principle of maximization of utility for individuals and returns for firms. The elementary kinds of change are the increase or decrease in utility and the greater or lesser availability of objects. The rule of composition states that the principle of maximization can be applied throughout the system in a manner independent of particular contexts.

Maximization provides the moving force of economics. It asserts that any unit of the system will move toward an equilibrium position as a consequence of universal efforts to maximize utility or returns. Maximization is a general basic law that applies to the elementary units and, by the rules of composition, to larger and more complicated collections of these units. The system is conceived as a mechanism of interdependent parts related by common laws. Particular contexts are introduced as sets of conditions when the system is applied. The outcome of the general laws in a particular context is thus deducible as a consequence of the operation of an equilibrating system. Thus, the equilibrating system permits us to describe the context and deduce the particular state of the system, or to state a desired outcome and deduce the particular values the variables must assume in order to produce that outcome. It also allows us to make general statements about the kinds of conditions that will produce one sort of outcome rather than another. Equilibrium analysis of this mechanistic sort is the basis of modern economic theory.

In mechanical theories the parts are assumed to be independent entities which are combined according to special rules to yield aggregates. These aggregates obey the same general laws that apply to the parts. Functional analysis, on the other hand, starts with the unity that goals give to the system. Functional theories postulate a general purpose for the system, and proceed to discriminate the component parts and subgoals of the parts. The goal of the system acts to bind the components in the same way that the general law and the rules of composition act to relate the variables of mechanistic systems. Thus, the goal of a functionalist theory is more than one postulate among other postulates. It gives the system a general direction and exerts a pulling force on all the components and functions within the system. The parts are related to each other through their goal-fulfilling properties. Changes in the units will usually be analyzed in terms of their differential consequence to the attainment of the system's goal.

Functionalist theories usually describe some of the relations within the system as self-regulating mechanisms. The "self" that is regulated is the system as a whole; the mechanism describes the way in which the dysfunctional movement of one variable stimulates a compensatory movement in another variable. In particular, some components are acted upon so that they tend to vary only within certain specified ranges. These mechanisms constrain and secure a chain of mutual adjustment among the variables, so that the system moves toward a given state of equilibrium and restores this state when it is disturbed. The desired state of equilibrum is identified as the system's goal. Thus, we may observe that the postulated goal is fundamental to the analysis of functionalism as an equilibrating system.

Equilibrating Systems[5]

Equilibrium Theory Defined

To be described as equilibrating, a system must provide orderly patterns of realignment among the dependent variables when changes are introduced into the system. Both functionalist and mechanistic theories present forms analogous to the equilibrating structure of economic theory.

The everyday notion of equilibrium will not be misleading as long as we remember that dynamic equilibrium is as possible as static equilibrium. Stability and instability both describe properties of equilibrating systems. The state of rest is a particular equilibrium state, and there are as many states of a system as there are sets of conditions for the system.

Equilibrating theories provide a conceptual framework for dealing with the various kinds of interdependence. They allow us to deal with interacting forces in a system and to analyze the effect of changes in conditions on an interacting system. The concept of equilibrium facilitates the examination of the properties of systems as these properties derive from different kinds of conditions, classes of forces, or ranges of particular variables. It permits the classification of relations and conditions into those which are capable of being controlled for policy purposes and those which are less amenable to control. It offers a method for contrasting ideal and observed systems.

Equilibrium analysis construes a system to be made up of relations and conditions. These relations and conditions may be theoretical, conjectural, normative, or observational. The particular mix will determine the general applicability of the system and the degree of realism and precision that it can attain. The relations provide the system with its forces, while the conditions interpret the special contexts and determine the scope of the system. Thus, the simplest equilibrium system requires that two variables, "x" and "y," be related in such a manner that there is a "y" or a class of "y's" associated with each "x." The relations of the system, constituted as its forces, provide the grounds for associating "y" with "x." A set of conditions specifies the range within which "x" will yield "y" and asserts the circumstances that will determine a particular "x." The equilibrium theory asserts that a change in "x" unleashes forces which bring about a change in "y," but "y" does not have to vary directly with "x." It is possible for "y" to vary as "x" changes within

[5] For further discussion of equilibrating systems the reader might refer to Samuelson 1953:7–23, 260–262; Frisch 1936:100–105; Myrdal 1958:198–205; Boulding 1950:3–29; Machlup 1963.

some specific range, and as "x" passes out of the designated range "y" may completely alter its direction.

What is essentially required of an equilibrating system is that it be capable of analyzing the forces at work and the conditions and scope of these forces. That is, when the conditions and forces are sufficient to explain or predict a particular outcome, equilibrium is said to be determined. If an entire class of outcomes is predictable, equilibrium is said to be indeterminate for any particular solution within that class. Such indeterminacy implies either that the forces and conditions have been inadequately stated, or that the interdependence itself does not permit an analyzable outcome.

This ambiguous implication of indeterminacy presents certain problems. For example, the existence of a self-regulating mechanism of the state of the variables. The manner of operation, the conditions, and the ranges within which the variables mutually function must be specified before a determinate solution can be reached. This requirement is especially important in functional analysis, where the forces at work are internal to the individual system and not generalized throughout the system, as in economics.

Stable Equilibrating Systems

A system may exhibit properties of stability or instability. If unstable, it may be cyclical or fluctuating. It can exhibit stability in a variety of ways. A system may be stable for changes in conditions of a certain magnitude and unstable when conditions change beyond some designated limit. A system may be stable only for certain ranges of a particular variable. The properties of a system may be such that large changes in conditions have little effect on outcome, or it may be such that small changes in conditions create important shifts in solutions. Internal changes may stay within some boundary, or may change the boundary conditions themselves. These properties of a system are not intrinsic to the system. They are introduced by the relations and conditions which constitute a particular application of a theoretical system.

The stability of an equilibrating system is established by the system's tendency to react in a constant way to a change introduced into the system. It moves to a new equilibrium position which persists unless—or until—there is another change in conditions. The persistence at an equilibrium position once established is basic to stability. It should be noted, however, that the equilibrium position achieved after the system has adjusted to changed conditions is not necessarily identical with the equilibrium position that had previously been established. Also, although the system has moved, its stability may remain unimpaired.

Special self-regulating mechanisms are sometimes present in systems exhibiting stability. They can also be introduced into systems to help create stability. These mechanisms operate by creating compensatory adjustments in some variables when disturbing changes occur in other parts of the system. In sociology, the increasing severity of penalties applied to infraction of the moral code acts in a self-regulatory manner to reinforce the given set of social values. In economics, where many of the self-regulating mechanisms are more clearly formulated, the stabilizers such as unemployment insurance, progressive income tax, or escalator clauses in wage contracts, are constantly being debated with regard to their effectiveness as stabilizing mechanisms. Self-regulatory mechanisms in the other social sciences are sometimes more difficult to evaluate than in economics, but theoretical precision about effectiveness, range of operation, and manner of influence has the salutary effect of making it possible to test and refine selected aspects of the system and its self-regulating mechanisms.

It is also possible for a system to remain stable even when some variables undergo large changes in magnitude. This suggests the distinction between the stability of a system and its shiftability. The degree to which a change in "x" effects a change in "y" is the system's shiftability. If a small change in "x" brings about a large change in "y," then the equilibrium is highly shiftable. However, this change in "y" can be realized at a new and stable equilibrium position. For example, if a small improvement in the grievance machinery ("x") resulted in a large reduction in internal conflict ("y"), the equilibrium would be shifted. In this case the new equilibrium might be even more stable than it was at the starting position.

Systems are shiftable but stable, then, when a change in "x" brings about a change in "y" but the change in "y" does not threaten the established boundary conditions or shift the system enough to create radically new relations between the variables. That is, the change will not shift the system so as to alter the character and direction of the forces.

A few examples may make these theoretical possibilities more vivid. In industrial relations a stable and unshiftable equilibrium would be one where every emergence of conflict is met by small changes in policy which are successful in reducing the conflict—for example, a human relations program. A stable but shiftable equilibrium would be one where a small increase in conflict results in a large increase in wages which is successful in reducing the conflict. An unstable equilibrium might be exemplified by a system where a small increase in conflict resulted in managerial policies aimed at reducing the conflict, but which succeeded only in creating further opposition. A system which is stable over some range but unstable for values of the variables beyond this range would be illustrated by an authoritarian management which succeeded in reducing all small conflict situations by the use of coercion. In the case of a major initial conflict, however, authoritarian sanctions would succeed mainly in deepening the conflict and promoting increasingly forceful reactions and counter-reactions—for example, a wildcat strike.

Unstable Equilibrating Systems

Stable equilibrating systems held the center of the stage in economics for a long time. The tradition of comparative statics analyzed the solutions of equilibrating systems under changing conditions of supply and demand.

Modern economics, however, has come to recognize the value of exploring unstable equilibrating systems.

The introduction of self-generating mechanisms permits us to describe systems in continuous change. All theories of economic fluctuations provide mechanisms by means of which a change introduced into a system generates further change. An important example of this is the multiplier-accelerator interaction in the theory of economic fluctuations. The multiplier is derived from the marginal propensity to consume; that is, the small rise in consumption resulting from a small rise in income. If the multiplier is small, large changes in investment will generate only modest changes in income. The accelerator refers to a relation between income and investment such that a change in income will generate changes in investment. If an initial change occurs in investment, income will rise. If the accelerator is positive and large, the increase in income will bring about a further increase in investment, and so on. The degree of instability depends upon the initial change in investment, the size of the multiplier and the accelerator, the level of income when the initial change was introduced, and other factors. By altering the relations between a change in income and its effect on consumption—the multiplier—or between investment and consumption—the accelerator—it is possible to create a system that is "dampened," explosive, or cyclically fluctuating. It is also possible to describe a system that is dampened—returns to the initial state—unless the initial change in investment is of some designated magnitude. If investment is below this amount, the level of income never will rise high enough to create a large accelerator. If, however, investment is above the critical amount, then the change in income that is generated may be reinforced by a constantly rising accelerator so that the system becomes explosive until it reaches certain limits, such as a full employment boundary.

Equilibrium technique may also be used to compare ideal and observed states, thus providing a tool for policy. The example of the multiplier-accelerator interaction implies that the speed and direction of a change may be varied by altering one of the relations. Thus a policy can be designed to raise the multiplier—for example, a tax cut—or to increase the size of the accelerator—for example, investment subsidy. More generally, it is possible to specify certain policy goals for a system as magnitudes or values. The real observed state of the system can then be compared with the idealized equilibrium values of the variables, and conclusions may be drawn about the kind of relations that are necessary to achieve the desired state. For example, welfare economics proceeds by describing the relations and conditions that might be considered ideal as a normative equilibrium. These are compared with observed relations and conditions, and policies are determined which will move the existing system in the direction of the normative equilibrium. At the extreme, an engineered equilibrium can be formulated in which conditions and relations are always being altered by systems of control to achieve desired states. Equilibrium theory encourages a careful distinction between those relations that can be altered by policy and those that are not amenable to control.

Functional Analysis as an Equilibrating System[6]

The systems described by functionalist theory tend to maintain their individual patterns and relations despite changes in conditions. This occurs because the parts are given goal-maintaining attributes and because special homeostatic mechanisms are introduced. Integration, the alignment of the parts with the goals of the system, and adaptation, the mutual adjustment of the variables toward the maintenance of some desired state, are characteristic properties of functionalist systems. As equilibrating systems, functional formulations emphasize the internal harmony of systems which are integrated, adaptive, goal-achieving, and environment-determined or -determining, although these qualities are present in various degrees and are achieved in different ways.

Ideal Functional Theory

An ideal for functional analysis could be outlined which would start with a system organized as a set of goals and conditions, relations, and variables. From these conditions and relations the state of the system could be deduced. The conditions would be specified by a set of goals both internal and external, by a set of environmental influences or constraints, by a set of boundaries on the values that the variables may assume within the system, and by explicit statement of the values the variables must have for the "proper" functioning of the system. The relations would specify the kind and range of effects of internal and environmental factors on the variables. The conditions would allow these to be specified as the kinds of changes possible for a single variable. Relations would be of two sorts: general relations for the system as a whole, and specific and contextual relations. The distinction between general and specific relations would be analogous to the general and contingent laws of mechanical systems. Goal-seeking properties, for example, might be general to the system. Subsystems such as departments in an organization or regional political parties might require special contextual relations.

The variables or parts would be sufficiently numerous to give the system adequate scope and completeness, but few enough so that the relations between the variables can be systematically explored. Variables which act to block goal-achievement would be included with the goal-maintaining variables. It is essential that the units be capable of expressing "more" or "less" of their imputed properties and of taking on different values for each set of influences or level of goal achievement. In that way a particular variable could be highly functional over some particular range, less functional over other ranges, and, perhaps, dysfunctional for values outside of these ranges. For example, cohesion within the work group yields increasing efficiency up to some point, but too much cohesion can create competing subgoals.

In principle, functional analysis, using equilibrium methods, can yield sig-

---

[6] My book, *Pattern in Organization Analysis: A Critical Examination* (1964), explores "organization theory" as a type of functional analysis. The equilibrating properties of organization theory and some of its characteristic limitations provide a central theme.

nificant explanations of certain classes of problems. This type of explanation has been extremely useful in dealing with the working of the human body and with some of the servo-mechanisms of cybernetics. Functionalist theory may be able to offer important insights in relation to certain kinds of social systems. The army, the church, small cohesive groups—in short, all institutions which by design or by nature are highly goal-oriented—are likely areas for functionalist investigation. Functional methods are particularly promising for analyzing systems which are self-contained and subject to relatively few environmental influences.

It is in relation to large social systems or groups which are minimally cohesive that functional analysis is likely to raise problems. Where common goals are weak or diffuse, conflict will probably play an important part in the social structure. The stress of functional theories on goal-maintenance markedly reduces their capacity for dealing with conflict-ridden systems.

Problems Relating to Goals in Functional Theories

The importance of goals in functional analysis is sometimes a source of theoretical difficulty. The following section discusses three of the problems which often affect the equilibrating character of functional systems: (1) the pulling force of the system is readily exaggerated; (2) the requirement for clearly specified goals may excessively narrow the scope and applicability of the system; (3) the logical role of the goal is unclear, so that behavioral and normative categories are not adequately distinguished.

The social sciences must often deal with situations in which the attitudes and beliefs of the participants vary. Ideally, the integrative force of the goal also varies from system to system as well as within a particular system. Minimally, there should be theoretical provision for expressing a range of effectiveness for the integrative force of the goal. This can be achieved by specifying resistance and countertendencies to goal achievement. The basic integrative and adaptive characteristics of functionally ordered systems facilitate the overstatement of cohesiveness in such systems, and this tendency must be guarded against.

In highly integrated systems with few but consistent goals—servo-mechanisms, for example—goals provide significant explanatory premises for the workings of the system. But in many social organizations the unifying power of goals is extremely difficult to assess. Consequently, it may remain unanalyzed or residual, and the description of a system as a goal-fulfilling entity becomes correspondingly vague.

It is generally desirable to provide clear formulations of the system's goal, since this facilitates the task of specifying variables and their relations. Unfortunately, systems with clearly articulated goals are usually very specific and confine themselves to the examination of a small number of variables. Unexamined variables tend to be left undefined or located among the conditions of the system. Highly constrained systems, such as the problem-solving teams in small groups, lend themselves to the analysis of a handful of variables in curiously sterilized situations. The removal of external and environmental influences from the field of enquiry entails serious risks for the theorist. He may easily neglect relevant data and end up with a seriously incomplete system.

Choosing one set of goals as the dominant goals for the system may create another problem. It may encourage the theorist to minimize or exclude the means developed by subsystems for the achievement of their subsidiary goals. In fact, secondary goals may modify the effectiveness of the primary goal in a variety of ways. They may reinforce it, shift its direction, or impede its operation (Gouldner 1959:241–266; Hempel 1959:271–302; Sayles 1958). This is particularly important in the context of the idea of consent, which is often a basic feature of social organization. The problem arises when individuals or groups are thought of as co-operating for the achievement of goals. Social organization conceived of as a system of co-operation, however, often exaggerates the voluntary and supportive role of the participants. This reduces the scope and relations of countertendencies to goal achievement and exaggerates the forces tending toward consensus. Managerial theories of organization have often shown this weakness, with the result that the problems of conflict in organization are often inadequately treated.

Functionalist theories are not always clear about the logical function of goals. The logical relationship of a goal to a system may be formulated in various ways: goals may describe boundary conditions of the system; they may define the behavioral relations or norms of the system; or they may state the limits which the system must attain for minimum performance—for example, survival.

If goals are limits, they merely confine the variables to some minimum range, and the particular value of a variable above this limit will depend upon influences other than goals. For example, an area of high co-operation between participants may exist in the region of minimum goal attainment while opposition to goals emerges for regions above this minimum. This situation is illustrated when workers take wage cuts in a failing firm. The same workers, if the firm were successful, might fight militantly for a wage increase.

Sometimes goals are forces conditioning the operations of the units. As criteria for work performance, however, goals will be perceived differently by different interest groups. An employer may have standards of performance which are not acceptable to the employee. Viewed from different goal perspectives, the standards of work exhibit different behavioral properties and, consequently, different equilibrating tendencies.

Sometimes a goal is an ideal, like harmony. When goals are ideals or criteria for judging the performance of a system, they must be separated from the forces that determine this performance. Ideals for system performance should not be confused with actual system tendencies. The formulation of ideal equilibrium values for the variables is a valid and useful practice, but it should obviously remain distinct from the observed values. In order to discuss a system as co-operative, co-operation must be stated as an interaction of forces which yields different degrees of co-operation, including conflict. High levels of integration should not result from the method of analysis itself. The equilibrium values for the variables in ideal systems should be so framed that there is no tendency to confuse an ideal state of the system with its observed state.

Problems of Variables and Relations in Functional Theories

Other theoretical difficulties arise when goal formation is a product of the elements of the system itself. This complex state of affairs arises within large systems which include diverse subgroups. In this case the goal of the system may be significantly influenced by conditions within the system and by compromises between subsets of rival social groups. Here the system's goal must be interpreted as a dependent variable, and the aims of the distinct subgroups must be recognized as creating a multiplicity of goals within the system.

Variables which are functional for one set of goals may be dysfunctional for another. Multiple goals will usually exhibit some contradictory solutions for the variables, and it is possible that the strains on the system may threaten its adaptive and integrative capacities, pushing it away from possible solutions. Moreover, the internal forces, as goal-creating rather than goal-maintaining influences, will constantly be changing the criteria of system performance and the criteria for selection of its variables. An integrating force for one goal may create a condition of instability for another goal. A highly co-ordinated machine process, for example, may rationalize production but disturb labor relations by imposing undesirable work routines.

Goal changes bring about shifts in the choice of variables, in conditions, in the nature of the relations of the system, and in its general behavioral characteristics. Unless special care is taken to isolate these shifts, they are likely to make the system incapable of generating determinate equilibrium solutions. Equally important, goal shifts may create a situation in which the range of indeterminacy in equilibrium solutions cannot be indicated.

Because the criteria for the selection of parts and relations derive from the definition of the system as a goal-maintaining framework, there is frequently a tendency to minimize the importance of external influence on the behavior of the variables. This emphasis on the internal properties of a system is reinforced by the self-regulating mechanisms which reduce the shock of external influence and prevent internal change from becoming disequilibrating. This bias was illustrated in the early human relationists who envisioned a system of internal mechanisms as a way of reducing tensions, even if these tensions were externally derived. Emphasis on self-regulating mechanisms predisposes a view of the system as stable by stressing the stability of equilibrium. Emphasis on these mechanisms in social theory—rewards and sanctions, laws, ethical traditions, and the like—produces a vision of an integrated society with a high degree of consensus. However, these mechanisms need not in fact be pervasive or powerful enough to create stability.

The very act of goal achievement may unleash feedback which creates instability. If the achievement of one set of goals by some members of a system implies a denial of goal realization for other members of the system, then goal achievement creates some internal instability. This tendency may intensify as the system fulfills its goals, and the ultimate stability of the system will depend upon the passivity or militancy of the disaffected groups.

Then again, if technology and innovation are crucial for economic growth, as economists believe them to be, progress may depend upon significant deviation from expected norms. The self-regulating mechanisms may be dysfunctional for social development. The study of the instability of systems, consequently, may be necessary to explain large sectors of human conduct and social progress.

Important sectors of stability and instability for a system are associated with the contradictions between individual and collective goals and with the degree of conflict generated by multiple goals. Complex differentiated systems such as our own, with widely divergent social groups, organizations, and ethical traditions, might be more adequately served by theoretical systems which systematically include instability and which start with the independence of the parts rather than with the consensus of the whole.

Conclusion

The power of equilibrium analysis lies in its general explanatory capability. This does not mean it is applicable to all problems. It is, however, a language that can be neutral with respect to variables, relations, and conditions. It permits us to develop systems in a manner that need not prejudice outcomes. Economics in particular among the social sciences has developed the concepts of equilibrating systems and has applied modern empirical methods to its theories. It seems probable that social scientists in other disciplines would find that the methods of economic theory can be fruitfully applied to the special substantive problems of their own sciences. The interchange between sociology, anthropology, and psychology has provided a major source of stimulation in the social sciences; economics, in contrast, has had practically no influence on the other social sciences. This is especially lamentable because the development of analytic and systematic methods has probably been more advanced in economics than in any of the other social sciences.[7]

[7] Gunnar Myrdal's great book, *An American Dilemma* (1944), superbly illustrates the possibilities for the use of the equilibrium technique of economic theory in other contexts. For a more limited application to the context of "authority," see Sherman Krupp and Eugene Schneider, "An Illustration of the Use of Analytical Theory in Sociology: The Application of the Economic Theory of Choice to Non-Economic Variables," a paper read at the annual meeting of the American Sociological Association in Montreal, September 1, 1964.

part three

CASES

16 SONJO BRIDE-PRICE AND THE QUESTION OF AFRICAN "WIFE PURCHASE"[1]
Robert F. Gray

Introduction

In the years from 1929 to 1931 a lively controversy appeared in the pages of *Man* concerning the best term to use for designating the transfer of property that frequently takes place at African marriages. A number of Africanists contributed to this discussion,[2] each suggesting a different term to indicate the function of the custom as he conceived it; but with one exception all agreed that the "bride-price" was an undesirable term. In attacking "bride-price" these writers believed themselves to be correcting a view of African marriage that was supposed to be current, especially among missionaries and administrators, in which marriage was wrongly represented as an essentially commercial transaction, with wives being treated as chattels. The prevailing sentiment of this symposium is fairly summed up in an article by Evans-Pritchard (1931:36) in which he writes of the term "bride-price" that

> it encourages the layman to think that "price" used in this context is synonymous with "purchase" in common English parlance. Hence we find people believing that wives are bought and sold in Africa in much the same manner as commodities are bought and sold in European markets. It is difficult to exaggerate the harm done to Africans by this ignorance.

The only dissenter in this concurrence of opinions was Lord Raglan (1931:75), who obstinately stuck to the view that "the payment of bride-price partakes of the character of a commercial transaction." Evans-Pritchard (1931:38), in the same article, proposed the term "bride-wealth" as being relatively neutral with respect to theories of function. Perhaps for this reason, and because it was less bizarre than the other proposed terms, "bride-wealth" came to prevail over alternative terms and was widely (though not universally) accepted by subsequent writers on the subject: the tendency has been to avoid "bride-price."

The choice of a term is not important in itself except insofar as it indicates

From American Anthropologist *62:34–47. Reprinted by permission.*

adherence to the doctrine, quoted above, that it is erroneous and harmful to describe certain marriage customs of some African societies as economic transactions akin to the sale and purchase of property. Actually, the doctrine soon hardened into dogma which few anthropologists have dared question, and then only hesitantly. If the doctrine is wrong, as I believe, it has retarded our understanding of both African marriage and African economic systems. As a result, evidently, of their tacit acceptance of this doctrine, anthropologists have tended to relate bride-price to almost every institution in society except the economic system. And yet in many of these tribes, marriages are major occasions for the exchange of property. Therefore an account of such an economic system can only be incomplete if bride-price transactions are excluded from it. On the other hand, an analysis of marriage customs in these societies which fails to recognize the economic character of the property exchanges must be one-sided.

While the argument may appear superficially to be concerned only with the ues of words, the consequences are serious and can result in faulty analysis of social systems. It may be that the terminology of our own economic system, carrying as it does the implication of a money economy, is inadequate when applied to primitive societies without money, and may even be misleading if used carelessly. However, satisfactory alternative terms have not yet been generally accepted by anthropologists, and I shall not attempt to introduce any such new terms in this paper. The real question at issue is not, as Evans-Pritchard's statement suggests, whether African wives are bought and sold in the same manner as commodities are bought and sold in European markets: it is whether women in some African societies are transferred as wives in a manner that has a basic resemblance to the manner in which other economic commodities are transferred in the same societies. Where this resemblance is found, then if economic terms are applied to dealings in other commodities, I shall argue that it is legitimate to apply them to dealings in wives as well. One might object that the words "bought" and "sold" are not entirely suitable for any of these dealings, and I shall discuss these words in a moment. In that case, it would be as legitimate to question whether African cows are bought and sold. But it is misleading to compare European cows and African wives, just as it would be to compare African cows and European wives. If we mean to demonstrate the differences between the two social and economic systems, we must first compare the manner in which European wives and European cows are dealt with and then African wives and African cows. From this would emerge two patterns which could be properly compared.

In the following pages I use the term *property* to mean something in which a person has certain exclusive *rights* with respect to its use or disposal, these rights being recognized as valid in his society. To *own* something is to possess these rights in it. By *purchase* I mean the acquisition of property by giving goods in exchange for it. *Selling* is the action of the person who delivers the property in exchange for other goods. *Price* is the amount of the goods asked or given for the property. Property may be termed a *commodity* when considered as goods which are bought and sold for a price. In thus defining these words, I have simply removed those implications relating to a money economy that inhere in their usual dictionary definitions or their use in "common English parlance." This is necessary if they are to be adapted to the economic systems of societies which lack money.

The critics of the term "bride-price," at least while writing on that subject, seem to have some misconceptions about these economic terms. They sometimes write as if property were a thing to which its owner is attached in some absolute way and which he can use or dispose of as he wishes without regard for the restrictions imposed by the society to which he belongs. This, admittedly, is never the situation of a wife, and therefore—they seem to argue— to say that a woman has a price and is bought and sold implies that she is owned as property, which, by this incorrect definition, is absurd. But an owner's rights in his property are not normally—in our society perhaps never—absolute. He is limited in his use and disposal of it by various laws and social conventions based on economic, moral, political, and religious considerations. In some societies, as I shall indicate later, certain defined rights in a woman are regularly sold and purchased for a price, and therefore it is not absurd to consider her as property. These rights, for convenience, may be termed *wife rights*, and may be regarded as a special form of property rights. The nature of wife rights will be discussed later.

The doctrine that African marriage must not be regarded as an economic transaction has been repeated in the literature from time to time, both in pure form and with variations. Thus:

> The idea that an African buys a wife in the way that an English farmer buys cattle is the result of ignorance, which may once have been excusable but is so no longer, or of blind prejudice, which is never excusable in those responsible for governing an African people (Radcliffe-Brown 1950:47).

> It is popularly supposed that the requirement of this *quid pro quo* [bride-price], when it consists in goods, is tantamount to the sale of a woman, and, in the early days of South Africa, the courts refused to recognize as valid a marriage in which cattle had passed. Closer acquaintance with the custom has shown that to regard it in this light is to misinterpret its meaning. . . .
> The term "bride-price," which was formerly used for the *quid pro quo*, has been rejected by many anthropologists because of its suggestion of a sale (Mair 1953:5).

In contradiction to all this, the Sonjo of Tanganyika regard bride-price unequivocally as an economic institution. Wives—that is to say, wife rights —are transferred among them according to the same basic rules as certain other forms of property. These transactions involve the exchange of relatively large amounts of goods, and the economic system could not possibly be described without including bride-price. In the remainder of this paper I shall describe Sonjo marriage customs in outline, and then discuss the question as to whether women are exchanged as property in other societies as well.

Background of Sonjo Marriage[3]

The Sonjo, a Bantu-speaking group with a total population of about 4,500, inhabit six villages in a rather inaccessible part of northern Tanganyika, east of Lake Natron and near the Kenya border. These villages, which are separated from one another by distances of up to sixteen miles, are located in the interior of Masai district, and until recently they were all fortified against Masai attacks with encircling palisades of thorn trees and could be entered only through stout gates which were easily defended. Each village is situated at a stream which supplies irrigation water, for the region is too arid for cultivation of crops by rainfall alone. The villages are politically and economically autonomous, but they all share the same tribal religion and age-grade system, and there is some intermarriage between villages. The economy is based upon goat herding and cultivation of sorghum and sweet potatoes, with other crops of less importance. Honey is also important economically, being made into beer which is used ritually and also drunk for pleasure by the older men. In the division of labor the older men operate the irrigation system, women till the fields with digging sticks, and the younger boys herd goats. Young men in the age-grades of junior and senior warriors traditionally took no part in exploitative activities and were not allowed to marry; they were responsible for defending the villages against Masai raids. Nowadays some of the warriors leave home for a year or two to work as migrant laborers. Pottery is made by the women and iron goods by the men of an endogamous pariah group who formerly lived at all the villages, but are now found at only two villages. Their marriage customs differ from those of other Sonjo, but they will not be discussed in this paper.

Political authority is in the hands of an hereditary council of elders, numbering from 16 to 18 members at different villages, who derive their power from control of irrigation water. The villages are segmented into four to six patrilineal exogamous clans, each occupying a separate ward. The clans control the building sites within their wards, but have almost no other powers or economic functions. The most important economic unit, which I term a "lineage group," is normally comprised of a father and his adult sons, together with their wives and children. Close unity is maintained within this group owing to the fact that the father retains control of all property possessed by the group as long as he lives. At his death, the property is divided among the adult sons, each of whom then starts to form a new lineage group. If a man's sons are still small when he dies, his brother takes over his role as father and also inherits his widow.

The Sonjo have a lively system of economic exchange in which goats play a prominent role. These animals possess utilitarian value as basic resources for food and garments, and they exist as conveniently discrete units which are equivalent in value, one with another. The economic value of other goods is normally measured in goats. Thus the exchange of honey, grain, beehives, pottery, iron goods, and irrigation rights all involve the transfer of goats or their equivalents in value. This exchange system also encompasses the sale and purchase of rights in women, who in their economic aspects are dealt with much like other commodities.

Betrothal and Bride-Price

Sonjo girls are customarily betrothed in childhood, sometimes even in infancy, so that betrothal often precedes marriage by a number of years. The bulk of the bride-price is paid at that time. A boy may also be quite young at his betrothal, and an effort is made to match the ages of the two children so that when the boy finally becomes an "elder" and thus qualified for marriage the girl will have just reached marriageable age herself. A father chooses a bride for his son mainly on the social status and personal characteristics of her family, since the girl herself may be still a child at that time. A girl's father accepts or rejects a suitor on similar grounds. The preliminary negotiations leading up to a betrothal may be carried out directly between the two fathers or indirectly by go-betweens, but both fathers consult with other members of their families before closing the deal.

The bride-price in 1955 ranged from 60 to 300 goats, the average being about 100 goats. To the Sonjo this represents a large amount of wealth and exceeds the number of goats possessed by an average owner at any one time. The collection of this sum is basically the responsibility of the lineage group of the suitor, though his mother's brothers are expected to make a small contribution of several animals. The manner in which contributions are apportioned among members of the lineage group is determined by the stage reached in the family cycle. If the suitor's grandfather is living, he still has legal control of all the wealth possessed by his married sons. He normally contributes substantially from his personal herd and requires the suitor's father to provide at least half the goats; the remainder are collected from the father's brothers. If the grandfather is dead, the father will have to provide a larger proportion of the total number, and in that case the contributions from his brothers are voluntary though the moral obligation is strong.

The dispersal of the bride-price among the bride's relatives follows a different principle from that governing its collection. If we assume that the bride-price amounts to 100 goats, the customary division, as computed from the marriage histories of informants, is as follows, listing the relatives of the betrothed girl and the number of goats that each will expect to receive:

Father	26
Father's father	12
Mother's father	12
Father's eldest brother	12
Mother's eldest brother	12
Father's second brother	6
Mother's second brother	6
Sisters and other brothers of father and mother—each	2

It will be noted that after the father's share has been subtracted, the remaining goats are divided equally among the girl's paternal and maternal relatives. That is, individuals of the same degree of relationship on either side of her family receive the same number of goats. This is the basic rule, but the proportions are sometimes altered in consideration of special circumstances.

This transaction involves the transfer of certain rights in a girl from one group to another, the two groups being quite different structurally. The original rights are vested in members of a group of bilateral kin who otherwise have no corporate existence. The girl's father is the leader and spokesman of the group, and possesses the largest share in the rights; the shares decrease with kinship distance as conceived by the Sonjo. These rights are exchanged for a sum of goats with the lineage group of the suitor—in this case a corporate group which at certain stages in its developmental cycle holds property rights communally. The rights in the girl remain latent until the marriage, after which the suitor can actively exercise his wife rights, and at that time he also acquires limited or full rights (depending on the family cycle) in property such as land and livestock belonging to the lineage group.

The suitor's father is expected to make full payment of the bride-price within two months after the final agreement with the girl's father, and he normally obtains promises for the necessary goats before making the agreement. It is a Sonjo rule of great consequence that *once paid, the bride-price is never re-funded*. This rule also applies to partial payments. If payment is not completed within the time limit, the girl's father is free to accept another suitor; therefore the bride-price is never paid in installments but always in full. This works to the disadvantage of a poor youth whose father may find it impossible to collect the bride-price. Such a man may have to wait many years for marriage, until he acquires the necessary goats through his own efforts.

The foregoing account applies to a man's first marriage. A second betrothal is not normally contracted until his first marriage has been completed, and seldom while his father is still alive. The husband himself then usually provides all or most of the bride-price, with his brothers helping him as they are able and wish to. There is no prolonged betrothal period with a second wife; the marriage generally follows soon after the payment of the bride-price.

Marriage

The first marriage of either a man or woman is nearly aways with a partner who comes from a different clan of the same village. In addition to clanmates, marriage is prohibited between first cousins. It is forbidden to marry the daughter of an age-mate, but there is no bar to marrying his sister. A man cannot marry the sister of his first wife, either contemporaneously as a second wife, or subsequently after his first wife has died or been divorced; nor can he marry the sister of a brother's wife. This follows logically: if brothers married sisters the brother would not be allowed to inherit his deceased brother's widow, to whom he might otherwise be entitled (cf. Evans-Pritchard 1949:88).

Polygyny is relatively rare. Preliminary returns of a government census at one of the villages (Soyetu) revealed that out of 157 married men, 140 (over 88 percent) had only one wife, 17 had two wives, and only one man had three wives. My own rougher estimates at other villages agreed with these figures. There are definite economic incentives for polygyny: a man with many goats has little opportunity to invest them except in multiple wives, while if he should inherit an excessive amount of land it cannot be fully utilized unless he has a second wife to help cultivate it. On the other hand, it is generally believed that strife and discord are inevitable in a polygynous household.

As the time for the marriage approaches, the prospective husband builds a house with help from his father-in-law and men of his own ward. When all is ready a final payment of ten goats is made to the bride's father. This sum, which is invariable at all first marriages, is divided among the bride's relatives along the same lines as the bride-price paid at the betrothal. The wedding events, which concern the relatives and neighbors of the bride and groom rather than the whole village, occupy four days. If a man marries a second wife—it being her first marriage—the payments are the same as for a first wife, but the ceremonies may be abridged. Each wife must be provided with her own house.

The wife rights that a husband obtains in exchange for bride-price entitle him to sexual access to his wife and to her labor in the home and in his fields, and he has paternal rights in her children. The wife's father, upon receiving the final payment of the bride-price, surrenders his rights in his daughter and thereafter has little control over her. The husband has certain obligations towards his wife and children which must be fulfilled as long as the marriage lasts, and the wife's father also has certain residual obligations. Should the husband fail in the duties normally expected of a family head, his wife and her children may return to the home of her father or a brother, and these men have the obligation of receiving her, at least temporarily. The daughter of an informant—an alert old woman named Gahamu, who knew some Swahili—developed pulmonary tuberculosis and, according to Sonjo belief, required some goats to be sacrificed for her. Her husband, realizing the hopeless prognosis—she was in a terminal condition when I first saw her—begrudged her the goats, and she returned with her young son to her parents' home, where her father vainly sacrificed six goats for her. The husband relinquished his rights in the woman and was therefore legally released from his obligations, but old Gahamu was fiercely indignant at his shoddy behavior and the community generally regarded it as morally reprehensible. The boy will be raised by his grandparents; he will take his grandfather's clan and inherit from him.

Death of a Marriage Partner

Since bride-price is never returned, and there is usually a long interval between betrothal and marriage, a man risks a complete loss of bride-price if his fiancée should die, or his young wife die before she has borne children. When a wife with children dies, the husband is left in possession of the children.

When a husband dies, his wife rights are inherited by his eldest surviving brother. In this respect wives are dealt with in a different manner from other forms of property, which are inherited by a man's sons. A brother may take the widow as his wife, whereas sons would not be allowed to do this. A brother may also sell the wife rights in the widow to another man, but in order to understand this transaction we must consider a mystical aspect of Sonjo marriage. It is believed that when a married person dies he will ultimately be reunited with his spouse in the spirit world. This belief is expressed in a myth: In former times the dead sometimes returned to earth to help their relatives here, but the last spirit to so materialize on earth was insulted and vowed that thereafter the dead would remain forever in the spirit world; she explained before departing that the spirits of dead husbands and wives waited in the spirit world for their spouses to die, and were then reunited with them there. This belief has a practical bearing on bride-price transactions. Thus when a husband dies, the brother who inherits the widow may sell his rights in her to another man for the fixed price of thirty goats. This relatively small sum of less than half the woman's normal bride-price is explained by the belief in spirit marriage, for the new husband only acquires full wife rights in the woman in this world; after she dies she will rejoin her original husband in the spirit world. A second husband loses possession of her ghost.

This reduced bride-price for a widow cannot be explained as resulting from a deterioration in her value as a wife. The mystical bond is formed at the time of the betrothal when the main bride-price is paid, and a bereaved fiancée is dealt with in the same way as a widow. Again the eldest brother inherits the right to marry the girl, and in that case he pays the girl's father twenty goats—double the usual final payment at marriage. Alternatively, the brother may sell his rights in the girl to another man, but for just thirty goats, even though she is still an untouched virgin. The buyer is then required to pay the twenty goats to the girl's father. After death the girl will become the spirit wife of her original fiancé.

Transfer of Wives between Husbands

The term "divorce" is singularly unsuitable for describing Sonjo customs, and I use it here in a restricted sense. In its usual sense the word suggests that a woman separates from her husband and reverts to a status that is essentially that of an unmarried woman, returning to her parental home or becoming independent. Situations of this kind occur only in exceptional circumstances among the Sonjo. In the case of Gahamu's daughter, a wife returned to her parents after her husband had failed in his obligations, but this happened because she no longer had economic value as a wife. If a husband dies leaving no suitable heir, his wife may come to the homestead of her brother, who adopts her children. A widow with older children does not as a rule become the wife of her husband's brother, but lives with her children as an independent family at her dead husband's homestead. The divorce of a young wife, however, is normally linked to her remarriage, the two actions representing two inseparable aspects of a single transaction which allows her no interim of independence.

In most respects a broken betrothal is dealt with by the Sonjo in the same manner as a divorce. If a young man does not wish to marry his fiancée he sends her a broken twig, which signifies his decision. The girl is then free to accept another suitor, who has only to pay the fiancé the original bride-price in order to marry the girl. The girl herself can also break the engagement if she can find an alternative suitor who is willing to pay back the bride-price. If the fiancé finds another man who is willing to buy his marriage rights, the girl is obliged to accept the change unless she can find someone more to her liking before the time set for her marriage. Whoever finally marries the girl must make the regular payment of ten goats to her father before the marriage, and he must also pay a fee of seven goats to the village council, which is customary at every divorce and remarriage.

Instead of selling the marriage rights of a girl, it is considered better form to exchange her with another man who also has a fiancée whom he does not want to marry. If the two bride-prices were the same, an even trade is made of the two girls. If one bride-price was larger, the difference in goats must be made good to the man with the more costly fiancée. When an exchange of brides is made in this manner, both men are taxed with a divorce fee by the village council, but only four goats are collected from each, the other three being waived on condition of good behavior; if either man is later guilty of transgressing customary law he is immediately required to pay the remaining three goats. The approval of the girls' fathers is normally obtained when there is an exchange of betrothal partners.

After her marriage a woman is comparatively free from the control of her father or other blood relatives, and they do not intervene in any divorce proceedings. The rules of divorce are essentially the same as those governing a broken engagement. A husband exchanges his wife rights with another man for a sum of goats. It is convenient to say that he "sells" his wife, because the form of the transaction is basically the same as those in which he exchanges or sells other goods. Thus a young wife is treated economically as a commodity. Later in life she outgrows this status, partly because her sexual attractions wane, but of more importance is the fact that her children grow up and are betrothed—bride-price is received for her daughters, and her sons reach the stage where they cannot break their clan affiliations. This stabilizes her position in the community, for a Sonjo mother cannot be separated from her children.

A young woman's value as a wife is not generally thought to be depreciated just because she was previously married, and a husband in selling a wife attempts to regain the same bride-price that he paid for her, which was originally based mainly on the social status of her parental family. How well he succeeds in this depends upon conditions of supply and demand at the time. The new husband must belong to a different clan from the first, and of course he cannot belong to the woman's clan. These restrictions limit the probability of finding a buyer in the same village, and it is usual for a woman's second husband to be from a different village. After a buyer has been found, the wife is always given a grace period for finding a more desirable second husband before she is required to marry the man found by her husband. No physical coercion on the part of the husband is involved in the sale of a wife. The compulsive factor resides in the social structure, in which there is no regular position except as a wife for a young woman who was once married. However, a Sonjo husband has a special power, sanctioned by the community, over a wife whom he wishes to sell: if no acceptable buyer can be found within the tribe, he can sell her to the Masai, whose demands for Sonjo women and children seem to provide an unfailing market. The father of my informant, Gidia, sold his second wife and her two children to the Masai in this way; his motive, which seemed to be socially approved, was to increase his holdings in goats for the benefit of his heirs— Gidia and his brothers.

If a woman herself is displeased with the marriage, she can take temporary refuge with her father or a brother, but it is understood that she will either return to her husband or accept another man as a husband within a reasonable time. If she behaves so as to make herself unsatisfactory as a wife she may induce her husband to sell her to another man of her choice, and thus has some means of protecting her own interest. This system of wife purchase is quite flexible in operation and seems to allow a woman as much freedom of choice— admittedly little—as is found in most other African societies.

According to Sonjo law, children must always stay with their mother; they go with her when she is sold and are adopted by her new husband. Children are priced at four goats apiece, which must be paid to their father by the new husband. These children break most of their agnatic kinship bonds. After the exchange they are not barred from marriage with people of their father's clan, but only with his close relatives. The father himself loses all rights in his children by a former wife and has no further obligations toward them. The second husband has full authority over his stepchildren. Property inheritance in these cases is through the stepfather. The children are assimilated to his clan and automatically acquire the same kinship bonds with his blood relatives as his other children have. Their relationships with their mother's family remain unchanged.

As in the case of betrothed couples, two husbands may exchange wives and adjust the difference in bride-price between them. Three-cornered exchanges of wives—with A marrying B's wife, B marrying C's wife, and C marrying A's wife—are also practiced, and again there is an adjustment in goats to even up the bride-prices. Sometimes men exchange wives and children, and then the number of children as well as the bride-prices of their wives must be taken into account in settling up. This exchange of wives is regarded as the ideal method of divorce and remarriage, but it is admitted that the necessary conditions for the transaction seldom arise.

Only young wives, childless or with young children, are normally considered saleable, and the price paid usually equals or is near the original bride-price, though that is never exceeded. In at least one case an older woman was sold by her husband for a considerably reduced price. This was a woman of about forty who knew a little Swahili and sometimes served as a guide for my wife. Coming originally from the village of Soyetu, she had recently been sold to a man at

Kheri, where our camp was located, and was disliked by her new neighbors because of her quarrelsome character. Informants from Kheri stated that her second price was only ten goats. The woman herself admitted it had been reduced, but denied it was so small.

In these divorces and remarriages no payment is made to the woman's father, but only to her original husband. The village council, however, levies a tax of seven goats on these transactions—which seems to contradict Radcliffe-Brown's (1950:46) statement, regarding African marriages, that "the marriage is not the concern of the political authorities. . . ." This fee or tax is no doubt indicative of some underlying disapproval of the selling of wives. Most of these goats, like those collected in fines, are sacrificed at communal rituals which are supposed to benefit the whole community. When wives are exchanged rather than sold, the tax is only four goats instead of seven, which accords with the general opinion that exchanging wives is preferable to selling them.

Extramarital Sex Relations

The public attitude of the Sonjo toward sex tends to be puritanical. Children, for example, are discouraged from indulging in any play or talk concerning sex, at least in the presence of adults. All extramarital intercourse is regarded as illicit and when discovered is dealt with as a public or private delict, depending upon the circumstances. Crosscutting this dichotomy is another one dividing sex offenses into secular and ritual. The principal offenses in these different categories are listed below with brief explanatory notes. In each case it is assumed that the charge was proved to the satisfaction of the village council.

I. *Secular Offenses*

A. *Public delict.* A senior warrior involved in any sex offense or scandal is fined one goat by the leader of his age-set. Junior warriors are said to lead strictly celibate lives.

B. *Private delict.* For intercourse with a married woman, not resulting in pregnancy, a man is required to pay one goat to her husband. It is said that a husband is justified in killing a man whom he catches with his wife in flagrante delicto.

II. *Ritual Offenses.* (These all involve illicit pregnancies.)

A. *Public delicts.*

1. Uncircumcised boy and girl. Circumcision and ritual purification must be performed before the birth. Previous betrothals are broken. The pair normally marry, as their permanent impurity prevents either from marrying another Sonjo. The boy expiates by clearing a patch of forest and planting grain, then leaving the crop unharvested.

2. Uncircumcised girl and initiated male. Dealt with as above, but in addition the man is fined twelve goats. If the putative father cannot be found, the girl is sold to the Masai.

B. *Combined public and private delicts.*

1. Initiated betrothed girl. A purification ceremony must be performed before the birth. The guilty man is fined six goats and required to pay compensation of six goats to the fiancé. The betrothal is not necessarily broken.
2. Married woman. The guilty man is fined six goats and pays six goats to the husband. It is believed childbirth will be difficult or the baby abnormal unless the woman confesses and undergoes purification ceremonies.

Without going into the explanatory myths supporting these laws, it should be evident that Sonjo religion is considerably preoccupied with sexual behavior. These rules, with their economic and ritual sanctions, tend to protect a husband's exclusive sexual rights in his wife and discourage other men from attempting to infringe on those rights.

Functions of Bride-Price

If a Sonjo were asked to explain the function of bride-price he would no doubt say that it enables men to obtain wives; he would be telling us its *manifest* function, which Merton (1949:61) defines as "conscious motivations for social behavior." Anthropologists, on the other hand, are more concerned with what Merton calls its *latent* functions—"its objective consequences." Sonjo bride-price has both noneconomic and economic functions of this kind; I will start with the first of these, because a great deal has been written about that subject (cf. the writers referred to in the introduction) but very little about the economic functions of bride-price.

Among the social functions which have been claimed for bride-price, perhaps the following are the most common: to create an alliance between the respective kinship groups of husband and wife, to legalize marriage, and to stabilize marriage. Sonjo marriage undoubtedly creates special affinal bonds between the two families concerned, though it would seem an exaggeration to term these bonds an "alliance" (cf. Radcliffe-Brown 1950:46). They are simply the minimal relationships existing between in-laws in almost all societies regardless of whether goods have been exchanged, and Sonjo bride-price does not specifically create or strengthen these bonds. It does function to prevent hostilities arising between the two groups over conflicting interests in the same woman. In accepting bride-price, the bride's family relinquishes all rights to the woman, and relations between the two families should thereafter simulate those of amicable neighbors. Thus we can say that bride-price among the Sonjo has a *disjunctive* rather than *conjunctive* function, to use Radcliffe-Brown's terms (1952:91–92).

One of the functions of Sonjo bride-price is certainly to legalize marriage; but if we view Sonjo marriage as an exchange of commodities, this is only to say that it gives legal sanction to the wife rights that a man has purchased, just as when a Sonjo acquires other goods through purchase or exchange his property rights are protected by Sonjo law. In this function we seem to have evidence establishing the essentially economic character of the transaction rather than disproving it. If bride-price failed to legalize marriage—if it were just a voluntary gesture of good will for establishing cordial relations—that would be a cogent argument against wife purchase.

Marriage stability is a somewhat vague term with several possible meanings (Schneider 1953). It is usually measured by frequency of divorce, which gives some indication of the duration of marriage. While divorce is not infrequent among the Sonjo, no exact figures are available. The chief argument advanced to show that bride-price stabilizes marriage does not apply to the Sonjo, namely that a wife's kinsmen will try to prevent a divorce in order to avoid refunding the bride-price. As the Sonjo do not require that the bride-price be refunded when there is a divorce, the wife's family has no economic motive for promoting the stability of her marriage. These social functions of bride-price, in any case, are really irrelevant to the question of wife purchase. Commodities in any economic system may or may not serve specific social functions, but we regard them as commodities because they are exchanged for other goods, not because of their social functions.

Without denying the importance of noneconomic functions, we turn now to the economic functions of bride-price, which I think stand out more clearly. Bride-price transactions are similar in form to other exchange transactions. The characteristic features of these transactions can be summed up by saying that in Sonjo exchanges goods are delivered with *quitclaims*. At a betrothal, the goats making up the bride-price are thus paid to the bride's father with a quitclaim, even though it may be far in advance of the marriage; and at the agreed time the woman is turned over to her husband, again with a quitclaim. No guarantee is given by either party as to the qualities or survival of the exchanged commodities: thereafter neither side can have recourse to total or partial refund or withdrawal of his property: the transaction is final. When a wife is transferred from husband to husband, again the woman and goats are exchanged with quitclaims. The same rule governs the exchange of other goods as well. This relatively simple form of exchange is by no means universal in Africa. For example, in East African societies such as the Kikuyu (Kenyatta 1953:218) and the Pakot (H. Schneider 1959:152) a common exchange form exists in which a male animal is exchanged for a female animal, with various rules governing the division of the offspring of the female and specifying responsibility for its care and welfare. The Sonjo have nothing like this.

Sonjo bride-price acts to stimulate the whole exchange system by providing an important incentive for economic activity. Nearly every family, once or oftener during the period when sons are growing up, has to collect a large number of goats for bride-price, and attempts to do this without completely depleting the family herds. At those times surplus goods such as honey, grain, and beehives are exchanged for goats. On the other side of the picture we find families acquiring goats paid as bride-price for their daughters, and if there is no immediate need to provide sons with wives, these goats are available to be exchanged for the necessities and luxuries of life. Even if the Sonjo had no bride-price, there would undoubtedly be some trade and exchange for the purpose of leveling off inequalities in different foodstuffs and other goods possessed by individuals. But there would be no incentive to raise the volume of this exchange above a bare minimum, for the Sonjo seem to lack any notion of trading for profit, that is, of buying cheap and selling dear. The necessity of raising bride-price from time to time creates an external incentive for producing surplus primary goods for exchange; while the acquisition of surplus goats as bride-price creates a demand for consumer goods over and above the minimum sub-sistence level.

The economic interpretation that has been presented in this paper runs counter to a widely held opinion concerning the nature and functions of bride-price. Sonjo marriage customs, it is true, seem to differ from those of other African societies that have been described in that the economic functions of bride-price are unusually prominent. Nevertheless, I do not consider the Sonjo to be really unique in this respect, and believe that the same basic economic pattern could be revealed in many other societies, though perhaps not as clearly. In order to illustrate this basic similarity I shall discuss bride-price in four other tribes from different parts of Africa and compare them with the Sonjo.

Thonga Bride-Price

Junod wrote his well-known monograph on the Thonga before the appearance of the manifesto against "bride-price" but he was already aware of the prevailing sentiment and attempted to interpret Thonga bride-price as a non-economic social institution.

> As we have said previously the only way of understanding the lobola . . . is to consider it *as a compensation given by one group to another group,* in order to restore the equilibrium between the various collective units composing the clan. The first group acquires a new member. The second groups feels itself diminished, and claims something which permits it to reconstitute itself, in its turn, by the acquisition of another woman. This collectivist conception alone explains all the facts [italics his] (Junod 1927:I,278).

He then goes on to tell us the functions ("advantages") of bride-price, of which he lists three (1927:I,279).

> 1) It strengthens the family, I mean the patriarchal family, the right of the father. 2) It marks the difference between a legitimate and an illegitimate marriage and, in this sense, takes the place of an official marriage register. 3) It puts hindrances in the way of dissolving the matrimonial union, as a wife cannot definitely leave her husband without her group returning the lobola. Therefore it obliges the married pair to have a certain regard, one for the other.

Thus Junod starts out by attributing noble functions to the bride-price, but as he observes the custom more closely it becomes tinged with commercialism. A little later he writes that

> Marriages concluded on the lobola basis are frequently dissolved. The tie being purely material, it is easy to sever it. [And again] . . . though she is not looked upon exactly as a head of cattle, a marriageable girl is in principle entirely at the mercy of her family as regards the choice of her husband. . . . It is true that she is not a *slave*. She is, however, owned (1927:I,280–1).

The way that lobola actually operates as an exchange transaction is revealed in a long footnote (1927:I,280), which must be quoted in full.

> I will give only one example which I witnessed among my neighbors and which shows that, with women of loose character, at any rate, the payment of lobola helps very little to strengthen the matrimonial tie. A girl named Hlapfuta, daughter of Bandi, married a first husband. The "Bukosi" (name commonly given to lobola money) was used to procure a wife for her brother. But she left her husband and was married by Nwamusi. This second husband paid the lobola, which was then returned to the first. But Hlapfuta ran away a second time and joined a man called Matshubele. She did the same thing five consecutive times, and finally she moved to Majlangaleu, to the suburb of Lorenzo Marques, the favorite quarter of the prostitutes. There she was lost, and the "Bukosi" also. Her paternal uncle who had been put to any amount of trouble to recover the "Bukosi" in order to give it back to the five abandoned husbands, seeing that it would be impossible to satisfy the last, could no longer bear the strain and committed suicide by hanging himself from a tree not far from my home in Rikatla. The debt remained with the girl's brother who "had eaten the bukosi."

Despite Junod's attempt to interpret bride-price as a "collectivist" institution for strengthening family and marriage, its economic character is just as evident among the Thonga as the Sonjo. Marriage transactions in the two tribes are similar in basic principle, but are governed by different rules. For example, Thonga husbands exchange wives and bride-price, not directly, but indirectly via the wife's family. Again, a Thonga father delivers his daughter to her husband with a money-back guarantee that she will stay with him, while no such guarantee is given by a Sonjo father. As for humanitarian considerations, it is doubtful if any Sonjo woman, living under a regime of outright purchase, has been passed from husband to husband as often as Hlapfuta. Moreover, the tragic suicide of her uncle, resulting from the complex debt that he had incurred, would not be likely to happen in the simple and direct exchange system of the Sonjo. Although Junod does not clearly explain how children are dealt with, he mentions that "If divorce takes place and the lobola is not returned to the husband, he keeps them [the children] and the mother will be separated from them forever" (1927:I,281). This implies that the possession of children is determined largely by property exchange.

Gusii Bride-Price

The bride-price customs of the Gusii of Kenya have been described and analyzed by Mayer (1950) in perhaps greater detail than those of any other African society. Again I shall attempt to demonstrate a basic similarity between Sonjo and Gusii bride-price when considered as exchange transactions, though at first sight the two institutions appear to be very unlike one another. Briefly stated, these are the most significant features of Gusii customs. The amount of the main bride-price (the "bridewealth proper"), consisting of cattle and goats in a set ratio, varies within certain limits at any one time. The Gusii themselves "can only explain the fluctuations in terms of what the European might call the price mechanism that governs the price of a commodity in a more or less perfect market" (Mayer 1950:16). In coming to an agreement as to the size and quality of the bride-price, the girl's father bargains for a high price and the suitor's father for a low price: "both donor and recipient approach *okomana* [negotiations] in a business-like spirit of hard bargaining" (Mayer 1950:7).

The bulk of the bride-price becomes the property of the bride's father or her brothers; these men normally use the animals to obtain wives for themselves. In a polygynous household the bride-price goes to the uterine brothers of the bride, with the father having rights to some of it. When there are many wives, the nuclear families belonging to a single man are linked in pairs: his first and second wives and their children form a linked pair, the third and fourth another pair, and so on. The linkage involves mutual responsibility for one another's bride-price debts.

A man who purchases a wife (and hereafter I shall use terms of economic exchange) is responsible for the survival of the animals constituting the bride-price. If any of these animals should die, he is given the carcass and must replace it with a live animal of equal quality. However, if he had originally received these animals as bride-price paid to him for a woman of his own family, then the man who purchased his sister or daughter is held responsible for replacing the animals when they die. This line of responsibility for the survival of the animals is traced back through successive owners for as far as the facts can be ascertained.

On the other hand, the father and brothers of a wife are held responsible for her survival, and if she dies the man who used her bride-price to buy himself a wife is required to refund it or supply another woman in her place. If he is no longer living, the responsibility for refunding the bride-price passes to his heir— to a son or a uterine brother or, if he has none, to a half-brother of a linked nuclear family. In theory, at least, these claims for repayment of bride-price are imperishable. Only in the death of a very old wife or one leaving married children is the repayment of bride-price not required. When young children survive their mother's death, a deduction is made from the bride-price that has to be refunded. Several different systems are in use for calculating the amount of the deduction. According to the system favored by the chiefs at present, ten percent of the bride-price is deducted for each surviving child.

Gusii divorce laws have recently been altered by the British administration, and I shall only refer here to the traditional laws as described by Mayer. As in the death of a wife, a divorce requires the repayment of the bride-price, only the total sum refunded is greater because the wedding gifts as well as the "bride-wealth proper" must be returned. Children accompany their mother, and when she marries again they become the legal children of her new husband. Unlike the Sonjo, the Gusii do not seem to require a man to make an additional payment for children when he purchases a divorced wife; it must be their legal principle that a man is entitled to all his wife's children while she remains his wife, and that whether they are born before or after he acquires her does not matter. If her bride-price is still in possession of her father or brothers, it should be repaid before she remarries.

> If, however, the bridewealth had already been handed on to a third party the husband will normally have to wait until his divorced wife re-marries; the father ought then to pass the new bridewealth on to the creditor immediately (Mayer 1950:55).

Thus when a wife is transferred from husband to husband among the Gusii, as in the case of the Thonga, the second husband pays bride-price indirectly to the first husband, with the woman's father acting as intermediary, rather than directly as among the Sonjo. Still a third form of transfer is practiced by the Gusii of Uganda, where the father must first refund the bride-price to the original husband, and only then may he accept a new bride-price from the second husband. "There must be two separate transactions and no man can give bridewealth for a divorced woman until it has been refunded to her ex-husband" (LaFontaine 1959:48).

Bride-price transactions among both the Gusii and Sonjo are integrated into the general system of economic exchange, though the two exchange systems differ markedly. Mayer understands and states this clearly, even though he prefers to analyze the institution for the most part in noneconomic terms. I quote his concise statement, which starts by emphasizing

> the strong resemblance between the marriage transaction and those other customary exchanges of animals which before the advent of Europeans took the place of buying and selling, there having been no exact counterpart of "purchase" and "sale" in the traditional economy. The Gusii system, placing women, cattle, goats, and grain in this order of descending value, regulates the exchange of any kind into the next less valuable kind by just the same set of principles.
>
> A single example may be given to illustrate the similarity. In the commonest economic exchange, *A* gives one cow or heifer for several goats of *B*'s; if one of the goats thereafter dies without progeny *B* must replace it upon return of the corpse, but if the cow itself dies without progeny *A* will not give another until he receives an extra goat from *B*. In just the same way, when *A* gives his daughter for several cows of *B*'s, if one of the cows dies without progeny *B* must replace it upon return of the corpse, but if

the woman herself dies without progeny *A* will not give another as *riika* [substitute wife] until he receives an extra cow from *B* (Mayer 1950:38–39).

Although Mayer writes in several places about the "equilibrium" that bride-price transactions are supposed to "maintain," to me it appears to be only the kind of equilibrium that is presupposed in any system of economic exchange. At any rate it has little effect on the stability of Gusii marriage, as indicated by this statement: "The living together of man and wife, and their sharing of the daily routine of the homestead, is regarded as a desirable and natural consequence of marriage, but the bridewealth system as such does nothing to secure it" (Mayer 1950:57).

This summary, I think, amply demonstrates that Gusii bride-price, like Sonjo bride-price, functions as an economic institution. The Gusii seem to recognize this, and according to Mayer (1950:39), "Gusii women say of themselves: 'We are bought like cattle'" (cf. Radcliffe-Brown's statement which was quoted earlier). If the institution in each of these two societies is considered in the context of its own exchange system, the fundamental similarities stand out clearly. The most striking difference between the two systems of exchange has to do with the relations between seller and buyer after an exchange has been made. A Gusii seller remains permanently responsible to the buyer for the quality and survival of the commodity that he has sold, while a Sonjo seller is relieved of all further responsibility. The basic principle of the Gusii system might be termed the rule of interminable guarantee, whereas the Sonjo system is governed by a principle of quitclaim exchange.

Tiv Bride-Price

The bride-price system of the Tiv of Nigeria, our third example, can be easily dealt with, because it has been described by Bohannan (1955:61) in almost purely economic terms. Among the Tiv, we are told,

> Everything, including women, which is exchanged has an exchange value or equivalent (*ishe*), whereas no gift has an exchange value. In a market situation *ishe* means vaguely "exchange equivalent"—one might even sometimes translate it "price."

Nowadays the Tiv purchase their wives with a cash bride-price, but the traditional system was more complex.

> A wife is traditionally acquired by being granted a sister or cousin . . . to exchange for a wife, either directly or by means of bride wealth. . . . A wife whom one acquires in any other way is not the concern of one's marriage-ward sharing group because the woman or other property exchanged for her did not belong to the marriage-ward group (Bohannan 1955:66).

From this it would appear that women were distributed in the main by means of a separate system of sister and cousin exchange, but that this system was inadequate for circulating enough women in the society; therefore additional transactions in women took place in the general exchange system. A similar situation exists among the Bwamba of western Uganda (Winter 1956:22). At any rate, Bohannan places women in one of the three categories into which exchangeable goods are classified.

> All exchanges within this category are exchanges of rights in human beings, usually dependent women and children, so that the category may be called the category of dependent persons, and many of its values are expressed in terms of kinship and marriage (1955:63).

Bohannan distinguishes between exchanges of goods within one of these categories and exchanges between categories; the first transaction he terms "conveyance" and the second "conversion": both kinds of exchange are practiced. The categories are "arranged in a hierarchy on the basis of moral values" (1955:64). This provides one of the dynamic factors which make the exchange system work.

> The drive towards success leads most Tiv, to the greatest possible extent, to convert food [the lowest category] into prestige items [middle category]; to convert prestige items into dependents—women and children (1955:64).

If the system is in equilibrium, there are presumably opposite drives of equal force impelling men to convert their women and prestige items into goods of lower categories, though the motives may be baser than those producing upward conversion. However, we are not concerned here with moral or intrinsic values of goods, but only with their economic values. Considered in that light, Tiv women, except for those who are exchanged as sisters and cousins, are dealt with in a relatively simple exchange system in which all commodities have a price.

Evidently Tiv women, like Sonjo women, are regarded as exchangeable commodities both before and after marriage. Thus we read that "individual items are removed from the third category [of exchangeable items]—that of rights in dependent persons—by death of human beings, and by death alone" (1955:64). Like the Sonjo, the Tiv exchange women with quitclaims, so far as their survival is concerned. "If a woman dies her husband cannot recover bridewealth from her guardian" (Bohannan 1957:88). When a wife is transferred from husband to husband, some form of indirect payment of bride-price seems to be the rule. Bohannan (1957:86) only describes the first phase of this transaction, that is, the divorce:

> If a woman leaves her husband the guardian (and some others) must refund certain parts of the bridewealth. . . . Sometimes there are disputes about which parts of the bridewealth are returnable. The amount paid for a woman is always returnable, less deductions for children she has borne.

Ganda Bride-Price

For our final example, we consider briefly the Ganda as described in the writings of Mair, whose stricture on the word "bride-price" and its implications was cited in the introduction. Actually, from the little information on economic functions that we are given, the Ganda appear to conform to the pattern of wife purchase found in the other tribes, and add some interesting features of their own.

Bride-price was an important component in the Ganda system of trade and exchange. We are told that men would go on "distant trading expeditions" to raise bride-price (Mair 1934:130). This is confirmed by Roscoe (1911:452) for an earlier period:

> The Baganda nation has an inbred love of trading and bartering, which seems to have increased owing to their custom of paying for their brides, and the difficulty in finding the amount demanded by the bride's clan.

Ganda fathers expect to be reimbursed for the trouble and expense of bringing up their daughters—a common native explanation of bride-price, rationalizing the economic interests which fathers have in daughters whom they later sell to husbands. So entrenched was this principle among the Ganda that it survived drastic culture changes and now appears in bizarre circumstances. Thus Mair (1934:100) tells of one of her informants:

> Kanywamagule refused to let his daughter become a nun for this reason, and when I told him that we had no bride-price in England, he asked, "Then do they bring up girls for nothing?"

The custom was formerly that bride-price was returned at a divorce. "Her [the wife's] family would naturally try to make the new husband's bride-price cover the amount that had to be refunded to the other" (Mair 1934:98). This is the usual pattern of indirect wife purchase. As Christianity became a power in Uganda, divorce was no longer legally recognized, and a husband then had no legal sanction supporting his demand for the refund of his bride-price. "The stages in the process by which the non-returnability of the bride-price came to be taken for granted can no longer be traced" (Mair 1940:20). At the final stage, it appears, a husband paid bride-price for a wife with no guarantee that she would stay with him, and with no legal confirmation of his wife rights. A father might sell his daughter to several consecutive husbands and pocket the bride-price each time, evidently without being accused of swindle.

> It would be quite unfair to say that fathers regard their daughters simply as a profitable commodity, but now that the bride-price is sheer gain to them they are rather more willing than otherwise to see a daughter change her husband three or four times . . . (Mair 1934:100).

It is hard to reconcile this state of affairs with the statement that "The transfer of the bride-price was, and still is, the essential act which legalizes marriage" (Mair 1934:81), no matter what construction is put on the word "legalize." These somewhat contradictory fragments of information suggest an extraordinary story concerning the evolution of an African economic system in which bride-price played a prominent role, and we would like to know more about it. However, an investigator who believes that Ganda bride-price customs "demonstrate the fallacy of arguing from this payment that women are bought and sold like chattels" (Mair 1934:98) might be inhibited from probing the economic system too deeply lest the practice of wife purchase be revealed even more clearly. It is safer to make the conventional assertion that "The bride-price in pre-European days was a guarantee for the stability of the marriage" (Mair 1934:99), particularly as this interpretation cannot now be either refuted or confirmed.

Conclusion

Although space does not permit further comparative observations, there is no doubt that exchange mechanisms similar to those operating in Sonjo, Gusii, and Tiv marriage underlie the bride-price transactions in many other African societies. These mechanisms can be discerned in published accounts, only they are often veiled; for anthropologists, with a few notable exceptions, have tended to ignore the economic implications in the facts which they set forth, owing to the pervasive influence of the doctrine denying the existence of wife purchase. As a result of this bias, the close interrelations between economic and marriage systems have been neglected, and our analyses of both systems have suffered.

In discussions of cattle-keeping tribes, the contrast is often drawn between the intense desire of these people to acquire cattle and the inefficiency of their utilization as subsistence resources. One of the chief incentives for acquiring cattle is undoubtedly to use them in obtaining wives for the individual or group possessing the cattle, but this tends to be overlooked by an investigator who conscientiously avoids treating bride-price as an economic transaction. Instead, the intrinsic or mystical value that cattle have for the people is stressed. "They are merely possessed and esteemed for the prestige their possession brings" (Herskovits 1952:265). This interpretation explains the desire for cattle, but fails to account for the exchange and circulation of cattle which certainly occurs in most of these societies. If cattle are frankly regarded as exchange commodities, having, in addition to their utilitarian and intrinsic values, economic or relative values (prices), then we have the means of analyzing the economic system and can better understand the social structure; but by giving absolute values to cattle at a premature stage in the investigation we are discouraged from further analysis. It is significant that in his recent study of the Jie and Turkana, Gulliver (1955) carefully investigated the various exchanges and transfers involving livestock and found no need in his analysis to fall back on absolute or prestige values for cattle.

In African societies with simple technologies and possessions, the material necessities of life are produced for the most part by the family groups that consume them, and there would be little incentive for the exchange of commodities unless an additional factor were introduced. Wives are not produced by the family group; they must be obtained from other groups, usually in exchange for goods which the family group itself produces. This seems to provide an incentive which sets in motion a chain of exchanges and creates an economic system where otherwise there would be merely a subsistence system. Thus bride-price occupies a crucial position in these exchange systems, and often reveals most clearly the prevailing forms of exchange—customary economic equivalents and the rules governing their exchange—which may differ from society to society, but which are susceptible of analysis and classification. In some societies, such as the Sonjo and Gusii, wives are exchanged in basically the same way as other commodities and may be subsumed under the general exchange system. In other societies exchanges of women may constitute a subsystem separate from the general exchange system. This may be true, for example, where sister exchange is practiced.

If the economic aspect of bride-price is neglected because of the conviction that wives are not bought and sold, a valuable aid in understanding marriage customs themselves is rejected. For this reason many accounts of African divorce are unsatisfactory. If we assume that a young divorced woman normally re-marries—because there is no permanent role for a single woman of this kind in most African societies—then a divorce can be regarded as only the first step in an exchange transaction that is completed when she remarries and the second husband directly or indirectly pays bride-price to the first. This transaction clearly has some resemblance to wife purchase, and evidently to avoid that diffi-culty anthropologists usually discuss divorce as if it were a social act complete in itself, as it is customarily considered in our society, forcing the facts into the mold of our conventional ideas about divorce. I cite one example of this kind of distortion, which is common in the literature. This is a recent study by Fallers (1957) of divorce among the Soga of Uganda. From his conventionally re-stricted viewpoint, the analysis is convincing enough as far as it goes. If it is unsatisfactory as a whole, this is not primarily because of vague concepts and inadequate statistics, as Fallers suggests (1957:121), but because it is incom-plete and one-sided. Despite his findings that between one-quarter and one-half of Soga marriages end in divorce, no consideration is given to the remarriage of divorced women or the bride-price adjustments.

All this is not to deny that bride-price has noneconomic functions and that it is of value to study them. These functions, however, have undoubtedly been exaggerated by anthropologists, in some cases evidently thinking thereby to dis-prove the existence of wife purchase. After making a broad survey of bride-price customs in some fifty tribes of the East African cattle area, Pearsall (1947:31) was not altogether convinced of the functions of bride-price which are usually put forward.

> The present study cannot demonstrate any reason for the origin of the bride-wealth complex. That the custom arose for the sole purpose of stabiliz-ing or legalizing marriage seems absurd, though, once established, it may well have served as a stabilizer. Nor does it seem that bride-wealth creates social relationships between the marrying families; rather it reflects social usages already established.

On the same page, however, Pearsall betrays her adherence to the prevailing doctrine and writes: "Wives are not bought. Wives can never be resold. . . ."

If bride-price thus has no definite social function, and if it is not an economic transaction, we are left with no explanation at all for these exchanges of large amounts of property, and it remains an inexplicable and meaningless custom.

It is beyond the scope of this discussion to trace the history of the bride-price confusion, but at the risk of oversimplifying what is obviously a complex problem, I suggest that it stems mainly from a single ethnocentric interpretation— namely, that wife purchase is necessarily debasing for the people who practice it. The early missionaries and government officials in Africa recognized that native marriage customs involved wife purchase, and felt obliged to condemn the custom as being morally repugnant (Phillips 1953:195). As anthoropologists studied and acquired a better understanding of African societies, they found no evidence that the payments made at marriage were demeaning or socially harmful. Therefore they opposed the official view, but with the wrong arguments: they resorted to the expedient of denying the existence of wife purchase, instead of setting about the job of analyzing it. Thus, by implication, they accepted uncritically and at face value the laymen's moral evaluation of wife purchase in general. Although the original purpose may have been to defend native customs against unjust condemnation, the result of carelessly planned counter-propaganda has been to create a selective ethnocentrism that has hobbled anthropology in its attempts to understand African marriage and economics.

Wife purchase, of course, is not practiced in our society and would be severely condemned if attempted, but neither is parallel cousin marriage or various other forms of preferential marriage which are certainly at variance with our ideals concerning human dignity and freedom of choice, but which are normally described by anthropologists without wincing. It should be the business of anthropologists to explain customs that differ from theirs, not to conceal them. African wives themselves do not seem to consider it debasing to be exchanged for cattle or other goods. On the contrary they often express approval of the custom, and I am sure that other anthropologists, like myself, have found Africans incredulous and even disapproving when told that we do not pay bride-price for our wives. A typical statement is the following by Smith and Dale (1920:II,49):

> . . . a woman among the Ba-ila has a certain pride in the amount of *chiko* given by her husband. . . . [One woman] said she would not stay with a man who had paid nothing for her.

Thus there appears to be little justification in native attitudes for expunging the word "bride-price" and substituting a euphemism.

This ethnocentric notion of wife purchase, once established in the literature, has tended to be self-perpetuating and has bred other mistakes. The meanings of economic terms, such as purchase, price, and property rights, are prejudiced when it is assumed that they can not be applied to wives. When wife purchase is defined hypothetically for the purpose of refuting it, as we noted earlier, African wives are compared with commodities in a European market or cattle at an English auction. This only shows that it is absurd to compare attitudes toward similar customs in different cultures, not that it is absurd to compare wives to other commodities in the same society. When the latter comparison was made we found wives, cattle, goats, and other commodities, being exchanged with one another according to the rules governing the economic system of the society. In many African societies, bride-price can hardly be analyzed thoroughly without revealing its integral position in the exchange system, which would make it clear that wives are dealt with economically like other commodities. This has been avoided at the expense of exaggerating its noneconomic functions. Thus bride-price tends to be pictured as a benevolent institution built into a society by folk wisdom for the purpose of protecting marriage and family, but existing in an economic vacuum.

In quoting Radcliffe-Brown several times in this paper, it was not meant to single him out for criticism, but only to show how an otherwise astute observer of primitive society was affected by the epidemic of resentment against the term "bride-price" and the viewpoint that it represents. In closing I quote from a more characteristic statement of his which was a stimulus to me in writing the paper: "Only when we have made a very extensive analysis and classification of all varieties of exchange or payment shall we be able to create a really scientific terminology" (Radcliffe-Brown 1929:132).

NOTES

[1] I am indebted to E. H. Winter for helpful suggestions during the drafting of this paper.

[2] A total of 22 items on this subject by 11 different authors may be found listed in the indexes of *Man*, vols. 29 to 31.

[3] The Sonjo material used in this paper was obtained in the field during the last half of 1955. The fieldwork was supported by a Ford Foundation research grant, administered by the Institute of Current World Affairs.

17 THE POTLATCH SYSTEM OF THE SOUTHERN KWAKIUTL: A NEW PERSPECTIVE[1]

Stuart Piddocke

This paper is, first, an attempt to reconstruct the potlatch system of Southern Kwakiutl society around the last decade of the eighteenth century, i.e. at the beginning of direct contact with Occidental civilization; and, second, an argument that in aboriginal times the potlatch had a very real pro-survival or subsistence function, serving to counter the effects of varying resource productivity by promoting exchanges of food from those groups enjoying a temporary surplus to those groups suffering a temporary deficit.[2] In making this reconstruction, I find myself forced by the data to depart from the orthodox portrait of the Kwakiutl potlatch and to develop another based on data rather neglected in the literature. At the same time, there is no need to reject the orthodox picture as at least an approximately accurate description of *later* Kwakiutl potlatching, because the later form can be deduced from the proposed model of the aboriginal potlatch when certain actual historical processes, i.e. the events of the contact period, are fed in as conditions disturbing the original state of equilibrium specified in the model. Therefore, although this paper is not intended as a reconstruction of Kwakiutl history, it does provide an explanation for some of the responses that actually occurred in the historic period.

In particular, I wish to present evidence for the following propositions:

(a) The Kwakiutl have been commonly described as having a "fantastic surplus economy" distinguished by a great abundance of food and other natural resources further maximized by efficient methods of exploiting and storing the various products; this great abundance, preserved in summer, fed the people throughout the winter, during which season an abundance of leisure time enabled the people to develop their extraordinary potlatches and winter ceremonials (Codere 1950:4–5, 14, 63–64, 68, 126; Ford 1941:8). What I hope to show is that, however true such a picture of abundance may have been for the Kwakiutl

From Southwestern Journal of Anthropology *21:244–264. Reprinted by permission.*

[1] This inquiry into the ecological relationships of the Kwakiutl potlatch was first started in 1959–60 as part of a seminar on Northwest Coast cultures conducted at the University of British Columbia by Dr. Wayne Suttles and Dr. A. P. Vayda, who must be regarded as the joint inspirers of this paper and for whom its first version was written. A second version was read in the late fall of 1960 at the London School of Economics seminar on anthropological theory conducted by Professor Raymond Firth, whose criticism has greatly benefited both this paper in particular and my own thinking in general. Reference to this unpublished second version is also made in a 1961 paper by Dr. Vayda; and the preparation and publication of this final version is therefore in the nature of a somewhat belated fulfillment of a scholastic obligation.

[2] Compare Suttles (1960:296–305), where he shows how the Coast Salish potlatch, status rivalry, subsistence activities, variations in production within the Coast Salish resources, and their system of exchanges between affinal relatives were all linked together as parts of a single socioeconomic system.

as a whole, it was less than true for the various individual local groups. For these latter, scarcity of food was an ever-present threat, depending on the varying productivity of sea and land; and without the distribution of food from wealthier local groups to poorer ones, the latter would often have died of hunger.

(b) The potlatch was in aboriginal times confined to the chiefs or headmen of the various localized kin-groups or numayms that made up the tribes or winter-village groups, and hence the series of potlatches between the various chiefs were in effect exchanges of food and wealth between tribes and numayms. Through this exchange system, the effects of variations in productivity were minimized, and a level of subsistence was maintained for the entire population.

(c) In this system food could be exchanged for wealth objects, such as blankets, slaves, and canoes; and wealth objects exchanged in turn for increased prestige.

(d) The desire for prestige and the status rivalry between chiefs directly motivated potlatching and so indirectly motivated the people to continue the system of exchanges; and the continuation of these practices ensured the survival of the population.

Kwakiutl history may be divided into four periods: the Aboriginal or Pre-Contact period, extending from the indefinite past to 1792; the Early Contact period, 1792 to 1849; the Potlatch period, 1849 to the early 1920's; and the Post-Potlatch period, from the early 1920's to the present. What I have here separated as the Aboriginal and Early Contact periods corresponds to the Pre-Potlatch period distinguished by Codere (1961:434); the two later divisions follow Codere exactly. In 1792, European civilization, in the persons of Captain Vancouver and his expedition, first made direct contact with the Kwakiutl at the place known as "Cheslakee's Village" (Vancouver 1801:268–73).[3] European influence thenceforward slowly but steadily increased until in 1849 the Hudson's Bay Company established their trading post of Fort Rupert (Dawson 1887:66), and shortly thereafter the four Kwakiutl tribes later to be known as the Fort Rupert tribes settled hard by the post. This marks the appearance in Kwakiutl country of a direct non-traditional source of wealth, as contrasted with indirect trade through Nootka or relatively inconstant trade with trading ships. And with this new source of wealth there came changes in Kwakiutl society, notably an intensification of status rivalry and an increase in the frequency and volume of potlatching, so much so that the potlatch became the predominant Kwakiutl institution. This Potlatch period ended in the early 1920's when the beginning of an economic depression for the Kwakiutl coincided with the first notable successes in the Government's campaign to stop the Indians from potlatching.

Subsistence

Sea-fishing, river-fishing, berry picking, and the hunting of land and sea animals were the chief subsistence activities. Reviewing the list of the fish, animals,

---

[3] Identified by Dawson (1887:72) with the Nimkish village of Whulk, at the mouth of the Nimkish River.

and plants eaten, one gets at first glance an impression of abundance: salmon, salmon-spawn, herring, herring-spawn, eulachen or candle-fish (notable for its oil), halibut, cod, perch, flounder, kelp-fish, devil fish, sea-slugs, barnacles, and winkles; seals, porpoises, and the occasional beach-stranded whale; mountain goats; elderberries, salalberries, wild currants, huckleberries, salmon-berries, viburnum berries, dogwood berries, gooseberries, and crabapples; clover roots, cinquefoil roots, sea-milkwort, bracken roots, fern-roots, erythronium roots, lupine roots, wild carrots, and lily-bulbs; eel-grass and some sea-weeds. Of these, some would be eaten in summer, and the rest preserved for use in winter (Boas 1921:173–514).

This impression of abundance is, however, not sustained by further examination. For instance, the various roots and berries did not grow everywhere. Good crabapples could be picked in only two places; elsewhere they were "rotten." Viburnum berries could be picked only at the end of summer at the head of Knight Inlet (Boas 1921:213, 216). And berries and roots, generally, could be picked only in season.

Similar restrictions governed the supply of fish. The several varieties of salmon ran only at certain seasons of the year and did not spawn in every stream. Herring did not spawn everywhere. The eulachen ran in spring (Boas 1921:198), and, according to Curtis (1915:22–23), in three streams only, namely those on Kingcome River, at the head of Knight Inlet, and at the head of Rivers Inlet; furthermore, "this fish cannot be taken for its oil above tidal water." Curtis (1915:24–25) also informs us that only the following groups specialized in halibut fishing (though others might fish for halibut also, their fishing was only occasional): four tribes of Quatsino, two tribes (one now extinct) at Cape Scott, the Newettee of Hope Island, the Goasila of Smith Inlet, the Naqoaqtoq of Seymour Inlet, and the Owikeno of Rivers Inlet; the principal halibut banks were near Hope Island, Galiano Island, the Gordon group, and certain islands of the larger inlets. Flounders had to be caught in calm weather, when the tide was coming in (Boas 1921:413). Winkles were collected only when they spawned (Boas 1921:509). Kelp-fish were not caught in large numbers, and there was in any one catch usually only enough for a family (Boas 1921:397, 400, 405, 408). Of this apparent abundance of products, only a few were staples; the rest were additions, very welcome and very necessary to the Kwakiutl, but still only supplementary to the main diet. These staples were salmon, herring, eulachen, berries, and, to a somewhat lesser extent, goats, seals, and porpoises.

The Kwakiutl quarrelled and fought amongst themselves over rights to hunting grounds, fishing stations on rivers, use of fish weirs and traps, and berrying grounds; trespassing was a frequent cause for conflict (Boas 1921:1345–1348; Curtis 1915:22). Wars were waged "to take the land away from people" (Boas 1935:60, 66–67).

Starvation was no stranger to the Kwakiutl. Stories of starvation were more numerous among the tribes living on the islands in Queen Charlotte and Johnstone Straits, but all experienced hunger. Reasons given for such starvation included prolonged periods of bad weather which prevented hunting and fishing, and the failure of fish runs. The tales emphasized the especial dependence of the people on the salmon (Boas 1935:24). People would eat fern-roots when they were hungry and lacking in other food or when they had to camp for a long time in bad weather. The lupine root when eaten caused dizziness and sleepiness; yet it would be eaten in spring "when the tribes are hungry" before the eulachen arrived in Knight Inlet (Boas 1921:196, 198). As we would expect in such circumstances, they wasted very little of what food there was; for instance, recipes are given for salmon tails and roasted salmon backbone (Boas 1921:329).

This evidence can only lead, I think, to the conclusion that the abundance of the resources of the Kwakiutl has been somewhat overestimated and its significance misinterpreted. It was great enough to support a population larger than the usual size reported for hunting and gathering societies; but this population lived sufficiently close to the margins of subsistence so that variations in productivity which fell below normal could threaten parts of the population with famine and death from starvation.

Thus the evidence in the ethnographic record. It describes the localization of Kwakiutl subsistence resources and indicates—but does not document—variations in productivity. Further evidence for variation, however, is to be found in fisheries statistics concerning production of salmon and herring.

Herring

Statistics on herring show great variations, some spawning grounds apparently not being continuously used. Times of spawning vary from place to place. Changes in population abundance, says Outram (1956:7; 1957:7; cf. also 1958), are due primarily to variations in environmental conditions which cause variations in the "relative strengths of the contributing year classes" rather than to inadequate spawning or over- or under-fishing.

The Kwakiutl ate both herring and herring-spawn, and caught both at the spawning grounds. Besides the variation from year to year in the absolute number of herring spawn deposited (measured in miles of spawn at some standard intensity of deposition), the intensity of spawn varied from ground to ground, and we might expect this to have some effect on the catch made by Kwakiutl.

Salmon

Considerable year-to-year variation is likewise shown in the statistics on the packs of canned sockeye and other salmon taken at Rivers Inlet from 1882 to 1954 (Cobb 1921:172–174; Godfrey 1958a:333; cf. also Hoar 1951, for a general survey of variations in abundances of pink salmon on the British Columbia coast). These variations in salmon packs are traced to variations in the actual size of the salmon populations, variations which are in turn due to several causes. Notable among these causes are variable water levels and temperatures in the spawning streams, variations in the permeability of the stream beds, occasional extreme floods, variable temperatures and salinity in the ocean, and the variable freshwater runoffs and the action of tides, currents, winds, and deep-water upwelling in the estuarine and inshore waters that are the habitat of the young salmon for weeks or perhaps months before they reach the open seas (Godfrey 1958b; Neave 1953, 1958; Rostlund 1952:16; Wickett 1958). These causes are likely to have operated in previous centuries as well as in the present, and therefore indicate the existence of variations before statistics began to be kept on the fish population.

Rostlund (1952:16–17) has suggested that Indian fishing, before the advent of commercial fishing, helped to maintain the optimum salmon population by preventing over-crowding of the salmon streams. This may have been so, and it is a possibility to be taken into account when evaluating the productivity of subsistence resources for the Kwakiutl. But the effect of the Indian fishing would nevertheless not eliminate variations due to the causes enumerated above.

In addition to the variation in actual numbers of fish and game available for food, we must take into consideration the effects of the weather in hindering or preventing hunting and fishing expeditions. This has already been referred to as one of the reasons for starvation among the Kwakiutl.

The evidence is, I think, sufficient. For the various local groups of the Kwakiutl, scarcity of food was an ever-present threat, depending on the varying production of sea and land. Oftentimes it fell out that a local group would have died of starvation if it had not acquired food from other groups. The remainder of this paper will now be devoted to showing how the exchange system of the Kwakiutl ensured a continual movement of food from those groups enjoying a temporary abundance to those groups suffering privation, and so contributed to the survival of the whole population involved in the exchange system.

Social Units

The basic unit of Kwakiutl society was the numaym, which may be summarily described as a named group associated mythologically with a traditional place of origin; it owned property consisting of fishing locations, hunting territory, and one or more houses in a winter village; and it was headed by a chief or headman descended, at least in theory, in the most senior genealogical line from a founding ancestor.[4] The members of the numaym consisted of people related, sometimes closely, sometimes distantly, usually patrilineally, but often through their mothers or wives, to the chief. There would at any time probably be a number of visitors dwelling with the people of the numaym, and some of the members of the numaym would also likely be away visiting. The numaym was in

---

[4] Succession to the chief's position could apparently go to a woman, if she were a chief's eldest child and on condition that she resided in her father's numaym. We can perhaps best describe the success as one of primogeniture with a patrilineal bias and a residence quali-fication. Since marriage seems to have been generally virilocal, at least for persons of high status, the residence qualification would tend to have ruled out most daughters, barring uxorilocal exceptions (which, of course, occurred). See also the section on rank, below.

pre-contact times the potlatching unit, resource-exploiting unit, and the unit of social control.[5]

The next larger unit of Kwakiutl society was the tribe. This was composed of a number of numayms which shared a common winter village site. In summer the villages dispersed and the various numayms departed for their fishing stations. At these summer grounds, groups living in separate winter villages would meet. This seasonal migration was an important feature of Kwakiutl life, and it involved both inter-tribal meetings and some sharing of access to resources (Curtis 1915:21–23, 108; Dawson 1887:64, 72).

Chieftainship

The position of the chief or numaym head among the Kwakiutl was described by the people themselves as "the office of giving potlatches among the tribes" (Boas 1925:91, 99, 105), an expression which points out the position of the chief as representative of his numaym and his special task of potlatch giving. In former times, potlatching was a chiefly prerogative. Dawson (1887:7) has a significant passage on this point:

> Mr. George Blenkinsop, who has been for many years among the Kwakiool, informs me that the custom [of the potlatch] was formerly almost entirely confined to the recognized chiefs, but that of late years it has extended to the people generally, and become very much commoner than before. The Rev. A. J. Hall bears testimony to the same effect. With the chiefs, it was a means of acquiring and maintaining prestige and power. It is still so regarded, but has spread to all classes of the community and become the recognized mode of attaining social rank and respect.

By the time Boas was making his studies of the Fort Rupert Kwakiutl and collecting and editing George Hunt's texts, the potlatch was no longer a chiefly prerogative alone, and it had also, perhaps, been modified with respect to the job it was performing in society. This change seems to have been due to the advent of European traders, bringing sources of wealth beyond those traditionally provided for by Kwakiutl culture, and to the decline of population, which led to some groups having more "seats" (see below) than members (cf. Codere 1961; Drucker 1955:121–122, Wike 1952:98–99).

The chief was the custodian or manager of the resources of the numaym. As such, it was his duty to perform the necessary rituals concerning the exploitation of these resources at the appropriate season. In this position, he received a certain portion (sometimes called "tribute" in the texts) of the fish, seals, goats, etc., caught by the men. His wife similarly received a portion of the berries and roots collected by the women. With this supply the chief could hold potlatches (though not always without further assistance) and could pay for the carving

[5] The whole question of the nature of the Kwakiutl numaym is still a thorny one. This brief sketch, based on Boas (1889:832; 1897:332–338; 1920:112ff; 1921:795ff; 1925:57–58, 91, 101; 1935:173), Curtis (1915:28, 132), and Ford (1941:15) should be considered still only approximate and provisional and should also be considered in relation to the portrait of Kwakiutl ranking (see below).

of totem poles, the construction of canoes, and the building of a new house (Boas 1921:1333–1340; 1925:311ff, 331; Curtis 1915:28).[6]

Rank

Three status levels have been distinguished among the Kwakiutl and are termed in the literature "nobles," "commoners," and "slaves." But the distinctions between them are not of the same sort. Slaves were not, writes Boas (1897: 338), strictly part of the numaym but were, rather, captives taken in war or people obtained by purchase; they might change ownership like any other piece of property, being, for instance, given away as marriage gifts (Boas 1921:856, 865–866, 881), presented to guests as a potlatch (Boas 1921:1027), or used as part of the purchase price of a copper (Boas 1921:1024). Indeed, according to one ancient account, a woman-slave was once killed and eaten in the cannibal dance (Boas 1921:1017). Marriages between free persons and slaves were possible, but they were considered disgraceful; and the stigma of having had slaves among one's ancestors descended to the children and grandchildren of the marriage, and beyond (Boas 1921:1094ff, 1104ff). Not even the accumulation (in later, post-contact times) of wealth and of names could remove it.

The distinction between "nobles" and "commoners" is of a different kind than that between free persons and slaves. Codere (1957:474–475) has summed it up in the following words:

> "Commoner" in Kwakiutl refers to a person who at the moment of speaking is either without a potlatch position, chief's position, or standing place— all these being interchangeable but "noble" terms—or applies to one who has low rank which is nevertheless a "standing place" or position. The man referred to at that moment might have passed on his position just the moment before, or he might just the next moment be a successor to a position. "Commoners" in Kwakiutl society cannot be considered a class, for they have no continuous or special function; they have no identity, continuity, or homogeneity as a group, and no distinguishing culture or subculture. Individuals can at will become commoners by retirement from potlatch positions, and they customarily did so; individuals are raised from a common to a noble position at the will of others; individuals chose to consider "common" the lower positions of noble social rank; brothers and sisters of the same parents were given positions greatly varying in social rank and the younger ones might receive a position so lowly as to be "common."

These potlatch positions, or "seats" as Boas (1897:338) called them, were

[6] It should be noted that the term "chief" in the literature denotes sometimes simply "numaym head" and at other times "numaym head and other high ranking nobles," but it is not always clear which usage is intended. That there is a distinction between the "numaym head" and the other "chiefs" seems to be indicated by the tenor of the various relevant texts. However, it does not matter much for my argument if nobles other than the headmen occasionally gave inter-numaym or even inter-tribal potlatches, as it is clear they gave them on behalf of their numayms. Nor would such other nobles constitute a very great part of the "nobility" as a whole.

ranked in serial order, the chief of the numaym occupying the position of highest rank. Boas described these seats as each having associated with it a tradition of origin ("which almost always concerns the acquisition of a manitou"), certain crests, and certain privileges which the holder of the seat may enjoy; the rank was recognized in the order of seating the holders at potlatches, whence the position with its privileges came to be referred to as a "seat." Curtis (1915:137–138) describes the properties of the seat as including "names, crests, special ceremonial privileges, and territorial rights as to fishing and gathering vegetal food."

Succession to rank was by succession to the name and crest and complex of associated privileges, which of course also included its ranking. According to Curtis (1915:139), this succession was

> . . . ordinarily reckoned directly through the male line from father to eldest son; but a childless man may transfer his rank to a younger brother by adopting him as a son. More commonly, if he has a daughter his seat goes to her eldest son, or to her in trust for her infant or expected son. Less important names, along with ceremonial privileges, are regularly given to the son-in-law as a part of the dowry, in trust for his children; in fact, the acquisition of titles and privileges for children yet unborn is the most important consideration in arranging a union. But the principal name and rank never thus pass out of the direct succession unless there is no direct male heir. If a man dies while his eldest son is too young for man's responsibilities, the seat may be given in trust to an elder sister of the boy, or to an uncle.

Though Boas in his earlier work (1897:338–340) does not mention this distinction between names and positions which could go out of the numaym and those which could not, he does recognize it in his later paper (1920:121) reviewing Kwakiutl social organization. The distinction is also repeatedly affirmed by the Kwakiutl themselves in the texts collected by Boas (1921:786–787, 824, 231; 1925:91, 101, 105), that only those names acquired from one's father-in-law can be given to one's son-in-law, and that certain names and positions, including that of headchief of the numaym, cannot be given away or go out of the numaym, daughters therefore inheriting when sons are not available. The distinction was sharper in principle than in practice, for, as might be expected, a few exceptions to the rule also did occur.

The numaym may be seen, then, not only as a kinship unit (as it was described earlier) but also as a collection of ranked positions, their incumbents, and persons related to these incumbents. As Codere (1957:479) has put it:

> A numaym is a lineage group consisting of a series of ranked social positions, plus children and adults who do not have one of the ranked positions but who may receive one as a relative of someone who has one to pass on to or who may have held one and retired from it.

The numayms within a tribe were also ranked in serial order, the head of the highest-ranking numaym being reckoned the head chief of the tribe, or village.

This seems also to have been true in aboriginal times. There is no evidence, however, that the villages or tribal groups were ranked prior to European contact; the ranking of villages is a later nineteenth century development (cf. Codere 1961:445).

Thus far in this paper we have examined subsistence, the basic social units, chieftainship, and rank, demonstrated the first of the four propositions of this paper, and laid the foundation for demonstrating the remaining three. If in aboriginal times only chiefs potlatched (the chiefs being the numaym headmen and possibly one or two other leading men in each numaym as well), and if chiefs were supported in their potlatching by their numayms and potlatched on behalf of their numayms, then potlatches could only be between different numayms and were in effect exchanges of gifts between these numayms. The evidence for the first part of the antecedent in this proposition has been given in the section on "Chieftainship," and the second part of the antecedent implicitly supported there also. The numaym has been described and its resource-exploiting function noted. Kwakiutl ranking and its relation to the numaym have also been described, and something of its importance to the social structure suggested. What remains to be described is the system of exchanges, the conversions between food, wealth, and prestige, and the motivating factor of "status rivalry." These come to a focus in the institution of the potlatch, and to this we must now turn.

The Potlatch

What may be called the orthodox[7] view of the Kwakiutl potlatch is based largely on the summary and analysis given by Helen Codere in *Fighting with Property* (1950:63–80), following in turn the interpretation given by Boas in his early study of Kwakiutl social organization and "secret societies" (1897: 341–358). As Codere has herself admitted (1950:89), however, her reconstruction does not apply to the *aboriginal* potlatch but to the potlatch of the later contact period. Between the aboriginal potlatch and the potlatch of Codere's reconstruction there are several very important differences.

The first point of difference concerns Codere's setting the potlatch "in the context of a fantastic surplus economy" (1950:63). There seems no valid reason to doubt the appearance among the Kwakiutl in the last quarter of the nineteenth century of a great surplus beyond the needs of subsistence. But in aboriginal times such a surplus did not exist. Earlier in this paper I assembled evidence to indicate that the "fantastic surpluses" of the Kwakiutl have been overestimated, and that they were much closer to the margins of survival than has commonly been thought. The appearance of great wealth and "surpluses above any conceivable need" in later, post-contact times was probably due (a) to the drastic population decline from smallpox, venereal diseases, etc., ensuring that the productivity of sea and land, variable or not, was more than ample for the survivors' needs; and (b) to the increase in wealth coming from the sale of sea-otter furs

---

[7] It has, for instance, been followed by Herskovits (1952:165, 225, 306) in his now classic work on economic anthropology, and by Bohannan in his recent textbook (1963:253–259).

to the fur traders and, later, to other non-traditional sources of wealth made possible by the contact situation. In aboriginal times, no such source of wealth was available, and it may also be presumed that the population was then at the limit of subsistence. Hence the threat of starvation, and in turn a very real pro-subsistence function for potlatch exchanges.

Secondly, Codere's account emphasizes not merely the giving away of gifts in the potlatch and the consequent accrual of honor to the giver, but also the obligation on the recipient to give a return potlatch or else lose prestige. She particularly writes (1950:68–69):

> The property received by a man in a potlatch was no free and wanton gift. He was not at liberty to refuse it, even though accepting it obligated him to make a return at another potlatch not only of the original amount but of twice as much, if this return was made, as was usual, in a period of about a year. This gave potlatching its forced loan and investment aspects, since a man was alternately debtor and creditor for amounts that were increasing at a geometric rate.

This passage links the obligatory nature of the return potlatch to the institution of borrowing-and-lending-at-interest. Following Boas (1897:341), Codere sees borrowing-and-lending-at-interest as an integral, indeed essential, part of potlatching, and a consequent continuous increase in the size of potlatch gifts as therefore also integrally part of the whole system.

This interpretation has, however, been vigorously denied by Curtis (1915: 143–144) whose account has been curiously neglected in the study of the Kwakiutl potlatch:[8]

> It has been said of the potlatch that "the underlying principle is that of the interest-bearing investment of property." This is impossible. A Kwakiutl would subject himself to ridicule by demanding interest when he received a gift in requital of one of like amount made by him. Not infrequently at a potlatch a guest calls attention to the fact that he is not receiving as much as he in his last potlatch gave to the present host; and he refuses to accept anything less than the proper amount. Even this action is likened to "cutting off one's own head," and results in loss of prestige; for the exhibition of greed for property is not the part of a chief; on the contrary he must show his utter disregard for it. But to demand interest on a potlatch gift is unheard of. Furthermore, a man can never receive through the potlatch as much as he disburses, for the simple reason that many to whom he gives will die before they have a potlatch, and others are too poor to return what he gives them. Thus, only a chief of great wealth can make a distribution

---

[8] It is very odd that though Codere in *Fighting with Property* (1950) relies very heavily on Curtis' accounts of Kwakiutl warfare, she makes absolutely no reference to Curtis' description of the potlatch, even though it is in the same volume as the war histories.

According to his book, Curtis gathered his data intermittently between 1910 and 1914 and was assisted by George Hunt; his inquiry was also facilitated by Boas' earlier work, especially *Social Organization and Secret Societies* (1897). Curtis' book contains Kwakiutl material which cannot be found in any other published source.

in which all the tribes participate and every person receives something; but all except a very few of these members of other tribes will never hold an intertribal potlatch, and consequently the man who gives presents to them cannot possibly receive any return for them. As to those who die, it may be said that theoretically a man's heir assumes his obligations, but he cannot be forced to do so, and if they far exceed the credits he is likely to repudiate them.

The potlatch and the lending of property at interest are two entirely distinct proceedings. Property distributed in a potlatch is freely given, bears no interest, cannot be collected on demand, and need not be repaid at all if the one who received it does not for any reason wish to requite the gift. When the recipient holds a potlatch he may return an equal amount or a slightly larger amount, or a smaller amount with perhaps the promise to give more at a future time.

The feeling at the bottom of the potlatch is one of pride rather than greed. Occasionally men have tried to accumulate wealth by means of the potlatch and of lending at interest, but the peculiar economic system has always engulfed them, simply because a man can never draw out all his credits and keep the property thus acquired. Before his debtors will pay, he must first call the people together and inaugurate a potlatch, thus ensuring an immediate redistribution.

This is a very different picture of the potlatch system. The practice of borrowing-and-lending-at-interest is both clearly distinct from and subordinated to the potlatch proper. The appearance of its being part of the potlatching is clearly due to the fact that debts were paid and could be called in only in connection with potlatching, often (Curtis 1915:144) only on the day of the potlatch itself.

The whole tone of the potlatch is different in Curtis' account—"one of pride rather than greed." This picture is much more consistent with data provided by Codere (1956:334ff) on the "amiable side" of Kwakiutl potlatching and by Boas himself (1925:249) in texts published at a later date, indicating that a chief should not be too proud or arrogant. The inability of creditors to enforce their claims unless they were intending to put on a potlatch—in which case their claims would be reinforced by public opinion—is in perfect accord with the lack of developed institutions of social control among the Kwakiutl. This institution of borrowing-and-lending-at-interest was, furthermore, by no means a universal Northwest Coast institution, apparently being confined to the Southern Kwakiutl (Barnett 1938:349ff; Olson 1940:173).

Curtis' report of potlatch gifts as not increasing in size but remaining about the same is, ironically, supported by Codere's own analysis of aboriginal potlatches (1950:90–94; 1961:446), where she notes that during the one hundred twenty years previous to 1849 the potlatches recorded in the texts involved relatively small distributions and showed no tendency to increase in size.

Finally, Curtis' account is more consistent with Dawson's report, already quoted in the section on chieftainship, that formerly only chiefs potlatched. In aboriginal times only chiefs would be able to assemble the wealth with which to hold a potlatch. For most people in the numaym the importance of having a position of rank would be in the receiving of gifts at potlatch distributions, not in having to validate these positions by potlatch giving—note Curtis' remark that many if not most of the persons receiving gifts in a potlatch, especially an intertribal one, would not be able to give potlatches in return.

For these reasons, the viewpoint followed in this paper in reconstructing the aboriginal potlatch is Curtis' rather than Boas' and Codere's.

Thirdly, we must also raise doubts about the aboriginal existence of the sacrifice potlatch, an institution which looms large in all the accounts of our authorities (Boas, Codere, *and* Curtis) on the post-contact potlatch. The sacrifice potlatch and the grease feast are not mentioned in Kwakiutl mythology, nor does their presence in aboriginal times seem indicated by any other evidence. Concerning the destruction of property in the context of public assemblies or feasts Boas (1935:68), in summing up Kwakiutl culture as reflected in mythology, has only the following to say:

> In myths the destruction of property occurs only in connection with the cannibal ceremony when the cannibal devours his own slaves or is given slaves to eat. Canoe breaking during a potlatch occurs in a tale on which the person who breaks canoes owned by others makes them whole again by his magical powers. A man pushes a copper under a mountain during a feast.

No sacrifice potlatch or grease feast here!

The destruction of property in aboriginal times is, however, clearly indicated in connection with the dead or dying. For example, food is burnt and so sent to a spirit in order to persuade him to spare the life of the dying child; spoons must be burnt by a woman visiting the ghost-country in order that the spirits of the dead may receive the gifts; and when a man has died, bundles of dried salmon, along with oil, fishing hooks, clothing and his canoe, are burnt to provide him with travelling provisions (Boas 1921:705–711, 1329). What we have, then, in historic times is a spread of the idea of the destruction of property from a funeral context to a context of potlatching and active status rivalry, with the idea of honoring the dead perhaps providing the semantic link between the two contexts, and the new wealth consequent upon contact providing the means. This would be part of the religious changes suggested by Wike (1952) as having taken place on the Northwest Coast during the nineteenth century, namely a transfer of interest and concern from practices linked with the dead to a more secular manipulation of wealth and prestige.

How, then, may we describe the potlatch of aboriginal or precontact times, taking into consideration the points debated above?

The Kwakiutl potlatch, during those early times, may be described as the giving by a numaym, represented by its chief or headman, of a feast and presents to other numayms and their chiefs, often from other villages. At these distributions the more generous the host was, the more prestige he received; and if his generosity was not matched by the guests when they gave their potlatches, the host and his numaym increased in prestige at the expense of the guests. Hence there was a competitive element necessarily present in the potlatch.

Potlatches were held on several occasions: following or during funerals, by the deceased's successor when he entered formally into his new position; when a man wished to make a public announcement of his successor; whenever a name was changed or a person took on a new status in the community, as when a boy attained puberty or a girl first menstruated; when a marriage was contracted, and at several points thereafter during the marriage cycle; during the winter ceremonials, when dances were given; when persons were initiated into the "secret societies" or dance-fraternities; at "house-warmings," given when one's new house had been completed; when a copper was sold or bought; whenever a man, having accumulated a lot of property, wished to do something for the honor of himself and his numaym; when a man wished to humiliate his rivals and elevate his rank at their expense; and, sometimes, when persons on ill terms with one another decided to make peace (Boas 1921:691; 1925:135–357; Curtis 1915:142; Ford 1941:17, 19–23, 31, 36ff, 49, 169, 184–185, 218ff).[9] Potlatching, that is to say, was not so much a special social event (though such purely potlatch events did occur) as an aspect or accompaniment of many social happenings.

At these potlatchings a great many people would be present, and these spectators would act as witnesses to the changes of status thus announced and to whatever other transactions also went on. Such memorable events therefore served the function of marking and validating changes in social status; in fact, Barnett (1938) saw in this task the especial function and underlying principle of the potlatch. In the old days, a numaym member who did not himself have sufficient wealth to hold a potlatch (and most numaym members would be in such a predicament) would give such wealth as he did have to the chief of his numaym, and the latter would put on the potlatch for him (Drucker 1955:125, 129).

In potlatching, a chief was assisted by the members of his numaym, who gave food, blankets, and other property in amounts dependent upon their means. They did not expect him to return to them what they had given him, but they would receive recognition of their services in intangible but no less important returns (Boas 1921:1340–1344; Drucker 1955:124–125, 129). This was in addition to the wealth received by the chief as "tribute"; and if he still did not have as much as he wanted, he could obtain it by borrowing from his friends and relatives in other numayms or by calling in what was owed him.

Blankets, as already intimated, were not the only gifts given in the potlaches. The guests were heavily feasted, the food being formally reckoned as worth a hundred blankets (Boas 1925:205); and the food they did not eat they would take home with them (Boas 1935:38) or their hosts take them afterwards, often

---

[9] Many of the occasions named here would be more important in the lives of nobles and their immediate relatives rather than in the lives of commoners. Potlatching was a responsibility of aristocrats.

with the very feast dishes as well (Boas 1921:768, 775). Canoes might be given away with or instead of blankets. "The potlatch which took place upon the occasion of the marriage payment by the bride's family a few years after the wedding invariably involved the distribution of such household articles as provisions, wooden boxes, mats, blankets . . ." (Ford 1941:19). At another form of the potlatch, known as the "grease feast," boxes of eulachen oil were given away.

Potlatches were given by one numaym to other numayms, or by one tribe to other tribes. In the light of the data presented on subsistence, the utility of intertribal distributions of food and wealth will be readily obvious. But the utility of distributions between the various numayms *within* a single tribe may not be obvious at first glance. However, the numaym and not the tribe was the land-owning, resource-exploiting unit, and in summer the various numayms of the tribe dispersed to different places. It might easily happen, therefore, that some of the numayms within the tribe had a more fruitful year than did the others; and in such circumstances, distributions of food and wealth between the numayms even within the same tribe would be advantageous to all.

The potlatch had not one essential function, but several. It redistributed food and wealth. It validated changes in social status. It converted the wealth given by the host into prestige for the host and rank for his numaym, and so provided motivation for keeping up the cycle of exchanges. The potlatch was, in fact, the linch-pin of the entire system.

Buying and Selling

But blankets, canoes, and boxes cannot be eaten. A starving numaym would find it very awkward if it could not convert into food the wealth it had received in potlatches. I have shown how, through the potlatch, wealth could be converted into prestige. Could food be exchanged for wealth, so that a starving numaym could sell blankets for the food it needed in order to subsist, and a wealthy numaym sell food in return for the blankets necessary to potlatch?

The answer is yes. In preparing to give a potlatch, the host, if he did not have sufficient food to feed his guests, could buy it with blankets (Boas 1897: 342). I have already noted that food given in a potlatch was reckoned as being worth one hundred blankets. In a short summary of accounts of buying and selling in the texts which he collected, Boas (1935:67) wrote:

> When a man catches many herrings at his beach, he sells them for slaves and becomes a rich man. People go out in canoes and buy food from another tribe. A chief goes out and buys many cherries from the neighbouring tribe. Starving people pay for food with dressed elkskins, slaves, canoes, and even their daughters.

Conclusions

In the beginning of this paper I set forth four propositions linking (a) variable productivity of food sources, (b) potlatch exchanges, (c) interconvertibility of food, wealth, and prestige, and (d) status rivalry among the Kwakiutl.

The rest of the paper has been devoted to presenting the evidence in support of these propositions. It remains simply to explain the picture of aboriginal Kwakiutl society that results.

Let us first consider a simplified system made up of only two numayms, A and B. This simplification is not wholly artificial, since the total Kwakiutl potlatch exchange system may be considered as being made up of combinations of such overlapping pairs. Let our pair, furthermore, start out evenly balanced in resources, food supply, wealth, and prestige. Both, however, are pressing in numbers upon the margins of their resources, so that a poor harvest for either one would result in its going hungry and, if the poor harvests continue, in eventual starvation, certain diminution, and possible extinction. Since the initial amount of wealth possessed by each is the same, at the end of a potlatch cycle each numaym has still about the same amount of wealth as it began with, and the prestige of the two numayms also remains alike.

Let A suffer a severe failure in food supply. To feed themselves, the members of A sell blankets to B in exchange for food. This increment of wealth enables B either to hold potlatches more frequently or to give bigger gifts in their pot-latches. And B does so, giving wealth to A in batches larger than before and so gaining increased prestige in return. Thus through the potlatch A recovers its wealth in return for granting more prestige to B. With this wealth A can either hold a return potlatch and regain its prestige by giving equally large gifts or use the wealth to purchase more food. If A uses some of this wealth to purchase more food, it will not be able to give a return potlatch of generosity equal to B's potlatch, and the increment in B's prestige will be more firmly established. If, sometime later, B suffers a deficiency in food supply, it can buy food from A, and this cycle will be repeated with the roles reversed.

Two consequences stand out from the above model: (a) if a numaym continually suffers from a failure of food supply, it will not be able to respond in potlatching with gifts of value equal to what it has received, and its prestige will steadily decline. Because the potlatch-system is also tied in with other aspects of society, such as marriage and war,[10] such a steady decline of prestige would probably have the effect of forcing the numaym in time out of the system entirely as an independent unit: it would either literally die out, or it would become a permanent dependency of its wealthy partner. (b) There will be, over time, a steady increment in the absolute size of potlatch gifts, regardless of which partner suffers food deficiencies. In fact, the more frequent such deficiencies are, the greater the rate of incrementation is likely to be. This does not, however, necessarily entail an increase in the number of actual wealth objects; tally sticks,

---

[10] Codere (1950) has shown how in historic times warfare declined as potlatching increased. We may further add that comparisons of the war histories and the marriage accounts suggest a tendency for the groups with which a given numaym warred not to be those with which it inter-married; war and marriage were alternate means of gaining new crests. Establishing new marriage links would also have had the effect of increasing the number of relatives, both affines and kinsfolk, with whom oneself and one's children and other relatives could visit.

such as the Kwakiutl did in fact use (e.g. Boas 1897:352), would serve the purpose adequately.

The institution of borrowing and lending can be seen as another way of acquiring blankets with which, in times of economic distress, to maintain one's level of potlatch giving and so maintain one's prestige.

This system would be more efficient the more units were involved. With many numayms selling food, the increment in wealth received by them would be for each much smaller than that if only one numaym was the seller, and the temptation to increase potlatch gifts would be correspondingly reduced. Consequently, with many numayms in the system, the rate of increase in sizes of potlatch gifts would be reduced. Further, the chances of many numayms all suffering deficient harvests simultaneously would be considerably less than the chances for two numayms being thus afflicted together.

If the food deficiencies be *short-term, intermittent,* and *not sustained,* the relative ranking of the numayms involved will over the long-run remain constant, whether or not one numaym is given to suffering more deficiencies than another. If the deficiencies be *long-term and sustained,* however, as pointed out above, the numaym so marked out will be forced in the long-run out of the system.

However, even a long-term run of bad luck, with continually deficient food supply and declining prestige, may be offset if the wealthier partner in its turn suffers a long-term deficiency while the food supply of the poorer improves, provided of course that the poorer numaym's run of misfortune has not been so prolonged as to drive it out of the system altogether. In such circumstances the *long-term* relative ranking of the numayms will oscillate about a constant level.

The model presupposes, therefore, an overall balance of resource productivity among the numayms involved in the system. No numaym, or at most only a few, suffers from long-term, sustained resource deficiencies which would take it out of the system: variations in resources tend to be short-term and intermittent. All groups are pressing on their resources, so that times of low productivity menace their existence; but the population/resource ratio for each is substantially the same. Indeed, we may suspect that a rough equality in population/resource ratios between numayms is necessary for this system to work.

This system, coping successfully with variable productivity and by its exchanges of food and wealth enabling a larger population to live in the Southern Kwakiutl country than would otherwise have lived there, is nevertheless vulnerable to the following:

(a) A change in the pattern of resource exploitation such that some numayms increase their food production consistently relative to the remainder: This change will change their population/resource ratio, enable them to sell more food for more wealth, and so, as has already been explained, by increased potlatching gain more prestige than can be matched by poorer numayms. Such a resource discrepancy may occur through some numayms decreasing their food production, through some increasing theirs, or through population decline in some numayms and not in others so that the former no longer press so closely on their resources. Changes in food production could in turn be due either to changes in the natural environment beyond human control or intent, or to changes in techniques of resource exploitation.

(b) The entry into the system of a new, non-traditional source of wealth: The general effect of this factor would be to promote more frequent potlatches and bigger potlatch gifts, and to permit persons other than the traditional chiefs to engage in potlatching. This in turn would promote an increase in competitive or rivalrous potlatching. Exchanges would become less between numayms and more between prestige-seeking individuals. The balance between food, wealth, and prestige would, I think, become more precarious, but, provided the effects were distributed evenly over the whole system, the system would still survive, though at a higher level of activity. Destruction of wealth, if adopted, would serve to take some of this new wealth out of the system and so serve to inhibit the increase in the velocity of circulation. And, finally, if the influx were only for a short time, the system could probably survive it without much change.

But if the influx of wealth were unevenly distributed among the numayms, benefiting some more than others, not only would potlatch rivalry be accentuated, but some groups would rapidly gain an ascendancy over the others, and the balance of the system would be upset. The groups having lost prestige would in one way or another eventually be forced out of the system. And through the decline in the number of potlatching social units, the system itself would become increasingly unstable. This instability would be further heightened by the increase in potlatching rivalry and by a concurrent increasing individualization of potlatching. The end result would, in time, be to destroy the system beyond recovery.

(c) A general decline in population, with the consequence that the population no longer presses on the margins of its resources, and the threat of starvation resulting from reduced harvests is removed: Assuming that the amount of wealth in the total system remains constant, this change would both free more wealth from food-purchasing for use in potlatching and increase the per capita wealth among the Kwakiutl. Frequency and size of potlatches would increase, and with this increased wealth the chances of more persons being engaged in it would also be increased. The effects of population decline would therefore be similar to those of the influx of new wealth.

In post-contact times we find the latter two changes taking place together and in marked degree, viz., an influx of new wealth, first from the fur-trade and later from other non-traditional sources, and a drastic decline in population, both prolonged for about a hundred years. The result was as would be expected if the construction proposed in this paper is correct: an increase in the size and frequency of potlatches, a general spread of potlatching to most persons in the Kwakiutl communities, an increase in rivalrous potlatches with a concomitant individualizing of potlatches, and the appearance of the "fantastic surplus economy" so marked in the later ethnographic record.

18 SOME PRINCIPLES OF EXCHANGE AND INVESTMENT AMONG THE TIV[1]

Paul Bohannan

Tiv are a pagan people numbering over 800,000 who live in the middle Benue Valley of northern Nigeria. The basis of their economy is subsistence agriculture, supplemented by an effective network of markets particularly in the southern and central portions of their country. Tiv pride themselves on their farming abilities and their subsistence wealth.

Today, however, their ideas of economic exchange and their traditional methods of investment and economic aggrandizement are being undermined by a new economic system which demands different actions, motives and ideas. This article deals with: (I) Tiv ideas of exchange as expressed in their language, (II) some traditional modes of investment and exchange, based on a ranked hierarchy of spheres or categories of exchangeable commodities, and (III) the impact of Western economy on such aspects of subsistence, exchange and investment which Tiv consider in terms of these spheres or categories.

I

Distribution of goods among Tiv falls into two spheres: a "market," on the one hand, and gifts, on the other.

The several words best translated "gift" apply—besides the cases which we in the West would recognize as "gift"—to exchange over a long period of time between persons or groups in a more or less permanent relationship. The gift may be a factor designed to strengthen the relationship, or even to create it. There are several Tiv words for "gift," the examination of which would require another article the length of this one. For our purposes, it is primary that any of these "gift" words implies a relationship between the two parties concerned which is of a permanence and warmth not known in a "market," and hence—though "gifts" should be reciprocal over a long period of time— it is bad form overtly to count and compute and haggle over gifts.

A "market" is a transaction which in itself calls up no long-term personal relationship, and which is therefore to be exploited to as great a degree as possible. In fact, the presence of a previous relationship makes a "good market" impossible: people do not like to sell to kinsmen since it is bad form to demand as high a price from a kinsman as one might from a stranger. Market behavior and kinship behavior are incompatible in a single relationship, and the individual must give way to one or the other.

The word "market" (*kasoa*) has several meanings in Tiv. It refers primarily to any transaction which is differentiated from gift exchange (and, as we shall see, from exchange marriage). It is also a meeting of people at a regular place

From American Anthropologist *57:60–70. Reprinted by permission.*

and time for the primary purpose of exchanging food and other items. One's "market" is also an aspect of one's luck (*ikôl*)—some people have "good market [luck]" and some have bad market [luck]." Therefore, one's market can be affected by one's ritual conditions, for fetishes (*akombo*)—not to mention witches (*mbatsav*)—can spoil a man's market (*vhi or kasoa*); indeed, curses and broken promises can also affect a person's market.

Everything, including women, which is exchanged has an exchange value or equivalent (*ishe*), whereas no gift has an exchange value. In a market situation *ishe* means vaguely "exchange equivalent"—one might even sometimes translate it "price"—though Tiv seldom ask or quote equivalents in their own trading. Rather, they effect bargains, usually without recourse to this word. An expensive item is a "thing of great value" or "thing of high equivalent" (*kwagh u kehe ishe*), and to haggle is to dispute the value or equivalent (*kperen ishe*). The general term both for economic trading and for exchange marriage can be translated roughly as "trading value" (*yamen ishe*).

In every market transaction, there is a man who sells (*te*) and a man who buys (*yam*). These words must be carefully examined for they do not exactly parallel their English equivalents. *Te* means to spread something out on the ground to the public view, as in a market place. By extension, it means "to sell"—there is no other way to say "to sell," and no other verb to designate that half of an exchange in which one releases or gets rid of an article. *Yam*, on the other hand, means "trade" in the widest sense, but refers primarily to that half of the exchange in which one takes or gains an article. It can, therefore, often be translated by the English word "buy." Its difference, however, can be seen in sentences such as "I bought money with it" (*m yam inyaregh a mi*— more accurately translated "I realized money on it," and still more accurately but less literally, "In this exchange what I received was money"). Activities of traders are called *yamen a yam*; exchange marriage is often called "woman trading" (*kwase yamen*) or, more politely, "value trading" (*ishe yamen*).

Although Tiv have a word which means approximately the same as the English word "exchange" (*musan*), which can sometimes be used to differentiate barter from money transactions, this word is not ordinarily used of trade or commerce.

II

Within the bounds of these words and basic concepts, Tiv image and communicate their ideas of economic transactions and investments. It is important to realize, however, that the ideas themselves may never be articulated as principles or as logical systems. The systematization may be, as in this case, the work of the ethnographer. Yet, this systematization is—or at least is consistent with—the Tiv covert ideology in the matter; its empirical validity is demonstrated when, in terms of it, the ethnographer can both sensibly discuss the ideas and images with Tiv in their language, and communicate them in another language to his colinguals and colleagues.

It is in these terms that we can say that in Tiv ideology it is neither usual nor desirable to exchange a commodity for just any other commodity. Rather, there are several different categories of interchangeable commodities and items, each of which is felt to be more or less exclusive. It seems to be necessary to distinguish three such categories.

The most apparent category of exchangeable items among Tiv consists primarily of foodstuffs (*yiagh*). All locally produced foodstuffs (imported, particularly European, food is not *yiagh*) are said by Tiv to be of a single economic kind, and immediately interchangeable. To trade pepper for locust-bean sauce or yams for guinea corn is a common transaction or "market" among Tiv. The quantities to be exchanged are never prescribed,[2] as they are in some societies—the bargain which any individual may drive within the sphere of foodstuffs is a reflection of the market aspect of his luck. If I, selling pepper, can get locust beans of a quality and quantity whose value I myself consider to be greater than the value of the pepper I gave for them, my market is good; if I get less, my market is bad—or, more commonly, the market of the other person is better than mine. The obvious advantage of such a line of reasoning is that, in really successful transactions, everybody's market is good.

Included within this same category are chickens and goats, as well as household utensils (mortars, grindstones, calabashes, baskets and pots) and some tools (particularly those used in agricultural pursuits), and also raw materials for producing any items in the category. For a woman to sell yams to buy a pot, for her to make a pot and sell it to buy yams—these are considered to be normal buying and selling (*yamen a yam*).

The second important category is that which includes slaves, cattle, that type of large white cloth known as *tugudu*, and metal bars. One is still entitled to use the present tense in this case, for ideologically the category still exists in spite of the fact that brass rods are today very rare, and that slavery has been legally abolished. Tiv still quote prices of slaves in cows and brass rods, and of cattle in brass rods and *tugudu* cloths. Akiga, in a hitherto untranslated part of his book, tells us that,

> You could buy one iron bar (*sokpo*) for a *tugudu* cloth. In those days five *tugudu* cloths were equivalent to a bull! A cow was worth ten *tugudu*. One brass rod (*bashi*) was worth about the same as one *tugudu* cloth; thus five brass rods were worth a bull.

Other Tiv would disagree about the actual values of these various commodities.[3] The value of the brass rod is said by all to have declined considerably just before the arrival of Europeans in Tivland. None, however, would disagree with Akiga's grouping of commodities.

This second category is associated with prestige (*shagba*) in the same way that the first category is associated with subsistence. Although slaves and brass rods, at least, had some economic value beyond their value as prestige-conferring property, this latter was their main use.

The supreme and unique category of exchange values contains only one item: rights in human beings other than slaves, and particularly rights in women. Even twenty-five years after official abolition of exchange marriage, it is this category of exchange in which Tiv are emotionally most entangled (L. and P. Bohannan 1953:69–71). All exchanges within this category are exchanges of rights in human beings, usually dependent women and children, so that the category may be called the category of dependent persons, and many of its values are expressed in terms of kinship and marriage.

This plan or scheme leaves out several important items of Tiv material culture: particularly weapons, specialists' tools like divining apparatus, etc., which do not, generally speaking, enter into exchange situations. Since I have no record of hearing these items discussed in a situation of exchange, I have no basis for assigning them to one category or another—indeed, I doubt that Tiv would do so. My purpose in reporting these categories is not the pedantic one of putting every commodity into one or the other; rather, the categories represent the fundamentals of Tiv notions of exchange and investment.

Further, several items which we consider as exchangeable wealth, and as bases for investment, are not included by Tiv in this system of thought. Services and labor, for example, are by and large reciprocal and form part of the age-set, kinship and domestic group structures and moralities. Tiv consider it rude and improper to discuss services in terms of "exchange" but insist rather that such matters be viewed as individual acts of generosity or as kinship or age-set obligations. They recognize the reciprocity, of course, but do not themselves cast it into terms which we would consider "economic." Land, which many peoples—including, perhaps, ourselves—consider to be the ultimate wealth, is not exchangeable among Tiv, not even for other land. Land is, to Tiv, the spatial aspect of social organization; land rights are conditions of agnation. It is impossible for a Tiv to invest in land, since his basic right in land is a right to sufficient land, and only secondarily a right to specific lands. No Tiv can control more land than he can use. (Both land rights and labor are discussed at some length in Bohannan 1954.) Therefore, it should be noted, we are dealing with Tiv exchange and investment, but Tiv notions cover only a part of the range to which the English words "exchange" and "investment" refer.

It is instructive of Tiv modes of thought about these three main categories of exchangeable items to note the manner in which individual items can be "removed" from the categories, or made incapable of further exchange. Individual items are removed from the category of subsistence by expenditure, including sacrifice to fetishes. Although yams have an exchange value as well as a utilitarian value, once eaten they no longer have either. Household equipment breaks or is worn out. All items which are removed from this sphere of exchangeable goods are removed either by being used up or by being sacrificed (and subsequently used up).

Removing individual items from the second category—that centering around prestige—is more complex, and its very complexity makes possible some of the characteristics of Tiv economy. Some individual items—cloth—can be removed by expenditure; other individual items—slaves—can be removed by death of human beings. Most of the items, however, are removed by an act which increases the prestige of the owner of the item by diminishing its utility or exchangeability. Thus, brass rods can be converted into jewelry, thereby increasing the prestige of ownership but diminishing the range of utility; cows can be butchered on festive occasions (cattle are never sacrificed for religious purposes among Tiv), thereby increasing the prestige of the owner but diminishing the utility of the commodity and nullifying its exchangeability.

Individual items are removed from the third category—that of rights in dependent persons—by death of the human beings, and by death alone.

The three chief categories of exchangeable items among Tiv, while considered of equal practical importance, are nevertheless arranged in a hierarchy on the basis of moral values. The category of prestige is superior to (but no more important than) the category of subsistence; great prestige assumes adequate or ample subsistence means. The category of dependent persons is superior to (but no more important than) the categories both of prestige and of subsistence. A large number of dependent persons, demonstrating success in attracting, getting, and keeping dependents, assumes adequate or ample prestige and subsistence goods. But, conversely, many dependents give one prestige and enable one to produce ample and generous amounts of subsistence wealth.

The moral basis of the hierarchy is evident in the fact that the ethics of kinship are more compelling than the ethics of mere prestige (and always take precedence—ideally one must always sacrifice prestige or hope of gain to aid a kinsman); the ethics of prestige are more compelling than the mores of markets and exchange of subsistence wealth—a man forgoes gain in subsistence wealth for the sake of prestige or to fulfill kinship obligations.

The hierarchal nature of the values involved in the three main categories of exchangeable goods provides a basis for investment and economic endeavor in Tiv society. The drive toward success leads most Tiv, to the greatest possible extent, to convert food into prestige items; to convert prestige items into dependents—wives and children. Tiv say that it is good (*do kwagh*) to trade food for brass rods, but that it is bad (*vihi kwagh*) to trade brass rods for food; that it is good to trade your cows or brass rods for a wife, but very bad to trade your marriage ward for cows or brass rods. Seen from the individual's point of view, it is profitable and possible to invest one's wealth only if one converts it into a higher category: to convert subsistence wealth into prestige wealth and both into women is the aim of the economic endeavor of individual Tiv.

That Tiv do conceptualize exchange articles as belonging to different categories, and that they rank the categories on a moral basis, gives rise to the fact that two different kinds of exchanges may be recognized: exchanges of items contained within a single category, and exchanges of items belonging to different categories. For Tiv, these two different types of exchange are marked by separate and distinct moral attitudes.

Exchanges within a category—particularly that of subsistence, the only one intact today—excite no moral judgments beyond comments regarding the "market" luck of one or both of the parties to the exchange. Exchanges between categories, however, excite a completely different sort of moral reaction: the man who exchanges lower category goods for higher category goods does not brag about his market luck but about his skill in investment, his personal magnetism, and his "strong heart." The man who exchanges high category goods for lower rationalizes his action in terms of high-valued motivation (most often the needs of his kinsmen).

To maintain this distinction between the two types of exchanges which Tiv mark by different behavior and different values, I shall use separate words. I shall call those exchanges of items within a single category "conveyances" and those exchanges of items from one category to another "conversions." (Steiner [1954] uses "translations" for what I have called conversions.) For purposes of analysis, I shall maintain the dichotomy between the two words representing types of exchanges more rigidly than would any Tiv between the two types of moral behavior in the normal course of living. Roughly, conveyances are—to Tiv—morally neutral; conversions have a strong moral quality in their rationalization.

The two institutions most intimately connected with conveyance are markets and marriage, particularly exchange marriage. Both these are special subjects and must be dealt with separately. The remainder of this section is concerned with conversion.

Conversion, unlike conveyance, is not mere exchange of equivalent goods. Because there is a definite moral dimension to conversion, it forms a strong source of motivation to individual action. It is in the light of such motivation that we must evaluate the fact that a very high percentage of autobiographies collected from Tiv contain variants of this story: "When I was a very small child, my kinsman gave me a baby chicken. I tended it carefully and when it grew up it laid eggs and hatched out more chickens; I exchanged these chickens for a young nanny goat, who bore kids, which I put out with various kinsmen until I could exchange them for a cow. The cow bore calves, and eventually I was able to sell the calves and procure a wife." Every successful man considers such a story one of the most important sequences of his biography; it proves that he has been successful.

Tiv say that it was often possible in the old days to buy brass rods for food, but usually only if the owner of the brass rods were short of food or required an unusually large amount to give a feast, making too heavy a drain on his wives' food supplies. They also say that no honorable man would exchange slaves for food—there were other means of getting food, especially along the extended web of kinship. Although all Tiv with whom I discussed the matter denied emphatically that Tiv would ever sell a kinsman, wife or ward to get food (there are other reasons for which such sales were made), Akiga—in an untranslated section of his book—mentions a famine which was so severe that, as a last resort, men sold their daughters to foreigners in exchange for food so that they could keep their sons alive.

Another conversion found among Tiv is marriage by bride wealth (which may be of several types, usually all lumped together and called *kem kwase*). Although some forms of marriage by bride wealth were in the past actually delayed exchanges (and today can be seen as substitutes for exchanges [L. and P. Bohannan 1953:71–73]), to "receive a woman" (*ngoho kwase*)—to get wife or marriage ward without giving one in exchange—is every man's goal. A wife is traditionally acquired by being granted a sister or cousin (any woman in one's marriage-ward sharing group—the *ingôl* group of Akiga 1939 and Abraham 1940) to exchange for a wife, either directly or by means of bride wealth. A wife whom one acquires in any other way is not the concern of one's marriage-ward sharing group because the woman or other property exchanged for her did not belong to the marriage-ward group. The daughters of such a wife are not divided among the members of a man's marriage-ward group, but only among his sons. Such a wife is not only indicative of a man's ability and success financially and personally, but rights in her are the only form of property which is not ethically subject to the demands of his agnates.

Wives may sometimes be acquired by means of much more elaborate conversions. We discovered one case (in the course of a witchcraft moot) in which a man two generations ago had traded a slave for a cow, which he in turn traded for a marriage-ward to exchange for a wife; the distribution, as marriage-wards, of the daughters of this marriage (among his sons rather than his marriage-ward group) was called into question. Sometimes Tiv acquire foreign wives for cattle, from tribes whose custom it is to marry with cattle; the daughters of such women are considered to be Tiv, and can be exchanged in regular Tiv fashion—they do not go into the "pool" of wards in the marriage-ward group unless a man's agnates force him by threats of witchcraft to share his "property" with them.

There are many social sanctions for conversion of one's wealth to higher categories: Tiv are very scornful of a man who is merely rich in subsistence goods (or, today, in money); they say that if he has not converted his goods the reasons must be personal inadequacy. Tiv also say that jealous kinsmen of a rich man will bewitch him and his people by means of certain fetishes in order to make him expend his wealth in sacrifices to "repair" the fetishes. Once the conversion is made, demands of kinsmen are no longer effective—at least, they must take a new form.

A man who persists in a policy of converting his wealth into higher categories instead of letting it be dispersed by his dependents and kinsmen is said to have a "strong heart" (*taver shima*). He is both feared and respected: because he is strong enough to resist the excessive demands of his kinsmen, but still fulfills his kinship obligations generously, he is feared as a man of special, potentially evil, talents (*tsav*).

III

Tiv notions of exchange and investment are among the hardest hit of all their ideas by impact of Western ideology and by colonial economy and social organization because these ideas are immediately and obviously in conflict with Western ideas and practice. Today, Tiv are concerned because their categories of exchangeable items cannot be maintained. There are three main reasons for this fact: (1) two of the categories today have no overt validity, (2) many new commodities have been introduced which do not belong to any category, and (3) money has provided a common denominator among the categories which was previously lacking.

A moment's consideration makes it obvious that the category of prestige goods, centering mainly about cattle, slaves and brass rods, has ceased to exist in material terms, although the category is maintained ideally. Slave dealing was prohibited from the first effective European control (about 1910); brass rods are no longer generally available because the Administration regarded them primarily as currency and "replaced" them with pounds, shillings and pence. Perhaps of even greater moment was the fact that in 1927 the highest exchange category, that of rights in women, was dealt a crippling blow by Administrative abolition of exchange marriage and substitution of marriage by bride wealth (payable in money) as the legal form. The category of subsistence items is the only one that today can still be found in anything like its original form.

European and African traders have introduced many new commodities to Tivland, both of Nigerian and European manufacture, and have increased many fold the quantity of some other commodities which were formerly present in small amounts or small numbers. These goods, particularly European goods, were introduced concurrently with money, and they are considered part of the money complex. They do not enter into any formerly existing category, but form their own category only very imperfectly. Thus, there are today many more commodities than ever before which do not fit precisely into traditionally structured exchange situations.

Finally, and perhaps more important, is the introduction of currency, the very nature of which is to standardize the exchangeability value of every item to a common scale. The introduction of currency was not only to be expected with the extension of Western economic ventures, it was hurried by the Administration in its desire to collect tax in a convenient and readily transportable form. A money tax, payable by all adult males, was imposed throughout Tivland by the end of the first World War. Imposition of this tax coincided with the initiation of large-scale growing of beniseed (*sesamum indicum*) as a cash crop. Beniseed, although long known to Tiv, is today often called by the word for "tax" or "tribute" (*kpandegh*).

Even though it is possible to consider brass rods as "currency" in the old system, because they were a commodity whose exchange value was more far-reaching than that of any other commodity and because they belonged to the intermediary category, the introduction of coinage was not a simple "substitution" of one form of currency for another as was thought at the time to be the case. Brass rods were, it is true, the main medium of conversion in the old days: brass rods could be and sometimes were used to buy food, they could be and often were used to get a wife. But the penetrability of brass rods into the other categories of exchange, while more pronounced than that of any other commodity, did have limitations. Brass rods never provided a standard gauge against which the exchangeability value of all commodities was reckoned, as is the case with the coinage issued by the West African Currency Board.

Today all conversions and most conveyances are made in terms of money. Yet Tiv constantly express their distrust of money. They compare the monetary system to the subsistence system at great length, always to the disfavor of the former. Money does not (they say) reproduce itself or bear seed. You spend (*vihi*, literally "spoil") money and it's gone—a man can't spend a field, and though he sacrifices a goat, it has already borne kids. Money, they feel, is the root of much of their trouble.

Tiv, both desiring and distrusting money as they do, have attempted at least in some contexts to relegate it to a fourth and lowest category of exchangeable goods. The logical end of such a classification, however, would be either that money is exchanged only for money, or that it is exchanged only for those European goods which were introduced more or less concurrently with it. This is precisely the view that many Tiv elders expound. It is a view, however, which cannot be maintained in the present situation in Tivland.

Concurrently with the introduction of money, pacification of the countryside and introduction of cash crops, a further factor arose: men's trading developed very rapidly. Men's trade, like women's, tends to be based on subsistence goods, but unlike women's, on goods which must be procured and traded over long distances: smoked fish from the Benue and Katsina Ala Rivers, camwood and kolas from Ogoja Province, and items such as cotton which are grown in some parts of Tivland and not in others. Today men up to the age of forty may carry their goods as much as 150 miles to market where it commands the highest price. This trade is usually carried out in terms of money, by semiprofessional traders. These men start with money and end with money; their purpose is to increase their money. Tiv consider this legitimate enterprise.

Tiv also say that women's trade is legitimate and sensible: a woman may sell one type of food to buy another, or sell food to buy a waist cloth for herself or small gifts and latter-day necessities for her children. All Tiv say that the fact that these transactions are carried out in money is beside the point: the woman has not made a conversion, for she has sold expendable subsistence goods and bought expendable subsistence goods.

The difficulty arises when the semiprofessional traders begin trading in the foodstuffs which were formerly the province solely of women. These men may invest sums of their capital in food for resale; in fact, these young semi-professional traders are the most active buyers and sellers of grain at Tiv markets today, although women also speculate in grain and in yams to a smaller extent. A young trader buys grain in small quantities—often in two- and three-penny lots—from women who are selling it in the market. He collects this grain, may hold it for a while and almost certainly will transport it to another market for sale either to another middleman or to the Hausa or Ibo lorry drivers who visit the larger markets to buy food for export to the over-populated areas of the Eastern Provinces or the new urban areas in Tivland.

Both the trade carried on by women and that carried on by these ambitious young professional traders are considered admirable by Tiv. The trader is not granted so favorable a position in Tiv society as he is in some other West African societies, and mere monetary or subsistence wealth is not sufficient in itself to afford great prestige. Trade of women stays within the category of subsistence (if one considers the end in view and discounts the presence of money, as Tiv do in the situation), while the trade of the professionals stays within the monetary category.

Yet Tiv see truckload after truckload of foodstuffs driven away from their large markets every fifth day. They say that food is less plentiful today than it was in the past, though more land is being farmed. Tiv elders deplore this situation and know what is happening, but they do not know just where to fix the blame. In attempts to do something about it, they sometimes announce that no women are to sell any food at all. But when their wives disobey them, men do not really feel that they were wrong to have done so. Tiv sometimes discriminate against non-Tiv traders in attempts to stop export of food, but their actions are seldom upheld by the courts to which the outsiders scurry, and in any case Tiv themselves are occupied in the export of food. In their condemnation of the situation which is depriving them of their food faster than they are able to increase production, Tiv elders always curse money itself. It is money which, as the instrument for selling one's life subsistence, is respon-sible for the worsened situation—money and the Europeans who brought it.

Yet they cannot fix the blame or stop the situation. When women sell to middlemen, Tiv class this exchange in the category of subsistence exchange. When middlemen sell to other middlemen or exporters, it falls within the ethics of money trade. That the two spheres have overlapped they find mysterious and frustrating, and in the nature of money. Yet, so long as a woman does not sell too much food, there is no feeling that she has done wrong; so long as a man buys a commodity with money and sells it for money, he has done nothing blameworthy.

Of even greater concern to Tiv is the influence money has had on marriage institutions, by affecting the interchange of rights in women. In response to what appeared superficially to be popular demand, the Administration (en-couraged by the Missions and with the apparent concurrence of the tribal councils) abolished exchange marriage and substituted for it a form of marriage by bride wealth. It is the writer's opinion that both Tiv and Administration today believe this action to have been precipitate and ill-advised. Today every woman's guardian, in accepting money as bride wealth, feels that he is converting down. Although attempts are made to spend money which is received in bride wealth to acquire brides for one's self and one's sons, it is in the nature of money, Tiv insist, that this is most difficult to accomplish. The good man still spends his bride wealth receipts for brides—but good men are not so numerous as would be desirable. Tiv deplore the fact that they are required to "sell" (*te*) their daughters and "buy" (*yam*, but more euphemistically *kem*, to accumulate) wives. It smacks, they tell the investigator in low tones, of slavery. There is no dignity in it since the possibility of converting a bride-wealth marriage into an exchange marriage has been removed.

The fact that Tiv, in the face of the introduction of a money economy, have retained the motivations commensurate with their old ideology of investment based on a scheme of the discreteness of several categories of exchangeable items, hierarchically arranged, has created several difficulties and inconsistencies. It is considered admirable to invest one's wealth in wives and children—the least expendable form of wealth traditionally known to Tiv, and that form most productive of further wealth.

But Tiv have come upon a simple paradox: today it is easy to sell subsistence goods for money to buy prestige articles and women, thereby aggrandizing oneself at a rapid rate. The food so sold is exported, decreasing the amount of subsistence goods available for consumption. On the other hand, the number of women is limited. The result is that bride wealth gets higher—the price of women becomes inflated. Under these conditions, as Tiv attempt to become more and more wealthy in people, they are merely selling more and more of their foodstuffs and subsistence goods, leaving less and less for their own consumption.

Indigenuous Tiv ideas of the sort we would call economic not only formed a basis for their intellectual ordering of their economic exchanges, but also supply motivation for their personal economic striving. These ideas are inconsistent with a monetary economy on the fringe of industrial society. Tiv, to whom these are not "economic ideas" but a "natural" ordering of phenomena and behavior, tend to see the difficulty as being with the monetary economy. The ethnographer can only look on and attempt to understand the ideas and motivations, knowing that the discrepancy between ideas and the actual situation will become greater until one is smashed and then adapted to suit the other—and he knows also that the conclusion is foregone.

NOTES

[1] Twenty-six months' research was carried out between July 1949 and January 1953 among the Tiv, under the auspices of the Social Science Research Council and the Wenner-Gren Foundation for Anthropological Research, with supplementary

grants from the Colonial Social Science Research Council and the Government of Nigeria, to all of which bodies grateful acknowledgment is made.

[2] This fact may be a function of the time observations were made, which was a time of inflation in Tivland as elsewhere.

[3] I believe Akiga to be giving examples of a category rather than quoting prices here. But the price stability may have been generally recognized in the pre-money days of stable exchange to which Akiga refers.

19 THE SOCIAL CONTEXT OF ECONOMIC CHOICE IN A SMALL SOCIETY*
Manning Nash

The distinctions between complex, monetized and civilized societies and the small-scale, non- or partially monetized peasant and primitive societies in economic life are startling, deeply rooted and easily apparent. These distinctions have frequently been laid to a special rationale of economic choice in small-scale non-Western societies. Boeke (1947:2) finds a cleavage so deep between the small-scale economy and the capitalistic organization of economic life that a new name is needed, and he suggests 'oriental economics' to account for the workings of non-Western economies. Polanyi (1957:46ff.) sees the essential difference in the 'absence of a motive of gain' from peasant and primitive societies, and of course from Maine onward there is a literature which claims that peasant values subordinate economic activity to social ends. It is the con—tention of this paper that the rationale of economic choice in peasant society follows the same general rule of maximization as economic activity does any-where, at any time. What is distinctive about peasant and primitive societies are not the habits of mind about advantage, nor an inability to calculate costs and benefits of a course of action, nor even an absence of a motive of gain; but rather the possession of a set of concrete social organizations which directly channel economic choice, on the one hand, and a set of sanctions which operate to keep economic deviants in physical as well as moral jeopardy on the other. A corollary of this contention is that debate of rules of choice or abstract principles of economic organization will be barren and lead only to a 'spectral dance of bloodless categories,' to the profusion of empty boxes of theory; while the emphasis on the stipulation of the economic consequences of concrete

From Man *LXI:186–191. Reprinted by permission.*

* I am indebted to the National Institute of Mental Health, the Department of Anthropology and the Graduate School of Business of the University of Chicago for financing the field work on which this paper is based. June Nash covers in detail the social structure of Amatenango in Social Relations in Amatenango: An Activity Analysis, unpublished Ph.D. thesis, University of Chicago. Miss Joan Ablon aided in some of the data here reported during her field work in the community.

social structures will generate an empirically powerful body of middle-range theory.

By an examination of the economy of peasant Indians in the state of Chiapas, Mexico, I hope to show how the structure and membership criteria of production units limit maximization; how the level and rhythm of output are consequences of the ceremonial cycle; and how notions of witchcraft and the supernatural combine to keep wealth from being used for economic ends and thus contribute to the steady state of small, reduplicative, productive units with little interest in, or incentive for, technological or social innovation.

In south-eastern Chiapas, Tzeltal- and Tzotzil-speaking Indians are the predominant population. These Indians live in communities whose general characteristics are familiar from work done with neighbouring highland Maya in Guatemala (Tax 1937). One Tzeltal community is that of Amatenango de Valle. Amatenango is a *municipio* (the administrative unit of Mexico, like a township, but tending to coincide with an Indian society in highland Chiapas and Guatemala) situated just off the Pan-American Highway some 44 kilometres south of the region's largest Mexican city. Amatenango, for an Indian community, has a reputation for wealth and independence. Its people call themselves *Tzontajal*; they wear a distinct costume; their mode of speech is dialectically distinct from neighbouring Tzeltal-speaking communities; they are nearly endogamous; they have economic skills not shared by neighbours; a local civil administration; a local set of sacred officials, and a particular calendar of sacred and secular festivals. They are a corporate community (Wolf 1954), united by blood and custom, living on their own territory, with an ethnic distinctiveness which sets them apart in their minds, and in fact, from their Indian neighbours and the superordinate communities of Mexicans which surround them.

Amatenango makes its living by cultivating the soil, by cattle-raising, and by producing pottery. The technology of agriculture is on a relatively low level. The ox-drawn plough, the machete, the digging stick, the sickle and a net bag make up the tool kit. A simple irrigation system of ditching serves some of the land, and the watered lands are rotated between milpa crops (corn, beans, squash) and a wheat cash crop. Fertilizer is not used. Soil-nutrient is added only by the burning of corn or wheat stubble and leaving the ash, or by turning animals loose in the fields after harvest. Seed-selection is not rigorous. And as in most peasant agriculture the vicissitudes of wind, rain, frost and sun make for wide swings in the annual harvest. Famine, or even real hunger, however, is not part of Amatenango experience, except in the days when the warring factions of the Mexican revolution swept through the region and disrupted life and devastated agriculture. The agricultural complex also includes garden plots near house sites, as distinct from field lands. Garden plots are used for some milpa, but their chief economic significance lies in the growing of *chayote*, a squash-like plant, and its root which are sold to other communities. The maguey plants, lima and avocado tree and some fruit trees supply domestically used produce. The agricultural complex is part of a system of regional interdependence based on ecological and traditional differences. Nearby communities specialize in other products, and there is a lively exchange of agricultural products between Amatenango, its neighbours and the nearby coastal 'hot' lands. The interpretation of the agricultural complex seems simple enough: ecological specialization on the base of natural resources combined with special agricultural skills and knowledge. The actual distribution of agricultural specialties results from the operation of comparative advantage over a long stretch of time.

Insight into the economic dynamics of the community and of the region may be had more clearly through the industrial rather than the agricultural organization of Amatenango. Agriculture does not, by itself, maintain Amatenango at its expected level of living. The making and selling of pottery is an important component in the meeting of the customary standard of life. Of the 280 households in the town centre of Amatenango (the peripheries of the community were recently settled either by Indians uprooted from other communities, or by poor Mexicans, and pose a special problem for social analysis) only two or three are not engaged in the production of pottery for sale. Pottery-making is a community specialization, not an individual skill. It is part of the socialization process for women in Amatengo. All women who are born and grow up in Amatenango know how to, and do, make pots. The striking nature of the community specialization comes home forcibly when it is observed that an adjoining community with virtually the same natural resources as Amatenango does not produce one single pot, and that in a region nearly 40 miles long and 30 across, there is no other Indian pottery-making community, although a few pottery-makers are scattered elsewhere in the region. In short, in a regionally diversified marketing area, only the people of Amatenango produce salable pottery, and all of the women produce it. The technique does not spread to other Indian communities, whatever the abstract profitability of such diffusion might be, because making pottery is part of a way of life, learned in the informal, intimate setting in which the basic parts of culture are acquired, and not a technique of production to be acquired by whoever sees the main chance.

Although women are the makers of pottery in Amatenango, pottery is not considered, and is not, strictly a woman's product. Men bring most of the firewood necessary for the firing of the pottery, and men take the pottery to the points of sale (now by bus and truck passage, but formerly on horseback), but the packing of pots in grass-padded net bags is still an arduous task. Pottery requires male and female co-operation, and single women make pots only if they live in a household with male members, or have male relatives who are willing to aid in the work.

The technology of pottery-making is simple and inexpensive. As the skills come to the women potters in the process of being socialized (there are, however, some women who do not know how to make the more specialized pottery like incense-burners and perforated pots, and 'on order' pottery sold exclusively to *Ladinos,* as the non-Indians are called, is made by very few families) and so provide every household with the art, so the technology, in terms of skill and materials, is within the reach of even the poorest household in the community. Pottery is a hand industry. No wheel, no mould, no oven are required. The shaping hand of the female potter, the open street firing of the ware, the slipping and decorating are ingenious skills, but technologically simple. Not even purchased, non-indigenous materials are necessary in pottery-production. The clay, the temper, the pigment, the scraping stone, the wood used in firing, the net bags used in packing, all come from communal resources and are open to every member of Amatenango equally. No payment or special permission is needed to use these resources. Community membership gives free (but not costless, since labour is involved) access to the materials of pottery-making. If one purchases part of the equipment (a steel blade for scraping, a smooth board for resting pot bases, a burlap bag or skirt under the potter's knees, nets, bags) the cost is under three dollars, and every household has that at its disposal.

There exists wide variations in the output of different pottery-making households. Estimating the range of variation in output and finding the reasons for output differences is, in a preliterate culture, a difficult task. In one household a daily record covering the entire annual production was obtained, and in three other households lesser periods, ranging from one to four months, were recorded. This information is supplemented by observations on pottery-making in several dozen households, and was checked against the complete field census of the community, so that the typicality of the sample can be judged. At any rate, the problem of measuring the gross community output of pottery was not the major research interest (though a reasoned and plausible estimate could be constructed from the data in hand). The problem was to assess the limits of output variability and to pin these down to a set of factors which were the determinants of production. The determinants of production would, when checked by micro-comparison between households in the community, indicate the 'controlling mechanism' regulating the pottery industry, and by extension the economic life of the community.

Figure 19–1 is a composite of the production of one of the most intensive pottery-producing households in the community. An inspection of this figure (the special ware represents pottery made only in a few households, the dash line is commonly but not universally made ware, and the solid is pottery made in all households) shows that pottery-making tends to reach its peak just before the major festive occasions in the community and in surrounding communities. This is explicable in terms of the nature of the ecological market situation. Pottery-making is a cash-raising activity. Ware is sold in an impersonal, free market with prices set by the interaction of supply and demand. The festal occasions are the times when Amatenangueros need money; they are also the periods when the largest demand from visitors to a local fiesta may be expected, so producers reach a maximum of output just prior to the festal times of heavy buying and selling. Production is maximized not at the time of highest prices on

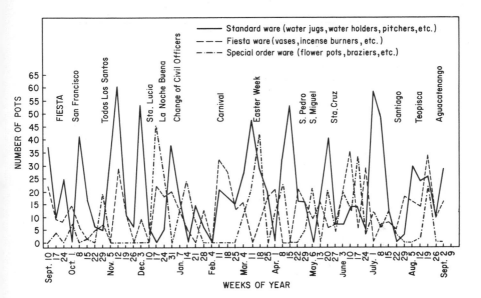

Figure 19–1   Annual production in household (4 women producers, no children).

the market, but rather in time with the rhythm of sacred and secular celebration which require cash outlay and provide opportunities for disposal without storage problems.

The peaks reached for fiestas are not of the same height. Two things operate here: the size or local importance of the given fiesta and whether it falls in the rainy or dry seasons. In the rainy months (from June to September, but heaviest from late July to mid September) less pottery is made than in the dry sunny times of the year. However, in January and February, dry sunny months, there is high wind which complicates the drying of pottery (because the pottery must be kept under leaves to keep moisture in it until it is ready for firing) and hence output is reduced. The general pattern of seasonal flux is common to all households, and so is the peak and trough pattern of production along with fiestas.

While Figure 19–1 establishes the rhythm of pottery-production common to the society by virtue of its technology and annual cycle, Figure 19–2 compares the differences in level of production among three households. Household No. 6 outproduces No. 14 and No. 13 outproduces both No. 6 and No. 14 (the numbers refer to a genealogical map and census of the community which is not here included). Each of the households is differently constituted in numbers of potters in it. Household No. 13 has four potters (two young women, one middle-aged and one old). Household No. 6 has two potters (one young and one middle-aged woman) and No. 14 has two potters (one young and one middle-aged). Therefore the sheer number of hands which can be mustered in No. 13 is greater and helps explain its greater output. Furthermore No. 14 and

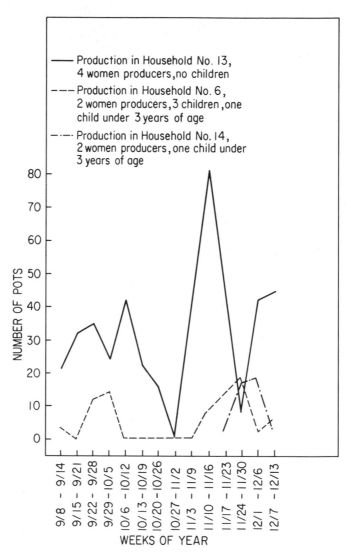

*Figure 19–2   Pottery production of all types of ware com-
pared for three households.*

No. 6 have small children under three years of age in the household, and No.
13 does not. Child care and household maintenance compete with pottery-making
for a woman's time, so the small child is a further brake on production in these
two households.

Inspection of Figure 19–2 shows that four women produce more than twice
as much as do two women (even adjusting for children). Part of this is an
'economy of scale.' Pottery-production has some assembly-line aspects. Women

work on a part of a pot, making bases, then they turn to making bodies, then to making necks, and finally to putting handles on the pot. Between these operations the pots are partially dried. If there are four women, the division of labour is better, and relative efficiency of the producing unit rises. Beyond four, not much increase occurs. But the differences in output between No. 6 and No. 14 are such that sheer numbers of hands will not serve as an explanation, and the factors of relative efficiency, or of skill, are so nearly matched in these households, that it does not really enter as a factor in the account of output differences. Explanation must be sought in the wider economic setting of the productive unit.

If all of the households in the community were ranked in terms of the major source of wealth—land at the disposal of the household—an immediate connexion would be noted between the wealth of the household and its level of output. The motivation to work at the top of the bent is stronger in poorer households, because alternative sources of income are less, and more of the family's subsistence must come from pottery-making. Land, of course, needs men to work it, and household No. 13 has but one old man, and he cannot work much land, nor lay claim to government-grant lands (*ejido*) of any considerable size. In richer households (in terms of land and cattle owned) there is sufficient milpa raised to ensure that corn need not be bought, and the need for continuous cash income is not so pressing. This also has a circular effect: richer households tend to be able to keep more children alive; with more children to care for, women devote less time to pottery. Conversely poorer households depend upon pottery income, have fewer living children, and hence have both the opportunity and the need to produce almost continuously.

The rate of output is determined on two levels:

(1) that common to the whole society (technology, resources, seasons and ceremonial cycle);

(2) the organization and wealth differences among producing units (number of women, number of children under three, number of men, and amount of land and cattle owned).

To understand why the second level of determinants of production continues to be operative, involves a move from the micro-structural analysis of producing units, to the macro-structural analysis of the whole social and economic organization of Amatenango. It moves the question from that of incentives and motivations of actors and producers to the plane of the structural sources of and constraints upon incentives and motivation. The units of production are households, and the households are kinship units. As a kinship unit, membership comes only by being born or marrying into the unit. The household unit, with its kinship of recruitment, sets the size of the 'labour force' available for pottery-making. No one hires out to do pottery for wages, since pottery-making is only part of a woman's job as a member of a household (and even if a wage were paid it could not cover all activities and still yield anything to an employer). Amatenango's kinship system is one of nearly perfectly balanced bilateralism. A combination of personal tastes and wealth of the household determines whether a married couple will live with his or her parents. Wealthier households can attract either sons-in-law or daughters-in-law to live with them, and have a slightly larger labour force potential. But the absence of wage labour in a household production system limits any given unit's ability to expand pottery activities. Expected, and, of course observed, is the common feature of peasant economic organization, a multiplicity of small reduplicative, productive units, with no tendency toward agglomeration or centralization. Furthermore, since pottery-production is household-organized, many activities compete with it for the time of the same set of personnel. Economic activities are but one field in which maintenance needs are met. Internal family social relations, the socialization of members, sickness and curing, religious activity, social status, and dispute settlement are tasks partly centred in the family, and in household organization. Economic activity, be it in the market, field, or handicraft, is a means to implement and provide facilities for other aspects of household activity. It is not an instance of conflicting standards when a woman with small children stops pottery-making, but rather a case of clear priorities.

This bears on an analogy sometimes used by anthropologists when a household is compared to a firm (Tax 1953). A household may be conceived of as a unit trying to maximize, given its resources and personnel. The analogy is misleading, not on the grounds of the kind of *rules* of allocation, but on the nature of the social structures involved. Firms are special organizations for economic activity in societies of highly differentiated structure based on complex technology, extensive social division of labour, large numbers of people, and deliberate, continual technical and economic innovation. Firms may or may not follow the rule of income-maximization depending upon the larger social structure (*viz.* the firm in the Soviet economy and the firm in the United States economy). But in peasant and primitive societies like Amatenango the context of economic choice is a multi-purposed social organization, which, unlike a firm, cannot liquidate if it makes poor calculations. Households, or more precisely the members of them, in Amatenango are as acutely aware as we are of relative costs and are keenly sensitive to economic gain. When marketing their pottery they go to Las Casas, or Comitán, or Las Rosas, or other points of sale in accord with price differentials. They closely question men returning from the various places as to prevailing prices and act accordingly. Price is on every tongue and is a topic of unending interest. Amatenangueros are 'rational' economic actors in the sense of bringing means and ends together, only their ends are values other than (or in addition to) maximization of a given single magnitude. The formal convergence of rules of choice in a household and in a firm does not lead to similar social arrangements or similar social consequences simply because the organization of personnel, resources and methods of role-recruitment form a different social structure.

The households, of course, form a social system. And the social system operates so that households orient to the prevailing value system, on the one hand, and remain fairly equivalent in wealth, on the other. Figure 19–3 gives a land-distribution chart based upon the informant's self-reported wealth (it does not include the two *tablones* of government land which most family heads have granted to them). This suffers from underestimation and deliberate concealment of assets, but serves to approximate the *shape* of the real distribution of land. Land is the best index to wealth. The features of social life which account for the shape of the curve, and the position of any given family at a point on the curve can be conceptualized as a levelling mechanism (Nash 1958; 1959). Levelling mechanisms are ubiquitous devices in peasant economies in this region (Wolf 1954). Not only do they ensure a 'democracy of poverty' but they serve to inhibit economic expansion of any given unit within the society under the threat of expulsion or sacral retribution. The levelling mechanism rests first on the absolute level of wealth in the community. Amatenango's low-level technology and its restricted land base impose severe limits on the wealth of the society as a whole, and for households and individuals a correspondingly low level. No household is so rich that the spectre of poverty is not a real possibility in the wake of long illness or a sustained run of bad luck. Given a relatively low level of absolute wealth, the inheritance mechanism tends to fracture such estates as are accumulated. In Amatenango inheritance is

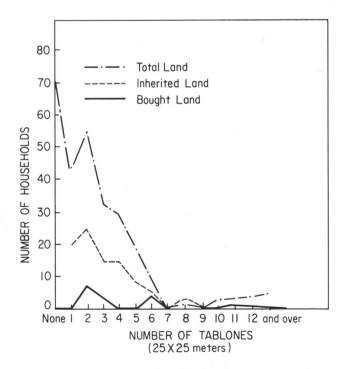

Figure 19–3   Size of landholdings, by households.

bilateral, with equal inheritance for all the offspring (although there are prerogatives of women in inheriting houses and house sites, and of men in receiving horses and cattle). The process of inheritance scrambles land-holdings among sons and daughters even before death of the head of a household. However, Figure 19–3 shows a skewed land-distribtuion, and this is a necessary part of Amatenango's social organization. The important point is that the rich, or large land-holders, change from generation to generation, and if the technical and economic levelling factors do not inhibit accumulation of wealth or capital, there are social means for ensuring that wealth does not adhere to family lines. There are a series of offices in which a man (as a representative of a family) must serve. This hierarchy of civil and religious offices is a drain on work time and uses up some of the resources of the household. Its offices are unpaid, and since a man must serve in 12 such offices before he is relieved of communal service, they are a continuing cost all through his adult, productive life.

Another social mechanism reducing accumulation is the institution of the *Alférez*. The Alférez office, of which there are four to be filled every year, is a ritual and sacred office filled by a younger man. The cost of this office is, in terms of Amatenango's wealth, exorbitant. An Alférez expends more than the annual income of even the richest Amatenanguero in feasting a group of neighbours, relatives and officers of the hierarchy, in the great consumption of liquor and the renting of the special costumes. Before the Alférez feasts weeks of preparation for it occupy the household. Women make pottery to use for the cooking of the larger amounts of special food, as well as pottery for sale. Men of the household spend their time making liquor in the hills near Amatenango, and chopping wood for the firing of pits and cooking of foods. They also make extra trips to sell pottery. Members of the bilateral kindred come in to aid in the pottery-making and liquor-distilling. Undertaking the post of Alférez leaves the family in reduced straits and with depleted assets.

Alfereces are selected by the officials of the civil and religious hierarchy, and the selection is almost strictly on ability to pay. The eligible households are few in number, and are those on the right-hand side of Figure 19–3. Richer households have a levy placed against them in consequence of their prosperity. In a community like Amatenango it is nearly impossible to conceal one's wealth— the cows and horses owned are visible, and the land cultivated is public knowledge, and the health of one's children is a reliable index of it. Strong negative sanctions—witchcraft, gossip and envy—would be consequent on a refusal to accept the post of Alférez when it was proffered. These things together—(1) low level of technology and limited land, (2) fracture of estate by bilateral inheritance, (3) expenditure of time and resources in communal office, (4) forced expenditure in ritual by the wealthy—combine to keep the fortunes of the various households nearly equivalent, and to maintain the shift of family fortunes throughout time. In addition, the business of marrying is expensive and uses household resources. Nobody gains goods in exchanges like marriage payment, or Alférez feasts or payments for dispute-settlement. The use of liquor as the medium of payment—the completely consumable good—precludes accumulation.

Not only are households in a situation where maximization of an output or income dimension is unfeasible because of their social structure, but should a given household decide on the course of maximization or be lucky or exceedingly skilled in its economic operations, the 'levelling mechanism' comes into play to minimize differences. In short, Amatenango presents a socio-economy where wealth is not easily turned to technical and economic uses, but is drained by the social and religious constitution of the culture.

Behind, and sanctioning, the social and religious organization of Amatenango is a pervasive system of belief in witchcraft. Witchcraft befalls those who violate the norms of familial and household harmony, who do not get along with neighbours, who are rich but not generous, who refuse communal obligations, who become outstanding in some dimension which violates the corporate nature of the community or upsets its tendency to economic homogeneity. Amatenangueros do not formulate the principles of witchcraft in this manner, but they behave as if their actions were governed by these premises. Witchcraft as a working means of sanctioning behaviour is not an easy thing to live with, and at least one man is killed every two months for being a practitioner of witchcraft. But the tension between economic expansion and social coercion is apparently not so strong that the system appears in immediate or even remote danger of falling under its own weight.

The economy of Amatenango, like the rest of the social structure, shows little dynamism, and change and innovation are not by-products of economic activity, as they are in the 'developed' industrial societies. The simple technology, the absence of literary skills, the shortage of capital, the lack of credit all help to explain this fact. But the social and cultural basis of Amatenango's indifference to finding means to economic change depends upon the twin facts of household organization of production and the social and religious system of witchcraft which inhibits accumulation and prevents the discovery or utilization of economic opportunity. No one can run the risks of wide economic differentials, and even if the risks were taken, membership in the community would require investment in social relations, not economic ones. Amatenango presents the paradox of a community whose market economy makes it aware of economic calculation and relative costs and benefits, but a social structure and value system which channels economic choice toward economic stability and social continuity. Communities like Amatenango develop in the face of great economic pressure from the superordinate society, or *via* the extension of economic links with persons and social systems in which the rules of choice and values, and organizations are congruent with sustained ability to seize or make economic opportunity.

In small-scale societies like Amatenango, the facts of interconnexion of economy and society and their reciprocal interaction are open to inspection. They need not be bracketed away in the abstract language of formal economic analysis. Anthropologists do not have to lose the advantages of small scale by following the trend to principle-construction at the level of the skeletal model, universal, beyond time and space, for the dubious benefits of elegance and easy manipulation. The task of understanding a representative series of social structures and their economic consequences and correlates is still to be done. With this intellectual task pursued, the making of 'principles' or the fashioning of 'models' will be only the happy task of summary and extrapolation.

20 THE LELE—RESISTANCE TO CHANGE
Mary Douglas

The Lele[1] and the Bushong[2] are separated only by the Kasai River. The two tribes recognize a common origin, their houses, clothes and crafts are similar in style, their languages are closely related.[3] Yet the Lele are poor, while the Bushong are rich. The Lele produce only for subsistence, sharing their goods, or distributing them among themselves as gifts and fees. The Bushong have long been used to producing for exchange, and their native economy was noted for its use of money and its specialists and markets. Everything that the Lele have or can do, the Bushong have more and can do better. They produce more, live better, and populate their region more densely.

The first question is whether there are significant differences in the physical environment of the two peoples. Both live in the latitude 5°, in the area of forest park merging into savannah, which borders the south of the Congo rain forest. They both have a heavy annual rainfall of 1400 to 1600 mm. (40 to 60 inches) per annum. The mean annual temperature is about 78°F. (25°C.). As we should expect from their proximity, the climatic conditions are much the same for both tribes.

Nonetheless, a curious discrepancy appears in their respective assessments of their climate. The Bushong, like the local Europeans, welcome the dry season of

From Markets In Africa *edited by Paul Bohannan and George Dalton, Evanston, Northwestern University Press, 1962, pp. 211–233. Reprinted by permission.*

[1] The Lele are a tribe, inhabiting the west border of the Bakuba Empire. They are divided into three chiefdoms, of which only the most westerly has been studied. The chief of the eastern Lele, at Perominenge, apes Kuba fashions in his little capital; the men wear basketry hats held on with metal pins, the chief has some of the dress and paraphernalia of the Nyimi. How much deeper this resemblance goes, it is impossible to say, since conditions at the time of field work were not favorable for study of this chiefdom. Everything that is said here concerning the Lele refers to the western Lele, whose chief, when visits were made in 1949–50 and 1953, was Norbert Pero Mihondo. The field work was carried out under the generous auspices of the International African Institute, and of the *Institut de Recherche Scientifique en Afrique Centrale.*

[2] The Bushong are the ruling tribe of the Kuba Kingdom. They were studied in 1953–56 by Dr. Vansina, to whom I am deeply indebted for his collaboration and for supplying unpublished information for this paper.

[3] According to the Lexico-statistical survey conducted by Dr. Vansina, there is an 80 per cent similarity between the two languages.

mid-May to mid-August as a cold season, whereas the Lele regard it as danger-
ously hot. The Bushong in the north tend to have a dry season ten days shorter
(Bultot 1954) than most of the Lele (see Figure 20–1), and the Lele soils retain
less moisture, and the vegetation is thinner, so that the impression of drought is
more severe, but otherwise there seems no objectively measurable difference in
the climate to account for their attitudes.

There are certainly important differences in the soil, drainage and vegetation.
The Lele are distinctly less fortunate. Their soils belong to the most easterly
extension of the Kwango plateau system, and to some extent share in the sterility
characteristic of that region. On that plateau, the soils are too poor to support
anything but a steppe-like vegetation in spite of the ample rainfall. The soils

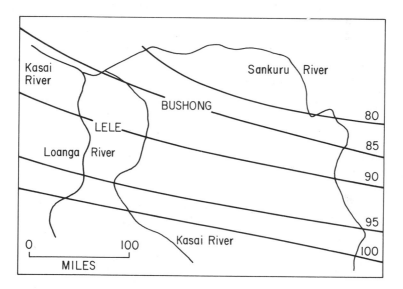

*Figure 20–1   Average length of dry season expressed in days (from
Bultot 1954).*

consist of sands, poor in assimilable minerals of any kind, lacking altogether in
ferro-magnates or heavy minerals, and so permeable that they are incapable of
benefiting from the heavy rainfall[4] (see Figure 20–2). On the Bushong side of
the Kasai River the soil is altogether richer, and mineral deposits, particularly
of iron ore, occur. Whereas Lele country is characterized by rolling grasslands
with forest galleries along the river banks, Bushong country is relatively well
forested, although the sketch map tends to exaggerate the forested area on their
side of the Kasai.

With such important differences in their basic natural resources, we are not

[4] We are very grateful to M. L. Cahen, Director of the *Musée du Congo Belge*, Tervuren,
for guidance on the physical environment of the two tribes.

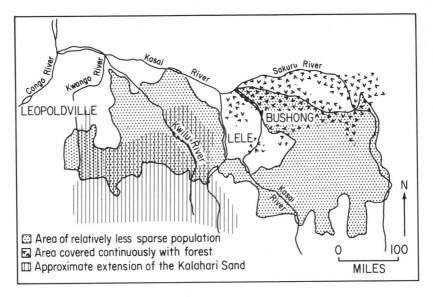

Figure 20–2   Population density and forest cover (Lele and Bushong)
(from N. Nicolai and J. Jacques 1954:112).

surprised that Lele country is poorer and more sparsely populated. But how much poverty and how low a density can be attributed to the environmental factor? Can we leave the matter here?

There is no certain method of estimating the extent to which environment itself limits the development of an area. The Pende of Gungu, immediate neighbors of the Lele, inhabit an area even poorer in soils than the Lele area, and as poor as those worked by the notoriously wretched Suku of Kahemba and Feshi. The Lele are poor, but the Suku are known as a miserable, dispirited people, incapable of exploiting to the full such resources as their poor environment offers. The Pende are famous as energetic cultivators, well nourished and industrious. All three peoples grow different staple crops; the Pende, millet; the Suku, manioc; the Lele, maize. There is obviously no end to the speculation one could indulge as to what the potentialities of the environment might be.

Congo geographers have been much occupied by the question of the relation between soil and population density. The whole Belgian Congo is an area of very low density. Fifty per cent of its surface has a population of less than 2.4 to the square kilometer (roughly 6 to the square mile) (Gourou 1955:4). It is generally agreed (Gourou 1955 cites Cohen; Nicolai 1952:247) that there is a rough correlation of poor sandy soils with low densities, insofar as the small stretch of relatively more populous country occurs in a favored gap between the Kwango "kalahari" plateau and sands to the north. However, it is also agreed that soil poverty in itself is not an adequate explanation of the pockets of extra low density which occur, especially on the second and fifth parallels of South latitude. Professor Gourou says emphatically and repeatedly that the sterility of the soils cannot be held to account for all the densities of less than 2 to the square kilometer (5 to the square mile) in the Belgian Congo (Gourou 1955:52, 57, 109; Nicolai 1952). In Northern Rhodesia we have an illuminating case. The Ndembu live at an average density of 6 to the square mile, in many areas at a density of only 3, but according to a careful calculation of the capacity of their land, worked according to their own methods, the area should be capable of supporting a population of from 17 to 38 to the square mile (6.8 to 15 per square kilometer) (Turner 1957).

In short, we cannot assume, as some have done, that there is any universal tendency to maximize food production (Harris 1959), or that the food resources of a region are the only factor limiting its population.

For the Lele and the Bushong the relative densities are as follows. The territory of Mweka, where the Bushong live, has an average density of 4–5 to the square kilometer (11 to the square mile). The BCK railway running through the area has attracted an immigrant population of Luba. If we abstract the railway zone from our figures, we find that the Bushong proper live at a density of (Gourou 1955:109) only 3 or 4 to the square kilometer (7–10 to the square mile). The Lele[5] inhabit Basongo territory, where the average density is from 2 to 4 to the square kilometer (5–7 to the square mile), but since the Lele account for only half the population (among recent immigrants of foreign tribesmen to work in the Brabanta oil concession, refinery and port, and among Cokwe hunters), we can suppose that until recently Lele themselves used to live at a mere 1.7 to the square kilometer (4 to the square mile).

When the geographers agree that poverty of soil is not a sufficient explanation for the degree of poverty prevailing in similar areas, we are justified in looking for a sociological explanation to supplement the effect of environmental factors. For one thing, it is obvious that the demographic factor works two ways. Low density is partly the result of inferior technology, applied to inferior resources, but it may also inhibit development by hampering enterprises which need large-scale collaboration.

If we now consider technology, we find many suggestive differences. In certain processes marked superiority would be likely to increase output. Others are proof of a higher standard of living. Surveying these, we find that in hunting, fishing and housebuilding, the Bushong worker uses more specialized materials and equipment than the Lele, and in cultivation he spends more energy and time.

Take hunting first, since the Lele are passionately interested in it and pride themselves on their skill (Douglas 1954). In the eyes of their neighbors, it seems that they are notorious as inefficient hunters, particularly because they do not use nets, and only rarely make pit traps.

Hunting is the only occupation in which large numbers of Lele men regularly

---

[5] According to P. Gourou, 1951, the average density of the population of all tribes for the Basongo-Port Francqui region, in which the Lele now account for only half, is 3 to 4 to the square kilometer. This agrees with calculations based on the total number of Lele in that area, about 26,000, and the extent of their territory, about 63 by 110 miles, which give a Lele density of roughly 4 to the square mile, or 1.7 to the sq. km.

combine. They reckon that fifteen to twenty men and ten dogs are necessary for a good hunt. Using nets, the Bushong need a team of only ten men, and can hope to do well with five. In short, the Bushong hunter uses better capital equipment, and his hours of hunting are more productive.

Why should the Lele not have nets? The materials are present in the forest on both sides of the river, and the Lele know what nets are. Making a net is presumably a long task. In view of the local deforestation and the resulting paucity of game, it may be a case in which costly capital equipment is simply not worth while. Bushong nets are made by their women. Perhaps the rest of the answer lies in the different division of labor between men and women in each tribe, and the larger proportion of the total agricultural work which Lele leave to their women. Whatever the reason, we note that the absence of nets is consistent with a general Lele tendency not to invest time and labor in long-term equipment.

The same applies to pit traps. Lele know how to make these, and frequently talk about them. The task requires a stay in the forest of several days and nights, or regular early dawn journeys and late returns. The traps are hard work to dig with only a blunt machete for spade, and once set, they need to be watched. In practice few men ever trouble to make them. I suspect that the reason in this case is again that the amount of game caught by pit traps tends to be disappointing in relation to the effort of making them, and that the Lele have felt discouraged when using a technique which is more productive in the thicker forests on the other side of the river.

Lest it be thought that the Lele neglect capital-intensive aids because hunting is a sport, a pleasure, and a religious activity, let me deny any parallel with English fox hunting. The Lele would have applauded the French brigadier of fiction who used his saber to slay the fox. Their eager purchase of firearms whenever they can get the money and the license shows that their culture does not restrict them to inferior techniques when these do not require long-term collaboration and effort.

In fishing the Lele are also inferior. Their country is well watered by streams and rivers, and bounded on two sides by the great Kasai, and on the west by the swift-flowing Loange. Along the banks of the Kasai are fishing villages, whose men dot the river with elaborate traps and fishing platforms. These fishermen are mostly Dinga, or Bushong, and not often Lele. In one northern village, near the Kasai, Lele women used to go every two days to the nearest Dinga village where, lacking claims of kinship, they obtained fish by bartering manioc. Compared with the Bushong the Lele as a whole are not good at fishing, or at canoe making. There is no need to describe in detail the diversity and elaborate character of Bushong fishing equipment, but it is worth noting that in some types of fishing, using several canoes trailing nets, the team may consist of twenty men or more. These skills may be a legacy from their distant past, since the Bushong claim to have entered their territory in canoes along the Kasai River, while the Lele claim to have traveled overland (Vansina 1956) and to have found the river banks already occupied by Dinga fishing villages.

If the Lele were originally landsmen, and the Bushong originally fishermen, this might account for more than the latter's present technical superiority in fishing. For primitive fishermen are necessarily more heavily equipped than are primitive hunters and cultivators. The need for fishing tackle, nets, lines, hooks, traps, curing platforms, and for watercraft as well as for weirs and dams makes quite a different balance in the allocation of time between consumers' and producers' goods. If they started in this area with the typical balance of a fishing economy, this may have meant an initial advantage for the Bushong in the form of a habit of working for postponed consumption.

Be that as it may, Lele mostly leave fishing to their women. Their simple method is to block a slow-moving stream, so as to turn the nearest valley into a marsh. In this they make mud banks and ponds, where they set traps for fish scarcely bigger than minnows. A morning's work draining out such a pond and catching the fish floundering in the mud yields a bare pint or so of fish. In the dry season they make a two-day expedition to the Lumbundji, where they spread a saponaceous vegetable poison over the low waters, and pull out the suffocated fish by hand, or in baskets.

As to housing, Lele and Bushong huts look much alike. They are low rectangular huts, roofed with palm thatch. The walls are covered with rows of split bamboos or palm ribs, lashed onto layers of palm-leaf, on a frame of strong saplings. Deceptive in appearance, Lele huts when new look much sturdier than those of the Bushong, but in practice they last less well: the Lele hut is more roughly and quickly made. A well-built one will last about six years without repair, and, as they are capable of being renewed piecemeal, by the substitution of new walls or roof thatch, they are not replaced until the whole village is moved to a new site, and the owner decides that he has neglected his hut so long that it will not stand removal. A hut in good condition is transported to a new site, with from six to eight men carrying the roof, and four at a time carrying the walls.

Bushong huts are also transportable. They are made with slightly different materials. For the roof thatch, they use the leaves of the raffia palm, as do the Lele. For the walls, they use the reputedly more waterproof leaves of a dwarf palm growing in the marshes. Over this, instead of palm ribs split in half, they sew narrow strips of bamboo, where available. Lele consider bamboo to be a tougher wood than palm, but it is rare in their region. The narrow strips are held in place by stitching in pleasing geometric patterns (Nicolai & Jacques 1954:272ff.). A rich Bushong man, who can command labor, can build a hut that will last much longer than the ordinary man's hut, up to fifteen years without major repairs. The palace of the Nyimi at Mushenge, which was still in good condition in 1956, had been originally built in 1920.

The Bushong use an ingenious technique of ventilation, a movable flap between the roof and the walls, which lets out smoke. It is impossible to say whether they do this because their building is too solid to let the smoke filter through the walls, or whether they are more fastidious and painstaking about their comfort than the Lele, whose huts do certainly retain some of the smoke of their fires.

Within the hut, the furnishings illustrate the difference in material wealth, for the Bushong have a much greater refinement of domestic goods. They sit on stools, lay their heads on carved neck rests (often necessary to accommodate an elaborate hair style). They eat from basketry plates, with iron or wooden spoons. They have a bigger range of specialized basketry or wooden containers for food, clothing, cosmetics. A man who has more than one hat needs a hat box and a place for his metal hat pins. Lele do not make fiber hats, and only a few men in a village may possess a skin hat. The beautiful Bushong caskets for cosmetics are prized objects in many European museums. When a Lele woman has prepared some cosmetic from camwood, she uses it at once, and there is rarely enough left over for it to be worth storing in a special container. Only a young mother who, being cared for by her own mother after her delivery, has nothing else to do but grind camwood for herself and the baby, stores the prepared ointment in a little hanging basket hooked into the wall, enough for a few days.

Dr. Vansina was impressed with the high protein content of the Bushong diet, with the large quantities of fish and meat they ate, and the variety in their food. The Lele give an impression of always being hungry, always dreaming of meat, often going to bed fasting because their stomach revolts at the idea of a vegetable supper. They talk a lot about hunger, and *ihiobe*, an untranslatable word for meatlessness and fishlessness. The Bushong cultivate a wider range of crops and also grow citrus fruits, pineapples, pawpaws, mangoes, sugar cane and bananas, which are either rare or completely absent in the Lele economy.

In short, the Bushong seem to be better sheltered, better fed, better supplied with goods, and with containers for storing what they do not immediately need. This is what we mean by saying that the Bushong are richer than the Lele. As to village crafts, such as carving and smithing, the best of the Lele products can compete in quality with Bushong manufacture, but they are much scarcer. The Lele are more used to eating and drinking out of folded green leaves than from the basket plates and carved beakers common among the Bushong. Their medical instruments, too, are simpler. If, instead of cutting down a gourd top, they carve a wooden enema funnel for a baby, they make it as fine and thin as they can, but do not adorn it with the elaborate pattern found on some Bushong examples.

Before considering agriculture, we should mention the method of storing grain, for this is a rough index of output. Both Lele and Bushong houses are built with an internal grain store, suspended from the roof or supported on posts over the hearth. Here grain and even fish and meat can be preserved from the ravages of damp and of insects by the smoke of the fire. Most Lele women have no other grain store. Bushong women find this too small and use external granaries, built like little huts, raised a few feet above ground. These granaries, of which there may be one or two in a Lele village, are particularly characteristic of the southern Bushong villages, while in the north the huts which are built in the fields for a man to sleep in during the period of heaviest agricultural work are used as temporary granaries. The Lele are not in the habit of sleeping in their fields, except to shoot wild pig while the grain is ripening. This may be another indication that they do less agricultural work than the Bushong.

When we examine the techniques of cultivation, we find many contrasts. The Bushong plant five crops in succession in a system of rotation that covers two years. They grow yams, sweet potatoes, manioc, beans, and gather two and some- times three maize harvests a year. The Lele practice no rotation and reap only one annual maize harvest. If we examine the two agricultural cycles, we see that the Bushong work continuously all the year, and that the Lele have one burst of activity, lasting about six weeks, in the height of the dry season.

Here is the probable explanation of their dread of the dry season. There is, in fact, surprisingly little range in the average monthly temperatures through the year. For the coldest month, July, it is only 2°C. less than the hottest month, January (Vandenplas 1947:33–38). Nonetheless, the Europeans and the Bushong welcome the period from mid-May to mid-August as the "cold season," probably because they enjoy the cooler nights and the freedom from humidity. But the Lele, enduring the sun beating on them from a cloudless sky while they are trying to do enough agricultural work for the whole year, suffer more from the dust and impurities in the atmosphere and from the greatly increased insolation. The relatively cooler nights may make them feel the day's heat even more intensely.

Apart from the differences in crops cultivated, we may note some differences in emphasis. Lele give hunting and weaving a high priority throughout the year, while the Bushong think of them as primarily dry-season activities. Traditionally, the Lele used to burn the grassland for big hunts (in which five or six villages combined for the day) at the end of the dry season, when the bulk of their agricultural work was done. If the first rains had already broken, so much the better for the prospects of the hunt, they said, as the animals would leave their forest watering places to eat the new shoots. As the end of the dry season is the time in which the firing could do the maximum damage to the vegetation, it has been forbidden by the administration, and if permission is given at all, the firing must be over by the beginning of July. The Bushong used to burn the grassland in mid-May or early June, at the beginning of the dry season, when the sap had not altogether died down in the grass.

The cycle of work described for the Lele is largely what the old men describe as their traditional practice. It was modified by the agricultural officers of the Belgian Congo. Lele are encouraged to sow maize twice, for harvesting in November, and in April. Manioc is now mainly grown in the grassland, instead of in the forest clearings. There are some changes in the plants cultivated. Voandzeia has been replaced by groundnuts, some hill rice is sown, and beans in some parts. These are largely treated as cash crops by the Lele, who sell them to the Europeans to earn money for tax. The other occupation which competes for their time is cutting oil-palm fruits to sell to the *Huileries du Congo Belge*, whose lorries collect weekly from the villages. Lele complain that they are now made to work harder than before, to clear more land, keep it hoed, grow more crops.

They never complain that cutting oil-palm fruits interferes with their agricultural program, only that the total of extra work interferes with their hunting.

This is not the place for a detailed study of Bushong agriculture. It is enough to have shown that it is more energetically pursued and is more productive. One or two details of women's work are useful indications of a different attitude to time, work and food. Lele like to eat twice a day: in the morning at about eleven o'clock or midday, and in the evening. They complain that their wives are lazy, and only too often the morning meal consists of cold scraps from the previous night; they compare themselves unfavorably with Cokwe, who are reputed to have more industrious wives. In practice the Lele women seem to be very hard-working, but it is possible that the absence of labor-saving devices may make their timetable more arduous.

For example, one of their daily chores is to fetch water from the stream. At the same time, they carry down a heavy pile of manioc roots to soak for a few days before carrying them back to the village. Bushong women, on the other hand, are equipped with wooden troughs, filled with rain water from the roofs, so that they can soak their manioc in the village without the labor of transporting it back and forth. Bushong women also cultivate mushrooms indoors for occasional relish, while Lele women rely on chance gathering.

Bushong women find time to do the famous raffia embroidery, perhaps because their menfolk help them more in the fields. Lele men admiring the Bushong velours were amazed to learn that women could ever be clever enough to use needle and thread, still less make this elaborate stitching. The Bushong culinary tradition is more varied than that of the Lele. This rough comparison suggests that Lele women are less skilled and industrious than Bushong women, but it is probable that a time-and-motion study of women's and men's work in the two economies would show that Lele men leave a relatively heavier burden of agricultural work to their women, for reasons which we shall show later.

Another difference between Bushong and Lele techniques is in the exploitation of palms for wine. Lele use only the raffia palm for wine. Their method of drawing it kills the tree; in the process of tapping, they cut out the whole of the crown of the palm just at the time of its first flowering. During the few years before the palm has matured to this point, they take the young yellow fronds for weaving, and after drawing the sap for wine, the stump is stripped and left to rot down. Lele have no use for a tree which has once been allowed to flower, except for fuel and building purposes. The life of a palm, used in this way, is rarely more than five years, although there seems to be some range in the different times at which individual palms mature.

The Bushong also use this method on raffia palms, but they have learnt to tap oil palms by making an incision at the base of the large inflorescene, a technique which does not kill the tree. Presumably this technique could be adapted to raffia palms, since the Yakö of Cross River, Nigeria use it (Forde 1937). But neither Lele nor Bushong attempt to preserve the raffia palm in this way, and Lele do not draw any wine from oil palms, although these grow plentifully in

TABLE 7 *Annual Cycle of Work*

	Bushong		Lele
	Dry Season		
Mid-May	Harvest beans, maize II, yams. Clear forest	Hunt, weave draw wine	Clear forest for maize
	Burn grassland for hunt		
June	Hunt, fish, weave, repair huts	" "	
Mid-July to Aug. 15	Burn forest clearings, gather bananas and pineapple. Plant hemp	" "	Women fish in low waters
	Hunt, fish, plant sugar cane and bananas		Burn forest clearings
	Send tribute to capital. Period of plenty		Sow maize
	Wet Season		
Mid-August	Lift groundnuts	" "	Fire grassland for hunting
Sept.	Sow groundnuts, sow maize I	" "	Sow voandzeia, plant manioc, bananas, peppers; s u g a r cane, pineapples (occasional) and raffia palms in forest clearings, with maize
	Collect termites		
Oct.		" "	
Nov.		" "	
Mid-Dec.		" "	
	Little Dry Season		
Mid-Dec.	Sow maize II; sow voandzeia	" "	Green maize can be plucked
Jan.	Sow tobacco, sow maize II	" "	Maize harvest
	Wet Season		
Feb.	Lift groundnuts, sow beans, collect termites and grubs	" "	Lift voandzeia
	Reap maize I (main crop)		
March	Reap maize I, sow tobacco, beans, yams, manioc	" "	
April to Mid-May	Gather beans, sow voandzeia and tobacco	" "	

the north of their territory. According to Lele traditions oil palms were very scarce in their country until relatively recently, and this may account for their not exploiting it for wine. But here again, consistently with other tendencies in their economy, their techniques are directed to short-term results, and do not fully use their resources.

To balance this picture of Lele inefficiency, we should mention the weaving of raffia, for here, at least, they are recognized as the better craftsmen. Their raffia cloth is of closer texture than Bushong cloth, because they use finer strands of raffia, produced by combing in three stages, whereas the Bushong only comb once. Incidentally, the fine Lele cloth is not suitable for velours embroidery.

Lele take pride in producing cloth of a regular and fine weave, and they refuse inferior cloth if it is proffered for payment. A length of woven raffia is their normal standard of value for counting debts and dues of all kinds. How little it has even now become a medium of exchange has been described elsewhere (Douglas 1958). Raffia cloth is not the medium of exchange for the Bushong, who freely used cowries, copper units, and beads before they adopted Congolese francs as an additional currency. Raffia cloth is the principal export for the Lele, whereby they obtain knives, arrowheads and camwood. This may explain why unadorned raffia cloth holds a more important place in the admittedly simpler economy of the Lele than its equivalent in the diversified economy of the Bushong.

If we ask now why one tribe is rich and the other poor, the review of technology would seem to suggest that the Lele are poorer not only because their soil is less fertile, but because they work less at the production of goods. They do not build up producer's capital, such as nets, canoes, traps and granaries. Nor do they work so long at cultivation, and their houses wear out quicker. Their reduced effort is itself partly a consequence of their poorer environment. It is probable that their soil could not be worked by the intensive methods of Bushong agriculture without starting a degenerative cycle. Hunting nets and pit traps are less worth while in an area poor in forest and game. But certain other features of their economy cannot be fully explained as adaptations to the environment.

When Lele timetables of work are compared with those of the Bushong, we see no heavy schedules which suggest that there would be any shortage of labor. Yet their economy is characterized paradoxically by an apparent shortage of hands, which confronts anyone who seeks collaborators. When a sick man wants to send a message, or needs help to clear his fields, or to repair his hut, or to draw palm wine for him, he will often be hard put to find anyone whose services he can command. *"Kwa itangu bo* [No time]*"* is a common reply to requests for help. His fields may lie uncleared, or his palm trees run to seed for lack of hands. This reflects the weakness of the authority structure in Lele society, and does not imply that every able-bodied man is fully employed from dawn to dusk.

Some anthropologists write as if the poorer the environment and the less efficient the techniques for exploiting it, the more the population is forced to work hard to maintain itself in existence; more productive techniques produce a surplus which enables a part of the population to be supported as a "leisure class."[6] It is not necessary to expose the fallacies of this approach, but it is worth pointing out that, poor as they are, the Lele are less fully employed than the Bushong. They do less work.

[6] For the most widely read statement of this view, see Herskovits 1952 (Part V, The Economic Surplus) and for a list of reputed subscribers to this view, see Harris 1959.

"Work," of course, is here used in a narrow sense, relevant to a comparison of material wealth. Warfare, raiding, ambushing, all planning of offensive and defensive actions, as also abductions, seductions, and reclaiming of women, making and rebutting of sorcery charges, negotiations for fines and compensations and for credit—all these absorbingly interesting and doubtless satisfying activities of Lele social life must, for this purpose of measuring comparative prosperity, be counted as alternatives to productive work. Whether we call them forms of preferred idleness, or leisure activities, or "non-productive work," no hidden judgment of value is implied. The distinction between productive work and other activities is merely used here as rough index of material output.

If we wish to understand why the Lele work less, we need to consider whether any social factors inhibit them from exploiting their resources to the utmost. We should be prepared to find in a backward economy (no less than in our own economy) instances of decisions influenced by short-term desires which, once taken, may block the realization of long-term interests.

First we must assess, in a very general way, the attitudes shown by the Lele towards the inconveniences and rewards of work.

For the Bushong, work is the means to wealth, and wealth the means to status. They strongly emphasize the value of individual effort and achievement, and they are also prepared to collaborate in numbers over a sustained period when this is necessary to raise output. Nothing in Lele culture corresponds to the Bushong striving for riches. The Bushong talk constantly and dream about wealth, while proverbs about it being the steppingstone to high status are often on their lips. Riches, prestige, and influence at court are explicitly associated together (Vansina 1954).

On the other hand, Lele behave as if they expect the most satisfying roles of middle and old age to fall into the individual's lap in the ripeness of time, only provided that he is a real man—that is, normally virile. He will eventually marry several wives, beget children, and so enter the Begetters' cult. His infant daughters will be asked in marriage by suitors bearing gifts and ready to work for him. Later, when his cult membership is bringing in a revenue of raffia cloth from fees of new initiates, his newborn daughter's daughters can be promised in marriage to junior clansmen, who will strengthen his following in the village. His wives will look after him in his declining years. He will have stores of raffia cloths to lend or give, but he will possess this wealth because, in the natural course of events, he reached the proper status for his age. He would not be able to achieve this status through wealth.

The emphasis on seniority means that, among the Lele, work and competitiveness are not geared to their longings for prestige. Among the Bushong, largely through the mechanism of markets, through money, and through elective political office, the reverse is true. It also means that Lele society holds out its best rewards in middle life and after. Those who have reached this period of privilege have an interest in maintaining the *status quo*.

All over the world it is common for the privileged sections of a community to adopt protective policies, even against their own more long-term interests. We find traces of this attitude among old Lele men. They tend to speak and behave as if they held, collectively, a position to be defended against the encroachments of the young men. Examples of this attitude have been published elsewhere (Douglas 1959). Briefly, secrets of ritual and healing are jealously guarded, and even knowledge of the debts and marriage negotiations of their own clans are deliberately withheld from the young men, as a technique for retarding their adulthood. The old are realistic enough to know that they are dependent ultimately on the brawn and muscle of the young men, and this thought is regularly brought up in disputes, when they are pressing defense of their privileges too far: "What would happen to us, if we chased away the young men? Who would hunt with us, and carry home the game? Who would carry the European's luggage?" The young men play on this, and threaten to leave the village until eventually the dispute is settled. Although it does not directly affect the levels of production that we have been discussing, this atmosphere of jealousy between men's age groups certainly inhibits collaboration and should probably not be underestimated in its long-term effects.

Lele also believe in restricting competition. At the beginning of the century, the Lele chief Ngoma Nvula tried to protect the native textile industry by threatening death for anyone who wore European cloth (Simpson 1911:310). If a Lele man is asked why women do not weave or sew, he instantly replies: "If a woman could sew her own clothes, she might refuse to cook for the men. What could we give them instead of clothes to keep them happy?" This gives a false picture of the male contribution to the domestic economy, but it is reminiscent of some modern arguments against "equal pay" for both sexes.

Within the local section of a clan, restrictions on entry into the skilled professions are deliberately enforced. A young boy is not allowed to take up a craft practiced by a senior clansman, unless the latter agrees to retire. In the same clan, in the same village, two men rarely specialize in the same skill. If a man is a good drummer, or carver, or smith, and he sees an aptitude for the same craft in his son or nephew, he may teach the boy all he knows and work with him until he thinks the apprenticeship complete. Then, ceremonially, he hands over his own position, with his tools, and retires in favor of the younger man. This ideal is frequently practiced. The accompanying convention, that a boy must not compete with his elder kinsman, is also strong enough to stop many a would-be specialist from developing his skill. Lele openly prefer reduced output. Their specialist craftsmen are few and far between because they are expected to make matters unpleasant for rivals competing for their business. Consequently the Lele as a whole are poorer in metal or wooden objects for their own use, or for export.

Lastly, it seems that Lele old men have never been able to rely on their junior clansmen for regular assistance in the fields. As a junior work mate, a son-in-law is more reliable than a fellow clansman. This is so for reasons connected with the pattern of residence and the weak definition of authority within the clan (Douglas

1957). An unmarried youth has no granary of his own to fill. Work which he does to help his maternal uncles, father, or father's brothers, is counted in his favor, but he can easily use the claims of one to refuse those of another, and escape with a minimum of toil. Boys would be boys, until their middle thirties. They led the good life, of weaving, drinking, and following the manly sports of hunting and warfare, without continuous agricultural responsibilities.

The key institution in which the old men see their interests as divorced from those of the young men is polygyny. Under the old system, since the young girls were pre-empted by the older men, the age of marriage was early for girls (eleven or twelve), and late for men (in their thirties). It would be superficial to suppose that these arrangements were solely for the sexual gratification of the old men. One should see them as part of the whole economic system, and particularly as one of the parts which provide social security of the old.

The division of labor between the sexes leaves the very old men with little they can do. An old woman, by contrast, can earn her keep with many useful services. But old men use their rights over women to secure necessary services, both from women and from men. Through polygyny, the principles of male dominance and of seniority are maintained to the end. To borrow an analogy from another sphere, we could almost say that the Lele have opted for an ambitious old-age pensions scheme at the price of their general standards of living. We shall see that the whole community pays for the security in old age which polygyny represents.

In the kingdom of ends peculiar to the Lele, various institutions seem to receive their justification because they are consistent with polygyny of the old men and delayed marriage of the young. The latter were reconciled to their bachelorhood, partly by the life of sport and ease, and partly by the institution of wife sharing by age sets. They were encouraged to turn their attention away from the young wives in their own villages by the related custom of abducting girls from rival villages (Douglas 1951). Intervillage feuding therefore appears to be an essential part of the total scheme, which furthermore commits the Lele to small-scale political life. The diversion of young men's energies to raiding and abducting from rival villages was a major cause of the low levels of production, for its effects were cumulative. The raiding gave rise to such insecurity that at some times half the able-bodied males were engaged in giving armed escort to the others. Men said that in the old days a man did not go to the forest to draw palm wine alone, but his age mate escorted him and stood with his back to the tree, bowstring taut, watching for ambush.

Coming from Bushong country in 1907, Torday was amazed at the fortified condition of Lele villages:

> Here, too, we found enclosures, but instead of the leaf walls which are considered sufficient among the Bushongo, the separations were palisades formed by solid stakes driven into the ground. Such a wall surrounded the whole village, and the single entrance was so arranged that no more than one person was able to enter at one time. (Torday 1925:231)

Simpson also remarked that Lele men, asked to carry his baggage from their own village to the next, armed as if going into strange country. Such insecurity is obviously inimical to trade.

We have started with polygyny as the primary value to which other habits have been adjusted, because the Lele themselves talk as if all relations between men are defined by rights to women.

The point is the more effective since the Bushong are monogamous. We know well that polygyny elsewhere does not give rise to this particular accumulation of effects. Are there any features peculiar to Lele polygyny? One is the proportion of polygynous old men, indicated by the high rate of bachelorhood. Another is in the solutions they have adopted for the problems of late marriage. In some societies with extensive polygyny, the institutions which exist for the sexual satisfaction of the young men[7] are either wholly peaceful, or directed to warfare with other tribes and not to hostilities between villages. Thirdly, where the chain of command is more sharply defined (as in patrilineal systems, or in matrilineal societies in which offices are elective or carry recognizable political responsibilities, as among the Bushong), then polygyny of older men is less likely to be accompanied by attitudes of suspicion and hostility between men's age groups.

Having started our analysis with polygyny and the high rate of bachelorhood, tracing the various interactions, we find the Lele economy constantly pegged down to the same level of production. Something like a negative feedback appears in the relations of old to young men: the more the old men reserve the girls for themselves, the more the young men are resentful and evasive; the more the young men are refractory, the more the old men insist on their prerogatives. They pick on the most unsatisfactory of the young men, refuse to allot him a wife, refuse him cult membership; the others note his punishment, and either come to heel or move off to another village. There cannot be an indefinite worsening in their relations because, inevitably, the old men die. Then the young men inherit their widows, and, now not so young, see themselves in sight of polygynous status, to be defended by solidarity of the old.

So we find the Lele, as a result of innumerable personal choices about matters of immediate concern, committed to all the insecurity of feuding villages, and to the frustrations of small-scale political life and ineffective economy.

If we prefer to start our analysis at the other end, not with polygyny but with scale of political organization, we come to the same results. For whatever reason, the Bushong developed a well-organized political system (Vansina 1957), embracing 70,000 people. Authority is decentralized from the Nyimi, or paramount chief, to minor chiefs, and from these to canton heads, and from these to village heads. Judicial, legislative, and administrative powers are delegated down these channels, with decisions concerning war and peace held

---

[7] For example, Tiv "sister marriage" or the "manyatta" of the Masai.

at the center by the Nyimi. Political office is elective or by appointment. Appropriate policing powers are attached to leaders at each point in the hierarchy. Leaders are checked by variously constituted councils, whom they must consult. The Nyimi maintains his own army to quell rebellions. Tribute of grain, salt, dried foods, and money is brought into the capitals, and redistributed to loyal subjects and officials. The chiefly courts provide well-rewarded markets for craftsmen's wares so that regional specialties are salable far from their sources. Even before the advent of Europeans there was a food market at Musenge, the Nyimi's capital. No doubt the Kasai River, protecting them from the long arm of the Bushong Empire, is partly responsible for the Lele's never having been drawn, willy-nilly, into its orbit, and accepting its values.

The Lele village, which is their largest autonomous unit, is not so big as the smallest political unit in the Bushong system. (The Lele villages average a population of 190, and the Bushong villages 210.) True, there are Lele chiefs, who claim relationship with Bushong chiefs. Each village is, indeed, found within a chiefdom—that is, an area over which a member of the chiefly clan claims suzerainty. But in practice his rights are found to be ritual and social. Each village is completely independent. The chief has no judicial or military authority. He claims tribute, but here we have no busy palace scene in which tribute payers flock in and are lavishly fed by the special catering system which chiefly polygyny so often represents.

When a chief visited a village, he was given raffia cloths, as many as could be spared. Then the villagers asked what woman he would give them in return. He named one of his daughters, and they settled a day to fetch her. The girl became the communal wife of one of the age sets, the whole village regarding itself as her legal husband and as son-in-law to the chief. Son-in-lawship expressed their relation to him until the day that he claimed the girl's first daughter in marriage. Then the relation became reversed, the chief being son-in-law to the village. The raffia gifts and women which went back and forth between the chief and village were not essentially different from those which linked independent villages to one another in peaceful exchange. None of this interfered with the autonomy of the village.

The simple factor of scale alone has various repercussions. There is no ladder of status up which a man may honorably climb to satisfy his competitive ambitions. There is no series of offices for which age and experience qualify a man, so that in his physical decline he can enjoy respect and influence and material rewards. The Bushong lay great emphasis on individual effort and achievement, but the Lele try to damp it down. They avoid overt roles of leadership and fear the jealousy which individual success arouses. Their truncated status system turns the Lele village in on itself, to brood on quarrels and sorcery accusations, or turns it, in hostility, against other villages, so promoting the general feeling of insecurity. The latter makes markets impossible, and renders pointless ambition to produce above home needs. The old, in such an economy, unable to save, or to acquire dignity in their declining years by occupying high political office, bolster their position by claiming the marriageable women, and building up a system of rewards reserved for those who begat in wedlock. And so we are back again to polygyny and prolonged bachelorhood.

This picture has been partly based on deductions about what Lele society must have been like twenty years before fieldwork was begun. Before 1930 they could still resort to ordeals, enslave, raid and counterraid, abduct women, and pursue blood vengeance with barbed arrows. They still needed to fortify their villages against attacks. By 1949 the scene had changed. The young men had broken out of their restraining social environment—by becoming Christians. They enjoyed protection, from mission and government, from reprisals by pagans. They could marry young Christian girls who, similarly, were able to escape their expected lot as junior wives of elderly polygynists. Raiding was ended, age sets were nearly finished. Old men had less authority even than before. The young Christian tended to seek employment with Europeans to escape the reproaches and suspicions which their abstention from pagan rituals engendered.[8]

It would be interesting to compare their performance as workers in the new and freer context. One might expect that, away from the influence of their old culture, Lele performance might equal or surpass that of Bushong. Unfortunately the framework for such a comparison is lacking. Neither tribe has a high reputation for industry with its respective employers, compared with immigrant Cokwe, Luba and Pende workers. This may simply be because the best reputations are earned by tribes which have longest been accustomed to wage labor.

One is tempted to predict that, in so far as it is due to social factors, Lele are likely to change their name for idleness and lack of stamina before long. In 1949–50 they were not forthcoming in numbers for plantation labor or for cutting oil-palm nuts. By 1954, when a scattering of small shops through the territory had put trade goods within their reach, they had become eager to earn money. The restrictive influence of the old social system was already weaker.

We may now look again at the demographic factor, and distinguish some effects on it of the economy and the political system. It is obvious that in different types of economy, the active male contribution may have different time spans according to the nature of the work. If there were a modern community whose breadwinners were international skating champions, footballers, or miners at the coal face, their period of active work would be briefer than in economies based on less physically exacting tasks. A primitive economy is, by definition, one based on a rudimentary technology, and the more rudimentary, the more the work consists of purely individual physical effort. Moreover, the simpler the economy, the smaller the scope for managerial roles and ancillary sedentary

[8] This process has been described in Douglas 1959b.

work. The result, then, is that the period of full, active contribution to the economy is shorter.[9]

If we compare Lele and Bushong economies on these lines, we see that the "age of retirement" is likely to be earlier for the Lele. The typical Bushong man is able, long after he has passed his physical prime, to make a useful contribution to production, either by using his experience to direct the collaboration of others or in various administrative roles which are important in maintaining the security and order necessary for prosperity. The Lele economy, on the other hand, with its emphasis on individual work, gives less weight to experience and finds less productive work for the older man to do. We can only guess at the differences, but it is worth presenting the idea visually, as in Figure 20–3.

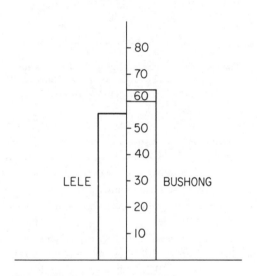

Figure 20–3 Age of retirement from work.

Furthermore, at the other end of the life span, the same trend is increased because of the late entry into agricultural work of Lele men. The young Lele is not fully employed in agriculture until he is at least thirty and married, the Bushong man when he is twenty.

Figure 20–4 illustrates the idea that the active labor force in the Lele economy, as a proportion of the total population, is on both scores smaller than it is with the Bushong. The total output of the economy has to be shared among a larger population of dependents.

The comparison of the two economies has shown up something like the

[9] This approach was suggested by Linton 1940.

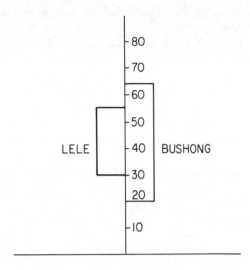

*Figure 20–4   Period of full work, show-
ing age of entry into full
agricultural responsibility.*

effects of "backwash" described by Professor Myrdal (1957). First we see
that in the environment there are initial disadvantages which limit development. Secondly, we find that in the social organization itself there are further
inhibiting effects which are cumulative, and which work one on another and
back again on the economy, technology and population, to intensify the initial
disadvantages. We have tried to present the interaction of these tendencies in a
simplified form in Figure 20–5.

"Nothing succeeds like success." Somehow, sometime, the Bushong took
decisions which produced a favorable turn in their fortunes and set off interactions which resulted in their political hegemony and their wealth. The Lele
missed the benefits of this civilization because of their location on the other
side of the Kasai River, their poorer soils, their history. The decisions they
took amounted to an accommodation of their life to a lower political and economic level. Their technology was inferior, so their efforts were backed with
less efficient equipment, and their economy was less productive. Their old
social system barred many of the chances which might have favored economic
growth.

Anthropologists sometimes tend to discuss the adoption or rejection of new
techniques in terms of a cultural mystique, as if dealing with irreducible principles, of which no analysis is feasible.[10] The Lele may be taken as a case

---

[10] See Benedict (1956:187): "Among primitive peoples, this lack of interest in 'progress'
has been proverbial . . . Every primitive tribe has its own cultural arrangements which
ensure its survival . . . They may be culturally uninterested in labor-saving devices. Often
the value they put on time is extremely low, and 'wisdom' is far more valued than efficiency.
Our cultural system and theirs are oriented around different ideals."

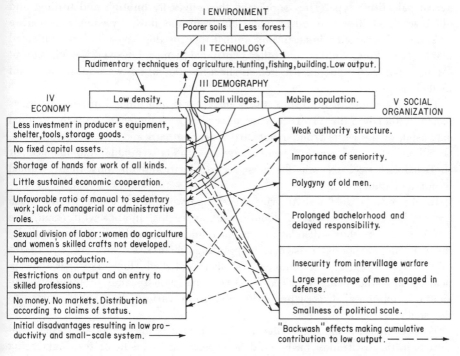

Figure 20–5 Lele economy and social organization.

in point. Their preference for their own inferior techniques, in spite of awareness of better methods used across the river, depend on certain institutions, and
these again on their history and environment. Through economic analysis we
can break down the effect of choices, each made reasonably enough in its own
restricted context. By following up the interactions of these choices, one upon
another, we can see how the highly idiosyncratic mold of Lele culture is related
to a certain low level of production.

21 STEEL AXES FOR STONE-AGE AUSTRALIANS

Lauriston Sharp

I

Like other Australian aboriginals, the Yir Yoront group which lives at the
mouth of the Coleman River on the west coast of Cape York Peninsula originally
had no knowledge of metals. Technologically their culture was of the old stone

From Human Organization, *Vol. 11, Summer 1952, pp. 17–22. Reprinted by permission of*
The Society for Applied Anthropology.

age or paleolithic type. They supported themselves by hunting and fishing, and obtained vegetables and other materials from the bush by simple gathering techniques. Their only domesticated animal was the dog; they had no cultivated plants of any kind. Unlike some other aboriginal groups, however, the Yir Yoront did have polished stone axes hafted in short handles which were most important in their economy.

Towards the end of the 19th century metal tools and other European artifacts began to filter into the Yir Yoront territory. The flow increased with the gradual expansion of the white frontier outward from southern and eastern Queensland. Of all the items of western technology thus made available, the hatchet, or short handled steel axe, was the most acceptable to and the most highly valued by all aboriginals.

In the mid 1930's an American anthropologist lived alone in the bush among the Yir Yoront for 13 months without seeing another white man. The Yir Yoront were thus still relatively isolated and continued to live an essentially independent economic existence, supporting themselves entirely by means of their old stone age techniques. Yet their polished stone axes were disappearing fast and being replaced by steel axes which came to them in considerable numbers, directly or indirectly, from various European sources to the south.

What changes in the life of the Yir Yoront still living under aboriginal conditions in the Australian bush could be expected as a result of their increasing possession and use of the steel axe?

II The Course of Events

Events leading up to the introduction of the steel axe among the Yir Yoront begin with the advent of the second known group of Europeans to reach the shores of the Australian continent. In 1623 a Dutch expedition landed on the coast where the Yir Yoront now live.[1] In 1935 the Yir Yoront were still using the few cultural items recorded in the Dutch log for the aboriginals they encountered. To this cultural inventory the Dutch added beads and pieces of iron which they offered in an effort to attract the frightened "Indians." Among these natives metal and beads have disappeared, together with any memory of this first encounter with whites.

The next recorded contact in this area was in 1864. Here there is more positive assurance that the natives concerned were the immediate ancestors of the Yir Yoront community. These aboriginals had the temerity to attack a party of cattle men who were driving a small herd from southern Queensland through the length of the then unknown Cape York Peninsula to a newly established government station at the northern tip (Jack 1921:298–335). Known as the "Battle of the Mitchell River," this was one of the rare instances in which Australian aboriginals stood up to European gunfire for any length of time. A diary kept by the cattle men records that: ". . . 10 carbines poured volley after volley into

[1] An account of this expedition from Amboina is given in Jack 1921:18–57.

them from all directions, killing and wounding with every shot with very little return, nearly all their spears having already been expended. . . . About 30 being killed, the leader thought it prudent to hold his hand, and let the rest escape. Many more must have been wounded and probably drowned, for 59 rounds were counted as discharged." The European party was in the Yir Yoront area for three days; they then disappeared over the horizon to the north and never returned. In the almost three-year long anthropological investigation conducted some 70 years later—in all the material of hundreds of free association interviews, in texts of hundreds of dreams and myths, in genealogies, and eventually in hundreds of answers to direct and indirect questioning on just this particular matter—there was nothing that could be interpreted as a reference to this shocking contact with Europeans.

The aboriginal accounts of their first remembered contact with whites begin in about 1900 with references to persons known to have had sporadic but lethal encounters with them. From that time on whites continued to remain on the southern periphery of Yir Yoront territory. With the establishment of cattle stations (ranches) to the south, cattle men made occasional excursions among the "wild black-fellows" in order to inspect the country and abduct natives to be trained at cattle boys and "house girls." At least one such expedition reached the Coleman River where a number of Yir Yoront men and women were shot for no apparent reason.

About this time the government was persuaded to sponsor the establishment of three mission stations along the 700-mile western coast of the Peninsula in an attempt to help regulate the treatment of natives. To further this purpose a strip of coastal territory was set aside as an aboriginal reserve and closed to further white settlement.

In 1915, an Anglican mission station was established near the mouth of the Mitchell River, about a three-day march from the heart of the Yir Yoront country. Some Yir Yoront refused to have anything to do with the mission, others visited it occasionally, while only a few eventually settled more or less permanently in one of the three "villages" established at the mission.

Thus the majority of the Yir Yoront continued to live their old self-supporting life in the bush, protected until 1942 by the government reserve and the intervening mission from the cruder realities of the encroaching new order from the south. To the east was poor, uninhabited country. To the north were other bush tribes extending on along the coast to the distant Archer River Presbyterian mission with which the Yir Yoront had no contact. Westward was the shallow Gulf of Carpentaria on which the natives saw only a mission lugger making its infrequent dry season trips to the Mitchell River. In this protected environment for over a generation the Yir Yoront were able to recuperate from shocks received at the hands of civilized society. During the 1930's their raiding and fighting, their trading and stealing of women, their evisceration and two- or three-year care of their dead, and their totemic ceremonies continued, apparently uninhibited by western influence. In 1931 they killed a

European who wandered into their territory from the east, but the investigating police never approached the group whose members were responsible for the act.

As a direct result of the work of the Mitchell River mission, all Yir Yoront received a great many more western artifacts of all kinds than ever before. As part of their plan for raising native living standards, the missionaries made it possible for aboriginals living at the mission to earn some western goods, many of which were then given or traded to natives still living under bush conditions; they also handed out certain useful articles gratis to both mission and bush aboriginals. They prevented guns, liquor, and damaging narcotics, as well as decimating diseases, from reaching the tribes of this area, while encouraging the introduction of goods they considered "improving." As has been noted, no item of western technology available, with the possible exception of trade tobacco, was in greater demand among all groups of aboriginals than the short handled steel axe. The mission always kept a good supply of these axes in stock; at Christmas parties or other mission festivals they were given away to mission or visiting aboriginals indiscriminately and in considerable numbers. In addition, some steel axes as well as other European goods were still traded in to the Yir Yoront by natives in contact with cattle stations in the south. Indeed, steel axes had probably come to the Yir Yoront through established lines of aboriginal trade long before any regular contact with whites had occurred.

III   Relevant Factors

If we concentrate our attention on Yir Yoront behavior centering about the original stone axe (rather than on the axe—the object—itself) as a cultural trait or item of cultural equipment, we should get some conception of the role this implement played in aboriginal culture. This, in turn, should enable us to foresee with considerable accuracy some of the results stemming from the displacement of the stone axe by the steel axe.

The production of a stone axe required a number of simple technological skills. With the various details of the axe well in mind, adult men could set about producing it (a task not considered appropriate for women or children). First of all a man had to know the location and properties of several natural resources found in his immediate environment: pliable wood for a handle, which could be doubled or bent over the axe head and bound tightly; bark, which could be rolled into cord for the binding; and gum, to fix the stone head in the haft. These materials had to be correctly gathered, stored, prepared, cut to size and applied or manipulated. They were in plentiful supply, and could be taken from anyone's property without special permission. Postponing consideration of the stone head, the axe could be made by any normal man who had a simple knowledge of nature and of the technological skills involved, together with fire (for heating the gum), and a few simple cutting tools—perhaps the sharp shells of plentiful bivalves.

The use of the stone axe as a piece of capital equipment used in producing other goods indicates its very great importance to the subsistence economy of the aboriginal. Anyone—man, woman, or child—could use the axe; indeed, it was used primarily by women, for their's was the task of obtaining sufficient wood to keep the family campfire burning all day, for cooking or other purposes, and all night against mosquitoes and cold (for in July, winter temperature might drop below 40 degrees). In a normal lifetime a woman would use the axe to cut or knock down literally tons of firewood. The axe was also used to make other tools or weapons, and a variety of material equipment required by the aboriginal in his daily life. The stone axe was essential in the construction of the wet season domed huts which keep out some rain and some insects; of platforms which provide dry storage; of shelters which give shade in the dry summer when days are bright and hot. In hunting and fishing and in gathering vegetable or animal food the axe was also a necessary tool, and in this tropical culture, where preservatives or other means of storage are lacking, the natives spend more time obtaining food than in any other occupation—except sleeping. In only two instances was the use of the stone axe strictly limited to adult men: for gathering wild honey, the most prized food known to the Yir Yoront; and for making the secret paraphernalia for ceremonies. From this brief listing of some of the activities involving the use of the axe, it is easy to understand why there was at least one stone axe in every camp, in every hunting or fighting party, and in every group out on a "walk-about" in the bush.

The stone axe was also prominent in interpersonal relations. Yir Yoront men were dependent upon interpersonal relations for their stone axe heads, since the flat, geologically-recent, alluvial country over which they range provides no suitable stone for this purpose. The stone they used came from quarries 400 miles to the south, reaching the Yir Yoront through long lines of male trading partners. Some of these chains terminated with the Yir Yoront men, others extended on farther north to other groups, using Yir Yoront men as links. Almost every older adult man had one or more regular trading partners, some to the north and some to the south. He provided his partner or partners in the south with surplus spears, particularly fighting spears tipped with the barbed spines of sting ray which snap into vicious fragments when they penetrate human flesh. For a dozen such spears, some of which he may have obtained from a partner to the north, he would receive one stone axe head. Studies have shown that the sting ray barb sprears increased in value as they move south and farther from the sea. One hundred and fifty miles south of Yir Yoront one such spear may be exchanged for one stone axe head. Although actual investigations could not be made, it was presumed that farther south, nearer the quarries, one sting ray barb spear would bring several stone axe heads. Apparently people who acted as links in the middle of the chain and who made neither spears nor axe heads would receive a certain number of each as a middleman's profit.

Thus trading relations, which may extend the individual's personal relationships beyond that of his own group, were associated with spears and axes, two of the most important items in a man's equipment. Finally, most of the exchanges took place during the dry season, at the time of the great aboriginal celebrations centering about initiation rites or other totemic ceremonials which attracted hundreds and were the occasion for much exciting activity in addition to trading.

Returning to the Yir Yoront, we find that adult men kept their axes in camp with their other equipment, or carried them when travelling. Thus a woman or child who wanted to use an axe—as might frequently happen during the day—had to get one from a man, use it promptly, and return it in good condition. While a man might speak of "my axe," a woman or child could not.

This necessary and constant borrowing of axes from older men by women and children was in accordance with regular patterns of kinship behavior. A woman would expect to use her husband's axe unless he himself was using it; if unmarried, or if her husband was absent, a woman would go first to her older brother or to her father. Only in extraordinary circumstances would she seek a stone axe from other male kin. A girl, a boy, or a young man would look to a father or an older brother to provide an axe for their use. Older men, too, would follow similar rules if they had to borrow an axe.

It will be noted that all of these social relationships in which the stone axe had a place are pair relationships and that the use of the axe helped to define and maintain their character and the roles of the two individual participants. Every active relationship among the Yir Yoront involved a definite and accepted status of superordination or subordination. A person could have no dealings with another on exactly equal terms. The nearest approach to equality was between brothers, although the older was always superordinate to the younger. Since the exchange of goods in a trading relationship involved a mutual reciprocity, trading partners usually stood in a brotherly type of relationship, although one was always classified as older than the other and would have some advantage in case of dispute. It can be seen that repeated and widespread conduct centering around the use of the axe helped to generalize and standardize these sex, age, and kinship roles both in their normal benevolent and exceptional malevolent aspects.

The status of any individual Yir Yoront was determined not only by sex, age, and extended kin relationships, but also by membership in one of two dozen patrilineal totemic clans into which the entire community was divided.[2] Each clan had literally hundreds of totems, from one or two of which the clan derived its name, and the clan members their personal names. These totems included natural species or phenomena such as the sun, stars, and daybreak, as well as cultural "species": imagined ghosts, rainbow serpents, heroic ancestors; such eternal cultural verities as fires, spears, huts; and such human

---

[2] The best, although highly concentrated, summaries of totemism among the Yir Yoront and the other tribes of north Queensland will be found in Sharp 1939:254–275; 439–461 and 1943:66–71.

activities, conditions, or attributes as eating, vomiting, swimming, fighting, babies and corpses, milk and blood, lips and loins. While individual members of such totemic classes or species might disappear or be destroyed the class itself was obviously ever-present and indestructible. The totems, therefore, lent permanence and stability to the clans, to the groupings of human individuals who generation after generation were each associated with a set of totems which distinguished one clan from another.

The stone axe was one of the most important of the many totems of the Sunlit Cloud Iguana clan. The names of many members of this clan referred to the axe itself, to activities in which the axe played a vital part, or to the clan's mythical ancestors with whom the axe was prominently associated. When it was necessary to represent the stone axe in totemic ceremonies, only men of this clan exhibited it or pantomimed its use. In secular life, the axe could be made by any man and used by all; but in the sacred realm of the totems it belonged exclusively to the Sunlit Cloud Iguana people.

Supporting those aspects of cultural behavior which we have called technology and conduct, is a third area of culture which includes ideas, sentiments, and values. These are most difficult to deal with, for they are latent and covert, and even unconscious, and must be deduced from overt actions and language or other communicating behavior. In this aspect of the culture lies the significance of the stone axe to the Yir Yoront and to their cultural way of life.

The stone axe was an important symbol of masculinity among the Yir Yoront (just as pants or pipes are to us). By a complicated set of ideas the axe was defined as "belonging" to males, and everyone in the society (except untrained infants) accepted these ideas. Similarly spears, spear throwers, and fire-making sticks were owned only by men and were also symbols of masculinity. But the masculine values represented by the stone axe were constantly being impressed on all members of society by the fact that females borrowed axes but not other masculine artifacts. Thus the axe stood for an important theme of Yir Yoront culture: the superiority and rightful dominance of the male, and the greater value of his concerns and of all things associated with him. As the axe also had to be borrowed by the younger people it represented the prestige of age, another important theme running through Yir Yoront behavior.

To understand the Yir Yoront culture it is necessary to be aware of a system of ideas which may be called their totemic ideology. A fundamental belief of the aboriginal divided time into two great epochs: (1) a distant and sacred period at the beginning of the world when the earth was peopled by mildly marvelous ancestral beings or culture heroes who are in a special sense the forebears of the clans; and (2) a period when the old was succeeded by a new order which includes the present. Originally there was no anticipation of another era supplanting the present. The future would simply be an eternal continuation and reproduction of the present which itself had remained unchanged since the epochal revolution of ancestral times.

The important thing to note is that the aboriginal believed that the present world, as a natural and cultural environment, was and should be simply a detailed reproduction of the world of the ancestors. He believed that the entire universe "is now as it was in the beginning" when it was established and left by the ancestors. The ordinary cultural life of the ancestors became the daily life of the Yir Yoront camps, and the extraordinary life of the ancestors remained extant in the recurring symbolic pantomimes and paraphernalia found only in the most sacred atmosphere of the totemic rites.

Such beliefs, accordingly, opened the way for ideas of what *should be* (because it supposedly *was*) to influence or help determine what actually *is*. A man called Dog-chases-iguana-up-a-tree-and-barks-at-him-all-night had that and other names because he believed his ancestral alter ego had also had them; he was a member of the Sunlit Cloud Iguana clan because his ancestor was; he was associated with particular countries and totems of this same ancestor; during an initiation he played the role of a dog and symbolically attacked and killed certain members of other clans because his ancestor (conveniently either anthropomorphic or kynomorphic) really did the same to the ancestral alter egos of these men; and he would avoid his mother-in-law, joke with a mother's distant brother, and make spears in a certain way because his and other people's ancestors did these things. His behavior in these specific ways was outlined, and to that extent determined for him, by a set of ideas concerning the past and the relation of the present to the past.

But when we are informed that Dog-chases-etc. had two wives from the Spear Black Duck clan and one from the Native Companion clan, one of them being blind, that he had four children with such and such names, that he had a broken wrist and was left handed, all because his ancestor had exactly these same attributes, then we know (though he apparently didn't) that the present has influenced the past, that the mythical world has been somewhat adjusted to meet the exigencies and accidents of the inescapably real present.

There was thus in Yir Yoront ideology a nice balance in which the mythical was adjusted in part to the real world, the real world in part to the ideal pre-existing mythical world, the adjustments occurring to maintain a fundamental tenet of native faith that the present must be a mirror of the past. Thus the stone axe in all its aspects, uses, and associations was integrated into the context of Yir Yoront technology and conduct because a myth, a set of ideas, had put it there.

IV   The Outcome

The introduction of the steel axe indiscriminately and in large numbers into the Yir Yoront technology occurred simultaneously with many other changes. It is therefore impossible to separate all the results of this single innovation. Nevertheless, a number of specific effects of the change from stone to steel axes may be noted, and the steel axe may be used as an epitome of the increasing quantity of European goods and implements received by the aboriginals and of their general influence on the native culture. The use of the steel axe to illustrate such influences would seem to be justified. It was one of the first European artifacts to be adopted for regular use by the Yir Yoront, and whether made of stone or steel, the axe was clearly one of the most important items of cultural equipment they possessed.

The shift from stone to steel axes provided no major technological difficulties. While the aboriginals themselves could not manufacture steel axe heads, a steady supply from outside continued; broken wooden handles could easily be replaced from bush timbers with aboriginal tools. Among the Yir Yoront the new axe was never used to the extent it was on mission or cattle stations (for carpentry work, pounding tent pegs, as a hammer, and so on); indeed, it had so few more uses than the stone axe that its practical effect on the native standard of living was negligible. It did some jobs better, and could be used longer without breakage. These factors were sufficient to make it of value to the native. The white man believed that a shift from steel to stone axe on his part would be a definite regression. He was convinced that his axe was much more efficient, that its use would save time, and that it therefore represented technical "progress" towards goals which he had set up for the native. But this assumption was hardly borne out in aboriginal practice. Any leisure time the Yir Yoront might gain by using steel axes or other western tools was not invested in "improving the conditions of life," nor, certainly, in developing aesthetic activities, but in sleep—an art they had mastered thoroughly.

Previously, a man in need of an axe would acquire a stone axe head through regular trading partners from whom he knew what to expect, and was then dependent solely upon a known and adequate natural environment, and his own skills or easily acquired techniques. A man wanting a steel axe, however, was in no such self-reliant position. If he attended a mission festival when steel axes were handed out as gifts, he might receive one either by chance or by happening to impress upon the mission staff that he was one of the "better" bush aboriginals (the missionaries definition of "better" being quite different from that of his bush fellows). Or, again almost by pure chance, he might get some brief job in connection with the mission which would enable him to earn a steel axe. In either case, for older men a preference for the steel axe helped change the situation from one of self-reliance to one of dependence, and a shift in behavior from well-structured or defined situations in technology or conduct to ill-defined situations in conduct alone. Among the men, the older ones whose earlier experience or knowledge of the white man's harshness made them suspicious were particularly careful to avoid having relations with the mission, and thus excluded themselves from acquiring steel axes from that source.

In other aspects of conduct or social relations, the steel axe was even more significantly at the root of psychological stress among the Yir Yoront. This was the result of new factors which the missionary considered beneficial: the simple numerical increase in axes per capita as a result of mission distribution, and distribution directly to younger men, women, and even children. By winning the favor of the mission staff, a woman might be given a steel axe which was clearly intended to be hers, thus creating a situation quite different from the previous custom which necessitated her borrowing an axe from a male relative. As a result a woman would refer to the axe as "mine," a possessive form she was never able to use of the stone axe. In the same fashion, young men or even boys also obtained steel axes directly from the mission, with the result that older men no longer had a complete monopoly of all the axes in the bush community. All this led to a revolutionary confusion of sex, age, and kinship roles, with a major gain in independence and loss of subordination on the part of those who now owned steel axes when they had previously been unable to possess stone axes.

The trading partner relationship was also affected by the new situation. A Yir Yoront might have a trading partner in a tribe to the south whom he defined as a younger brother and over whom he would therefore have some authority. But if the partner were in contact with the mission or had other access to steel axes, his subordination obviously decreased. Among other things, this took some of the excitement away from the dry season fiesta-like tribal gatherings centering around initiations. These had traditionally been the climactic annual occasions for exchanges between trading partners, when a man might seek to acquire a whole year's supply of stone axe heads. Now he might find himself prostituing his wife to almost total strangers in return for steel axes or other white man's goods. With trading partnerships weakened, there was less reason to attend the ceremonies, and less fun for those who did.

Not only did an increase in steel axes and their distribution to women change the character of the relations between individuals (the paired relationships that have been noted), but a previously rare type of relationship was created in the Yir Yoront's conduct towards whites. In the aboriginal society there were few occasions outside of the immediate family when an individual would initiate action to several other people at once. In any average group, in accordance with the kinship system, while a person might be superordinate to several people to whom he could suggest or command action, he was also subordinate to several others with whom such behavior would be tabu. There was thus no overall chieftainship or authoritarian leadership of any kind. Such complicated operations as grass-burning animal drives or totemic ceremonies could be carried out smoothly because each person was aware of his role.

On both mission and cattle stations, however, the whites imposed their conception of leadership roles upon the aboriginals, consisting of one person in a controlling relationship with a subordinate group. Aboriginals called together to receive gifts, including axes, at a mission Christmas party found themselves facing one or two whites who sought to control their behavior for the occasion, who disregarded the age, sex, and kinship variables of which the aboriginals were so conscious, and who considered them all at one subordinate level. The white also sought to impose similar patterns on work parties. (However, if he placed an aboriginal in charge of a mixed group of post-hole diggers, for example, half of the group, those subordinate to the "boss," would work while the other half, who were superordinate to him, would sleep.) For the aboriginal, the steel axe and other European goods came to symbolize this new and uncomfortable form of social organization, the leader-group relationship.

The most disturbing effects of the steel axe, operating in conjunction with other elements also being introduced from the white man's several sub-cultures, developed in the realm of traditional ideas, sentiments, and values. These were undermined at a rapidly mounting rate, with no new conceptions being defined to replace them. The result was the erection of a mental and moral void which foreshadowed the collapse and destruction of all Yir Yoront culture, if not, indeed, the extinction of the biological group itself.

From what has been said it should be clear how changes in overt behavior, in technology and conduct, weakened the values inherent in a reliance on nature, in the prestige of masculinity and of age, and in the various kinship relations. A scene was set in which a wife, or a young son whose initiation may not yet have been completed, need no longer defer to the husband or father who, in turn, became confused and insecure as he was forced to borrow a steel axe from them. For the woman and boy the steel axe helped establish a new degree of freedom which they accepted readily as an escape from the unconscious stress of the old patterns—but they, too, were left confused and insecure. Ownership became less well defined with the result that stealing and trespassing were introduced into technology and conduct. Some of the excitement surrounding the great ceremonies evaporated and they lost their previous gaiety and interest. Indeed, life itself became less interesting, although this did not lead the Yir Yoront to discover suicide, a concept foreign to them.

The whole process may be most specifically illustrated in terms of totemic system, which also illustrates the significant role played by a system of ideas, in this case a totemic ideology, in the breakdown of a culture.

In the first place, under pre-European aboriginal conditions where the native culture has become adjusted to a relatively stable environment, few, if any, unheard of or catastrophic crises can occur. It is clear, therefore, that the totemic system serves very effectively in inhibiting radical cultural changes. The closed system of totemic ideas, explaining and categorizing a well-known universe as it was fixed at the beginning of time, presents a considerable obstacle to the adoption of new or the dropping of old culture traits. The obstacle is not insurmountable and the system allows for the minor variations which occur in the norms of daily life. But the inception of major changes cannot easily take place.

Among the bush Yir Yoront the only means of water transport is a light wood log to which they cling in their constant swimming of rivers, salt creeks, and tidal inlets. These natives know that tribes 45 miles further north have a bark canoe. They know these northern tribes can thus fish from midstream or out at sea, instead of clinging to the river banks and beaches, that they can cross coastal waters infested with crocodiles, sharks, sting rays, and Portuguese men-of-war without danger. They know the materials of which the canoe is made exist in their own environment. But they also know, as they say, that they do not have canoes because their own mythical ancestors did not have them. They assume that the canoe was part of the ancestral universe of the northern tribes. For them, then, the adoption of the canoe would not be simply a matter of learning a number of new behavioral skills for its manufacture and use. The adoption would require a much more difficult procedure; the acceptance by the entire society of a myth, either locally developed or borrowed, to explain the presence of the canoe, to associate it with some one or more of the several hundred mythical ancestors (and how decide which?), and thus establish it as an accepted totem of one of the clans ready to be used by the whole community. The Yir Yoront have not made this adjustment, and in this case we can only say that for the time being at least, ideas have won out over very real pressures for technological change. In the elaborateness and explicitness of the totemic ideologies we seem to have one explanation for the notorious stability of Australian cultures under aboriginal conditions, an explanation which gives due weight to the importance of ideas in determining human behavior.

At a later stage of the contact situation, as has been indicated, phenomena unaccounted for by the totemic ideological system begin to appear with regularity and frequency and remain within the range of native experience. Accordingly, they cannot be ignored (as the "Battle of the Mitchell" was apparently ignored), and there is an attempt to assimilate them and account for them along the lines of principles inherent in the ideology. The bush Yir Yoront of the mid-thirties represent this stage of the acculturation process. Still trying to maintain their aboriginal definition of the situation, they accept European artifacts and behavior patterns, but fit them into their totemic system, assigning them to various clans on a par with original totems. There is an attempt to have the myth-making process keep up with these cultural changes so that the idea system can continue to support the rest of the culture. But analysis of overt behavior, of dreams, and of some of the new myths indicates that this arrangement is not entirely satisfactory, that the native clings to his totemic system with intellectual loyalty (lacking any substitute ideology, but that associated sentiments and values are weakened. His attitudes towards his own and towards European culture are found to be highly ambivalent.

All ghosts are totems of the Head-to-the-East Corpse clan, are thought of as white, and are of course closely associated with death. The white man, too, is closely associated with death, and he and all things pertaining to him are naturally assigned to the Corpse clan as totems. The steel axe, as a totem, was thus associated with the Corpse clan. But as an "axe," clearly linked with the stone axe, it is a totem of the Sunlit Cloud Iguana clan. Moreover, the steel axe, like most European goods, has no distinctive origin myth, nor are mythical ancestors associated with it. Can anyone, sitting in the shade of a *ti* tree one afternoon, create a myth to resolve this confusion? No one has, and the horrid suspicion arises as to the authenticity of the origin myths, which failed to take into account this vast new universe of the white man. The steel axe, shifting hopelessly between one clan and the other, is not only replacing the stone axe physically, but is hacking at the supports of the entire cultural system.

The aboriginals to the south of the Yir Yoront have clearly passed beyond this stage. They are engulfed by European culture, either by the mission or cattle station sub-cultures or, for some natives, by a baffling, paradoxical combination of both incongruent varieties. The totemic ideology can no longer support the inrushing mass of foreign culture traits, and the myth-making process in its native form breaks down completely. Both intellectually and emotionally a saturation point is reached so that the myriad new traits which can neither be ignored nor any longer assimilated simply force the aboriginal to abandon his totemic system. With the collapse of this system of ideas, which is so closely related to so many other aspects of the native culture, there follows an appallingly sudden and complete cultural disintegration, and a demoralization of the individual such as has seldom been recorded elsewhere. Without the support of a system of ideas well devised to provide cultural stability in a stable environment, but admittedly too rigid for the new realities pressing in from outside, native behavior and native sentiments and values are simply dead. Apathy reigns. The aboriginal has passed beyond the realm of any outsider who might wish to do him well or ill.

Returning from the broken natives huddled on cattle stations or on the fringes of frontier towns to the ambivalent but still lively aboriginals settled on the Mitchell River mission, we note one further devious result of the introduction of European artifacts. During a wet season stay at the mission, the anthropologist discovered that his supply of tooth paste was being depleted at an alarming rate. Investigation showed that it was being taken by old men for use in a new tooth paste cult. Old materials of magic having failed, new materials were being tried out in a malevolent magic directed towards the mission staff and some of the younger aboriginal men. Old males, largely ignored by the missionaries, were seeking to regain some of their lost power and prestige. This mild aggression proved hardly effective, but perhaps only because confidence in any kind of magic on the mission was by this time at a low ebb.

For the Yir Yoront still in the bush, a time could be predicted when personal deprivation and frustration in a confused culture would produce an overload of anxiety. The mythical past of the totemic ancestors would disappear as a guarantee of a present of which the future was supposed to be a stable continuation. Without the past, the present could be meaningless and the future unstructured and uncertain. Insecurities would be inevitable. Reaction to this stress might be some form of symbolic aggression, or withdrawal and apathy, or some more realistic approach. In such a situation the missionary with understanding of the processes going on about him would find his opportunity to introduce his forms of religion and to help create a new cultural universe.

22 TIWI MARRIAGE

C. W. M. Hart and Arnold R. Pilling

Cultural Isolation

People who live in the congested cities and towns of the modern world have difficulty in realizing how different life can be at the hunting and gathering level of human existence. The basic fact about the life of hunters and gatherers is the thinly spread-out manner in which they live and the isolation of families and households from each other. In the case of the Tiwi, these conditions of isolation and dispersal were accentuated by their island habitat. Melville and Bathurst Islands lie off the northern coast of Australia some fifty to eighty miles from Darwin, which is the administrative capital of the empty north. They are separated from the mainland by about twenty-five miles of open sea at the narrowest part. This distance is slightly greater than the distance that separates England from France at the Straits of Dover, and just as the dim outline of coastal France can be seen from England on clear days, so the dim outline of the Australian mainland can be seen from the southern edges of the islands. However, Tiwi tradition is firm and certain that before the white man's arrival there was no contact between the islands and the mainland. To them, the dimly seen coastline of Australia was *Tibambinumi*, the home of the dead, to which all Tiwi souls went after death. It follows from this that they regarded the inhabited world as composed of their own two islands, and on those islands they lived a self-contained and exclusive existence. Occasionally outsiders appeared, either castaways from surrounding areas, including presumably the Australian mainland, and in recent centuries, fishing boats and pirates from Indonesia, loosely called "Malays" in the literature. To such visitors from outside, the Tiwi were consistently and implacably hostile. Their own traditions and what little written history there is of "Malay" penetration into the Arafura Sea both tell the same story. Outsiders who landed on the islands were massacred or vigorously resisted. Whether they were classified as *Malai-ui* ("Malays") or *Wona-rui* (Australian aborigines from the mainland) they were not Tiwi and hence not real people, or at least not human enough to share the islands with the chosen people who owned them.

Thus, the word "Tiwi" did not mean "people" in the sense of all human beings, but rather "we, the only people," or the chosen people who live on and own the islands, as distinct from any other alleged human beings who might show up from time to time on the beaches. This exclusion of outsiders from real "us-ness" and hence from real "human-ness" was continued when the Europeans began to arrive in the early nineteenth century, and certainly as late as 1930 the Tiwi continued to call and think of themselves as Tiwi, *the* people, and to use other words for all non-Tiwi, whether they were mainland aborigines, Malay fishermen, Japanese pearl-divers, French priests, or British officials, who penetrated into their exclusive little cosmos.

Their firm tradition that the twenty-five miles of ocean were adequate to isolate them from the mainland is confirmed by certain objective distributional evidence. Several characteristic features of mainland native technology were absent on Melville and Bathurst Islands, notably the spear thrower and the curved (or return) boomerang. To anthropologists, the idea of an Australian tribe lacking spear throwers and curved boomerangs is almost a contradiction in terms, and the only feasible explanation is isolation and hence failure of these mainland traits to diffuse to the islands.[1]

That no culture stands absolutely still in its technology no matter how isolated it may be is suggested by the fact that the Tiwi, while lacking the spear thrower and curved boomerang of the mainland, elaborated their wooden spears to a complexity of design and a degree of decoration unknown on the mainland, and also developed a much greater assortment of straight throwing sticks, made of hardwood, than any mainland tribe. Moreover, their carved and elaborately painted grave posts are unique among Australian tribes, and point up both the Tiwi isolation from the mainland and the favorable food situation which permitted the leisure time necessary to manufacture the elaborate posts as well as the elaborate ceremonial spears. In the nontechnological aspects of their culture we find in many respects the same absence of mainland traits and the same elaboration of traits that were distinctively or even uniquely Tiwi. Male initiation ceremonies on the mainland focus upon circumcision or subincision or both; neither custom was practiced by the Tiwi, who instead included in their initiation ritual the forcible plucking out of the pubic hair of the novice. The degree of plural marriages achieved under their marriage rules was far greater than anything reported for the mainland; the absolute prohibition of any female, regardless of age, being without a husband was unknown elsewhere in Australia; certain features of the kinship system fail to conform to any of the mainland norms, and so on. Wherever we look in their culture we get the strong impression of an Australian tribe that was able to develop within the general Australian type of culture a number of distinct features, some of them unique, while at the same time lacking entirely other features which were widespread on the mainland. Tiwi isolation from the mainland explains the differences and the lacks; their favorable environment explains why they were able to develop certain traits along their own unique lines.

The Tribe and the Bands

Because they were isolated and few outsiders came near them, they did very little as a united tribe. Everybody on the two islands was a Tiwi, and the Tiwi world stopped at the water's edge. Fuzziness on the edges of tribal terri-

---

[1] A toy spear thrower, played with by children, was in use, but this may be the result of post-white contact. Its native name—*pani*—seems most un-Tiwi, and a likely guess is that it was introduced by Cooper's mainlanders, being accepted as a toy for children but scorned as childish by the adult men.

tory—a chronic headache to anthropologists working with mainland tribes—did not exist, nor did the problem of marriage outside the tribe. All Tiwi, of course, spoke the same language and practiced the same customs and regarded themselves as *the* people; these were almost the only respects in which they could be said to do anything as a tribal unit. There was no tribal government, there were no tribal officials, and no occasions which required the whole tribe to assemble together as a collective entity. For daily and yearly living, the important group was the band or horde,[2] of which there were nine. The total area of the two islands is about 3000 square miles, but some of this is swampy, some of it waterless, some of it mosquito-infested mangrove jungle, and the suitability of the rest for native living varies a good deal. Hence, the actively used and lived-in areas for each band probably averaged about two hundred square miles each and, in any case, there was not a very close relationship between band size and area occupied. Details of band size at various times are given in a later chapter, but, typically, Tiwi bands probably varied in size between a hundred and three hundred people.

The band was the territorial group with which a man most closely identified himself. Though the band lived from day to day spread out over a wide area and a man might not see many of his fellow band-members for weeks at a time, the average Tiwi thought of the two or three hundred square miles of band territory as his "own country" and of his fellow members as his own people. This is why the tribal name—Tiwi—so seldom needed to be used at home on the islands. It did not identify one group as distinct from another, since all locals were Tiwi. Just as in a New York suburb one does not say that there are some Americans in the house next door, but may say that there are some Texans or some Californians or some people from Michigan next door, so a Tiwi, seeing a group of visitors arriving in his band territory, would immediately identify them as Malauila or Rangwila or by whatever band they belonged to. A father would say casually, "I have betrothed my daughter to a Tiklauila" or "My wife is a Munupula woman"; a mourner would say, "He died when visiting the Munupula and therefore we will have to go to Munupi for the funeral"; an old man would reminisce about being brought up as a youth by his mother's brother, who was a Turupula, and the good times he had in Turupi; and another would recount details of big battles between the Munupula and the Malauila. All of these were band names or band territories. The nine bands thus acted, psychologically, as small tribelets or semisovereign groups, since it was with one of them that every Tiwi most closely identified in his day-to-day life on the islands. It is only when, as nowadays, he leaves the islands to go to work for the white man in Darwin that he has to think of himself as a Tiwi, since there he mingles with men of other tribes. Even then,

[2] Radcliffe-Brown, the great authority on Australian tribal society, tried to introduce the word "horde" for the Australian local group, but probably because of its suggestion to the popular mind of a dense concentration of people, it has never become established and in these pages we have used the more neutral word "band."

work and residence in the white man's town does not entirely obliterate band identification. A Tiklauila in Darwin prefers to work with and to consort in the evenings with other Tiklauila, and Malauila with Malauila.[3]

Because of certain peculiar features of Tiwi domestic life, to be discussed below, it is difficult to sum up the Tiwi band in any simple formula. People, especially women, changed their band residence frequently in the course of their lives, and being born into a band did not at all require permanent residence with that band, either for males or for females. Thus the district (for example, Tiklaru or Malau) was a firm, fixed, known quantity, but the people who "owned" the district (for example, Tiklauila or Malauila) were a flexible and constantly shifting collection of individuals.

The territorial boundaries between bands were clear and well known to everybody, though they were not the sharp lines on a map such as we regard as essential for a frontier or a land boundary. All pieces of country—clumps of jungle, stretches of grassland, sections of thick woods—had names. One such piece of country, say a thickly wooded area, belonged to one band, while the more open country that began where the woods thinned out belonged to another; thus the boundary was not a sharp line but a transitional zone— perhaps of several miles—where the change from trees to open savannah became noticeable, with the band territories thus fusing into one another rather than being separated by sharp lines. The Tiwi, so to speak, thought of the landscape as a sort of spectrum where a man moved gradually out of one district into another as he passed from one type of horizon to the next. Since rivers, and even Apsley Strait, a very narrow arm of the sea separating Melville from Bathurst Island, usually have similar types of vegetation on *both* sides or banks, none of the island rivers nor Apsley Strait was a boundary or frontier between bands. The Mandiimbula, predominantly a Melville Island tribe, owned also the country on the opposite side of Apsley Strait at the southeast corner of Bathurst, while the Malauila, the band in the northern half of Bathurst Island, conversely overlapped their ownership across the strait to take in a thin strip of coastline on the northwest corner of Melville.

These details illustrate the fact that the band was the land-owning, workaday, territorially organized group which controlled the hunting, the food supply, and the warfare. Until the white man arrived in force in the coastal waters of North Australia, the average Tiwi regarded the nine bands as the main functional units of his existence, and his loyalty to and identification with his band were given much greater opportunity for exercise than any loyalty to or identification

---

[3] In the early 1930's the situation at the Government Hospital in Darwin offered a good illustration of this. The hospital authorities said they gave preference for house-boy jobs to "Melville Islanders because of their greater intelligence and reliability." In point of fact, some of the younger Tiklauila had established a monopoly on hospital jobs and no Tiwi other than a Tiklauila was ever hired there. The whites thought they were hiring Tiwi but the Tiklauila saw to it that they hired only Tiklauila and felt no vestige of obligation to other Tiwi to help them get these desirable jobs. The alleged greater intelligence of the islanders was undoubtedly due to the fact that the Tiklauila, having had a Catholic mission in their territory since 1911, were more used to white requirements.

with the whole Tiwi tribe. He did many things as a member of a band, but he did little as a member of a tribe. Only when an outsider turned up did he need to think of himself as a Tiwi, and outsiders were very rare. For the rest of the time he thought of himself as a member of his band, thought of his band as his people, and of his band territory as his country.

The Household

Since the band consisted of anything from one hundred to three hundred people, it could not live together in one place, except for very short periods of time. Hunting and gathering in almost any part of the world (except the north-west coast of America in pre-white times) require the human population to disperse itself very thinly over the countryside and live from day to day in small hunting and camping units. Such small primary groups are usually in one sense families and in another sense households, and this is the case among the Tiwi. We propose to call such units households rather than families for reasons that will soon become apparent. It is true that Tiwi "houses," especially in the long dry season (from March to October), were the flimsiest and most temporary of structures, but the group of people in question was the group who lived together day after day, hunted as a unit, pooled the results of their food getting, and ate and slept together. Functionally this group is identical with an American household, even though the "house" they used was nothing more than a few piled-up tree branches, used as shelter for a night or two and then abandoned. Like the American household also, the Tiwi household usually consisted of a man, his wife (or wives), and their children, though in many would also be included a few leftovers or extras, common to all cultures, such as bachelor uncles, visiting cousins, ancient widowers, and ambiguous "men who came to dinner" and were still there. (Tiwi households did not, however, include maiden aunts, female orphans, or ancient widows, since these could not exist in Tiwi culture.)

Thus the Tiwi household was more or less the same thing as the Tiwi family group, but Tiwi family organization had such a number of unusual twists that we find it desirable to insist upon calling such a group the household rather than the family. There was no ambiguity about its "living together" aspect; there were many ambiguities about its kinship aspects. To some of these unusual domestic usages we now turn.

Marriage by Betrothal

In many nonliterate societies, including most, if not all of the mainland Australian tribes, there is a tendency to believe that the main purpose in life for a female is to get married. The Tiwi subscribed to this idea, but firmly carried it to its logical conclusion; namely, that all females must get married, regardless of age, condition, or inclination. They (and they almost alone among human societies) took the very slight step from saying "All females *should* be married" to saying "All females *must* be married." As a result, in aboriginal times there was no concept of an unmarried female in Tiwi ideology, no word for such a condition in their language, and in fact, no female in the population without at least a nominal husband. Their own explanation of this unique situation was connected with their beliefs about conception and where babies come from. Anthropologists have long been aware that the Australian aborigines generally (and indeed some of the Melanesians, such as the famous case of the Trobriand Islands) ignored the role of the male in human conception and firmly believed that a woman becomes pregnant because a spirit has entered into her body. The Tiwi were no exception, but went a step further than the mainlanders in dealing with the dangerous situation created by the unpredictability of the spirits. Since any female was liable to be impregnated by a spirit at any time, the sensible step was to insist that every female have a husband *all the time* so that if she did become pregnant, the child would always have a father. As a result of this logical thinking, all Tiwi babies were betrothed before or as soon as they were born; females were thus the "wives" of their betrothed husbands from the moment of birth onward. For similar reasons, widows were required to remarry at the gravesides of their late husbands, and this rule applied even to ancient hags who had already buried half a dozen previous husbands in the course of a long life. It can readily be seen that these rules—prenatal betrothal of female infants and immediate remarriage of all widows—effectively eliminated all possibility of an unmarried female from Tiwi society. They also eliminated any possibility of an unmarried mother or a fatherless child. No matter where the unpredictable spirit chose to create a baby, whether it was in the body of a pretty young woman, a toothless old hag, or a little girl of six or seven, the pregnant female would have a husband, and the children when born would have a father. The Tiwi were thus probably the only society in the world with an illegitimacy rate of zero.

The practical application of these two unusual rules had certain unusual consequences. The rule of prenatal betrothal obviously gave a great deal of power to the person with the right to betroth, and in Tiwi this right belonged to the husband of the pregnant woman. We carefully say "the husband of the pregnant woman" rather than "the father of the child" because the right resided in the male head of the household at the time of the birth. Although he was ordinarily both the father of the child and the husband of its mother, there were naturally occasions when a child was born after the death of its father, in which case the right of betrothal unquestionably belonged to the mother's new husband. The clearest statement of this rule is to say that the right of betrothal of all newly born females resided in the husband of the mother at the time of the girl's birth. "He who named the child bestowed it."

In most human societies the proportion of males and females in the population is approximately equal, except in the older age-groups where women predominate owing to their tendency to live longer than men. The Tiwi conformed to this norm biologically, but their cultural insistence that all females of every age be married resulted in further unusual features of the domestic situation.

No such compulsory marriage was required or expected of males. Hence, the total female population, but only part of the male population, was married. Mathematically this permitted, indeed required, a high degree of plural marriage. The men who held the right to betroth—namely, the fathers of the female babies—could, within certain limits imposed by the kinship system, bestow their about-to-be-born or newly born daughters where they wished, and they certainly did not bestow them on about-to-be-born or newly born males. On the contrary, they bestowed them, generally speaking, where some tangible return was to be anticipated. Put bluntly, in Tiwi culture daughters were an asset to their father, and he invested these assets in his own welfare. He therefore bestowed his newly born daughter on a friend or an ally, or on somebody he wanted as a friend or an ally. Such a person was apt to be a man near his own age or at least an adult man, and hence perhaps forty years or so older than the newly born baby bestowed upon him as a wife. Or, the father might bestow an infant daughter on a man—or some close relative of such a man— who had already bestowed an infant daughter upon him, thus in effect swapping infant daughters. Obviously, the fathers who did the swapping, even if they were not quite the same age themselves, were bound to be many years older than the infant wives they thus received from each other. Or, thirdly, a father looking for a suitable male upon whom to bestow his infant daughter's hand might decide to use her as old-age insurance—in which case he selected as her future husband not one of the older adult men who would be old when he himself was old, but a likely looking youngster "with promise"; that is, a youth in his late twenties or thirties who showed signs of being a good hunter and a good fighting man, and who was clearly on his way up in tribal power and influence. Such a youth, in his late twenties at the time of betrothal, would, with luck, be in his prime as "a big man" in about twenty years—a time when the father of the infant daughter would be getting old and decrepit and much in need of an influential son-in-law who was obligated to him.

There were other bases upon which infant daughters were betrothed, and indeed the father was seldom an entirely free agent, since he not only had to make his choices for his daughters within the limits imposed by the kinship system, but he was also caught in an intricate network of previous commitments, residual interests, and contingent promises made by other men who had had some prior interest in the baby or the mother of the baby. To mention only the most common limiting situation of this sort, the mother of the baby might have been given to him in the first place on the understanding that when she grew up and had a female baby it was to be bestowed on so-and-so or even returned as a *quid pro quo* to its mother's father, either as wife or as ward.

We have oversimplified the situation, but it should be clear that Tiwi fathers, in an overwhelming number of cases, bestowed their infant daughters on husbands a great deal older than those daughters. It is hard to strike an average, but the overall situation is best expressed by saying that no Tiwi father, except in the most unusual cases, ever thought of bestowing an infant daughter upon any male below the age of at least twenty-five. Taking this lowest limit for illustration, this meant that a youth of twenty-five had his first wife betrothed or promised to him at that age but had to wait another fourteen years or so before she was old enough to leave her father's household and take up residence and marriage duties with him. By this time he was about forty and she was fourteen. An age gap between husband and wife at least as great as this, but usually greater, was a necessary and constant result of the Tiwi betrothal system.

No Tiwi young man, then, could expect to obtain his first resident wife through betrothal until he was well into his thirties, at which time this first resident wife would be around fourteen, having been betrothed to him at her birth or before. But it was likely that his first wife's father, who spotted him in his twenties as a "comer," was not the only older man to want him as a son-in-law. As in our own culture, where the first million is the hardest to make, so in Tiwi the first bestowed wife was the hardest to get. If some shrewd father with a daughter to invest in a twenty-year-old decided to invest her in you, his judgment was likely to attract other fathers to make a similar invest-ment. As a result, for *some* Tiwi men, the arrival in residence of the first wife, an event for which they had to wait until their late thirties, was quickly followed by the arrival in residence of a second, third, and fourth (at least), all of them bestowed very shortly after the bestowal of the first. Thus a successful Tiwi, having had no resident wife at all until his late thirties, would accumulate perhaps half a dozen between his late thirties and his late forties as his various betrothed wives reached the age of puberty and joined his household, and from then on he was practically certain to accumulate still more wives as later bestowals grew up and as he was able to invest the daughters borne by his first crop of young wives in transactions which brought in a later crop.

That this is not an exaggerated or overdrawn picture of the number of wives that could be accumulated in the course of a long life by a successful Tiwi household head is shown by the genealogies of the grandfathers of the present generation. Turimpi, who was born in the 1830's and died in the early 1900's, was at his death the most powerful old man among the Tiklauila. Some of his sons are still alive, and all of them were in the prime of life around 1930.[4] A complete list of Turimpi's wives, not all of them living in his house-hold at the same time or necessarily alive at the same time, contains more than twenty names. But Turimpi was outshone in this regard by several of his con-temporaries in other bands. A prominent Turupula of the same generation had a list of twenty-five; the father of Finger of the Wilrangwila had twenty-nine; the father of Tamboo and Puti had twenty-two. As late as 1930, men with lists of ten, eleven, and twelve wives were still plentiful, and Tu'untalumi, who was aged about seventy in that year and was a man of great influence, had by then accumulated no less than twenty-one.[5]

---

[4] See Hart 1954.
[5] Finger, Tamboo, and Puti were elders prominent in tribal affairs at the time of Hart's fieldwork. Puti was still alive in 1953–54 and well known to Pilling. Tu'untalumi, held in great affection by Hart, but anathema to the Mission Station, died in 1935.

Such numbers of wives as these per husband are very much higher than usually prevail even among the most polygynous hunting tribes. Obviously, a domestic unit with twelve or more wives in it makes for a very large household. Among the Tiwi, a household even of such men as those just named did not contain all these wives at the same time, mainly because of the very great variation in the ages of a man's wives. As far as bestowed or betrothed wives were concerned, such wives arrived at their husband's household to take up wifely duties therein when they reached the age of about fourteen. Hence the first of them to arrive (typically when their husband was nearly forty) would be women of nearly forty by the time the latest of them arrived (typically when the husband was well into his sixties). Even when the husband died, let us say at the ripe old age of seventy-five, there would probably be some of his bestowed wives still under the age of fourteen who were as yet too young to join his household. Tu'untalumi, the man of twenty-one wives, was already about seventy in 1930, yet in his list of twenty-one wives five were still *ali'inga*— that is, little girls not yet approaching puberty—and two were still babies at their mothers' breast. On the other hand, some of his earliest bestowed wives, who had taken up residence with him when he was in his late thirties, were already dead.

Because of this wide variation in the ages of a man's wives, it is necessary to distinguish between a "list" of a man's wives and those actually in residence in his household at any given time. The resident or active wives—one might almost say the working wives—were always fewer than the listed wives. This would necessarily be so even if marriage by betrothal were the only way by which a Tiwi man could obtain a wife. But while it was the most prestigeful form of marriage and the only respectable way in which a man could obtain a *young* wife, there were other ways of setting up a household. The most important way is one which we have already mentioned—namely, widow remarriage.

Widow Remarriage

To become "a big man" a Tiwi had, among other things, to accumulate a lot of wives. This required time, in addition to everything else. A rising star who accumulated by bestowal seven or eight wives by his middle forties and then died, merely left a lot of widows to be redistributed at his graveside, and by the process of wealth attracting more wealth, or capital creating more capital, these widows were most likely to be redistributed among his rivals and competitors of his own age group or among men even older than he. Hence, the largest number of wives ultimately accrued to the successful man who lived longest, since he was likely to gather up at least a few of the widows of each of his contemporaries or seniors as they predeceased him.

There was thus a close correlation between increasing age and the number of wives a man had, and the largest households belonged to a few surviving old men in each band. The two conditions, therefore, which were necessary to accumulate a large household were (1) to attract prospective fathers-in-law to invest their infant daughters in you while you were a young man, and then

(2) to live long enough to reap the dividends. The longer you lived, the more dividends would accrue to you from one source or another, provided you started off right by attracting betrothals in your twenties and thirties.

But what about the unimpressive young men, the "noncomers," who somehow failed as young men to attract any prospective fathers-in-law to invest an infant daughter in them? As we have seen, even the most highly regarded and well-connected Tiwi young man had to wait until his late thirties or longer before his first bestowed wife was old enough to join him in domestic bliss, but at least while waiting he knew the time was coming. The overlooked or unbetrothed young man had no such prospects. Since the only source of supply of new females was through the birth of female infants whose hands only their fathers could bestow, it would appear as if a young Tiwi male overlooked or ignored by all fathers of bestowable daughters had no alternative except permanent bachelorhood. Doubtless Tiwi fathers, as a class, would have regarded this as an ideal situation and would have said that permanent bachelorhood was a proper fate for such friendless and hence useless young men, but no social system of such rigidity has ever been discovered by anthropologists. Tiwi fathers were able rigidly to control the marriages of their infant daughters, but they were not able to control with the same rigidity the remarriages of their own widows, and it was widow remarriage that supplied the loophole in the system, or the cultural alternative that took care of young men.

A Tiwi husband was unavoidably and necessarily always much older than a bestowed wife. Therefore he usually died much earlier than she. A girl of fourteen who entered into residence with her first husband when he was fifty was likely to be left a widow by him within the next fifteen years, and even if she remarried a man of the same age as her first husband, she could easily be widowed for the second time while still herself a comparatively young woman. There were several different patterns, most of them intermingled in the same household, for a female matrimonial career, but the situation may be illustrated by the concrete case of one of Turimpi's widows, an ancient crone (in 1930) named Bongdadu. Born about 1865, she was betrothed at birth to a powerful old man named Walitaumi who was at least the same age as her father, if not older. Not unnaturally, he died while she was still a child and well before she was old enough to join his household. Her betrothal was then reassigned, so to speak, to Walitaumi's half-brother, Turimpi, then in his early forties. About seven years later, she joined Turimpi's household as a blushing bride of fourteen, her husband then being close to fifty. In the next twenty years she became Turimpi's most prolific wife and bore numerous children, three of whom, Antonio, Mariano, and Louis, all born between 1883 and 1900, were men of importance in Tiwi politics in 1930, and one of whom, Louis, is still alive today.[6]

---

[6] Tiwi personal names are polysyllabic and hard for the reader to remember; hence, wherever possible, we have used "whiteman names" for individuals. The frequency of Spanish names among these "whiteman names," such as Mariano or Dominico, derives from the fact that the original buildings for the Mission Station were built by a number of Filipino workmen whom the priests brought with them.

Around 1900, when Bongdadu was still only about thirty-five, she passed to M., a middle-aged Tiklauila, and was his wife until his death around 1925. By this date, Bongdadu was over sixty and had borne ten children, four of whom died young. Not unnaturally, she was beginning to approach the hag or crone stage of Tiwi womanhood. Nonetheless, she had to remarry, but by now all of the people who might have claimed any rights of bestowal in her were long since dead, her eldest sons were adult men of some importance and able to protect their mother's interests, and clearly she was unlikely to produce any more children.[7] Her chief value was as a food producer and housekeeper and female politician, roles for which she had been well trained in her long years as wife of Turimpi and M.

Old women in Bongdadu's position had to remarry, but they were in a good position to exercise some choice of their own as to whom they remarried, especially if they had strong influential sons to support them in their wishes. There was a frequent pattern in such cases for the widow, aided and abetted (or perhaps even forced) by her sons, to arrange a marriage of convenience with some obscure nonentity much younger than herself and usually a friend or contemporary of her sons. In 1925, then, Bongdadu, widowed three times already, married as her fourth husband one Dominico, a man of no importance whatever, as was shown by the fact that at this time he was nearly forty and had not been able to attract even one bestowed wife. He had, however, already married one widow, so that his marriage to Bongdadu gave him a second wife, also, of course, a widow. This marriage is of further interest when we discover that Antonio, Mariano, and Louis, the main sons of Bongdadu by a previous marriage, had some influence in arranging this marriage of their mother to a contemporary and satellite of theirs, and that a year or two before, Antonio had married the ancient mother of Dominico when *she* became a widow. In other words, Antonio and Dominico had married each other's mothers; Antonio while waiting for his oldest bestowed wife to grow up, Dominico with no bestowed wife in sight. The approximate ages of the parties at the time of these marriages were:

Antonio	37	Dominico's mother	55
Dominico	38	Bongdadu (Antonio's mother)	60+

Earlier, we mentioned the practice of fathers swapping their daughters within the infant bestowal system; here we find sons swapping their mothers within the widow remarriage system.

This is a relatively simple example of the complexity of Tiwi domestic arrangements, and we hesitate to complicate matters further. But clearly the last remarriage of Bongdadu (to Dominico) and the remarriage around the same time of Dominico's mother to one of Bongdadu's sons, a friend of Dominico, raise some

---

[7] The Tiwi saw no inconsistency between believing in spirit impregnation and believing at the same time that an old woman was unlikely to bear children. It was to them a matter of probabilities, and of course with them as with us, occasionally an elderly lady did— disconcertingly—have a baby, proving the logic of their position.

important issues of social structure, particularly the question of whether widow remarriages of this type are to be regarded as a sub-species of bestowal marriages, with the sons having a right of bestowal over their mothers parallel or similar to the right of bestowal possessed by fathers over their infant daughters. Space does not permit any adequate discussion of this fascinating theoretical issue, but we can point out two factors which strongly deter us from regarding Tiwi widow remarriage as a special case of bestowal marriage. One is the self-evident and empirically observed fact that Tiwi widows, who remarried as Bongdadu and Dominico's mother remarried in the quoted case, were usually highly vocal and pretty tough old ladies who were not easily pushed around by anybody, even by their adult and ambitious sons. Whom they remarried in their old age was a matter upon which they had themselves a good deal to say. Secondly, to any anthropologist familiar with the kinship structures of Southeast Asia and the Pacific countries, there is a great deal of difference, in a society with matrilineal clans such as the Tiwi had, between a father making marriage decisions for his daughters, who do not belong to his clan, and sons making marriage decisions for their widowed mothers, who do belong to the same clan as their sons. We prefer, therefore, to view the overall Tiwi marriage situation and the interrelationship of their two forms of marriage as essentially a system wherein the matrilineal clan had lost its right to make marriage decisions for its female children, that right having been taken over (usurped) by the fathers of those children. The daughters of the clan were disposed of, not where fellow clansmen decided, but where an outsider (the father) decided—thus, bestowal or betrothal marriage. But when the female no longer had a father—that is, when she was old and could only be remarried through widow remarriage— then the right of her clansmen and more specifically her sons (in consultation with her own wishes) to arrange her remarriage became restored as a sort of residual or reanimated right. Moreover, as we shall see, it was in line with their own political interests for the sons to insist on exercising such a right.

Naming Rules

Such a way of integrating the two forms of marriage is supported by the Tiwi rules for naming children, which are very relevant to the issue. We mentioned earlier that the right to bestow a daughter was vested, strictly speaking, not in the actual father, but in the man who named her. Personal names were important in the Tiwi value system[8] and were given to every child a few weeks after its birth by its father or the man currently married to its mother. But whenever a husband died and the widows remarried, all the personal names given to their children by the dead man became strictly taboo, and the new husbands of the widows had the duty (or right) of providing all the children with new names. Since most women were widowed several times in their lives, most children were thus renamed several times in *their* lives, and the names given them by the earlier husbands of their mother dropped completely out of

[8] See Hart 1931.

use.[9] Logically under this system nobody would get a permanent name until his or her mother was dead, since as long as she were alive she would remarry and her new husband would rename all her children, no matter how aged they might be. The Tiwi insisted that logically this was how the naming system was supposed to work, and, in fact, the personal names of even prominent senior men did become taboo whenever their mothers' current husbands died. But convenience proved stronger than logic and the personal names of most men and women became well established in their early adulthood as people became used to them. While such names did become taboo when the man who had given them died, the taboo in such cases was temporary rather than permanent, and after a decent interval the name would creep back into use replacing some new and unfamiliar one which might be bestowed by the widow's new husband. In general, the name which thus became permanently or irrevocably attached to a person was the name which a person held when he or she first emerged into tribal prominence or first began to get talked about. For a male, this was most usually the name he was bearing in his late twenties and early thirties; for a female, the name she was known by in her early adolescence when she first left her father's household to take up residence with her earliest husband.

That convenience thus overbore logic in the Tiwi naming system by attaching some one semipermanent name to a person despite the rules of name taboo should not cause us to overlook the importance of these rules. In theory, at least, every new husband renamed all his wives' children by all their previous marriages—thus, at least symbolically, canceling out the signs of title of all the previous "fatherhoods" in those children and asserting his own fatherhood right as a new and exclusive one. A widow's new husband was the new household head for all her children, and he took over this position by renaming them all, thus becoming their legal father. If we can stop thinking of "father" as a biological or kin relationship, and think of the word as meaning only "head of the household," the Tiwi concept will become understandable. We will also realize that there is no contradiction or illogic involved in the Tiwi beliefs that male parents were not necessary for conception, but that every child born must be born to a woman with a husband. All they meant was that every child must be born into a household with a male at its head who belonged to a different clan from its mother—in other words, a "father," in Tiwi context.

The renaming of the children by the new household head was not, of course, sufficient to wipe out the commitments made by previous titleholders. Although the new father could and did change his step-daughters' names, he could not change their bestowals. The men upon whom the daughters had been bestowed by the previous father made sure of this. The new father was compelled to carry out the marriage arrangements for the daughters made by his predecessors in

---

[9] It can easily be seen what headaches this naming system created for an anthropologist trying to collect genealogies. Individuals would occur in one genealogy under one name and in another under another name, making the task of cross-indexing and cross-checking enormously difficult.

the fatherhood role, and there was sure to be a terrific row if he tried to alter them. Nevertheless, he acquired some power over the future of the daughters. The man to whom one of them had been promised by the previous father might die, thus making redisposal of the girl possible for him, or some new deal might be arrangeable in which he could use his new assets—for these new step-daughters were assets, regardless of the fact that their immediate matrimonial future was already settled. The new father could delay his decision as to whether they were yet old enough to join their betrothed husband or even drop a few hints that he did not think the betrothed husband's right to them was quite as certain as was generally believed. Such actions, of course, were liable to lead to violent reprisals by the betrothed husband, but there was always a chance that he would be open to a deal; for example, by giving an option on one of the women in whom he had an interest, he would seek to hasten the appearance of the girl in his own household or seek to clear whatever shadow upon his title to her the step-father sought to cast. Even the last husband of an elderly widow who had already passed through the hands of six or eight husbands and all of whose daughters were grown up and married two or three times already, gained some shadowy rights in the future remarriages of those daughters by marrying their ancient mother. And the validation of these shadowy rights was the fact that as their mother's new husband he had renamed the daughters and he who named them could bestow them. The only catch was, that while he could wipe out all the names bestowed by his predecessors, he could not equally readily wipe out their commitments. All he could do was maneuver within the network created by their commitments so as to try and advantage himself as much as possible by a skillful use of whatever shadowy right in the daughters he had obtained by becoming their current "father."

It is within such a context that the apparent swapping of mothers by Dominico and Antonio must be viewed. By marrying Bongdadu in her dotage, Dominico had acquired some rights in the future remarriages of her daughters, the sisters of Antonio, but since his marriage to her had been, partly at least, arranged by Antonio and her other sons, he would have to share with them his disposal rights to their sisters. Similarly, the marriage of Dominico's ancient mother to Antonio (part, so to speak, of the same "package deal") meant that Antonio as current father had some say in the future disposal of Dominico's sisters when they became widowed, since he had the power of renaming them.

What in effect occurred in this, as in many other cases, was that men of different clans and of about the same age formed a partnership or close alliance wherein "sons" and "husbands" cooperated in arranging the remarriages of their "mothers" and "sisters" by acting as quasi-fathers and treating their mothers and sisters as "quasi-daughters." The partnership or "firm" of Dominico (of the Crane clan) and Antonio, Mariano, and their brothers (of the Red Paint clan) had already arranged the remarriages of Bongdadu (Red Paint clan) and of Dominico's mother (Crane clan), and stood ready to take care of all future remarriages of any of Bongdadu's daughters (Red Paint) or Dominico's sisters (Crane) whenever any of these women became widowed. Each member of the firm was trying to maximize his own self-interest in this and all the other alliances he had a share in, but operations had to be carried out in this partnership form because the marriage of any woman had to be arranged by her "father," and the father, in the Tiwi rules, had to be a nonclansman of the woman whose marriage he arranged. Hence the Red Paint men needed Dominico, a Crane, as a front man to arrange the remarriages of their sisters, and he in turn used Antonio, a Red Paint man, to arrange the remarriages of his sisters. When clansmen made decisions about the remarriages of their sisters, they could only do it by using agreeable nonclansmen as nominal "fathers" and cooperating with them—and the agreeable nonclansmen would of course only come in on the deal if there was something in it for them, as there was for the obscure and unimportant Dominico in the present case. In return for acting as a front for the Red Paint brothers, he got himself a second wife, an excellent food provider though no longer beautiful; he became the ally, even if junior, of some men with assured futures; and he acquired some shadowy residual rights in the future remarriages of several potential widows. Dominico did himself a lot of good by marrying Bongdadu; if he hadn't married her, he would never have attracted much tribal notice and hence would not have warranted mention in these pages.

We find that the whole complex situation makes most theoretical sense if we see it as essentially an institutional struggle between clan rights and the father's rights in women. Tiwi fathers, as suggested above, had taken away from the clan the right to make marriage decisions for newly born female members of the clan. As mechanisms validating this success of father's rights against clan rights there existed two rules: he who bestowed the name had the right to dispose in marriage; and all names given by a woman's previous husband were cancelled by his death and a new set of names given to all her children by her new husband. Strictly and universally enforced, such rules would put *all* control over the marriages of *all* women, of every age, in the hands of their mother's husbands—that is, men from outside the clan of the women being disposed of, in other words, fathers in the Tiwi sense. But the Tiwi system failed to achieve such a result though their rules are pointed toward it. They achieved something close to it as far as infant or even young girls were concerned, since the fellow clansmen of such girls were either (as brothers) too young and unimportant to have any power to resist this alien control over their sisters' hands, or (as mothers' brothers and hence older men) too involved and absorbed in their own activities *as fathers* to take any position asserting clan rights as against fathers' rights. To be successful in tribal life, an ambitious young Tiwi male was best advised to forget his mother and his sisters' daughters (all members of his clan) and concentrate on getting wives for himself. Only by getting wives could he have daughters, and only by having daughters could he build alliances and obtain influence, power, and move wives. To get wives for himself, he could not use his mother or his sisters or his sisters' daughters, since their disposal was in the hands of the men who had named them—that is, their fathers. But there came a time in the life of an older man when his mother was old, and *her* mother was dead, and therefore the rights of the last man to name his mother had lapsed. And a similar situation would arise in the case of his sisters when their mother's last husband died. By this age, a man so situated was likely to be powerful enough and skilled enough in the rules of the game to exert some control over the late remarriages of his elderly sisters and even of his mother, were she still alive. Whenever this occurred, although the resulting situation might have the superficial appearance of clan solidarity—with sons, mothers, brothers, and sisters all acting and planning together as a partnership—such a surface appearance was illusory. The motivations involved in it were scarcely altruistic desires on the part of the brothers to look after their mothers and elderly sisters, but rather efforts by the brothers to use to advantage, in their intricate political schemes, some women of their own clan (their mothers and elderly sisters). Earlier in life these men had been prevented from such manipulation by the control over those women exercised by nonclansmen (their husbands or fathers) through the naming rules. Put another way, we might say that Tiwi men as a group had acquiesced to the system wherein "the father" had control over all marriages of his "daughters," because every Tiwi man hoped to be a "father" himself; but having acquiesced, every Tiwi male tried to beat the system, especially as he became older and more influential, by intriguing in the remarriages of his mother and elderly sisters—matters in which, according to the strict letter of the law, he had no right to interfere, since bestowal rights resided with the "father" or "fathers" of these women. One factor which greatly contributed to the setting aside of the rights involved in the naming system was the fact that since, on the whole, old men married young women and young men married old women, in many cases the nominal "father" of an elderly woman was very much younger and less influential than were her brothers, or her sons by an earlier husband. The brothers and/or sons, therefore, were able to override the wishes of their sisters' nominal father since the seniority system was on their side in such contests, even though the renaming rules were not.

Although it was very rare indeed for any Tiwi male to have a resident young wife until he was nearly forty, long before that age he was likely to acquire an ancient widow or two. In at least ninety out of every hundred cases a man's first resident wife was a widow very much older than himself. According to a complete genealogical census carried out in 1928–29, nearly every man in the tribe in the age group from thirty-two to thirty-seven was married to an elderly widow. Many of them had two elderly widows and a few had three. But very few of them, and certainly not more than one out of five of them, had a resident *young* wife. About half of them had bestowed wives, but these were mostly toddling infants who would not come into residence with them for another ten years or more. Even for the most promising and rapidly rising young man, the first young bestowed wife was not likely to arrive until several years after his marriage to a widow.

To get a start in life as a household head and thus to get his foot on the first rung of the prestige ladder, a Tiwi man in his thirties had first of all to get himself married to an elderly widow, preferably one with married daughters. This was the beginning of his career as a responsible adult. The widow did several things for him. She became his food provider and housekeeper. She served as a link to ally him with her sons. As her husband, he acquired some rights in the future remarriages of her daughters when they became widowed. And she, as the first resident wife in his household, stood ready to be the teacher, trainer, and guardian of his young bestowed wives when they began to join him after they reached puberty.

Levirate, Sororate, and Cross-Cousin Marriage

We have emphasized infant bestowal and widow remarriage because it was the elaborate development of these two matrimonial mechanisms that brought about the unusual, perhaps unique, character of the Timi household. Other matrimonial mechanisms, more usual in preliterate societies, were also used by the Tiwi but always in combination with or as minor adjuncts to the two basic mechanisms. Thus, a man often remarried his dead brother's wives, or at least some of them, within the institution of widow remarriage. Such a practice is known to anthropologists as the levirate, and tribes are said "to have" the levirate or "not to have" it. The Tiwi, with their pluralistic approach to the whole area of marriage relationships, can hardly be said to fall into either category. To them, every widow had to remarry and among the many possible candidates for her, the brothers of the dead husband were recognized as having a reasonable, but far from automatic, claim. Whether the brothers jointly, or any one of them singly, were able to translate that claim into marriage depended on the other claims. Brotherhood in itself gave no exclusive right to widows, but of course a brother, being necessarily of the same clan and frequently of the same band as the deceased husband, was well in line to assert a claim to the widow if he could make the claim good. Cursory inspection of the genealogies reveals, however, a surprisingly small number of cases of men taking over the widows of their deceased brothers. At best it was a very minor factor in Tiwi marriage customs.

The parallel custom of the sororate—that is, of sisters being married to the same husband—was more common. It occurred both in connection with infant bestowal, by a father promising *all* his daughters by a particular wife to the same husband, or in connection with widow remarriage, whereby two or more full sisters, previously married to the same husband, passed together on his death to the same new husband. The sororate occurred more frequently in the first form than in the second, largely because, as already mentioned, widows had more say in their own marriages than baby girls had, but there was nothing obligatory nor required about it, as is shown by the frequent cases in which a father bestowed all his daughters by one wife on the same man but on the early death of that man rebestowed them *seriatim* on several different husbands. One got the impression, though no Tiwi ever made the point explicit, that within the Tiwi bestowal system the prevailing high rate of infantile and child mortality was an important factor in sustaining the sororate principle to the extent that it did exist. A father who bestowed upon a man the first daughter borne by a certain wife was almost obliged to bestow upon the same man the second daughter of the same wife if the first one died in infancy. Moreover, since most fathers bestowed their daughters with an eye to their own advantage, it was clearly desirable if he wanted to cement the goodwill of a prospective son-in-law, to promise him *all* the daughters produced by a certain wife, so that even though most of them died in infancy, at least one or two would be delivered in good condition at the age of puberty. The aim of bestowal was to win friends and influence people, and a bestowal of a child who died before she reached the son-in-law did a father little good. A shrewd father could avoid this risk by following the sororate principle; a stupid or feckless father who scattered his daughters widely could well end up with as many disappointed sons-in-law as friendly ones, as the infantile and child mortality took its heavy toll of his young daughters. In the genealogies, sororate marriages in some form occur much more frequently than levirate marriages, but nonetheless their incidence is such as to indicate that they were a relatively minor feature in Tiwi marriages and that their occurrence was most frequently due to careful fathers trying to insure sons-in-law against disappointment, and themselves against charges of non-delivery.

No account of marriage in any Australian tribe can go very far without raising the difficult matter of the kinship system, since all the accounts we have of mainland Australian tribes tell us that all marriages there took place within a rigid kinship framework which required everybody to marry somebody who was automatically his or her cross-cousin (for example, a man and a daughter of his mother's brother).[10] Enough has been said already to indicate that in Tiwi marriage nothing was automatic. Females were given in marriage by their fathers, or (to a lesser extent) by their brothers, or (to a still lesser extent) by their sons. But fathers died and were succeeded by the men their widows remarried, and these men renamed all the widow's children, and by renaming them established some rights to make marriage decisions for the females. Therefore, cross-cousin marriage in Tiwi was merely part of the total system of marriage and had to adjust itself to the rest of the system. In theory, fathers could only bestow their infant daughters on men who stood to them in the relation of sisters' sons. Conversely, every man who received a bestowed wife received her from a man who was technically his mother's brother and of course the girl's father. To this extent the Tiwi were a tribe who practiced cross-cousin marriage and their kinship system belonged to one of the commonest Australian types, that which Radcliffe-Brown called Type I, having investigated it among

10 The definitive work on Australian kinship systems is Radcliffe-Brown 1930–31, and there is a large technical literature on the subject. See also Elkin 1951; Berndt 1955 and 1957; Murdock 1949.

the mainland tribe called the Kariera.[11] But a kinship system of the Kariera type could not accommodate all the complexities that had been introduced into Tiwi life by the emphasis on infant bestowal and widow remarriage. In particular, the generations kept getting badly mixed up, as for instance in the very common case of old men bestowing their infant daughters on other old men of their own age group, and in return receiving as infant wives (or wards) daughters of those old men. With this happening constantly, it was difficult to maintain the kinship principle that recipients of wives were always sons of the donor's sister and donors were always brothers of the recipient's mother. Which was mother's brother and which was sister's son in the case of two old men busily swapping daughters was a problem that put a severe strain on a Kariera-type kinship system. And widow remarriage introduced further complexities. We have already mentioned the case of two young men, Antonio and Dominico, who through a judicious use of widow-remarriage had ended up married to each other's elderly mothers. This was no isolated case; many pairs of men of like age were married to each other's mothers. Who called whom "father" and who called whom "son" became an insoluble riddle in such cases.

To avoid further involvement in the labyrinthine complexities of Australian kinship organization, all that we need say here is that the Tiwi had unscrambled the potential confusion introduced into their kinship categories by inventing a few new terms which, superimposed upon their Kariera-type system, kept everything straight. In Kariera, and generally among all the mainland tribes, no kinship distinction was made between potential wife and actual wife or between potential "in-laws" and actual "in-laws." A Kariera male called all the girls who were eligible for marriage to him by the same term (*Nuba*, usually translated mother's brother's daughter); all the fathers of such girls by the same term (*Kaga*, usually translated as mother's brother); and all the mothers of such girls by the same term (*Toa*, usually translated father's sister or mother's brother's wife). When he married one of these girls he still called her *Nuba*, he still called his wife's father *Kaga*, and still called his wife's mother *Toa*. But not in Tiwi. For them, all potential wives were, in theory, mothers' brothers' daughters and all potential wives' fathers were mothers' brothers. But when a man married any such girl, he immediately called her by a new and different kinship term which can only be translated as "wife," and corresponding new and separate terms were used for the actual wife's father, actual wife's mother, and even for the actual wife's father's sister. Thus marriage introduced for a Tiwi a new set of relatives with new kinship terms different from those he used toward his general run of cross-cousins, mother's brothers, father's sisters, and so on, and these "relatives by actual marriage" terms, being based on actual marriages rather than kinship categories, were capable of handling in a fairly orderly manner all the complexities introduced into Tiwi domestic life by such customs as old men exchanging infant daughters or young men marrying each other's

[11] See Radcliffe-Brown 1913.

mothers. We may sum it up briefly by saying that Tiwi marriages operated within a general framework of cross-cousin marriage kinship categories identical with the categories of the Kariera, but that females had become such important assets in power and prestige relationships among the senior men—marriage had become, so to speak, such a political affair—that a new set of kinship terms based on actual marriages had to be superimposed on the terms geared to cross-cousin marriage; in cases of conflict or anomaly or confusion in the cross-cousin terms, the terms based on actual marriages were controlling or took precedence. Which is only another way of saying that in theory all Tiwi marriages were rather idealistically approximated to marriages between cross-cousins, but in practice they departed quite far from such an ideal; so far, in fact, that extra kinship terms had been introduced to take care of the relationships created by such departures.

"Disputed" Wives

There is still one more category of wives to be mentioned, a category for which the Tiwi had no name in their own language but which in pidgin English they referred to as "stolen" wives. A few women so labeled were likely to turn up in the "list" of the wives of most big men, but analysis of the circumstances in each case makes it clear that "stolen" was an unsuitable label and that wives so designated were most often in a status that should be called either "disputed" or "shared." In legal terms they were wives in which there was or had been a divided interest. To explain fully the nature of these cases would carry us over into both the Tiwi legal and sexual systems, and here we are trying to confine our analysis to those aspects of marriage that have consequences for household organization. Since these disputed or shared wives had to at least reside in some household and had at least a nominal current husband at any given moment of time, all we need to note about them at this point is that in any listing of a man's wives we have to include "disputed" wives in addition to all the other categories of wives mentioned previously.

The Household: An Overview

In the discussion so far we have selected only those aspects of the Tiwi family complex that had close bearing on the nature of the household. These aspects can be briefly summarized as follows:

1. the high number of wives per husband that a successful man was likely to acquire if he lived long enough.

2. the two distinct mechanisms by which wives were acquired—infant bestowal and widow remarriage.

3. the operation of the bestowal system in such a way as to prevent even the most promising young man from achieving coresidence with a bestowed wife until he was at least nearly forty years old.

4. the tendency for success to lead to more success, whereby *some* astute men

received into their households a number of young wives in rapid succession after the age of forty.

5. the tendency of younger men and of nonbetrothed younger men in particular to marry elderly widows while waiting for betrothed wives to grow up or, in the case of those with no bestowals in sight, to enable them to start a household of their own.

6. as a result of the integrated operation of all these customs, the strong tendency in Tiwi households for husbands to be very much older than their wives (as a result of infant bestowal) or very much younger than their wives (as a result of widow remarriage) or—what was commonest of all in the bigger households—some combination of both. Hence many a Tiwi husband had some wives much older than himself, including some already dead (but still counted), and some very much younger than himself, including some who were still babies in their mothers' wombs (with their sex still undetermined). All these dead wives, current wives, nominal wives, "disputed" wives, not-yet-joined-the-household wives, and not-yet-born wives were still counted in a husband's list, and the length of his list was a measure of his influence, power, and importance as a household head.

It is now perhaps clear why we chose to begin our account of Tiwi culture with some discussion of Tiwi marriage. Compulsory marriage for all females, carried out through the twin mechanisms of infant bestowal and widow remarriage, resulted in a very unusual type of household, in which old successful men had twenty wives each, while men under thirty had no wives at all and men under forty were married mostly to elderly crones. This unusual household structure was the focal point of Tiwi culture. It linked together in an explicable unity the kinship system, the food-gathering system, the political and prestige system, the totemic system, the seniority system, the sexual system, and the legal-moral-religious system of the tribe. Or perhaps all these should be labeled as subsystems under the household structure, the master system which unified them.

23   MAKING MONEY

H. G. Barnett

Being Palauan is being interested in money, in the same sense that being American is being interested in money. It is not the whole of existence, but it strikes the outsider as commanding or coloring a great part of it. There are Palauans, as there are Americans, who deliberately reject a materialistic defini-

From Being a Palauan *by H. G. Barnett, pp. 37–43, copyright © 1960 by Holt, Rinehart and Winston, Inc. Reprinted by permission.*

tion of success and the competition that goes with it. There are others who disclaim the ambition to be measured in these terms while at the same time they are motivated by it. But whether they like it or not, none can deny or escape the impress that the striving for wealth gives to his life.

This is not a recent development, for Palauans had several forms of money when they were visited by Captain Wilson in 1783. All are quite different from the coin and currency of modern nations. They do not have the seal of government on them and the supply of the most important kind, so-called "men's money," can never be increased because its source is unknown. All of it came to the islands centuries ago, presumably through trade with people to the west. When the traffic that brought it ceased, mystery and legend began to replace whatever facts might have been known about its origins.

Men's money is composed of three materials: a hard, glassy pottery, a variegated porcelain, and old imperfect glass. There are a large number of types within each of these categories: bars, discs, spheres, and tubes. They range in size from 1/4 to 3 inches. Most of them are perforated for stringing. All except the glass pieces are still in use, so much so that social position and political power depend on the possession of a certain number of them. American money is now acceptable in part as a substitute, but by no means wholly so. Crucial events, such as births, marriages, and deaths, must still be socially validated by a transfer of native money from the male to the female side of the family.

The names of the shapes and sizes of these many bits of pottery and glass, and the values attached to them, make little sense to an outsider and only slightly more to the average Palauan. The mystery is not entirely due to the confusion of accident or practical necessity. It is in part a deliberate complication, for knowledge of the different classes and grades of money is a cultivated art. It is, moreover, a jealously guarded prerogative of chiefs and specialists; few ordinary people even know the names of the various denominations. The system is not uncontrolled, but it operates to the advantage of the few who are in a position to manipulate it. For them, the circulation of money is an exciting game wherein salesmanship, social dominance, and deception are assets.

Women have their own kind of money. It is subsidiary to and less valuable than men's. It is made of turtle shell, cut and molded to form small trays not more than 10 inches in length. The material for them is near at hand, though not easy to get. Theoretically the supply is unlimited, and trays continue to be made now as in the past. The increase resulting from more efficient means of capturing turtles has not seriously inflated the value of the trays, for the older ones are rated above recent products much for the same reason that individual pieces of men's money have acquired distinction.

Turtle-shell trays and fragments of foreign pottery and glass have never been indispensable to life in Palau. Plenty of food, good shelter, and a rich variety of useful goods have always been available to anyone who has wanted to produce them himself. Nevertheless, both men's and women's money have been geared into the subsistence economy in such a way as to stimulate it to an output beyond the essentials of a livelihood, and even beyond a modest luxury and surplus production level. The stimulation is in the interest of gaining prestige, and very often it operates to produce a wasteful excess of labor and goods. In addition, money has been injected into social, political, and religious affairs to such an extent that the Palauan outlook on life has a distinctive materialistic bent. Everything owned by others must be paid for; and many things are paid for in Palau that people in other parts of the world take or use as a natural right. As a result, the whole superstructure of purpose, attitude, and social interaction would collapse if by some selective catastrophe all Palauan money were suddenly to disappear.

Since money has this importance, it is essential that every person have a certain amount of it to his credit, even though he may never see it or know just how much of the family reserve is his. There are several ways that a credit can be built up today, and still others that have been outlawed or discarded under German and Japanese rule.

One of the approved ways of making money, of course, is to earn it. In aboriginal times the exercise of talent had a greater scope than it now has. It also commanded a better price. There were, for example, professional canoe makers, tatooers, song composers, carvers, healers, and priests as well as house builders such as there are today. They profited from their abilities in two ways: by selling their services and by accepting apprentices who paid them for instruction. Their earning power was greater than that of the few remaining specialists for another reason: they enjoyed a virtual monopoly of their craft. There were, presumably, a certain number of amateurs, because not everyone could afford to pay for everything he wanted. They must have been few, however, because every person had the help of his relatives and they collectively could provide the prestige necessities. In any event, no one with pretensions to rank would think of making his own canoe or building his own house. This is still true with respect to house building.

All service for pay operates on the cardinal rule that, for corporate benefit, it must be performed for someone outside the lineage. No one collects money from a maternal kinsman. The rule holds and is most evident in the case of routine, unprofessional services and physical labor. At this point it gears into a complex system of work and compensation that is channeled through the domestic unit of man, wife, and child. To put it starkly—as few Palauans put it to themselves—the ordinary domestic duties of a woman and her children are conceived as work done for her husband and their father. He or his heir pays for this service, when either he or they die, with pieces of money given to their closest male relative, who retains and uses the money in their names. The husband and father is therefore a key outsider for the maternal kinsmen. He is a more constant and certain source of income to a group of such kinsmen than are others who have only an occasional or single professional service to offer.

This system of pay for domestic service, which is called *omulu'ul*, requires that food and labor be exchanged for money and, at times, land. The exchange is regularized by the further requirement that a wife, her children, and others in her lineage always tender food and labor to her husband and he always compensates them with money or land, never the reverse. A money debt is not paid with money nor a food or work debt in kind. There are other kinds of exchanges outside this system, as when a personal service is paid with service, and when borrowed food is returned. These reciprocations are between relatives, occasionally between very good friends and neighbors. They never involve Palauan money.

The *omulu'ul* system is best explained by stating the three principles on which it operates. The first is that only the oldest male in a group of maternal lineage mates can actually hold and control his own money and land. He also controls the money and land of his siblings and that of his sister's children. Younger brothers do not administer the wealth that they have inherited and that is considered to be theirs. As young men, they neither hold nor control the money that they earn from their own efforts. As they grow older they may, with the consent of their lineage head, gradually assume more control.

The second principle is that individuals owe their services and the products of their labor to their lineage head in return for his guidance, protection, and financial support. They are obliged to supply him with food derived from their fishing activities or, in the case of women, from their work in the taro fields and other agricultural activities. Not only do they supply food for his household needs; they are also obliged to work for their lineage head when he is called upon to serve others as a result of demands upon him through the system of exchanging money for services. These are obligations that they inherit by reason of their birth in his matrilineal group. In return for their services, the lineage head is obliged to support them and maintain their social position. He is therefore responsible for making arrangements and payments at the times of their births, marriages, and deaths. In short, the mother's brother is the financial agent and administrator for his immediate matrilineal kinship group.

The third principle, and one likely to lead to misunderstanding of the system unless it is grasped, is that the fundamental prerogative of a lineage head to act as agent for his dependents can be transferred. This must be done by a well-understood agreement. By such an agreement a man renounces his right to administer the affairs of a given dependent, but he does not break off his kinship ties with him. There is not even a complete denial of financial interest in such a former dependent. The mother's brother, in effect, simply sells his dependent's services for a period of time, normally for the lifetime of the latter. In the end he must be compensated for this loan of his relative.

The relinquishment of control by the mother's brother is by no means uncommon. In fact, it is so routine as to be the rule rather than the exception, because the person who normally takes over the control of a dependent is his own father. It is not only regular procedure for a mother's brother to relinquish his prerogative in this respect; it is expected that the father will substitute for him.

The prerogative of a mother's brother to administer the fortunes of his dependents is normally relinquished in part also to husbands. When a woman gets married it is with the implicit assumption that she owes food and service to her husband. She is not freed of her obligation to help her mother's brother, but she is expected to divert most of her energies toward the service of her husband. In this she is encouraged and aided by her uncle and her brothers because they, through her, are entitled to a money return, and sometimes compensation in land. By the same token, a man also diverts a part of his energies from the service of his mother's brother to that of his sister's husband in return for money paid either directly to him or to his uncle.

In this game the wife has little or nothing to say. Her allegiance is naturally, as the Palauans see it, to her brothers and to her mother's brother—not to her husband. She is, in fact, in conspiracy with her blood relatives to get the most money possible out of her husband and his relatives. If she were to be lax in this respect she would be regarded as ungrateful to her relatives. The ideal type of woman is one who works hard in the interests of her brothers and sisters. Her labor is only indirectly for the benefit of her husband, since the primary objective is to get money for her kin group. It is for this reason that Palauan women are said to be the source of money.

Women carry on exchanges among themselves. Their activities in this respect parallel those of the men but the two systems do not overlap. Women always deal in only their kind of money—that is, in turtle-shell trays. A woman never gives or receives pieces of men's money. Their exchanges take place on the same occasions as those of the men, but they are subordinate to the men's activities. Just as a husband owes only money to his wife's brother in compensation for food and service, so his sister is required to pay his wife so many shell trays for her share of the same food and service. Similarly, just as a man is obliged to give money to the brother of his daughter-in-law, so a woman gives shell trays to her daughter-in-law. In all instances, money and trays are classed together, and both are set over against food and service.

Most men are financially dependent on their fathers or lineage heads all of their lives. There is one way, however, that an ambitious man can achieve some measure of independence. He can, with the consent of his father or uncle, hold an *o'oraul* for the purpose of receiving contributions of money from his friends and relatives. He also takes care to invite his sisters' husbands, for they are expected to contribute most liberally. The contributions of these men and those of friends are considered to be loans. Those of the host's own relatives were once regarded as gifts; now they too tend to be treated as loans. The host's wife and her relatives, as usual, are the suppliers of the feast that must precede the collection of money.

Men never release their money willingly or graciously but cling to it as if it were a part of them. This tenacity exists not only because money is dear but also because a generous man could not long survive the many pressures put upon him. Every transfer entails prolonged negotiations and various gambits and counter-strategies. The two parties to the negotiations do not confront each other face to face but use intermediaries. The intermediaries are chosen for their ability to use flattery, persuasive arguments, and clever interpretations to induce acceptance of the offers made by their group.

Bargaining takes place at any time there is a transfer of money, regardless of the nature of the occasion. The same reluctance to pay for a bride at marriage prevails at death, when the husband's relatives must join together in paying a respectable sum of money to the wife's male relatives. No payment is settled in advance. The price of a canoe or a house is what the workman can force or wheedle out of the buyer after the job is completed. The reluctance to part with money is also displayed when a man borrows money from his invited guests at an *o'oraul*. Each person, on all of these occasions, holds back what he must pay for a seemingly interminable time before he finally hands it over with great deliberation in movement.

When the floor of the club house in Adas had to be replaced it was rumored that Menglo, the father of the carpenter, was going to demand $800 for the job. This was an extravagant charge, for the work could have been done with a fair profit for $200. But the building is claimed by the titled men of the village, and chiefs always have to pay more than common men. Their solution to the problem of paying this amount was to request all of the middle-aged men of the district to consider themselves chiefs for the occasion. All were addressed by the honorific term *rupak* and they had no option but to submit to the flattery and the request. This meant that they had to raise money fast, and the way to do this is by holding an *o'oraul*. Everybody, including the chiefs, took this course. On one day five were held in the same village. Since many of the same men were involved each time, the tangle of debts and counter-debts almost produced a financial crisis.

When the day for settlement arrived, thirty-nine men of varying ranks were assembled in the club house by 10 o'clock in the morning. The first chief of the district sat in his accustomed place by the first door on the right. Honored guest chiefs from two other villages sat on each side of the front entrance. Other titled men occupied the places assigned by tradition to their rank on either side of a doorway. The "chiefs for a day" filled in wherever there was a space. Menglo was one of these, and he sat at the end of the building farthest away from the first chief, who was the strategist for the buyers of the floor and his principal adversary in the bargaining maneuvers to come. Because of the differences in their rank, the interplay could not be so straightforward as to directly involve these two men.

There is no rule against a man speaking for himself in opposition to a chief, but it is better not to. Low rank talking to high rank calls for reserve and acquiescence. Furthermore, a low-ranking man is a novice in the protocol of dealing with chiefs. He feels tongue tied and powerless. Like the lay citizen in court, he may lose his case by saying the right thing at the wrong time. He needs a skilled advocate. Following custom, Menglo had therefore brought with him a spokesman who held a title and by good fortune was also the maternal uncle of the carpenter, Menglo's son. As speaker for his side, the first chief designated a chief of approximately the same rank as Menglo's spokesman. All cross-communication, from one end of the house to the other, was between these two intermediaries, one of whom was higher in rank than the man he represented, the other lower.

Before they could begin the negotiations, the buyers (the "chiefs") had to assess their resources. Ordinarily this would have been done before the appearance of the other party; otherwise the procedure was the usual one. Middle-aged subordinate relatives crouched before their family representatives to offer them one or two dollars; young men and women handed their contributions in the doorways to be passed to their leaders. The first chief placidly but firmly directed the canvass, having at his command three attendants who quietly and deferentially shuttled between him and the other chiefs, carrying information and directions. Two men busy with paper and pencil sat at his side, setting down names and sums. Finally they arrived at the conclusion that $621 was all they could count on.

Menglo never spoke aloud. When the negotiations opened, the chief who represented him requested $800. This initiated an exchange of repartee between the two spokesmen, most of which was designed to draw laughter and relieve the tension. The chiefs had the advantage, not only because of rank and numbers, but also because each, as he thought of it, passed along an intimidating witticism to their spokesman who embellished it as he saw fit.

By one o'clock it was evident that Menglo was ready to accept the chiefs' offer, and their spokesman was sent to huddle with him in private. He returned to his place to announce that a price of $600 was agreed upon. The messengers then collected the individual contributions on platters and the tellers verified their count. After the money had been given to Menglo, the first chief directed his spokesman to make a laudatory speech commending Menglo for his reasonable attitude and announcing that an extra $21 was being given to him by way of appreciation.

It was about 2:30 when the first chief directed that the food be served. Women brought it on trays to the doorways and attendants placed it before the men, following the chief's instructions. Several times there were mutterings about who should receive what, especially when it came to serving the untitled "chiefs." Quietly and decisively the first chief asserted that he was the "master of the way" and proceeded to direct the placement of the food trays and the sprigs of betel nut.

The men ate quickly and silently. The chiefs were given very large portions from which they took what they wanted and then handed their trays to their relatives outside. Everyone got something in proportion to his rank, down to Nial, a forlorn old widower who had been able to contribute only $.50. After the food had been cleared away, the lesser men unobtrusively drifted off. This was really not their party. The rest remained to talk until almost dark, as is the custom among important men.

24 THE KAPAUKU INDIVIDUALISTIC MONEY ECONOMY

Leopold Pospisil

In Western society we are accustomed to think in terms of dichotomies and contrasts. The field of anthropology and economics has not escaped this tendency. We classify the various peoples of the world either as civilized or as primitive societies. While civilized people are popularly regarded as logical, having a complex technology, and an economy characterized by true money and by markets, primitive people have been credited with only a prelogical mentality, and a crude technology that has as its "logical" consequence a simple, nonmonetary type of economy. Their economy has been considered by various writers to be either overindividualistic or communistic. As will be apparent, the Kapauku society does not fit such oversimplified generalizations. It combines, strangely enough, one of the world's most primitive technologies with a rather sophisticated and complex economic system. The latter in its main features resembles a simplified version of capitalism rather than any sort of primitive communism.

MONEY AND MARKETS.   Contrary to many generalizations about the nature of exchange in primitive societies, barter plays a minor role among the Kapauku. Despite their simple technology, sales (the acquisition of goods by money) are the regular means of exchange on the inter- as well as intratribal level; barter and gifts are always secondary to trade.

One of the major pillars on which the Kapauku economy stands is the use of true money. Cowrie shell and two types of necklaces function in this society as the common medium of exchange and the common measure of value. For this money one can buy not only food, domesticated animals, growing crops, land, and artifacts, but one can also use it as payment for labor in the gardens, for various services (such as surgery, magical curing, breeding of pigs), for the lease of land, and for damages and fines that originate from criminal as well as contractual delicts. Only money enables a man to get married, to gain prestige and become an influential individual, to conclude best-friendship unions with respected individuals, and to achieve the highest status of the political leadership and legal authority. Without money one is called *daba*—poor, idle, a not respected individual, who has no standing in the native society. The closest translation of this word is "tramp."

As in modern monetary systems the Kapauku cowrie shell money comes in various "denominations." The cheapest is a shell type called *kawane*, which is of eliptical shape with a smooth surface. Five such shells equal the value of one *tuanika mege*, a cowrie recently introduced from the coast that, except for its newness, has all the characteristics of a precious cowrie called *bomoje*. This valuable shell is the most frequent type of native money encountered in the Papuan trade. It has an angular outline and an uneven surface with occasional depressions and bumps. There are two types of these shells: *dege bomoje*, which is yellowish-white in color and is worth 15 *kawane*, and *buna bomoje* of darker, bluish or white color whose value is approximately 20 *kawane*. In addition the Kapauku have two other types of high-value shell: the *epaa mege* and the *bodija*. Both of these closely resemble the *bomoje* except that they are much larger. Whereas *epaa mege* is usually worth 2 *bomoje*, the value of *bodija* varies with its size. It is always valued more than *epaa mege*, and it may even reach the exchange rate of 10 or 12 *bomoje*. With the introduction of European glass beads of cylindrical shape and light blue color, the value of a Kapauku *bomoje* was set at 30 such beads in 1955. Besides the cowrie shell the natives also use as money necklaces of tiny cowrielike shells (*Nassarius* sp.) called *dedege*, and necklaces of small glass beads of various colors called *pagadau*. Both of these necklaces are standardized at the length of a human arm and are worth 1 *bomoje*.

Since none of the Kapauku shell money is produced by the people themselves, but has to be acquired through trade from the coastal lowland Papuans, the amount in circulation is limited. Indeed, the trade relations with the Kapauku lowlanders were, prior to the white man's pacification of the area, very irregular because of the dangers involved in this enterprise, since the lowland Papuans were not only keen traders but also expert headhunters and cannibals. Exchanges occasionally ended in unexpected ways, with the Kapauku traders themselves taken as a commodity for which no price was paid. Because of the uncertainties involved in this trade the coastal cowries have been always relatively scarce in the highlands and the demand for them great. It is my impression that prior to the contact with the white man the amount of cowries in circulation was almost static; the cowries lost, and through normal wear destroyed (split by the string), about equaled the import of these treasures. Thus the supply of old Kapauku money was about fixed and the value of the currency, determined by its scarcity, was generally stable.

MARKET AND PRICES.   There are several interdependent factors in the price-making process. The relative scarcity of cowrie shell and long practice have established a scale of customary prices for commodities—that is, a set of ideals to which the actually charged prices "ought to conform." These customary prices are regarded by the people as ethically justifiable and fair, and the man who demands them is considered honest. There is seldom a dispute after a customary price has been charged and paid. When people are asked in general about prices of various commodities they always cite these ideals. Accordingly, the people quote 5 *bomoje* shell as the price for 900 square meters of land or for a crop growing on the same area. Lease of the same land costs 1 *bomoje*. A piece of pork of about 2 kilograms should sell for 1 *bomoje*; an introduced steel ax costs 5 *bomoje* and a steel machete 3 *bomoje*. A male pig of approximately 90 kilograms' weight which is destined for slaughter sells for 20 *bomoje;* seven large marsupials should cost 2 *bomoje,* and the customary price for 30 rats is 1 *bomoje,* and so on. However, the actual prices charged on specific occasions may, and often actually do, differ from the quoted ideals. Lacking an authority or a binding custom that could determine and fix the value of certain commodities, the Kapauku market relies heavily upon free and automatic adjustment of prices to the supply and demand. But this does not mean that the idea of a customary price would have no effect upon the actual price; indeed, it still remains an ideal. To pay the customary price means security for both parties to the contract. Sales of land especially conform to the ideal because if a price lower than customary has been charged for a plot of land, the seller or his heirs can always ask for the difference under the threat of repossessing the land after repayment of what they originally received.

Sales of other commodities are usually heavily influenced by the law of supply and demand. Although payment of a customary price also provides security here, since these goods, unlike land, are perishable, the security is not so desirable. This is especially so because Kapauku law guarantees no annulment of contract in case a lower than customary price has been charged for such commodities. Also, any security obtained from conforming to the ideal is almost always obtained at the expense of a greater financial profit to one of the parties of the sale. As consequence the ideals are frequently disregarded, and for the Kapauku market it is generally true that the higher the supply the lower the prices, and vice versa. The fluctuation of prices on the native market may often be so considerable as to dwarf the elasticity of prices in the Western economic system. For example, in February 1955 at a pig feast in Egebutu 2-kilogram pieces of pork were being sold for 2 *bomoje,* in other words for 100 percent more than the customary price. At another time there was such a high demand for pigs in the Kamu Valley that Ijaaj Amoje of Aigii succeeded in selling a pig, customarily worth 12 *bomoje* shell, for a price three times as high. On the other hand prices may fall well below the customary ones. In 1953 Pigome Ipouga of Obajbegaa, capitalizing on a large supply of pork, brought from Pigome Gaajabii of the same village 4 kilograms of pork for only 1 *bomoje,* which is exactly one half of the customary price.

In addition to the force of the ideal customary price and the law of supply and demand, the prices on the Kapauku market are influenced to some degree by particular relationships between the trading partners, by the force of competition, and by the status of the buyer. Often, but not as a rule, prices tend to be lower if the parties to the sale are close relatives. Also, prices charged between best friends, and between a debtor and a creditor may disregard to some extent the law of supply and demand. However, such a disregard is an exception rather than a regular occurrence when one takes into consideration the Kapauku market as a whole. More frequently the prices are depressed below the customary level by a competition among several vendors of the same type of commodity who are eager to sell, even if it means a loss with regard to the customary value of the merchandise. The status of the buyer may also influence the prices of commodities that he buys. A rich man or a political leader is especially likely to be offered "bargains" either because the seller expects future favors or because he feels grateful for past financial or legal aid.

Marketing of the Kapauku commodities takes place daily in an inconspicuous, unceremonial way. However, the native "businessmen" do most of their selling and buying on special occasions of a ceremonial nature. There are three types of such occasions: *juwo*, the pig feast, *tapa*, the fund-gathering ceremony, and *dedomai*, the pig market. The pig feast is the most elaborate and conspicuous ceremony in the Kapauku culture. Its nature and structure, together with those of the other two ceremonies, are explained in some detail in the fifth chapter. Here we may limit ourselves to a few statements concerning its marketing function. Besides other important roles, such as entertainment, feasting, settling of political affairs, and dating, during its last day, called *juwo degii naago*, the Kapauku pig feast is a huge market. Often well over a 1000 sellers and buyers gather in order to offer their produce for sale or to make necessary purchases with their shell money. Usually hundreds of pigs are slaughtered during this day and the meat is distributed through sales, loans, and repayment of debts. The trading is, of course, not limited to pork and pigs. People offer for sale many other products of their labor such as salt, bamboo and gourd containers, bundles of bowstrings made of rattan, packs of native tobacco, pandanus leaves for wrapping the native cigarettes, bows, arrows, net carrying bags, chickens, bundles of dried inner bark, axes, knives, and necklaces. Since a pig feast attracts people from faraway places, even from other Papuan tribes, this feast functions also as an important institution of interregional as well as intertribal trade.

The fund-gathering ceremony is far less conspicuous than the pig feast; its economic role dominates this event, while the social functions are only secondary and often incidental. The major objective of the sponsors of this event is to gather funds through loans or collection of debts. In addition to these financial transactions the ceremony functions, like the pig feast as a large market. However, the volume of trade concluded at a *tapa* ceremony is far smaller than at a pig feast. The last of the ceremonies that supplies a market place for the Kapauku trade, *dedomai*, is the least ceremonial, its purpose being almost entirely economic. This occasion is devoted entirely to business. No dancing takes place and no ceremonial structures are erected. All people from the region as well as from other tribes are invited to participate in selling and buying the various produce. Since this event does not involve any conspicuous ceremonial processions, dances, or other performances, and because its only function is an informal redistribution of goods and shell money, *dedomai* may be regarded as a market place or a fair, and is comparable to the same institutions in the Western civilization.

EXCHANGE AND TRANSFER OF PROPERTY. Among the Kapuku an overwhelming amount of goods is exchanged through sales. Although Papuans do not discriminate against sale contracts concluded between strangers (which occur in large numbers at the markets just described), more sales are concluded within local patrilineal kin groups, and therefore between closely related people, than between complete strangers, because of their physical proximity. In their selling and buying most of the Kapauku are strictly profit motivated. Often they invest money in pigs, chickens, large *woti* (bailer shell), inner bark, or animal teeth, for the purpose of breeding the animals for profit, speculating in sales of the bailer shell, or for making artifacts for sale. In its emphasis on sales this primitive economy resembles the modern Western economic system. Besides the necessity of having to buy with money such commodities as land, manufactured products, labor, and services such as surgery, curing, and midwifery, the Kapauku have to pay for favors and acts for which even in our capitalistic society there is no charge. For example, one pays a bride price for a wife, the services of a foster father have to be paid for by the grown boy, a grief expressed by strangers or distantly related people over the death of a close relative has to be recompensed in money, and almost all crimes can be settled through a proper transfer of shell currency. The dominant position of sales in the native economy has pushed barter into an insignificant position. Barter, in addition, is provided with so many restrictions of a legal and traditional nature that it has become not only exceptional but also a means of exchange to be avoided if possible.

There is a major difference between the concept of the sale contract in Roman law and its counterpart in the Kapauku society. Among these natives a mutual agreement does not seal a sale. Not until the buyer receives the sold object and the seller his full payment does the transfer of ownership take place. Also a tacit underselling of nonreal property (less than the customary price), which is not accompanied by an explicit statement as to the finality of the transaction, allows the seller or his main heir to invalidate the deal at any time in the future. In other respects the Kapauku sale resembles our idea of this type of contract. Bargaining is acceptable, and the price and quality of the commodity are often hotly disputed. To almost every sale there are witnesses so that a possible future dispute can be adjudicated on the basis of objective evidence. Usually merchandise need not be advertised. It can simply be displayed at a market place or, if such a facility is not readily available, the news about a commodity for sale spreads by means of local gossip.

The Kapauku have designed many types of sale contracts to fit the various types of commodities; the contracts vary in their complexity according to the value of the merchandise. The sale of land is provided with several restrictions of a legal nature: if less than the customary price (5 *bomoje* for 900 square meters) is charged for the property, the sellers of the real estate, or his heirs, can at any time either annul the agreement or ask for the difference in price. An old man cannot sell his land validly without the consent of his sons; if he should do so, his heirs can always repossess the land against a return of the purchase price. Growing crops are also subject to sale. For a payment of 5 *bomoje* shell the buyer receives the right to harvest a crop of sweet potatoes on an area of about 900 square meters. The vendor is always responsible should the crop be damaged by weather or a pig; part of the price is returned, in proportion to the damage. Sale of a house is rather rare but involves a simple contract; the price varies with the size of the structure (from 3 to 5 *bomoje*), and the new owner is often expected to move the property to another site.

Since pigs are fundamental to the Kapauku culture, it is not surprising that their sale is elaborately regulated. There are basically two types of pig-selling contracts, one for a male pig, the other for a sow. A male piglet may be bought simply by paying the full price (6 to 7 *bomoje*) or by a down payment of 1 *bomoje* and a final payment (usually about 10 *bomoje*) at the time the animal is slaughtered. For an older pig one usually has to pay 1 *bomoje* shell for each 2-kilogram piece of pork that (it is estimated) can be cut from its carcass. In contrast to this simple transaction, selling a small sow is very complex. First, the buyer has to pay *bo badii*, a down payment that varies from 3 to 10 *bomoje*, at the time of purchase. Later, when the sow has had piglets and has been fattened, she is killed with some of her offspring. The buyer must then deliver to the seller a large payment called *epaawa*, which varies from 60 to 180 *bomoje*. The final payment for a sow is called *ijobai* and consists, according to the original agreement, of one or several female piglets of the sow. If, however, the sold female pig dies prematurely, the buyer is not only absolved from the subsequent payments, but he may actually request the return of the whole *bo badii* (down payment) against delivery of the carcass of the dead pig. Also, if the female pig proves to be sterile, the buyer is absolved from delivering the two subsequent payments. Thus the risk in the trade of a female pig rests on the shoulders of the seller.

Sales of chickens in many respects parallel those of pigs. Whereas a small rooster can usually be purchased for a simple payment of 1 *bomoje*, a hen is sold for a down payment of 1 *bomoje* and, if she lays eggs and hatches chicks, for an additional payment of 3 *bomoje*. As in the case of a sow, an *ijobai*, consisting of one or two female chicks, has to be paid later.

Of the various types of food sales, by far the most frequent are those of pieces of pork. The meat comes to the market in the form of *kado*, a piece of about 2 kilograms in weight and usually costs 1 *bomoje*; but the price, as has been already indicated, can vary greatly with supply and demand.

Next in importance in the trade of food comes salt. This mineral comes into the Kamu Valley through trade with neighboring regions, or special expeditions are undertaken by the inhabitants of the Kamu to the distant salt springs in the north (Moni country), where they themselves burn the leaves and wood soaked in the salt water and make "bundles of salt" from the ashes. The weight of these pieces of salt is about 2 kilograms each. The salt, which is stone hard and blackened from a high content of ashes, is wrapped in banana leaves and tied with rattan vine so as to form an elongated bundle that can be carried by a rattan strap. During an eight-month period in 1955 the 180 inhabitants of the village of Botukebo imported about 34.25 kilograms of salt. Except for 2 kilograms that were traded to outsiders, all the salt was locally consumed.

Game, especially rats and marsupials, is also traded between the natives. Because of the scarcity of wild life in the Kamu Valley, the region relies heavily on imports of roasted carcasses of these animals from the southern Pona Valley. For example, inhabitants of Botukebo village purchased from the outside, in 51 separate transactions, 160 rats and 38 marsupials in eight months in 1955. The customary price for 30 rats is 1 *bomoje*, and for seven marsupials it is 2 *bomoje*.

Trade of raw material for the manufacture of artifacts, as well as of the finished products, is very active. Although influenced by the ideal "customary prices" the actual payments for bundles of inner bark, bowstrings, bamboo containers, fire saws, net bags, fishing nets, bows, arrows, axes, introduced machetes, and so forth are influenced by supply and demand. Thus a net carrying bag, whose price should be 1 *bomoje* shell is often sold for twice the amount when the supply of new products becomes low. There is one commodity that is deliberately bought for speculation; this is the large bailer shell, called by the natives *woti* (*Melo hunteri* Perry), supply and demand of which depends on irregular trade with the coast and therefore varies so remarkably in price from time to time, that the shell has become an article of great speculation among the natives. Many a wise Kapauku businessman buys a large quantity of these shells when their price is low and the supply high. He hides them (usually in one of the numerous holes and cavities in the limestone cliffs) until the price rises, when he may sell his shell for a profit as high as 200 percent.

The following figures represent the imports and exports for intervillage trade of the Botukebo community that occurred during an eight-month period in 1955. They sold their goods and services to outsiders for an amount equivalent to 6519 glass beads (or 317 *bomoje* shell, which may purchase double the amount of kilograms of pork); they expended 45,328 glass beads (or 1511 *bomoje* shell) on imports. As a result their balance of trade was strongly negative. The figures are somewhat distorted as the inhabitants of the village had a large pig feast in 1953 that left the livestock depleted although it brought lots of cash into the community. Because they planned another pig feast for 1957, during the eight-month period in 1955 they made disproportionately more purchases than would have been the case otherwise.

In their trading Kapauku do not limit themselves to partners of their own tribe. Indeed, the Kamu Valley constitutes but a segment in a chain of intertribal trade that starts in the south at the Mimika coast of New Guinea and continues through the Kapauku territory into the interior, at least as far as the Baliem Valley, or even farther. The whole intertribal trade resembles a chain reaction in which traders from many regions and tribes participate by exchanging their commodities, carrying the newly acquired ones for a relatively short distance and trading them again for other goods to their neighbors on the other side of their territory. In this way bailer shell, necklaces of the small *dedege* shell, iron axes, and machetes move along the route from the Mimika coast into the interior toward the northeast. From the northeast come red ochre, palm wood, stone axes, and stone knives. The stone tools, made of a fine serpentine and green jadeite, are manufactured by the Dani people. From the Moni Papuan country the southbound trade takes bundles of native salt as far as to the Mapia region of the Kapauku country. There, on the southern periphery of the Kapauku territory, all articles that arrive from the north are traded for dogs, net bags, and tobacco, which finally reach the Mimika coast of New Guinea.

In comparison to sales, barter in the Kapauku economy is far less important. For example, during the eight-month period in 1955 the value of bartered goods in the village of Botukebo amounted to only one tenth of the sales. However, if we include under sales any transaction by which one receives for money a commodity, a service, or a wife, then the volume of barter amounted to only 1 percent of the sales. Unlike sales, barter of various goods is subject to customary regulations that group the commodities into spheres of exchange. This means that only certain types of goods are mutually exchangeable. To exchange items belonging to two different spheres is not only improper, but appears to be legally invalid and is consequently not practiced. Needless to say, such rules necessarily restrict exchange through the channels of barter. The four spheres of exchange allow: (1) an exchange of pork for land, growing crops, steel axes, bows, net carrying bags, and salt; (2) bailer shell, bows, and net carrying bags to be bartered for growing crops and for pork; (3) a man to receive for his agricultural labor a reduction of the price to be paid for his wife, a free lease of land, or a growing crop; (4) artifacts, except canoes and planks, to be mutually exchanged.

In one respect the Kapauku distribution of goods appears more capitalistic than our own. The natives do not have the institution of gift, by which ownership of an item is transferred to a recipient who is not legally obligated to reciprocate with an equivalent value. In other words, a Kapauku cannot forfeit, even by an explicit declaration, his legal right to request a return of something that has been given to another person. To a Kapauku the concept of *jegeka* means "a donation to be repaid in the distant future." If a "gift giving" occurs among good friends and relatives, "distant future" often means the lifetime of the donor or the recipient. Since debts are inherited, and an unreciprocated gift is regarded by a Kapauku as a debt, the repayment of gifts is promptly requested by the main heir as soon as the donor dies. In practice, repayment of a gift is usually asked at the time that the beneficiary acquires a substantial sum of money (from the sale of a pig, from a bride price paid for his sister and so on), or on the death of either the donor or the recipient. Although from the Kapauku legal point of view, little difference is made between debt and gift, the two concepts are not really identical. Whereas it is legal and moral to request repayment of a loan at any time, it is regarded as highly immoral to ask for a reciprocation of a gift shortly after it has been made. Consequently, Kapauku distinguish the concepts of loan and gift on the moral rather than legal plane.

As in our modern economy, Kapauku know the institutions of lease, rent, and loan. A plot of agricultural land of approximately 900 square meters is customarily leased for 1 cowrie. Lease of land for a monetary compensation is, however, not too frequent. Of all cultivated land of the residents of Botukebo

(172,480 square meters) only 6.8 percent (11,800 square meters) was leased to their cultivators for a specific monetary compensation in 1955. Far more popular than leasing land for cash is to acquire it for cultivation as a "land grant in exchange." Kapauku refer to such a grant as *jegeka*, a gift. What is actually given is not the land, of course, but only the use of it, usually for one crop only. The natives request such grants because the plots they have in mind are bordered on one or several sides by gardens already made, thus saving the construction of fences and drainage ditches on those sides. Also, because of their promise of high fertility, plots that have lain fallow for a long time are in great demand. The land grant in exchange closely resembles a loan. In other words the recipient of the grant not only has an obligation to return the favor in kind, but the reciprocation of it is often requested within a short period of time. The grantee is required to return the "borrowed" land to its owner after he has harvested his crops from it. He is liable for all changes to the plot incurred by an improper use of it. In 1955 the cultivators of the village of Botukebo made about 34 percent of their gardens (57,900 square meters) on land obtained from others as grants in exchange. Movables, such as axes, adzes, machetes, and canoes are also loaned by their owners to others. If the borrower uses the tools for economic gain a small charge is invariably made for the loan. On the other hand, loans of necklaces and net carrying bags are free of any payment because they do not give a man any economic profit.

Extension of credit is another very important means of redistributing money among the Kapauku. It has greater importance in this society than in Western capitalism. Among the Kapauku the role of credit is not limited to the economic sphere only. Through a proper allocation of credit, which in itself is regarded by the Kapauku (who have no gift proper) as the highest expression of generosity and the safest way to acquire great prestige, a rich man assumes political leadership and also becomes a legal authority and judge in his group. The political and legal roles of credit will be fully treated in Chapter 3. The discussion here will be limited and will give the reader only one example of the importance of credit in the political sphere.

The Kapauku economy does not recognize the legal enforcement of interest on loan payments. Debtors often promise to pay a few extra shell for the favor of borrowing money, but this promise, if not kept, cannot become a cause for legal complaint. It is always entirely up to the debtor whether he will pay the extra sum; but if he refuses to do so, he faces a severe loss of prestige and will be regarded as an untrustworthy, dishonest individual. Ultimately this informal moral sanction carries with it economic repercussions; people hesitate to loan money to an individual who has broken his promise in the past.

The extent of credit may be illustrated by quantitative data on 170 cases of monetary loans involving 55 males as creditors or debtors. The total value of loans equaled 170,382 glass beads, an amount that could purchase 11,358 kilograms of pork. Fifty-one percent of all the loans were extended internally—that is within the village. External credits to outsiders accounted for 35 percent, and external debts amounted to the remaining 14 percent. The balance of external debts and credits proved to be favorable to the residents of Botukebo; the surplus of external credits equaled 66,379 glass beads, an amount capable of purchasing 4425 kilograms of pork. As for the relationship of the parties to these contracts, it was interesting to note that 46 percent of all cases of monetary loans were between paternal-parallel kinsmen.

The broad significance of credits can be described by demonstrating the consequences of an acculturation situation in the Kamu Valley that by severely reducing the amount of borrowing among the natives, profoundly changed the political structure of the region. Upon my second return to the Kamu Valley in 1962 a spectacular loss of power and influence of most of the native headmen was observed. Strangely enough, however, the Dutch Administration had shown a deep interest in preserving the old system of political leadership. A review of the outstanding debts and credits in 1962, compared with those of 1959 and 1955, explained the loss of power of the local headmen. Most Kapauku follow the decisions of the local headmen because they are indebted to them and are afraid of being asked to repay what they owe, because they feel grateful for past loans, or because they expect some future monetary favors. Comparison of the total of credits in the three years revealed that in 1962 the natives owed their rich headmen only about one fourth of what they did in 1955. It was therefore obvious that the disintegration of the headmen's power and, ultimately, the complete collapse of their leadership resulted from the spectacular decrease of indebtedness of the common native to his leader. The young men, who in former times had to borrow heavily from the headman in order to buy themselves wives or pigs, found, with the advent of the white man, a way to escape indebtedness. They secured remunerative employment at Moanemani, a government outpost where the Administration was building an airstrip. This construction had an unexpected effect upon the native Kapauku culture: by eliminating the necessity to borrow it caused the native political structure to disintegrate.

Intestate as well as testamentary inheritance plays an important role in the Kapauku system of redistribution of property. In their regulations of intestate inheritance Kapauku distinguish three different situations that determine the allocation of property in absence of a testament. Accordingly, different rules apply to the distribution of property left by a man or by a woman; the rules are again modified if the main heir is a minor. To every inheritance there is a main heir who is identified by a combination of the principles of primogeniture and patriparallel descent. Thus it is first the eldest son of the deceased who is the main heir to the estate. In the absence of sons the eldest living brother is the heir; in the absence of brothers the eldest son of the eldest brother inherits. If no first fraternal nephews survive, the father of the deceased inherits. In the absence of the father, the father's eldest brother becomes the main heir. In his deficiency the title to the estate passes to the eldest son of the father's oldest brother, and so on. Consequently, the difference between the three inheritance situations does not lie in the fact that different people would be designated as main heirs.

Indeed, in all three situations he is the same person. Rather it is the degree of inclusiveness of the main heir's siblings in sharing the estate that marks the difference.

When a man dies, his eldest son or in his absence another main heir has an exclusive right to inherit the following objects: bows and arrows, net carrying bags, necklaces, charm stones, the main house as well as *tone* (the woman's house), dogs, chickens, all cowrie shell money and glass beads, and all pigs. If during his life the deceased had imposed a taboo on himself not to use certain cowrie shell, glass beads, and bead and *dedege* shell necklaces, but to leave them intact as an inheritance for his sons, all these become the property of the main heir. However, the heir has a legal duty to distribute some portion of them among his siblings. If these currencies have been kept during the life of the deceased by his wives, the sons of every wife are entitled to shares of those cowries kept by their mothers. All land, salt, and stone and iron axes are divided among the main heir and his siblings on the basis of mutual agreement.

From a woman her eldest son (or in his absence her husband or another main heir) inherits her shell necklaces and her net carrying bags. Although glass beads and *dedege* shell necklaces become the property of the main heir, he has a duty to give a portion of them to his siblings. Iron and stone machetes and stone knives should be distributed among the sons on the basis of common agreement. The eldest daughter inherits only her mother's fishing net and large net carrying bag. If the deceased woman had no daughters, these articles become the property of her eldest sister.

When the main heir is a minor, his older brother (or father if he is not a son of the deceased) becomes a trustee of the inheritance and guardian of the minor. The guardian has the duty to bring up the boy properly and to help him with a loan in the purchase of a wife. In return the guardian is later paid *mune*, a fee for bringing up the child. Upon his coming of age the boy receives his father's land and all the tabooed currency that the guardian had kept for him. Of other inherited money the boy receives only a part; the rest is kept by the guardian. The latter also becomes the owner of all pigs of the estate and has no duty to return any of the animals to the main heir. Tools, necklaces, and weapons are also taken by the guardian who may keep most of them as his own property.

Every Kapauku who feels that he is going to die soon has the moral duty to make an oral testament in the presence of several witnesses. Most of these declarations simply dispose of the property according to the rules of intestate inheritance. Nevertheless, an explicit statement about the disposal eliminates possible uncertainties and difficulties pertaining to the division of the estate. Some testaments, of course, differ markedly from the laws of intestate inheritance. In order to protect the interests of legal heirs who might be unjustly eliminated, Kapauku law sets up certain restrictions to the free testamentary dispositions of a dying man. It categorically states that no sons, brothers, fathers, or nephews can be deprived of their share of land under any circumstances. A son, however, may be denied money and pigs if he abused or insulted the testator without a serious reason or neglected him in disease or old age. In the absence of sons these restrictions apply to any other type of heir. Bows and arrows, necklaces, net carrying bags, and fishing nets can be willed freely without restrictions.

The last type of redistribution of property is that which occurs by forceful seizure. The Kapauku law states that a man's property may be seized against his will if he has failed or refused to meet his obligations originating from a contract or from a damage he has caused. A successful seizure of the liable person's property, which inevitably takes the form of capturing a pig, absolves the debtor from any further obligation irrespective of the value of the seized property. The natives usually resort to forceful seizure in cases that cannot be legally adjudicated. This happens when the debtor and creditor belong to two different political confederacies in which case no single legal system applies. As will be demonstrated later, in the Kapauku society law exists only within a political confederacy that forms, politically speaking, a completely independent unit. Beyond the boundaries of this group affairs are settled either through diplomatic negotiations or violence, which takes the form of forceful seizure or war.

ECONOMIC INDIVIDUALISM. These capitalistic features of the Kapauku economy, such as the existence of true money, savings, and speculation, a market regulated by the law of supply and demand, an emphasis on wealth that surpasses in its magnitude that encountered in our own society, the dominant position of sales in the exchange of commodities, the use of paid labor and of lease contracts, are combined with a strong indigenous version of individualism. This manifests itself especially in the Kapauku system of ownership. Every material item that the natives possess is owned individually, a common ownership being simply inconceivable. They claim that two men cannot own a plot of land together because they would try to exploit each other by stealing from each other's crops and by avoiding work as much as possible. Thus money, movables, canoes, houses, and land have always only one owner. Even tracts of virgin forest belong to individual Kapauku. There is no common property of a group such as a lineage, village, or family. Even large structures erected for the benefit of a whole village are not, strictly speaking, owned by the residents in common. A main drainage ditch, or a large fence that protects an area consisting of gardens of numerous owners is, legally speaking, composed of many segments owned by specific individuals who care for the upkeep of only their particular property. Even a bridge across a river does not belong to a village as a whole. This becomes obvious if the structure collapses or if, for any reason, it has to be taken apart. Individuals who have built the structure come to claim the logs and poles that they contributed to its construction. Wife and husband also possess separate property, as does even a boy only twelve years old. It is a frequent occurrence that spouses or father and son are indebted to each other and that debts are payable upon request.

The notion of individualism and a relative financial independence are inculcated into the Papuans at a very early age. When a boy is about ten years old his father gives him a garden plot and encourages him to work on it for his own benefit. The boy gradually develops its production and begins his own financial career. He often plays the role of creditor or debtor to his father, older brother, or cousin. I was once a witness to a very interesting and amusing lesson on individualism that a young boy received from his father. While walking through the village of Botukebo I heard a loud howling and lamentation coming from one of the houses. When I entered the structure I found to my surprise a middle-aged, muscular man squatting in the middle of the room, crying and yelling while a boy, about eleven years old, was screaming at him and hitting him with a stick. The man was being beaten by his own son. The reason for the excitement was that the father owed his son 2 *bomoje* shell which he refused to pay back. Thus the boy had a right to punish his debtor. However, by the beating he abrogated his right to the debt, in other words the father's obligation to repay was annulled. After the beating was over and the enraged boy departed, the father wiped away his tears and smiled with great satisfaction: "My boy will be quite a businessman, but he must learn not to trust anybody." In addition to the lesson in commerce the whole affair proved to be most satisfactory to the happy father, as he assured me. Not only had he gained 2 cowries, but the beating administered by his son, he insisted, was so painless that he received the wealth for practically nothing.

Native individualism also affects the cooperation in a household, as well as the pattern of work in general. The people do not like to, and actually do not, work together on the same plot of land. Co-wives, for example, will never till land as a group; a plot is subdivided into *medeke*, individual sections, which are then entrusted to the care of individual women. Men also make gardens individually. If a helper is required in order to clear a large tract of forest, the area is invariably subdivided and each man works in his own section alone. Kapauku firmly believe that an individual should be free to make his own decisions and organize his work according to his own wishes.

Even eating does not escape this pronounced individualism. Unlike many primitive societies, Kapauku, in a strict sense, do not share their food in common in any social group. There are always individuals who own the food and function as hosts to the rest of the household. Those men who were treated to a meal by one of their coresidents have a duty to reciprocate in kind, and they are hosts in turn. Since women eat separately in their small rooms they do not participate directly in this distribution. The food that is customarily harvested by the men they receive from their husbands. They reciprocate those gifts of pork, game, sugar cane, bananas, and so on by supplying their spouses daily with sweet potatoes. In his work *Trade and Market in the Early Empires* (1957:46) Polanyi generalizes for "tribal societies" and claims that a community "keeps all its members from starving unless it is itself borne down by catastrophe in which case interests are again threatened collectively, not individually." This theme of collectivism is certainly not applicable to the Kapauku situation. Among these Papuans there exists no collective action that would keep individuals from starving. The individual differences in wealth and consumption of food are striking. The Kapauku individualism indeed permits the natives, particularly children from poor homes, to develop severe symptoms of undernourishment, while the residents of the neighboring prosperous households are well fed. The village of Botukebo may serve us again as an example. There, members of the household of the old Kamutaga certainly starved, while their neighbors from the house of Timaajjokainaago lived in plenty. This difference in the state of economic affairs was plainly visible in the physical appearance of the residents of the two households.

Cooperation, to be sure, does exist among the Kapauku, but its pure form, which de-emphasizes individualism, is limited to a few activities. Thus people work together when erecting a building either for habitation or for festivity, when they pull a canoe to a lake, or when they are fighting a war. In other events that require the joint effort of several people, their activity appears to be somehow autonomous. Although several persons may work on the same project, their tasks are so defined that the contribution of an individual is readily perceivable and separable from that of others. In this way the work is either easily remunerable, or the fruits of the cooperation are retained by the workers.

Although the Kapauku economic system resembles in so many ways Western capitalism, there exists one important difference. The system is not combined with the sociological phenomenon that Veblen calls conspicuous consumption. In contrast to our own civilization, the rich men among the Kapauku dress as the commoners do. If they have some special food they tend to be secretive about its consumption, so as to avoid a possible sharing with others. Very often rich men's elaborate necklaces are loaned to the poorer people to wear, while the owners remain undecorated. Kapauku, of course, display their wealth, but through the channels of conspicuous generosity. Since these people do not know the gift proper, generosity may take the form of loans, or lavish distribution of food free of charge on such occasions as birth ceremonies or *putu duwai naago*, the opening day of the cycle of dances connected with a pig feast. There exists almost a compulsion for extension of credit in this native society. In some regions, such as that of the Paniai Lake, rich people who prove to be stingy with their credits are even punished by execution.

The wealth of a native, and therefore also his prestige and political status, changes with his successes and losses in pig breeding and trading. Consequently, the economic as well as the political structure is constantly undergoing change. New and successful pig breeders are elevated to the position of *tonowi*, the rich headmen, only to lose their positions later to younger and more successful businessmen. More so than in Western society the rich men among the Kapauku are self-made, thus testifying to the great vertical mobility in their economic and social system.

25 THE SINHALESE OF THE DRY ZONE OF NORTHERN CEYLON

E. R. Leach

The concept of social structure, as it is used by British social anthropologists, is closely linked with the notion of social continuity. It is an established convention among anthropologists that a "people" can survive the most startling changes of external circumstance. The Iroquois who build skyscrapers in New York are "the same" Iroquois that introduced Morgan to the mysteries of matrilineal kinship organization. Clearly, if we use such a terminology, the notion of sameness requires cautious analysis.

Over a period of time the actual composition of any "society" changes; the old die, children grow old, and new children are born. Customs change too, in primitive as well as in sophisticated cultures; in a single generation the headhunters of Sarawak have become prosperous rubber planters touring their rivers in outboard motorboats. In the face of such change, what is it that persists? The total situation is plainly very complex, for the perpetuation of language alone entails the maintenance of an elaborate mesh of "tradition" which is, to a high degree, impervious to immediate changes in the local situation. In developing their special theory of social structure the British social anthropologists have laid stress on only one particular aspect of this total problem.

If we consider a community of people at any given point in time, we can readily see that most interpersonal relations are governed by conventional rules which, in themselves, apply to statuses rather than to individuals. There are rules about how the young should respect the old, how men should treat women, how parents should deal with their children, and so on. Such rules, as a whole, can be said to form a "system." In principle, the system will not be altered by any mere progression of time, for at every point in time there will always be old and young, men and women, parents and children.

Going further, the British social anthropologists have claimed that, in societies where unilineal descent is given marked cultural emphasis, the continuing system of jural relationships to which I have referred turns out to be very largely a matter of kinship organization. The continuity of the society as a whole rests on the continuity of the system of lineages, each of which is a "corporation," the life span of which is independent of the individual lives of its individual members.

This mode of analysis has proved so fruitful, particularly with regard to African materials, that it has been easy to overlook its limitations. The argument

From Social Structure in Southeast Asia *edited by George P. Murdock, pp. 116–127. Published by Quadrangle Books for The Viking Fund Publications in Anthropology, 1960. Reprinted by permission.*

is one which has developed specifically with regard to societies possessing clear-cut unilineal descent groups (Fortes, 1953), and this poses two questions. First, what kind of ongoing corporation takes the place of the lineage in societies which lack unilineal descent groups? Second, if we are to distinguish societies with unilineal descent groups as a special type, where do we draw the line? For, considered as an organizing principle, unilineal descent is never simply present or absent; it can be present in varying degrees.

The justification for including a paper on Ceylon in a symposium on Southeast Asia is precisely that Sinhalese society may be considered a marginal case. Generally speaking, the tribal peoples of Borneo and the Philippines have kinship systems which are fully cognatic. Nothing could be more "bilateral" than the pattern described by Barton (1949) for the Kalinga or by Freeman (1958) for the Iban. Sinhalese society, however, though broadly speaking cognatic in type, also contains marked elements of unilinearity, and one authority (Ryan 1953: 26) has even alleged that the Sinhalese have a lineage system. A discussion of the nature of structural continuity in the Sinhalese case may therefore serve to discriminate some of the critical issues.

The notion of a corporation, as derived from Maine, is that an estate comprises a "bundle of rights" over persons and things. At any one time the corporation embraces a number of individuals who share in the assets of the estate according to their particular relative status. Recruitment to such a property-owning corporation may be acquired in a variety of ways, e.g., by purchase, by initiation, or by inheritance. It is the general characteristic of unilineal descent groups that a child automatically inherits corporation membership from one or the other of its recognized parents, but not from both.

Clearly the principle of unilineal descent is a convenient one, but this should not blind us to the fact that several other kinds of "inheritance" are theoretically possible. A system in which all children inherited equal rights from both parents would plainly lead to total confusion, but a system in which children could choose to take particular rights from either the father or the mother (though not from both at once) would not, in principle, lead to a structure any more complex than one of straight unilineal descent. Alternatively, the status might depend not so much upon parentage as one place of residence. Ethnographic examples of both these alternatives have been recorded. The Sinhalese case contains something of both.

Sinhalese culture is by no means uniform. Common usage distinguishes the low-country Sinhalese of southwestern Ceylon from the Kandyans of the central and north central areas. Within the Kandyan category it is useful to distinguish further the population of the mountainous, and relatively densely populated, Central Province from that of the flat Dry Zone lying to the north and east. The reasons for cultural differences here are partly historical, partly ecological. European colonialism made its impact upon the coastal regions and upon the southwest several centuries before the Kandyan kingdom was subjugated. Within the Kandyan area, on the other hand, the climatic contrast between the Dry Zone and the rest is very great, and in consequence quite different residential patterns have developed in different sections.

Formally considered, the whole Kandyan area possesses a unified system of customary law, much of which now has judicial sanction. The principles of this law, especially as regards matters of marriage and inheritance, have been described in a number of textbooks, notably that of Hayley (1923). Patterns of residence in relation to kinship have received less attention, but Tambiah (1958) has recently published an excellent account of the situation prevailing in hill villages close to Kandy itself. Still more recently Yalman (1960) has reported on other Kandyan hill communities.

Kandyan hill communities are mostly of substantial size, with populations exceeding 1,000 individuals. They usually include members of a number of different castes, and there is wide economic differentiation between rich and poor. The wealthier sections of the society set considerable value on the maintenance of the family estate as an intact entity. The *gedera*, i.e., the family house and its associated lands, is looked upon as a patrimony to be handed down mainly to the male heirs, who should ideally continue to reside in, or close to, the parental home. With this patrilineal ideology, however, is associated a bilateral principle of inheritance. Daughters as well as sons inherit from both parents, and in equal degree. The patrimonial landed estate can therefore be conserved on behalf of the sons only if the daughters can take their share of the inheritance in some other form, usually that of money or other movable assets given as a dowry at the time of the daughter's marriage.

Although the same ideology concerning property rights prevails throughout the community, it is in general only the wealthier families that are able to provide their daughters with cash dowries. Hence it is only among the wealthy that the *gedera* emerges as a named group with many of the attributes of a corporate patrilineage. Among poorer families, property in land, such as it is, is dispersed among both sons and daughters, and the appearance of unilinearity disappears.

The situation in the northern Dry Zone is rather different. The general region of Anuradhapura has a very long history of human occupation. It was the site of the classical kingdom of Ceylon, the virtues of which are extolled in the Mahavamsa. What is relevant in a highly complex history is only that a sophisticated civilization flourished there from the third century B.C. until the thirteenth century after Christ. It was a "hydraulic civilization" in the sense in which Wittfogel (1957) uses the term; the whole countryside was very intensively developed by a great variety of irrigation works of various types and sizes.

In later centuries the more elaborate of these works fell into decay, but village life continued to be possible on a limited scale. If we ignore the consequences of the intensive reconstruction work over the past thirty years, the general ecological pattern of the North Central Province today may be summarized as follows. Each village constitutes a separate economic entity. Its population subsists by the cultivation of irrigated rice in a small permanent field which is watered from a rain-fed reservoir (tank) which is particular to that village alone. The villagers are alone responsible for the maintenance of the tank and, subject to certain supervisory governmental controls, have sole rights in its water.

The village field necessarily lies below the level of the tank where it is easily irrigated with a controlled water supply. The houses of the village are clustered together immediately below the earthwork of the tank, where water seepage makes it possible to grow fruit trees and moisture-demanding vegetables. Although the total annual precipitation is considerable—50 to 75 inches—it is concentrated in brief periods, and the rate of evaporation in dry weather is very high. Some cultivation in unirrigated areas is possible, but only erratically so. Generally speaking, permanent human habitation is impossible without irrigation.

It follows that there is a peculiarly intimate relationship between any particular tank and the village and field that are associated with it. The size of any tank depends upon its position. Once the main earthwork has been constructed the capacity of the tank is fixed within quite narrow limits. This sets consequential limits on the size of the field which can be irrigated, and more indirectly on the size of the village population which can derive its subsistence from that field.

Since the field is fixed in size and position, it is not surprising to find that land is owned according to rules which we might describe as "freehold private tenure," i.e., which allow land to be bought and sold, leased, and mortgaged. Such a description, however, masks the really crucial element in the situation. The scarce valuable is not land but water. Although the villagers appear at first sight to be concerned with the ownership of land, closer investigation shows that land is measured in terms of the water to which it is entitled. This fact has considerable social implications.

While plots of land can be divided, the unity of the tank is permanent and inescapable. The villagers who derive their sustenance from a single tank may have their petty rivalries, but in larger matters, such as the maintenance of the tank earthwork and the proper operation of the tank sluices, they must cooperate closely lest disaster befall them all. We consequently find that, although the ownership of land (i.e., water) is meticulously fragmented into small individual parcels, the work of the agricultural cycle is closely coordinated and operated according to a strict collective timetable. We find too that the villagers who derive their sustenance from a single tank are almost invariably members of a single small sub-caste (*variga*), that they tend strongly to be endogamous, and that they are consequently all close kin.

Although both men and women own and inherit property, it is the husband who is normally its manager. Since it is humiliating for a man to be exclusively dependent upon his wife's property, every man endeavors to marry virilocally (*diga*). If he must marry uxorilocally (*binna*), he looks for a girl from his own village, where he is likely to have assets of his own. While the ideal preference for *diga* as opposed to *binna* marriage is quite explicit, the actual numerical proportion of *binna* marriages may be 40 per cent or more.

Binna marriages belong to several clearly defined types. There is the *binna* husband who is himself landless and makes himself the servile dependent of his father-in-law; there is the *binna* heiress who has no brothers and whose parents have insisted that she stay at home to maintain the family estate; and there is the *binna* marriage where the spouses are cross-cousins. In this last instance there is again an economic motive. Since a man normally inherits land both from his father and from his mother, he may be co-heir with his mother's brother's daughter of land located in his mother's village of birth, so that by marrying her he consolidates the estate. Sinhalese even say that a man has a "right" to marry his mother's brother's daughter for this purpose. In practice, although cross-cousin marriages occur quite frequently, they are in no special sense preferred or prescribed.

Properly speaking there is no dowry system. What is sometimes called a dowry (*dävädda*) is simply an advance of inheritance in the form of land. There is in this region no technique of preserving the patrimonial estate for males by giving movable assets to the daughters. Nevertheless, since it is the more prosperous families who marry *diga*, there is observable among them a statistical tendency in the direction of patrilineal rather than cognatic inheritance. What happens is roughly as follows. Both the male head of a household and his wife may separately own property in land. Both parcels will be separately inherited by the sons and daughters. Those who remain resident in the village will all receive equal shares, but those who marry far away will, in practice, get smaller shares or even nothing at all.

It is mainly a question of the practicability of fragmentation. A poor man with several children can not in practice divide his assets equally, and the family usually disperses, leaving a single son to inherit the patrimony and buy out his co-heirs as the occasion demands. A wealthy household with only one son and one daughter, on the other hand, is likely to arrange an exchange marriage with some equally wealthy household in a nearby village or even in the same village. The property may be fragmented for the time being, but the possibility, indeed the probability, exists that it will be brought together again by further marriages between the same two families at a later date. Such procedures do not have the effect of conserving property within a patrilineage, but they do tend, in the long run, to conserve property within particular co-resident compound groups. The heads of such groups are normally male and are usually descended from previous owners by male rather than female links.

If the total population of a cluster of closely adjacent villages is analyzed over a period of time, it will be found that, in each village, the occupants of a small number of particular compounds (*watte*) persistently retain most of the economic and political influence. None of the various positions of influence and title which villagers can hold, either by governmental appointment or in their own private affairs, are hereditary, but the constancy with which such positions remain within a narrow circle of kin plainly demonstrates that, among the wealthy, the strategy of marriage can be used to circumvent the apparently disruptive influence of bilateral inheritance.

In one village studied, for example, the leadership over a period of about half a century was transmitted successively (the dates are approximations) as follows:

In 1905 to A, a resident in Compound 1;
In 1925 to B, a resident in Compound 2, son-in-law to A;
In 1938 to C, a resident in Compound 1, son of a cross-cousin of A's wife;
In 1948 to D, a resident in Compound 2, sister's son to C and cross-cousin's son to B;
In 1952 to E, a resident in Compound 1, cross-cousin to D and son to C.

There were nine compounds in the village, but the other seven were entirely excluded from positions of influence during the period in question. This was not because Compounds 1 and 2 had any special hereditary right but was directly due to the fact that A and B arranged a series of highly astute marriages both for themselves and for their descendants. In 1886 the occupants of Compounds 1 and 2 had both been nearly bankrupt; by 1954 their successors owned all the best land in the village.

It is against this background of property maneuver that we can best understand the peculiar attitude of the Dry-Zone Sinhalese toward marriage. By European standards the villagers are scandalously promiscuous. A girl ordinarily starts having love affairs as soon as she reaches puberty, and most women have been pregnant at least once by the time they reach sixteen. According to customary law the resulting children are always legitimate, provided always that the girl is not foolish enough to have a liaison with a man of the wrong sub-caste.

This kind of "marriage" can be entered into in the most casual manner. Any woman who cooks for a man is considered to be his wife for the time being, and the relationship can be broken off as easily as it is started. When a child is born, the villagers go to great pains to see that the birth is registered and that the father's name appears on the birth certificate, for this may potentially affect the child's ultimate status as an heir. The ordinary obligations of parents toward children, however, are treated in a highly casual way. It is quite common to find that a man and woman who are living together and rearing a family have each had several other children by several different spouses. One consequence of this is that half-brother and step-brother relationships are extremely common.

In addition to these casual "common-law" marriages, we find that the villagers sometimes turn a wedding into a ceremony of the utmost elaboration. Ceremonial weddings are the occasion for expensive feasting and the demonstrative gathering of rival groups of kinsmen. From a legal point of view the formal wedding is no more binding than an informal liaison, though in practice the collapse of a formally established marriage is likely to lead to bitter recriminations. The formal marriages, as one might expect, are mainly those of influential people, or of those who are seeking to gain influence. In terms of village politics they represent treaties of alliance between potentially hostile groups of kinsmen. The two types of marriage are identical from the point of view of the children, who are legitimate in either case. They differ in the fact that, whereas informal marriage is a private affair between husband and wife, a formal marriage is arranged by the parents. Formal unions are part of the long-term strategy whereby property and influence are conserved within particular compound groups.

Since all the inhabitants of a Sinhalese Dry-Zone village are likely to be related to one another in several different ways, it would be misleading to suppose that kinship behaviors conform to rigid stereotypes. Nevertheless, some general tendencies deserve to be noted. Relations between a man and his children are never close. As soon as a young man marries he begins to be treated as a separate householder, and his relations with his parents become increasingly formal and remote. Separation of the sexes is extreme. Although men and women sometimes work together in the field, there are few other occasions when they can, with propriety, be seen close together.

Relations between co-resident siblings, who are likely to be heirs to the same property, are formal rather than friendly. In contrast, the relationship between brothers-in-law, which is assimilated to that of cross-cousins, is characteristically one of cooperative equality. Where brothers-in-law reside in the same compound their friendship often assumes the form of a joking relationship. This stereotyped pattern is, however, complicated by the high incidence of half-sibling and step-sibling relationships alluded to above. Since the total area of irrigated land available to the villagers is unalterable, the inheritance of land inevitably becomes a source of bitter jealousy. The restrained formality with which a younger brother is expected to treat an elder brother is in accord with this. Co-resident "brothers," however, may well be of partly or completely different parentage, so that their potential rights of inheritance are quite different. In such cases much of the potential strain inherent in the sibling relationship disappears, and half-brothers who are not co-heirs to the same property are often close allies.

Neat summary of these facts is difficult, but underlying the whole complex one can discern two contradictory, yet complementary, structural principles. On the one hand there is the principle of bilteral inheritance by all sons and all daughters in roughly equal proportions. While property can be transmitted in other ways, e.g., by will or by sale, inheritance remains the main process by which rights in land are transferred from one generation to another. Considered simply in kinship terms, bilateral inheritance must lead to the fragmentation of holdings and to rivalry between co-heirs. It thus stands in contradiction to the ideology which requires the co-heirs of an estate to remain co-resident in the same ancestral compound, and which presupposes that a band of brothers will always act together as a united family.

On the other hand, the principle that women, despite their inferior political status, have rights to land means that the transmission of property to children serves to unite disparate holdings as well as to fragment them, for the separate properties of a man and his wife are unified in their children. Heirship separates property; marriage brings it together. It is a reflection of this that full brothers, though formally united, seldom cooperate, whereas brothers-in-law, though formally opposed, are characteristically close allies.

Space is lacking for more than the barest outline of the system of land tenure which provides the economic basis for Sinhalese Dry-Zone society, but its essence can be briefly summarized. The village field is not only fixed in size; it is also fixed in layout. It consists of a set number of permanent shares (*pangu*), which are so laid out on the ground that each share receives a precisely equal proportion of the total available tank water. One share may be divided among several owners, or one owner may possess several shares, but the layout of the field, which is plain for all to see, remains the same from generation to generation.

Let me sum up. The study of social structure in societies organized according to unilineal descent has not only thrown the emphasis on kinship but has given the impression that kinship structures can be considered in isolation, without reference to the economic background. It has also suggested that social structure is a matter of clearly defined rules, e.g., of descent, of inheritance, and of preferential marriage. In the society considered in this essay social structure is likewise a matter of kinship, but kinship arrangements are not clearly constrained by rules. In all issues of inheritance, succession, marriage, and residence the individual is faced with choice. It is not implied that choice is random, but by and large choices are governed by economic ends.

In such a society the continuing entity is the pattern of the man-made economic context—the village tank, the compounds, the layout of the village field. Within narrow limits these are unalterable facts to which each generation of inhabitants must adjust their domestic lives. Although, as in other primitive and peasant societies, the language of kinship plays a dominating role in the expression of social relationships, social behavior is not constrained by the prior existence of kinship corporations. It is not so much that the Sinhalese order their economic lives in accord with kinship relations as that their kinship relations are an expression of the way in which they order their economic lives.

The relevance of this analysis in the present context of a survey of Southeast Asian societies is that it should make us cautious of embarking upon typological generalizations. Freeman's analysis of Iban society might, on first inspection, suggest a polarization of types—the social structure of bilateral societies in contrast to the social structure of societies with unilineal descent groups. But we need to be careful. My analysis of Sinhalese social structure has followed lines closely analogous to those of Freeman for the Iban, even though less quantitative evidence has been provided. But Sinhalese society, though lacking a fully developed lineage system, is by no means fully cognatic in a sense applicable to the Iban and the Kalinga. More important than typology is the implication, in both Freeman's work and my own, that social structures are sometimes best regarded

as the statistical outcome of multiple individual choices rather than a direct
reflection of jural rules. For this approach both of us are indebted to a highly
germinal essay by Fortes (1949).

26 THE ECONOMIC ORGANISATION OF A P.O.W. CAMP

R. A. Radford

Introduction

After allowance has been made for abnormal circumstances, the social institutions, ideas and habits of groups in the outside world are to be found reflected in
a Prisoner of War Camp. It is an unusual but a vital society. Camp organisation
and politics are matters of real concern to the inmates, as affecting their present
and perhaps their future existences. Nor does this indicate any loss of proportion.
No one pretends that camp matters are of any but local importance or of more
than transient interest, but their importance there is great. They bulk large in a
world of narrow horizons and it is suggested that any distortion of values lies
rather in the minimisation than in the exaggeration of their importance. Human
affairs are essentially practical matters and the measure of immediate effect on
the lives of those directly concerned in them is to a large extent the criterion of
their importance at that time and place. A prisoner can hold strong views on
such subjects as whether or not all tinned meats shall be issued to individuals
cold or be centrally cooked, without losing sight of the significance of the
Atlantic Charter.

One aspect of social organisation is to be found in economic activity, and
this, along with other manifestations of a group existence, is to be found in any
P.O.W. camp. True, a prisoner is not dependent on his exertions for the provision of the necessaries, or even the luxuries of life, but through his economic
activity, the exchange of goods and services, his standard of material comfort
is considerably enhanced. And this is a serious matter to the prisoner: he is not
"playing at shops" even though the small scale of the transactions and the simple
expression of comfort and wants in terms of cigarettes and jam, razor blades
and writing paper, make the urgency of those needs difficult to appreciate, even
by an ex-prisoner of some three months' standing.

Nevertheless, it cannot be too strongly emphasised that economic activities do
not bulk so large in prison society as they do in the larger world. There can be
little production; as has been said the prisoner is indepedent of his exertions for
the provision of the necessities and luxuries of life; the emphasis lies in exchange
and the media of exchange. A prison camp is not to be compared with the
seething crowd of higglers in a street market, any more than it is to be compared
with the economic inertia of a family dinner table.

From Economica, *November 1945, pp. 189–201. Reprinted by permission.*

Naturally then, entertainment, academic and literary interests, games and discussions of the "other world" bulk larger in everyday life than they do in the life of more normal societies. But it would be wrong to underestimate the importance of economic activity. Everyone receives a roughly equal share of essentials; it is by trade that individual preferences are given expression and comfort increased. All at some time, and most people regularly, make exchanges of one sort or another.

Although a P.O.W. camp provides a living example of a simple economy which might be used as an alternative to the Robinson Crusoe economy beloved by the text-books, and its simplicity renders the demonstration of certain economic hypotheses both amusing and instructive, it is suggested that the principal significance is sociological. True, there is interest in observing the growth of economic institutions and customs in a brand new society, small and simple enough to prevent detail from obscuring the basic pattern and disequilibrium from obscuring the working of the system. But the essential interest lies in the universality and the spontaneity of this economic life; it came into existence not by conscious imitation but as a response to the immediate needs and circumstances. Any similarity between prison organisation and outside organisation arises from similar stimuli evoking similar responses.

The following is as brief an account of the essential data as may render the narrative intelligible. The camps of which the writer had experience were Oflags and consequently the economy was not complicated by payments for work by the detaining power. They consisted normally of between 1,200 and 2,500 people, housed in a number of sparate but intercommunicating bungalows, one company of 200 or so to a building. Each company formed a group within the main organisation and inside the company the room and the messing syndicate, a voluntary and spontaneous group who fed together, formed the constituent units.

Between individuals there was active trading in all consumer goods and in some services. Most trading was for food against cigarettes or other foodstuffs, but cigarettes rose from the status of a normal commodity to that of currency. RMk.s existed but had no circulation save for gambling debts, as few articles could be purchased with them from the canteen.

Our supplies consisted of rations provided by the detaining power and (principally) the contents of Red Cross food parcels—tinned milk, jam, butter, biscuits, bully, chocolate, sugar, etc., and cigarettes. So far the supplies to each person were equal and regular. Private parcels of clothing, toilet requisites and cigarettes were also received, and here equality ceased owing to the different numbers despatched and the vagaries of the post. All these articles were the subject of trade and exchange.

The Development and Organisation of the Market

Very soon after capture people realised that it was both undesirable and unnecessary, in view of the limited size and the equality of supplies, to give away or to accept gifts of cigarettes or food. "Goodwill" developed into trading as a more equitable means of maximising individual satisfaction.

We reached a transit camp in Italy about a fortnight after capture and received ¼ of a Red Cross food parcel each a week later. At once exchanges, already established, multiplied in volume. Starting with simple direct barter, such as a non-smoker giving a smoker friend his cigarette issue in exchange for a chocolate ration, more complex exchanges soon became an accepted custom. Stories circulated of a padre who started off round the camp with a tin of cheese and five cigarettes and returned to his bed with a complete parcel in addition to his original cheese and cigarettes; the market was not yet perfect. Within a week or two, as the volume of trade grew, rough scales of exchange values came into existence. Sikhs, who had at first exchanged tinned beef for practically any other foodstuff, began to insist on jam and margarine. It was realised that a tin of jam was worth ½ lb. of margarine plus something else; that a cigarette issue was worth several chocolate issues, and a tin of diced carrots was worth practically nothing.

In this camp we did not visit other bungalows very much and prices varied from place to place; hence the germ of truth in the story of the itinerant priest. By the end of a month, when we reached our permanent camp, there was a lively trade in all commodities and their relative values were well known, and expressed not in terms of one another—one didn't quote bully in terms of sugar—but in terms of cigarettes. The cigarette became the standard of value. In the permanent camp people started by wandering through the bungalows calling their offers—"cheese for seven" (cigarettes)—and the hours after parcel issue were Bedlam. The inconveniences of this system soon led to its replacement by an Exchange and Mart notice board in every bungalow, where under the headings "name", "room number", "wanted" and "offered" sales and wants were advertised. When a deal went through, it was crossed off the board. The public and semi-permanent records of transactions led to cigarette prices being well known and thus tending to equality throughout the camp, although there were always opportunities for an astute trader to make a profit from arbitrage. With this development everyone, including nonsmokers, was willing to sell for cigarettes, using them to buy at another time and place. Cigarettes became the normal currency, though, of course, barter was never extinguished.

The unity of the market and the prevalence of a single price varied directly with the general level of organisation and comfort in the camp. A transit camp was always chaotic and uncomfortable: people were overcrowded, no one knew where anyone else was living, and few took the trouble to find out. Organisation was too slender to include an Exchange and Mart board, and private advertisements were the most that appeared. Consequently a transit camp was not one market but many. The price of a tin of salmon is known to have varied by two cigarettes in 20 between one end of a hut and the other. Despite a high level of organisation in Italy, the market was morcellated in this manner at the first transit camp we reached after our removal to Germany in the autum of 1943. In this camp—Stalag VIIA at Moosburg in Bavaria—there were up to 50,000 prisoners of all nationalities. French, Russians, Italians and Jugo-Slavs were free to move about within the camp: British and Americans were confined to their compounds, although a few cigarettes given to a sentry would always procure permission for one or two men to visit other compounds. The people who first visited the highly organised French trading centre, with its stalls and known prices, found coffee extract—relatively cheap among the tea-drinking English— commanding a fancy price in biscuits or cigarettes, and some enterprising people made small fortunes that way. (Incidentally we found out later that much of the coffee went "over the wire" and sold for phenomenal prices at black market cafés in Munich: some of the French prisoners were said to have made substantial sums in RMk.s. This was one of the few occasions on which our normally closed economy came into contact with other economic worlds.)

Eventually public opinion grew hostile to these monopoly profits—not everyone could make contact with the French—and trading with them was put on a regulated basis. Each group of beds was given a quota of articles to offer and the transaction was carried out by accredited representatives from the British compound, with monopoly rights. The same method was used for trading with sentries elsewhere, as in this trade secrecy and reasonable prices had a peculiar importance, but as is ever the case with regulated companies, the interloper proved too strong.

The permanent camps in Germany saw the highest level of commercial organisation. In addition to the Exchange and Mart notice boards, a shop was organised as a public utility, controlled by representatives of the Senior British Officer, on a no profit basis. People left their surplus clothing, toilet requisites and food there until they were sold at a fixed price in cigarettes. Only sales in cigarettes were accepted—there was no barter—and there was no higgling. For food at least there were standard prices: clothing is less homogeneous and the price was decided around a norm by the seller and the shop manager in agreement; shirts would average say 80, ranging from 60 to 120 according to quality and age. Of food, the shop carried small stocks for convenience; the capital was provided by a loan from the bulk store of Red Cross cigarettes and repaid by a small commission taken on the first transactions. Thus the cigarette attained its fullest currency status, and the market was almost completely unified.

It is thus to be seen that a market came into existence without labour or production. The B.R.C.S. may be considered as "Nature" of the text-book, and the articles of trade—food, clothing and cigarettes—as free gifts—land or manna. Despite this, and despite a roughly equal distribution of resources, a market came into spontaneous operation, and prices were fixed by the operation of supply and demand. It is difficult to reconcile this fact with the labour theory of value.

Actually there was an embryo labour market. Even when cigarettes were not scarce, there was usually some unlucky person willing to perform services for them. Laundrymen advertised at two cigarettes a garment. Battle-dress was scrubbed and pressed and a pair of trousers lent for the interim period for twelve. A good pastel portrait cost thirty or a tin of "Kam". Odd tailoring and other jobs similarly had their prices.

There were also entrepreneurial services. There was a coffee stall owner who sold tea, coffee or cocoa at two cigarettes a cup, buying his raw materials at market prices and hiring labour to gather fuel and to stoke; he actually enjoyed the services of a chartered accountant at one stage. After a period of great prosperity he overreached himself and failed disastrously for several hundred cigarettes. Such large-scale private enterprise was rare but several middlemen or professional traders existed. The padre in Italy, or the men at Moosburg who opened trading relations with the French, are examples: the more subdivided the market, the less perfect the advertisement of prices, and the less stable the prices, the greater was the scope for these operators. One man capitalised his knowledge of Urdu by buying meat from the Sikhs and selling butter and jam in return: as his operations became better known more and more people entered this trade, prices in the Indian Wing approximated more nearly to those elsewhere, though to the end a "contact" among the Indians was valuable, as linguistic difficulties prevented the trade from being quite free. Some were specialists in the Indian trade, the food, clothing or even the watch trade. Middlemen traded on their own account or on commission. Price rings and agreements were suspected and the traders certainly co-operated. Nor did they welcome newcomers. Unfortunately the writer knows little of the workings of these people: public opinion was hostile and the professionals were usually of a retiring disposition.

One trader in food and cigarettes, operating in a period of dearth, enjoyed a high reputation. His capital, carefully saved, was originally about 50 cigarettes, with which he bought rations on issue days and held them until the price rose just before the next issue. He also picked up a little by arbitrage; several times a day he visited every Exchange or Mart notice board and took advantage of every discrepacy between prices of goods offered and wanted. His knowledge of prices, markets and names of those who had received cigarette parcels was phenomenal. By these means he kept himself smoking steadily—his profits— while his capital remained intact.

Sugar was issued on Saturday. About Tuesday two of us used to visit Sam and make a deal; as old customers he would advance as much of the price as he could spare then, and entered the transaction in a book. On Saturday morning he left cocoa tins on our beds for the ration, and picked them up on Saturday afternoon. We were hoping for a calendar at Christmas, but Sam failed too. He was left holding a big black treacle issue when the price fell, and in this weakened state was unable to withstand an unexpected arrival of parcels and the consequent price fluctuations. He paid in full, but from his capital. The next Tuesday, when I paid my usual visit he was out of business.

Credit entered into many, perhaps into most, transactions, in one form or another. Sam paid in advance as a rule for his purchases of future deliveries of sugar, but many buyers asked for credit, whether the commodity was sold spot or future. Naturally prices varied according to the terms of sale. A treacle ration might be advertised for four cigarettes now or five next week. And in the future market "bread now" was a vastly different thing from "bread

Thursday." Bread was issued on Thursday and Monday, four and three days' rations respectively, and by Wednesday and Sunday night it had risen at least one cigarette per ration, from seven to eight, by supper time. One man always saved a ration to sell then at the peak price: his offer of "bread now" stood out on the board among a number of "bread Monday's" fetching one or two less, or not selling at all—and he always smoked on Sunday night.

The Cigarette Currency

Although cigarettes as currency exhibited certain peculiarities, they performed all the functions of a metallic currency as a unit of account, as a measure of value and as a store of value, and shared most of its characteristics. They were homogeneous, reasonably durable, and of convenient size for the smallest or, in packets, for the largest transactions. Incidentally, they could be clipped or sweated by rolling them between the fingers so that tobacco fell out.

Cigarettes were also subject to the working of Gresham's Law. Certain brands were more popular than others as smokes, but for currency purposes a cigarette was a cigarette. Consequently buyers used the poorer qualities and the Shop rarely saw the more popular brands: cigarettes such as Churchman's No. 1 were rarely used for trading. At one time cigarettes hand-rolled from pipe tobacco began to circulate. Pipe tobacco was issued in lieu of cigarettes by the Red Cross at a rate of 25 cigarettes to the ounce and this rate was standard in exchanges, but an ounce would produce 30 home-made cigarettes. Naturally, people with machine-made cigarettes broke them down and re-rolled the tobacco, and the real cigarette virtually disappeared from the market. Hand-rolled cigarettes were not homogeneous and prices could no longer be quoted in them with safety: each cigarette was examined before it was accepted and thin ones were rejected, or extra demanded as a make-weight. For a time we suffered all the inconveniences of a debased currency.

Machine-made cigarettes were always universally acceptable, both for what they would buy and for themselves. It was this intrinsic value which gave rise to their principal disadvantage as currency, a disadvantage which exists, but to a far smaller extent, in the case of metallic currency—that is, a strong demand for non-monetary purposes. Consequently our economy was repeatedly subject to deflation and to periods of monetary stringency. While the Red Cross issue of 50 or 25 cigarettes per man per week came in regularly, and while there were fair stocks held, the cigarette currency suited its purpose admirably. But when the issue was interrupted, stocks soon ran out, prices fell, trading declined in volume and became increasingly a matter of barter. This deflationary tendency was periodically offset by the sudden injection of new currency. Private cigarette parcels arrived in a trickle throughout the year, but the big numbers came in quarterly when the Red Cross received its allocation of transport. Several hundred thousand cigarettes might arrive in the space of a fortnight. Prices soared, and then began to fall, slowly at first but with increasing rapidity as stocks ran out, until the next big delivery. Most of our economic troubles could be attributed to this fundamental instability.

Price Movements

Many factors affected prices, the strongest and most noticeable being the periodical currency inflation and deflation described in the last paragraphs. The periodicity of this price cycle depended on cigarette and, to a far lesser extent, on food deliveries. At one time in the early days, before any private parcels had arrived and when there were no individual stocks, the weekly issue of cigarettes and food parcels occurred on a Monday. The non-monetary demand for cigarettes was great, and less elastic than the demand for food: consequently prices fluctuated weekly, falling towards Sunday night and rising sharply on Monday morning. Later, when many people held reserves, the weekly issue had no such effect, being too small a proportion of the total available. Credit allowed people with no reserves to meet their non-monetary demand over the week-end.

The general price level was affected by other factors. An influx of new prisoners, proverbially hungry, raised it. Heavy air raids in the vicinity of the camp probably increased the non-monetary demand for cigarettes and accentuated deflation. Good and bad war news certainly had its effect, and the general waves of optimism and pessimism which swept the camp were reflected in prices. Before breakfast one morning in March of this year, a rumour of the arrival of parcels and cigarettes was circulated. Within ten minutes I sold a treacle ration, for four cigarettes (hitherto offered in vain for three), and many similar deals went through. By 10 o'clock the rumour was denied, and treacle that day found no more buyers even at two cigarettes.

More interesting than changes in the general price level were changes in the price structure. Changes in the supply of a commodity, in the German ration scale or in the make-up of Red Cross parcels, would raise the price of one commodity relative to others. Tins of oatmeal, once a rare and much sought after luxury in the parcels, became a commonplace in 1943, and the price fell. In hot weather the demand for cocoa fell, and that for soap rose. A new recipe would be reflected in the price level: the discovery that raisins and sugar could be turned into an alcoholic liquor of remarkable potency reacted permanently on the dried fruit market. The invention of electric immersion heaters run off the power points made tea, a drug on the market in Italy, a certain seller in Germany.

In August, 1944, the supplies of parcels and cigarettes were both halved. Since both sides of the equation were changed in the same degree, changes in prices were not anticipated. But this was not the case: the non-monetary demand for cigarettes was less elastic than the demand for food, and food prices fell a little. More important however were the changes in the price structure. German margarine and jam, hitherto valueless owing to adequate supplies of Canadian butter and marmalade, acquired a new value. Chocolate, popular and a certain seller, and sugar, fell. Bread rose; several standing contracts of bread for cigarettes were broken, especially when the bread ration was reduced a few weeks later.

In February, 1945, the German soldier who drove the ration wagon was found to be willing to exchange loaves of bread at the rate of one loaf for a bar of chocolate. Those in the know began selling bread and buying chocolate, by then almost unsaleable in a period of serious deflation. Bread, at about 40, fell slightly; chocolate rose from 15; the supply of bread was not enough for the two commodities to reach parity, but the tendency was unmistakable.

The substitution of German margarine for Canadian butter when parcels were halved naturally affected their relative values, margarine appreciating at the expense of butter. Similarly, two brands of dried milk, hitherto differing in quality and therefore in price by five cigarettes a tin, came together in price as the wider substitution of the cheaper raised its relative value.

Enough has been cited to show that any change in conditions affected both the general price level and the price structure. It was this latter phenomenon which wrecked our planned economy.

Paper Currency—Bully Marks

Around D-Day, food and cigarettes were plentiful, business was brisk and the camp in an optimistic mood. Consequently the Entertainments Committee felt the moment opportune to launch a restaurant, where food and hot drinks were sold while a band and variety turns performed. Earlier experiments, both public and private, had pointed the way, and the scheme was a great success. Food was bought at market prices to provide the meals and the small profits were devoted to a reserve fund and used to bribe Germans to provide greasepaints and other necessities for the camp theatre. Originally meals were sold for cigarettes but this meant that the whole scheme was vulnerable to the periodic deflationary waves, and furthermore heavy smokers were unlikely to attend much. The whole success of the scheme depended on an adequate amount of food being offered for sale in the normal manner.

To increase and facilitate trade, and to stimulate supplies and customers therefore, and secondarily to avoid the worst effects of deflation when it should come, a paper currency was organised by the Restaurant and the Shop. The Shop bought food on behalf of the Restaurant with paper notes and the paper was accepted equally with the cigarettes in the Restaurant or Shop, and passed back to the Shop to purchase more food. The Shop acted as a bank of issue. The paper money was backed 100 per cent by food; hence its name, the Bully Mark. The BMk. was backed 100 per cent by food: there could be no over-issues, as is permissible with a normal bank of issue, since the eventual dispersal of the camp and consequent redemption of all BMk.s was anticipated in the near future.

Originally one BMk. was worth one cigarette and for a short time both circulated freely inside and outside the Restaurant. Prices were quoted in BMk.s and cigarettes with equal freedom—and for a short time the BMk. showed signs of replacing the cigarette as currency. The BMk. was tied to food, but not to cigarettes: as it was issued against food, say 45 for a tin of milk and so on, any reduction in the BMk. prices of food would have meant that there were unbacked BMk.s in circulation. But the price of both food and BMk.s could and did fluctuate with the supply of cigarettes.

While the Restaurant flourished, the scheme was a success: the Restaurant bought heavily, all foods were saleable and prices were stable.

In August parcels and cigarettes were halved and the Camp was bombed. The Restaurant closed for a short while and sales of food became difficult. Even when the Restaurant reopened, the food and cigarette shortage became increasingly acute and people were unwilling to convert such valuable goods into paper and to hold them for luxuries like snacks and tea. Less of the right kinds of food for the Restaurant were sold, and the Shop became glutted with dried fruit, chocolate, sugar, etc., which the Restaurant could not buy. The price level and the price structure changed. The BMk. fell to four-fifths of a cigarette and eventually farther still, and it became unacceptable save in the Restaurant. There was a flight from the BMk., no longer convertible into cigarettes or popular foods. The cigarette re-established itself.

But the BMk. was sound! The Restaurant closed in the New Year with a progressive food shortage and the long evenings without lights due to intensified Allied air raids, and BMk.s could only be spent in the Coffee Bar—relict of the Restaurant—or on the few unpopular foods in the Shop, the owners of which were prepared to accept them. In the end all holders of BMk.s were paid in full, in cups of coffee or in prunes. People who had bought BMk.s for cigarettes or valuable jam or biscuits in their heyday were aggrieved that they should have stood the loss involved by their restricted choice, but they suffered no actual loss of market value.

Price Fixing

Along with this scheme came a determined attempt at a planned economy, at price fixing. The Medical Officer had long been anxious to control food sales, for fear of some people selling too much, to the detriment of their health. The deflationary waves and their effects on prices were inconvenient to all and would be dangerous to the Restaurant which had to carry stocks. Furthermore, unless the BMk. was convertible into cigarettes at about par it had little chance of gaining confidence and of succeeding as a currency. As has been explained, the BMk. was tied to food but could not be tied to cigarettes, which fluctuated in value. Hence, while BMk. prices of food were fixed for all time, cigarette prices of food and BMk.s varied.

The Shop, backed by the Senior British Officer, was now in a position to enforce price control both inside and outside its walls. Hitherto a standard price had been fixed for food left for sale in the Shop, and prices outside were roughly in conformity with this scale, which was recommended as a "guide" to sellers, but fluctuated a good deal around it. Sales in the Shop at recommended prices were apt to be slow though a good price might be obtained: sales outside could be made more quickly at lower prices. (If sales outside were to be at higher prices, goods were withdrawn from the Shop until the recommended price rose: but the recommended price was sluggish and could not follow the market closely by reason of its very purpose, which was stability.) The Exchange and Mart notice boards came under the control of the Shop: advertisements which exceeded a 5 per cent departure from the recommended scale were liable to be crossed out by authority: unauthorised sales were discouraged by authority and also by public opinion, strongly in favour of a just and stable price. (Recommended prices were fixed partly from market data, partly on the advice of the M.O.)

At first the recommended scale was a success: the Restaurant, a big buyer, kept prices stable around this level: opinion and the 5 per cent tolerance helped. But when the price level fell with the August cuts and the price structure changed, the recommended scale was too rigid. Unchanged at first, as no deflation was expected, the scale was tardily lowered, but the prices of goods on the new scale remained in the same relation to one another, owing to the BMk., while on the market the price structure had changed. And the modifying influence of the Restaurant had gone. The scale was moved up and down several times, slowly following the inflationary and deflationary waves, but it was rarely adjusted to changes in the price structure. More and more advertisements were crossed off the board, and black market sales at unauthorised prices increased: eventually public opinion turned against the recommended scale and authority gave up the struggle. In the last few weeks, with unparalleled deflation, prices fell with alarming rapidity, no scales existed, and supply and demand, alone and unmellowed, determined prices.

Public Opinion

Public opinion on the subject of trading was vocal if confused and changeable, and generalisations as to its direction are difficult and dangerous. A tiny minority held that all trading was undesirable as it engendered an unsavoury atmosphere; occasional frauds and sharp practices were cited as proof. Certain forms of trading were more generally condemned; trade with the Germans was criticised by many. Red Cross toilet articles, which were in short supply and only issued in cases of actual need, were excluded from trade by law and opinion working in unshakable harmony. At one time, when there had been several cases of malnutrition reported among the more devoted smokers, no trade in German rations was permitted, as the victims became an additional burden on the depleted food reserves of the Hospital. But while certain activities were condemned as antisocial, trade itself was practised, and its utility appreciated, by almost everyone in the camp.

More interesting was opinion on middlemen and prices. Taken as a whole, opinion was hostile to the middleman. His function, and his hard work in bringing buyer and seller together, were ignored; profits were not regarded as a reward for labour, but as the result of sharp practices. Despite the fact that his very existence was proof to the contrary, the middleman was held to be redundant in view of the existence of an official Shop and the Exchange and Mart. Appreciation only came his way when he was willing to advance the price of a sugar ration, or to buy goods spot and carry them against a future sale. In these cases the element of risk was obvious to all, and the convenience of the service was felt to merit some reward. Particularly unpopular was the middleman with an element of monopoly, the man who contacted the ration wagon driver, or the man who utilised his knowledge of Urdu. And middlemen as a group were blamed for reducing prices. Opinion notwithstanding, most people dealt with a middleman, whether consciously or unconsciously, at some time or another.

There was a strong feeling that everything had its "just price" in cigarettes. While the assessment of the just price, which incidentally varied between camps, was impossible of explanation, this price was nevertheless pretty closely known. It can best be defined as the price usually fetched by an article in good times when cigarettes were plentiful. The "just price" changed slowly; it was unaffected by short-term variations in supply, and while opinion might be resigned to departures from the "just price", a strong feeling of resentment persisted. A more satisfactory definition of the "just price" is impossible. Everyone knew what it was, though no one could explain why it should be so.

As soon as prices began to fall with a cigarette shortage, a clamour arose, particularly against those who held reserves and who bought at reduced prices. Sellers at cut prices were criticised and their activities referred to as the black market. In every period of dearth the explosive question of "should non-smokers receive a cigarette ration?" was discussed to profitless length. Unfortunately, it was the non-smoker, or the light smoker with his reserves, along with the hated middleman, who weathered the storm most easily.

The popularity of the price-fixing scheme, and such success as it enjoyed, were undoubtedly the result of this body of opinion. On several occasions the fall of prices was delayed by the general support given to the recommended scale. The onset of deflation was marked by a period of sluggish trade; prices stayed up but no one bought. Then prices fell on the black market, and the volume of trade revived in that quarter. Even when the recommended scale was revised, the volume of trade in the Shop would remain low. Opinion was always overruled by the hard facts of the market.

Curious arguments were advanced to justify price fixing. The recommended prices were in some way related to the calorific values of the foods offered: hence some were overvalued and never sold at these prices. One argument ran as follows:—not everyone has private cigarette parcels: thus, when prices were high and trade good in the summer of 1944, only the lucky rich could buy. This was unfair to the man with few cigarettes. When prices fell in the following winter, prices should be pegged high so that the rich, who had enjoyed life in the summer, should put many cigarettes into circulation. The fact that those who sold to the rich in the summer had also enjoyed life then, and the fact that in the winter there was always someone willing to sell at low prices were ignored. Such arguments were hotly debated each night after the approach of Allied aircraft extinguished all lights at 8 p.m. But prices moved with the supply of cigarettes, and refused to stay fixed in accordance with a theory of ethics.

Conclusion

The economic organisation described was both elaborate and smooth-working in the summer of 1944. Then came the August cuts and deflation. Prices fell, rallied with deliveries of cigarette parcels in September and December, and fell again. In January, 1945, supplies of Red Cross cigarettes ran out: and prices slumped still further: in February the supplies of food parcels were exhausted and the depression became a blizzard. Food, itself scarce, was almost given away in order to meet the non-monetary demand for cigarettes. Laundries ceased to operate, or worked for £s or RMk.s: food and cigarettes sold for fancy prices in £s, hitherto unheard of. The Restaurant was a memory and the BMk. a joke. The Shop was empty and the Exchange and Mart notices were full of unaccepted offers for cigarettes. Barter increased in volume, becoming a larger proportion of a smaller volume of trade. This, the first serious and prolonged food shortage in the writer's experience, caused the price structure to change again, partly because German rations were not easily divisible. A margarine ration gradually sank in value until it exchanged directly for a treacle ration. Sugar slumped sadly. Only bread retained its value. Several thousand cigarettes, the capital of the Shop, were distributed without any noticeable effect. A few fractional parcel and cigarette issues, such as one-sixth of a parcel and twelve cigarettes each, led to momentary price recoveries and feverish trade, especially when they coincided with good news from the Western Front, but the general position remained unaltered.

By April, 1945, chaos had replaced order in the economic sphere: sales were difficult, prices lacked stability. Economics has been defined as the science of distributing limited means among unlimited and competing ends. On 12th April, with the arrival of elements of the 30th U.S. Infantry Division, the ushering in of an age of plenty demonstrated the hypothesis that with infinite means economic organisation and activity would be redundant, as every want could be satisfied without effort.

27 CAPITAL, INVESTMENT AND THE SOCIAL STRUCTURE OF A PASTORAL NOMAD GROUP IN SOUTH PERSIA

Fredrik Barth

In this essay, I shall present a summary analysis of some aspects of the pastoral nomad economy of the Basseri tribe of Fars, South Persia. I shall discuss the nature of pastoral capital and its implications for the social structure of the nomads, granted certain cultural premises current among the Basseri. In this discussion I shall draw on material collected in the field during the winter and spring of 1958.

The Basseri are a tribe of 15,000–20,000 pastoral nomads, divided residentially into camps of ten to fifty tents, who migrate between winter pastures in the steppes and deserts of southern Fars and summer pastures in the high mountains 300 miles farther north. A general picture of this tribe has been presented elsewhere (Barth 1961), and certain aspects of the prevailing system of land use and migration have been analysed (Barth 1960). In general, the following description may be taken as representative of conditions among the pastoral nomads of the whole South Persian area, a population of about half-a-million nomads.

A pastoral nomadic subsistence is based on assets of two main kinds: domesticated animals, and grazing rights. The recognition by the sedentary authorities of traditional grazing rights vested in distinct tribes is basic to the pastoral adaptation in Fars. Such tribes mostly have centralized political organizations based on chiefs, as do the Basseri, and are further united into large confederacies, which were formerly integrated into the semi-feudal traditional organization of Persia, and which are still recognized by the authorities. The association of every tribe with a corporate estate in the form of shared grazing rights has important implications for the political forms developed in the area. But in this essay I shall concentrate on the internal organization of the tribe, particularly the structure of local camp units. Within camps, all members share equal access to *pastures*; so for my present purposes I shall concentrate my analysis on the other main form of asset, the *herds*, and try to show the connection between features of this form of capital, and the internal structure of camps and of the tribe.

Capital Form

Animals are individually owned private property, and a Basseri household makes its livelihood from the production of the animals owned by its members.

From Raymond Firth and B. S. Yamey (eds.): Capital Saving and Credit in Peasant Societies, *Chicago, Aldine Publishing Company and London, George Allen & Unwin Ltd. Copyright © 1964 by George Allen & Unwin Ltd. Reprinted by permission.*

A certain minimum of additional property is necessary in a nomadic adaptation, mainly a tent, bedding, saddlebags, ropes, and leather sacks for milk and water, all produced by household members, and clothes, shoes, cooking and eating utensils, obtained from the towns. The total value of such equipment is slight compared to that represented by the animals. Of them the most important producers are sheep, subsidiarily goats, while donkeys are necessary for transport. Every household also has a watchdog.

In South Persia in 1958, the market value of a live adult female sheep was around 80 Tomans (£4). Its product per annum was estimated at:

clarified butter	c. 25 T.
wool	20 T.
lamb: skin	15 T.
total	60 T. or £3.

In addition, there were the lambs' meat, buttermilk and curds, to which the nomads could not give a money value of any meaning since these products are not regularly marketed. The corresponding values for goats are somewhat lower, and there is no market for their hides. On the other hand, twinning is much more frequent among them. The main reason why some goats are kept in every herd, however, is to provide goat-hair for the production of tent cloth.

The productive capital on which the pastoral adaptation is based is thus a large herd of sheep and goats. Of these a 10 per cent population of rams and he-goats is sufficient to ensure the fertility of the ewes and she-goats.

Certain features of this form of capital appear to have fundamental implications for the economic and social organization of the nomads:

(a) *Essentially all productive capital is in consumable form.* The livestock may at any time be slaughtered and eaten; and thus the main productive asset of a household may be consumed without the necessity of conversion through a market.

(b) *A significant fraction of the income is in the form of capital gains.* Lambs reach maturity in two years, and a female sheep is estimated by the Basseri to have a productive period of about seven years. To maintain the full capital value of the herd, about 15 per cent of the lambs must thus be set aside each year to ensure replacement of stock; the remaining female lambs and a proportionate fraction of male lambs may be regarded as capital gains and give a possible capital increase rate of nearly 40 per cent per annum. As in the case of point (a), no market mechanism is necessary to effect a conversion from consumable product to productive capital.

(c) *There is a continual risk of total or partial loss of capital.* Since all nomadic property is movable, total loss through robbery or warfare is a continual and real danger in the weakly administered areas frequented by the nomads. Furthermore various other disasters may strike the herd: accidents and predatory animals threaten the sheep, particularly when they stray from the main flock, so constant vigilance is required to keep the animals together and protect them; and at times epidemic disease, drought or famine may strike the herds, reducing the total animal population by as much as 50 per cent.

(d) *The rate of income decreases with increased capital.* This is mainly a consequence of the herding and management techniques known to the Basseri. Unassisted by dogs, a shepherd cannot control a flock larger than about 400 head; the man who owns more animals is forced to divide his flock and entrust other persons with shepherding duties. In fact, since shepherding is a strenuous and exacting occupation, owners of herds larger than about 200 animals already tend to hire a shepherd. A recognized consequence of this is somewhat less careful herding and more frequent losses, as well as a continual pilfering of the produce. The larger the total number of animals, the less effective is the owner's supervision of his shepherds, and the greater is the decrease in the rate of income. Standard shepherding contracts, especially the long-term ones in which there is no supervision, reflect these expectations in their stipulations:

(i) *dandune* contract: the shepherd pays 10–15 Tomans per animal per year and takes all produce. At the expiration of the contract period, he returns a flock of the same number and age composition as he originally received;

(ii) *nimei* contract: the shepherd pays 30 Tomans per animal per year for a period of 3–5 years. He takes all produce, and at the expiration of the contract returns half the herd as it stands, and keeps the other half (cf. Lambton 1953:351 ff.; Barth 1961).

In addition to these characteristics of the pastoral form of capital, certain other aspects of the economic situation of the Basseri should be described before discussing social implications, namely consumption patterns, borrowing, and investment.

A striking feature of the consumption patterns is the importance of agricultural produce to a nomad household. Wheat is the main staple; rice, dates, sugar and tea are also consumed in large quantities. Together with the considerable needs for cloth and clothing, various equipment, and luxuries, this implies a strong productive specialization and a dependence on market exchanges. A few family budgets in the nomad camp best known to me suggest an average rate of consumption in agricultural and industrial products to a value of more than 3,000 Tomans, or nearly £200, per annum per household of about six persons.

These products are paid for by the marketing of pastoral products, which only among the very poor is augmented by seasonal labour. Marketing and purchases usually take place through the medium of 'village friends'—small peddlers who live in predominantly agricultural villages where they sell industrial goods to the peasants, while supplying nomads with both agricultural and industrial produce. A nomad householder establishes a relation with such a village friend in every area where he spends a long period; during his time there he is provisioned by the peddler, and before his departure he usually settles the accumulated debt by delivery of butter, wool and hides. Though money is rarely used in these transactions, all values are estimated in terms of fluctuating current market prices.

Where the nomad does not have accumulated stores to cover his purchases, he is usually granted a half-year's or one year's credit. While such debts are usually paid for by villagers at a rate of 5 per cent per month, nomads are rarely charged more than 20–30 per cent per annum, and this is often waived when payment is made. Some nomads' debts run up to 4,000 to 5,000 Tomans.

Though this would appear to represent borrowing for current consumption, such credit serves in fact to conserve the productive asset represented by the herd: payment could be made by delivery of livestock, but by obtaining credit with security in the flock, this loss of productive animals is prevented. With a rate of income on mature sheep of nearly 100 per cent per annum (value: 80 T., product: 60 T. plus various foodstuffs), such borrowing is clearly advantageous for the nomad even when full interest is charged; and nomads often succeed in recouping in the course of a year or two in spite of heavy indebtedness.

There are thus outside sources of credit available to members of a nomadic group; likewise, outside investments are open to them. There is, in Fars, an open market in land, and standard land tenancy contracts secure a considerable income for the absentee landowner (one-sixth to two-thirds of the crop, according to the quality of the land). However, there are difficulties in converting capital in herds into capital in land which partially prevent such investments. Animals may be freely sold, but the market for livestock is severely restricted. The strains of sheep owned by the nomads, though larger and more productive than those of the villagers, are less robust, and experience shows that only some 30 per cent survive if kept in one locality through the whole year. Old sheep are of course sold for slaughter to the villages, but they fetch only a small price; animals for breeding and use can only be sold to other nomads. But since fellow nomads have very few sources of income other than their own herds, those who wish to increase their flocks by purchase have relatively limited means and represent only a very small market. The marketing of livestock is thus inevitably a rather slow process.

On the other hand, income from the sale of wool, butter and hides beyond what is required to pay for the household's consumption may freely be accumulated in the form of money, and can be invested in land. The advantages offered by this investment are security, in that the land cannot be lost through epidemics or the negligence of herdsmen, and the fact that income from land is in the form of the very agricultural products which a nomad household requires.

Social Implications

The above sketch of some relatively simple features of the economic situation of the Basseri pastoral nomads highlights factors of relevance to the economic choices faced by nomadic householders. I shall now try to show the social implications which they have for (a) the family development cycle, (b) processes which maintain social homogeneity within the nomad camp, and (c) attitudes and practices with respect to saving and investment.

(a) FAMILY DEVELOPMENT CYCLE. A pastoral household requires flocks to subsist as an independent productive unit; among the Basseri at the time of my visit the nomads estimated that a herd of sixty adult sheep/goats was about the minimum required by an elementary family, while the average size of flock was at that time nearly 100 head. But a pastoral adaptation also implies certain labour requirements, and the tasks that are necessary are among the Basseri traditionally divided in such a way as to require the co-operation of at least three persons: a male head of the household, who loads the pack animals and directs the migration, erects the tent, fetches water and wood, and keeps most equipment in repair; a woman who does the cooking and housework, assists in packing and camping, and milks the flock; and a man who herds the animals, driving them to camp to be milked at about 12 a.m. and 5 p.m.

These capital and labour requirements define conditions which a family must satisfy if it is to live as an independent household. It is immediately apparent that an elementary family can only expect to satisfy these conditions with regard to labour force for a limited period of its natural development cycle, i.e. from the time the first son reaches the age of about eight to ten years, till the last son marries; and that it can obtain the necessary capital, if not on credit, then only through inheritance, i.e., normally at the dissolution of the parental household(s). Yet the value placed in Basseri culture on the elementary family as an independent household has called forth certain standardized adjustments, the forms and wider consequences of which may be analysed as social implications of pastoral capital forms and uses, granted the ideal of elementary family households.

The labour requirements of such small households are safeguarded among the Basseri by the formation of co-operative herding units of two to five tents. Since a single shepherd, as noted above, can control a herd of up to 400 head, several households can usually combine their flocks and still remain below this critical number, thus together requiring only one shepherd. Families which are short on personnel establish herding co-operation with families with several adolescent sons, thereby securing the additional labour assistance they need. The increased work involved in shepherding a flock say of 300 instead of 100 is negligible, and so the payments for this service are small: a household which supplies no herdsman for the flock of its co-operative herding unit generally gives the boys from the other tents who perform this duty one or two lambs a year and occasional small presents.

The capital requirements of a newly established family, on the other hand, are obtained by a different pattern, essentially a pattern of anticipatory inheritance. Only sons, subsidiarily collateral agnates or adopted sons, receive a share of their father's flock. This share they are given at the time of their marriage, thereby losing further claims on the estate. Each son receives at the time of his marriage the share which he would have received if his father had died at that moment, with no subsequent adjustments. An example will illustrate this: A man had 200 sheep when the eldest of his three sons married. He first paid the brideprice of 20 sheep, leaving 180; of this estate the groom received his rightful third, or 60 head, leaving 120 for the father and remaining two sons. If the father's flock subsequently increases to 200 again before the next son marries, that son will, assuming the same brideprice, receive 90 sheep at his marriage; and there is no attempt to correct the disparity between the 60 and 90 sheep received respectively by the first and second son—because, the Basseri argue, his 60 sheep may meanwhile have grown to 600, or have been lost. The marriage of the last son is usually delayed until the parents are old, or one parent dies, so the son can become head of the new household in which the old parent(s) are permitted to live. If the son or only son reaches maturity while the father is still in his prime, the two often divide the flock 'as brothers' and separate.

In a culture where elementary families should live apart in separate tents, the capital forms and management patterns described above thus have clear social implications: certain technical patterns of herding co-operation and inheritance rules are developed, and these again have wider implications. Since the establishment of a household unit depends on the allocation to it of independent productive capital, the separation of men from their fathers and brothers is already completed when they marry—no vested economic or managerial interest ties them to their parental household. They are free to join whichever co-operative herding unit they wish, for personal or economic reasons—the practices prevent the formation of minimal or potential patrilineal nuclei on the basis of shared economic interests.

(b) SOCIAL HOMOGENEITY. The Basseri constitute a population of striking social homogeneity—apart from the unique position occupied by the quite small chiefly dynasty, which is based on a number of unique features such as private title to lands, political functions, and taxation rights. Nearly all Basseri commoners are independent small herd owners, and this homogeneity of the population has extensive implications for the political organization of the tribe. There is no effective hierarchy of authority in camps or sections, and groups of every size experience great difficulties when trying to reach corporate decisions, unless these are dictated by the tribal chief (cf. Barth 1960). This basic social homogeneity may be analysed as the result of a number of processes, to a large extent implicit in the economic features I have outlined. I shall try to show (i) that these features are such as to inhibit the concentration of wealth, and thus the emergence of status differences based on wealth, and furthermore (ii) that they tend to encourage the elimination from the group of persons who deviate significantly in wealth from the average.

(i) A number of different factors tend to inhibit the accumulation of capital in the form of large herds. The continual risk of capital losses has been noted: epidemics, famines, and losses of young animals in case of late frost may all strike as sudden disasters and reduce the herd in a fashion which is unpredictable, and which thus the herd owner cannot anticipate in his stock management. All herds will thus experience intermittent setbacks, sometimes gross reductions.

While this control on herd growth strikes large and small flocks alike, other controls, implicit in Basseri consumption patterns, have increased effects with growing herds. The household with larger herds not only increases its consumption of luxuries and of foodstuffs—that is lambs, as well as tea, sugar, rice, etc. With greater capital in herds, an increasing amount of the wealthy household's labour is also diverted from pastoral production and management to other pursuits: the men require greater leisure, and their efforts are taken up by training and tending horses, hunting, and political activity; the women weave and tie rugs (which are never marketed); and the increased weight of household belongings and larger tents requires more beasts of burden, including camels, which again means a need for a separate camel herder. All these activities and persons depend on the herd without significantly contributing to its care and production; their presence will serve as a brake on the rate of herd increase.

Greater wealth also generally leads to an earlier fragmentation of the household. The pattern of anticipatory inheritance noted above means that the marriage of sons effects a dispersal of the household's capital; furthermore, such a marriage is only possible if the son can be equipped with a share of animals sufficient to support his wife and himself—i.e. about fifty animals or more. The expected marriage age of men is in their twenties; among poor people it may be postponed till the man is as much as thirty-five to permit the necessary accumulation of capital. Wealthy people, on the other hand, have no reason for such delay; and pressure from the boy and the community at large assure a marriage age of eighteen to twenty for the sons of the large herd owners. In other words, within about twenty years of his own marriage, the dispersal of the successful herder's flock commences, giving only a brief period of accumulation for the wealthy, and nearly twice that time for the poorer and less successful. For the wealthy this means also an early loss of the cheap and dependable labour represented by adult, unmarried sons.

Finally, it is common for wealthy herd owners to contract plural marriages; they may after some years take a second, younger wife, and sometimes even a third and fourth. This means a significant increase in the size of household which must be supported by the flock, and the increased consumption will represent a drain on that flock. Furthermore, since plural marriage extends the herd owner's fertile period, it affects the distribution of wealth by inheritance. The elder sons will wish to be married at a time when their father's younger wife is still bearing children—this means that they will receive unduly large shares of their father's estate, since the shares of as-yet unborn half-brothers will not be deducted. In short, the effects of all these different and partly interconnected factors—accidental capital losses, differential consumption rates and the diversion of labour from pastoral production, accelerated division of household and capital, polygyny and increased family size without corresponding reduction of the inheritance shares of elder sons—these all act together to inhibit the concentration of wealth in the form of large herds.

(ii) These factors are not, however, completely effective checks on the accumulation of wealth. Even less are they an effective guarantee against impoverishment, though reduced consumption, postponement of the fragmentation caused by the marriage of sons, etc., will facilitate cases of rehabilitation, just as their obverse hampers accumulation. The homogeneity of the tribe with respect to wealth will not result from these processes alone. But there are other features of the economic situation which also tend to produce homogeneity, though by a different process: there is a distinct tendency and clearly observable frequency of elimination from the tribe of households with unusually great and unusually small capital. This is possible because the Basseri, like other Persian nomads, are but a segment of a larger population where assimilation by sedentarization into peasant villages and urban centres is possible and frequent, and for different reasons sedentarization is the normal result of great capital accumulation, or capital losses.

Firstly in the case of accumulation: factors which tend to reduce the rate of income with increased size of herd have been noted. This means that while the risk of capital losses remains or increases, the increment to a large herd owner's income which results from the addition of further animals to his flocks decreases significantly. Consider, then, the possibilities of alternative investment. In nomadic activities they are nil; but the possibility of investment in agricultural land is always present. I should emphasize the sedentarization is never regarded as an ideal among the nomads; they value their way of life more highly than life in a village. But the economic advantages of land purchase are palpable: the risk of capital loss is eliminated, the profits to an absentee landowner are large, and they are in the form of products useful in a nomadic household. There is thus no feeling that land purchase implies sedentarization—a small plot of land can be let out on tenancy contracts and is merely a source of economic security and useful products. The difficulty in such investment is to convert the capital in animals to money capital by which land may be purchased. As noted, this is a relatively slow process, unless the owner is willing to take a considerable loss; none the less, with some patience it may be done, and banking facilities are available in the towns for accumulating savings, though no credit is available to nomads for investment in land.

Once a piece of land has been bought, the wealthy herd owner's money income increases rapidly, since production in a marketable goods such as wool, butter and hides continues while expenses for the purchase of agricultural produce are reduced or eliminated. If a herd owner continues to be successful, he will thus accumulate wealth more rapidly, with little promise of profit through further investment in herds, but increasingly in a form which may be directly invested in land. Furthermore, title to land is held in a sedentary legal system where sons upon their marriage have no rights to anticipatory inheritance—which makes it an attractive form of capital from the owner's point of view and prevents a premature dispersal of the wealth.

This gradual process of land accumulation was observed in the field in its various stages. Only towards the very end do informants see sedentarization as its natural end result: they have a house built on their property and become increasingly concerned with the need for management of house and land, they develop a taste for many comforts that can only be satisfied by sedentary residence, etc. Sudden stock losses at this stage seem to be a common precipitating factor which drives them into the village; and even when they are well established as petty landowners they generally erect their old tent in their compound, and reside in it in the summer months.

Cases of sedentarization through capital accumulation and land purchase are by the nature of things relatively rare, and my material for the above description consists mainly of a handful of life histories. Sedentarization through impoverishment, on the other hand, is a constant threat for many and has a high empirical frequency, of the order of one person in every three in the groups of my censuses. Here the process is very simple: accident, sickness or poor management of a small herd leads to losses, and thus to an annual production below what is required for the purchase of food and clothing. But the herd itself is a large food store, and hunger easily drives the nomad to invade this his only productive capital, reducing the pastoral output further, in a vicious circle. The only alternative is to seek additional sources of income. Since shepherding contracts are relatively few (because they are, as we have seen, unprofitable for the herd owner), such sources are mainly found in sedentary society: as seasonal labourer, shepherd for the village flocks, doing local transport with donkeys, etc. To be successful, these activities must give the nomad income both to support his household *and* to increase his flock (thereby constituting a market for rich herd owners who wish to buy land). But frequently such work for a village community disturbs the nomad's migratory cycle, and thus leads only to reduced pastoral production and further animal losses, which makes him all the more dependent on sedentary sources of income. The Basseri feel that once a household's flock falls significantly below the minimal level of sixty adult head, this downward spiral is pretty inevitable and quite rapid; and there is a steady flow of impoverished settlers from every South Persian tribe to the villages and towns of their area.

These features of capital form and management thus tend, in the wider economic situation of the Basseri, to maintain a general economic homogeneity among the nomads, both by inhibiting the concentration of pastoral wealth, and by a constant elimination through sedentarization of the top and the bottom of the economic spectrum. As a consequence, social differentiation based on, or accompanied by, economic differences becomes impossible; and the nomad population becomes characterized by a striking social homogeneity, consisting of independent, economically self-sufficient small herd owners.

(c) SAVING AND INVESTMENT.   A final implication of these features may be seen in attitudes and practices relating to saving, thrift, and capital accumulation. I have noted the fact that pastoral capital is in a directly consumable form and consists of animals with a short life span. This creates a situation where a certain minimum of thrift is necessary in capital management—the capital can only be maintained through a systematic policy of reserving lambs for the replacement of stock. Whereas in agriculture the distinction between produce and land is clearly apparent, among pastoralists nearly every instance of consumption threatens the productive capital itself, and must be considered and evaluated by the nomad. What is more, many of the factors involved are unknown. Disease may strike so that even a conservative policy of slaughter of lambs and yearlings still results in a reduction of stock. Milking practice is also a field of continual economic choice: not only the question of how many sheep should be left with lambs, but also how much sheep with lambs should be milked, and how much should be left to those lambs. In a good year, near-starvation of lambs gives a greater yield in butter to the nomad and does not appear to have great ill effects; on the other hand, if such lambs are subject to special strain or mild disease, they are lost in much higher frequency than are well-fed, robust lambs. In short, the management of pastoral capital requires a constant awareness of savings and investment policy; it breeds an attitude of continual and thrifty concern for the herd in its practitioners.

The Basseri are very aware of the economics involved in these choices, and discuss such policy at length within the household, though rarely in public, except in the form of gossip about third persons. The basic guiding principle which they adopt comes out in an almost obsessive desire to postpone every incident of consumption—to let each lamb gain weight one more day, or week, or season, to have one more lamb from an old sheep, to make a worn-out pair of shoes last till the next market town, or till arrival in the summer area, or till next spring equinox (the Persian New Year, when it is customary to put on new clothes).

Yet—or perhaps precisely as a correlate of these interests—hospitality is a highly valued virtue. The hospitable man is admired and people speak highly of him whether he is present or absent. Men seek his company and flock to his tent, though without importunity. By their own standards, then, most Basseri are miserly; and a few glaring examples are held up for public ridicule. Thus one of the largest herd owners in the group is popularly known as D.D.T. Khan because, they say, he is such a miser he eats his own lice.

But this failure in good manners (by Basseri canons) caricatured by some and prevalent in most need not be explained only in terms of the special habits of thrift developed as a result of pastoral life. There are also clear social reasons why a pattern of conspicuous consumption and hospitality is not only economically unwise, but also socially and politically unprofitable—in contrast to most of the local societies in the Middle East. These are found in the very features of social structure described in the previous section: the great economic and social homogeneity within Basseri camps. Where wealth differences are small, a policy of social aggrandizement through public consumption of wealth is bound to bring very limited returns. Nearly all the tents of a camp remain independent and self-supporting units; a hospitable man may gain influence in his camp through hospitality, but never to the extent of being able to dominate his camp fellows, or to expect economic support or advantage from them at a later date. On the contrary, the homogeneity itself is valued, and lampoons are sung about anyone who puts on airs and assumes an authoritative manner. For the Basseri commoner, there is little to gain by spendthriftness, and thus few inducements, but many controls, on the practice of hospitality.

Conclusion

The material presented in this brief paper can hardly be drawn together further, since the paper itself is already a summary of select features of the economic and social organization of a pastoral tribe which show a clear relation to certain features of sheep and goat herds as a form of capital. As noted in the introduction, other economic features (e.g. relating to pasture rights and the organization of migrations) have not been discussed, though they appear to have methodologically analogous implications for centralized authority and other features of the political organization of the tribe. In the present essay I have merely attempted to show how certain elementary characteristics of capital in the form of herds are related to a limited range of features of family organization, social homogeneity within camps, and common saving and consumption patterns—granted certain cultural values and conceptions held by the Basseri people. The characteristics of pastoral capital which I have discussed are, I believe, of a type familiar in conventional economic analysis, though here admittedly in a very elementary and rough form. What is interesting, and perhaps surprising, to a social anthropologist is the fact that it should be possible at all to show their social implications by a discussion involving relatively few 'cultural' facts—that the processes by which they are made relevant to social action and features of a local social system seem to implicate few of the other basic premises of Basseri culture. Admittedly, some of these premises are contained in the specific economic definitions and characterizations used; and it would seem a hopeless, and perhaps fundamentally impossible, task to state them all in a manner so that their implications would have the form of a deductive system. But it does seem possible to show how specific social forms are related as a product to simple constellations of determining factors, and thus how partial features of Basseri social structure are directly related to specific characteristics of pastoral capital and other economic facts.

28 ECONOMICS IN EAST AFRICAN ABORIGINAL SOCIETIES
Harold K. Schneider*

> *The distinctions to be drawn between literate and nonliterate economies are . . . those of degree rather than kind (Herskovits 1952:488.)*

Scarcely anyone who has ever had contact with the so-called cattle-keeping peoples of East Africa has failed to comment on their admiration for cattle, and the prestige that possession of them gives their holders. They seem to be principally stores of value outside normal market processes. To those concerned with the economic future of Africa, this matter naturally requires attention because of its implications for economic development, since a very considerable number of people, from the Sudan to South Africa, in what I shall call East Africa, possess great numbers of these animals.

I have placed the quotation from Herskovits at the head of the paper to set the mood, because the attempt will be made here to show that the function of cattle as a symbol of status is dependent on their economic use. It will be shown that the Wanyaturu, whose economy will be most extensively discussed, have a market or money economy, or something very like a market economy in which livestock, not just cattle, are the items most frequently traded, so that they are more or less standardized media of exchange. It will be further shown that livestock seem to be used in the same general way over most of East Africa and that this fact, contradicting the impression that they are merely stores of value, explains to a large extent the comparatively unusual attitude toward and use of cattle in this part of the world.

It is not intended here to describe the actual working of these economies, except incidentally, for though this would be ideal, the recognition that they are pecuniary type economies has only just begun to bear fruit. The paper will merely support my assertion while all the multitude of questions that are fostered about the operation of the systems will have to wait for future investigation.

We shall begin with some relevant aspects of Turu (or Wanyaturu) economics, follow with a discussion of the concepts of money as applied to this area, and conclude with a comparative discussion of the phenomenon in other East African societies.

From Economic Transition in Africa *edited by Melville J. Herskovits and Mitchell Harwitz,* Evanston, Northwestern University Press 1964:53–75. Reprinted by permission.
* I wish to express gratitude to the National Science Foundation for a grant which made possible field work among the Wanyaturu in 1959–1960.

2

Cattle in Turu economics play three roles: they are *real capital, money* and, at times, *consumption goods.* In contrast it will be recognized that cattle in Euroamerican economies are principally real capital, as in the case of milk production, and consumption goods, as with beef and hides. The failure to see this distinction has been at the core of a great deal of misunderstanding of East African people by outsiders.

The most obvious role of cattle is that of capital. Among the Turu and other people of the Turu cluster, return on this capital is predominantly found in the production of manure. While milk is a fundamental element of subsistence in the Nilotic societies to the North, such as the Masai, Suk, Turkana and Nandi, the Turu use it only to feed children and as a luxury for adults. Among the Turu, production of an adequate supply of grain is normally impossible without manure to fertilize the crops. This means that all people who start independent homesteads must have cattle, and the economy is "arranged" to see that they get them through the cattle loaning system called *uriha* if they are not otherwise available. One way or another Turu have much meat to eat—all animals that die are eaten unless contaminated—but purposeful slaughter of livestock for food is avoided except for various sacrificial rites; thus livestock are only incidentally to be regarded as a consumption good.

Whether cattle are money is a subject of much debate. In Turu, cattle, together with small stock, are media of exchange and standards of value as well as stores of value, and they can be converted into wives, grain, honey, iron goods, land, services and many other less important items. But cattle are the "big notes" of the system, and since in themselves they lack divisibility, small stock rest in a standardized ratio to them, so that three smaller animals always equal a young bull or steer, or five head of small stock equal a heifer. Because of this it is possible to translate a man's livestock wealth into livestock units, each unit being one small animal. This system of equivalents is overtly known to the people and is so used that, for example, when discussing the inheritance of one heifer by two sons, it will be converted into five small animals. In a similar way, when explaining bridewealth payments a person will speak of having paid an *njiku* (steer) when in fact he actually paid three small animals. Von Sick recorded the prevailing system of equivalents at the time of the German conquest:

1 goat equals an iron hoe, or a spear, or one bow and five arrows, or the *honga* shield.
2 goats equal an ostrich feather headdress.
3 goats equal a Colobus monkey skin.

(Von Sick 1916:25–26)

It seems clear that the equation within the indigenous economy between small stock and cattle was the same as later, so that the last item, the Colobus monkey skin, could be priced at 1 steer, which is the equivalent of 3 goats, the word "goat" being interchangeable with "sheep" since there is no difference in the economic value of these two kinds of animals.

Thus Turu are accustomed to think in terms of standardized values. Von Sick notes that a knife was priced at one hen; for trading grain, not only did they have a standardized ox-hide bag (*musuta*), which holds about 200 pounds of millet, but they had standardized wooden troughs used to measure the contents of the bag so that the *sori ya ngombe* ("cow trough"), three of which filled a musuta, held an amount equivalent in value to a male calf. Even arrows, which are used as a means of payment in some aspects of marriage, are occasionally generalized as a measure of value in relation to other things. Indeed, the term *muyi*, arrow, has come to mean "fee" when the price is very small. It must be noted that the value of cows as capital for producing calves normally outweighs their use as money, such animals never being slaughtered or sold if it is possible to avoid it. Since Von Sick's day, the commodities traded have changed somewhat, but the basic structure of the indigenous economy remains the same. War helmets, spears and shields are now unimportant, and the export of salt to the Iramba or trading beads and cloth from the Gogo for cattle has stopped, while Arab, Indian and other foreign traders have come to be middlemen for the import and export of goods even, in certain cases, between Turu groups themselves.

The first goal of Turu economic activity is, of course, to provide a sufficient supply of food for the family; the ultimate goal is to accumulate as many cattle as possible. The method of achieving this, a norm followed in some degree by all, is to grow a surplus of grain, the staple food, which can be sold for livestock. In order to do this it is necessary to capitalize production with land on which to grow a crop and graze the livestock, and wives to do the necessary productive work. The system is so composed as to make it possible for individual households to control these variable to a sufficient degree in order to increase their number of livestock.

The Turu live in compact villages composed of homesteads situated on the arable land, each of which is headed by a male, or in rare cases a female, all of whom are related through a common ancestor about five generations removed from the adult men. Though land can be and is sold, its saleability is hedged about by restrictions which serve to preserve it to the occupying lineage. That is, a father must pass on his land to his sons, and all sales are reversible on demand by the seller or his descendants who must, however, pay twice the original selling price. This right, however, weakens with time, so that it is unenforceable in most instances after the original parties and witnesses to the transaction are dead.

Marsh land adjoining the village, crucial for reserve grazing, is more frequently sold than arable land. In fact, such land is valued for the prestige it brings and because it is a good investment, being relatively scarce and in great demand. Those who own it, however, would not normally entirely exclude dependable fellow-members of the village from its use, though grazing fees are often charged. Since sale seldom occurs, it is difficult to obtain a clear picture of its price, but it seems that one heifer will buy about 5 to 10 acres.

Polygyny is possible and desirable. The average initial disbursement for a wife, four or five head of cattle, or about three heifers and one or two steers, seems to be in recompense for the services of the woman, who runs her own house, produces and processes grain and provides firewood, water and the like. Though the husband theoretically has exclusive sexual rights to his wife, he is expected to allow her a lover, from whom he can extract a fine of six goats if he catches the pair *in flagrante delicto*. Her child-bearing function is taken into account in the bridewealth only indirectly; initially bridewealth merely compensates the bride's mother for loss of her services. An extra payment of a heifer for a girl or a steer for a boy, levied at a later date when the woman has borne two children, is determined by the sex of the first child.

Other rights in a woman are retained by her father and brothers. They may fine the husband for badly beating her, or for any act on his part which can be claimed to have shortened her life. Turu bridewealth, indeed, is technically a part of a reciprocal loan, since the father reserves rights in his daughter while the husband reserves rights in the cattle of the bridewealth.

Millet of either of two varieties is the staple food; in "normal" years it is exchangeable for livestock, when a seller can be found, at the rate of four *debes*— that is, four gasoline tins, the unit of measuring grain—for one small animal, twenty debes for a heifer, and twelve debes for a steer. This rate is correlated with sterling, so that one debe is worth five shillings (East African) and one goat shs. 20, with four debes thus equaling one goat. Prices in the European market are similar, a debe of grain in normal times costing four or five shillings, a goat averaging about shs. 17 and a heifer selling for about shs. 105. It is thus evident that the Turu take account of the prices in both indigenous and induced systems, but fix them at standard rates. That is, the sterling equivalents have risen over the years with the inflation of prices in the European economy, but the ratio of value of the goods in the European market is very close to that in the Turu indigenous economy.

It is the exchange of grain for livestock and vice versa that comprises the main sector of the Turu economic system. The prices quoted above for grain are those expected in normally productive years. In a bad year, when production of grain falls off markedly, the price of grain goes up so that in some instances, as in 1937, one could buy a heifer for only three debes, or 120 lbs. of grain. It is for this that the enterprising Turu waits. Normally a Turu who produces an excess of grain stores it in his house sealed with ant-hill clay in bark vats (*kiu*), carefully attended so that it will last two or three years or more. But it has a regular turn-over, achieved by lending it in small quantities to members of the village who run short before the harvest, so that it is returned fresh. No interest is paid on such loans, the freshness of the grain which is returned being regarded as sufficient payment. If the owner can hold on to his stocks, the grain is sold at the optimum time and a large profit made in the acquisition of livestock.

Livestock are essential because of the need for manure. But since many people do not own enough animals to provide sufficient manure, the economy would be seriously imbalanced without the system of loaning cattle. Almost anyone who is not totally unreliable can get someone to provide him with animals on loan, if not from a non-kinsman, then from a relative on whose sense of obligation he can play. The desire always is first for female animals which will produce not only manure but milk for the children, though male animals are acceptable. The care given to the animals is considered to balance the service rendered, but the recipient is usually insecure because the owner can legally remove the animals at any time.

It is important to recognize also that because of the system of loaning cattle, the number of these animals it is theoretically possible for a Turu to own is for all practical purposes unlimited. The number of wives he may have is limited by his ability to cope with them, availability of land, permission of a previous wife to use her cattle for another marriage, and the like, though some men have managed to have more than ten. The amount of grain one can possess is limited by the physical limits to the size of houses, danger of deterioration and the fact that grain can not usually be stored anywhere but in one's home. The amount of land one can get is limited by its availability. But the number of livestock a man may own is limited only by his ability to get them.

Therefore, individual Turu homesteads may be thought of as small firms. The head of the household manages all external buying and selling while the wives exchange goods within the household. Technically the male household head owns none of the wealth of the house which is all in the names of his various wives whose obligation is to increase it and pass it on to their sons, but from the outside he is seen as the owner because it is his prerogative to handle all exchanges or disbursements in the market of the wealth of his wives. Sharing and mutual aid are important among men of the same village, but this does not by any means exclude private enterprise, expressed in wide variations in wealth even among full brothers. This is best shown in Table 28–1 which records the economic positions of most of the homesteads in one village, and in which number five is the younger brother of number twenty-four. In Table 28–1 the households are arranged in terms of the amount of manure produced, a "manure index" being obtained by counting the number of animals actually in the corral and assigning a figure to each in terms of a goat as 1, a calf 2 and each full-grown cow or bull 5 (column 4). The other columns show the amount of land available for production in 1958–1959 (column 1), the number of women heading individual houses in a household, both wives and mothers (column 2), the number of cattle actually held in the corral whether they are owned or borrowed (column 3), the number of livestock actually owned by members of the household expressed in livestock units, i.e., the "wealth index" (column 5), and the number of debes of grain produced in the 1959 harvest (column 6). While the number of livestock units producing manure in the homestead does not represent the "wealth index," which derives from the actual number owned,

TABLE 28–1   *Relation between Grain Production and the Variables of Manure, Acres Cultivated and Numbers of Wives in Thirty Farmsteads in a Turu Village*

Farmstead	1 Acres	2 Women	3 Cattle Present	4 Manure Index	5 Wealth Index	6 Grain Production
1. Muhomi	4.1	4	34	187	315+	189
2. Sunas	4.7	3	35	177	160	95
3. Nkango	6.4	3	25	148	272	335
4. Kinyisi	5+	3	23	130	336	150
5. Ikoti	4.6	1	22	130	268	57
6. S. Masaka	6.8	5	30	127	188	195
7. Lisu	3.5	2	24	113	156	205
8. Mudemis	5.2	2	16	98	31	72
9. Petero	3.1	3	18	90	28	90
10. Sunja	2.6	1	16	87	57	75
11. Ibi	8.8	4	18	85	92	163
12. S. Mosi	2.6	1	16	82	109	53
13. Chima	2.7	1	20	79	179	96
14. Mtinangi	4.3	2	11	71	66	95
15. Mutinda	2+	3	10	70	28	55
16. Nkuwi	2.6	1	18	69	27	75
17. M. Mpondo	6.7	3	16	69	1	58
18. Mutatuu	2.3	1	9	61	75	36
19. Ghula K.	4.2	1	13	56	17	76
20. Ikita	4.0	1	13	54	2	125
21. Samahii	4.0	1	6	54	40	45
22. Msumari	6.1	3	11	51	45	90
23. Ibunka	2.7	1	9	50	22	37
24. Ntui	2.6	1	10	41	15+	35
25. Nkongolo	4.1	2	6	39	14	41
26. M. Sinda	1.8	1	6	35	8	40
27. Mujou	2.0	2	8	34	33	61
28. Bula	3.0	2	8	34	5	49
29. Ngua	3.3	1	4	17	0	40
30. M. Nkese	1+	0	0	0	0	4

since most homesteads have loaned some livestock out and borrowed others, actual wealth correlates with the number held in the homestead as may be seen in Figure 28–1, which shows the correlation between the manure index, productivity of grain in debes and the wealth index. The wealth index skews upward away from the manure index at the top and downward and away from the manure index at the bottom as we would expect if the rich loan out excess livestock and the poor borrow these animals.

The graph shows the interplay of the important variables in production and the wide variations in wealth that are possible in the Turu system through the manipulation of the variables. It is generally clear that there is a correlation between the amount of manure available and the amount of grain produced. It

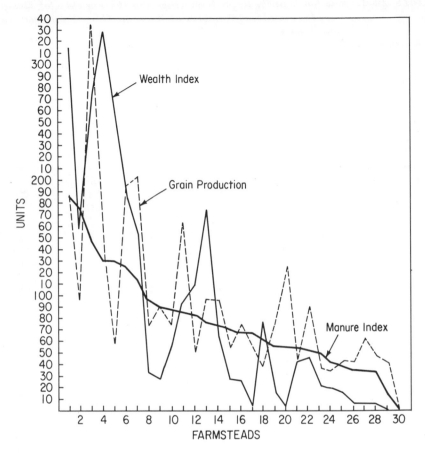

Figure 28–1   Graph showing actual livestock wealth (wealth index) in relation to livestock held (implied by manure index) and grain production in thirty farmsteads in a Turu village.

is also apparent that productivity is markedly affected by the number of workers available, who are principally the women. The amount of land available, while quite important in a few cases, such as No. 11, where it apparently allows the four women of the homestead wide latitude, on the whole has less significance. Other variables are at work in this system, but cannot be shown in quantitative terms. A very important one is incentive. No. 24, an old man with an old wife, is unwilling to try to excell. Those Turu who work hard to get ahead tend to view those who fall behind as lazy, though they recognize that other factors may enter.

This graph, treating of the main elements of the economy, suggests its dynamics, which may be more explicitly detailed. For one thing, the matter of loaning out cattle creates a network of ties within and without the village that affects almost everyone in some way. The rich men, at the top of the table, have multiple ties. These relations are constantly being reviewed, with cattle passing back and forth. Additionally, when the census on which these data are based was taken, the total cattle population of this village was about 550. During the preceding year about 110 head of cattle were born while about 80 animals died or were disposed of by slaughter. The number of cattle transferred on loan was relatively small; about 40 were sold during the year, most of which were sent to the government livestock markets for a total of about shs. 4100, or $575. This represents a 7 per cent takeoff, which is about average for all of Turu. Thirty-one head of cattle were involved in bridewealth transactions, of which 12 were gained and nineteen lost. But at the core of the dynamics is the fact that in this village, out of a total of about seventy independent productive units—that is, the houses composing each homestead, each of which is autonomous as concerns production and consumption—twenty-nine did not produce enough grain for normative subsistence, which is 18 debes per year per adult. Because of the large degree of unpredictability of success in production, many of the inferior producers own livestock while many of the surplus producers do not. The incentive for the circulation of livestock and grain derives from this fact, though, as has been pointed out, the expectation of periodic droughts and other natural impediments to production also provide an incentive to surplus producers of grain to hold on to it to sell at a high price. Thus while there is a correlation between wealth reckoned in livestock and wealth reckoned in amount of grain stored, there is enough lack of a relationship between the two to keep the economy viable.

When the Germans imposed their rule on Turu country, there was an immediate influx of traders—Arabs, Wanyamwezi and others—who were interested in the surpluses of grain and the large number of livestock. It is noteworthy that the Turu entered the livestock export market almost immediately, showing their familiarity with market processes. Von Sick (1916:60) noted that during the first year of the establishment of a German military post in the area, in 1909, livestock were sold to traders at the post in the amount of 50,000 rupees, or about shs. 100,000. While the introduction of taxation had something to do with this, it is an undeniable fact that the Turu took immediately to clothing and certain other imported items. This has continued so that clothing is still the most important general item imported. Limitation in the demand for imports, shown by the continued use of indigenously made iron goods, pots, stools and the like, reflects the continued importance of this indigenous economy. That is, the livestock and grain markets introduced by outsiders are a source of cash for items which have come to serve as prestige symbols, but this external economy does not substitute for the indigenous one, because it cannot sufficiently guarantee subsistence security.

In Turu society prestige derives from a number of sources. A *muhomi*, a man who has killed a lion, a woman who has borne twins, a feat considered equal to killing a lion, a *muxai*, or courageous and aggressive person, all receive the deference due them. Skill, intelligence and cleverness of all kinds, especially in human relations, are admired. On this list the possession of wealth in live-stock ranks high. In former times men used to keep the especially large and handsome steers out of the market because of the prestige they conferred. Even today a man may acquire prestige by being the keystone in a voluntary herding group which is identified by his name.

It has been suggested above that the prestige associated with cattle, or rather livestock, is a result of the role of livestock as a medium of exchange. That is, the owner of many animals is admired for his control of resources. He may be called *mnyampa*, "sir," and will be offered a stool to sit on when he visits, even if he is a young man. He is given the better beer and otherwise favored, espe-cially if he is not of the particular village in which he is visiting and is thus outside the local system of stratification based on age. If we consider the first three men listed in Table 28–1, the richest in the village, it is significant that all three are strongly disliked. The one thing they all have in common is a callous attitude toward others. In another village, the two richest men were also strongly disliked, and for the same reason. In contrast, Nos. 4 and 5 in Table 28–1 are considered to be "good" men, in that they are quiet and apparently unaggressive. This points to a paradox in Turu economic psychology: to become wealthy necessitates aggressiveness, which brings on dislike while also leading to the deference that derives from wealth in livestock which, as we have seen, more than any other single fact confers prestige. Prestige is thus separable from respect. The envy and hatred generated by the possession of wealth is a normal risk. "It is god's will that a man seek riches," said one old man, "so that a man must try to get it despite its hazards."

3

Dalton (1961:10), in a recent article on market economies and "primitive" economics asserts that a market economy *is* a money economy. Contrary to Goodfellow's position (Goodfellow 1939), he holds that there is no market economy in East African societies. To Dalton a market economy is a specific kind of economy which occurs only in industrialized nations, all other economies being different from it *in kind*. In these terms, Goodfellow is accused of applying market concepts to an area where they are not applicable because there is no money. Yet is it not possible that in East Africa we have something which, while not a market economy in this restricted sense of the term, does not differ from it in kind?

Turu livestock may be considered money because animals are standards of value, media of exchange and stores of value. Livestock are normally used for purchasing goods priced in terms of them, and they are the supreme stores of value, the end of all economic pursuits. Thus, however strange a form of money they may appear to be, they are functionally equivalent to money as defined by economists.

Here another question arises. We have seen that in the Turu system the exchange rate between livestock and grain is usually stable. Why, then, should we not also regard grain as a medium of exchange? It is true that in some instances Turu price commodities other than livestock in terms of the number of debes of grain they are worth. In some instances they may make payments in grain. Von Sick, in 1910, told of a Turu who bought a "cow trough" for the amount of grain it would hold. Yet, significantly enough, the price of the trough could be stated as one calf. Moreover, the deficiencies of grain as a medium of exchange are apparent. Grain, in any appreciable amount of value, has little portability. To carry an amount equivalent in value to a heifer, some twenty containers, would mean that a bridegroom going to claim his bride would in most cases be faced with the problem of transporting grain in the amount of one ton! Again, grain is highly perishable and must be carefully protected, whereas with luck a man can expect his livestock to exist for many years with a minimum of care. Third, livestock retain significantly high value no matter what the condition of an animal may be, short of severe sickness or death, whereas the value of grain fluctuates with the state of the crops in a given year so that at times there is no demand for it. Finally, livestock holdings increase by themselves through natural processes, whereas the amount of grain a man owns can be increased only through the expenditure of labor.

The reason why goats and sheep have become standardized in relation to cattle is perhaps due to the fact that, except in unusual conditions, the ratio of small stock to cattle in a given area and to the human population seems to remain constant. What would kill cattle in exceptional numbers would also kill the small animals, notably severe drought. The tendency for bridewealth to remain relatively constant may also perhaps be explained this way. In 1910 Von Sick's census of the Turu showed about 102,000 human beings and about 173,000 head of cattle (1916:4). In 1958 there were about 150,000 human beings and slightly over 200,000 head of cattle. The bridewealth has also remained about the same.

The Turu must be thought of as possessing money and a market system which are not different in kind from those of Europe and America, even though limited in terms of the variety of goods exchanged. Differences must be sought in such things as their social orientation and cultural values, which lead to different emphases, and in the differing degrees of technological complexity their culture manifests.

4

When we examine the economic systems of other East African societies, we find that livestock tend to monopolize exchange at all levels above the value of a single goat, and are everywhere used as media of exchange, standards of value and stores of value. It may even be possible to construct a general economic model for these societies showing the interplay of such important variables as women, livestock, grain and land in the socio-cultural setting in which they occur. Such a model would enable us to predict, for example, that bridewealth rates rise with the increase of livestock proportionately with the population, and in relation to other variables, such as the value in terms of potential productivity held to be paid for by the bridewealth. It is not without significance that while no one has suggested a regular system of standards of value in East African economies, almost every observer has recorded some data indicating the existence of such a system. A partial survey of these data may be given, beginning with the Suk of Kenya, among whom I gathered the following information in 1951–1952. Among the *Suk*, bridewealth varies in proportion to the general wealth of the subarea from about one cow in the cattle-poor hills to more than 20 in the cattle-rich plains (Schneider 1953:272ff.). Other than this:

10 goats = 1 steer
40 goats = 1 camel (hence four steers equal one camel)
  4 bags of grain (100–150 lb.) = 1 load of meat (two legs and a few other parts)
  1 goat = 2 axes
  1 goat = 1 spear
  1 goat = a small irrigated plot; 2 goats = a large plot
  1 goat = 1 pot of honey
  1 steer = about shs. 100 (in internal trade)
  1 goat = about shs. 10 (hence shs. 100 = 10 goats = 1 steer)

Grain is also exchanged for live cattle, but the equivalents could not be determined.

According to Wagner (1956:102, 109, 161, 162 and *passim*), bridewealth in the *Vugusu* cattle-rich area in the region inhabited by the Bantu of North Kavirondo is six head and up, much less in the south. The exchange system is as follows:

4 or 5 goats   = 1 steer
1 heifer   = 25–30 bundles of eleusine grain
1 basket of grain = 1 basket of meat
50 lb. of grain   = 1 sword or 1 chicken
1 pot   = 1 spear head

Wagner also refers to grain and hoes as the "currency" of the *Logoli*, the cattle-poor group south of the Vugusu. Otherwise cattle, goats and sheep are exchanged on "an economic basis" for grain, iron work, and other goods and services including payment with steers or heifers, depending on the service, for the work of diviners. Grain is loaned out before harvest at an interest rate of 25–30 per cent for a period of about two months and chickens are sold.

Kikuyu (Middleton 1953:19–20) commodity values were traditionally reckoned in goats since they far outnumber cattle, there being only a few of the latter. A rich man might possess only 10–12 head. Beads were once used as "currency" in the regular markets and there was trade with Masai from whom, for swords, tobacco, honey and ochre, they obtained livestock. In times of shortage livestock were exchanged between tribes for grain. Among the *Nandi* (Huntingford 1950:40, 59, 68, 81, 82) one axe equaled one full bag of honey in 1938 and one arrow head was equal to one gourd of honey. Steers are traded for various commodities; they are also used for bridewealth. There was trade with the Bantu of Kavirondo for grain, while pottery and iron goods were exchanged with the Dorobo for baskets of honey. Land with an unripe crop on it was sold.

Iteso (Lawrance 1957:93, 143, 148, 202) bridewealth varies from 10–15 head, though after the rinderpest epidemic of 1890, it fell to 1 cow and 30 goats. The government set the legal rate at five head, but this is systematically violated. Cattle have come to be sold in large numbers, to obtain cash for luxuries, at a legal price for a "cow" of shs. 100. In 1920, except for the final item in the following list, the system of values in exchange was recorded as follows:

1 basket of millet = a pot, or "iron work," or a plaited door, or a basket, a hoe handle, sandals, a chair, or a mortar
25 baskets of unthreshed millet = 1 heifer
10 baskets of unthreshed millet = 1 bull
2–3 baskets of unthreshed millet = 1 goat or sheep
1 bull = 1 large drum
"goats" = 1 small drum
2 goats = 1 ostrich-feather headdress
2 heifers and 1 bull = 1 live ostrich
1 "cow" = 1 donkey
2 hoes = 1 heifer
1 "cow" = shs. 600 (but regularly exchange for bicycles worth shs. 300)

Turkana (Gulliver 1951:164) livestock are used for exchange, particularly with other tribes, but also in internal trading for grain and other goods. It is recorded by Huntingford (1953:109) that the *Masai* trade with the Bantu for grain and other goods, using livestock as "media of exchange." Cattle are regularly sold on the livestock markets in large numbers. *Gusii* (Mayer 1950: 38) bridewealth fluctuates, being equated by the people with change in prices in European market economics. Cattle and goats, equated in set ratio, are used to price other goods. Most valued, in order, are women, cattle, goats, grain.

Duruma (Prins 1952:57) are said to "invest" their money in sheep and goats, which are then exchanged for cattle at the following rates:

8 small animals = 1 steer
4 small animals and 1 steer (or 12 small animals) = 1 cow

The main items of exchange are grain and cattle.

As concerns the *Sonjo* (Gray 1960:37–38), bridewealth varies between sixty and three hundred goats, with an average of 100. Goats are otherwise used as measures of value for honey, grain, beehives, pottery, iron goods and irrigation rights. Among the *Sukuma* (Malcolm 1953:44, 50, 70, 81), bridewealth varies across the country from none in districts having no cattle to over 10 in richer areas. Few actual examples of the monetary structure are given, but it is apparent that one exists. Cattle were formerly rare all over the country but have been introduced in most places and now replace hoes, small stock and grain as symbols of wealth. Grain is used to purchase cloth, hoes and the like. Cattle are "capital"; they are seen as grain stored in another form. Land rights were sold in marshes where sorghum was grown, the price being "1 or 2 cattle," while slaughtered cows are used to pay those who work the fields. Grain is customarily exchanged for livestock in good times, the animals being reconverted to grain in bad times.

Data from people living south of central Tanganyika show the same pattern of economic organization that exists in the North. The *Tonga* (Colson 1951:27) exchanged livestock for grain; Goodfellow, in discussing the economics of the Bantu of the South, states, "it is still evident that . . . cattle are managed on precisely the same lines as grain" (1939:67). The *Sotho* have always recognized the exchange value of one steer for 2 calves or 4 bags of grain. "The esteem in which the Basuto hold cattle is closely related to the superior facilities for storing and investing wealth that cattle provide in such an economy" (Sheddick 1953:21). As concerns the *Tswana*, Schapera tells us that cattle and small animals were and still are the "standard medium of exchange" (1953:23). Other instances could be cited, but these suffice to make the point.

In the facts recorded above we see examples of how values vary, though apparently in terms of similar economic models. There is a noticeable tendency to use grain to pay for small items but grain seems universally to be traded for livestock. It is noteworthy, in this context, that a number of investigators have seen the signs of a market economy, and have referred to cattle and goats as "capital," "investments" and "currency," terms also applied in some cases to hoes and grain. Finally, while valuation between livestock and other goods is usually given as though prices are stabilized, the information generally suggests that the prices fluctuate with market conditions.

With the gradual intrusion of the Euroamerican economy, a shift seems to be occurring all over East Africa to the use of cash as a medium of exchange. The use of cash, however, does not displace cattle, since these continue to be depositories of value which earn superior interest by bearing calves and solidify capital. This is additive to the indigenous functions of cattle, making it impossible to dispense with cattle even if money is present. Cash pays taxes, and is convenient for purchasing trade goods; it is even useful within the indigenous systems for some exchanges. But this only masks the continued operation of indigenous economies. In Suk the process takes the form of selling cattle to Somali traders and using the money to buy grain; this renders unnecessary the older system of exchanging cattle for surplus grain directly with hill Suk. Probably a strong reason for the rise of cash dealings is the greater precision in pricing that is made possible, for though differences in the qualities of animals are recognized, it is not always possible to express this in fine terms with indigenous media of exchange.

The relative dependence on grain and livestock is a critical factor in determining the nature of the exchange economy in East Africa. The staple food is ordinarily grain, or milk, or both. Other foods, such as meat, blood and various vegetables, are important to varying degrees, but seldom compete with the two principal items. In general, it seems that all people depend on grain to some extent, the more the better, for milk does not by itself seem to satisfy and meat, though much is consumed, is in most places of limited importance because of prohibitions against slaughter; eating cows is the most inefficient way of economizing them. Turu, Sukuma, Logoli and probably most Bantu have grain as their staple, while milk and meat are of varying but lesser importance. Among the Turu milk is of little importance, but in some of the more arid regions of East Africa it is crucial for subsistence, at least during parts of the year when grain supplies are low. The Nilotics, who are most dependent on milk, seem to try to grow or buy grain to economize their livestock. Among the Nilotic Suk the greatest dependence on milk is during the period of a few months before the harvest, when the only available plant foods are wild, when the rains have freshened the grass and so brought the cattle to their best milk productivity. During this time, however, they also sell meat and livestock for grain and slaughter animals for food. For both groups, Bantu and Nilotics, except for the Turu, milk is therefore important at some time.

Despite the predominant value of grain and milk, one should not underestimate the importance of meat. All these peoples like meat; its nutritional values are everywhere recognized. Under economic acculturation, consumption grows as traders buy cattle to slaughter and sell back to the people, so that the situation arises whereby the Vugusu, because of the meat markets that have grown up in Kenya, may be consuming less meat than their cattle-poor cousins, the Logoli (Wagner 1956:61). Contrariwise, consumption of meat has fallen among the Turu, since mature steers and smaller animals are no longer so extensively slaughtered, but are sold to other groups.

Throughout East Africa one finds a norm relating to slaughter which may be summed up in the statement, "One should not kill an animal without a good reason." Understandably, this often is taken to mean that killing occurs only at funerals, ancestral sacrifices, and other ritual observances. This interpretation, however, places too much emphasis on ritual as a determinant of economic behavior. The meaning is rather that there is nothing wrong with slaughtering animals if this is the most economic thing to do. This interpretation is supported by the Turu attitude toward eating eggs, which is precisely the same as the reason given for not eating meat. Chickens are almost never used in rituals, but are a supplementary food; what is meant is that it is foolish to eat an egg when it can grow into a chicken.

Land is often a commodity, but as such has a particular character. The sale of rights in land, as among the Turu, Sukuma and Logoli, seems to depend on whether the land has intrinsic worth for production over a significant period of time; in areas where it has no worth beyond the work put into it each year, it has no value. But transfer of land is frequently hedged with restrictions which derive from the feeling that land is essential for the continuation of the social group. A common example is the right of a seller to redeem his land at will. The fact that Suk sell "freeholds" on irrigation plots seems to be a function of the lack of strong, permanently localized kin groups. In general, even when intrinsically valuable, land is too immobile to participate to an appreciable extent in market processes.

5

The relation between grain and livestock is, as we have seen, the central fact in most of the economies of Eastern Africa. There is a general tendency for emphasis to be laid on the production of grain but for this to decline as numbers of livestock rise. The Sukuma offer a test case. Malcolm reports that in South Sukuma there are thirty or forty men who have managed to acquire herds of one thousand head of cattle or more (Malcolm 1953:70). These men have entirely dispensed with agriculture, depending for subsistence on grain bought with their cattle. The reason for this does not seem to be lack of interest in agriculture but abandonment of one type of productivity for a superior one. Grain can always be purchased; if not, one can live off the cattle.

Between north and south North Kavirondo, the amount of grain produced is in inverse ratio to wealth in livestock. This is also true in Suk where there are at least four stages, ranging from the extreme pastoralism of the far plains where no grain is produced, through a second stage of balance between the two forms, to the high hills where few animals are owned and grain is the most important form of wealth, and finally to the irrigated subdistrict of Wei Wei where there are no cattle whatever, and a good surplus of grain is grown.

It is easy to overlook a fact of fundamental importance, that the universal desirability of livestock in East Africa is such that they can be employed for trading both internally and externally. Thus to specialize in cattle it is not necessary for some part of each society to produce a surplus of grain. In general the Turkana produce little grain and internal trade seems weak, as is the case in other Nilotic groups, but they conduct external trade with people who have grain, in contrast to the Turu for whom both internal and external trade flourish. Where in normal times in a Bantu society like the Turu the market consists most importantly of internal redistribution of grain between variably producing units, in times of drought the same process occurs between tribes variously affected by the drought. Indeed, in pre-contact days the surrounding tribes seem to have looked on Turu district as a "bread basket."

It is possible that some misunderstanding about the role of cattle in these economies might derive from the idea that individual freedom in the market is greatly limited. It is true that the systems of reciprocity and joint rights that operate to one degree or another in all areas are factors that must be considered to understand market processes. Among the Turu a younger son's freedom to dispose of his animals is to some degree limited by his subordination to his eldest brother. But despite this, someone always has sufficient rights in livestock to be able to dispose of them if market conditions make this reasonable.

If there is one thing East Africanists seem to agree on it is that livestock are individually owned. By the same token, men are everywhere much more interested in livestock than are the women, because only men are allowed to buy and sell them.

This leads us to the factor of profit orientation, a subject on which there is by no means agreement. Gray argues that the Sonjo have no profit orientation at all, which is why he speaks of bridewealth as being so important in stimulating their economy (1960:46). But his notion of profit orientation, the attempt to buy cheap and sell dear in a dramatic fashion, would seem to be too narrow. The slow, unromantic accumulation of grain and its conversion to livestock when possible is as much profit seeking as is long term investment in pecuniary economies. It may be assumed that Wagner's assertion that the Kavirondo Bantu only exceptionally used cattle in economic exchange in pre-contact days also implies a lack of profit orientation (1956:104). Huntingford strongly infers a non-profit orientation when he says that Nandi in the past did not engage in trade (Huntingford 1950:81).

As long as livestock are not perceived as a form of money, the functioning of the profit motive is beclouded. This becomes clear if the thesis of this paper, that everywhere people tend to try to amass livestock in as great an amount as possible, because livestock are money, is kept in mind. We have seen the profit motive at work in Turu. Everywhere manipulations designed to increase livestock are most apparent, including the widespread method of robbing one's neighbors. Except for Audrey Butt in her description of the Nuer (1952:41), no one has asserted that in East Africa all members of a given society are equally rich or poor. Our information is rather that wealth varies, and that maximization of herds is a central aim.

East Africans seem normally to be oriented toward making profit. In Suk some men express it in a new way by going to a part of the district where goats and sheep are cheap, buying them in large quantities, and taking them to parts of the district where they are scarce to sell them dear for a cash profit.

It is not just in terms of livestock, however, that the profit motive operates. We have seen that the Logoli charge what would elsewhere be considered exorbitant rates of interest for the loan of grain. The fundamental reason for polygyny, besides the desire to perpetuate the family, seems usually to be the desire to increase the surplus production of grain. In short, the assumption of an intimate association of money and profit orientation is, if anything, strengthened in these societies. This does not mean that methods of making a profit do not vary. The custom of selling dear is represented in some places, as among the Suk, in haggling over everything, including bridewealth, while among the Turu prices are simply stated and either accepted or rejected without further discussion.

The prestige that derives from the ownership of cattle is everywhere based on the feeling that a man who has many animals is to be admired for his superior control of resources. While it is not possible to say that the prestige inherent in the possession of cattle is nothing but pecuniary, it does not seem possible any longer to entertain the notion that it is purely non-economic. And though in accord with Herskovits' discussion of prestige economies (1952: 461ff.), we find that there are various techniques for impressive display of their wealth, the mere marshalling of numbers of cattle is not one of these. The total number of animals a man owns is everywhere concealed, this in the main being based on a desire to avoid the envy of others.

Conspicuous display is, however, not absent. It is seen in the slaughter of numerous head of livestock at the funerals of chiefs and important men, so that we may say that funerals tend to be the occasion for reasserting the status of the family of the deceased. In Turu, normally, two or three cows are slaughtered by the family of a man who has died, while additional animals are killed by his sons-in-law to show their respect. Since status is intimately connected with control of resources, when is the need greater to display wealth and thus assert status than when the head of the house dies?

One of the most impressive kinds of conspicuous display in East Africa, and one of the most misleading, is the singling out of an ox for special attention by each man who can afford it, thereby impressing others while deriving emotional satisfaction himself. This custom seems to have led to the belief that such affectionate attention extends to all livestock; but nothing could be farther from the truth. Even in the case of such prize oxen, we should remember that frequently a most impressive act of conspicuous consumption is to kill one for a feast for members of the community. Among the Turu, the significance of the adulation of the ox is to be seen in a new light; to a great extent, such animals are sold on the induced livestock market to buy the new symbols of status— clothing, bicycles, radios and the like. However, it should be noted that the man working within the strict confines of the indigenous system considers such things useless.

The sacrificial role of cattle varies greatly. In many places men tend to identify cattle with themselves, and show this in sacrifices where the animals act as surrogates for men, as among the Nuer. But the logic behind this for the Nuer is explained in a passage that has ambiguous meaning, one ritual and the other "economic": "In the time of the ancestor of his clan the 'cow' gave her life for his salvation, and so it is with his descendants today and so it will be with their descendants tomorrow. Whence springs the identification of man with ox, of lineage with herd, and of men with cattle" (Evans-Pritchard 1953: 197).

It is not necessary to take an exclusive position in the matter of whether cattle are economically valued or ritually valued. They are both. They can be used to gain pecuniary ends while still being "gods with wet noses," as Schapera puts it (1937:138). The only thing to be insisted on is that for the most part the one objective is integral to the other, ritual status being intimately tied in with economic value, just as pecuniary use is integral with subsistence use.

6

We are thus led to the final segment of this comparative survey. Lest it be thought that in this paper market economics is emphasized at the expense of all else, we may recall the fundamental principle that the working out of any element in a given culture, including the economy, will depend upon the total setting of which it is a part. For example, the degree of individualism permitted is to be associated with the type of society. Among the Turu localized lineages act as corporations, in which joint ownership of livestock and other goods is recognized. Within the corporation, exchange of goods and services is in some respects achieved by reciprocity rather than open trade. Contrariwise, in Suk, the obligations of kin toward each other are greatly lessened and hardly extend outside the group of full brothers. It is possible that in the Kavirondo area the greater part of exchange is also achieved in the localized lineages through the means of mutual obligations and to a much greater degree than among Turu.

It has already been noted that bridewealth seems to be affected by ideas concerning what is being contracted for; it should further be noted that though no mention has been made in this paper of the non-economic aspects of marriage, such as assuaging of the feelings of a mother-in-law for the loss of her daughter or the love that the bride and groom often feel for each other, they nonetheless enter. Furthermore, the values of a people may intrude on the processes of exchange, so that, for example, among the Suk a person who grossly deceives another in a transaction can be made to rectify the wrong. Everywhere a significant number of animals is constantly being drawn off for rituals, gifts, and fines for ritual offenses which are necessary to the mental well-being of the people.

But despite these things, which are normally sufficiently emphasized, the very fact of variations in wealth and the existence of systems of valuation and exchange among people in these different societies proves that nowhere are cultural and social factors so overwhelming as to eliminate market behavior or make impossible economic analysis without taking them fully into account. Herskovits notes,

> . . . it must . . . be understood that economic problems may be studied without the need to give a complete account of all the interrelations between an economic system and other aspects of social life, or the need to consider all the sanctions on which a given body of economic custom rests (1952: 502).

With this statement, as a methodological principle, we must agree; this survey suggests that a general theory of economics in East African societies is possible on this basis.

If Gray is right when he comments that anthropologists have overplayed their hand with regard to bridewealth by insisting that it is not an economic

transaction, presumably because if it were it would be offensive (1960:34),
I suggest further that it is an error to think that social mechanisms must take
precedence over or completely negate individual marketing behavior. Too often
students have been content with mere assertion as to the economic component
in marriage, ritual, exchange, and the like. Yet this is not a matter for assertion
but investigation and, in particular, for the collection of statistical, quantitative
data. If reciprocity and other comparable methods of exchange are important, it
must be shown in what respect, and to what degree. Among the Turu mutual
obligations are seldom so diffuse as to be undefinable or make other kinds of
exchange unimportant. When a Turu gives his brother a cow for his marriage,
this is an obligation so well understood that he can verbalize it and document
his statement. And if his brother comes to him for another cow for another
marriage, it is as well understood that he has no moral right to the animal and
will not get it unless he contracts to pay it back. In fact it may be argued that,
as in all human societies, throughout East Africa the social obligations imposed
on people are constantly at war with their individual desires.

We have argued that among the cattle-keeping people of East Africa we find
market economies in which the main elements of trade are women, grain, land
and livestock, the exchange of which is achieved by the use of livestock as
money. Livestock are to be thought of as the functional equivalents of money
because they have the properties of a standard of value, constitute a medium of
exchange and are a store of value. Thus, with some variations, the fundamental
orientation of the economic systems is toward maximization of livestock,
usually through the conversion of surplus grain to livestock and subsequent
promotion of natural increase, with further investment in women and land to
increase grain supplies and thus increase wealth in livestock. It was pointed
out in the opening paragraphs of this essay that the great value assigned to
cattle has been widely interpreted as being a function of their ritual worth,
deriving from their role as symbols of status. A more adequate interpretation
would seem to be that the prestige of livestock wealth is of the same order as
the prestige gained through the control of resources in any market economy.

The recognition of the existence of indigenous market systems gives promise
of working out development in the future because we are dealing with peoples
who are not unfamiliar with the kind of economic thinking and processes
which will be essential to national development. They should be sympathetically
consulted when changes are proposed. When destocking was imposed on the
Turu, they complained that its effect would simply be to make the rich richer
and the poor poorer. While this sounded like merely an emotional reaction,
it was in fact a reasonable prediction. By arbitrarily reducing the number of
livestock across the board, the currency was in effect inflated in value while
the price of grain accordingly fell. The chance for the "poor" to convert their
holdings of grain into livestock was thus reduced and market viability reduced
as if, in our economy, Federal Reserve interest rates were increased. But the
future is not all promising. It will not be easy to find a new focus of economic

life which will provide as much productivity and security as livestock. The resistence of many herding peoples to change is based on reluctance to forsake a proven system for others which are less certain.

29 ECONOMIC VARIATIONS ON A THEME BY SCHNEIDER *

Benton F. Massell

In a recent paper (Schneider 1964),† Harold K. Schneider provides an interesting and provocative analysis of the economic activities of the Turu, an aboriginal tribe in the central part of Tanganyika. He provides evidence that the Turu are, to a large extent, motivated by economic considerations, notably, maximization of profit and accumulation of wealth. While he stops short of a quantitative analysis of the Turu economy, Professor Schneider does provide us with some excellent data relating to agricultural production, the principal Turu occupation.

The present paper presents an analysis of these data, using elementary econometric techniques. Thus Schneider's qualitative observations on the relationship among the variables will be supplemented here by a more formal treatment that involves fitting a production function to cross-section data, using multiple regression analysis.

Choice of a Production Function

The functional form which comes most readily to mind is, of course, the Cobb-Douglas function, which has gained respectability through its widespread use by economists (which is explained as much by analytical convenience as by the plausibility of the assumptions underlying the function). For comparison, we shall also fit a simple linear production function.

There has been considerable controversy concerning the estimation of the coefficients in a Douglas function, using either time series or cross-section data (see Menderhausen 1938; Reder 1943; Bronfenbrenner 1941; Marschak and Andrews 1944). With regard to cross-section data, where the observations relate

Reprinted from Economic Development and Culture Change, *Volume XII,* No. 1, October, 1963, pp. 33–41, by permission of The University of Chicago Press. Copyright 1963 by The University of Chicago.

* The author is with The RAND Corporation. Any views expressed in this paper are those of the author. They should not be interpreted as reflecting the views of The RAND Corporation or the official opinion or policy of any of its governmental or private research sponsors.

† The material used by Massell in his analysis was contained in an unpublished paper originally presented at the SSRC Conference on Indigenous and Induced Elements in the Economics of Subsaharan Africa, Northwestern University, November, 1961. The paper was subsequently published and is reprinted above, pp. 426–445 (eds.).

to firms within an industry, all in the same economy (as is the case here), it is argued that either the firms are operating on different production functions, in which case the coefficients are meaningless, or else the firms should all be operating on the same point of the curve. Thus, the variation in output that one observes, in the latter case, is accounted for largely by variables which have not been explicitly considered in the model, rather than by variation in the observed inputs. I do not believe that the present study is subject to this criticism. While there is reason to expect the "firms" to be operating on the same production function, there is no presumption of the sort of rational economic behavior which would lead all Turu households to the same point on the function.

The Cobb-Douglas function can be written:

$$(1) \quad Q = e^{\alpha 0} K^{\alpha 1} N^{\alpha 2} L^{\alpha 3}$$

where Q = output, K = capital input, N = labor input, L = land under cultivation, and $e^{\alpha 0}$ = a multiplicative constant. Transforming (1) to logs, we have:

$$(2) \quad \ln Q = a_0 + a_1 \ln(K) + a_2 \ln(N) + a_3 \ln(L)$$

It is straightforward to estimate the coefficients in (2), using the least squares method.

Estimation of the Coefficients

We have 29 observations on the set of four variables, each observation relating to a Turu household.[1] Output is measured in *debes* of grain; in other words, it is a physical measure. Capital refers to an index of fertilizer, constructed with reference to the number and type of animals in the household's corral.[2] As farm labor is performed by the women in the Turu economy (as in many African societies), labor input refers to the number of adult women in the household.[3] Finally, land is measured as the number of acres under cultivation by the household. The data are presented in Table 29–1.

The production function (2) was fitted, yielding the following estimates:

$$\ln (Q) = .673 + .523 \cdot n(K) + .267 \ln(N) + .330 \ln(L)$$
$$\quad\quad\quad (.158) \quad\quad (.174) \quad\quad (.321)$$

The standard errors are presented in parentheses beneath their respective coefficients. The coefficient of multiple correlation, R, is .785, and the F ratio is 13.4, with 3 and 25 degrees of freedom. This value of F is significant at the .01 level. While a_1 is significantly greater than zero (using a one-tailed test) at the .01 level, a_2 and a_3 fail to be significant even at the .05 level; however, they are significant at the .10 level.

The large standard errors associated with a_2 and a_3 can be explained in terms

---

[1] A thirtieth observation had to be discarded, as two variables took on zero values (and the log of zero, of course, does not exist).

[2] Thus, a goat counts as one unit, a calf as two, and adult cattle as five each (Schneider 1964:54).

[3] Thus, for our purposes, women are assumed to be homogeneous. Differences in skill are ignored.

TABLE 29–1   ***Output and Inputs in a Sample***
of Turu Farmsteads

Fertilizer index (K)	Acres (L)	Women (N)	Grain production (Q)
187	4.1	4	189
177	4.7	3	95
148	6.4	3	335
130	5.0	3	150
130	4.6	1	57
127	6.8	5	195
113	3.5	2	205
98	5.2	2	72
90	3.1	3	90
87	2.6	1	75
85	8.8	4	163
82	2.6	1	53
79	2.7	1	96
71	4.3	2	95
70	2.0	3	55
69	2.6	1	75
69	6.7	3	58
61	2.3	1	36
56	4.2	1	76
54	4.0	1	125
54	4.0	1	45
51	6.1	3	90
50	2.7	1	37
41	2.6	1	35
39	4.1	2	41
35	1.8	1	40
34	2.0	2	61
34	3.0	2	49
17	3.3	1	40
2,338	115.8	59	2,733

Source: Adapted from Schneider 1964:58.

of multicollinearity. In the sample used, there is a high degree of intercorrelation between land and labor. Hence it was decided to delete these variables, one at a time, and regress output against the remaining variables. The production function then can be rewritten (with land deleted):

(3) $\ln(Q) = \beta_\Omega + B_1 \ln(K) + \beta_2 \ln(N)$

Again, estimating the coefficients by least squares, we have:

$$\ln(Q) = .740 + .573 \ln(K) + .386 \ln(N)$$
$$(.157) \qquad (.156)$$

with $R = .765$ and $F = 18.36$, with 2 and 26 degrees of freedom. Again, F is significant at the .01 level.

Now the partial coefficient associated with labor is significantly positive at the .01 level, while the coefficient for capital remains significant as well. Both coefficients have a slightly higher value than the corresponding a's, as one would expect.

Next, deleting labor from equation (2), we write:

(4) $\ln(Q) = \gamma_0 + \gamma_1 \ln(K) + \gamma_3 \ln(L)$

The coefficients are given by:

$$\ln(Q) = .504 + \underset{(.154)}{.598 \ln(K)} + \underset{(.208)}{.499 \ln(L)}$$

with $R = .762$ and $F = 18.01$. Thus, both coefficients and the over-all regression (as measured by F) are significant at the .01 level. Again, the γ's are somewhat larger than the corresponding a's. In both (3) and (4), R is only slightly less than in equation (2), suggesting that addition of a third independent variable makes only a marginal contribution to explaining the variation in grain output.

Turning now to the coefficients themselves, we note that

$$\sum_{i=1}^{3} a_i = 1.120, \quad \sum_{i=1}^{2} \beta_i = .959, \text{ and } \sum_{i=1,3} \gamma_i = 1.097.$$

In none of these cases is the sum of the coefficients significantly different from zero (at even the .10 level); in other words, there is no evidence of either increasing or decreasing returns to scale.

The Economic Basis of Turu Agriculture

It is well known that the coefficients in a Cobb-Douglas function signify the elasticity of production of the respective inputs—that is, the ratio of the factor's marginal product to its average product. Under competitive factor pricing, this would represent the factor's share of the product. Returning to the equation (2) estimates, we see that capital's elasticity of production is approximately one-half, that of land one-third, and that of labor one-fourth.

Next, we note that it is possible to compute the marginal productivities of the factors, i.e., letting f_i = the marginal product of the ith factor:

(5) $f_K = a_1 \dfrac{Q}{K}$

$f_N = a_2 \dfrac{Q}{N}$

$f_L = a_3 \dfrac{Q}{L}$

The values of Q, K, N, and L are, of course, the column totals shown in Table 1. The marginal productivities, then, are

$f_K = .611$

$f_N = 12.37$

$f_L = 7.78$

These are marginal physical products. Noting that a *debe* of grain is worth Shs. 5 (Schneider 1964:52), the marginal value products, in shillings, can be obtained by multiplying the respective marginal physical products by 5. Thus, the marginal value product of a woman is Shs. 62, that of an acre of land Shs. 39, and that of a cow (= 5 fertilizer units) Shs. 15. In other words, the marginal product of a woman is approximately four times that of a cow and 50 percent greater than that of an acre of land.

Fortunately, Schneider has also provided us with the factor prices. Thus, a cow is worth Shs. 100 (IBID.) and a woman (i.e., the bride price) Shs. 400;[4] cultivatable land is seldom sold, but swamp land, which we may take to be roughly comparable in value to land under cultivation, when sold, brings in up to Shs. 20 (Schneider 1964:56). Thus, we shall say that cultivable land is worth approximately Shs. 20. Dividing the marginal value product of each factor by its price, P_i, and letting the subscript, C, refer to cow, we have:

$$\frac{f_C}{P_C} = .155$$

$$\frac{f_N}{P_N} = .150$$

$$\frac{f_L}{P_L} = 1.95$$

Interestingly enough, in the Turu community, the marginal contribution to output (or revenue) of a shilling spent on capital (cattle) is just about equal to that of a shilling spent on labor (women) and substantially less than the marginal contribution to output of a shilling's worth of land. Thus, given the institutional factors which help determine the price of land, it is quite understandable, in purely economic terms, for a man not to want to sell land. Moreover, the community has set the relative prices of cattle and women in such a way as to reflect their relative marginal contribution to grain output.[5]

---

[4] "The average initial contract for a wife consists of four or five head of cattle (about 3 heifers and 1 or 2 steers). This seems to be for the services of the woman, who runs the household, which encompasses producing grain, processing it, and providing firewood, water, and so forth. The husband also has theoretical exclusive sexual rights to his wife, but in fact he is expected to allow her a lover from whom the husband can extract a fine of six goats if he catches the pair *en flagrante delicto*." (Schneider 1964:56. Phrasing in the published version is slightly altered—Eds.)

[5] This is not quite correct; the relevant economic cost of the factors is, strictly speaking, the annual rent. This would consist of interest on the initial investment, maintenance expenses (e.g., subsistence costs), and depreciation. Actually, with cattle, depreciation is negative, as the net reproduction rate exceeds zero. Women also bear children, but the offspring technically belong to the bride's father, necessitating a payment by the husband for each child born. Thus depreciation on women is positive. It is interesting to note, however, that when a woman dies, part of the bride price is likely to be returned— the amount returned, which we may term the "salvage value," is typically a decreasing function of the woman's useful economic life.

As an alternative to the model employed thus far, we turn now to a linear production function, which is written:

(6) $Q = \xi_0 + \xi_1 K + \xi_2 N + \xi_3 L$

Again estimating the coefficients by least squares, we have:

$$Q = 25.304 + .755 K + 9.105 N + 10.055 L$$
$$\quad\quad\quad\;\; (.257) \quad (11.93) \quad\quad (7.23)$$

with $R = .735$ and $F = 9.79$, which is significant at .01. We note that, comparing the standard errors and the F ratio in (6) with the corresponding figures in (2), the Cobb-Douglas appears to give a somewhat better fit. In (6), the coefficients signify the marginal productivities; these turn out to be roughly the same as those estimated with equations (2) and (5).

The question arises, can the results of the regressions be accepted as evidence of the economic "rationality" of the Turu? Schneider has in fact argued that to a considerable extent Turu behavior *can* be explained in rational economic terms. And one might argue that the pricing of women relative to cattle (and refusal to sell cultivable land at the institutionally fixed price) lends support to his thesis. However, it is worth noting that this "rationality" applies to the aggregate while not to the individual farmsteads. For, given the relative factor prices, those producers with a high capital-labor ratio could increase profits by acquiring more wives, whereas producers with a low capital-labor ratio would do well to acquire more cattle. In other words, all households could improve their performance by moving closer to the point at which the relative marginal productivities equal the relative factor prices.

The Rate of Interest on Cattle

One can carry the analysis a step further and compute an own rate of interest on cattle in Turu society. We note that production is characterized by joint processes, one process producing grain and the other cattle. The first of these processes is given by:

(7) $Q = e^{\alpha_0} K^{\alpha_1} N^{\alpha_2} L^{\alpha_3}$

and the other process can be represented

(8) $\triangle K = g(K)$

where $\triangle K =$ the net annual increase in livestock (measured in fertilizer units) from natural causes. If it is assumed that cattle reproduce at a constant annual percentage rate, η, we can write:

(9) $\triangle K = \eta K$

Now, the total value of output (of both grain and cattle) V, can be written:

(10) $V = PQ + \triangle K P_K$

Now write:

(11) $\quad Y = \dfrac{V}{P} = Q + \delta \, \triangle K,$

where $\delta = \dfrac{P_K}{P} = \dfrac{P_C}{5P}$

Then, substituting (1) into (10) and differentiating with respect to cattle, we have:

(12) $\quad \dfrac{dY}{dK} = f_K + \delta \eta$

The rate of interest, ρ, is then given by:[6]

(13) $\quad \rho = \dfrac{P \dfrac{dY}{dK}}{P_K} = \dfrac{f_K}{\delta} + \eta$

Now, we know that $f_K = .6$, and $\delta = \dfrac{P_C}{5P} = 4$, so that $\rho = .15$.

We do not know η, but we do know the birth and death rate of cattle for one year (Schneider 1954:61) ; and, assuming this year to be typical, we can compute the net reproduction rate. This procedure gives $\eta = .06$, and $\rho = .21$.

[6] Assuming maintenance costs on cattle are negligible.

part four

SOME
FURTHER
THEORETICAL
ISSUES

As was pointed out in the introduction, not all the theoretical issues which exist in economic anthropology have been touched upon in the selections of readings which constitute the core of this book. In addition, some issues which have been discussed need further elaboration. We shall take up these matters here.

On the Scope of Economics

We accept as a definition of economics that it is the study of the allocation of scarce resources among alternative ends (see above, p. 197). Such a definition seems to many to be too broad. If the terms are defined as broadly as they need to be defined, almost every human action can be seen as involving a decision concerning the allocation of scarce resources among alternative ends; every human act is then an economic act.

Does this mean, then, that anthropology must be reduced to nothing more than a specialized branch of economics? The answer is an unqualified negative. In the first place, economists themselves are not interested in studying all of human behavior. In the second place, economics—or whatever might grow out of it in a purely anthropological context—is a shoe which needs to be worn, if it needs to be worn at all, only when it fits. There is much with which the anthropologist concerns himself which cannot be explained or accounted for in terms of the theory of choice. For example, while a specific act of a man toward a particular kinsman might be usefully analyzed in terms of the theory of choice, it seems highly unlikely that a kinship system per se can be accounted for in terms of the theory of choice or the theory of maximization or anything growing out of it.

Similarly, and more fundamentally, while choices are made in terms of culturally determined values, it again seems highly unlikely that those values can be accounted for wholly in terms of the theory of choice.

In short, the theory of choice cannot explain everything about a society or culture, although more might be explainable in these terms than now seems possible.

At the same time, it would seem that until we have gained more experience in the use of this theory in the analysis of social processes and structure, it would be wise to confine it to some fairly traditional areas of investigation—not quite to those areas which are the concern of the substantivists, but perhaps something like them.

In the light of this, it would seem that debates about whether or not some particular kind of cultural phenomenon, for example, bride price, is or is not "economic," are rather fruitless. They are certainly fruitless unless the debaters agree on what they mean by "economic." More than this, the only question is whether the concepts of economics can be fruitfully used in analyzing the phenomena in question. We would be inclined, in cases of doubt, to argue for assuming that economic analysis would be fruitful, until the contrary is demonstrated. More precisely, we would argue that anyone interested in using this point of departure for analysis is perfectly entitled to do so, without imposing upon others the obligation to do so.

"Economic Man" and the Relativity of Values

One of the tired old chestnuts of controversy over economic theory is the concept of "economic man." It has been one of the favorite whipping boys of anthropologists since Malinowski, and of nonanthropological critics of conventional economic theory since Thorstein Veblen. But they have been flogging a dead horse for more than half a century.

The concept was implicit in much early economic writing, and was finally given explicit definition in the writings of John Stuart Mill as early as 1844, although he did not use the phrase himself. Mill argued that the economist did not concern himself with the whole conduct of man in society. Rather, Mill said, the economist was concerned with only that aspect of man's behavior which is concerned with the acquisition and possession of wealth. Thus did Mill, who was a "classical" economist, anticipate what Polanyi was to later offer as a "substantive" definition of "economic."

Mill's idea was picked up and elaborated by later writers who postulated not merely that the economist was concerned with the acquisition of wealth, but that men themselves were concerned with nothing else. This is obviously a far different notion than that advanced by Mill.

It is part of the genius of theoretical economics that it has continually buried its theoretical mistakes in theoretical refinements and advances. The nineteenth-century, simplistic concept of an economic man motivated only by money gains—a useful simplifying assumption in the state of economic art at the time—gave way to a more sophisticated concept, and had done so long before Malinowski wrote his acid comments on the subject (see above, pp. 17–49).

What survives of the concept of economic man is the concept of a satisfaction-maximizing individual, or of a rational man who makes decisions on the basis of the calculus of maximization. Yet there are those who find it difficult to accept even this much. It is no longer as fashionable as it once was for anthropologists to call attention to examples of "noneconomic"—or nonrational—

behavior, but this sort of thing has not entirely disappeared from anthropological thinking.

Interestingly enough, such efforts violate a cardinal principle of modern anthropological thought and practice: cultural relativism. Cultural relativism implicitly raises the question, rational according to what scale of values.

In the light of the doctrine of cultural relativism, many judgements to the effect that particular choices are "noneconomic," are seen to be nothing more than cases of a peculiar kind of ethnocentrism on the part of the person making the judgement. Even Herskovits, usually so careful in these matters, sometimes falls into this trap, as in a discussion of the "wastefulness" of certain funerary rites (Herskovits 1952:492). The question which must be asked is, wasteful according to what standards of what constitutes proper use of materials. Such practices are not wasteful according to the standards of the people concerned. And it does no good to argue that the living may starve because the departing spirits have been blessed with gifts of food. To the people concerned, it may be preferable that the living starve rather than incur the wrath of the spirit of the dead ancestor. Only a people who care little for the spirits of dead ancestors and much for the comfort of their own flesh could make the judgement that the burial of material goods with the corpse of the deceased is wasteful.

In the end, acceptance of the validity of the principle of maximization involves acceptance of the modern concept of economic man and vice versa. The two are opposite sides of the same coin.

The Notion of Maximization

With all that has been said here, the words "maximize" and "maximization" are being more frequently used by anthropologists. But it is by no means always clear that those who use the terms have a full understanding of what they mean. It is hardly within the scope of this book to attempt a full-scale exposition of maximization theory. Any theoretically oriented introductory economics text does the job more effectively than we possibly could in the space we have available (Samuelson remains the most popular such text). However, some general comments seem in order.

When reference is made to conventional economic theory, a large part of what is being referred to is what we may call the neoclassical model or models. Models is the more accurate term since neoclassical theory has several parts to it.

The core of neoclassical theory is what is usually called the theory of the firm. The theory of the firm, along with other aspects of neoclassical theory, evolved slowly but reached substantially its present form in the late 1920s. Closely related to the theory of the firm (and here "firm" means any business enterprise, no matter how organized, not merely a corporation) were additional models covering the "factor markets"—theories of wages, interest and rent.

In addition, neoclassical theory made some ritual obeisance to the phenomenon of consumer demand, though this part of neoclassical theory was not developed to as high a degree as was the theory of the firm and its related theories.

Key elements in neoclassical theory are the notion of rationality as defined by the calculus of maximization, and the notion of equilibrium of "forces" as the operating principle in translating the individual calculus into a social calculus of maximization.

To the initiated, these central elements in neoclassical theory often have something of the quality of "revealed truth"; for uninitiated skeptics, they often seem meaningless, particularly in view of the fact that it is virtually impossible to demonstrate their validity empirically.

Just what is the "calculus of maximization?" In its purest theoretical form, it is just what it says it is, a calculus, or *the* calculus, in the strict mathematical sense of the term. Maximization problems always involve, at least in principle, maximizing the sum of two or more functions which have a common independent variable, or maximizing the difference between two functions which have a common variable.

As an example of the latter situation, we may refer to a simple profit maximization model. We start with a basic equation which defines profit: $P = R - C$; profit equals revenue minus cost. All three items in the equation are presumed to be functions (again in the mathematical rather than the sociological sense) of a single independent variable: quantity of output (Q). This statement can be expressed algebraically in three new equations, as follows: $P = f_p(Q)$; $R = f_r(Q)$; $C = f_c(Q)$. The subscripts are intended to indicate that the mathematical functions are different in each case.

Having postulated that some functional relationship exists and having expressed the fact algebraically, we can substitute the new terms into the original equation so that it now reads as follows: $f_p(Q) = f_r(Q) - f_c(Q)$. The problem now is to find a value for Q at which profit, or $f_p(Q)$, is at a maximum. This is an elementary problem in differential calculus. With calculus it can readily be shown that the maximum value for $f_p(Q)$ occurs at a value of Q such that another expression: $f_p'(Q) = 0$. The expression: $f_p'(Q)$, is called the "first derivative" of $f_p(Q)$, and may be thought of rather roughly as describing the rate of change of P as Q changes. If you imagine P increasing as Q increases (the more you sell, at least for a while, the greater your profit), reaching a maximum, and then beginning to fall as Q continues to increase (you may have to lower your price to sell more; costs of operations may increase as you begin to exceed the design capacity of your plant and for other reasons) you should readily see that at that value of Q when P is maximum, P is neither increasing nor decreasing. This is what leads to the proposition that P_{max} when $f_p'(Q) = 0$.

We may now return to our earlier profit equation as expressed in functional form: $f_p(Q) = f_r(Q) - f_c(Q)$. It can be shown that given this equation, the following equation is also true: $f_p'(Q) = f_r'(Q) - f_p'(Q)$. Now if P_{max} when $f_p'(Q) = 0$, it follows by substitution that P_{max} when $0 = f_r'(Q) - f_c'(Q)$. It then follows that P_{max} when $f_r'(Q) = f_c'(Q)$. The first derivatives of the revenue and cost functions are called, in neoclassical economics, "marginal revenue" and "marginal cost" respectively. The last equation given then leads to the statement that "profit is at a maximum when marginal cost equals marginal revenue"; this, at least, is the way the whole line of mathematical reasoning is usually summed up in introductory economics texts.

So far, we have been talking in bare-bones abstractions. To put some analytical flesh on those bones, we need to go still further. When we say, for example, that $y = f(x)$, we are simply stating that some relationship exists between y and x, but we have said nothing about what the relationship is. If we then say that $y = 2x^2 + 3x + 4$, we have defined the function, we have defined the relationship between our y of the moment and our x of the moment. We might, on another occasion, say that there is another function, which we may call $y = f_1(x)$. This function may be definable as $y = 9x^3 + 4x - 10$; here we have defined a new relationship between y and x—we have defined a new function.

In applying the maximization principle to human affairs we need not only to work out the relationship among functions, but we must also define the functions, or at least specify their character. For example, neoclassical economic theory holds that for a business firm operating under conditions of perfect competition, the revenue function: $R = f_r(Q)$, is definable as $R = aQ$, where *a* is the prevailing market price per unit of the commodity in question. This is a precise definition of a function. Cost functions are seldom defined in this way except perhaps in very advanced treatments; usually economists are content to specify the general character of the function graphically; the specification is a U-shaped curve of unit costs where Q (quantity) is the horizontal axis and unit cost is the vertical axis.

The heart and soul of neoclassical economic theory is precisely the specification of, usually, the general character of relevant functions under varying conditions.

And this leads us to a very general proposition: the heart and soul of any systematic application of maximization theory in economic anthropology must consist first in working out the relationships among the relevant functions, and second in defining, or at least specifying the general characteristics of the relevant functions. To the best of our knowledge, no efforts of this kind have yet appeared in print. But to use terms like maximize and maximization in any other context or way is to resort to nothing more than impressive but meaningless jargon.

The Concept of "Equilibrium"

The second cardinal element, along with maximization theory, in neoclassical economic theory is the notion of equilibrium. Maximization theory by itself can be thought of as a theory of individual behavior. Equilibrium theory moves economic theory into a social context, translating the individual calculus of maximization into a social calculus of maximization.

Many humanistically oriented people find the notion of equilibrium uncongenial, largely, it would seem, because it appears to suggest that people are the victims of mysterious forces beyond their control. When someone describes the equilibrium models of economics as "mechanistic models" (as opposed to the teleological models of sociology) as is done by Krupp in the paper reprinted above (see pp. 243–256), the belief in "mysterious forces" is perhaps enhanced. However, it is certainly true of the equilibrium situations with which the economist deals, and should in principle be true in any other case of social equilibrium, that the "mysterious forces" which seem to be pushing people around are nothing more or less than their free choices within the framework of the constraints of their physical and social environment.

The simplest example of an equilibrium model is the classical supply-demand model. All that the supply-demand model purports to show is what two groups of people, a supply group and a demand group, will do under particular conditions, namely under different conditions of market price. What must be understood is that a supply schedule (or curve, that bane of beginning students in economics) simply is the analyst's effort to describe what the supply group will do under specified varying conditions. It says that the supply group will want to sell large quantities of something at high prices, and small quantities of the same thing at low prices. It also says that if the price is high and the supply group is not selling as much as it would like to sell at that price, at least some members of the supply group would offer to sell at a lower price rather than see goods remain on their hands.

Again, it is important to recognize that this pattern of behavior is not something which is imposed upon the supply group by the supply schedule. Rather, the supply schedule is a description of what the intentions and wishes of the supply group are.

By the same token, the demand schedule says that the demand group would like to buy a large quantity at a low price and a small quantity at a high price. If the price is low and the demand group is unable to buy as much as it would like to buy at that price, then at least some members of the demand group would offer to buy at a higher price rather than do without. Once again, the demand schedule merely reflects their intentions.

If an appropriate relationship exists between the intentions of the supply group on the one hand and the demand group on the other, there is some one price at which the supply group is selling all its wants to sell at that price and the demand group is buying all it wants to buy at that price. Buyers are not motivated to offer higher prices to get more; sellers are not motivated to offer lower prices to sell more.

The reference above to "an appropriate relationship" can be and should be expressed in mathematical terms, much along the lines of our earlier discussion of the maximization model. Then the "supply schedule" can be expressed as a function: $Q = f_s(P)$: the quantity which sellers will wish to sell is a function of price, and the "demand schedule" can be expressed as a function: $Q = f_d(P)$: the quantity which buyers will wish to purchase is a function of price. Since these functions are functions in two variables, they can also be expressed as lines on a graph. It is generally assumed that the supply is a line sloping downward from right to left, while the demand schedule is a line sloping downward from left to right. An appropriate relationship exists if the two lines intersect, and the equilibrium price and quantity exists at the point of intersection; all this on a graph where price is on the vertical axis, and quantity is on the horizontal axis. If the prevailing market price is either above or below the equilibrium price, then either the supply group or the demand group will be motivated to change their behavior by making different price offers, until the price gradually returns to the equilibrium level. If the price is above or below the equilibrium price, then the situation is said to be in disequilibrium.

One question which arises is whether, when in the disequilibrium state, the alterations in behavior which are motivated by the disequilibrium condition are in the direction of equilibrium behavior. In economics, it is possible to specify conditions in some kinds of complex models in which the motivated behavior is away from rather than toward the equilibrium position. When a real society gets into this kind of situation, and it is possible, the result is likely to be some kind of social collapse. One example of such a situation was the runaway inflation that occurred in Germany after World War I. A second example was the deep economic depression in the United States in the 1930s.

Once again, in applying equilibrium theory to social situations, the trick is to work out the relationships among the relevant functions and then either to define those functions, or at least to specify their general character.

On the Definition of "an Economy"

The question of what we mean by "an economy" or an "economic system," although it has received some attention, has perhaps not received the attention it deserves. Among other things, it is not clear enough that "an economy" and an "economic system" might very well be two different things.

In considering this question, it is well that we give explicit consideration to an important notion: that is the distinction to be made between "that which exists in the real world" and descriptions of "that which exists in the real world." No scientist of any sophistication, be he of the natural, social, or physical variety, confuses the two. It is widely recognized that descriptions of reality, however precise and detailed, are no more than approximations of reality itself.

Under prevailing usages in anthropology, the anthropologist would be tempted to use the term "economy" to refer to whatever it is in the real world that we are concerned with, and to use the term "the economic system" to refer to the description of the economy. This is not, however, in agreement with the usage in economics. In economics "the economic system" is the term used to refer to the real world phenomenon; the description of that phenomenon is called an "economic model."

Our impulse is to follow the usage of economics; indeed, this usage becomes a handy key to analysis in one of the papers reprinted above (see pp. 199–200).

We need now to say something about the general character of this "economic system" viewed as something which exists in the real world and the operations of which might be describable in an economic model. Economizing can be seen as involving purely private choices among alternatives, but it can also be seen as involving social choices as well. One can imagine situations in which the "social choice" is no more than a kind of sum of individual choices. But in all societies known to us, the idea of social choice involves something more than just this; it involves certain social mechanisms (the market is such a mechanism) by which individual choices are translated into a collective choice. The "economic system," viewed as a social phenomenon in the real world, would consist of these mechanisms. The only such system which has been analyzed in any detail is the market system. Other systems are possible, since market systems are not universal. One major untouched task of economic anthropology must be the exploration of alternative systems.

What then of the term "the economy," which seems to have no referent in this scheme? We do not feel under any obligation to provide employment for unemployed words. But there is something else of relevance to economic analysis for which the term "the economy" or "an economy" seems ready-made. What we are concerned with here grows out of the definition of economics which we accepted earlier (see pp. 197, 455), that it is the study of the allocation of scarce resources among alternative ends. With this in mind, it seems convenient to define an "economy" as a universe or set of ends which are mutual alternatives, whether directly or indirectly, together with the resources which may or must be allocated among them. Since the first part of the definition, relating to "ends," necessarily implies the second part, relating to "resources," an "economy" might be more simply defined as a universe of ends among which choices must be made.

This formulation, it should be said, is not common in economics; the term "an economy" is usually used interchangeably with "an economic system" in our definition of the term. But we are moved in this direction by certain speculations of anthropologists in recent years, which we will discuss presently.

It must be emphasized that our present proposal to group or classify ends according to whether they are or are not mutual alternatives rests on criteria which are relevant for the sort of economic analysis ordinarily pursued by professional economists. It would be possible to establish different criteria for classifying ends, criteria which might be useful for other purposes. We might further subdivide these into ends relating to hunger, fatigue, and the desire for sexual fulfillment, or to the desire for religious experience or self-esteem. We might even find it convenient to refer to these as "hunger economies," or "sex economies," or "religious economies," as some have referred to "subsistence economies" or "prestige economies." But when we do so refer to them, it must be understood that it merely means that we are referring to those aspects of behavior which are exclusively or primarily concerned with the drives in question.

With this established, it is useful to consider the idea of "multicentric economies." The term seems to have originated with Bohannan, who has discussed
the concept at some length (see above, pp. 300–311, and also Bohannan 1963:
246–265).

Bohannan's current ideas rest on an earlier theoretical base. A Dutch economist
named Boeke first talked about "dual economies" or "dual societies" apparently
as early as 1910, although his ideas on the subject did not see print in English
until as late as 1947 (Boeke 1947). Boeke's "dual economies" were to be found
in colonial situations (his immediate reference point was the Dutch East Indies).
One of the two "economies" consisted on the traditional peasant "economy"
of the colony, the other consisted of an intrusive, European based commercial
"economy."

In 1948, Herskovits used the term "dual economy" to refer to a far different
notion, that of a cleavage *within* a traditional economic system. The cleavage
noted by Herskovits was between what he called the "prestige economy" and
the "subsistence economy." Bascom later expanded the idea to postulate, in at
least one case, a "three centered economy" on Ponape (1948). There Bascom
found the two traditional "economies" postulated by Herskovits, together with
a third, intrusive, commercial "economy" rooted in Western contacts with
Ponape. This third "economy" is, of course, similar to one of Boeke's two
"economies," but Bascom's idea owes more to Herskovits' formulation than it
does to that of Boeke.

Bohannan in his study of the Tiv found at least three traditional "economies"
together with an intrusive commercial "economy." With the numbers piling up,
it makes sense to talk of "multicentric economies." Once again, this description
is rather more in the Herskovits than the Boeke tradition.

This idea of "multicentric economies" in the Herskovits tradition grows out
of the perception that in many economic systems there appear to be two or
more autonomous spheres of exchange. If there were a pure form of "multicentric economy," goods in one category could not be exchanged for goods
in another category.

The question which has to be raised is a simple one. What is the significance
of this distinction for economic analysis, as opposed to any descriptive value it
might have? Moreover, does emphasis on the "separateness" of the various
"centers" possibly hide some fundamental unity in the economic system being
considered?

As we have defined the term economy, the various "centers" do not constitute autonomous "economies." Bohannan makes it clear that in the case of
the Tiv, goods do move across the boundaries of the "centers," although this
movement does occur against ideological resistance in the case of the individual
who is "trading down." (See above, pp. 304–307.)

At first glance, the "valuables" of the Trobriand *kula* might seem to constitute
an example of a completely autonomous "center" since, so far as we can tell,
valuables are traded only for each other and never for other things. But even

here, the Trobriander must make choices involving the allocation of his labor between *kula* activities on the one hand and other activities, including subsistence activities, on the other. Thus the *kula* activities are part of a single economy, not an autonomous one (see above, pp. 17–39).

Since there is one resource which is necessarily common to all "ends" in a given society (labor, or human effort, or man hours) it is impossible for two or more completely autonomous "economies" to exist in a single society, in the strict sense. At the same time, it is essential to recognize that the behavioral patterns of the people in question may argue for the existence of what we might call "semiautonomous centers of activity." In this sense, the Herskovits-Bascom-Bohannan concepts have some validity.

Keynesian Economics

While we have said that equilibrium theory in neoclassical economics translates the individual calculus of maximization into a social calculus of maximization, it is also true that neoclassical theory was a theory of parts rather than of the whole. It is this which led it to be referred to as "microeconomic theory." It is a theory of the behavior of individuals (in groups) and of "firms" (or groups of firms). There were some notions about the consequences of the interactions of individuals and firms, to be sure, but they had some of the quality of afterthoughts and had not been very carefully worked out.

This gap in economic theory was brilliantly filled by a British economist named John Maynard Keynes (pronounced to rhyme with "pains") in a book first published in 1936. His was a theory of how the whole system worked. There have been many developments and refinements in "Keynesian theory" since 1936, but the core of Keynes' contribution remains intact.

What is of interest here is that with one notable exception, not even the most ardent proponents of the doctrine of the applicability of economic theory to the problem of analyzing primitive economic systems have said anything about the applications of Keynesian theory in these situations.

In our view, this is due neither to oversight nor to ignorance. It hardly seems possible that those anthropologists who have familiarized themselves at least to some degree with neoclassical economics should not have at least some acquaintance with Keynesian economics as well. Why then has it not been used? The answer may very well be that it is not applicable in those situations with which the anthropologist typically deals.

In its simplest form, Keynesian theory postulates a particular relationship among the following: aggregate national income, aggregate national consumption, aggregate savings, aggregate investment, and the ratio of change in aggregate income and the associated changes in aggregate savings. The ratio: change in income/change in savings, is known as the "multiplier." Again in its simplest form, Keynesian theory holds that for any given change in the level of aggregate investment, there will be a change in investment multiplied by the "multiplier."

A slightly more complex version of the theory takes account of the influence of changes in government spending and taxation. This elaboration makes it clear that the level of aggregate income (gross national product) can be closely controlled by governmental manipulation of the relation between government spending and taxation. Other refinements of the theory can take account of the postulated influence of changes in income on levels of investment and so on.

The general validity of the Keynesian relationships has been demonstrated empirically, and have achieved broad acceptance not only within the ranks of professional economists but by the community at large as well. It is broadly accepted as the basis for fiscal policy making in the United States and elsewhere, although some politicians sometimes sound as if they do not accept it.

It can thus be seen that Keynesian theory stands on much firmer empirical ground than does so-called "classical theory." Why, then, has it failed to arouse much interest among economic anthropologists? The answer seems to be that the Keynesian model is more completely culture bound than are the fundamental elements of neoclassical theory.

The validity of the Keynesian model as a description of what happens in a complex industrial society such as ours depends on the fact that consumption and savings decisions on the one hand, and investment decisions on the other (leaving out of consideration government spending and taxes) are made independently of each other. Consumption and savings decisions are made by consumers, most of whom are not businessmen and most of whom are not concerned with making net investments. Investment decisions are made by businessmen who could not possibly personally accumulate all of the savings required to meet their investment needs. Paradoxically, while savings and investment decisions are made by two different groups of people, aggregate savings and aggregate investment must always be equal. The genius of Keynes lay in his ability to resolve this paradox and to show how its resolution affected the economic system as a whole.

In any case, a crucial element in the Keynesian model is the fact that in our own economic system, savings decisions and investment decisions are made separately by two different groups of people. This being the case, Keynesian theory applies, in its present form, only to those situations in which this is true.

But in most simple economic systems, this seems not to be true. A decision to "invest," let us say by accumulating yams, directly and automatically involves a corresponding decision to "save" by refraining from consuming yams. Or a decision to "invest," let us say by making a capital good in the form of a dugout canoe, directly and automatically involves a decision to "save" by refraining from using that production time for the production of a consumption good. Thus, savings and investment decisions are made by the same persons and are indeed opposite sides of the same coin. In such situations, Keynesian theory has no relevancy.

On the other hand, this does not say that Keynesian theory is totally inapplicable in all societies other than our own. There is another reason why Keynesian theory has not been attractive to economic anthropologists. Because the time dimension of anthropological field work is usually relatively short, and perhaps for other reasons, anthropologists have tended neither to look for nor to perceive variations in the "gross national product" of the societies they have studied. Phenomena which are not perceived do not have to be explained. Therefore Keynesian theory has had nothing to do in economic anthropology, at least so far.

The one exception to our general observation that Keynesian theory has not been used by anthropologists is to be found in a work by Salisbury (1962). He uses Keynesian theory to help explain the consequences of the advent of "hoardable liquid means of exchange" (money) in a previously nonmonetized society. At the same time, he argues that technological and organizational changes can produce major changes in "gross national product" outside the framework of the Keynesian relationships. In general, this seems to support our argument that Keynesian theory is relatively culture bound.

Money

To the economist, money is pretty clear-cut and its character is not often debated. Among anthropologists, it is a matter of no little debate and some confusion. Some anthropologists find it necessary or useful to talk of "general purpose money" and "special purpose money," and to debate such issues as whether cattle are money in East Africa or whether Yapese stone money is "really" money and so on. What follows may not end the debate, but it is hoped that it may clarify some of the issues.

In large part, and as so often in dealing with cross cultural situation, the basic problem arises out of the effort to apply a concept from one cultural context to other cultural contexts. This is not necessarily a practice to be avoided; to avoid it entirely would deny anthropology the status of a generalizing science.

A further difficulty arises from the fact that the concept of money, like many concepts, is not an entirely simple one. "Money" as it is normally understood, involves a combination of elements or properties. There is no problem if this constellation of elements or properties is found exactly duplicated in the new setting. The problem arises when a close approximation, but not an exact duplicate is found. This is a general problem in classification and does not involve money alone. Do you, in this case, strictly construe the original concept, and thus deny the affinity of the new phenomenon with the old? Or do you modify the concept so that it includes both phenomena?

There is danger in both courses. In the one case, you may ignore fundamental similarities, and make the world seem more complex than it really is. The danger in the second case is that you might, by a series of successive steps, so broaden the original concept that it eventually loses all meaning.

At the same time, it must be made clear that what we call money today in our society is, in some ways, perhaps not fundamental, a quite different thing from what was called money in this society as recently as 150 years ago. And it must also be said that what the economist and the banker calls money today may be somewhat different from what the noneconomist or nonbanker ordinarily thinks of when the term money is used.

Everyone will agree that coins and currency are money. As the economist and the banker sees it, checking account balances are also money, though many people do not think of them as such. One hundred and fifty years ago, checking accounts had not been invented, although there were some banking practices which were rather similar. Indeed, checking accounts as we know them today did not come into general use in the United States until just about one hundred years ago.

Conceptually, practically, and historically, money is initially and primarily a *medium of exchange*. What this originally meant in the evolution of money was some commodity of sufficiently wide appeal—*for reasons other than exchange value or in its ordinary uses*—that people were always or usually ready to accept it in exchange for something else even though they had no immediate direct need for it in its ordinary use. For any commodity to serve this purpose, there has to be a consensus about it. When such a consensus arises, the acceptability of the exchange commodity begins to turn as much on its exchange function as it does on its original function. One man accepts it in exchange partly or entirely because he knows that he can readily give it in exchange for something else he might want. There is nothing in the nature of the general idea of a medium of exchange which places any limitation on the character of the commodity which might receive this consensus, although there are certain kinds of practical limits, such as divisibility, portability, and preservability.

Once money as a medium of exchange is established, it is not a very long step to consider its usefulness in other ways. Out of this initial function or use very naturally grows the other uses: as a standard of value, unit of account, store of value, and standard of deferred payments.

These last turn out, on examination, to be subsidiary functions of the medium of exchange where it exists—useful extensions of the initial phenomenon. This is not to say that it would not be possible to invent other ways of performing the subsidiary functions, ways which had nothing to do with the medium of exchange. But this would be clumsy, and whatever serves as the medium of exchange serves the subsidiary functions so admirably well that they are ordinarily all linked together.

Until very recently in the lives of men—the turning point in the United States came less than forty years ago—it was the height of fiscal orthodoxy to insist that money was fundamentally a commodity. Whatever bankers and governments might do with bits of paper in the name of money, the bits of paper had to be exchangeable for the money commodity at will—the will of whoever happened to be holding the bits of paper. Until thirty years ago in the United States, the money commodity was gold, and under certain restricted conditions, silver. And in those days, the fiscally orthodox thought that the money commodity for any civilized nation should be gold, and any country where this was not so was not really very respectable. And it was further thought, and this was how things worked out or were made to work out, that the commodity value of the money commodity should be the same as the money value, so that a five-dollar gold piece was literally five dollars worth of gold. If the gold in a five-dollar gold piece came to be worth more than five dollars when used for making rings, let us say, then five-dollar gold pieces would disappear. If it came to be worth less than five dollars for making rings, this was considered immoral, and was called a financial crisis.

Although we, in our present sophistication, no longer insist on the right to convert our bits of paper into gold—we are not allowed to do so except under special license—this is a very recent development in the economic history of this country (and in most of the rest of the "civilized" world, it might be said). But our money is still tied to gold in ways that need not detain us here. And there still remains a lurking suspicion that money is really a commodity, although we have released ourselves from the necessity of lugging the stuff around, leaving that aspect of things to certain nameless employees of the Federal Reserve Bank of New York.

What does all of this tell us about cattle in East Africa, glassy beads on Palau, and stone wheels in Yap?

What it says, quite simply, is that if any of these commodities—and we are using this term somewhat loosely all along—are used as a medium of exchange, then they are money. If they also happen to be used as standards of value, units of account, stores of value, or standards of deferred payment—any one or any combination of these—so much the better.

But what of the objection that five-dollar gold pieces and Federal Reserve Notes are "general purpose money" while these other things might be special purpose money?

But how general is this general purpose money? Pretty general, we must admit. But it can't buy you love, though it might buy you the services of a woman; it can't buy you happiness, though some insist it can help make your misery more comfortable; there's some question as to whether it can buy you the esteem of your neighbors; and you can't take it with you. Nor, in principle, at least in American culture, can it buy you a wife. In short, it can be exchanged for lots of things, some ersatz, but not for everything.

How many things does a commodity have to be exchangeable for before it can be considered to be money? This is a question for which no precisely meaningful answer can be given.

In the end, the judgment concerning whether to refer to something as money must rest with the ethnographer. If calling something money, or calling something money with appropriate qualifications, facilitates discussion without being too misleading, the term should be used. If these conditions cannot be met, then it should not be used. After all, phenomena are not altered by the labels we pin on them, though our conception of phenomena might be powerfully influenced by our labels. This is the real issue.

"Economic Surplus"

The concept of economic surplus, defined as some portion of total output which is in excess of the requirements of subsistence, is at least as old as David Ricardo's *Principles of Political Economy and Taxation* (1817). The concept, along with Ricardo's notion of wages, which a later writer called the "Iron Law of Wages," played an important part in Marxian theory. It was also an important element in the economic and social theories of Thorstein Veblen.

It was introduced into anthropological thought mainly by Melville J. Herskovits, who was perhaps inspired more by Veblen than by Marx. While there are elements of a theory of exploitation in Herskovits' use of the concept, a notion which has Marxian overtones, this is a less prominent feature of his thought on the subject than is the concept of conspicuous consumption and its influence on prestige. This latter emphasis owes much more to Veblen and his *Theory of the Leisure Class.*

Still another implication, found to some degree in Herskovits, but developed more thoroughly by V. Gordon Childe, sees surplus as a kind of motive power in cultural development.

Stated simply, the "surplus theory of cultural development" argues that an economic surplus is necessary before cultural development can take place. What is argued is that some people must produce a surplus of food above their own needs in order for other portions of the population to specialize in nonfood-producing activities.

In a rather polemical essay in *Trade and Market in the Early Empires,* Harry W. Pearson attacks the very concept of a surplus, and along with it, the "surplus theory of cultural development" (Pearson 1957b). His basic argument is that the concept of an economic surplus cannot be given operational meaning, that it is impossible to measure such a surplus cross-culturally, and that it has nothing to do with cultural development in any case.

Marvin Harris replied to Pearson's argument in a long and almost equally polemical essay a few years later (1959). He was answered in turn by George Dalton, in two papers (1960, 1963), who first tried to analyze the possible meanings of the term, and then followed Pearson in dismissing it.

Current thinking among many economic anthropologists is that the whole debate is pointless, though it continues (see Orans 1966).

No debate ever seems pointless at the time it is going on, at least to those involved. Much debate may be necessary before it becomes apparent that a particular concept can be shown to lead to an analytical dead end. And while anthropologists may have wearied over the dispute about the concept of surplus, which is a slippery concept at best, one central issue in the debate has remained unsettled. The problem here is that the issue has never been properly stated, and the debate, in consequence, has set the hounds baying after the wrong fox.

Success in science often rests on asking the right question. If one wishes to consider whether there is any "economic" basis for cultural development, asking questions about "surplus" leads us only into an exercise in futility. The right question to ask is as follows: As the average productivity of a society rises, what forms will the increased product take? When we ask this question, meaningful comparative study can be readily undertaken, both in the perspective of history and cross-culturally.

The first production requirement for any society is subsistence, a notion dear to the hearts of the surplus theorists. No society can survive as a society unless its members can feed themselves at some physiologically minimum level. And there is ample evidence in ethnography that the "poorest" societies, defined as those with the most minimally elaborated cultures, are those whose energies are largely taken up with the task of basic subsistence.

However, it is not necessary to define this notion of "basic subsistence"— and it is upon this rock that the subsistence theorists have foundered—to deal meaningfully with the problem posed here.

The question can be treated in this way. Granting that some people have solved the problem of feeding themselves, what do they do with their time. "Solving the problem of feeding themselves" means simply that they do not have to spend as much time, on the average, in getting food and other necessities as those less fortunately placed. One thing is clear. People who can produce a great deal of food and other necessities simply do not eat more and more without limit. No precise limits on the amount of food that a society can *directly* consume can be set (this merely turns the problem of defining minimum subsistence around). But there is clearly a limit, or a range of limits, or a zone of limitation.

What happens is that as food production becomes easier, people begin to devote less of their energy to food production and start doing other things. The question is what do they do instead.

This question can be answered without trying to answer the vexing question of what "minimum subsistence" is. The question can be answered in much more objective terms. It can be answered in terms of the number of man-hours, or man-days, or man-weeks, or man-years or any other convenient units which are devoted to what kinds of activities. Every ethnography at least implicitly contains at least a rough quantitative answer to this question.

So we should forget surplus and focus our attention on productivity and on "product mix," if we want to get any meaningful insights into the economic basis of cultural development.

On the Relation between "The Economic System" and "Other Sectors"

One question which is not infrequently raised in one context or another and in one phrasing or another is the question of the relationship which exists between "the economy" (for which read "the economic system") and other sectors of the society or culture. Unless there is some prior specification of what is meant by "the economy" and by "other sectors," indeed, unless there is some prior specification of how the various sectors are bounded, the question is incapable of being answered in any meaningful way.

On the whole, we would be inclined to argue that in the present state of conceptual and theoretical development in anthropology, it is rather doubtful that any very solid consideration can be given to the question.

Anthropologists have used a variety of ways of separating certain foci of interest from the totality of culture, social structure (in the broadest sense) or behavior patterns. One major difficulty in comparing foci is that they tend to slice the cultural pie in a number of different ways. Language is one order of phenomenon, material culture is another order of phenomenon, kinship structures are still another order of phenomenon and possibly the economic system is still another order. To try to compare them or establish relationships among them is rather like trying to compare a rock with a bird and both in turn with a petunia.

At the same time, one would intuitively feel that these various realms or foci are not completely autonomous or independent of each other. Language, for example, is at once the most autonomous and the most dependent of the branches of culture. Its structure seems to be dependent only upon its past; its content is a reflection of the rest of culture. At the same time, if we accept the Whorfian thesis, that part of language which is the most dependent upon culture nevertheless does condition culture and even perception.

If we ask, then, what is the relationship between "the economy" and language, or material culture, or kinship structures, we may get a variety of answers or no answer at all. In the first place, there are at least three kinds of definitions of "economy" as some of the readings in this volume will testify. They are the definitions implied by the distinction made by Polanyi and others, between "substantive" and "formal" meanings of "economic." In addition, there is a definition which lies somewhere between the two and which reflects the ad hoc decisions made by economists regarding their spheres of interest. Answering "relation" questions would depend, in the first instance, on which of these orientations we chose. It would depend, furthermore, on what we are seeking a "relation" with. And finally, it would surely depend upon the culture being studied.

The questions raised here have been more often raised than explored. We may not yet be ready to explore them systematically.

Deduction versus Induction as Scientific Method

One incidental consequence of the publication of Herskovits' *Economic Life Of Primitive People* in 1940 was a notable "debate" between Frank Knight, an eminent theoretical economist, who wrote a lengthy review of the Herskovits book, and Herskovits, who was invited to write a reply to the review. The review and the reply appeared in the same issue of the journal and were subsequently reprinted, with slight modifications, as an appendix to *Economic Anthropology*, the revision of Herskovits' earlier work (1952:508–531).

In this review, Knight extolled the virtues of deduction as scientific method, Herskovits replying by warning against the dangers of deduction and supporting the merits of induction as method, particularly in anthropology.

The Knight-Herskovits debate places in the context of economic anthropology a philosophical quarrel which goes back at least to Sir Francis Bacon and to René Descartes, the one the philosopher of induction as scientific method, the other the philosopher of deduction. The debate is roughly four hundred years old.

Under the impact of Boasian historicism, and in a necessary reaction against the theoretical excesses of the evolutionist and diffusionist schools, anthropology has tended to be suspicious of the deductive method and to glorify induction. Economics, on the other hand, has been the most gloriously deductive of the social sciences, Knight arguing in the debate that deduction was all that was needed and even denying any necessity for referring the products of deduction to the real world. (For a comment on this peculiarity in the thought of some economists, see above, LeClair, footnote 3, p. 206.)

In one very fundamental sense, the debate is a fruitless one. In practice, scientific method is, or should be, determined pragmatically rather than dogmatically and philosophically. Any kind of examination of a comprehensive sample of the literature of the natural and physical sciences indicates quite clearly that deduction and induction are both reputable and productive procedures. Some fields tend to be dominated by one or the other method. Physics is probably the field which has made the widest and best use of deduction as method. Relativity theory is a triumph of deduction. Biology, on the other hand, is more characteristically inductive in its method. The Watson-Crick model of the DNA molecule is a triumph of induction. Yet neither field is exclusively one nor the other, and frequently inductive and deductive methods interact, as when induction provides the premises from which deductive reasoning may produce new hypotheses.

At the same time, no practicing scientist would accept the Knight position that deduction is sufficient unto itself. Deduction divorced from the empirical world has to be classed as speculative mathematics or philosophy, an intellectual parlor game carried on for its own sake. For the deductive scientist, the acid test of any deduction is the referral of the products of deduction to the empirical world.

There have been many formulations of the essentials of deductive procedure. The following one by Hermann Bondi is as precisely concise as any:

The investigation proceeds in three stages:

> a. A set of assumptions is formulated whose fruitfulness and plausibility is tested in stages (b) and (c). These assumptions need not (and generally will not) be susceptible to direct observational check.
>
> b. Observable consequences are deduced from the assumptions.
>
> c. The empirical connection is established by comparing the consequences of the assumptions with the actual observations. If there is disagreement, the (a) has been disproved. If there is no disagreement then (a) remains

tenable pending the exploration of further observable consequences. A set of assumptions that does not lend itself to (c) and hence cannot be disproved is empty and scientifically futile (1955:89).

The inductively oriented anthropologist, plagued by the memory of G. Elliott Smith and his Mayan statues of "elephants," characteristically raises the spectre of observation "distorted" by prior conceptions. At worst, however, this argues for care in the use of the deductive method, not its rejection. Diffusionism was not essentially deductive in its method in any case. It was inductive in origin if it was anything at all and was subsequently misapplied by bad science or bad scientists. And diffusionist excesses were subsequently struck down by the only test that has any meaning in science: the empirical test, the test of hard data.

It can be argued that at the present juncture in anthropology, the opportunities for truly deductive methods in the study of man and his works may be limited. Perhaps we have not progressed far enough in our grasp of fundamental human and social processes to select meaningful premises, to make appropriate deductions, and to refer them reliably to the empirical world. Indeed, it is possible that because of the character of its material, anthropology will remain primarily an inductive rather than a deductive science, as has been the case with biology. But if this is the case, it should be a matter of pragmatics rather than philosophy. And on the other side, it must be said that deductive methods, where appropriate, have been so demonstrably powerful in generating new insights that they should be part of the scientific arsenal of any anthropologist and should be abandoned, not in principle, but in the specific application, only when they are clearly inappropriate.

Whatever the philosophers of science might say (and what they say is often confusing and contradictory) scientific method includes any process, mode of thought, operation or activity which will successfully lead to verifiable and verified propositions about the world around us. Anthropology is or is not a science. It is if its objective is to formulate verifiable and verified propositions about man and his ways of life. And if it is a science, it must necessarily use "scientific method," which includes whatever methods that enable it to reach these objectives.

part five

ECONOMIC ANTHROPOLOGY:
RETROSPECT AND PROSPECT

· section I
ANTHROPOLOGY AND ECONOMICS

30 ANTHROPOLOGY AND ECONOMICS
Richard F. Salisbury

A review of the relations between Anthropology and Economics is made easier[1] by the existence of an excellent summary of their relationship, through 1960, written by Joseph Berliner (1962). Since the state of the two disciplines has changed considerably from 1960, a stock-taking of these changes is in order. For the first principles, the reader is referred to Berliner's work.

Berliner's major analysis showed that all social science data can be visualized as a matrix with rows representing particular societies and columns standing for such entities as 'economy' and 'religion.' Anthropology has involved mainly the comparison of all cells in a column (i.e., cross-cultural studies of single institutions) or of all cells in a row (i.e., studies of functional relationships between institutions of a single society). Berliner showed the strength of Economics, as a discipline, to be the intensity of its study of relationships within the single cell of "Western economies," and called for much more intra-cell studies of non-Western economies. The attempt to demonstrate that non-Western economies had the same institutions as Western economies had doomed earlier economic anthropology to sterility; Berliner felt that the suggested intra-cell studies might bring about a revitalized anthropology.

To anticipate some of the conclusions of this paper, Berliner's predictions would seem to be borne out by the currently healthy state of economic anthropology (if economic anthropology was not already more healthy in 1960 than

From Anthropology and the Neighboring Disciplines, *edited by Otto von Mering and Leonard Kasdan, Chapter 2, Pittsburgh,* © *1968 Pittsburgh University Press. Reprinted by permission.*

[1] It would also have been made easier if Nash's textbook (1966) had appeared before rather than after its writing, as the lines of thought in both are parallel. The reader is referred to Nash for a fuller documentation of much descriptive material mentioned below; the present article presents a somewhat more developed stand on the nature of formal analysis and models than Nash might agree with. The author wishes to acknowledge how his thinking has developed in the course of discussions, not only with Nash, but with, among others: C. S. Belshaw, R. Crocombe, A. G. Frank, L. Hazelhurst, L. Kasdan, M. Sahlins and Mrs. G. Sankoff.

Berliner knew). Currently the major issue in economic anthropology is not whether non-Western Economics have different substantive economic institutions, for it is now accepted that they do, but to what extent different formal calculuses of rationality or of "economizing" can be isolated in non-Western conditions. Before considering the anthropological work that has led to this point of development, let us review some of the last decade's changes in economic thinking.

The Economic Side

In 1960, Berliner could still generalize plausibly about main trends in economic thinking as comprising Marshallian (or classical) theory, Keynesian theorizing about cyclical changes in national economies, and institutional Economics and economic history. However, by 1966, the unmentioned infant economic fields of 1960 seem to have effected a revolution in Economics. Neo-Keynesian thinking no longer studies regular cyclical fluctuations but focuses on how to induce continued expansion and secular change. Development Economics in 1960 was concerned with transplanting Western Economics to underdeveloped areas, it now studies and generalizes about the form of developing economies in their own right, and theorizes about sequences within the developmental process. "Structural transformation" is now a respectable term in Economics and not merely a use of social-anthropological jargon. Even though economists focus on such readily quantifiable topics as changing patterns of income distribution, and wage differentials between export and internal sectors, they are closely concerned with the same problems as anthropologists who study the breakdown of caste barriers in plural societies. In 1962, Hagen was avant-garde in proposing an individual psychological explanation of the emergence of entrepreneurship; in 1966, he is more concerned with how entrepreneurial behavior relates to (or is irrelevant in) the context of economic choice for peasant farmers. Economists, in short, are emerging from their private "Western-economies" cell. They are going up and down columns into different societies and along rows into other institutions, and they are increasingly concerned with secular change.

Another, not unrelated trend in Economics has been the study of decision-making at the levels of individuals, business firms and nations, and outside the classical context of supply-price-demand balancing. Von Neumann's invention of game theory was one initiator of this trend and the use of computers for playing simulated economic "games" has been another stimulus. Linear programming is perhaps the most mathematically advanced branch of this type of study. The effort is not to disprove the "maximizing" assumption of classical economic theory, but to demonstrate how most rationally to maximize specific magnitudes under various conditions of risk, where differing time spans exist or one decision is contingent on other people's decisions. Economics has moved far from the classical *homo oeconomicus* position, based on hypothetical Robinson Crusoes, ridiculed in anthropological literature from Malinowski to Polanyi.

Another closely related and expanding economic field is business administration. For the anthropologist this field is perhaps most accessible through the works of sociologists such as Mason Haire with his studies (1959) on growth of business organizations. Such works enable economists to conceive of alternative total organizations, and to compare the efficiency of overall structures in terms of their ability to respond to particular environmental problems and their eventual outputs. In short, this enables economists to see "organization" and "managerial skills" as factors of production to be measured and considered in general analysis.

The Anthropological Side

Ethno-Economics

As economists have escaped from their cell, anthropologists have become more focused on the internal analysis of single cells. Starting with Bohannan's study of the Tiv (1955), there have been several studies of the economic categories used in non-Western societies, which are intra-cell studies of single economic systems. My own study of categories used in relatively affluent tribal societies (Salisbury 1962) would serve as another example. Foster's (1964) discussion of the concept of "the limited good" is a major comparative summary of a form of conceptualization that would appear to be prevalent in many societies. This important new sub-field may be labelled "ethno-economics" insofar as it aims merely at the description of single economies. As description, it undoubtedly benefits from the refined methodology of the "new ethnography." I would maintain, however, that its major theoretical importance has been the advances it has permitted in the field of formal analysis. I will return to ethno-economics when I deal with formal analysis.

Substantivism

Achieving greater prominence in the period 1957–1966, the so-called substantivist school generalizes about the channels through which goods flow in total economies. This school stems largely from Polanyi's (1957) seminal *Trade and Markets in the Early Empires* which introduced a typology of societies "integrated by reciprocity, redistribution, and market exchanges." Considering the lack of quantitative studies then available, this was a remarkable synthesis. Unfortunately, most of the subsequent work of the school has involved the application of labels from Polanyi's typology, rather than the detailed investigation of the underlying processes which generate the social types Polanyi discussed. The major finding of Bohannan and Dalton's (1962) 800-page compilation of studies of African marketplace trade is that societies where trade is "imbedded" in other institutions and which do not use cash differ from those which form some system of "market exchange."

"Redistributive," as a label, has been applied to societies such as those in Polynesia and West African kingdoms. This use seems indiscriminate in the light of quantitative studies. Nadel's excellent early study of the Nupe economy (1942) shows that only a small portion of the total flow of goods and services is channeled through the king, and even where guilds nominally operate as agents for the king, the degree to which they organize production in terms of private customers is mainly determined by the size of the private market. Village self-sufficiency, trade partnerships, and open market trading are more common. What substantivists have done is to seize upon some rare, but distinctive, features—a court, guilds, tribute payments, and negotiated foreign trade between the court and foreigners—and to use a label based on these features to characterize the total economy.

Polanyi's own posthumous work on Dahomey (1966) does indeed get away from the rigidity of regarding reciprocity, redistribution and market exchange as mutually exclusive and as characterizing entire economies or integrating entire societies. He sees all three principles as operating together, each in a different domain within the single society. Yet, at the same time, he sees the main achievements of the book as the classification of institutions as "primitive" (i.e., found in reciprocative societies), "archaic" (i.e., characteristic of redistributive societies), or "market." Thus, Polanyi goes to great lengths (pp. 141–169) to unravel the difficulties Europeans had in balancing their bookkeeping in the 17th and 18th century slave trade, resulting from empirically fluctuating and varied, but nominally fixed, units used in different areas and times in West Africa. He concludes that West Africa had "archaic money," incompatible with a modern monetary system. Polanyi then isolates the characteristics of "archaic money" in terms of its status-building function in the emergence of state systems (p. 192). To an audience that accepts the fact of "trade in equivalencies," mere classification appears sterile. The identification of what caused the changes in exchange rates—such as differences of power balance, numbers of slaves, or availability of manufactures—becomes the interesting problem.

In short, "redistribution" or "archaic economy" may be useful labels for summarizing the way emergent national polities centralize certain services and organize taxation and the production of specialized commodities by infant industries by providing stability in market, raw materials, and labor. But such concepts would appear equally useful for analyzing the actions of newly independent, but fully monetized, nation states. They are not terms that characterize "entire economies" or "modes of integration," nor are they terms which fit economies into a unilineal progression from "primitive" to "archaic" to "market."

The same is true of the concept "reciprocity." Analyses of the actual working of societies crudely labelled as "reciprocative" (Salisbury 1960, Sahlins 1963, 1965) have shown that inter-individual transactions are always unbalanced and involve a continual struggle to obtain as much advantage over an 'opponent' as possible, short of breaking off the relationship and establishing new relationships with another partner. Each relationship between a pair implies a series of other relationships by each of them, and the terms of trade between one pair can be understood only against a background of their other relationships. The same generalization could be made about exchanges between partners in a monetary economy. The differences between "reciprocal" and "market" exchanges are not sufficiently clarified by attempts to characterize total systems of which they are parts. Rather, they are better understood through closer analysis of the specific situations, in both monetary and tribal societies, where it is mutually advantageous to use recurrent rather than isolated exchanges, or where imbalances in volumes tendered can be, or must be, tolerated for long periods. Such studies consider "markets" as general economic phenomena, not as the peculiar institution of localized "marketplaces"; the recent proliferation of such studies indicates the decline of the "anti-market mentality" (Cook 1966).

Specific Institutional Studies

In practice, most descriptive anthropological work has been more specific in its aim. An impressive literature has been emerging regarding the types of exchange and marketing behavior found under different conditions of risk, volume of the total market, relative numbers of buyers and sellers, knowledge of the market, and the power positions of parties to the exchanges. This has been extensively summarized elsewhere (e.g., Belshaw 1965, Salisbury NDa), and further review of the findings is not needed here. It will suffice to mention, as outstanding examples, Dewey's (1963) full length discussion of *Peasant Marketing in Java*, and of Nash's (1961) analyses of the calculations involved in the marketing of pottery in Chiapas. In terms of the trends in Economics there has been a convergence of interest here, with both disciplines focusing more precisely on how the context of economic choice can influence the nature of the choices actually made.

Spheres of activity other than marketing have not received such close scrutiny. Ethnobotanists and geographers have encouraged anthropologists to record how far considerations of plant varieties, soil types, or micro-climatic variation enter into the calculations of bushfallow agriculturalists (Conklin 1961). Agricultural economists too have often done studies that could be considered anthropological in the same way. Edwards' (1962) study of why Jamaican small farmers often rejected agricultural officers' advice led him to ask for their evaluations of land types and crop species. Returning later to the area, he found that peasant evaluations, initially at variance with agronomists' orthodoxy, had often become orthodox after research led agronomists to change their minds.

A relatively small number of anthropologists have collected labor input figures for different crops or techniques of cultivation and have investigated the extent to which agriculturalists make choices on this basis. But those few studies—for example, Pospisil (1963b) comparing labor inputs and yields for field and mound cultivation of sweet potatoes in New Guinea, and Nash (1965) comparing them for various crops and techniques in Burma—indicate the value of investigating this variable. Such studies also need to be linked to a treatment of how variations in labor demand correlate with different patterns of choice in production—of how, for example, different labor demands affect deep-sea and inshore fishing.

The use of capital, and its accumulation in peasant societies, has been the focus of less analysis than would appear from the publication of Firth and Yamey's (1964) *Capital, Savings and Credit in Peasant Society*. Most of the authors in this volume were social anthropologists who proudly vaunted their ignorance of economic analysis and merely described how different social groupings accumulated cash in particular societies. Little attention was devoted to the use made of such accumulations or to the nature of "capital." Among the exceptions to this general criticism of the 1964 volume was Barth's analysis of the capital needs and flows among South Persian nomads, and of the ways in which needs are related to the arrangements for meeting them. And Firth's own classic study of Malay Fishermen (1946) still stands out as an examination of the relation of credit to production.

Again, agricultural economists have contributed to this sub-field of study. Besides Edwards' previously cited study, Polly Hill's (1956, 1963) discussion of how Ghanaian cocoa farmers accumulated capital and land, and how different organizational forms were used to facilitate investment at different stages in the growth of the cocoa industry, is outstanding. Many anthropologists in the South Pacific have similar interests. Belshaw's study (1964) of Fiji, studies by the Australian National University's New Guinea Research Unit (e.g., Crocombe and Hogbin, 1964), and my own study of the New Britain Tolai (NDb) could be cited. The focus in all these is the forms of organization used in capital holding groups.

Entrepreneurship is another aspect of economic process that has been studied. Many descriptive studies of social change have listed the forms of cash-earning businesses that have emerged in formerly subsistence agricultural societies, and have classed all such businessmen as "entrepreneurs." Relatively few (e.g., Hazelhurst, 1966) have gone back to theoretical treatments of entrepreneurship, notably to Schumpeter, to consider the various roles focal to the concept. These roles include risk-taking, the middleman bringing together production factors, and the organizational innovator who exploits technological innovations made by others by bringing together new groupings. Yet the study of such roles would seem to be of primary interest to classical anthropological theory. It would seem that consideration of the nature of organizational innovation would be a major area, where new developments within Economics could parallel and fructify developments in formal organization theory and in economic anthropology.

Organization theory regarding both entrepreneurship and capital use constitutes a common thread to the studies above. Organization of production, generally, needs to be given greater consideration. Udy, in 1959, surveyed cross-cultural anthropological evidence on production organization, comparing such activities as "hunting, fishing, collection, animal husbandry, construction, and manufacturing." His conclusion, that technological demands were highly significant up to a certain level of social complexity with a widely varying range of organizational types thereafter, demands closer analysis to explain the residual variance in organizational forms. The ethnographers' laboratory of variant forms and variant social and physical environments should be exploited to provide information on the relative efficiency of particular forms. On the one hand, existing ethnographic descriptions need comparison and analysis in terms of a consistent theoretical viewpoint—Barth (1963b) has analyzed a series of field studies in Norway in this way and Sankoff (1965) has begun such work using published sources. On the other hand, more ethnographic studies are needed in which investigators trained in organization theory can ask appropriate questions about organizational efficiency in both traditional and cash activities. Such studies, like Erasmus' (1956) early study of the advantages and disadvantages of work bees and hired labor in Meso-America, should give much greater insight into the process of economic development than do analyses couched in terms of all-or-none "value changes."

Model Building

Anthropological economic studies have not been confined entirely to specific institutions and increasingly detailed studies of relationships between even smaller segments of social and economic activity. Just as input-output economists have interested themselves in constructing models of total economies, seeing the total system as the outcome of the flows and transactions between sectors, so some anthropologists have also begun to visualize entire economies as the resultant effects of flows between particular sectors. Development economists have proposed models of economic change which involve phase sequences. For example, infrastructure development at one phase leads to increased profitability of later industrial investments, and so to mass marketing. So anthropologists (and ethnohistorians) have proposed models of local economic development in terms of phase sequences and have looked for the causative relationship between phases.

The differences between economists' and anthropologists' models has largely been the different range of included phenomena. Economists tend to include such factors as demography, technology, organizational techniques or political controls only as boundary conditions for their models, making such simplistic assumptions as they remain constant, or they increase at steady rates. These assumptions are often disguised. A simple statement that it is "assumed that the marginal product of labor is positive" or that "it may be assumed that in a period of growth there is some organizational slack," implies questionable assumptions about the nature of technology or organization. However, making such assumptions, the economist can clarify the logic of his model and can proceed immediately to quantification.

The anthropologist is more concerned with building relationships between technology, organization or politics, and the economic activities *into* his models.

Thus, Geertz' (1963) model involves technology as a major variable in the interactions of labor-intensive monocrop agriculture in Java with foreign exchange-earning, cash-cropping and multicrop bush-fallow agriculture in outer Indonesia. The model shows the long-term prospect of impoverishing and 'peasantizing' the outer islands. In my own model (1962, NDb) organization is the major variable. It shows how in New Guinea surpluses are created by technological change funneled into the creation of more complex political organizations and how such political change permits the organizational change for the establishment of new types of productive activity.

It could be argued such models represent a return to many of the fundamental concerns of anthropology—the problems of social evolution and cultural change. Leslie White pioneered the return to interest in these problems, but his unidimensional scheme relating social development to the availability of energy sources was too simplistic. It may now be hoped that general models of a Leslie White type may become increasingly available. In such models technology levels, communication technology levels, and organizational variables may be given quantitative forms, visualized as forms of entropy (Adams 1960) —in order to consider types of society in terms of evolutionary dimensions.

Formal Analysis

Such a Utopian idea would see anthropologists returning closer to the traditional interests of their own discipline. But then, where does the future for a relationship between anthropology and Economics lie? Here I would return to my earlier analysis of substantivism and of current trends in economic anthropology. As I see it, where the substantivists attempted to classify total economies and came up with static models, more recent workers have tried to see the low level relationships which generate the eventual form of total economies. The models they build inevitably include a dynamic element. Yet to arrive at the relationships occurring at low levels, they have used the *tool* of economic analysis which substantivists scorned—that is, formal analysis. The formal approach of economists have involved seeing economic magnitudes as the primary data, and by comparing magnitudes, has demonstrated inductively the relationships among numbers of variables, each of them impinging, at a low level, on vast numbers of economic choices. Only when the formal analyses have been undertaken and the variables isolated, have dynamic models of the interplay of multiple variables been constructed.

Ethnoeconomists may take a short cut. Instead of isolating variables by the mathematical analysis of quantitative data, they may consider the economic concepts given them by informants as close approximations to the operating variables. But they then should consider deductively how the systematic use in the society of such concepts would give rise to overall patterns. They should construct models based on ethnoeconomic concepts. While it may be untrue to say that goods are absolutely limited in peasant society, it may be useful to consider what would happen if all (or many) members of a society believed that life were a zero-sum game. Game theory (or formal economic theory) could then be used to make predictions about such matters as the size of coalitions found, or the degree of tolerance of income inequalities. Anthropologists have been generally averse to such "as if" deductive theorizing, preferring to "stick to the facts." Exposure to economists and their methods could be invaluable in correcting this bias and in making deductive model-building familiar.

At the same time as ethno-economic description of the principles of choice verbalized by informants is leading to the formulation of ideal or hypothetical models, behavioral analysis must also be progressing. It must determine principles of choice from a consideration of transactions actually occurring and test the fit of hypothetical models against quantitative reality. Here, too, anthropologists have much to learn from working with economists and their tools. In the 1950's, Gluckman argued (1964) that it is better to remain naive about other disciplines, even when intruding on fields which they cover. I do not feel that this is true for anthropology and Economics in the 1960's. Anthropologists should study Economics and vice versa. I do agree with Gluckman that this should be done not to make the anthropologist an economist, but a better anthropologist. Given economic tools, he will improve anthropology. Give an economist the anthropological tools of sensitivity to what people say and of readiness to try to see order in different conceptual systems, and he may improve economics.

· section II
SOME FINAL WORDS

Science is a process, never a state of affairs. "Where we stand" can never be more than a kind of snapshot recording and fixing some instant in a pell-mell rush toward greater understanding. As this is being written, economic anthropology is in a state of great flux. More people are devoting more attention to it than ever before. At least two of the papers included in this reader were published after the general plan of the book had been pretty firmly established. The original plan was altered to include them. Other statements have since seen print and might have been included but for the fact that we had to stop somewhere.

The dominant fact of the sixties in economic anthropology has been adequately documented in these pages. It is the substantivist-formalist controversy. An emerging fact of 1967 is a tendency on the part of some anthropologists to pronounce a plague on both houses. Cancian, in a selection reproduced above (see pp. 228–233) suggests that there is no inconsistency between LeClair's "Economics is the study of economizing" (see p. 197) and Polanyi's "The economy is an instituted process" (see p. 126).

Perhaps. Indeed, probably. But the substantivist's first commandment seems to be "Thou shalt not study economizing." Still, no supernatural sanctions will be visited upon those who violate the commandment. There is no high court to enforce the law.

Who, then, shall win the debate? Probably nobody, certainly not in any dramatic way. There will be no public recantations, no decisive, crucial experiments. It seems unlikely then, that the two schools shall become reconciled.

Interestingly enough, there is some precedent for all of this in the history of conventional economics. There was a "substantive revolution" of a sort led by Veblen at the turn of the century. Veblen's early works had at least as great an impact as did Polanyi's fifty years later.

The Veblenian revolution culminated in the emergence of a distinct school in economics, the so-called "institutional economics." Institutional economics was descriptive rather than analytical and had its greatest success in the field of labor economics and in the field of business cycles, which, until the emergence of Keynesian economics in the late 1930s, had been notably short of adequate theoretical explanation.

Today, institutional economics has virtually disappeared as a separate movement, having merged back into the mainstream of economic thought, although there remain a few economists of a broadly institutionalist persuasion who are uncomfortable with formal economic theory and who doubt its validity. (See above, p. 206, fn. 3 for some references.) At the same time, some of Veblen's criticisms of the theory of his day formed the basis for revisions in neoclassical theory. Most notable among these was the emergence of the modern concept of "economic man" as a rational rather than merely a money-grubbing individual.

It seems likely to us that somewhat similar developments will occur in economic anthropology. Substantivist economic anthropology is already emerging as descriptive, almost empiricist. Part of its popularity is no doubt due to the fact that in this it is in keeping with the oldest traditions of anthropology in general. Along with this empiricist tendency, substantivist economic anthropology will become, indeed already is, a kind of economic sociology, something which labor economics did become in its institutionalist heyday. (This term is used here in a different sense from the economic sociology of Parsons and Smelser, which is more analytical in character.) The focus will be and is on economic institutions as functioning social structures. Again, this is in keeping with the oldest traditions of anthropology.

Meanwhile, there is no reason to suppose that formalist economic anthropology will not continue on its own course. It is a hard course and much needs to be done. The complex body of theory which explains the functioning of a more or less free enterprise market economic system such as our own obviously cannot be transposed in all of its details to explain any other type of economic system. It will take new, but presumably related bodies of theory to explain other types of systems. The development of such a body of theory for any given economic system is a task of considerable magnitude, and has not, as yet, been completed for any system, much less for systems in the plural. But if formalist economic anthropology is to have any future it is precisely this which must be done.

At some time in the future, the substantivist-formalist controversy will appear merely quaint to anthropologists who are wrestling with problems we cannot anticipate today. At that time, economic anthropology will hopefully long since have matured. Substantivists and formalists will have disappeared, perhaps by merger and interbreeding, and a new kind of economic anthropology will have emerged. We believe that the elements of today's formal theory will be an essential part of the economic anthropology of the future, and that in consequence, our understanding of man and his works will be considerably enhanced.

REFERENCES CITED

REFERENCES CITED

The majority of the items listed in the following bibliography are references cited in the readings which comprise the core of this book. Most authors, happily, followed contemporary anthropological style and usage in providing bibliographic information; some did not. Where bibliographic information was incomplete in the original source, we have attempted to supply the missing information. Often we were unable to do so, however, and so not all entries in this list are as complete as we would like them to be.

This is a "citation bibliography." Numbers printed in boldface type after each entry are the numbers of the pages on which references to the work in question may be found. Citations are not indexed in the General Index.

Abraham, R. D., 1940, *The Tiv People*, 2d ed. London: Crown Agents. **306.**

Adams, R. N., 1960, "Energy and Expanding Systems." Paper presented at the American Association for the Advancement of Science Meeting, New York, December 31, 1960. **484.**

Akiga (B. Akiga Sai), 1939, *Akiga's Story*, trans. by Rupert East. London: Oxford. International African Institute. **306.**

Amonn, *Objekt und Grundbegriffe der theoretischen Nationalökonomie.* **97, 99.**

Arensberg, Conrad, 1957, "Anthropology as History," in *Trade and Market in the Early Empires*, K. Polanyi, C. W. Arensberg, and H. W. Pearson (eds.). New York: Free Press. **163–164.**

Armstrong, W. E., 1924, "Shell Money from Rossell Island, Papua," *Man*, 24:119. **5.**

————, 1928, *Rossell Island*. London: Cambridge. **5.**

Arnold, Rosemary, 1957, "A Port of Trade: Whydah on the Guinea Coast," in *Trade and Market in the Early Empires*, K. Polanyi, C. W. Arensberg, and H. W. Pearson (eds.). New York: Free Press. **157.**

Ashby, W. Ross, 1958, "General Systems Theory as a New Discipline," in *General Systems*, 3:1–6. **101, 102.**

Back, K. W., 1950, "The Exertion of Influence through Social Communication," in *Theory and Experiment in Social Communication*, L. Festinger, K. Back, S. Schacter, H. H. Kelley, and J. Thibault (eds.). Ann Arbor, Mich.: Research Center for Dynamics, University of Michigan. **113.**

Bales, R. F., 1953, "The Equilibrium Problem in Small Groups," in *Small Groups*, A. P. Hare, E. F. Borgatha, and R. F. Bales (eds.). New York: Knopf. **114.**

Barnett, H. G., 1938, "The Nature of the Potlatch," *American Anthropologist*, 40:349–358. **293, 295.**

————, 1960, *Being a Palauan*, New York: Holt, Rinehart and Winston, Inc. **374–380.**

Barth, F., 1960, "The Land Use Pattern of Migratory Tribes of South Persia," *Norsk Geografisk Tidsskrift*, 17. **415, 420.**

———, 1961, *Nomads of South Persia.* Oslo: Norwegian University Press; New York: Humanities Press. **415, 417.**

——— (ed.), 1963, *The Role of the Entrepreneur in Social Change in Northern Norway.* Oslo: Norwegian University Press. **483.**

———, 1964, "Capital, Investment and the Social Structure of a Pastoral Nomad Group in South Persia," in *Capital, Savings and Credit in Peasant Societies,* Raymond Firth and B. S. Yamey (eds.). London: G. Allen. **415–425, 482.**

Barton, F., 1910, "The Annual Trading Expedition to the Papuan Gulf," in *The Melanesians of British New Guinea,* C. G. Seligman. Cambridge. (Chap. 8) **17.**

Barton, R. F., 1922, "Ifugao Economics," *University of California Publications in American Archeology and Ethnology,* 15:385–446. **3.**

———, 1949, *The Kalingas.* Chicago: University of Chicago Press. **396.**

Bascom, William R., 1948, "Ponapean Prestige Economy," *Southwestern Journal of Anthropology,* 4:211–221. **463.**

Beals, Ralph L., and Harry Hoijer, 1959, *An Introduction to Anthropology.* New York: Macmillan. **207.**

Belshaw, Cyril S., 1955, *In Search of Wealth.* American Anthropological Association Memoir No. 80. **188.**

———, 1964, *Under the Ivi Tree.* Berkeley, Calif.: University of California Press. **482.**

———, 1965, *Traditional Exchange and Modern Markets.* Englewood Cliffs, N.J.: Prentice-Hall. **v, 481.**

Bendix, R., 1956, *Work and Authority in Industry.* New York: Wiley. **166.**

Benedict, Ruth, 1956, "The Growth of Culture," in *Man, Culture and Society,* H. Shapiro (ed.). New York: Oxford. **340.**

Benham, Frederic, 1936, *Economics.* London. **40.**

Berliner, Joseph S., 1962, "The Feet of the Natives are Large: an Essay on Anthropology by an Economist," *Current Anthropology,* 3:47–61. **223, 477, 478.**

Berndt, R. M., 1955, " 'Murugiu' (Wulamba) Social Organization," *American Anthropologist,* 57:84–106. **371.**

———, 1957, "In Reply to Radcliffe-Brown on Australian Local Organization," *American Anthropologist,* 59:346–351. **371.**

Beveridge, Sir William, 1921, "Economics as a Liberal Education," *Economica,* 1:2–19. **88.**

Blau, Peter M., 1955, *The Dynamics of Bureaucracy.* Chicago: University of Chicago Press. **119, 120.**

———, 1964, *Exchange and Power in Social Life.* New York: Wiley. **214.**

Boas, Franz, 1889, *First General Report on the Indians of British Columbia.* Report of the British Association for the Advancement of Science, pp. 801–893. **288.**

———, 1897, *The Social Organization and the Secret Societies of the Kwakiutl Indians.* United States National Museum, Report for 1895, pp. 311–338. **288, 289, 290, 291, 292, 296, 298.**

———, 1920, "The Social Organization of the Kwakiutl," *American Anthropologist,* 22:111–126. **288, 290.**

———, 1921, *Ethnology of the Kwakiutl.* Thirty-fifth Annual Report, Bureau of American Ethnology. **285, 286, 288, 289, 290, 294, 295, 296.**

———, 1925, *Contributions to the Ethnology of the Kwakiutl.* Columbia University Contributions to Anthropology, 3. **288, 289, 290, 293, 295.**

———, 1935, *Kwakiutl Culture as Reflected in Mythology.* American Folklore Society, Memoir 28. **285, 286, 288, 294, 295, 296.**

Boeke, J. H., 1947, *Oriental Economics.* New York: Institute of Pacific Relations. **311.**

———, 1953, *Economics and Economic Policy of Dual Societies.* New York: Institute of Pacific Relations. **463.**

Bober, M. M., 1955, *Intermediate Price and Income Theory.* New York: Norton. **220, 225.**

Bohannan, Laura, and Paul Bohannan, 1953, *The Tiv of Central Nigeria.* London: International African Institute. **303, 306.**

Bohannan, Paul, 1954, *Tiv Farm and Settlement.* London: H. M. Stationery Office. **303.**

———, 1955, "Some Principles of Exchange and Investment among the Tiv," *American Anthropologist*, 57:60–70. **176, 276, 277, 300–311, 479.**

———, 1957, *Justice and Judgement Among the Tiv.* New York: Oxford. **165, 277.**

———, 1958, *Problems in Studying Primitive and Changing Economies.* Paper read at the American Anthropological Association meeting. **155.**

———, 1959, "The Impact of Money on an African Subsistence Economy," *The Journal of Economic History*, 19:491–503. **154, 157, 158, 164.**

———, 1963, *Social Anthropology.* New York: Holt, Rinehart and Winston, Inc. **13, 209, 210, 224, 291, 463.**

Bohannan, Paul, and George Dalton, 1962, *Markets in Africa.* Evanston, Ill.: Northwestern University Press; New York: Doubleday-Anchor (abridged edition), 1964. **209, 479.**

Bondi, Hermann, 1955, "Astronomy and Cosmology," in *What is Science?*, James R. Newman (ed.). New York: Simon and Schuster; also, 1961, New York: Washington Square Press. **473.**

Boulding, Kenneth E., 1941, *Economic Analysis.* New York: Harper & Row. **52.**

———, 1950, *A Reconstruction of Economics.* New York: Wiley. **248.**

———, 1956, "General System Theory—the Skeleton of Science," in *General Systems*, 1:11–17, reprinted from *Management Science*, 2:197–208. **101.**

———, 1957, "The Parsonian Approach to Economics," *Kyklos*, 10:317–319. **154.**

———, 1958, *The Skills of the Economist.* Toronto: Clarke, Irwin. **226.**

———, 1961, *The Image.* Ann Arbor, Mich.: University of Michigan Press. **225.**

———, 1962, "An Economist's View: Critique of Homan's *Social Behavior: Its Elementary Forms*," *American Journal of Sociology*, 67:458–461. **225.**

Braithwaite, R. B., 1953, *Scientific Explanation.* London: Cambridge. **110.**

Brinton, Crane, 1948, "Utilitarianism," in *Encyclopedia of the Social Sciences*, 15:197. **190.**

Broad, Charles Dunbar, 1925, *The Mind and its Place in Nature.* New York: Harcourt. **246.**

Bronfenbrenner, M., 1941, "Production Functions: Cobb-Douglas, Interfirm, Intrafirm," *Econometrica*, 9:35–44. **445.**

Brutzkus, Boris, 1935, *Economic Planning in Soviet Russia.* London: Routledge. **98.**

Bücher, Karl, 1901, *Industrial Evolution.* New York: Holt, Rinehart and Winston, Inc. **23.**

Bultol, F., 1954, *Saisons et Périodes Sèches et Pluvieuses au Congo Belge.* Brussels, Publications de l'Institut National pour l'étude agronomique du Congo Belge. **323.**

Burling, Robbins, 1962, "Maximization Theories and the Study of Economic Anthropology," *American Anthropologist*, 64:802–821. **12, 168–187, 217, 224, 231, 233.**

Butt, Audrey, 1952, *The Nilotes of the Anglo-Egyptian Sudan and Uganda.* London: International African Institute. **441.**

Cancian, Frank, 1966, "Maximization as Norm, Strategy, and Theory: a Comment on Programmatic Statements in Economic Anthropology," *American Anthropologist*, 68:465–470. **228–233.**

Cannan, Edwin, 1903a, *Elementary Political Economy*, 3d ed. London: H. Frowde. **88.**

———, 1903b, *History of the Theories of Production and Distribution*, in *English Political Economy*, reprinted 1967. New York: A. M. Kelly. **92.**

———, 1914, *Wealth, A Brief Explanation of the Causes of Economic Welfare.* London: King. **90, 93, 100.**

———, 1927, *An Economist's Protest.* London: King. **91.**

———, 1929, *A Review of Economic Theory.* London: King. **89, 92.**

Cassel, Gustav, 1925, *Fundamental Thoughts in Economics.* New York: Harcourt; London: T. F. Unwin. **98.**

Chalk, Alfred F., 1964, "Economic Man," in *Dictionary of the Social Sciences,* J. Gould and W. Kolb (eds.). New York: Free Press. **224, 225.**

Chapman, Sir Sidney, 1946, "The Profit Motive and the Economic Incentive," *The Economic Journal,* 56:51–56. **78.**

Clark, J. B., 1886, *The Philosophy of Wealth.* Boston: Ginn. **90.**

———, 1909, *Essentials of Economic Theory.* New York: Macmillan. **90.**

Cobb, John N., 1921, "Pacific Salmon Fisheries," 3d ed., Appendix I. U.S. Bureau of Fisheries: *Reports of U. S. Commission of Fisheries for the Fiscal Year 1921.* **286.**

Codere, Helen S., 1950, *Fighting with Property: a Study of Kwakiutl Potlatching and Warfare, 1792–1930.* Monographs of the American Ethnological Society, XVIII, New York. **52, 283, 291, 292, 293, 297.**

———, 1956, "The Amicable Side of Kwakiutl Life: the Potlatch and the Play-Potlatch," American Anthropologist, 58:334–351. **293.**

———, 1957, "Kwakiutl Society: Rank Without Class," *American Anthropologist,* 59:473–486. **289, 290.**

———, 1961, "Kwakiutl," in *Perspectives in American Indian Culture Change,* E. H. Spicer (ed.), pp. 431–516. Chicago: University of Chicago Press. **284, 288, 291, 293.**

Cole, Fay-Cooper, 1922, *The Tinguian.* Chicago, Field Museum of Natural History, Publication 209, Anthropological Series XIV, No. 2. **3, 71.**

Collins, O., M. Dalton, and D. Roy, 1946, "Restriction of Output and Social Cleavage in Industry," *Applied Anthropology,* 513:1–14. **78.**

Colson, E., 1951, "The Role of Cattle Among the Plateau Tonga," *The Rhodes-Livingstone Journal,* No. 11. **438.**

Conklin, Harold C., 1961, "The Study of Shifting Cultivation," *Current Anthropology,* 2:27–61. **207, 481.**

Cook, Scott, 1966, "The Obsolete 'Anti-Market' Mentality: A Critique of the Substantive Approach to Economic Anthropology," *American Anthropologist,* 68:323–345. **vii, 11, 208–228, 233, 481.**

Crocombe, R. G., and G. R. Hogbin, 1963, *The ERAP Mechanized Farming Project.* New Guinea Research Unit Bulletin No. 1, Canberra, Australian National University. **482.**

Curtis, E., 1915, "The Kwakiutl," in *The North American Indian,* Vol. 10. Norwood, Mass.: Plimpton Press. **285, 288, 289, 290, 292, 293, 295.**

Dalton, George, 1959a, *Robert Owen and Karl Polanyi as Socio-economic Critics and Reformers of Industrial Capitalism.* Unpublished Ph.D. dissertation, University of Oregon. **166, 167.**

———, 1959b, Review of *Trade and Market in the Early Empires, Boston University Graduate Journal,* 7:156–159. **167.**

———, 1960, "A Note of Clarification on Economic Surplus," *American Anthropologist,* 62:483–490. **165, 469.**

———, 1961, "Economic Theory and Primitive Society," *American Anthropologist,* 63:1–25. **11, 143–167, 186, 187, 188, 189, 190, 192, 193, 194, 195, 206, 209, 211, 216, 217, 219, 220, 223, 226, 233, 434.**

———, 1962, "Traditional Production in Primitive African Economies," *The Quarterly Journal of Economics,* 76:360–378. **209, 219.**

———, 1963, "Economic Surplus, Once Again," *American Anthropologist,* 65:389–394. **469.**

———, 1964, "The Development of Subsistence and Peasant Economies in Africa," *International Social Science Journal,* 16:378–389. **209, 210, 219, 225.**

———, 1965a, "Primitive Money," *American Anthropologist,* 67:44–65. **219, 224.**

————, 1965b, Review of *Capital, Saving, and Credit in Peasant Societies*, by R. Firth and B. S. Yamey (eds.), *American Anthropologist*, 67:121–122. **210.**

————, 1967, *Tribal and Peasant Economies: Readings in Economic Anthropology*. Garden City, N.Y.: Natural History Press. **v, 6, 7.**

Davenport, Herbert Joseph, 1913, *The Economics of Enterprise*. New York: Macmillan. **88, 89.**

Davis, R. C., 1958, "The Domain of Homeostasis," *Psychological Review*, 65:8–13. **106.**

Dawson, G. M., 1887, "Notes and Observations on the Kwakiool [sic] People of the Northern Part of Vancouver Island and Adjacent Coasts Made During the Summer of 1885, etc." *Proceedings and Transactions*, Royal Society of Canada, First Series, Vol. 5, No. 2: 63–98. **284, 288.**

Dewey, A., 1963, *Peasant Marketing in Java*. New York: Free Press. **481.**

Diamond, Stanley, 1964, "A Revolutionary Discipline," *Current Anthropology*, 5:432–437. **212.**

Diesing, Paul, 1950, "The Nature and Limitations of Economic Rationality," *Ethics*, 61: 12–26. **55, 236.**

Dolmatoff, Gerardo Reichel, 1950, *Los Kogi, una Tribu de la Sierra Nevada, en Colombia*. Bogotá. **42.**

Douglas, Mary, 1951, "A Form of Polyandry Among the Lele," *Africa*, 21:1–12. **335.**

————, 1954, "The Lele of the Kasai," in *African Worlds*, D. Forde (ed.). London: Oxford. **325.**

————, 1957, "The Pattern of Residence Among the Lele," *Zaïre*, 11:818–843. **334–335.**

————, 1958, "Raffia Distribution in the Lele Economy," *Africa*, 28:2. **332.**

————, 1959a, "Age Status Among the Lele," *Zaïre*, 13:386–413. **334.**

————, 1959b, "The Lele of the Kasai," in *The Church and the Nations*, A. Hastings (ed.). London: Sheed and Ward. **338.**

————, 1962, "The Lele—Resistance to Change," in *Markets in Africa*, Paul Bohannan and George Dalton (eds.). Evanston, Ill.: Northwestern University Press. **322–341.**

Drucker, Philip, 1955, *Indians of the Northwest Coast*. New York: McGraw-Hill. **288, 295.**

DuBois, Cora, 1936, "The Wealth Concept as an Integrative Factor in Tolowa-Tututni Culture," in *Essays in Anthropology Presented to A. L. Kroeber*, R. H. Lowie (ed.). Berkeley, Calif.: University of California Press. **154.**

Edwards, D., 1961, *An Economic Study of Small Farming in Jamaica*. Jamaica: Institute of Social and Economic Research. **481.**

Elkin, A. P., R. M. and C. M. Berndt, 1951, "Social Organization of Arnhem Land," *Oceania*, XXX, No. 4:253–301. **371.**

Erasmus, Charles, 1956, "Culture Structure and Process Occurrence and Disappearance of Reciprocal Labor," *Southwestern Journal of Anthropology*, 12:444–469. **483.**

Evans, George Heberton, Jr., 1950, *Basic Economics*. New York: Knopf. **194–195.**

Evans-Pritchard, E. E., 1931, "An Alternative Term for 'Bride Price'," *Man*, 31:36–39. **259.**

————, 1949, "Nuer Rules of Exogamy and Incest," in *Social Structure: Studies Presented to A. R. Radcliffe-Brown*, M. Fortes (ed.). Oxford: Clarendon. **264.**

————, 1953, "The Sacrificial Role of Cattle Among the Nuer," *Africa*, 23:3. **442.**

————, 1954, "Introduction," in *The Gift*, Marcel Mauss. New York: Free Press. **155, 163.**

Fairchild, F. R., E. S. Furniss, and N. S. Buck, 1936, *Elementary Economics*, 3d ed. New York: Macmillan. **172, 185, 187.**

Fallers, L. A., 1957, "Some Determinants of Marriage Stability in Busoga: a Reformulation of Gluckman's Hypothesis," *Africa*, 27:106–121. **280.**

Festinger, L., S. Schecter, and K. Back, 1950, *Social Pressures in Informal Groups*. New York: Harper & Row. **114.**

Fetter, Frank A., *Economic Principles* (Possibly 1915–1916, *Economics*, 2 vols., New York: Century). **96.**

Firth, G. G., 1964, "The Frontiers of Economics," *The Economic Record*, 40:33–45. **226.**

Firth, Raymond, 1929, *Primitive Economics of the New Zealand Maori.* New York: Dutton. **5, 69.**

———, 1939, *Primitive Polynesian Economy.* London: Routledge. **6, 8, 46, 69, 188, 196, 225.**

———, 1946, *Malay Fishermen: Their Peasant Economy.* London: Routledge. **83, 482.**

———, 1948, "Anthropological Background to Work," *Occupational Psychology*, 22:94–102. **78.**

———, 1951, *The Elements of Social Organization.* London: Watts (1961, Boston: Beacon Press). **165, 221.**

———, 1952, *The Elements of Social Organization*, 2d ed. London: Watts (1961, Boston: Beacon Press). **3, 6, 7.**

———, 1958, *Human Types*, rev. ed. New York: Mentor Books. **143, 153, 157, 158–159.**

———, 1959, *Economics of the New Zealand Maori*, R. E. Owen, Government Printer, Wellington, New Zealand. **176, 187.**

———, 1964, "The Place of Malinowski in the History of Economic Anthropology," in *Man and Culture: An Evaluation of the Work of Bronislaw Malinowski*, Raymond Firth (ed.). New York: Harper Torchbooks. **4.**

———, 1965, Review of *Kapauku Papuan Economy*, by L. Pospisil. *American Anthropologist*, 67:122–125. **224.**

Firth, Raymond, and B. S. Yamey (eds.), 1963, *Capital, Savings and Credit in Peasant Societies.* London: Allen. **482.**

Fisher, Irving, 1897, "Senses of Capital," *Economic Journal*, 7:199–213. **97.**

———, 1906, *The Nature of Capital and Income.* New York: Macmillan. **92.**

Ford, Clellan, S., 1941, *Smoke From Their Fires.* New Haven, Conn.: Yale University Press. **283, 288, 295, 296.**

Forde, Daryll, 1937, "Land and Labor in A Cross River Village," *Geographical Journal*, 40:1. **330.**

Fortes, M., 1949, "Time and Social Structure: An Ashanti Case Study, in *Social Structure*, M. Fortes (ed.), Oxford. **403.**

———, 1953, "The Structure of Unilineal Descent Groups," *American Anthropologist*, 55: 17–41. **396.**

Foster, George M., 1942, *A Primitive Mexican Economy.* Monographs of the American Ethnological Society, 5. **188.**

———, 1965, "Peasant Society and the Image of Limited Good," *American Anthropologist*, 67:293–315. **479.**

Frank, Gunder, n.d., "Soviet and American Economic Organization." (Processed.) **207.**

Freeman, J. D., 1958, "The Family System of the Iban of Borneo," *Cambridge Papers in Social Anthropology*, 1:15–52. **396.**

Freud, Sigmund, 1925, "Formulations Regarding the Two Principles in Mental Functioning," *Collected Papers*, Vol. 4, pp. 13–21. **180.**

Frisch, R., 1936, "On the Notion of Equilibrium and Disequilibrium," *Review of Economic Studies*, III. **248.**

Fusfeld, D. B., 1957, "Economic Theory Misplaced: Livelihood in Primitive Society," in *Trade and Market in the Early Empires*, K. Polanyi, C. W. Arensberg, and H. W. Pearson (eds.). New York: Free Press. **148, 150, 222.**

Geertz, C. S., 1963, *Agricultural Involution.* Berkeley, Calif.: University of California Press. **484.**

Gerard, H. B., 1954, "The Anchorage of Opinions in Face-to-Face Groups," *Human Relations*, 7:313–325. **115.**

Gide, Charles, 1930, "Economic Man," in *Encyclopedia of the Social Sciences.* New York: Macmillan. **224.**

Gluckman, M. (ed.), 1964, *Closed Systems and Open Minds.* Chicago: Aldine. **485.**

Godfrey, H., 1958a, "A Comparison of Sockeye Salmon Catches at Rivers Inlet and Skeena River, B.C., with Particular Reference to Age at Maturity," *Journal of the Fisheries Research Board of Canada*, 15:331–354. **286.**

———, 1958b, "Comparison of the Index of Return for Several Stocks of British Columbia Salmon to Study Variations in Survival," *Journal of the Fisheries Research Board of Canada*, 15:891–908. **287.**

Goldman, Irving, 1937, "The Kwakiutl of Vancouver Island," in *Co-operation and Competition Among Primitive Peoples*, M. Mead (ed.). New York: McGraw-Hill. **161, 162.**

Goodfellow, D. M., 1939, *Principles of Economic Sociology.* London: Routledge. **6, 8, 46, 55–65, 159, 162, 163, 224, 434, 438.**

Gouldner, Alvin, 1959, "Reciprocity and Autonomy in Functional Theory," in *Symposium on Sociological Theory*, Llewellyn Gross (ed.), pp. 241–266. New York: Harper & Row. **255.**

———, 1960, "The Norm of Reciprocity: A Preliminary Statement," *American Sociological Review*, 25:161–178. **214.**

Gourou, P., 1951, *Notice de la Carte de la Densité de la Population au Congo Belge et au Ruanda-Urundi.* Brussels: Institute Royal Colonial Belge. **325.**

———, 1955, *La Densité de la Population Rurale du Congo Belge*, etc., Brussels: Acad. Roy. Sci. Col. Mem., 8:1–2. **324, 325.**

Grampp, William D., 1948, "Adam Smith and the Economic Man," *Journal of Political Economy*, 61:315–336. **224.**

Gray, Robert F., 1960, "Sonjo Bride-price and the Question of African 'Wife Purchase'," *American Anthropologist*, 62:34–57. **187, 259–282, 437, 441, 444.**

Gulliver, P. H., 1951, *A Preliminary Survey of the Turkana.* Capetown: School of African Studies. **437.**

———, 1955, *The Family Herds; a Study of Two Pastoral Tribes in East Africa, the Jie and Turkana.* London: Routledge. **279.**

Hagen, Everett E., 1961, "Analytical Models in the Study of Social Systems," *The American Journal of Sociology*, LXII, Sept. 1961:144–151. Also reprinted in Hagen 1962. **9, 12, 100–109.**

———, 1962, *On the Theory of Social Change.* Homewood, Ill.: Dorsey Press. **223, 478.**

Haire, M. (ed.), 1959, *Modern Organization Theory.* New York: Wiley. **479.**

Hall, A. D., and R. E. Fagen, 1956, "Definition of System," in *General Systems*, 1:18–28. **101.**

Harris, Marvin, 1959, "The Economy Has No Surplus?" *American Anthropologist*, 61:185–200. **325, 332, 469.**

Harriss, C. Lowell, 1959, *The American Economy.* Homewood, Ill.: Irwin. **195, 207.**

Hart, C. W. M., 1931, "Personal Names among the Tiwi," *Oceania*, 1:280–290. **365.**

———, 1954, "The Sons of Turimpi," *American Anthropologist*, 56:242–261. **361.**

Hart, C. W. M., and Arnold R. Pilling, 1960, *The Tiwi of North Australia.* New York: Holt, Rinehart and Winston, Inc. **354–374.**

Hayley, F. A., 1923, *A Treatise on the Laws and Customs of the Sinhalese.* Colombo. **397.**

Hazelhurst, L. W., 1966, *Entrepreneurship and the Merchant Castes in a Punjabi City.* Durham, N.C.: Duke University Press. **482.**

He'mann, Eduard, 1945, *History of Economic Doctrine.* New York: Oxford. **225, 227.**

Hempel, Carl, 1959, "The Logic of Functional Analysis," in *Symposium on Sociological Theory*, Llewellyn Gross (ed.), pp. 271–302. Evanston, Ill.: Harper & Row. **254.**

Henderson, Lawrence J., 1937, *Pareto's General Sociology.* Cambridge, Mass.: Harvard University Press. **102.**

Herskovits, Melville J., 1938, *Dahomey: An Ancient West African Kingdom*. New York: Augustin. **195.**

——, 1940, *The Economic Life of Primitive Peoples*. New York: Knopf. **v, 6, 8, 69, 123, 143, 188, 471.**

——, 1941, "Economics and Anthropology: a Rejoinder," *Journal of Political Economy*, 49:269–278. Also reprinted in Herskovits 1952, Appendix. **143, 150, 188.**

——, 1948, *Man and His Works*. New York: Knopf. **53, 54.**

——, 1952, *Economic Anthropology*. New York: Knopf. **v, 6, 7, 8, 40–55, 123, 144, 148, 149, 152, 153, 156, 157, 161, 165, 166, 169, 174, 176, 187, 188, 206, 210, 211, 220, 223, 279, 291, 332, 426, 442, 443, 457, 471.**

Hicks, J. R., 1939, *Value and Capital*. Oxford: Clarendon Press. **70.**

Higgins, Benjamin, 1947, "The Economic Man and Economic Science," *Canadian Journal of Economics and Political Science*, 13:587–598. **225.**

——, 1959, *Economic Development*. New York: Norton. **221, 223, 226.**

Hill, P., 1956, *The Gold Coast Cocoa Farmer: A Preliminary Survey*. New York: Oxford. **482.**

——, 1963, *Migrant Cocoa Farmers of Southern Ghana*. Cambridge: University Press. **482.**

H. M. Agent and Consul General, 1902, "Report, 1901," in *Accounts and Papers*, Vol. CXXX. **84.**

Hoar, W. S., 1951, "The Chum and Pink Salmon Fisheries of British Columbia 1917–1947," *Fisheries Research Board of Canada, Bulletin 90*. **286.**

Homans, G. C., 1950, *The Human Group*. New York: Harcourt. **114, 115.**

——, 1953, "Status Among Clerical Workers," *Human Organization*, 12:5–10. **118.**

——, 1958, "Social Behavior as Exchange," *American Journal of Sociology*, 63:597–606. **109–121, 185.**

——, 1961, *Social Behavior: Its Elementary Forms*. New York: Harcourt. **214, 231, 233.**

Honigman, John J., 1949, "Incentives to Work in a Canadian-Indian Community," *Human Organization*, 8, 4:23–28. **82.**

Hopkins, Terence K., 1957, "Sociology and the Substantive View of the Economy," in *Trade and Market in the Early Empires*, K. Polanyi, C. W. Arensberg, and H. W. Pearson (eds.). New York: Free Press. **166, 243.**

Hoselitz, Bert F., 1960, *Sociological Aspects of Economic Growth*. New York: Free Press. **223.**

Huntingford, G. W. B., 1950, *Nandi Work and Culture*. London: Colonial Office. **436–437, 441.**

——, 1953, *The Southern Nilo-Hamites*. London: International African Institute, Ethnographic Survey of Africa. **437.**

Hutchison, T. W., 1938, *The Significance and Basic Postulates of Economic Theory*. London: Macmillan. **226.**

Jack, R. Logan, 1921, *Northmost Australia*, 2 vols. London: Simpkin, Marshall, Hamilton, Kent and Co. **342.**

Junod, H. A., 1927, *The Life of a South African Tribe*. London: Macmillan. **272, 273.**

Kaberry, Phyllis M., 1939, *Aboriginal Woman, Sacred and Profane*. London: The Blakiston Co. **47.**

Kenyatta, Jomo, 1953, *Facing Mount Kenya: The Tribal Life of the Gikuyu*. London: Secker and Warburg. **271.**

Keyfitz, N., 1959, "The Interlocking of Social and Economic Factors in Asian Development," *The Canadian Journal of Economics and Political Science*. 25:34–46. **165.**

Keynes, John Maynard, 1926, *The End of Laissez-Faire*. London: Hogarth. **166.**

——, 1936, *The General Theory of Employment, Interest and Money*. New York: Harcourt. **464.**

Keynes, John Neville, 1897, *The Scope and Method of Political Economy,* 2d ed. London. **54.**

Kluckhohn, Clyde, 1950, Review of *Human Behavior and the Principle of Least Effort,* G. K. Zipf, *American Anthropologist,* 52:268–270. **181.**

Knight, Frank H., 1933, *The Economic Organization,* Chicago. **40, 44.**

———, 1941, "Anthropology and Economics," *Journal of Political Economy,* 49:247–268. Also reprinted in Herskovits 1952: Appendix. **52, 143, 150, 186, 226, 471.**

———, 1951, *The Economic Organization.* New York: Augustus M. Kelley. **172.**

Koppers, Pater W., "Die Ethnologische Wirtschaftsforschung," *Anthropos,* 10:611–651. **23.**

———, 1916, "Die Ethnologische Wirtschaftsforschung," (continued), *Anthropos,* 11:971–1079. **23.**

Krupp, Sherman Roy, 1964, *Pattern in Organization Analysis: A Critical Examination.* New York: Holt, Rinehart and Winston, Inc. **252.**

———, 1965, "Equilibrium Theory in Economics and in Functional Analysis as Types of Explanation," in *Functionalism in the Social Sciences.* Philadelphia: The American Academy of Political and Social Science, Monograph No. 5. **9, 12, 243–256, 460.**

Krupp, Sherman, and Eugene Schneider, 1964, "An Illustration of the Use of Analytical Theory in Sociology: The Application of the Economic Theory of Choice to Noneconomic Variables." Paper read at the annual meeting of the American Sociological Association, Montreal, September 1, 1964. **256.**

Lambton, A. K. S., 1953, *Landlord and Peasant in Persia.* London: Oxford. **417.**

La Fontaine, J. S., 1959, "The Gisu of Uganda," *Ethnographic Survey of Africa,* East Central Africa, Part X. London: International African Institute. **275.**

Landry (not otherwise identified). **99.**

Lasswell, Harold, 1948, *Power and Personality.* New York: Norton. **181.**

Lawrance, J. C. D., 1957, *The Iteso.* London: Oxford. **437.**

Leach, E. R., 1954, *Political Systems of Highland Burma.* Cambridge, Mass.: Harvard University Press. **180–181.**

———, 1960, "The Sinhalese of the Dry Zone of Northern Ceylon," in *Social Structure in Southeast Asia,* George P. Murdock (ed.). Chicago: Quadrangle Books for Viking Fund Publications in Anthropology, pp. 116–127. **395–403.**

LeClair, Edward E., Jr., 1953, *Economic Values in Nonliterate Cultures.* Ph.D. dissertation. Ann Arbor, Mich.: University Microfilms. **207.**

———, 1959, "A Minimal Frame of Reference for Economic Anthropology." Paper presented to the Workshop in Economic Anthropology, Chicago, September 1959 (processed). **207.**

———, 1960, "A New Approach to Economic Anthropology." Paper read at the 59th annual meeting of the American Anthropological Association, Minneapolis, Minnesota, November 1960. **207.**

———, 1962, "Economic Theory and Economic Anthropology," *American Anthropologist,* 64:1179–1203. **12, 187–207, 217, 224, 227, 231, 232, 233.**

Leeds, Anthony, 1961, "Yaruro Incipient Tropical Forest Horticulture—Possibilities and Limits," *Anthropologica,* No. 10, Caracas. **207.**

Lester, R. A., 1946, "Shortcomings of Marginal Analysis for Wage-Employment Problems," *American Economic Review,* 36:63–82. **206.**

Levi-Strauss, Claude, 1944, *The Social and Psychological Aspects of Chieftainship in a Primitive Tribe: The Nambikuara.* Transactions of the New York Academy of Sciences, Series 2, VII, No. 1. **214, 225.**

Levy, Marion J., Jr., 1952, *The Structure of Society.* Princeton, N.J.: Princeton University Press. **107.**

Lewis, W. A., 1954, *The Theory of Economic Growth.* London: G. Allen. **223.**

Linton, Ralph, 1940, "A Neglected Aspect of Social Organization," *American Journal of Sociology,* 45. **339.**

Macfie, A. L., 1949, "What Kind of Experience is Economizing?" *Ethics,* 60:19–34. **41, 236.**

Machlup, Fritz, 1946, "Marginal Analysis and Empirical Research," *American Economic Review,* 36:519–554. **190, 206.**

————, 1963, *Essays in Economic Semantics.* Englewood Cliffs, N.J.: Prentice-Hall. **248.**

Mair, L. P., 1934, *An African People in the Twentieth Century.* London: Routledge. **278, 279.**

————, 1940, *Native Marriage in Buganda,* International Institute of African Languages and Cultures, Memorandum No. 19. London: Oxford. **278.**

————, 1953, "African Marriage and Social Change," in *Survey of African Marriage and Family Life,* Arthur Phillips (ed.). London: Oxford. **261.**

Malcolm, D. W., 1953, *Sukumaland.* London: Oxford. **437, 440.**

Malinowski, B., 1915, "The Mailu," in *Transactions of the Royal Society of South Australia,* 4:612–629. **17.**

————, 1921, "The Primitive Economics of the Trobriand Islanders," *The Economic Journal,* 31:1–16. **19, 23.**

————, 1922, 1961, *Argonauts of the Western Pacific.* London: Routledge; also New York: Dutton, 1932, 1961. **v, 3, 4, 5, 8, 17–39, 79, 153, 157, 187, 195.**

————, 1926, *Crime and Custom in Savage Society.* London: Routledge; New York: Harcourt. **79.**

Marschak, J., and W. H. Andrews, Jr., 1944, "Random Simultaneous Equations and the Theory of Production," *Econometrica,* 12:143–205. **445.**

Marshall, Alfred, 1920, *Principles of Economics,* various editions from 1890 to 1920. London: Macmillan. **88, 90.**

Marwick, Brian Allan, 1940, *The Swazi.* Cambridge: Cambridge. **47.**

Massell, Benton F., 1963, "Econometric Variations on a Theme by Schneider," *Economic Development and Cultural Change,* 12:1:34–41. **445–451.**

Mauss, Marcel, 1925, *The Gift: Forms and Functions of Exchange in Archaic Society,* 1954. New York: Free Press. **110, 153, 160–161, 162.**

Mayer, Hans, "Untersuchungen zu dem Grundgesetze der wirtschaftlichen Wertrechnung," *Zeitschrift für Volkwirtschaft und Sozialpolitik.* **95, 96.**

Mayer, Philip, 1950, *Gusii Bridewealth Law and Custom,* Rhodes-Livingstone Papers, No. 18. London: Oxford. **274, 275, 276, 437.**

Mead, Margaret, 1937, "Interpretive Statement," in *Cooperation and Competition among Primitive Peoples,* M. Mead (ed.). New York: McGraw-Hill. **148.**

Meade, J. E., 1948, "Planning Without Prices," *Economica,* 15:34. **72.**

Menderhausen, H., 1938, "On the Significance of Professor Douglas' Production Function," *Econometrica,* 6:143–154. **445.**

Menger, Karl, *Grundsaetze der Volkswirtschaftslehre.* **96.**

Merton, R. K., 1949, *Social Theory and Social Structure; Toward the Codification of Theory and Research.* New York: Free Press. **108, 270.**

————, 1957, *Social Theory and Social Structure,* rev. ed. New York: Free Press. **107, 108.**

Middleton, J. F. M., 1953, *The Kikuyu and the Kamba of Kenya.* London: International African Institute. **436.**

Mill, John Stuart, 1844, *Unsettled Questions of Political Economy.* London: J. W. Parker. **89, 456.**

Miller, James G., 1955, "Toward a General Theory for the Behavioral Sciences," *American Psychologist,* 10:513–531. Reprinted in *The State of the Social Sciences,* Leonard White (ed.). Chicago: University of Chicago Press. **109.**

Mitchell, Wesley C., 1949, *Lecture Notes on Types of Economic Theory.* New York: Kelley. **147.**

Moore, W. E., 1955a, *Economy and Society.* New York: Random House, Inc., **220.**

——, 1955b, "Labor Attitudes Toward Industrialization in Underdeveloped Countries," *American Economic Review,* 45:156–165. **151, 165, 166.**

Moos, S., 1945, "Laissez-faire Planning and Ethics," *The Economic Journal,* 55:17–27. **78.**

Mukerjee, Radhakamal, 1921, *Principles of Comparative Economics,* Vol. I. **54.**

——, 1922, *Principles of Comparative Economics,* Vol. II, London. **68–69.**

Murdock, George Peter, 1949, *Social Structure.* New York: Macmillan. **371.**

Myrdal, Gunnar, 1944, *An American Dilemma.* New York: Harper & Row. **256.**

——, 1957, *Rich Lands and Poor.* New York: Harper & Row. **165, 340.**

——, 1958, *Value in Social Theory.* London: Routledge. **248.**

Nadel, S. F., 1942, *A Black Byzantium.* London: Oxford. **479.**

Nagel, Ernst, 1961, *The Structure of Science.* New York: Harcourt. **244.**

Nash, Manning, 1958, *Machine Age Maya.* New York: Free Press, and American Anthropological Association Memoir 87. **319.**

——, 1959, "Some social and cultural aspects of economic development," *Economic Development and Cultural Change,* 7:137–150. **319.**

——, 1961, "The Social Context of Economic Choice in a Small Society," *Man,* 219:186–191. **v, 9, 228, 311–322, 481.**

——, 1965, *The Golden Road to Modernity.* New York: Wiley. **481.**

——, 1966, *Primitive and Peasant Economic Systems.* San Francisco: Chandler Publishing Co. **v, 477.**

Neale, Walter C., 1957, "Reciprocity and Redistribution in the Indian Village," in *Trade and Market in the Early Empires,* K. Polanyi, C. W. Arensberg, and H. W. Pearson (eds.). New York: Free Press. **150, 158, 167.**

——, 1959, "Discussion of Problems of Economic Development in Non-industrialized Areas," *The Journal of Economic History,* 19:525–527. **165.**

——, 1962, "On Defining 'Labor' and 'Services' for Comparative Studies," *American Anthropologist,* 64:1300–1307. **226.**

Neave, Ferris, 1953, "Principles Affecting the Size of Pink and Chum Salmon Populations in British Columbia," *Journal of the Fisheries Research Board of Canada,* 9:450–491. **287.**

——, 1958, "Stream Ecology and Production of Anadromous Fish," in *The Investigation of Fish-Power Problems—A Symposium Held at the University of British Columbia April 28 and 30, 1957,* P. A. Larkin (ed.), pp. 43–48. Vancouver: U.B.C. Institute of Fisheries. **287.**

Newcomb, T. M., 1956, "The Prediction of Interpersonal Attraction," *American Psychologist,* 11:575–586. **111.**

Nicolai, H., 1952, *Problèmes du Kwango.* Bulletin de la societé Belge d'Etudes Géographiques, 25:2. **324, 325.**

Nicolai, N., and J. Jacques, 1954, *La Transformation du Paysage Congolais par Chemin de Fer, L'example du B.C.K.* Acad. Roy. Sci. Col. Brussels, Sect. des Sci. Natu. et Med. Mem. in 8, XXIV, L. **324, 327.**

Northrup, F. S. C., 1948, *The Logic of the Sciences and Humanities.* New York: Macmillan. **206.**

Oliver, Douglas L., 1949, *Economic and Social Uses of Domestic Pigs in Siuai Southern Bougainville, Solomon Islands.* Papers, Peabody Museum of American Ethnology and Archeology, Vol. XXXIX, No. 4. **42.**

Olson, Ronald L., 1940, "The Social Organization of the Haisla of British Columbia," *Anthropological Records,* 2. **293.**

Orans, Martin, 1966, "Surplus," *Human Organization,* 25, 1:24–32. **469.**

Outram, D. H., 1956, *Amount of Herring Spawn Deposited in British Columbia Coastal Waters in 1956*, Fisheries Research Board of Canada, Pacific Biological Station, Nanaimo, B.C., Circular 42. **286.**

———, 1957, *Extent of Herring Spawning in British Columbia in 1957*, Fisheries Research Board of Canada, Pacific Biological Station, Nanaimo, B.C., Circular 46. **286.**

———, 1958, *The 1958 Herring Spawn Deposition in British Columbia Coastal Waters*, Fisheries Research Board of Canada, Pacific Biological Station, Nanaimo, B.C., Circular 50. **286.**

Pareto, Vilfredo, *Cours d'Economie Politique.* **90.**

Parsons, Talcott, 1934, "Some Reflections on 'The Nature and Significance of Economics'," *Quarterly Journal of Economics*, 47:522–529. **238.**

———, 1935, "Sociological Elements in Economic Thought," *Quarterly Journal of Economics*, 49:421. **238.**

———, 1949, *The Structure of Social Action*. New York: Free Press. **236, 237.**

———, 1951, *The Social System*. New York: Free Press. **107, 108.**

Parsons, T., and E. A. Shils, 1951, *Toward A General Theory of Action*. Cambridge, Mass.: Harvard University Press. **107, 108, 112, 243.**

Parsons, Talcott, Robert F. Bales, and Edward Shils, 1953, *Working Papers in the Theory of Action*. New York: Free Press. **243.**

Parsons, Talcott, and Robert F. Bales, 1954, *Family, Socialization and Interaction Process*. New York: Free Press. **107.**

Parsons, Talcott, and Neil Smelser, 1956, *Economy and Society*. New York: Free Press. **9, 234–243.**

Paulme, Denise, 1940, Organization Sociale des Dogon, Paris. **43.**

Pearsall, Marion, 1947, "Distributional Variations of Bride-wealth in the East African Cattle Area," *Southwestern Journal of Anthropology*, 3:15–31. **280.**

Pearson, Harry W., 1957a, "Parsons and Smelser on the Economy," in *Trade and Market in the Early Empires*, K. Polanyi, C. W. Arensberg, and H. W. Pearson (eds.), pp. 307–319. New York: Free Press. **9, 234–243.**

———, 1957b, "The Economy has no Surplus: Critique of a Theory of Development," in *Trade and Market in the Early Empires*, K. Polanyi, C. W. Arensberg, and H. W. Pearson (eds.), pp. 320–341. New York: Free Press. **469.**

———, 1957c, "The Secular Debate on Economic Primitivism," in *Trade and Market in the Early Empires*, K. Polanyi, C. W. Arensberg, and H. W. Pearson (eds.), pp. 3–11. New York: Free Press. **167.**

Phillips, Arthur, 1953, "Marriage Laws in Africa," in *Survey of African Marriage and Family Life*, Arthur Phillips (ed.). London: Oxford. **281.**

Piddocke, Stuart, 1965, "The Potlatch System of the Southern Kwakiutl: A New Perspective," *Southwestern Journal of Anthropology*, 21:244–264. **283–299.**

Pigou, A. C., 1935, "The Need for Money in Voluntary Private Dealings," in *Economics of Stationary States*. London: Macmillan. **72, 99.**

———, 1962, *Economics of Welfare*, 4th ed. London: Macmillan. **88, 99.**

Polanyi, Karl, 1944, *The Great Transformation*. New York: Holt, Rinehart and Winston, Inc.; Boston: Beacon Press, 1957. **11, 43, 146, 147, 166, 213, 225, 226.**

———, 1947, "Our Obsolete Market Mentality," *Commentary*, 13:109–117. **11, 166, 213, 214, 215, 225.**

———, 1957a, "Aristotle Discovers the Economy," in *Trade and Market in the Early Empires*, K. Polanyi, C. W. Arensberg, and H. W. Pearson (eds.), pp. 64–94. New York: Free Press. **154, 156, 157, 158, 166, 209.**

———, 1957b, "The Economy as Instituted Process," in *Trade and Market in the Early Empires*, K. Polanyi, C. W. Arensberg, and H. W. Pearson (eds.), pp. 243–270. New York:

Free Press. **10, 122–143, 157, 166, 170, 171, 186, 187, 209, 213, 214, 217, 218, 225, 226, 232, 233, 311, 393.**

——, 1959, "Anthropology and Economic Theory," in *Readings in Anthropology* II, Morton H. Fried (ed.). New York: Crowell. **166, 190, 191, 209, 211, 213, 218, 226, 227.**

Polanyi, K., C. W. Arensberg, and H. W. Pearson (eds.), 1957, *Trade and Market in the Early Empires.* New York: Free Press. **10, 151, 170, 187, 208, 209, 211, 218, 479.**

Polanyi, Karl, and A. Rotstein, 1966, *Dahomey and the Slave Trade.* Seattle: University of Washington Press. **11, 480.**

Pospisil, Leopold, 1963a, *Kapauku Papuan Economy.* New Haven, Conn.: Yale University Press. **222, 224, 225.**

——, 1963b, *The Kapauku Papuans of West New Guinea.* New York: Holt, Rinehart and Winston, Inc. **381–394, 481.**

Prins, A. H. J., 1952, *The Coastal Tribes of the North-eastern Bantu.* London: International African Institute. **437.**

Qureshi, Anwar Iqbal, 1945, *Islamand the Rate of Interest,* Lahore. **83, 85.**

Radcliffe-Brown, A. R., 1913, "Three Tribes of Western Australia," *J.A.I.,* 63:143–194. **372.**

——, 1929, "Bride-price, Earnest or Indemnity," *Man,* 29:131–132. **282.**

——, 1930–1931, "The Social Organization of Australian Tribes," *Oceania Monographs,* No. 1. **371.**

——, 1935, "On the Concept of Function in Social Science," *American Anthropologist,* 37:394–402; reprinted in *Structure and Function in Primitive Society: Essays and Addresses* by A. R. Radcliffe-Brown. New York: Free Press. **108.**

——, 1949, "White's View of a Science of Culture," *American Anthropologist,* 51:503–512. **71.**

——, 1950, "Introduction," in *African Systems of Kinship and Marriage,* A. R. Radcliffe-Brown and Daryll Forde (eds.). London: Oxford. **269, 270.**

——, 1952a, "On Social Structure," in *Structure and Function in Primitive Society.* New York: Free Press; reprinted from *Journal of the Royal Anthropological Institute,* 1940; Vol. LXX. **71.**

——, 1952b, *Structure and Function in Primitive Society, Essays and Addresses.* New York: Free Press. **108, 270.**

Radford, Richard A., 1945, "The Price System in a Prison Camp," *Economica,* Nov. 1945: 189–201. **403–414.**

Raglan, Lord, 1931, "Bride Price," *Man,* 31:75. **259.**

Razi, Imam, n.d., *Tafsir Kabir,* Cairo. As quoted in *Islam and the Rate of Interest,* A. I. Qureshi, Lahore, 1945. **83.**

Reder, M. W., 1943, "An Alternative Interpretation of the Cobb-Douglas Function," *Econometrica,* 11:259–264. **445.**

Ricardo, David, 1817, 1933, *Principles of Political Economy and Taxation.* New York: Dutton. **469.**

Richard, A. I., 1939, *Land, Labor and Diet in Northern Rhodesia.* London: Oxford. **82.**

Riecken, H. W., and G. C. Homans, 1954, "Psychological Aspects of Social Structure," in *Handbook of Social Psychology,* G. Lindzey (ed.). Cambridge, Mass.: Addison-Wesley. **114.**

Robbins, Lionel, 1932, 1935, "The Subject Matter of Economics," in *An Essay on the Nature and Significance of Economic Science.* London: Macmillan; New York: St. Martin's. **10, 78, 88–100, 123, 150, 169, 170, 172, 176, 177, 225, 226.**

Roll, Eric, 1937, *Elements of Economic Theory.* London: Oxford. **220, 225.**

Roscoe, John, 1911, *The Baganda; an Account of their Native Customs and Beliefs.* London: Macmillan. **278.**

Rostlund, Erhard, 1952, *Freshwater Fish and Fishing in Native North America,* University of California Publications in Geography, 9. **287.**

Rottenberg, Simon, 1958, Review of *Trade and Market in the Early Empires, American Economic Review,* 48:675–678. **152, 159, 218, 219, 224.**

Ryan, B., 1953, *Caste in Modern Ceylon.* New Brunswick, N.J.: Rutgers University Press. **396.**

Sahlins, Marshall D., 1960, "Political Power and the Economy in Primitive Society," in *Essays in the Science of Culture,* R. Carneiro and G. Dole (eds.). New York: Crowell. **225.**

———, 1962, Review of *Sociological Aspects of Economic Growth* by Bert Hoselitz, *American Anthropologist,* 64:1063–1073. **214, 225, 226.**

———, 1963, "On the Sociology of Primitive Exchange," in *The Relevance of Models for Social Anthropology,* pp. 139–227, Association of Social Anthropologists Monographs No. 1. London: Tavistock Publications. **214, 225, 480.**

———, 1965, "Exchange Value and the Diplomacy of Primitive Trade," in *Proceedings of the American Ethnological Society,* Spring Meetings, pp. 95–129. Seattle: University of Washington Press. **480.**

Samuelson, Paul A., 1953, *Foundations of Economic Analysis.* Cambridge, Mass.: Harvard University Press. **248.**

———, 1958, *Economics: An Introductory Analysis.* New York: McGraw-Hill. **192, 207, 457.**

Salisbury, R. F., 1960, "Ceremonial Exchange and Political Equilibrium," in *Proceedings of the 5th International Congress of Anthropological and Ethnological Sciences,* Paris, 2:255–260. **480.**

———, 1962, *From Stone to Steel.* Melbourne: University of Melbourne Press. **13, 222, 224, 225, 466, 479.**

———, 1968, "Anthropology and Economics," in *Anthropology and the Neighboring Disciplines,* Otto von Mering and Leonard Kasdan (eds.). Pittsburgh: Pittsburgh University Press. **427–485.**

———, n.d.(a), "Trade and Markets," in *Encyclopedia of the Social Sciences,* rev. ed., in press. **481.**

———, n.d.(b), *Vunamami: A Traditional Society in Economic Take-off,* forthcoming. **482, 484.**

Sankoff, G., 1965, *The Organizational Factor in the Economic Development of Traditional and Peasant Societies.* M. A. Thesis, McGill University. **483.**

Sayles, Leonard, 1958, *The Behavior of the Industrial Work Group.* New York: Wiley. **254.**

Schachter, S., 1951, "Deviation, Rejection and Communication," *Journal of Abnormal and Social Psychology,* 65:190–207. **113.**

Schachter, S., N. Ellerston, D. McBride, and D. Gregory, 1951, "An Experimental Study of Cohesiveness and Productivity," *Human Relations,* 4:229–238. **113.**

Schapera, I., 1937, *The Bantu-Speaking Tribes of South Africa.* London: Routledge. **442.**

———, 1953, *The Tswana.* London: International African Institute. **438.**

Schneider, D. M., 1953, "A Note on Bridewealth and the Stability of Marriage," *Man,* 53:55–57. **271.**

Schneider, Harold K., 1953, *The Pakot (Suk) of Kenya with Special Reference to the Role of Livestock in their Subsistence Economy,* Publication No. 7064. Ann Arbor, Mich.: University Microfilms. **436.**

———, 1959, "Pakot Resistance to Change," in *Continuity and Change in African Cultures,* William Bascom and Melville J. Herskovits (eds.). Chicago: University of Chicago Press. **271.**

———, 1961, "Economics in East African Aboriginal Societies," Paper presented at S.S.R.C. Conference on Indigenous and Induced Elements in the Economies of Subsaharan Africa, Northwestern University, November 1961. (See Schneider, 1964). **445.**

———, 1964, "Economics in East African Aboriginal Society," in *Economic Transition in Africa*, Melville J. Herskovits and Mitchell Harwitz (eds.). Evanston, Ill.: Northwestern University Press. **426–445, 445, 446, 447, 449.**

Schönfeld, *Grenznutzen und Wirtschaftsrechnung.* **95.**

Schumpeter, Joseph A., 1954, *History of Economic Analysis.* New York: Oxford. **208, 215, 216, 217, 226.**

———, *Epochen der Methoden- und Dogmengeschichte.* **89.**

———, *Wesen und Hauptinhalt der theoretischen Nationalökonomie.* **99.**

Seligman, C. G., 1910, *The Melanesians of British New Guinea.* London: Cambridge University Press. **3, 17, 18, 23, 34.**

Sharp, R. Lauriston, 1939, "Tribes and Totemism in Northeast Australia," *Oceania*, 8:254–275. **346.**

———, 1943, "Notes on Northeast Australian Totemism," *Studies in the Anthropology of Oceania and Asia*, Papers of the Peabody Museum of American Archeology and Ethnology, 20:66–71. **346.**

———, 1952, "Steel Axes for Stone-Age Australians," *Human Organization*, 11, Summer 1952:17–22. **341–353.**

Shea, Thomas W., Jr., 1959, "Barriers to Economic Development in Traditional Societies: Malabar, a Case Study," *The Journal of Economic History*, 19:504–522. **165.**

Sheddick, U. G. J., 1953, *The Southern Sotho.* London: International African Institute. **438.**

Shils, Edward, 1948, "Some Remarks on 'The Theory of Social and Economic Organization'," by Max Weber, *Economica*, 15:36–50. **72.**

Simpson, 1911, (not otherwise identified). **334, 336.**

Skinner, B. F., 1953, *Science and Human Behavior.* New York: Macmillan. **111, 112, 113.**

Smelser, Neil J., 1959, "A Comparative View of Exchange Systems," *Economic Development and Cultural Change*, 7:173–182. **164, 219, 224, 227.**

———, 1963, *The Sociology of Economic Life.* Englewood Cliffs, N.J.: Prentice-Hall. **vi.**

Smith, Adam, 1904, *Wealth of Nations*, Cannan's edition. London: Methuen and Co. **92.**

Smith, J. A., and D. P. Chase, trans., 1950, *The Ethics of Aristotle.* New York: Dutton. **225.**

Smith, Edwin W., and A. M. Dale, 1920, *The Ila-Speaking People of Northern Rhodesia.* London: Macmillan. **281.**

Stanner, W. E. H., 1962, "Foreword," in *From Stone to Steel*, R. F. Salisbury. Melbourne: Melbourne University Press. **225.**

Steiner, Franz, 1954, "Notes on Comparative Economics," *British Journal of Sociology*, 5:118–129. **154, 305.**

Stigler, George J., 1946, *The Theory of Price.* New York: Macmillan. **190.**

———, 1952, *The Theory of Price*, rev. ed. New York: Macmillan. **117.**

Stonier, Alfred W., and Douglas C. Hague, 1957, *A Textbook of Economic Theory*, 2d ed. London: Longmans. **219.**

Streeten, Paul, 1954, "Programs and Prognosis," *Quarterly Journal of Economics*, 68. **236.**

Strigl, *Die ökonomischen Kategorien und die Organisation der Wirtschaft.* **96, 98.**

Survey Research Center, 1953, *The White Collar Job.* Ann Arbor, Mich.: University of Michigan. **121.**

Suttles, Wayne, 1960, "Affinal Ties, Subsistence, and Prestige among the Coast Salish," *American Anthropologist*, 62:296–305. **283.**

Tambiah, S. J., 1958, "The Structure of Kinship and its Relationship to Land Possession and Residence in Pata Dumbara, Central Ceylon," *Journal of the Royal Anthropological Institute*, 88:21–44. **397.**

Taussig, Frank W., 1896, *Wages and Capital.* New York: Appleton. **92.**

Tawney, R. H., 1926, *Religion and the Rise of Capitalism.* New York: Harcourt. **83, 84.**

Tax, Sol, 1937, "The Municipios of the Midwestern Highlands of Guatemala," *American Anthropologist,* 39:423–444. **312.**

———, 1953, *Penny Capitalism: a Guatemalan Indian Economy.* Washington: Smithsonian Institute, Institute of Social Anthropology, Publication No. 16. **8, 188, 195, 318.**

Tax, Sol, and Lois Mednick, 1960, " 'Primitive' Peoples," *Current Anthropology,* 1:441–444. **189.**

Thrall, R. M., C. H. Coombs, and R. L. Davis, 1954, *Decision Processes.* New York: Wiley. **101.**

Thurnwald, Richard C., 1932, *Economics in Primitive Communities.* London: Oxford. **5, 153.**

Torday, E., 1925, *On the Trail of the Bushongo.* London: Seeley, Service and Co., Ltd. **335.**

Townsend, 1786, (not otherwise identified). **146.**

Turner, V. W., 1957, *Schism and Continuity in an African Society.* Manchester: Manchester University Press. **325.**

Udy, Stanley H., Jr., 1959, *Organization of Work.* New Haven, Conn.: HRAF Press. **207, 482.**

Usher, Abbott Payson, 1920, *An Introduction to the Industrial History of England.* Boston: Houghton. **47.**

———, 1949, "The Significance of Modern Empiricism for History and Economics," *The Journal of Economic History,* 9:137–155. **50.**

Vancouver, George, 1801, *A Voyage of Discovery to the North Pacific Ocean . . . ,* vol. 2. London: John Stockdale. **284.**

Vandenplas, A., 1947, *La Température au Congo Belge,* Pub. Minis. Colon. **329.**

Vansina, Jan, 1954, "Les Valeurs Culturelles des Bushong," *Zaïre,* 9:900–910. **333.**

———, 1956, "Migration dans la Province du Kasai," *Zaïre,* 10:69–85. **326.**

———, 1957, "L'État Kuba dans le Cadre des Institutions Politiques Africaines," *Zaïre,* 11:485–492. **336.**

Vayda, Andrew P., 1961, "A Re-examination of Northwest Coast Economic Systems," *Transactions of the New York Academy of Sciences,* Series II, 23:618–624. **283.**

Veblen, Thorstein, 1899, 1953, *The Theory of the Leisure Class.* New York: New American Library. **469.**

von Bertalanffy, Ludwig, 1956, "General System Theory," in *General Systems,* 1:1–10. **101.**

von Mises, Ludwig, *Die Gemeinwirtschaft.* **96, 98.**

Von Sick, E., 1916, "Die Waniaturu Walimi," in *Baessler Archiv,* 5:25–26. **427, 433, 435.**

Wagner, Günter, 1956, *The Bantu of North Kavirondo,* Vol. II, *Economic Life.* London: Oxford. **436, 439, 441.**

Walker, R. F., 1943, "The Study of Primitive Economics," *Oceania,* 13:131–142. **220, 225.**

Watson, William, 1958, *Tribal Cohesion in a Money Economy.* Manchester: Manchester University Press. **158.**

Weber, Max, 1923, *General Economic History.* New York: Free Press, 1950. **167.**

———, 1930, *The Protestant Ethic and the Rise of Capitalism,* trans. by Talcott Parsons. New York: Scribner's. **83.**

———, 1947, *Theory of Social and Economic Organization,* trans. by H. L. Henderson and Talcott Parsons. New York: Oxford. **69, 72, 226, 227.**

———, *Die Objektivität sozialwissenschaftlicher und sozialpolitischer Erkenntnis, Gesammelte Aufsätze zur Wissenschaftslehre.* **89.**

Wickett, W. P., 1958, "Review of Certain Environmental Factors Affecting the Production of Pink and Chum Salmon," *Journal of the Fisheries Research Board of Canada,* 15:1103–1126. **287.**

Wicksteed, (not otherwise identified). **58.**

Wike, Joyce, 1952, "The Role of the Dead in Northwest Coast Culture," in *Indian Tribes of Aboriginal America: Selected Papers of the XXIXth International Congress of Americanists,* Sol Tax (ed.) pp. 97–103. Chicago: University of Chicago Press. **288, 294.**

Winter, E. H., 1956, *Bwamba: a Structural-Functional Analysis of a Patrilineal Society.* Cambridge: W. Heffer. **277.**

Wittfogel, Karl A., 1957, *Oriental Despotism.* New Haven, Conn.: Yale University Press. **397.**

Wolf, Eric R., 1955, "Types of Latin American Peasantry," *American Anthropologist,* 57:452–459. **312, 319.**

———, 1964, *Anthropology.* Englewood Cliffs, N.J.: Prentice-Hall. **212.**

Workshop in Economic Anthropology, 1960, "Conference Report," *Current Anthropology,* 1:149–150. **207.**

Yalman, N., 1960, "The Flexibility of Caste Principles in a Kandyan Community," *Cambridge Papers in Social Anthropology,* 2:78–112. **397.**

Zipf, George Kingsley, 1949, *Human Behavior and the Principle of Least Effort.* Cambridge, Mass.: Addison-Wesley. **181, 182–183.**

INDEX

INDEX